Python Object-Oriented Programming

Fourth Edition

Build robust and maintainable object-oriented Python applications and libraries

Steven F. Lott

Dusty Phillips

BIRMINGHAM – MUMBAI

Python Object-Oriented Programming
Fourth Edition

Copyright © 2021 Packt Publishing

Producer: Dr. Shailesh Jain
Acquisition Editor – Peer Reviews: Saby D'silva
Project Editor: Parvathy Nair
Content Development Editor: Lucy Wan
Copy Editor: Safis Editor
Technical Editor: Aditya Sawant
Proofreader: Safis Editor
Indexer: Tejal Daruwale Soni
Presentation Designer: Pranit Padwal

First published: July 2010
Second edition: August 2015
Third edition: October 2018
Fourth edition: June 2021

Production reference: 2281221

Published by Packt Publishing Ltd.
Livery Place
35 Livery Street
Birmingham
B3 2PB, UK.

ISBN 978-1-80107-726-2

www.packt.com

Contributors

About the authors

Steven Lott has been programming since computers were large, expensive, and rare. Working for decades in high tech has given him exposure to a lot of ideas and techniques — some bad, but most are useful and helpful to others.

Steven has been working with Python since the '90s, building a variety of tools and applications. He's written a number of titles for Packt Publishing, including *Mastering Object-Oriented*, *Modern Python Cookbook*, and *Functional Python Programming*.

He's a technomad, and lives on a boat that's usually located on the east coast of the US. He tries to live by the words "Don't come home until you have a story."

Dusty Phillips is a Canadian author and software developer. His storied career has included roles with the world's biggest government, the world's biggest social network, a two person startup, and everything in between. In addition to *Python Object-Oriented Programming*, Dusty wrote *Creating Apps In Kivy* (O'Reilly) and is now focused on writing fiction.

Thank you to Steven Lott, for finishing what I started, to all my readers for appreciating what I write, and to my wife, Jen Phillips, for everything else.

About the reviewer

Bernát Gábor, originally from Transylvania, works as a senior software engineer at Bloomberg in London, UK. During his day job, he primarily focuses on improving the quality of the data ingestion pipeline at Bloomberg with predominant use of the Python programming language and paradigms. He's been working with Python for over ten years and is a major open-source contributor in this domain, with a particular focus on the packaging area. He's also the author and maintainer of high-profile projects such as `virtualenv`, `build`, and `tox`. For more information, see `https://bernat.tech/about`.

I would like to express my very great appreciation to Lisa, my fiancée, for her invaluable support on a daily basis. Love you!

Table of Contents

Preface   **xi**

Chapter 1: Object-Oriented Design   **1**

Introducing object-oriented   **2**

Objects and classes   **4**

Specifying attributes and behaviors   **6**

Data describes object state   7

Behaviors are actions   9

Hiding details and creating the public interface   **10**

Composition   **13**

Inheritance   **16**

Inheritance provides abstraction   18

Multiple inheritance   19

Case study   **20**

Introduction and problem overview   22

Context view   23

Logical view   26

Process view   28

Development view   30

Physical view   32

Conclusion   33

Recall   **34**

Exercises   **34**

Summary   **35**

Chapter 2: Objects in Python   **37**

Introducing type hints   **37**

Type checking   40

Creating Python classes — **43**
Adding attributes — 44
Making it do something — 45
Talking to yourself — 46
More arguments — 48
Initializing the object — 49
Type hints and defaults — 52
Explaining yourself with docstrings — 53
Modules and packages — **56**
Organizing modules — 59
Absolute imports — 60
Relative imports — 61
Packages as a whole — 62
Organizing our code in modules — 63
Who can access my data? — **68**
Third-party libraries — **69**
Case study — **71**
Logical view — 71
Samples and their states — 74
Sample state transitions — 75
Class responsibilities — 80
The TrainingData class — 81
Recall — **84**
Exercises — **85**
Summary — **86**
Chapter 3: When Objects Are Alike — **87**
Basic inheritance — **88**
Extending built-ins — 90
Overriding and super — 94
Multiple inheritance — **95**
The diamond problem — 99
Different sets of arguments — 105
Polymorphism — **109**
Case study — **112**
Logical view — 114
Another distance — 119
Recall — **121**
Exercises — **122**
Summary — **123**
Chapter 4: Expecting the Unexpected — **125**
Raising exceptions — **126**

Raising an exception   128
The effects of an exception   130
Handling exceptions   132
The exception hierarchy   138
Defining our own exceptions   139
Exceptions aren't exceptional   142
Case study   **146**
Context view   147
Processing view   148
What can go wrong?   149
Bad behavior   150
Creating samples from CSV files   151
Validating enumerated values   155
Reading CSV files   157
Don't repeat yourself   159
Recall   **160**
Exercises   **160**
Summary   **162**
Chapter 5: When to Use Object-Oriented Programming   **163**
Treat objects as objects   **164**
Adding behaviors to class data with properties   **170**
Properties in detail   174
Decorators – another way to create properties   176
Deciding when to use properties   177
Manager objects   **180**
Removing duplicate code   185
In practice   187
Case study   **191**
Input validation   192
Input partitioning   194
The sample class hierarchy   195
The purpose enumeration   197
Property setters   200
Repeated if statements   200
Recall   **201**
Exercises   **201**
Summary   **203**
Chapter 6: Abstract Base Classes and Operator Overloading   **205**
Creating an abstract base class   **207**
The ABCs of collections   210

Abstract base classes and type hints   212
The collections.abc module   213
Creating your own abstract base class   220
Demystifying the magic   224
Operator overloading   **226**
Extending built-ins   **232**
Metaclasses   **235**
Case study   **241**
Extending the list class with two sublists   242
A shuffling strategy for partitioning   244
An incremental strategy for partitioning   246
Recall   **249**
Exercises   **250**
Summary   **251**

Chapter 7: Python Data Structures   **253**
Empty objects   **253**
Tuples and named tuples   **255**
Named tuples via typing.NamedTuple   258
Dataclasses   **261**
Dictionaries   **265**
Dictionary use cases   271
Using defaultdict   272
Counter   275
Lists   **276**
Sorting lists   279
Sets   **285**
Three types of queues   **290**
Case study   **294**
Logical model   294
Frozen dataclasses   298
NamedTuple classes   301
Conclusion   304
Recall   **304**
Exercises   **305**
Summary   **306**

**Chapter 8: The Intersection of Object-Oriented
and Functional Programming**   **307**
Python built-in functions   **308**
The len() function   308
The reversed() function   309

The enumerate() function   310
An alternative to method overloading   **312**
    Default values for parameters   314
     Additional details on defaults   317
    Variable argument lists   319
    Unpacking arguments   326
Functions are objects, too   **327**
    Function objects and callbacks   329
    Using functions to patch a class   335
    Callable objects   337
File I/O   **339**
    Placing it in context   342
Case study   **346**
    Processing overview   347
    Splitting the data   348
    Rethinking classification   349
    The partition() function   352
    One-pass partitioning   353
Recall   **356**
Exercises   **357**
Summary   **358**
Chapter 9: Strings, Serialization, and File Paths   **359**
Strings   **360**
    String manipulation   361
    String formatting   364
     Escaping braces   365
     f-strings can contain Python code   366
     Making it look right   368
     Custom formatters   372
     The format() method   373
    Strings are Unicode   374
     Decoding bytes to text   375
     Encoding text to bytes   376
     Mutable byte strings   379
Regular expressions   **380**
    Matching patterns   382
     Matching a selection of characters   384
     Escaping characters   386
     Repeating patterns of characters   387
     Grouping patterns together   389
    Parsing information with regular expressions   390
     Other features of the re module   392
     Making regular expressions efficient   393

Filesystem paths	**394**
Serializing objects	**398**
Customizing pickles	401
Serializing objects using JSON	403
Case study	**407**
CSV format designs	407
CSV dictionary reader	408
CSV list reader	411
JSON serialization	413
Newline-delimited JSON	415
JSON validation	416
Recall	**419**
Exercises	**419**
Summary	**421**
Chapter 10: The Iterator Pattern	**423**
Design patterns in brief	**423**
Iterators	**424**
The iterator protocol	425
Comprehensions	**428**
List comprehensions	428
Set and dictionary comprehensions	431
Generator expressions	432
Generator functions	**434**
Yield items from another iterable	439
Generator stacks	441
Case study	**446**
The Set Builder background	446
Multiple partitions	448
Testing	452
The essential k-NN algorithm	454
k-NN using the bisect module	455
k-NN using the heapq module	456
Conclusion	457
Recall	**459**
Exercises	**460**
Summary	**462**
Chapter 11: Common Design Patterns	**463**
The Decorator pattern	**464**
A Decorator example	465
Decorators in Python	472

The Observer pattern	**476**
An Observer example	477
The Strategy pattern	**481**
A Strategy example	483
Strategy in Python	486
The Command pattern	**487**
A Command example	488
The State pattern	**493**
A State example	494
State versus Strategy	502
The Singleton pattern	**503**
Singleton implementation	504
Case study	**509**
Recall	**517**
Exercises	**518**
Summary	**519**
Chapter 12: Advanced Design Patterns	**521**
The Adapter pattern	**522**
An Adapter example	523
The Façade pattern	**527**
A Façade example	528
The Flyweight pattern	**532**
A Flyweight example in Python	534
Multiple messages in a buffer	542
Memory optimization via Python's __slots__	543
The Abstract Factory pattern	**545**
An Abstract Factory example	547
Abstract Factories in Python	552
The Composite pattern	**553**
A Composite example	555
The Template pattern	**561**
A Template example	562
Case study	**567**
Recall	**570**
Exercises	**570**
Summary	**572**
Chapter 13: Testing Object-Oriented Programs	**573**
Why test?	**573**
Test-driven development	575
Testing objectives	576

Testing patterns	577
Unit testing with unittest	**578**
Unit testing with pytest	**581**
pytest's setup and teardown functions	583
pytest fixtures for setup and teardown	586
More sophisticated fixtures	591
Skipping tests with pytest	597
Imitating objects using Mocks	**599**
Additional patching techniques	603
The sentinel object	606
How much testing is enough?	**608**
Testing and development	**612**
Case study	**613**
Unit testing the distance classes	613
Unit testing the Hyperparameter class	620
Recall	**623**
Exercises	**624**
Summary	**626**
Chapter 14: Concurrency	**627**
Background on concurrent processing	628
Threads	**629**
The many problems with threads	632
Shared memory	632
The global interpreter lock	633
Thread overhead	634
Multiprocessing	**634**
Multiprocessing pools	637
Queues	640
The problems with multiprocessing	645
Futures	**646**
AsyncIO	**650**
AsyncIO in action	652
Reading an AsyncIO future	654
AsyncIO for networking	655
Design considerations	661
A log writing demonstration	662
AsyncIO clients	665
The dining philosophers benchmark	**668**
Case study	**673**
Recall	**678**
Exercises	**679**

Summary   **680**

Other Books You May Enjoy   **683**

Index   **687**

Preface

The Python programming language is extremely popular and used for a variety of applications. The Python language is designed to make it relatively easy to create small programs. To create more sophisticated software, we need to acquire a number of important programming and software design skills.

This book describes the **object-oriented** approach to creating programs in Python. It introduces the terminology of object-oriented programming, demonstrating software design and Python programming through step-by-step examples. It describes how to make use of inheritance and composition to build software from individual elements. It shows how to use Python's built-in exceptions and data structures, as well as elements of the Python standard library. A number of common design patterns are described with detailed examples.

This book covers how to write automated tests to confirm that our software works. It also shows how to use the various concurrency libraries available as part of Python; this lets us write software that can make use of multiple cores and multiple processors in a modern computer. An extended case study covers a simple machine learning example, showing a number of alternative solutions to a moderately complicated problem.

Who this book is for

This book targets people who are new to object-oriented programming in Python. It assumes basic Python skills. For readers with a background in another object-oriented programming language, this book will expose many distinctive features of Python's approach.

Because of Python's use for data science and data analytics, this book touches on the related math and statistics concepts. Some knowledge in these areas can help to make the applications of the concepts more concrete.

What this book covers

This book is divided into four overall sections. The first six chapters provide the core principles and concepts of object-oriented programming and how these are implemented in Python. The next three chapters take a close look at Python built-in features through the lens of object-oriented programming. *Chapters 10, 11,* and *12* look at a number of common design patterns and how these can be handled in Python. The final section covers two additional topics: testing and concurrency.

Chapter 1, Object-Oriented Design, introduces the core concepts underlying object-oriented design. This provides a road map through the ideas of state and behavior, attributes and methods, and how objects are grouped into classes. This chapter also looks an encapsulation, inheritance, and composition. The case study for this chapter introduces the machine learning problem, which is an implementation of a *k*-nearest neighbors (*k*-NN) classifier.

Chapter 2, Objects in Python, shows how class definitions work in Python. This will include the type annotations, called type hints, class definitions, modules, and packages. We'll talk about practical considerations for class definition and encapsulation. The case study will begin to implement some of the classes for the *k*-NN classifier.

Chapter 3, When Objects Are Alike, addresses how classes are related to each other. This will include how to make use of inheritance and multiple inheritance. We'll look at the concept of polymorphism among the classes in a class hierarchy. The case study will look at alternative designs for the distance computations used to find the nearest neighbors.

Chapter 4, Expecting the Unexpected, looks closely at Python's exceptions and exception handling. We'll look at the built-in exception hierarchy. We'll also look at how unique exceptions can be defined to reflect a unique problem domain or application. In the case study, we'll apply exceptions to data validation.

Chapter 5, When to Use Object-Oriented Programming, dives more deeply into design techniques. This chapter will look at how attributes can be implemented via Python's properties. We'll also look at the general concept of a **manager** for working with collections of objects. The case study will apply these ideas to expand on the *k*-NN classifier implementation.

Chapter 6, Abstract Base Classes and Operator Overloading, is a deep dive into the idea of abstraction, and how Python supports abstract base classes. This will involve comparing **duck typing** with more formal methods of Protocol definition. It will include the techniques for overloading Python's built-in operators. It will also look at metaclasses and how these can be used to modify class construction. The case study will redefine some of the existing classes to show how abstraction must be used carefully to lead to simplification of a design.

Chapter 7, Python Data Structures, examines a number of Python's built-in collections. This chapter examines tuples, dictionaries, lists, and sets. It also looks at how dataclasses and named tuples can simplify a design by providing a number of common features of a class. The case study will revise some earlier class definitions to make use of these new techniques.

Chapter 8, The Intersection of Object-Oriented and Functional Programming, looks at Python constructs that aren't simply class definitions. While all of Python is object-oriented, function definitions allow us to create callable objects without the clutter of a class definition. We'll also look at Python's context manager construct and the with statement. In the case study, we'll look at alternative designs that avoid some class clutter.

Chapter 9, Strings, Serialization, and File Paths, covers the way objects are serialized as strings and how strings can be parsed to create objects. We'll look at several physical formats, including Pickle, JSON, and CSV. The case study will revisit how sample data is loaded and processed by the *k*-NN classifier.

Chapter 10, The Iterator Pattern, describes the ubiquitous concept of iteration in Python. All of the built-in collections are iterable, and this design pattern is central to a great deal of how Python works. We'll look at Python comprehensions and generator functions, also. The case study will revisit some earlier designs using generator expressions and list comprehensions to partition samples for testing and training.

Chapter 11, Common Design Patterns, looks at some common object-oriented design. This will include the Decorator, Observer, Strategy, Command, State, and Singleton design patterns.

Chapter 12, Advanced Design Patterns, looks at some more advanced object-oriented design. This will include the Adapter, Façade, Flyweight, Abstract Factory, Composite, and Template patterns.

Chapter 13, Testing Object-Oriented Programs, shows how to use unittest and pytest to provide an automated unit test suite for a Python application. This will look at some more advanced testing techniques, like using mock objects to isolate the unit under test. The case study will show how to create test cases for the distance computations covered in *Chapter 3*.

Chapter 14, Concurrency, looks at how we can make use of multi-core and multi-processor computer systems to do computations rapidly and write software that is responsive to external events. We'll look at threads and multiprocessing, as well as Python's `asyncio` module. The case study will show how to use these techniques to do hyperparameter tuning on the *k*-NN model.

To get the most out of this book

All of the examples were tested with Python 3.9.5. The *mypy* tool, version 0.812, was used to confirm that the type hints were consistent.

Some of the examples depend on an internet connection to gather data. These interactions with websites generally involve small downloads.

Some of the examples involve packages that are not part of Python's built-in standard library. In the relevant chapters, we note the packages and provide the install instructions. All of these extra packages are in the Python Package Index, at https://pypi.org.

Download the example code files

The code bundle for the book is also hosted on GitHub at https://github.com/PacktPublishing/Python-Object-Oriented-Programming---4th-edition.

We also have other code bundles from our rich catalog of books and videos available at https://github.com/PacktPublishing/. Check them out!

Download the color images

We also provide a PDF file that has color images of the screenshots/diagrams used in this book. You can download it here: https://static.packt-cdn.com/downloads/9781801077262_ColorImages.pdf

Conventions used

There are a number of text conventions used throughout this book.

`CodeInText`: Indicates code words in text, database table names, folder names, filenames, file extensions, pathnames, dummy URLs, user input, and Twitter handles. For example: "You can confirm Python is running by importing the `antigravity` module at the `>>>` prompt."

A block of code is set as follows:

```
class Fizz:
    def member(self, v: int) -> bool:
        return v % 5 == 0
```

When we wish to draw your attention to a particular part of a code block, the relevant lines or items are set in bold:

```
class Fizz:
    def member(self, v: int) -> bool:
        return v % 5 == 0
```

Any command-line input or output is written as follows:

```
python -m pip install tox
```

Bold: Indicates a new term, an important word, or words that you see on the screen, for example, in menus or dialog boxes. For example: "Formally, an object is a collection of **data** and associated **behaviors**."

 Warnings or important notes appear like this.

 Tips and tricks appear like this.

Get in touch

Feedback from our readers is always welcome.

General feedback: Email feedback@packtpub.com, and mention the book's title in the subject of your message. If you have questions about any aspect of this book, please email us at questions@packtpub.com.

Errata: Although we have taken every care to ensure the accuracy of our content, mistakes do happen. If you have found a mistake in this book, we would be grateful if you would report this to us. Please visit http://www.packtpub.com/submit-errata, selecting your book, clicking on the Errata Submission Form link, and entering the details.

Piracy: If you come across any illegal copies of our works in any form on the internet, we would be grateful if you would provide us with the location address or website name. Please contact us at copyright@packtpub.com with a link to the material.

If you are interested in becoming an author: If there is a topic that you have expertise in and you are interested in either writing or contributing to a book, please visit http://authors.packtpub.com.

Share Your Thoughts

Once you've read *Python Object-Oriented Programming, Fourth Edition*, we'd love to hear your thoughts! Scan the QR code below to go straight to the Amazon review page for this book and share your feedback.

https://packt.link/r/1-801-07726-6

Your review is important to us and the tech community and will help us make sure we're delivering excellent quality content.

1

Object-Oriented Design

In software development, design is often considered as the step that's done *before* programming. This isn't true; in reality, analysis, programming, and design tend to overlap, combine, and interweave. Throughout this book, we'll be covering a mixture of design and programming issues without trying to parse them into separate buckets. One of the advantages of a language like Python is the ability to express the design clearly.

In this chapter, we will talk a little about how we can move from a good idea toward writing software. We'll create some design artifacts – like diagrams – that can help clarify our thinking before we start writing code. We'll cover the following topics:

- What object-oriented means
- The difference between object-oriented design and object-oriented programming
- The basic principles of object-oriented design
- Basic **Unified Modeling Language** (**UML**) and when it isn't evil

We will also introduce this book's object-oriented design case study, using the "4+1" architectural view model. We'll touch on a number of topics here:

- An overview of a classic machine learning application, the famous Iris classification problem
- The general processing context for this classifier
- Sketching out two views of the class hierarchy that look like they'll be adequate to solve the problem

Introducing object-oriented

Everyone knows what an object is: a tangible thing that we can sense, feel, and manipulate. The earliest objects we interact with are typically baby toys. Wooden blocks, plastic shapes, and over-sized puzzle pieces are common first objects. Babies learn quickly that certain objects do certain things: bells ring, buttons are pressed, and levers are pulled.

The definition of an object in software development is not terribly different. Software objects may not be tangible things that you can pick up, sense, or feel, but they are models of something that can do certain things and have certain things done to them. Formally, an object is a collection of **data** and associated **behaviors**.

Considering what an object is, what does it mean to be object-oriented? In the dictionary, *oriented* means *directed toward*. Object-oriented programming means writing code directed toward modeling objects. This is one of many techniques used for describing the actions of complex systems. It is defined by describing a collection of interacting objects via their data and behavior.

If you've read any hype, you've probably come across the terms *object-oriented analysis*, *object-oriented design*, *object-oriented analysis and design*, and *object-oriented programming*. These are all related concepts under the general *object-oriented* umbrella.

In fact, analysis, design, and programming are all stages of software development. Calling them object-oriented simply specifies what kind of software development is being pursued.

Object-oriented analysis (OOA) is the process of looking at a problem, system, or task (that somebody wants to turn into a working software application) and identifying the objects and interactions between those objects. The analysis stage is all about *what* needs to be done.

The output of the analysis stage is a description of the system, often in the form of *requirements*. If we were to complete the analysis stage in one step, we would have turned a task, such as *As a botanist, I need a website to help users classify plants so I can help with correct identification*, into a set of required features. As an example, here are some requirements as to what a website visitor might need to do. Each item is an action bound to an object; we've written them with *italics* to highlight the actions, and **bold** to highlight the objects:

- *Browse* **Previous Uploads**
- *Upload new* **Known Examples**

- *Test* for **Quality**
- *Browse* **Products**
- *See* **Recommendations**

In some ways, the term *analysis* is a misnomer. The baby we discussed earlier doesn't analyze the blocks and puzzle pieces. Instead, she explores her environment, manipulates shapes, and sees where they might fit. A better turn of phrase might be *object-oriented exploration*. In software development, the initial stages of analysis include interviewing customers, studying their processes, and eliminating possibilities.

Object-oriented design (OOD) is the process of converting such requirements into an implementation specification. The designer must name the objects, define the behaviors, and formally specify which objects can activate specific behaviors on other objects. The design stage is all about transforming *what* should be done into *how* it should be done.

The output of the design stage is an implementation specification. If we were to complete the design stage in a single step, we would have turned the requirements defined during object-oriented analysis into a set of classes and interfaces that could be implemented in (ideally) any object-oriented programming language.

Object-oriented programming (OOP) is the process of converting a design into a working program that does what the product owner originally requested.

Yeah, right! It would be lovely if the world met this ideal and we could follow these stages one by one, in perfect order, like all the old textbooks told us to. As usual, the real world is much murkier. No matter how hard we try to separate these stages, we'll always find things that need further analysis while we're designing. When we're programming, we find features that need clarification in the design.

Most 21st century development recognizes that this cascade (or waterfall) of stages doesn't work out well. What seems to be better is an *iterative* development model. In iterative development, a small part of the task is modeled, designed, and programmed, and then the product is reviewed and expanded to improve each feature and include new features in a series of short development cycles.

The rest of this book is about object-oriented programming, but in this chapter, we will cover the basic object-oriented principles in the context of design. This allows us to understand concepts without having to argue with software syntax or Python tracebacks.

Objects and classes

An **object** is a collection of data with associated behaviors. How do we differentiate between types of objects? Apples and oranges are both objects, but it is a common adage that they cannot be compared. Apples and oranges aren't modeled very often in computer programming, but let's pretend we're doing an inventory application for a fruit farm. To facilitate this example, we can assume that apples go in barrels and oranges go in baskets.

The problem domain we've uncovered so far has four kinds of objects: apples, oranges, baskets, and barrels. In object-oriented modeling, the term used for a *kind of object* is **class**. So, in technical terms, we now have four classes of objects.

It's important to understand the difference between an object and a class. Classes describe related objects. They are like blueprints for creating an object. You might have three oranges sitting on the table in front of you. Each orange is a distinct object, but all three have the attributes and behaviors associated with one class: the general class of oranges.

The relationship between the four classes of objects in our inventory system can be described using a **Unified Modeling Language** (invariably referred to as **UML**, because three-letter acronyms never go out of style) class diagram. Here is our first *class diagram*:

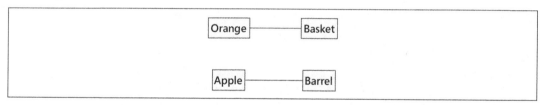

Figure 1.1: Class diagram

This diagram shows that instances of the **Orange** class (usually called "oranges") are somehow associated with a **Basket** and that instances of the **Apple** class ("apples") are also somehow associated with a **Barrel**. *Association* is the most basic way for instances of two classes to be related.

The syntax of a UML diagram is generally pretty obvious; you don't have to read a tutorial to (mostly) understand what is going on when you see one. UML is also fairly easy to draw, and quite intuitive. After all, many people, when describing classes and their relationships, will naturally draw boxes with lines between them. Having a standard based on these intuitive diagrams makes it easy for programmers to communicate with designers, managers, and each other.

Note that the UML diagram generally depicts the class definitions, but we're describing attributes of the objects. The diagram shows the class of Apple and the class of Barrel, telling us that a given apple is in a specific barrel. While we can use UML to depict individual objects, that's rarely necessary. Showing these classes tells us enough about the objects that are members of each class.

Some programmers disparage UML as a waste of time. Citing iterative development, they will argue that formal specifications done up in fancy UML diagrams are going to be redundant before they're implemented, and that maintaining these formal diagrams will only waste time and not benefit anyone.

Every programming team consisting of more than one person will occasionally have to sit down and hash out the details of the components being built. UML is extremely useful for ensuring quick, easy, and consistent communication. Even those organizations that scoff at formal class diagrams tend to use some informal version of UML in their design meetings or team discussions.

Furthermore, the most important person you will ever have to communicate with is your future self. We all think we can remember the design decisions we've made, but there will always be *Why did I do that?* moments hiding in our future. If we keep the scraps of papers we did our initial diagramming on when we started a design, we'll eventually find them to be a useful reference.

This chapter, however, is not meant to be a tutorial on UML. There are many of those available on the internet, as well as numerous books on the topic. UML covers far more than class and object diagrams; it also has a syntax for use cases, deployment, state changes, and activities. We'll be dealing with some common class diagram syntax in this discussion of object-oriented design. You can pick up the structure by example, and then you'll subconsciously choose the UML-inspired syntax in your own team or personal design notes.

Our initial diagram, while correct, does not remind us that apples go in barrels or how many barrels a single apple can go in. It only tells us that apples are somehow associated with barrels. The association between classes is often obvious and needs no further explanation, but we have the option to add further clarification as needed.

The beauty of UML is that most things are optional. We only need to specify as much information in a diagram as makes sense for the current situation. In a quick whiteboard session, we might just draw simple lines between boxes. In a formal document, we might go into more detail.

In the case of apples and barrels, we can be fairly confident that the association is **many apples go in one barrel**, but just to make sure nobody confuses it with **one apple spoils one barrel**, we can enhance the diagram, as shown here:

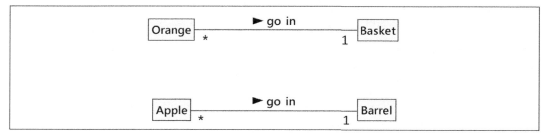

Figure 1.2: Class diagram with more detail

This diagram tells us that oranges **go in** baskets, with a little arrow showing what goes in what. It also tells us the number of that object that can be used in the association on both sides of the relationship. One **Basket** can hold many (represented by a *) **Orange** objects. Any one **Orange** can go in exactly one **Basket**. This number is referred to as the *multiplicity* of the object. You may also hear it described as the *cardinality*; it can help to think of cardinality as a specific number or range, and what we're using here, multiplicity, as a generalized "more-than-one instance".

We may sometimes forget which end of the relationship line is supposed to have which multiplicity number. The multiplicity nearest to a class is the number of objects of that class that can be associated with any one object at the other end of the association. For the apple goes in barrel association, reading from left to right, many instances of the **Apple** class (that is, many **Apple** objects) can go in any one **Barrel**. Reading from right to left, exactly one **Barrel** can be associated with any one **Apple**.

We've seen the basics of classes, and how they specify relationships among objects. Now, we need to talk about the attributes that define an object's state, and the behaviors of an object that may involve state change or interaction with other objects.

Specifying attributes and behaviors

We now have a grasp of some basic object-oriented terminology. Objects are instances of classes that can be associated with each other. A class instance is a specific object with its own set of data and behaviors; a specific orange on the table in front of us is said to be an instance of the general class of oranges.

The orange has a state, for example, ripe or raw; we implement the state of an object via the values of specific attributes. An orange also has behaviors. By themselves, oranges are generally passive. State changes are imposed on them. Let's dive into the meaning of those two words, *state* and *behaviors*.

Data describes object state

Let's start with data. Data represents the individual characteristics of a certain object; its current state. A class can define specific sets of characteristics that are part of all objects that are members of that class. Any specific object can have different data values for the given characteristics. For example, the three oranges on our table (if we haven't eaten any) could each weigh a different amount. The orange class could have a weight attribute to represent that datum. All instances of the orange class have a weight attribute, but each orange has a different value for this attribute. Attributes don't have to be unique, though; any two oranges may weigh the same amount.

Attributes are frequently referred to as **members** or **properties**. Some authors suggest that the terms have different meanings, usually that attributes are settable, while properties are read-only. A Python property can be defined as read-only, but the value will be based on attribute values that are – ultimately – writable, making the concept of *read-only* rather pointless; throughout this book, we'll see the two terms used interchangeably. In addition, as we'll discuss in *Chapter 5, When to Use Object-Oriented Programming*, the property keyword has a special meaning in Python for a particular kind of attribute.

In Python, we can also call an attribute an **instance variable**. This can help clarify the way attributes work. They are variables with unique values for each instance of a class. Python has other kinds of attributes, but we'll focus on the most common kind to get started.

In our fruit inventory application, the fruit farmer may want to know what orchard the orange came from, when it was picked, and how much it weighs. They might also want to keep track of where each **Basket** is stored. Apples might have a color attribute, and barrels might come in different sizes.

Some of these properties may also belong to multiple classes (we may want to know when apples are picked, too), but for this first example, let's just add a few different attributes to our class diagram:

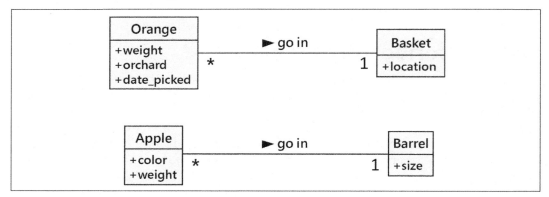

Figure 1.3: Class diagram with attributes

Depending on how detailed our design needs to be, we can also specify the type for each attribute's value. In UML, attribute types are often generic names common to many programming languages, such as integer, floating-point number, string, byte, or Boolean. However, they can also represent generic collections such as lists, trees, or graphs, or most notably, other, non-generic, application-specific classes. This is one area where the design stage can overlap with the programming stage. The various primitives and built-in collections available in one programming language may be different from what is available in another.

Here's a version with (mostly) Python-specific type hints:

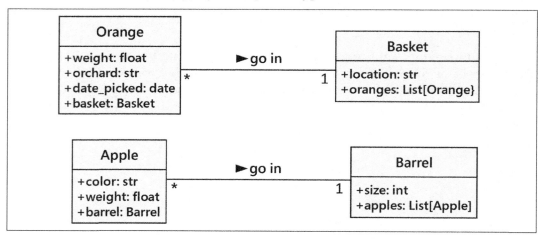

Figure 1.4: Class diagram with attributes and their types

Usually, we don't need to be overly concerned with data types at the design stage, as implementation-specific details are chosen during the programming stage. Generic names are normally sufficient for design; that's why we included `date` as a placeholder for a Python type like `datetime.datetime`. If our design calls for a list container type, Java programmers can choose to use a `LinkedList` or an `ArrayList` when implementing it, while Python programmers (that's us!) might specify `List[Apple]` as a type hint, and use the `list` type for the implementation.

In our fruit-farming example so far, our attributes are all basic primitives. However, there are some implicit attributes that we can make explicit – the associations. For a given orange, we have an attribute referring to the basket that holds that orange, the `basket` attribute, with a type hint of `Basket`.

Behaviors are actions

Now that we know how data defines the object's state, the last undefined term we need to look at is *behaviors*. Behaviors are actions that can occur on an object. The behaviors that can be performed on a specific class of object are expressed as the **methods** of the class. At the programming level, methods are like functions in structured programming, but they have access to the attributes – in particular, the instance variables with the data associated with this object. Like functions, methods can also accept **parameters** and return **values**.

A method's parameters are provided to it as a collection of objects that need to be **passed** into that method. The actual object instances that are passed into a method during a specific invocation are usually referred to as **arguments**. These objects are bound to **parameter** variables in the method body. They are used by the method to perform whatever behavior or task it is meant to do. Returned values are the results of that task. Internal state changes are another possible effect of evaluating a method.

We've stretched our *comparing apples and oranges* example into a basic (if far-fetched) inventory application. Let's stretch it a little further and see whether it breaks. One action that can be associated with oranges is the **pick** action. If you think about implementation, **pick** would need to do two things:

- Place the orange in a basket by updating the **Basket** attribute of the orange.
- Add the orange to the **Orange** list on the given **Basket**.

So, **pick** needs to know what basket it is dealing with. We do this by giving the **pick** method a **Basket** parameter. Since our fruit farmer also sells juice, we can add a **squeeze** method to the **Orange** class. When called, the **squeeze** method might return the amount of juice retrieved, while also removing the **Orange** from the **Basket** it was in.

The class **Basket** can have a **sell** action. When a basket is sold, our inventory system might update some data on as-yet unspecified objects for accounting and profit calculations. Alternatively, our basket of oranges might go bad before we can sell them, so we add a **discard** method. Let's add these methods to our diagram:

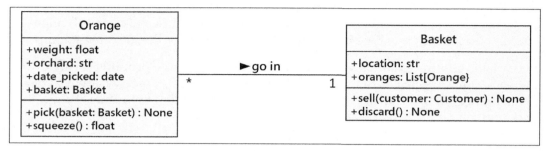

Figure 1.5: Class diagram with attributes and methods

Adding attributes and methods to individual objects allows us to create a **system** of interacting objects. Each object in the system is a member of a certain class. These classes specify what types of data the object can hold and what methods can be invoked on it. The data in each object can be in a different state from other instances of the same class; each object may react to method calls differently because of the differences in state.

Object-oriented analysis and design is all about figuring out what those objects are and how they should interact. Each class has responsibilities and collaborations. The next section describes principles that can be used to make those interactions as simple and intuitive as possible.

Note that selling a basket is not unconditionally a feature of the **Basket** class. It may be that some other class (not shown) cares about the various Baskets and where they are. We often have boundaries around our design. We will also have questions about responsibilities allocated to various classes. The responsibility allocation problem doesn't always have a tidy technical solution, forcing us to draw (and redraw) our UML diagrams more than once to examine alternative designs.

Hiding details and creating the public interface

The key purpose of modeling an object in object-oriented design is to determine what the public **interface** of that object will be. The interface is the collection of attributes and methods that other objects can access to interact with that object. Other objects do not need, and in some languages are not allowed, to access the internal workings of the object.

A common real-world example is the television. Our interface to the television is the remote control. Each button on the remote control represents a method that can be called on the television object. When we, as the calling object, access these methods, we do not know or care if the television is getting its signal from a cable connection, a satellite dish, or an internet-enabled device. We don't care what electronic signals are being sent to adjust the volume, or whether the sound is destined for speakers or headphones. If we open the television to access its internal workings, for example, to split the output signal to both external speakers and a set of headphones, we may void the warranty.

This process of hiding the implementation of an object is suitably called **information hiding**. It is also sometimes referred to as **encapsulation**, but encapsulation is actually a more encompassing term. Encapsulated data is not necessarily hidden. Encapsulation is, literally, creating a capsule (or wrapper) on the attributes. The TV's external case encapsulates the state and behavior of the television. We have access to the external screen, the speakers, and the remote. We don't have direct access to the wiring of the amplifiers or receivers within the TV's case.

When we buy a component entertainment system, we change the level of encapsulation, exposing more of the interfaces between components. If we're an Internet of Things maker, we may decompose this even further, opening cases and breaking the information hiding attempted by the manufacturer.

The distinction between encapsulation and information hiding is largely irrelevant, especially at the design level. Many practical references use these terms interchangeably. As Python programmers, we don't actually have or need information hiding via completely private, inaccessible variables (we'll discuss the reasons for this in *Chapter 2*, *Objects in Python*), so the more encompassing definition for encapsulation is suitable.

The public interface, however, is very important. It needs to be carefully designed as it can be difficult to change when other classes depend on it. Changing an interface can break any client objects that depend on it. We can change the internals all we like, for example, to make it more efficient, or to access data over the network as well as locally, and the client objects will still be able to talk to it, unmodified, using the public interface. On the other hand, if we alter the interface by changing publicly accessed attribute names or the order or types of arguments that a method can accept, all client classes will also have to be modified. When designing public interfaces, keep it simple. Always design the interface of an object based on how easy it is to use, not how hard it is to code (this advice applies to user interfaces as well). For this reason, you'll sometimes see Python variables with a leading _ in their name as a warning that these aren't part of the public interface.

Remember, program objects may represent real objects, but that does not make them real objects. They are models. One of the greatest gifts of modeling is the ability to ignore irrelevant details. The model car one of the authors built as a child looked like a real 1956 Thunderbird on the outside, but it obviously didn't run. When they were too young to drive, these details were overly complex and irrelevant. The model is an **abstraction** of a real concept.

Abstraction is another object-oriented term related to encapsulation and information hiding. Abstraction means dealing with the level of detail that is most appropriate to a given task. It is the process of extracting a public interface from the inner details. A car's driver needs to interact with the steering, accelerator, and brakes. The workings of the motor, drive train, and brake subsystem don't matter to the driver. A mechanic, on the other hand, works at a different level of abstraction, tuning the engine and bleeding the brakes. Here's an example of two abstraction levels for a car:

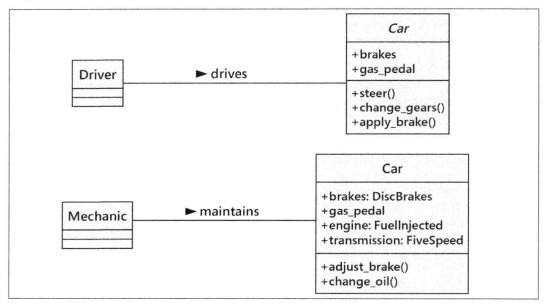

Figure 1.6: Abstraction levels for a car

Now, we have several new terms that refer to similar concepts. Let's summarize all this jargon in a couple of sentences: abstraction is the process of encapsulating information with a separate public interface. Any private elements can be subject to information hiding. In UML diagrams, we might use a leading – instead of a leading + to suggest it's not part of a public interface.

The important lesson to take away from all these definitions is to make our models understandable to other objects that have to interact with them. This means paying careful attention to small details.

Ensure methods and properties have sensible names. When analyzing a system, objects typically represent nouns in the original problem, while methods are normally verbs. Attributes may show up as adjectives or more nouns. Name your classes, attributes, and methods accordingly.

When designing the interface, imagine you are the object; you want clear definitions of your responsibility and you have a very strong preference for privacy to meet those responsibilities. Don't let other objects have access to data about you unless you feel it is in your best interest for them to have it. Don't give them an interface to force you to perform a specific task unless you are certain it's your responsibility to do that.

Composition

So far, we have learned to design systems as a group of interacting objects, where each interaction involves viewing objects at an appropriate level of abstraction. But we don't yet know how to create these levels of abstraction. There are a variety of ways to do this; we'll discuss some advanced design patterns in *Chapters 10, 11,* and *12*. But even most design patterns rely on two basic object-oriented principles known as **composition** and **inheritance**. Composition is simpler, so let's start with that.

Composition is the act of collecting several objects together to create a new one. Composition is usually a good choice when one object is part of another object. We've already seen a first hint of composition when talking about cars. A fossil-fueled car is composed of an engine, transmission, starter, headlights, and windshield, among numerous other parts. The engine, in turn, is composed of pistons, a crank shaft, and valves. In this example, composition is a good way to provide levels of abstraction. The **Car** object can provide the interface required by a driver, while also giving access to its component parts, which offers the deeper level of abstraction suitable for a mechanic. Those component parts can, of course, be further decomposed into details if the mechanic needs more information to diagnose a problem or tune the engine.

A car is a common introductory example of composition, but it's not overly useful when it comes to designing computer systems. Physical objects are easy to break into component objects. People have been doing this at least since the ancient Greeks originally postulated that atoms were the smallest units of matter (they, of course, didn't have access to particle accelerators). Because computer systems involve a lot of peculiar concepts, identifying the component objects does not happen as naturally as with real-world valves and pistons.

The objects in an object-oriented system occasionally represent physical objects such as people, books, or telephones. More often, however, they represent concepts. People have names, books have titles, and telephones are used to make calls. Calls, titles, accounts, names, appointments, and payments are not usually considered objects in the physical world, but they are all frequently-modeled components in computer systems.

Let's try modeling a more computer-oriented example to see composition in action. We'll be looking at the design of a computerized chess game. This was a very popular pastime in the 80s and 90s. People were predicting that computers would one day be able to defeat a human chess master. When this happened in 1997 (IBM's Deep Blue defeated world chess champion, Gary Kasparov), interest in the problem of chess waned. Nowadays, the descendants of Deep Blue always win.

A *game* of chess is **played** between two *players*, using a chess set featuring a *board* containing 64 *positions* in an 8×8 grid. The board can have two sets of 16 *pieces* that can be **moved**, in alternating *turns* by the two players in different ways. Each piece can **take** other pieces. The board will be required to **draw** itself on the computer *screen* after each turn.

I've identified some of the possible objects in the description using *italics*, and a few key methods using **bold**. This is a common first step in turning an object-oriented analysis into a design. At this point, to emphasize composition, we'll focus on the board, without worrying too much about the players or the different types of pieces.

Let's start at the highest level of abstraction possible. We have two players interacting with a **Chess Set** by taking turns making moves:

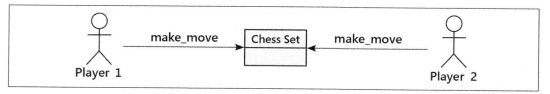

Figure 1.7: Object/instance diagram for a chess game

This doesn't quite look like our earlier class diagrams, which is a good thing since it isn't one! This is an **object diagram**, also called an **instance diagram**. It describes the system at a specific state in time, and is describing specific instances of objects, not the interaction between classes. Remember, both players are members of the same class, so the class diagram looks a little different:

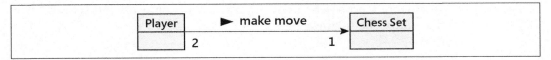

Figure 1.8: Class diagram for a chess game

This diagram shows that exactly two players can interact with one chess set. This also indicates that any one player can be playing with only one **Chess Set** at a time.

However, we're discussing composition, not UML, so let's think about what the **Chess Set** is composed of. We don't care what the player is composed of at this time. We can assume that the player has a heart and brain, among other organs, but these are irrelevant to our model. Indeed, there is nothing stopping said player from being Deep Blue itself, which has neither a heart nor a brain.

The chess set, then, is composed of a board and 32 pieces. The board further comprises 64 positions. You could argue that these pieces are not part of the chess set, because you could replace the pieces of a chess set with a different set of pieces. While this is unlikely or impossible in a computerized version of chess, it introduces us to **aggregation**.

Aggregation is almost exactly like composition. The difference is that aggregate objects can exist independently. It would be impossible for a position to be associated with a different chess board, so we say the board is composed of positions. But the pieces, which might exist independently of the chess set, are said to be in an aggregate relationship with that set.

Another way to differentiate between aggregation and composition is to think about the lifespan of the object:

- If the composite (outside) object controls when the related (inside) objects are created and destroyed, composition is most suitable.
- If the related object is created independently of the composite object, or can outlast that object, an aggregate relationship makes more sense.

Also, keep in mind that composition is aggregation; aggregation is simply a more general form of composition. Any composite relationship is also an aggregate relationship, but not vice versa.

Let's describe our current **Chess Set** composition and add some attributes to the objects to hold the composite relationships:

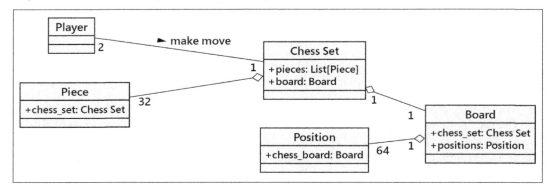

Figure 1.9: Class diagram for a chess game

The composition relationship is represented in UML as a solid diamond. The hollow diamond represents the aggregate relationship. You'll notice that the board and pieces are stored as part of the **Chess Set** in exactly the same way a reference to them is stored as an attribute on the chess set. This shows that, once again, in practice, the distinction between aggregation and composition is often irrelevant once you get past the design stage. When implemented, they behave in much the same way.

This distinction can help you differentiate between the two when your team is discussing how the different objects interact. You'll often need to distinguish between them when talking about how long related objects exist. In many cases, deleting a composite object (like the board) deletes all the locations. The aggregated objects, however, are not deleted automatically.

Inheritance

We discussed three types of relationships between objects: association, composition, and aggregation. However, we have not fully specified our chess set, and these tools don't seem to give us all the power we need. We discussed the possibility that a player might be a human or it might be a piece of software featuring artificial intelligence. It doesn't seem right to say that a player is *associated* with a human, or that the artificial intelligence implementation is *part of* the player object. What we really need is the ability to say that *Deep Blue is a player*, or that *Gary Kasparov is a player*.

The *is a* relationship is formed by **inheritance**. Inheritance is the most famous, well-known, and overused relationship in object-oriented programming. Inheritance is sort of like a family tree. Dusty Phillips is one of this book's authors.

His grandfather's last name was Phillips, and his father inherited that name. Dusty inherited it from him. In object-oriented programming, instead of inheriting features and behaviors from a person, one class can inherit attributes and methods from another class.

For example, there are 32 chess pieces in our chess set, but there are only six different types of pieces (pawns, rooks, bishops, knights, king, and queen), each of which behaves differently when it is moved. All of these classes of piece have properties, such as color and the chess set they are part of, but they also have unique shapes when drawn on the chess board, and make different moves. Let's see how the six types of pieces can inherit from a **Piece** class:

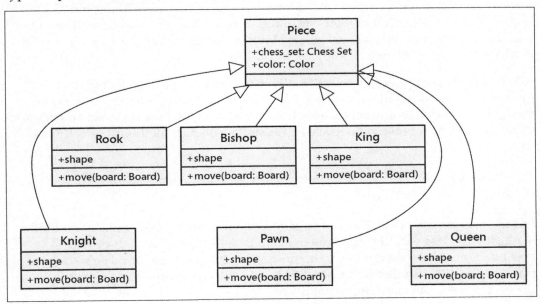

Figure 1.10: How chess pieces inherit from the Piece class

The hollow arrows indicate that the individual classes of pieces inherit from the **Piece** class. All the child classes automatically have a **chess_set** and **color** attribute inherited from the base class. Each piece provides a different shape property (to be drawn on the screen when rendering the board), and a different **move** method to move the piece to a new position on the board at each turn.

We actually know that all subclasses of the **Piece** class need to have a **move** method; otherwise, when the board tries to move the piece, it will get confused. It is possible that we would want to create a new version of the game of chess that has one additional piece (the wizard). Our current design will allow us to design this piece without giving it a **move** method. The board would then choke when it asked the piece to move itself.

We can fix this by creating a dummy move method on the **Piece** class. The subclasses can then **override** this method with a more specific implementation. The default implementation might, for example, pop up an error message that says **That piece cannot be moved**.

Overriding methods in subclasses allows very powerful object-oriented systems to be developed. For example, if we wanted to implement a **Player** class with artificial intelligence, we might provide a **calculate_move** method that takes a **Board** object and decides which piece to move where. A very basic class might randomly choose a piece and direction and move it accordingly. We could then override this method in a subclass with the Deep Blue implementation. The first class would be suitable for play against a raw beginner; the latter would challenge a grand master. The important thing is that other methods in the class, such as the ones that inform the board as to which move was chosen, need not be changed; this implementation can be shared between the two classes.

In the case of chess pieces, it doesn't really make sense to provide a default implementation of the move method. All we need to do is specify that the move method is required in any subclasses. This can be done by making **Piece** an **abstract class** with the **move** method declared as **abstract**. Abstract methods basically say this:

"We demand this method exist in any non-abstract subclass, but we are declining to specify an implementation in this class."

Indeed, it is possible to make an abstraction that does not implement any methods at all. Such a class would simply tell us what the class *should* do, but provides absolutely no advice on how to do it. In some languages, these purely abstract classes are called **interfaces**. It's possible to define a class with only abstract method placeholders in Python, but it's very rare.

Inheritance provides abstraction

Let's explore the longest word in object-oriented argot. **Polymorphism** is the ability to treat a class differently, depending on which subclass is implemented. We've already seen it in action with the pieces system we've described. If we took the design a bit further, we'd probably see that the **Board** object can accept a move from the player and call the **move** function on the piece. The board need not ever know what type of piece it is dealing with. All it has to do is call the **move** method, and the proper subclass will take care of moving it as a **Knight** or a **Pawn**.

Polymorphism is pretty cool, but it is a word that is rarely used in Python programming. Python goes an extra step past allowing a subclass of an object to be treated like a parent class. A board implemented in Python could take any object that has a **move** method, whether it is a bishop piece, a car, or a duck. When **move** is called, the **Bishop** will move diagonally on the board, the car will drive someplace, and the duck will swim or fly, depending on its mood.

This sort of polymorphism in Python is typically referred to as **duck typing**: *if it walks like a duck or swims like a duck, we call it a duck*. We don't care if it really *is a* duck (*is a* being a cornerstone of inheritance), only that it swims or walks. Geese and swans might easily be able to provide the duck-like behavior we are looking for. This allows future designers to create new types of birds without actually specifying a formal inheritance hierarchy for all possible kinds of aquatic birds. The chess examples, above, use formal inheritance to cover all possible pieces in the chess set. Duck typing also allows a programmer to extend a design, creating completely different drop-in behaviors the original designers never planned for. For example, future designers might be able to make a walking, swimming penguin that works with the same interface without ever suggesting that penguins have a common superclass with ducks.

Multiple inheritance

When we think of inheritance in our own family tree, we can see that we inherit features from more than just one parent. When strangers tell a proud mother that her son has *his father's eyes*, she will typically respond along the lines of, *yes, but he got my nose*.

Object-oriented design can also feature such **multiple inheritance**, which allows a subclass to inherit functionality from multiple parent classes. In practice, multiple inheritance can be a tricky business, and some programming languages (most famously, Java) strictly prohibit it. However, multiple inheritance can have its uses. Most often, it can be used to create objects that have two distinct sets of behaviors. For example, an object designed to connect to a scanner to make an image and send a fax of the scanned image might be created by inheriting from two separate scanner and faxer objects.

As long as two classes have distinct interfaces, it is not normally harmful for a subclass to inherit from both of them. However, it gets messy if we inherit from two classes that provide overlapping interfaces. The scanner and faxer don't have any overlapping features, so combining features from both is easy. Our counterexample is a motorcycle class that has a move method, and a boat class also featuring a move method.

If we want to merge them into the ultimate amphibious vehicle, how does the resulting class know what to do when we call move? At the design level, this needs to be explained. (As a sailor who lived on a boat, one of the authors really wants to know how this is supposed to work.)

Python has a defined **method resolution order** (**MRO**) to help us understand which of the alternative methods will be used. While the MRO rules are simple, avoiding overlap is even simpler. Multiple inheritance as a "mixin" technique for combining unrelated aspects can be helpful. In many cases, though, a composite object may be easier to design.

Inheritance is a powerful tool for extending behavior and reusing features. It is also one of the most marketable advancements of object-oriented design over earlier paradigms. Therefore, it is often the first tool that object-oriented programmers reach for. However, it is important to recognize that owning a hammer does not turn screws into nails. Inheritance is the perfect solution for obvious *is a* relationships. Beyond this, it can be abused. Programmers often use inheritance to share code between two kinds of objects that are only distantly related, with no *is a* relationship in sight. While this is not necessarily a bad design, it is a terrific opportunity to ask just why they decided to design it that way, and whether a different relationship or design pattern would have been more suitable.

Case study

Our case study will span many of the chapters of this book. We'll be examining a single problem closely from a variety of perspectives. It's very important to look at alternative designs and design patterns; more than once, we'll point out that there's no single right answer: there are a number of good answers. Our intent here is to provide a realistic example that involves realistic depth and complications and leads to difficult trade-off decisions. Our goal is to help the reader apply object-oriented programming and design concepts. This means choosing among the technical alternatives to create something useful.

This first part of the case study is an overview of the problem and why we're tackling it. This background will cover a number of aspects of the problem to set up the design and construction of solutions in later chapters. Part of this overview will include some UML diagrams to capture elements of the problem to be solved. These will evolve in later chapters as we dive into the consequences of design choices and make changes to those design choices.

As with many realistic problems, the authors bring personal bias and assumptions. For information on the consequences of this, consider books like *Technically Wrong*, by Sara Wachter-Boettcher.

Our users want to automate a job often called **classification**. This is the underpinning idea behind product recommendations: last time, a customer bought product X, so perhaps they'd be interested in a similar product, Y. We've classified their desires and can locate other items in that class of products. This problem can involve complex data organization issues.

It helps to start with something smaller and more manageable. The users eventually want to tackle complex consumer products, but recognize that solving a difficult problem is not a good way to learn how to build this kind of application. It's better to start with something of a manageable level of complexity and then refine and expand it until it does everything they need. In this case study, therefore, we'll be building a classifier for iris species. This is a classic problem, and there's a great deal written about approaches to classifying iris flowers.

A training set of data is required, which the classifier uses as examples of correctly classified irises. We will discuss what the training data looks like in the next section.

We'll create a collection of diagrams using the **Unified Modeling Language (UML)** to help depict and summarize the software we're going to build.

We'll examine the problem using a technique called **4+1 Views**. The views are:

- A **logical view** of the data entities, their static attributes, and their relationships. This is the heart of object-oriented design.
- A **process view** that describes how the data is processed. This can take a variety of forms, including state models, activity diagrams, and sequence diagrams.
- A **development view** of the code components to be built. This diagram shows relationships among software components. This is used to show how class definitions are gathered into modules and packages.
- A **physical view** of the application to be integrated and deployed. In cases where an application follows a common design pattern, a sophisticated diagram isn't necessary. In other cases, a diagram is essential to show how a collection of components are integrated and deployed.
- A **context view** that provides a unifying context for the other four views. The context view will often describe the actors that use (or interact) with the system to be built. This can involve human actors as well as automated interfaces: both are outside the system, and the system must respond to these external actors.

It's common to start with the context view so that we have a sense of what the other views describe. As our understanding of the users and the problem domain evolves, the context will evolve also.

It's very important to recognize that all of these 4+1 views evolve together. A change to one will generally be reflected in other views. It's a common mistake to think that one view is in some way foundational, and that the other views build on it in a cascade of design steps that always lead to software.

We'll start with a summary of the problem and some background before we start trying to analyze the application or design software.

Introduction and problem overview

As we mentioned previously, we'll be starting with a simpler problem – classifying flowers. We want to implement one popular approach called *k*-**nearest neighbors**, or *k*-**NN** for short. We require a training set of data, which the classifier algorithm uses as examples of correctly classified irises. Each training sample has a number of attributes, reduced to numeric scores, and a final, correct, classification (i.e. iris species). In this iris example, each training sample is an iris, with its attributes, such as petal shape, size, and so on, encoded into a numeric vector that is an overall representation of the iris, along with a correct species label for that iris.

Given an unknown sample, an iris whose species we want to know, we can measure the distance between the unknown sample and any of the known samples in the vector space. For some small group of nearby neighbors, we can take a vote. The unknown sample can be classified into the sub-population selected by the majority of the nearby neighbors.

If we only have two dimensions (or attributes), we can diagram the *k*-NN classification like this:

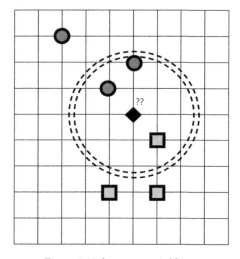

Figure 1.11: k-nearest neighbors

Our unknown sample is a diamond tagged with "??". It's surrounded by known samples of the square and circle species. When we locate the three nearest neighbors, shown inside the dashed circle, we can take a vote and decide that the unknown is most like the Circle species.

One underpinning concept is having tangible, numeric measurements for the various attributes. Converting words, addresses, and other non-ordinal data into an ordinal measurement can be challenging. The good news is that the data we're going to start with data that already has properly ordinal measurements with explicit units of measure.

Another supporting concept is the number of neighbors involved in the voting. This is the k factor in k-nearest neighbors. In our conceptual diagram, we've shown $k=3$ neighbors; two of the three nearest neighbors are circles, with the third being a square. If we change the k-value to 5, this will change the composition of the pool and tip the vote in favor of the squares. Which is right? This is checked by having test data with known right answers to confirm that the classification algorithm works acceptably well. In the preceding diagram, it's clear the diamond was cleverly chosen to be a midway between two clusters, intentionally creating a difficult classification problem.

A popular dataset for learning how this works is the Iris Classification data. See `https://archive.ics.uci.edu/ml/datasets/iris` for some background on this data. This is also available at `https://www.kaggle.com/uciml/iris` and many other places.

More experienced readers may notice some gaps and possible contradictions as we move through the object-oriented analysis and design work. This is intentional. An initial analysis of a problem of any scope will involve learning and rework. This case study will evolve as we learn more. If you've spotted a gap or contradiction, formulate your own design and see if it converges with the lessons learned in subsequent chapters.

Having looked at some aspects of the problem, we can provide a more concrete context with actors and the use cases or scenarios that describe how an actor interacts with the system to be built. We'll start with the context view.

Context view

The context for our application that classifies iris species involves these two classes of actors:

- A "Botanist" who provides the properly classified training data and a properly classified set of test data. The Botanist also runs the test cases to establish the proper parameters for the classification. In the simple case of k-NN, they can decide which k value should be used.

- A "User" who needs to do classification of unknown data. The user has made careful measurements and makes a request with the measurement data to get a classification from this classifier system. The name "User" seems vague, but we're not sure what's better. We'll leave it for now, and put off changing it until we foresee a problem.

This UML context diagram illustrates the two actors and the three scenarios we will explore:

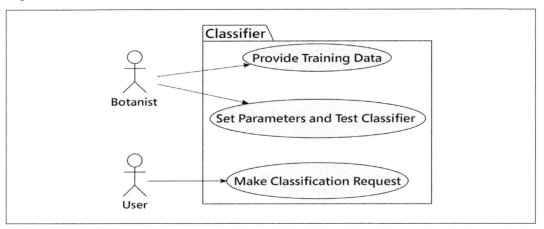

Figure 1.12: UML context diagram

The system as a whole is depicted as a rectangle. It encloses ovals to represent user stories. In the UML, specific shapes have meanings, and we reserve rectangles for objects. Ovals (and circles) are for user stories, which are interfaces to the system.

In order to do any useful processing, we need training data, properly classified. There are two parts to each set of data: a training set and a test set. We'll call the whole assembly "training data" instead of the longer (but more precise) "training and test data."

The tuning parameters are set by the botanist, who must examine the test results to be sure the classifier works. These are the two parameters that can be tuned:

- The distance computation to use
- The number of neighbors to consider for voting

We'll look at these parameters in detail in the *Processing view* section later in this chapter. We'll also revisit these ideas in subsequent case study chapters. The distance computation is an interesting problem.

We can define a set of experiments as a grid of each alternative and methodically fill in the grid with the results of measuring the test set. The combination that provides the best fit will be the recommended parameter set from the botanist. In our case, there are two choices, and the grid is a two-dimensional table, like the one shown below. With more complex algorithms, the "grid" may be a multidimensional space:

		Various k factors		
		k=3	k=5	k=7
Distance computation algorithms	Euclidean	Test results…		
	Manhattan			
	Chebyshev			
	Sorensen			
	Other?			

After the testing, a User can make requests. They provide unknown data to receive classification results from this trained classifier process. In the long run, this "User" won't be a person – they'll be a connection from some website's sales or catalog engine to our clever classifier-based recommendation engine.

We can summarize each of these scenarios with a **use case** or **user story** statement:

- As a Botanist, I want to provide properly classified training and testing data to this system so users can correctly identify plants.
- As a Botanist, I want to examine the test results from the classifier to be sure that new samples are likely to be correctly classified.
- As a User, I want to be able to provide a few key measurements to the classifier and have the iris species correctly classified.

Given the nouns and verbs in the user stories, we can use that information to create a logical view of the data the application will process.

Logical view

Looking at the context diagram, processing starts with training data and testing data. This is properly classified sample data used to test our classification algorithm. The following diagram shows one way to look at a class that contains various training and testing datasets:

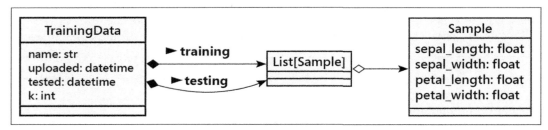

Figure 1.13: Class diagram for training and testing

This shows a Training Data class of objects with the attributes of each instance of this class. The TrainingData object gives our sample collection a name, and some dates where uploading and testing were completed. For now, it seems like each TrainingData object should have a single tuning parameter, k, used for the *k*-NN classifier algorithm. An instance also includes two lists of individual samples: a training list and a testing list.

Each class of objects is depicted in a rectangle with a number of individual sections:

- The top-most section provides a name for the class of objects. In two cases, we've used a type hint, List[Sample]; the generic class, list, is used in a way that ensures the contents of the list are only Sample objects.

- The next section of a class rectangle shows the attributes of each object; these attributes are also called the instance variables of this class.

- Later, we'll add "methods" to the bottom section for instances of the class.

Each object of the Sample class has a handful of attributes: four floating-point measurement values and a string value, which is the botanist-assigned classification for the sample. In this case, we used the attribute name class because that's what it's called in the source data.

The UML arrows show two specific kinds of relationships, highlighted by filled or empty diamonds. A filled diamond shows **composition**: a TrainingData object is composed – in part – of two collections. The open diamond shows **aggregation**: a List[Sample] object is an aggregate of Sample items. To recap what we learned earlier:

- A **composition** is an existential relationship: we can't have `TrainingData` without the two `List[Sample]` objects. And, conversely, a `List[Sample]` object isn't used in our application without being part of a `TrainingData` object.

- An **aggregation**, on the other hand, is a relationship where items can exist independently of each other. In this diagram, a number of `Sample` objects can be part of `List[Sample]` or can exist independently of the list.

It's not clear that the open diamond to show the aggregation of `Sample` objects into a `List` object is relevant. It may be an unhelpful design detail. When in doubt, it's better to omit these kinds of the details until they're clearly required to ensure there's an implementation that meets the user's expectations.

We've shown a `List[Sample]` as a separate class of objects. This is Python's generic `List`, qualified with a specific class of objects, `Sample`, that will be in the list. It's common to avoid this level of detail and summarize the relationships in a diagram like the following:

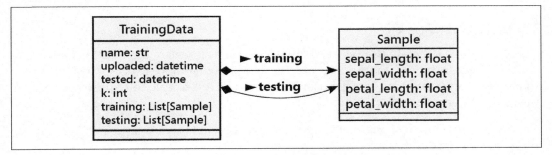

Figure 1.14: Condensed class diagram

This slightly abbreviated form can help with doing analytical work, where the underlying data structures don't matter. It's less helpful for design work, as specific Python class information becomes more important.

Given an initial sketch, we'll compare this logical view with each of the three scenarios mentioned in the context diagram, shown in *Figure 1.12* in the previous section. We want to be sure all of the data and processing in the user stories can be allocated as responsibilities scattered among the classes, attributes, and methods in the diagram.

Walking through the user stories, we uncover these two problems:

- It's not clear how the testing and parameter tuning fit with this diagram. We know there's a *k* factor that's required, but there are no relevant test results to show alternative *k* factors and the consequence of those choices.

- The user's request is not shown at all. Nor is the response to the user. No classes have these items as part of their responsibilities.

The first point suggests we'll need to re-read the user stories and try again to create a better logical view. The second point is a question of boundaries. While the web request and response details are missing, it's more important to describe the essential problem domain – classification and *k*-NN – first. The web services for handling a user's requests is one (of many) solution technologies, and we should set that aside when getting started.

Now, we'll turn our focus to the processing for the data. We're following what seems to be an effective order for creating a description of an application. The data has to be described first; it's the most enduring part, and the thing that is always preserved through each refinement of the processing. The processing can be secondary to the data, because this changes as the context changes and user experience and preferences change.

Process view

There are three separate user stories. This does not necessarily force us to create three process diagrams. For complex processing, there may be more process diagrams than user stories. In some cases, a user story may be too simple to require a carefully designed diagram.

For our application, it seems as though there are at least three unique processes of interest, specifically these:

- Upload the initial set of `Samples` that comprise some `TrainingData`.
- Run a test of the classifier with a given *k* value.
- Make a classification request with a new `Sample` object.

We'll sketch activity diagrams for these use cases. An activity diagram summarizes a number of state changes. The processing begins with a start node and proceeds until an end node is reached. In transaction-based applications, like web services, it's common to omit showing the overall web server engine. This saves us from describing common features of HTTP, including standard headers, cookies, and security concerns. Instead, we generally focus on the unique processing that's performed to create a response for each distinct kind of request.

The activities are shown in round-corner rectangles. Where specific classes of objects or software components are relevant, they can be linked to relevant activities.

What's more important is making sure that the logical view is updated as ideas arise while working on the processing view. It's difficult to get either view done completely in isolation. It's far more important to make incremental changes in each view as new solution ideas arise. In some cases, additional user input is required, and this too will lead to the evolution of these views.

We can sketch a diagram to show how the system responds when the Botanist provides the initial data. Here's the first example:

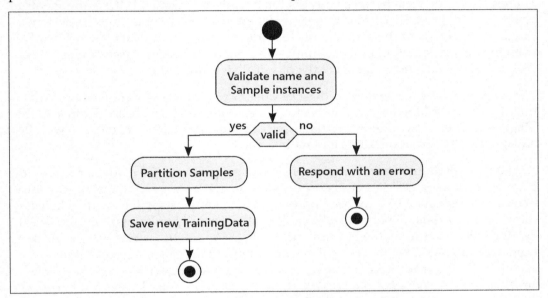

Figure 1.15: Activity diagram

The collection of KnownSample values will be partitioned into two subsets: a training subset and a testing subset. There's no rule in our problem summary or user stories for making this distinction; the gap shows we're missing details in the original user story. When details are missing from the user stories, then the logical view may be incomplete, also. For now, we can labor under an assumption that most of the data – say 75% - will be used for training, and the rest, 25%, will be used for testing.

It often helps to create similar diagrams for each of the user stories. It also helps to be sure that the activities all have relevant classes to implement the steps and represent state changes caused by each step.

We've included a verb, Partition, in this diagram. This suggests a method will be required to implement the verb. This may lead to rethinking the class model to be sure the processing can be implemented.

We'll turn next to considering some of the components to be built. Since this is a preliminary analysis, our ideas will evolve as we do more detailed design and start creating class definitions.

Development view

There's often a delicate balance between the final deployment and the components to be developed. In rare cases, there are few deployment constraints, and the designer can think freely about the components to be developed. A physical view will evolve from the development. In more common cases, there's a specific target architecture that must be used, and elements of the physical view are fixed.

There are several ways to deploy this classifier as part of a larger application. We might build a desktop application, a mobile application, or a website. Because of the ubiquity of internetworked computers, one common approach is to create a website and connect to it from desktops and mobile apps.

A web services architecture, for example, means requests can be made to a server; the responses could be HTML pages for presentation in a browser, or JSON documents that can be displayed by a mobile application. Some requests will provide whole new sets of training data. Other requests will be seek to classify unknown samples. We'll detail the architecture in the physical view below. We might want to use the Flask framework to build a web service. For more information on Flask, see *Mastering Flask Web Development*, https://www.packtpub.com/product/mastering-flask-web-development-second-edition/9781788995405, or *Learning Flask Framework*, https://www.packtpub.com/product/learning-flask-framework/9781783983360.

The following diagram shows some of the components we need would need to build for a Flask-based application:

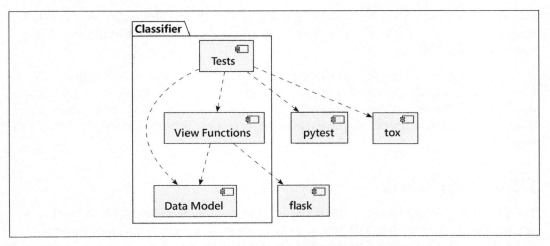

Figure 1.16: Components to be built

This diagram shows a Python package, `Classifier`, that contains a number of modules. The three top-level modules are:

- **Data Model**: (Since this is still analysis time, the name here is not properly Pythonic; we'll change it later as we move into implementation.) It's often helpful to separate the classes that define the problem domain into modules. This makes it possible for us to test them in isolation from any particular application that uses those classes. We'll focus on this part, since it is foundational.

- **View Functions**: (Also an analysis name, not a Pythonic implementation name.) This module will create an instance of the `Flask` class, our application. It will define the functions that handle requests by creating responses that can be displayed by a mobile app or a browser. These functions expose features of the model, and don't involve the same depth and complexity of the model itself; we won't focus on this component in the case study.

- **Tests**: This will have unit tests for the model and view functions. While tests are essential for being sure the software is usable, they are the subject of *Chapter 13, Testing Object-Oriented Programs*.

We have included dependency arrows, using dashed lines. These can be annotated with the Python-specific "imports" label to help clarify how the various packages and modules are related.

As we move through the design in later chapters, we'll expand on this initial view. Having thought about what needs to be built, we can now consider how it's deployed by drawing a physical view of the application. As noted above, there's a delicate dance between development and deployment. The two views are often built together.

Physical view

The physical view shows how the software will be installed into physical hardware. For web services, we often talk about a **continuous integration and continuous deployment (CI/CD)** pipeline. This means that a change to the software is tested as a unit, integrated with the existing applications, tested as an integrated whole, then deployed for the users.

While it's common to assume a website, this can also be deployed as a command-line application. It might be run on a local computer. It might also be run on a computer in the cloud. Another choice is to build a web application around the core classifier.

The following diagram shows a view of a web application server:

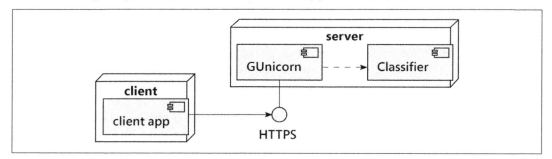

Figure 1.17: Application server diagram

This diagram shows the client and server nodes as three-dimensional "boxes" with "components" installed on them. We've identified three components:

- A Client running the **client app** application. This application connects to the classifier web service and makes RESTful requests. It might be a website, written in JavaScript. It might be a mobile application, written in Kotlin or Swift. All of these frontends have a common **HTTPS** connection to our web server. This secure connection requires some configuration of certificates and encryption key pairs.

- The **GUnicorn** web server. This server can handle a number of details of web service requests, including the important HTTPS protocol. See `https://docs.gunicorn.org/en/stable/index.html` for details.

- Our **Classifier** application. From this view, the complexities have been omitted, and the entire `Classifier` package is reduced to a small component in a larger web services framework. This could be built using the Flask framework.

Of these components, the Client's **client app** is not part of the work being done to develop the classifier. We've included this to illustrate the context, but we're not really going to be building it.

We've used a dotted dependency arrow to show that our `Classifier` application is a dependency from the web server. **GUnicorn** will import our web server object and use it to respond to requests.

Now that we've sketched out the application, we can consider writing some code. As we write, it helps to keep the diagrams up-to-date. Sometimes, they serve as a handy roadmap in a wilderness of code.

Conclusion

There are several key concepts in this case study:

1. Software applications can be rather complicated. There are five views to depict the users, the data, the processing, the components to be built, and the target physical implementation.

2. Mistakes will be made. This overview has some gaps in it. It's important to move forward with partial solutions. One of Python's advantages is the ability to build software quickly, meaning we're not deeply invested in bad ideas. We can (and should) remove and replace code quickly.

3. Be open to extensions. After we implement this, we'll see that setting the k parameter is a tedious exercise. An important next step is to automate tuning using a grid search tuning algorithm. It's often helpful to set these things aside and get something that works first, then extend working software later to add this helpful feature.

4. Try to assign clear responsibilities to each class. This has been moderately successful, and some responsibilities are vague or omitted entirely. We'll revisit this as we expand this initial analysis into implementation details.

In later chapters, we'll dive more deeply into these various topics. Because our intent is to present realistic work, this will involve rework. Some design decisions may be revised as the reader is exposed to more and more of the available objected-oriented programming techniques in Python. Additionally, some parts of the solution will evolve as our understanding of design choices and the problem itself evolves. Rework based on lessons learned is a consequence of an agile approach to development.

Recall

Some key points in this chapter:

- Analyzing problem requirements in an object-oriented context
- How to draw **Unified Modeling Language** (**UML**) diagrams to communicate how the system works
- Discussing object-oriented systems using the correct terminology and jargon
- Understanding the distinction between class, object, attribute, and behavior
- Some OO design techniques are used more than others. In our case study example, we focused on a few:
    - Encapsulating features into classes
    - Inheritance to extend a class with new features
    - Composition to build a class from component objects

Exercises

This is a practical book. As such, we're not assigning a bunch of fake object-oriented analysis problems to create designs for you to analyze and design. Instead, we want to give you some ideas that you can apply to your own projects. If you have previous object-oriented experience, you won't need to put much effort into this chapter. However, they are useful mental exercises if you've been using Python for a while, but have never really cared about all that class stuff.

First, think about a recent programming project you've completed. Identify the most prominent object in the design. Try to think of as many attributes for this object as possible. Did it have the following: Color? Weight? Size? Profit? Cost? Name? ID number? Price? Style?

Think about the attribute types. Were they primitives or classes? Were some of those attributes actually behaviors in disguise? Sometimes, what looks like data is actually calculated from other data on the object, and you can use a method to do those calculations. What other methods or behaviors did the object have? Which objects called those methods? What kinds of relationships did they have with this object?

Now, think about an upcoming project. It doesn't matter what the project is; it might be a fun free-time project or a multi-million-dollar contract. It doesn't have to be a complete application; it could just be one subsystem. Perform a basic object-oriented analysis. Identify the requirements and the interacting objects. Sketch out a class diagram featuring the highest level of abstraction on that system. Identify the major interacting objects. Identify minor supporting objects. Go into detail for the attributes and methods of some of the most interesting ones. Take different objects to different levels of abstraction. Look for places where you can use inheritance or composition. Look for places where you should avoid inheritance.

The goal is not to design a system (although you're certainly welcome to do so if inclination meets both ambition and available time). The goal is to think about object-oriented design. Focusing on projects that you have worked on, or are expecting to work on in the future, simply makes it real.

Lastly, visit your favorite search engine and look up some tutorials on UML. There are dozens, so find one that suits your preferred method of study. Sketch some class diagrams or a sequence diagram for the objects you identified earlier. Don't get too hung up on memorizing the syntax (after all, if it is important, you can always look it up again); just get a feel for the language. Something will stay lodged in your brain, and it can make communicating a bit easier if you can quickly sketch a diagram for your next OOP discussion.

Summary

In this chapter, we took a whirlwind tour through the terminology of the object-oriented paradigm, focusing on object-oriented design. We can separate different objects into a taxonomy of different classes and describe the attributes and behaviors of those objects via the class interface. Abstraction, encapsulation, and information hiding are highly-related concepts. There are many different kinds of relationships between objects, including association, composition, and inheritance. UML syntax can be useful for fun and communication.

In the next chapter, we'll explore how to implement classes and methods in Python.

2

Objects in Python

We have a design in hand and are ready to turn that design into a working program! Of course, it doesn't usually happen this way. We'll be seeing examples and hints for good software design throughout the book, but our focus is object-oriented programming. So, let's have a look at the Python syntax that allows us to create object-oriented software.

After completing this chapter, we will understand the following:

- Python's type hints
- Creating classes and instantiating objects in Python
- Organizing classes into packages and modules
- How to suggest that people don't clobber an object's data, invalidating the internal state
- Working with third-party packages available from the Python Package Index, PyPI

This chapter will also continue our case study, moving into the design of some of the classes.

Introducing type hints

Before we can look closely at creating classes, we need to talk a little bit about what a class is and how we're sure we're using it correctly. The central idea here is that everything in Python is an object.

When we write literal values like `"Hello, world!"` or `42`, we're actually creating instances of built-in classes. We can fire up interactive Python and use the built-in `type()` function on the class that defines the properties of these objects:

```
>>> type("Hello, world!")
<class 'str'>
>>> type(42)
<class 'int'>
```

The point of *object-oriented* programming is to solve a problem via the interactions of objects. When we write `6*7`, the multiplication of the two objects is handled by a method of the built-in `int` class. For more complex behaviors, we'll often need to write unique, new classes.

Here are the first two core rules of how Python objects work:

- Everything in Python is an object
- Every object is defined by being an instance of at least one class

These rules have many interesting consequences. A class definition we write, using the `class` statement, creates a new object of class `type`. When we create an **instance** of a class, the class object will be used to create and initialize the instance object.

What's the distinction between class and type? The `class` statement lets us define new types. Because the `class` statement is what we use, we'll call them classes throughout the text. See *Python objects, types, classes, and instances - a glossary* by Eli Bendersky: `https://eli.thegreenplace.net/2012/03/30/python-objects-types-classes-and-instances-a-glossary` for this useful quote:

> *"The terms "class" and "type" are an example of two names referring to the same concept."*

We'll follow common usage and call the annotations **type hints**.

There's another important rule:

- A variable is a reference to an object. Think of a yellow sticky note with a name scrawled on it, slapped on a thing.

This doesn't seem too earth-shattering but it's actually pretty cool. It means the type information – what an object is – is defined by the class(es) associated with the object. This type information is not attached to the *variable* in any way. This leads to code like the following being valid but very confusing Python:

```
>>> a_string_variable = "Hello, world!"
>>> type(a_string_variable)
<class 'str'>
>>> a_string_variable = 42
>>> type(a_string_variable)
<class 'int'>
```

We created an object using a built-in class, str. We assigned a long name, a_string_variable, to the object. Then, we created an object using a different built-in class, int. We assigned this object the same name. (The previous string object has no more references and ceases to exist.)

Here are the two steps, shown side by side, showing how the variable is moved from object to object:

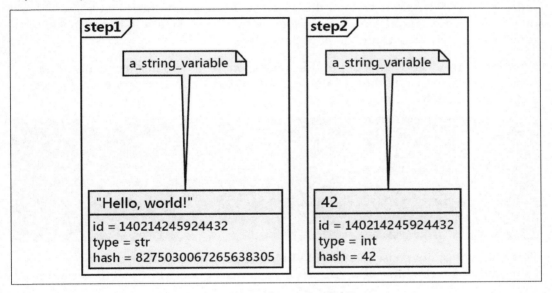

Figure 2.1: Variable names and objects

The various properties are part of the object, not the variable. When we check the type of a variable with type(), we see the type of the object the variable currently references. The variable doesn't have a type of its own; it's nothing more than a name. Similarly, asking for the id() of a variable shows the ID of the object the variable refers to. So obviously, the name a_string_variable is a bit misleading if we assign the name to an integer object.

Type checking

Let's push the relationship between object and type a step further, and look at some more consequences of these rules. Here's a function definition:

```
>>> def odd(n):
...     return n % 2 != 0

>>> odd(3)
True
>>> odd(4)
False
```

This function does a little computation on a parameter variable, n. It computes the remainder after division, the modulo. If we divide an odd number by two, we'll have one left over. If we divide an even number by two, we'll have zero left over. This function returns a true value for all odd numbers.

What happens when we fail to provide a number? Well, let's just try it and see (a common way to learn Python!). Entering code at the interactive prompt, we'll get something like this:

```
>>> odd("Hello, world!")
Traceback (most recent call last):
  File "<doctestexamples.md[9]>", line 1, in <module>
odd("Hello, world!")
  File "<doctestexamples.md[6]>", line 2, in odd
    return n % 2 != 0
TypeError: not all arguments converted during string formatting
```

This is an important consequence of Python's super-flexible rules: nothing prevents us from doing something silly that may raise an exception. This is an important tip:

 Python doesn't prevent us from attempting to use non-existent methods of objects.

In our example, the % operator provided by the str class doesn't work the same way as the % operator provided by the int class, raising an exception. For strings, the % operator isn't used very often, but it does interpolation: "a=%d" % 113 computes a string 'a=113'; if there's no format specification like %d on the left side, the exception is a TypeError. For integers, it's the remainder in division: 355 % 113 returns an integer, 16.

This flexibility reflects an explicit trade-off favoring ease of use over sophisticated prevention of potential problems. This allows a person to use a variable name with little mental overhead.

Python's internal operators check that operands meet the requirements of the operator. The function definition we wrote, however, does not include any runtime type checking. Nor do we want to add code for runtime type checking. Instead, we use tools to examine code as part of testing. We can provide annotations, called **type hints**, and use tools to examine our code for consistency among the type hints.

First, we'll look at the annotations. In a few contexts, we can follow a variable name with a colon, :, and a type name. We can do this in the parameters to functions (and methods). We can also do this in assignment statements. Further, we can also add -> syntax to a function (or a class method) definition to explain the expected return type.

Here's how type hints look:

```
>>> def odd(n: int) -> bool:
...      return n % 2 != 0
```

We've added two type hints to our odd() little function definition. We've specified that argument values for the n parameter should be integers. We've also specified that the result will be one of the two values of the Boolean type.

While the hints consume some storage, they have no runtime impact. Python politely ignores these hints; this means they're optional. People reading your code, however, will be more than delighted to see them. They are a great way to inform the reader of your intent. You can omit them while you're learning, but you'll love them when you go back to expand something you wrote earlier.

The *mypy* tool is commonly used to check the hints for consistency. It's not built into Python, and requires a separate download and install. We'll talk about virtual environments and installation of tools later in this chapter, in the *Third-party libraries* section. For now, you can use python -m pip install mypy or conda install mypy if you're using *the conda tool*.

Let's say we had a file, bad_hints.py, in a src directory, with these two functions and a few lines to call the main() function:

```
def odd(n: int) -> bool:
    return n % 2 != 0

def main():
    print(odd("Hello, world!"))

if __name__ == "__main__":
    main()
```

When we run the mypy command at the OS's terminal prompt:

```
% mypy -strict src/bad_hints.py
```

The *mypy* tool is going to spot a bunch of potential problems, including at least these:

```
src/bad_hints.py:12: error: Function is missing a return type
annotation
src/bad_hints.py:12: note: Use "-> None" if function does not return a
value
src/bad_hints.py:13: error: Argument 1 to "odd" has incompatible type
"str"; expected "int"
```

The def main(): statement is on *line 12* of our example because our file has a pile of comments not shown above. For your version, the error might be on *line 1*. Here are the two problems:

- The main() function doesn't have a return type; *mypy* suggests including -> None to make the absence of a return value perfectly explicit.

- More important is *line 13*: the code will try to evaluate the odd() function using a str value. This doesn't match the type hint for odd() and indicates another possible error.

Most of the examples in this book will have type hints. We think they're always helpful, especially in a pedagogical context, even though they're optional. Because most of Python is generic with respect to type, there are a few cases where Python behavior is difficult to describe via a succinct, expressive hint. We'll steer clear of these edge cases in this book.

Python Enhancement Proposal (PEP) 585 covers some new language features to make type hints a bit simpler. We've used *mypy* version 0.812 to test all of the examples in this book. Any older version will encounter problems with some of the newer syntax and annotation techniques.

Now that we've talked about how parameters and attributes are described with type hints, let's actually build some classes.

Creating Python classes

We don't have to write much Python code to realize that Python is a very *clean* language. When we want to do something, we can just do it, without having to set up a bunch of prerequisite code. The ubiquitous *hello world* in Python, as you've likely seen, is only one line.

Similarly, the simplest class in Python 3 looks like this:

```
class MyFirstClass:
    pass
```

There's our first object-oriented program! The class definition starts with the class keyword. This is followed by a name (of our choice) identifying the class and is terminated with a colon.

 The class name must follow standard Python variable naming rules (it must start with a letter or underscore, and can only be comprised of letters, underscores, or numbers). In addition, the Python style guide (search the web for *PEP 8*) recommends that classes should be named using what PEP 8 calls **CapWords** notation (start with a capital letter; any subsequent words should also start with a capital).

The class definition line is followed by the class contents, indented. As with other Python constructs, indentation is used to delimit the classes, rather than braces, keywords, or brackets, as many other languages use. Also, in line with the style guide, use four spaces for indentation unless you have a compelling reason not to (such as fitting in with somebody else's code that uses tabs for indents).

Since our first class doesn't actually add any data or behaviors, we simply use the `pass` keyword on the second line as a placeholder to indicate that no further action needs to be taken.

We might think there isn't much we can do with this most basic class, but it does allow us to instantiate objects of that class. We can load the class into the Python 3 interpreter, so we can interactively play with it. To do this, save the class definition mentioned earlier in a file named `first_class.py` and then run the `python -i first_class.py` command. The `-i` argument tells Python to *run the code and then drop to the interactive interpreter*. The following interpreter session demonstrates a basic interaction with this class:

```
>>> a = MyFirstClass()
>>> b = MyFirstClass()
>>> print(a)
<__main__.MyFirstClass object at 0xb7b7faec>
>>> print(b)
<__main__.MyFirstClass object at 0xb7b7fbac>
```

This code instantiates two objects from the new class, assigning the object variable names a and b. Creating an instance of a class is a matter of typing the class name, followed by a pair of parentheses. It looks much like a function call; **calling** a class will create a new object. When printed, the two objects tell us which class they are and what memory address they live at. Memory addresses aren't used much in Python code, but here, they demonstrate that there are two distinct objects involved.

We can see they're distinct objects by using the `is` operator:

```
>>> a is b
False
```

This can help reduce confusion when we've created a bunch of objects and assigned different variable names to the objects.

Adding attributes

Now, we have a basic class, but it's fairly useless. It doesn't contain any data, and it doesn't do anything. What do we have to do to assign an attribute to a given object?

In fact, we don't have to do anything special in the class definition to be able to add attributes. We can set arbitrary attributes on an instantiated object using dot notation. Here's an example:

```
class Point:
    pass

p1 = Point()
p2 = Point()

p1.x = 5
p1.y = 4

p2.x = 3
p2.y = 6

print(p1.x, p1.y)
print(p2.x, p2.y)
```

If we run this code, the two `print` statements at the end tell us the new attribute values on the two objects:

```
5 4
3 6
```

This code creates an empty `Point` class with no data or behaviors. Then, it creates two instances of that class and assigns each of those instances x and y coordinates to identify a point in two dimensions. All we need to do to assign a value to an attribute on an object is use the `<object>.<attribute> = <value>` syntax. This is sometimes referred to as **dot notation**. The value can be anything: a Python primitive, a built-in data type, or another object. It can even be a function or another class!

Creating attributes like this is confusing to the *mypy* tool. There's no easy way to include the hints in the `Point` class definition. We can include hints on the assignment statements, like this: `p1.x: float = 5`. In general, there's a much, much better approach to type hints and attributes that we'll examine in the *Initializing the object* section, later in this chapter. First, though, we'll add behaviors to our class definition.

Making it do something

Now, having objects with attributes is great, but object-oriented programming is really about the interaction between objects. We're interested in invoking actions that cause things to happen to those attributes. We have data; now it's time to add behaviors to our classes.

Let's model a couple of actions on our `Point` class. We can start with a **method** called `reset`, which moves the point to the origin (the origin is the place where x and y are both zero). This is a good introductory action because it doesn't require any parameters:

```
class Point:
    def reset(self):
        self.x = 0
        self.y = 0

p = Point()
p.reset()
print(p.x, p.y)
```

This `print` statement shows us the two zeros on the attributes:

```
0 0
```

In Python, a method is formatted identically to a function. It starts with the `def` keyword, followed by a space, and the name of the method. This is followed by a set of parentheses containing the parameter list (we'll discuss that `self` parameter, sometimes called the instance variable, in just a moment), and terminated with a colon. The next line is indented to contain the statements inside the method. These statements can be arbitrary Python code operating on the object itself and any parameters passed in, as the method sees fit.

We've omitted type hints in the `reset()` method because it's not the most widely used place for hints. We'll look at the best place for hints in the *Initializing the object* section. We'll look a little more at these instance variables, first, and how the `self` variable works.

Talking to yourself

The one difference, syntactically, between methods of classes and functions outside classes is that methods have one required argument. This argument is conventionally named `self`; I've never seen a Python programmer use any other name for this variable (convention is a very powerful thing). There's nothing technically stopping you, however, from calling it `this` or even `Martha`, but it's best to acknowledge the social pressure of the Python community codified in PEP 8 and stick with `self`.

The `self` argument to a method is a reference to the object that the method is being invoked on. The object is an instance of a class, and this is sometimes called the instance variable.

We can access attributes and methods of that object via this variable. This is exactly what we do inside the reset method when we set the x and y attributes of the self object.

> Pay attention to the difference between a **class** and an **object** in this discussion. We can think of the **method** as a function attached to a class. The self parameter refers to a specific instance of the class. When you call the method on two different objects, you are calling the same method twice, but passing two different **objects** as the self parameter.

Notice that when we call the p.reset() method, we do not explicitly pass the self argument into it. Python automatically takes care of this part for us. It knows we're calling a method on the p object, so it automatically passes that object, p, to the method of the class, Point.

For some, it can help to think of a method as a function that happens to be part of a class. Instead of calling the method on the object, we could invoke the function as defined in the class, explicitly passing our object as the self argument:

```
>>> p = Point()
>>> Point.reset(p)
>>> print(p.x, p.y)
```

The output is the same as in the previous example because, internally, the exact same process has occurred. This is not really a good programming practice, but it can help to cement your understanding of the self argument.

What happens if we forget to include the self argument in our class definition? Python will bail with an error message, as follows:

```
>>> class Point:
...     def reset():
...         pass
...
>>> p = Point()
>>> p.reset()
Traceback (most recent call last):
  File "<stdin>", line 1, in <module>
TypeError: reset() takes 0 positional arguments but 1 was given
```

The error message is not as clear as it could be ("Hey, silly, you forgot to define the method with a `self` parameter" could be more informative). Just remember that when you see an error message that indicates missing arguments, the first thing to check is whether you forgot the `self` parameter in the method definition.

More arguments

How do we pass multiple arguments to a method? Let's add a new method that allows us to move a point to an arbitrary position, not just to the origin. We can also include a method that accepts another `Point` object as input and returns the distance between them:

```python
import math

class Point:
    def move(self, x: float, y: float) -> None:
        self.x = x
        self.y = y

    def reset(self) -> None:
        self.move(0, 0)

    def calculate_distance(self, other: "Point") -> float:
        return math.hypot(self.x - other.x, self.y - other.y)
```

We've defined a class with two attributes, x, and y, and three separate methods, move(), reset(), and calculate_distance().

The move() method accepts two arguments, x and y, and sets the values on the self object. The reset() method calls the move() method, since a reset is just a move to a specific known location.

The calculate_distance() method computes the Euclidean distance between two points. (There are a number of other ways to look at distance. In the *Chapter 3, When Objects Are Alike*, case study, we'll look at some alternatives.) For now, we hope you understand the math. The definition is $\sqrt{(x_s - x_o)^2 + (y_s - y_o)^2}$, which is the math.hypot() function. In Python we'll use `self.x`, but mathematicians often prefer to write x_s.

Here's an example of using this class definition. This shows how to call a method with arguments: include the arguments inside the parentheses and use the same dot notation to access the method name within the instance. We just picked some random positions to test the methods. The test code calls each method and prints the results on the console:

```
>>> point1 = Point()
>>> point2 = Point()

>>> point1.reset()
>>> point2.move(5, 0)
>>> print(point2.calculate_distance(point1))
5.0
>>> assert point2.calculate_distance(point1) ==
point1.calculate_distance(
...     point2
... )
>>> point1.move(3, 4)
>>> print(point1.calculate_distance(point2))
4.47213595499958
>>> print(point1.calculate_distance(point1))
0.0
```

The assert statement is a marvelous test tool; the program will bail if the expression after assert evaluates to False (or zero, empty, or None). In this case, we use it to ensure that the distance is the same regardless of which point called the other point's calculate_distance() method. We'll see a lot more use of assert in *Chapter 13, Testing Object-Oriented Programs*, where we'll write more rigorous tests.

Initializing the object

If we don't explicitly set the x and y positions on our Point object, either using move or by accessing them directly, we'll have a broken Point object with no real position. What will happen when we try to access it?

Well, let's just try it and see. *Try it and see* is an extremely useful tool for Python study. Open up your interactive interpreter and type away. (Using the interactive prompt is, after all, one of the tools we used to write this book.)

The following interactive session shows what happens if we try to access a missing attribute. If you saved the previous example as a file or are using the examples distributed with the book, you can load it into the Python interpreter with the `python -i more_arguments.py` command:

```
>>> point = Point()
>>> point.x = 5
>>> print(point.x)
5
>>> print(point.y)
Traceback (most recent call last):
  File "<stdin>", line 1, in <module>
AttributeError: 'Point' object has no attribute 'y'
```

Well, at least it threw a useful exception. We'll cover exceptions in detail in *Chapter 4, Expecting the Unexpected*. You've probably seen them before (especially the ubiquitous `SyntaxError`, which means you typed something incorrectly!). At this point, simply be aware that it means something went wrong.

The output is useful for debugging. In the interactive interpreter, it tells us the error occurred at *line 1*, which is only partially true (in an interactive session, only one statement is executed at a time). If we were running a script in a file, it would tell us the exact line number, making it easy to find the offending code. In addition, it tells us that the error is an `AttributeError`, and gives a helpful message telling us what that error means.

We can catch and recover from this error, but in this case, it feels like we should have specified some sort of default value. Perhaps every new object should be `reset()` by default, or maybe it would be nice if we could force the user to tell us what those positions should be when they create the object.

Interestingly, ***mypy*** can't determine whether y is supposed to be an attribute of a `Point` object. Attributes are – by definition – dynamic, so there's no simple list that's part of a class definition. However, Python has some widely followed conventions that can help name the expected set of attributes.

Most object-oriented programming languages have the concept of a **constructor**, a special method that creates and initializes the object when it is created. Python is a little different; it has a constructor and an initializer. The constructor method, `__new__()`, is rarely used unless you're doing something very exotic. So, we'll start our discussion with the much more common initialization method, `__init__()`.

The Python initialization method is the same as any other method, except it has a special name, __init__. The leading and trailing double underscores mean this is a special method that the Python interpreter will treat as a special case.

 Never name a method of your own with leading and trailing double underscores. It may mean nothing to Python today, but there's always the possibility that the designers of Python will add a function that has a special purpose with that name in the future. When they do, your code will break.

Let's add an initialization function on our Point class that requires the user to supply x and y coordinates when the Point object is instantiated:

```
class Point:
    def __init__(self, x: float, y: float) -> None:
        self.move(x, y)

    def move(self, x: float, y: float) -> None:
        self.x = x
        self.y = y

    def reset(self) -> None:
        self.move(0, 0)

    def calculate_distance(self, other: "Point") -> float:
        return math.hypot(self.x - other.x, self.y - other.y)
```

Constructing a Point instance now looks like this:

```
point = Point(3, 5)
print(point.x, point.y)
```

Now, our Point object can never go without both x and y coordinates! If we try to construct a Point instance without including the proper initialization parameters, it will fail with a not enough arguments error similar to the one we received earlier when we forgot the self argument in a method definition.

Most of the time, we put our initialization statements in an __init__() function. It's very important to be sure that all of the attributes are initialized in the __init__() method. Doing this helps the *mypy* tool by providing all of the attributes in one obvious place. It helps people reading your code, also; it saves them from having to read the whole application to find mysterious attributes set outside the class definition.

While they're optional, it's generally helpful to include type annotations on the method parameters and result values. After each parameter name, we've included the expected type of each value. At the end of the definition, we've included the two-character -> operator and the type returned by the method.

Type hints and defaults

As we've noted a few times now, hints are optional. They don't do anything at runtime. There are tools, however, that can examine the hints to check for consistency. The *mypy* tool is widely used to check type hints.

If we don't want to make the two arguments required, we can use the same syntax Python functions use to provide default arguments. The keyword argument syntax appends an equals sign after each variable name. If the calling object does not provide this argument, then the default argument is used instead. The variables will still be available to the function, but they will have the values specified in the argument list. Here's an example:

```python
class Point:
    def __init__(self, x: float = 0, y: float = 0) -> None:
        self.move(x, y)
```

The definitions for the individual parameters can get long, leading to very long lines of code. In some examples, you'll see this single logical line of code expanded to multiple physical lines. This relies on the way Python combines physical lines to match ( )'s. We might write this when the line gets long:

```python
class Point:
    def __init__(
        self,
        x: float = 0,
        y: float = 0
    ) -> None:
        self.move(x, y)
```

This style isn't used very often, but it's valid and keeps the lines shorter and easier to read.

The type hints and defaults are handy, but there's even more we can do to provide a class that's easy to use and easy to extend when new requirements arise. We'll add documentation in the form of docstrings.

Explaining yourself with docstrings

Python can be an extremely easy-to-read programming language; some might say it is self-documenting. However, when carrying out object-oriented programming, it is important to write API documentation that clearly summarizes what each object and method does. Keeping documentation up to date is difficult; the best way to do it is to write it right into our code.

Python supports this through the use of **docstrings**. Each class, function, or method header can have a standard Python string as the first indented line inside the definition (the line that ends in a colon).

Docstrings are Python strings enclosed within apostrophes (') or quotation marks ("). Often, docstrings are quite long and span multiple lines (the style guide suggests that the line length should not exceed 80 characters), which can be formatted as multi-line strings, enclosed in matching triple apostrophe (''') or triple quote (""") characters.

A docstring should clearly and concisely summarize the purpose of the class or method it is describing. It should explain any parameters whose usage is not immediately obvious, and is also a good place to include short examples of how to use the API. Any caveats or problems an unsuspecting user of the API should be aware of should also be noted.

One of the best things to include in a docstring is a concrete example. Tools like **doctest** can locate and confirm these examples are correct. All the examples in this book are checked with the doctest tool.

To illustrate the use of docstrings, we will end this section with our completely documented `Point` class:

```python
class Point:
    """
    Represents a point in two-dimensional geometric coordinates

    >>> p_0 = Point()
    >>> p_1 = Point(3, 4)
    >>> p_0.calculate_distance(p_1)
    5.0
    """

    def __init__(self, x: float = 0, y: float = 0) -> None:
        """
        Initialize the position of a new point. The x and y
```

```
        coordinates can be specified. If they are not, the
        point defaults to the origin.

        :param x: float x-coordinate
        :param y: float x-coordinate
        """

        self.move(x, y)

    def move(self, x: float, y: float) -> None:
        """
        Move the point to a new location in 2D space.

        :param x: float x-coordinate
        :param y: float x-coordinate
        """

        self.x = x
        self.y = y

    def reset(self) -> None:
        """
        Reset the point back to the geometric origin: 0, 0
        """

        self.move(0, 0)

    def calculate_distance(self, other: "Point") -> float:
        """
        Calculate the Euclidean distance from this point
        to a second point passed as a parameter.

        :param other: Point instance
        :return: float distance
        """

        return math.hypot(self.x - other.x, self.y - other.y)
```

Try typing or loading (remember, it's `python -i point.py`) this file into the interactive interpreter. Then, enter `help(Point)<enter>` at the Python prompt.

You should see nicely formatted documentation for the class, as shown in the following output:

```
Help on class Point in module point_2:

class Point(builtins.object)
 |  Point(x: float = 0, y: float = 0) -> None
 |
 |  Represents a point in two-dimensional geometric coordinates
 |
 |  >>> p_0 = Point()
 |  >>> p_1 = Point(3, 4)
 |  >>> p_0.calculate_distance(p_1)
 |  5.0
 |
 |  Methods defined here:
 |
 |  __init__(self, x: float = 0, y: float = 0) -> None
 |      Initialize the position of a new point. The x and y
 |      coordinates can be specified. If they are not, the
 |      point defaults to the origin.
 |
 |      :param x: float x-coordinate
 |      :param y: float x-coordinate
 |
 |  calculate_distance(self, other: 'Point') -> float
 |      Calculate the Euclidean distance from this point
 |      to a second point passed as a parameter.
 |
 |      :param other: Point instance
 |      :return: float distance
 |
 |  move(self, x: float, y: float) -> None
 |      Move the point to a new location in 2D space.
 |
 |      :param x: float x-coordinate
 |      :param y: float x-coordinate
 |
 |  reset(self) -> None
```

```
|       Reset the point back to the geometric origin: 0, 0
|
|       --------------------------------------------------------
|   Data descriptors defined here:
|
|   __dict__
|       dictionary for instance variables (if defined)
|
|   __weakref__
|       list of weak references to the object (if defined)
```

Not only is our documentation every bit as polished as the documentation for built-in functions, but we can run python -m doctest point_2.py to confirm the example shown in the docstring.

Further, we can run *mypy* to check the type hints, also. Use mypy --strict src/*.py to check all of the files in the src folder. If there are no problems, the *mypy* application doesn't produce any output. (Remember, *mypy* is not part of the standard installation, so you'll need to add it. Check the preface for information on extra packages that need to be installed.)

Modules and packages

Now we know how to create classes and instantiate objects. You don't need to write too many classes (or non-object-oriented code, for that matter) before you start to lose track of them. For small programs, we generally put all our classes into one file and add a little script at the end of the file to start them interacting. However, as our projects grow, it can become difficult to find the one class that needs to be edited among the many classes we've defined. This is where **modules** come in. Modules are Python files, nothing more. The single file in our small program is a module. Two Python files are two modules. If we have two files in the same folder, we can load a class from one module for use in the other module.

The Python module name is the file's *stem*; the name without the .py suffix. A file named model.py is a module named model. Module files are found by searching a path that includes the local directory and the installed packages.

The import statement is used for importing modules or specific classes or functions from modules. We've already seen an example of this in our Point class in the previous section. We used the import statement to get Python's built-in math module and use its hypot() function in the distance calculation. Let's start with a fresh example.

If we are building an e-commerce system, we will likely be storing a lot of data in a database. We can put all the classes and functions related to database access into a separate file (we'll call it something sensible: database.py). Then, our other modules (for example, customer models, product information, and inventory) can import classes from the database module in order to access the database.

Let's start with a module called database. It's a file, database.py, containing a class called Database. A second module called products is responsible for product-related queries. The classes in the products module need to instantiate the Database class from the database module so that they can execute queries on the product table in the database.

There are several variations on the import statement syntax that can be used to access the Database class. One variant is to import the module as a whole:

```
>>> import database
>>> db = database.Database("path/to/data")
```

This version imports the database module, creating a database namespace. Any class or function in the database module can be accessed using the database.<something> notation.

Alternatively, we can import just the one class we need using the from...import syntax:

```
>>> from database import Database
>>> db = Database("path/to/data")
```

This version imported only the Database class from the database module. When we have a few items from a few modules, this can be a helpful simplification to avoid using longer, fully qualified names like database.Database. When we import a number of items from a number of different modules, this can be a potential source of confusion when we omit the qualifiers.

If, for some reason, products already has a class called Database, and we don't want the two names to be confused, we can rename the class when used inside the products module:

```
>>> from database import Database as DB
>>> db = DB("path/to/data")
```

We can also import multiple items in one statement. If our database module also contains a Query class, we can import both classes using the following code:

```
from database import Database, Query
```

We can import all classes and functions from the database module using this syntax:

```
from database import *
```

 Don't do this. Most experienced Python programmers will tell you that you should never use this syntax (a few will tell you there are some very specific situations where it is useful, but we can disagree). One way to learn why to avoid this syntax is to use it and try to understand your code two years later. We can save some time and two years of poorly written code with a quick explanation now!

We've got several reasons for avoiding this:

- When we explicitly import the database class at the top of our file using from database import Database, we can easily see where the Database class comes from. We might use db = Database() 400 lines later in the file, and we can quickly look at the imports to see where that Database class came from. Then, if we need clarification as to how to use the Database class, we can visit the original file (or import the module in the interactive interpreter and use the help(database.Database) command). However, if we use the from database import * syntax, it takes a lot longer to find where that class is located. Code maintenance becomes a nightmare.

- If there are conflicting names, we're doomed. Let's say we have two modules, both of which provide a class named Database. Using from module_1 import * and from module_2 import * means the second import statement overwrites the Database name created by the first import. If we used import module_1 and import module_2, we'd use the module names as qualifiers to disambiguate module_1.Database from module_2.Database.

- In addition, most code editors are able to provide extra functionality, such as reliable code completion, the ability to jump to the definition of a class, or inline documentation, if normal imports are used. The import * syntax can hamper their ability to do this reliably.

- Finally, using the import * syntax can bring unexpected objects into our local namespace. Sure, it will import all the classes and functions defined in the module being imported from, but unless a special __all__ list is provided in the module, this import will also import any classes or modules that were themselves imported into that file!

Every name used in a module should come from a well-specified place, whether it is defined in that module, or explicitly imported from another module. There should be no magic variables that seem to come out of thin air. We should *always* be able to immediately identify where the names in our current namespace originated. We promise that if you use this evil syntax, you will one day have extremely frustrating moments of *where on earth can this class be coming from?*

 For fun, try typing import this into your interactive interpreter. It prints a nice poem (with a couple of inside jokes) summarizing some of the idioms that Pythonistas tend to practice. Specific to this discussion, note the line "Explicit is better than implicit." Explicitly importing names into your namespace makes your code much easier to navigate than the implicit from module import * syntax.

Organizing modules

As a project grows into a collection of more and more modules, we may find that we want to add another level of abstraction, some kind of nested hierarchy on our modules' levels. However, we can't put modules inside modules; one file can hold only one file after all, and modules are just files.

Files, however, can go in folders, and so can modules. A **package** is a collection of modules in a folder. The name of the package is the name of the folder. We need to tell Python that a folder is a package to distinguish it from other folders in the directory. To do this, place a (normally empty) file in the folder named __init__.py. If we forget this file, we won't be able to import modules from that folder.

Let's put our modules inside an ecommerce package in our working folder, which will also contain a main.py file to start the program. Let's additionally add another package inside the ecommerce package for various payment options.

We need to exercise some caution in creating deeply nested packages. The general advice in the Python community is "flat is better than nested." In this example, we need to create a nested package because there are some common features to all of the various payment alternatives.

The folder hierarchy will look like this, rooted under a directory in the project folder, commonly named `src`:

```
src/
  +-- main.py
  +-- ecommerce/
      +-- __init__.py
      +-- database.py
      +-- products.py
      +-- payments/
      |   +-- __init__.py
      |   +-- common.py
      |   +-- square.py
      |   +-- stripe.py
      +-- contact/
          +-- __init__.py
          +-- email.py
```

The `src` directory will be part of an overall project directory. In addition to `src`, the project will often have directories with names like `docs` and `tests`. It's common for the project parent directory to also have configuration files for tools like *mypy* among others. We'll return to this in *Chapter 13, Testing Object-Oriented Programs*.

When importing modules or classes between packages, we have to be cautious about the structure of our packages. In Python 3, there are two ways of importing modules: absolute imports and relative imports. We'll look at each of them separately.

Absolute imports

Absolute imports specify the complete path to the module, function, or class we want to import. If we need access to the `Product` class inside the `products` module, we could use any of these syntaxes to perform an absolute import:

```
>>> import ecommerce.products
>>> product = ecommerce.products.Product("name1")
```

Or, we could specifically import a single class definition from the module within a package:

```
>>> from ecommerce.products import Product
>>> product = Product("name2")
```

Or, we could import an entire module from the containing package:

```
>>> from ecommerce import products
>>> product = products.Product("name3")
```

The `import` statements use the period operator to separate packages or modules. A package is a namespace that contains module names, much in the way an object is a namespace containing attribute names.

These statements will work from any module. We could instantiate a `Product` class using this syntax in `main.py`, in the `database` module, or in either of the two payment modules. Indeed, assuming the packages are available to Python, it will be able to import them. For example, the packages can also be installed in the Python `site-packages` folder, or the `PYTHONPATH` environment variable could be set to tell Python which folders to search for packages and modules it is going to import.

With these choices, which syntax do we choose? It depends on your audience and the application at hand. If there are dozens of classes and functions inside the `products` module that we want to use, we'd generally import the module name using the `from ecommerce import products` syntax, and then access the individual classes using `products.Product`. If we only need one or two classes from the `products` module, we can import them directly using the `from ecommerce.products import Product` syntax. It's important to write whatever makes the code easiest for others to read and extend.

Relative imports

When working with related modules inside a deeply nested package, it seems kind of redundant to specify the full path; we know what our parent module is named. This is where **relative imports** come in. Relative imports identify a class, function, or module as it is positioned relative to the current module. They only make sense inside module files, and, further, they only make sense where there's a complex package structure.

For example, if we are working in the `products` module and we want to import the `Database` class from the `database` module next to it, we could use a relative import:

```
from .database import Database
```

The period in front of `database` says *use the database module inside the current package*. In this case, the current package is the package containing the `products.py` file we are currently editing, that is, the `ecommerce` package.

If we were editing the `stripe` module inside the `ecommerce.payments` package, we would want, for example, to *use the database package inside the parent package* instead. This is easily done with two periods, as shown here:

```
from ..database import Database
```

We can use more periods to go further up the hierarchy, but at some point, we have to acknowledge that we have too many packages. Of course, we can also go down one side and back up the other. The following would be a valid import from the `ecommerce.contact` package containing an `email` module if we wanted to import the `send_mail` function into our `payments.stripe` module:

```
from ..contact.email import send_mail
```

This import uses two periods indicating *the parent of the payments.stripe package,* and then uses the normal `package.module` syntax to go back down into the `contact` package to name the `email` module.

Relative imports aren't as useful as they might seem. As mentioned earlier, the *Zen of Python* (you can read it when you run `import this`) suggests "flat is better than nested". Python's standard library is relatively flat, with few packages and even fewer nested packages. If you're familiar with Java, the packages are deeply nested, something the Python community likes to avoid. A relative import is needed to solve a specific problem where module names are reused among packages. They can be helpful in a few cases. Needing more than two dots to locate a common parent-of-a-parent package suggests the design should be flattened out.

Packages as a whole

We can import code that appears to come directly from a package, as opposed to a module inside a package. As we'll see, there's a module involved, but it has a special name, so it's hidden. In this example, we have an `ecommerce` package containing two module files named `database.py` and `products.py`. The `database` module contains a `db` variable that is accessed from a lot of places. Wouldn't it be convenient if this could be imported as `from ecommerce import db` instead of `from ecommerce.database import db`?

Remember the `__init__.py` file that defines a directory as a package? This file can contain any variable or class declarations we like, and they will be available as part of the package. In our example, if the `ecommerce/__init__.py` file contained the following line:

```
from .database import db
```

We could then access the db attribute from `main.py` or any other file using the following import:

```
from ecommerce import db
```

It might help to think of the `ecommerce/__init__.py` file as if it were the `ecommerce.py` file. It lets us view the `ecommerce` package as having a module protocol as well as a package protocol. This can also be useful if you put all your code in a single module and later decide to break it up into a package of modules. The `__init__.py` file for the new package can still be the main point of contact for other modules using it, but the code can be internally organized into several different modules or subpackages.

We recommend not putting much code in an `__init__.py` file, though. Programmers do not expect actual logic to happen in this file, and much like with `from x import *`, it can trip them up if they are looking for the declaration of a particular piece of code and can't find it until they check `__init__.py`.

After looking at modules in general, let's dive into what should be inside a module. The rules are flexible (unlike other languages). If you're familiar with Java, you'll see that Python gives you some freedom to bundle things in a way that's meaningful and informative.

Organizing our code in modules

The Python module is an important focus. Every application or web service has at least one module. Even a seemingly "simple" Python script is a module. Inside any one module, we can specify variables, classes, or functions. They can be a handy way to store the global state without namespace conflicts. For example, we have been importing the `Database` class into various modules and then instantiating it, but it might make more sense to have only one `database` object globally available from the `database` module. The `database` module might look like this:

```python
class Database:
    """The Database Implementation"""

    def __init__(self, connection: Optional[str] = None) -> None:
        """Create a connection to a database."""
        pass

database = Database("path/to/data")
```

Then we can use any of the import methods we've discussed to access the `database` object, for example:

```
from ecommerce.database import database
```

A problem with the preceding class is that the `database` object is created immediately when the module is first imported, which is usually when the program starts up. This isn't always ideal, since connecting to a database can take a while, slowing down startup, or the database connection information may not yet be available because we need to read a configuration file. We could delay creating the database until it is actually needed by calling an `initialize_database()` function to create a module-level variable:

```
db: Optional[Database] = None

def initialize_database(connection: Optional[str] = None) -> None:
    global db
    db = Database(connection)
```

The `Optional[Database]` type hint signals to the *mypy* tool that this may be `None` or it may have an instance of the `Database` class. The `Optional` hint is defined in the `typing` module. This hint can be handy elsewhere in our application to make sure we confirm that the value for the `database` variable is not `None`.

The `global` keyword tells Python that the database variable inside `initialize_database()` is the module-level variable, outside the function. If we had not specified the variable as global, Python would have created a new local variable that would be discarded when the function exits, leaving the module-level value unchanged.

We need to make one additional change. We need to import the `database` module as a whole. We can't import the `db` object from inside the module; it might not have been initialized. We need to be sure `database.initialize_database()` is called before `db` will have a meaningful value. If we wanted direct access to the database object, we'd use `database.db`.

A common alternative is a function that returns the current database object. We could import this function everywhere we needed access to the database:

```
def get_database(connection: Optional[str] = None) -> Database:
    global db
    if not db:
        db = Database(connection)
    return db
```

As these examples illustrate, all module-level code is executed immediately at the time it is imported. The `class` and `def` statements create code objects to be executed later when the function is called. This can be a tricky thing for scripts that perform execution, such as the main script in our e-commerce example. Sometimes, we write a program that does something useful, and then later find that we want to import a function or class from that module into a different program. However, as soon as we import it, any code at the module level is immediately executed. If we are not careful, we can end up running the first program when we really only meant to access a couple of functions inside that module.

To solve this, we should always put our startup code in a function (conventionally, called `main()`) and only execute that function when we know we are running the module as a script, but not when our code is being imported from a different script. We can do this by **guarding** the call to `main` inside a conditional statement, demonstrated as follows:

```python
class Point:
    """
    Represents a point in two-dimensional geometric coordinates.
    """

    pass


def main() -> None:
    """
    Does the useful work.

    >>> main()
    p1.calculate_distance(p2)=5.0
    """

    p1 = Point()
    p2 = Point(3, 4)
    print(f"{p1.calculate_distance(p2)=}")


if __name__ == "__main__":
    main()
```

The `Point` class (and the `main()` function) can be reused without worry. We can import the contents of this module without any surprising processing happening. When we run it as a main program, however, it executes the `main()` function.

This works because every module has a __name__ special variable (remember, Python uses double underscores for special variables, such as a class' __init__ method) that specifies the name of the module when it was imported. When the module is executed directly with python module.py, it is never imported, so the __name__ is arbitrarily set to the "__main__" string.

 Make it a policy to wrap all your scripts in an
if __name__ == "__main__": test, just in case you write a
function that you may want to be imported by other code at some
point in the future.

So, methods go in classes, which go in modules, which go in packages. Is that all there is to it?

Actually, no. This is the typical order of things in a Python program, but it's not the only possible layout. Classes can be defined anywhere. They are typically defined at the module level, but they can also be defined inside a function or method, like this:

```python
from typing import Optional

class Formatter:
    def format(self, string: str) -> str:
        pass

def format_string(string: str, formatter: Optional[Formatter] = None)
-> str:
    """
    Format a string using the formatter object, which
    is expected to have a format() method that accepts
    a string.
    """

    class DefaultFormatter(Formatter):
        """Format a string in title case."""

        def format(self, string: str) -> str:
            return str(string).title()

    if not formatter:
        formatter = DefaultFormatter()

    return formatter.format(string)
```

We've defined a `Formatter` class as an abstraction to explain what a formatter class needs to have. We haven't used the abstract base class (abc) definitions (we'll look at these in detail in *Chapter 6, Abstract Base Classes and Operator Overloading*). Instead, we've provided the method with no useful body. It has a full suite of type hints, to make sure *mypy* has a formal definition of our intent.

Within the `format_string()` function, we created an internal class that is an extension of the `Formatter` class. This formalizes the expectation that our class inside the function has a specific set of methods. This connection between the definition of the `Formatter` class, the `formatter` parameter, and the concrete definition of the `DefaultFormatter` class assures that we haven't accidentally forgotten something or added something.

We can execute this function like this:

```
>>> hello_string = "hello world, how are you today?"
>>> print(f" input: {hello_string}")
 input: hello world, how are you today?
>>> print(f"output: {format_string(hello_string)}")
output: Hello World, How Are You Today?
```

The `format_string` function accepts a string and optional `Formatter` object and then applies the formatter to that string. If no `Formatter` instance is supplied, it creates a formatter of its own as a local class and instantiates it. Since it is created inside the scope of the function, this class cannot be accessed from anywhere outside of that function. Similarly, functions can be defined inside other functions as well; in general, any Python statement can be executed at any time.

These inner classes and functions are occasionally useful for one-off items that don't require or deserve their own scope at the module level, or only make sense inside a single method. However, it is not common to see Python code that frequently uses this technique.

We've seen how to create classes and how to create modules. With these core techniques, we can start thinking about writing useful, helpful software to solve problems. When the application or service gets big, though, we often have boundary issues. We need to be sure that objects respect each other's privacy and avoid confusing entanglements that make complex software into a spaghetti bowl of interrelationships. We'd prefer each class to be a nicely encapsulated ravioli. Let's look at another aspect of organizing our software to create a good design.

Who can access my data?

Most object-oriented programming languages have a concept of **access control**. This is related to abstraction. Some attributes and methods on an object are marked private, meaning only that object can access them. Others are marked protected, meaning only that class and any subclasses have access. The rest are public, meaning any other object is allowed to access them.

Python doesn't do this. Python doesn't really believe in enforcing laws that might someday get in your way. Instead, it provides unenforced guidelines and best practices. Technically, all methods and attributes on a class are publicly available. If we want to suggest that a method should not be used publicly, we can put a note in docstrings indicating that the method is meant for internal use only (preferably, with an explanation of how the public-facing API works!).

We often remind each other of this by saying "We're all adults here." There's no need to declare a variable as private when we can all see the source code.

By convention, we generally prefix an internal attribute or method with an underscore character, _. Python programmers will understand a leading underscore name to mean *this is an internal variable, think three times before accessing it directly*. But there is nothing inside the interpreter to stop them from accessing it if they think it is in their best interest to do so. Because, if they think so, why should we stop them? We may not have any idea what future uses our classes might be put to, and it may be removed in a future release. It's a pretty clear warning sign to avoid using it.

There's another thing you can do to strongly suggest that outside objects don't access a property or method: prefix it with a double underscore, __. This will perform **name mangling** on the attribute in question. In essence, name mangling means that the method can still be called by outside objects if they really want to do so, but it requires extra work and is a strong indicator that you demand that your attribute remains **private**.

When we use a double underscore, the property is prefixed with _<classname>. When methods in the class internally access the variable, they are automatically unmangled. When external classes wish to access it, they have to do the name mangling themselves. So, name mangling does not guarantee privacy; it only strongly recommends it. This is very rarely used, and often a source of confusion when it is used.

 Don't create new double-underscore names in your own code, it will only cause grief and heartache. Consider this reserved for Python's internally defined special names.

What's important is that encapsulation – as a design principle – assures that the methods of a class encapsulate the state changes for the attributes. Whether or not attributes (or methods) are private doesn't change the essential good design that flows from encapsulation.

The encapsulation principle applies to individual classes as well as a module with a bunch of classes. It also applies to a package with a bunch of modules. As designers of object-oriented Python, we're isolating responsibilities and clearly encapsulating features.

And, of course, we're using Python to solve problems. It turns out there's a huge standard library available to help us create useful software. The vast standard library is why we describe Python as a "batteries included" language. Right out of the box, you have almost everything you need, no running to the store to buy batteries.

Outside the standard library, there's an even larger universe of third-party packages. In the next section, we'll look at how we extend our Python installation with even more ready-made goodness.

Third-party libraries

Python ships with a lovely standard library, which is a collection of packages and modules that are available on every machine that runs Python. However, you'll soon find that it doesn't contain everything you need. When this happens, you have two options:

- Write a supporting package yourself
- Use somebody else's code

We won't be covering the details about turning your packages into libraries, but if you have a problem you need to solve and you don't feel like coding it (the best programmers are extremely lazy and prefer to reuse existing, proven code, rather than write their own), you can probably find the library you want on the **Python Package Index (PyPI)** at `http://pypi.python.org/`. Once you've identified a package that you want to install, you can use a tool called `pip` to install it.

You can install packages using an operating system command such as the following:

```
% python -m pip install mypy
```

If you try this without making any preparation, you'll either be installing the third-party library directly into your system Python directory, or, more likely, will get an error that you don't have permission to update the system Python.

The common consensus in the Python community is that you don't touch any Python that's part of the OS. Older Mac OS X releases had a Python 2.7 installed. This was not really available for end users. It's best to think of it as part of the OS; and ignore it and always install a fresh, new Python.

Python ships with a tool called `venv`, a utility that gives you a Python installation called a **virtual environment** in your working directory. When you activate this environment, commands related to Python will work with your virtual environment's Python instead of the system Python. So, when you run `pip` or `python`, it won't touch the system Python at all. Here's how to use it:

```
cd project_directory
python -m venv env
source env/bin/activate      # on Linux or macOS
env/Scripts/activate.bat     # on Windows
```

(For other OSes, see `https://docs.python.org/3/library/venv.html`, which has all the variations required to activate the environment.)

Once the virtual environment is activated, you are assured that `python -m pip` will install new packages into the virtual environment, leaving any OS Python alone. You can now use the `python -m pip install mypy` command to add the *mypy* tool to your current virtual environment.

On a home computer – where you have access to the privileged files – you can sometimes get away with installing and working with a single, centralized system-wide Python. In an enterprise computing environment, where system-wide directories require special privileges, a virtual environment is required. Because the virtual environment approach always works, and the centralized system-level approach doesn't always work, it's generally a best practice to create and use virtual environments.

It's typical to create a different virtual environment for each Python project. You can store your virtual environments anywhere, but a good practice is to keep them in the same directory as the rest of the project files. When working with version control tools like **Git**, the `.gitignore` file can make sure your virtual environments are not checked into the Git repository.

When starting something new, we often create the directory, and then `cd` into that directory. Then, we'll run the `python -m venv env` utility to create a virtual environment, usually with a simple name like `env`, and sometimes with a more complex name like `CaseStudy39`.

Finally, we can use one of the last two lines in the preceding code (depending on the operating system, as indicated in the comments) to activate the environment.

Each time we do some work on a project, we can `cd` to the directory and execute the `source` (or `activate.bat`) line to use that particular virtual environment. When switching projects, a `deactivate` command unwinds the environment setup.

Virtual environments are essential for keeping your third-party dependencies separate from Python's standard library. It is common to have different projects that depend on different versions of a particular library (for example, an older website might run on Django 1.8, while newer versions run on Django 2.1). Keeping each project in separate virtual environments makes it easy to work in either version of Django. Furthermore, it prevents conflicts between system-installed packages and `pip`-installed packages if you try to install the same package using different tools. Finally, it bypasses any OS permission restrictions surrounding the OS Python.

There are several third-party tools for managing virtual environments effectively. Some of these include `virtualenv`, `pyenv`, `virtualenvwrapper`, and `conda`. If you're working in a data science environment, you'll probably need to use `conda` so you can install more complex packages. There are a number of features leading to a lot of different approaches to solving the problem of managing the huge Python ecosystem of third-party packages.

Case study

This section expands on the object-oriented design of our realistic example. We'll start with the diagrams created using the **Unified Modeling Language** (**UML**) to help depict and summarize the software we're going to build.

We'll describe the various considerations that are part of the Python implementation of the class definitions. We'll start with a review of the diagrams that describe the classes to be defined.

Logical view

Here's the overview of the classes we need to build. This is (except for one new method) the previous chapter's model:

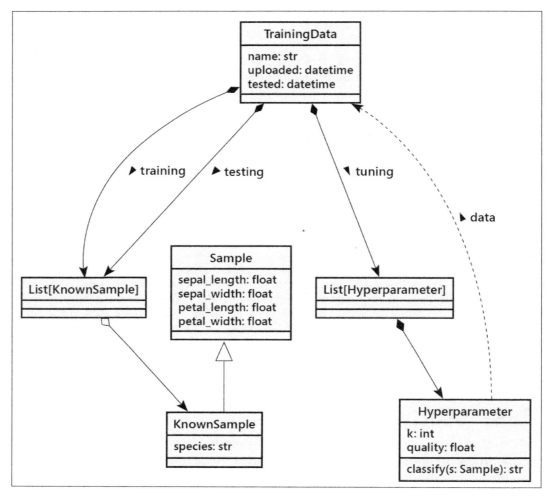

Figure 2.2: Logical view diagram

There are three classes that define our core data model, plus some uses of the generic list class. We've shown it using the type hint of List. Here are the four central classes:

- The TrainingData class is a container with two lists of data samples, a list used for training our model and a list used for testing our model. Both lists are composed of KnownSample instances. Additionally, we'll also have a list of alternative Hyperparameter values. In general, these are tuning values that change the behavior of the model. The idea is to test with different hyperparameters to locate the highest-quality model.

We've also allocated a little bit of metadata to this class: the name of the data we're working with, the datetime of when we uploaded the data the first time, and the datetime of when we ran a test against the model.

- Each instance of the Sample class is the core piece of working data. In our example, these are measurements of sepal lengths and widths and petal lengths and widths. Steady-handed botany graduate students carefully measured lots and lots of flowers to gather this data. We hope that they had time to stop and smell the roses while they were working.

- A KnownSample object is an extended Sample. This part of the design foreshadows the focus of *Chapter 3, When Objects Are Alike*. A KnownSample is a Sample with one extra attribute, the assigned species. This information comes from skilled botanists who have classified some data we can use for training and testing.

- The Hyperparameter class has the *k* used to define how many of the nearest neighbors to consider. It also has a summary of testing with this value of *k*. The quality tells us how many of the test samples were correctly classified. We expect to see that small values of *k* (like 1 or 3) don't classify well. We expect middle values of *k* to do better, and very large values of *k* to not do as well.

The KnownSample class on the diagram may not need to be a separate class definition. As we work through the details, we'll look at some alternative designs for each of these classes.

We'll start with the Sample (and KnownSample) classes. Python offers three essential paths for defining a new class:

- A class definition; we'll focus on this to start.

- A @dataclass definition. This provides a number of built-in features. While it's handy, it's not ideal for programmers who are new to Python, because it can obscure some implementation details. We'll set this aside for *Chapter 7, Python Data Structures*.

- An extension to the typing.NamedTuple class. The most notable feature of this definition will be that the state of the object is immutable; the attribute values cannot be changed. Unchanging attributes can be a useful feature for making sure a bug in the application doesn't mess with the training data. We'll set this aside for *Chapter 7*, also.

Our first design decision is to use Python's class statement to write a class definition for Sample and its subclass KnownSample. This may be replaced in the future (i.e., *Chapter 7*) with alternatives that use data classes as well as NamedTuple.

Samples and their states

The diagram in *Figure 2.2* shows the Sample class and an extension, the KnownSample class. This doesn't seem to be a complete decomposition of the various kinds of samples. When we review the user stories and the process views, there seems to be a gap: specifically, the "make classification request" by a User requires an unknown sample. This has the same flower measurements attributes as a Sample, but doesn't have the assigned species attribute of a KnownSample. Further, there's no state change that adds an attribute value. The unknown sample will never be formally classified by a Botanist; it will be classified by our algorithm, but it's only an AI, not a Botanist.

We can make a case for two distinct subclasses of Sample:

- UnknownSample: This class contains the initial four Sample attributes. A User provides these objects to get them classified.
- KnownSample: This class has the Sample attributes plus the classification result, a species name. We use these for training and testing the model.

Generally, we consider class definitions as a way to encapsulate state and behavior. An UnknownSample instance provided by a user starts out with no species. Then, after the classifier algorithm computes a species, the Sample changes state to have a species assigned by the algorithm.

A question we must always ask about class definitions is this:

Is there any change in behavior that goes with the change in state?

In this case, it doesn't seem like there's anything new or different that can happen. Perhaps this can be implemented as a single class with some optional attributes.

We have another possible state change concern. Currently, there's no class that owns the responsibility of partitioning Sample objects into the training or testing subsets. This, too, is a kind of state change.

This leads to a second important question:

What class has responsibility for making this state change?

In this case, it seems like the TrainingData class should own the discrimination between testing and training data.

One way to help look closely at our class design is to enumerate all of the various states of individual samples. This technique helps uncover a need for attributes in the classes. It also helps to identify the methods to make state changes to objects of a class.

Sample state transitions

Let's look at the life cycles of `Sample` objects. An object's life cycle starts with object creation, then state changes, and (in some cases) the end of its processing life when there are no more references to it. We have three scenarios:

1. **Initial load**: We'll need a `load()` method to populate a `TrainingData` object from some source of raw data. We'll preview some of the material in *Chapter 9, Strings, Serialization, and File Paths*, by saying that reading a CSV file often produces a sequence of dictionaries. We can imagine a `load()` method using a CSV reader to create `Sample` objects with a species value, making them `KnownSample` objects. The `load()` method splits the `KnownSample` objects into the training and testing lists, which is an important state change for a `TrainingData` object.

2. **Hyperparameter testing**: We'll need a `test()` method in the `Hyperparameter` class. The body of the `test()` method works with the test samples in the associated `TrainingData` object. For each sample, it applies the classifier and counts the matches between Botanist-assigned species and the best guess of our AI algorithm. This points out the need for a `classify()` method for a single sample that's used by the `test()` method for a batch of samples. The `test()` method will update the state of the `Hyperparameter` object by setting the quality score.

3. **User-initiated classification**: A RESTful web application is often decomposed into separate view functions to handle requests. When handling a request to classify an unknown sample, the view function will have a `Hyperparameter` object used for classification; this will be chosen by the Botanist to produce the best results. The user input will be an `UnknownSample` instance. The view function applies the `Hyperparameter.classify()` method to create a response to the user with the species the iris has been classed as. Does the state change that happens when the AI classifies an `UnknownSample` really matter? Here are two views:

   - Each `UnknownSample` can have a `classified` attribute. Setting this is a change in the state of the `Sample`. It's not clear that there's any behavior change associated with this state change.

   - The classification result is not part of the `Sample` at all. It's a local variable in the view function. This state change in the function is used to respond to the user, but has no life within the `Sample` object.

There's a key concept underlying this detailed decomposition of these alternatives:

There's no "right" answer.

Some design decisions are based on non-functional and non-technical considerations. These might include the longevity of the application, future use cases, additional users who might be enticed, current schedules and budgets, pedagogical value, technical risk, the creation of intellectual property, and how cool the demo will look in a conference call.

In *Chapter 1, Object-Oriented Design*, we dropped a hint that this application is the precursor to a consumer product recommender. We noted: "The users eventually want to tackle complex consumer products, but recognize that solving a difficult problem is not a good way to learn how to build this kind of application. It's better to start with something of a manageable level of complexity and then refine and expand it until it does everything they need."

Because of that, we'll consider a change in state from UnknownSample to ClassifiedSample to be very important. The Sample objects will live in a database for additional marketing campaigns or possibly reclassification when new products are available and the training data changes.

We'll decide to keep the classification and the species data in the UnknownSample class.

This analysis suggests we can coalesce all the various Sample details into the following design:

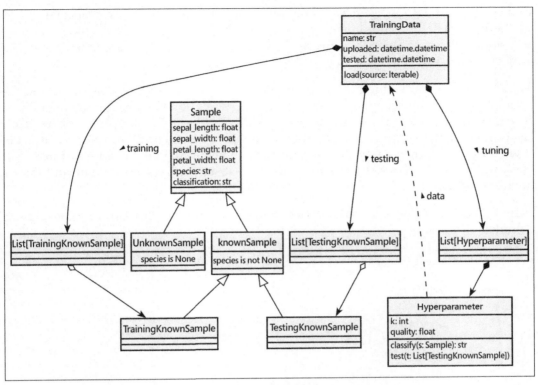

Figure 2.3: The updated UML diagram

This view uses the open arrowhead to show a number of subclasses of Sample. We won't directly implement these as subclasses. We've included the arrows to show that we have some distinct use cases for these objects. Specifically, the box for KnownSample has a condition **species is not None** to summarize what's unique about these Sample objects. Similarly, the UnknownSample has a condition, **species is None**, to clarify our intent around Sample objects with the species attribute value of None.

In these UML diagrams, we have generally avoided showing Python's "special" methods. This helps to minimize visual clutter. In some cases, a special method may be absolutely essential, and worthy of showing in a diagram. An implementation almost always needs to have an __init__() method.

There's another special method that can really help: the __repr__() method is used to create a representation of the object. This representation is a string that generally has the syntax of a Python expression to rebuild the object. For simple numbers, it's the number. For a simple string, it will include the quotes. For more complex objects, it will have all the necessary Python punctuation, including all the details of the class and state of the object. We'll often use an f-string with the class name and the attribute values.

Here's the start of a class, Sample, which seems to capture all the features of a single sample:

```python
class Sample:

    def __init__(
        self,
        sepal_length: float,
        sepal_width: float,
        petal_length: float,
        petal_width: float,
        species: Optional[str] = None,
    ) -> None:
        self.sepal_length = sepal_length
        self.sepal_width = sepal_width
        self.petal_length = petal_length
        self.petal_width = petal_width
        self.species = species
        self.classification: Optional[str] = None

    def __repr__(self) -> str:
        if self.species is None:
            known_unknown = "UnknownSample"
        else:
            known_unknown = "KnownSample"
        if self.classification is None:
            classification = ""
        else:
            classification = f", {self.classification}"
```

```
            return (
                f"{known_unknown}("
                f"sepal_length={self.sepal_length}, "
                f"sepal_width={self.sepal_width}, "
                f"petal_length={self.petal_length}, "
                f"petal_width={self.petal_width}, "
                f"species={self.species!r}"
                f"{classification}"
                f")"
            )
```

The __repr__() method reflects the fairly complex internal state of this Sample object. The states implied by the presence (or absence) of a species and the presence (or absence) of a classification lead to small behavior changes. So far, any changes in object behavior are limited to the __repr__() method used to display the current state of the object.

What's important is that the state changes do lead to a (tiny) behavioral change.

We have two application-specific methods for the Sample class. These are shown in the next code snippet:

```
    def classify(self, classification: str) -> None:
        self.classification = classification

    def matches(self) -> bool:
        return self.species == self.classification
```

The classify() method defines the state change from unclassified to classified. The matches() method compares the results of classification with a Botanist-assigned species. This is used for testing.

Here's an example of how these state changes can look:

```
>>> from model import Sample
>>> s2 = Sample(
...     sepal_length=5.1, sepal_width=3.5, petal_length=1.4, petal_
width=0.2, species="Iris-setosa")
>>> s2
KnownSample(sepal_length=5.1, sepal_width=3.5, petal_length=1.4, petal_
width=0.2, species='Iris-setosa')
>>> s2.classification = "wrong"
```

```
>>> s2
KnownSample(sepal_length=5.1, sepal_width=3.5, petal_length=1.4, petal_
width=0.2, species='Iris-setosa', classification='wrong')
```

We have a workable definition of the Sample class. The __repr__() method is quite complex, suggesting there may be some improvements possible.

It can help to define responsibilities for each class. This can be a focused summary of the attributes and methods with a little bit of additional rationale to tie them together.

Class responsibilities

Which class is responsible for actually performing a test? Does the Training class invoke the classifier on each KnownSample in a testing set? Or, perhaps, does it provide the testing set to the Hyperparameter class, delegating the testing to the Hyperparameter class? Since the Hyperparameter class has responsibility for the *k* value, and the algorithm for locating the *k*-nearest neighbors, it seems sensible for the Hyperparameter class to run the test using its own *k* value and a list of KnownSample instances provided to it.

It also seems clear the TrainingData class is an acceptable place to record the various Hyperparameter trials. This means the TrainingData class can identify which of the Hyperparameter instances has a value of *k* that classifies irises with the highest accuracy.

There are multiple, related state changes here. In this case, both the Hyperparameter and TrainingData classes will do part of the work. The system – as a whole – will change state as individual elements change state. This is sometimes described as **emergent behavior**. Rather than writing a monster class that does many things, we've written smaller classes that collaborate to achieve the expected goals.

This test() method of TrainingData is something that we didn't show in the UML image. We included test() in the Hyperparameter class, but, at the time, it didn't seem necessary to add it to TrainingData.

Here's the start of the class definition:

```
class Hyperparameter:
    """A hyperparameter value and the overall quality of the
classification."""

    def __init__(self, k: int, training: "TrainingData") -> None:
```

```
        self.k = k
        self.data: weakref.ReferenceType["TrainingData"] =
weakref.ref(training)
        self.quality: float
```

Note how we write type hints for classes not yet defined. When a class is defined later in the file, any reference to the yet-to-be-defined class is a *forward reference*. The forward references to the not-yet-defined TrainingData class are provided as strings, not the simple class name. When *mypy* is analyzing the code, it resolves the strings into proper class names.

The testing is defined by the following method:

```
def test(self) -> None:
    """Run the entire test suite."""
    training_data: Optional["TrainingData"] = self.data()
    if not training_data:
        raise RuntimeError("Broken Weak Reference")
    pass_count, fail_count = 0, 0
    for sample in training_data.testing:
        sample.classification = self.classify(sample)
        if sample.matches():
            pass_count += 1
        else:
            fail_count += 1
    self.quality = pass_count / (pass_count + fail_count)
```

We start by resolving the weak reference to the training data. This will raise an exception if there's a problem. For each testing sample, we classify the sample, setting the sample's classification attribute. The matches method tells us if the model's classification matches the known species. Finally, the overall quality is measured by the fraction of tests that passed. We can use the integer count, or a floating-point ratio of tests passed out of the total number of tests.

We won't look at the classification method in this chapter; we'll save that for *Chapter 10, The Iterator Pattern*. Instead, we'll finish this model by looking at the TrainingData class, which combines the elements seen so far.

The TrainingData class

The TrainingData class has lists with two subclasses of Sample objects. The KnownSample and UnknownSample can be implemented as extensions to a common parent class, Sample.

We'll look at this from a number of perspectives in *Chapter 7*. The `TrainingData` class also has a list with `Hyperparameter` instances. This class can have simple, direct references to previously defined classes.

This class has the two methods that initiate the processing:

- The `load()` method reads raw data and partitions it into training data and test data. Both of these are essentially `KnownSample` instances with different purposes. The training subset is for evaluating the *k*-NN algorithm; the testing subset is for determining how well the *k* hyperparameter is working.

- The `test()` method uses a `Hyperparameter` object, performs the test, and saves the result.

Looking back at *Chapter 1*'s context diagram, we see three stories: *Provide Training Data, Set Parameters and Test Classifier,* and *Make Classification Request*. It seems helpful to add a method to perform a classification using a given `Hyperparameter` instance. This would add a `classify()` method to the `TrainingData` class. Again, this was not clearly required at the beginning of our design work, but seems like a good idea now.

Here's the start of the class definition:

```
class TrainingData:
    """A set of training data and testing data with methods to load and
test the samples."""

    def __init__(self, name: str) -> None:
        self.name = name
        self.uploaded: datetime.datetime
        self.tested: datetime.datetime
        self.training: List[Sample] = []
        self.testing: List[Sample] = []
        self.tuning: List[Hyperparameter] = []
```

We've defined a number of attributes to track the history of the changes to this class. The uploaded time and the tested time, for example, provide some history. The `training`, `testing`, and `tuning` attributes have `Sample` objects and `Hyperparameter` objects.

We won't write methods to set all of these. This is Python and direct access to attributes is a huge simplification to complex applications. The responsibilities are encapsulated in this class, but we don't generally write a lot of getter/setter methods.

In *Chapter 5, When to Use Object-Oriented Programming*, we'll look at some clever techniques, like Python's property definitions, additional ways to handle these attributes.

The `load()` method is designed to process data given by another object. We could have designed the `load()` method to open and read a file, but then we'd bind the `TrainingData` to a specific file format and logical layout. It seems better to isolate the details of the file format from the details of managing training data. In *Chapter 5*, we'll look closely at reading and validating input. In *Chapter 9, Strings, Serialization, and File Paths*, we'll revisit the file format considerations.

For now, we'll use the following outline for acquiring the training data:

```python
def load(
        self,
        raw_data_source: Iterable[dict[str, str]]
) -> None:
    """Load and partition the raw data"""
    for n, row in enumerate(raw_data_source):
        ... filter and extract subsets (See Chapter 6)
        ... Create self.training and self.testing subsets
    self.uploaded = datetime.datetime.now(tz=datetime.timezone.utc)
```

We'll depend on a source of data. We've described the properties of this source with a type hint, `Iterable[dict[str, str]]`. The `Iterable` states that the method's results can be used by a `for` statement or the `list` function. This is true of collections like lists and files. It's also true of generator functions, the subject of *Chapter 10, The Iterator Pattern*.

The results of this iterator need to be dictionaries that map strings to strings. This is a very general structure, and it allows us to require a dictionary that looks like this:

```python
{
    "sepal_length": 5.1,
    "sepal_width": 3.5,
    "petal_length": 1.4,
    "petal_width": 0.2,
    "species": "Iris-setosa"
}
```

This required structure seems flexible enough that we can build some object that will produce it. We'll look at the details in *Chapter 9*.

The remaining methods delegate most of their work to the Hyperparameter class. Rather than do the work of classification, this class relies on another class to do the work:

```python
def test(
        self,
        parameter: Hyperparameter) -> None:
    """Test this Hyperparameter value."""
    parameter.test()
    self.tuning.append(parameter)
    self.tested = datetime.datetime.now(tz=datetime.timezone.utc)

def classify(
        self,
        parameter: Hyperparameter,
        sample: Sample) -> Sample:
    """Classify this Sample."""
    classification = parameter.classify(sample)
    sample.classify(classification)
    return sample
```

In both cases, a specific Hyperparameter object is provided as a parameter. For testing, this makes sense because each test should have a distinct value. For classification, however, the "best" Hyperparameter object should be used for classification.

This part of the case study has built class definitions for Sample, KnownSample, TrainingData, and Hyperparameter. These classes capture parts of the overall application. This isn't complete, of course; we've omitted some important algorithms. It's good to start with things that are clear, identify behavior and state change, and define the responsibilities. The next pass of design can then fill in details around this existing framework.

Recall

Some key points in this chapter:

- Python has optional type hints to help describe how data objects are related and what the parameters should be for methods and functions.
- We create Python classes with the class statement. We should initialize the attributes in the special __init__() method.

- Modules and packages are used as higher-level groupings of classes.

- We need to plan out the organization of module content. While the general advice is "flat is better than nested," there are a few cases where it can be helpful to have nested packages.

- Python has no notion of "private" data. We often say "we're all adults here"; we can see the source code, and private declarations aren't very helpful. This doesn't change our design; it simply removes the need for a handful of keywords.

- We can install third-party packages using PIP tools. We can create a virtual environment, for example, with venv.

Exercises

Write some object-oriented code. The goal is to use the principles and syntax you learned in this chapter to ensure you understand the topics we've covered. If you've been working on a Python project, go back over it and see whether there are some objects you can create and add properties or methods to. If it's large, try dividing it into a few modules or even packages and play with the syntax. While a "simple" script may expand when refactored into classes, there's generally a gain in flexibility and extensibility.

If you don't have such a project, try starting a new one. It doesn't have to be something you intend to finish; just stub out some basic design parts. You don't need to fully implement everything; often, just a print("this method will do something") is all you need to get the overall design in place. This is called **top-down design**, in which you work out the different interactions and describe how they should work before actually implementing what they do. The converse, **bottom-up design**, implements details first and then ties them all together. Both patterns are useful at different times, but for understanding object-oriented principles, a top-down workflow is more suitable.

If you're having trouble coming up with ideas, try writing a to-do application. It can keep track of things you want to do each day. Items can have a state change from incomplete to completed. You might want to think about items that have an intermediate state of started, but not yet completed.

Now try designing a bigger project. A collection of classes to model playing cards can be an interesting challenge. Cards have a few features, but there are many variations on the rules. A class for a hand of cards has interesting state changes as cards are added. Locate a game you like and create classes to model cards, hands, and play. (Don't tackle creating a winning strategy; that can be hard.)

A game like Cribbage has an interesting state change where two cards from each player's hand are used to create a kind of third hand, called "the crib." Make sure you experiment with the package and module-importing syntax. Add some functions in various modules and try importing them from other modules and packages. Use relative and absolute imports. See the difference, and try to imagine scenarios where you would want to use each one.

Summary

In this chapter, we learned how simple it is to create classes and assign properties and methods in Python. Unlike many languages, Python differentiates between a constructor and an initializer. It has a relaxed attitude toward access control. There are many different levels of scope, including packages, modules, classes, and functions. We understood the difference between relative and absolute imports, and how to manage third-party packages that don't come with Python.

In the next chapter, we'll learn more about sharing implementation using inheritance.

3

When Objects Are Alike

In the programming world, duplicate code is considered evil. We should not have multiple copies of the same, or similar, code in different places. When we fix a bug in one copy and fail to fix the same bug in another copy, we've caused no end of problems for ourselves.

There are many ways to merge pieces of code or objects that have a similar functionality. In this chapter, we'll be covering the most famous object-oriented principle: inheritance. As discussed in *Chapter 1*, *Object-Oriented Design*, inheritance allows us to create "is-a" relationships between two or more classes, abstracting common logic into superclasses and extending the superclass with specific details in each subclass. In particular, we'll be covering the Python syntax and principles for the following:

- Basic inheritance
- Inheriting from built-in types
- Multiple inheritance
- Polymorphism and duck typing

This chapter's case study will expand on the previous chapter. We'll leverage the concepts of inheritance and abstraction to look for ways to manage common code in parts of the *k*-nearest neighbors computation.

We'll start by taking a close look at how inheritance works to factor out common features so we can avoid copy-and-paste programming.

Basic inheritance

Technically, every class we create uses inheritance. All Python classes are subclasses of the special built-in class named `object`. This class provides a little bit of metadata and a few built-in behaviors so Python can treat all objects consistently.

If we don't explicitly inherit from a different class, our classes will automatically inherit from `object`. However, we can redundantly state that our class derives from `object` using the following syntax:

```
class MySubClass(object):
    pass
```

This is inheritance! This example is, technically, no different from our very first example in *Chapter 2, Objects in Python*. In Python 3, all classes automatically inherit from `object` if we don't explicitly provide a different **superclass**. The superclasses, or *parent* classes, in the relationship are the classes that are being inherited from, `object` in this example. A subclass – `MySubClass`, in this example – inherits from a superclass. A subclass is also said to be *derived from* its parent class, or the subclass *extends* the parent class.

As you've probably figured out from the example, inheritance requires a minimal amount of extra syntax over a basic class definition. Simply include the name of the parent class inside parentheses between the class name and the colon that follows. This is all we have to do to tell Python that the new class should be derived from the given superclass.

How do we apply inheritance in practice? The simplest and most obvious use of inheritance is to add functionality to an existing class. Let's start with a contact manager that tracks the names and email addresses of several people. The `Contact` class is responsible for maintaining a global list of all contacts ever seen in a class variable, and for initializing the name and address for an individual contact:

```python
class Contact:
    all_contacts: List["Contact"] = []

    def __init__(self, name: str, email: str) -> None:
        self.name = name
        self.email = email
        Contact.all_contacts.append(self)

    def __repr__(self) -> str:
        return (
            f"{self.__class__.__name__}("
```

```
            f"{self.name!r}, {self.email!r}"
            f")"
    )
```

This example introduces us to **class variables**. The all_contacts list, because it is part of the class definition, is shared by all instances of this class. This means that there is only one Contact.all_contacts list. We can also access it as self.all_contacts from within any method on an instance of the Contact class. If a field can't be found on the object (via self), then it will be found on the class and will thus refer to the same single list.

 Be careful with the self-based reference. It can only provide access to an existing class-based variable. If you ever attempt to *set* the variable using self.all_contacts, you will actually be creating a *new* instance variable associated just with that object. The class variable will still be unchanged and accessible as Contact.all_contacts.

We can see how the class tracks data with the following example:

```
>>> c_1 = Contact("Dusty", "dusty@example.com")
>>> c_2 = Contact("Steve", "steve@itmaybeahack.com")
>>> Contact.all_contacts
[Contact('Dusty', 'dusty@example.com'), Contact('Steve',
'steve@itmaybeahack.com')]
```

We created two instances of the Contact class and assigned them to variables c_1 and c_2. When we looked at the Contact.all_contacts class variable, we saw that the list has been updated to track the two objects.

This is a simple class that allows us to track a couple of pieces of data about each contact. But what if some of our contacts are also suppliers that we need to order supplies from? We could add an order method to the Contact class, but that would allow people to accidentally order things from contacts who are customers or family friends. Instead, let's create a new Supplier class that acts like our Contact class, but has an additional order method that accepts a yet-to-be-defined Order object:

```
class Supplier(Contact):
    def order(self, order: "Order") -> None:
        print(
            "If this were a real system we would send "
            f"'{order}' order to '{self.name}'"
        )
```

Now, if we test this class in our trusty interpreter, we see that all contacts, including suppliers, accept a name and email address in their __init__() method, but that only Supplier instances have an order() method:

```
>>> c = Contact("Some Body", "somebody@example.net")
>>> s = Supplier("Sup Plier", "supplier@example.net")
>>> print(c.name, c.email, s.name, s.email)
Some Body somebody@example.net Sup Plier supplier@example.net

>>> from pprint import pprint
>>> pprint(c.all_contacts)
[Contact('Dusty', 'dusty@example.com'),
 Contact('Steve', 'steve@itmaybeahack.com'),
 Contact('Some Body', 'somebody@example.net'),
 Supplier('Sup Plier', 'supplier@example.net')]

>>> c.order("I need pliers")
Traceback (most recent call last):
  File "<stdin>", line 1, in <module>
AttributeError: 'Contact' object has no attribute 'order'
>>> s.order("I need pliers")
If this were a real system we would send 'I need pliers' order to 'Sup Plier'
```

Our Supplier class can do everything a contact can do (including adding itself to the list of Contact.all_contacts) and all the special things it needs to handle as a supplier. This is the beauty of inheritance.

Also, note that Contact.all_contacts has collected every instance of the Contact class as well as the subclass, Supplier. If we used self.all_contacts, then this would *not* collect all objects into the Contact class, but would put Supplier instances into Supplier.all_contacts.

Extending built-ins

One interesting use of this kind of inheritance is adding functionality to built-in classes. In the Contact class seen earlier, we are adding contacts to a list of all contacts. What if we also wanted to search that list by name? Well, we could add a method on the Contact class to search it, but it feels like this method actually belongs to the list itself.

The following example shows how we can do this using inheritance from a built-in type. In this case, we're using the list type. We're going to inform *mypy* that our list is only of instances of the Contact class by using list["Contact"]. For this syntax to work in Python 3.9, we need to also import the annotations module from the __future__ package. The definitions look like this:

```python
from __future__ import annotations
class ContactList(list["Contact"]):
    def search(self, name: str) -> list["Contact"]:

        matching_contacts: list["Contact"] = []
        for contact in self:
            if name in contact.name:
                matching_contacts.append(contact)
        return matching_contacts


class Contact:
    all_contacts = ContactList()

    def __init__(self, name: str, email: str) -> None:
        self.name = name
        self.email = email
        Contact.all_contacts.append(self)

    def __repr__(self) -> str:
        return (
            f"{self.__class__.__name__}("
            f"{self.name!r}, {self.email!r}" f")"
        )
```

Instead of instantiating a generic list as our class variable, we create a new ContactList class that extends the built-in list data type. Then, we instantiate this subclass as our all_contacts list. We can test the new search functionality as follows:

```python
>>> c1 = Contact("John A", "johna@example.net")
>>> c2 = Contact("John B", "johnb@sloop.net")
>>> c3 = Contact("Jenna C", "cutty@sark.io")
>>> [c.name for c in Contact.all_contacts.search('John')]
['John A', 'John B']
```

We have two ways to create generic list objects. With type hints, we have another way of talking about lists, separate from creating actual list instances.

First, creating a list with [] is actually a shortcut for creating a list using list(); the two syntaxes behave identically:

```
>>> [] == list()
True
```

The [] is short and sweet. We can call it **syntactic sugar**; it is a call to the list() constructor, written with two characters instead of six. The list name refers to a data type: it is a class that we can extend.

Tools like *mypy* can check the body of the ContactList.search() method to be sure it really will create a list instance populated with Contact objects. Be sure you've installed a version that's 0.812 or newer; older versions of *mypy* don't handle these annotations based on generic types completely.

Because we provided the Contact class definition after the definition of the ContactList class, we had to provide the reference to a not-yet-defined class as a string, list["Contact"]. It's often more common to provide the individual item class definition first, and the collection can then refer to the defined class by name without using a string.

As a second example, we can extend the dict class, which is a collection of keys and their associated values. We can create instances of dictionaries using the {} syntax sugar. Here's an extended dictionary that tracks the longest key it has seen:

```
class LongNameDict(dict[str, int]):
    def longest_key(self) -> Optional[str]:
        """In effect, max(self, key=len), but less obscure"""
        longest = None
        for key in self:
            if longest is None or len(key) > len(longest):
                longest = key
        return longest
```

The hint for the class narrowed the generic dict to a more specific dict[str, int]; the keys are of type str and the values are of type int. This helps *mypy* reason about the longest_key() method. Since the keys are supposed to be str-type objects, the statement for key in self: will iterate over str objects. The result will be a str, or possibly None. That's why the result is described as Optional[str]. (Is None appropriate? Perhaps not. Perhaps a ValueError exception is a better idea; that will have to wait until *Chapter 4, Expecting the Unexpected*.)

We're going to be working with strings and integer values. Perhaps the strings are usernames, and the integer values are the number of articles they've read on a website. In addition to the core username and reading history, we also need to know the longest name so we can format a table of scores with the right size display box. This is easy to test in the interactive interpreter:

```
>>> articles_read = LongNameDict()
>>> articles_read['lucy'] = 42
>>> articles_read['c_c_phillips'] = 6
>>> articles_read['steve'] = 7
>>> articles_read.longest_key()
'c_c_phillips'
>>> max(articles_read, key=len)
'c_c_phillips'
```

 What if we wanted a more generic dictionary? Say with either strings *or* integers as the values? We'd need a slightly more expansive type hint. We might use dict[str, Union[str, int]] to describe a dictionary mapping strings to a union of either strings or integers.

Most built-in types can be similarly extended. These built-in types fall into several interesting families, with separate kinds of type hints:

- Generic collections: set, list, dict. These use type hints like set[something], list[something], and dict[key, value] to narrow the hint from purely generic to something more specific that the application will actually use. To use the generic types as annotations, a from __future__ import annotations is required as the first line of code.

- The typing.NamedTuple definition lets us define new kinds of immutable tuples and provide useful names for the members. This will be covered in *Chapter 7*, *Python Data Structures*, and *Chapter 8*, *The Intersection of Object-Oriented and Functional Programming*.

- Python has type hints for file-related I/O objects. A new kind of file can use a type hint of typing.TextIO or typing.BinaryIO to describe built-in file operations.

- It's possible to create new types of strings by extending typing.Text. For the most part, the built-in str class does everything we need.

- New numeric types often start with the numbers module as a source for built-in numeric functionality.

We'll use the generic collections heavily throughout the book. As noted, we'll look at named tuples in later chapters. The other extensions to built-in types are too advanced for this book. In the next section, we'll look more deeply at the benefits of inheritance and how we can selectively leverage features of the superclass in our subclass.

Overriding and super

So, inheritance is great for *adding* new behavior to existing classes, but what about *changing* behavior? Our Contact class allows only a name and an email address. This may be sufficient for most contacts, but what if we want to add a phone number for our close friends?

As we saw in *Chapter 2, Objects in Python*, we can do this easily by setting a phone attribute on the contact after it is constructed. But if we want to make this third variable available on initialization, we have to override the __init__() method. Overriding means altering or replacing a method of the superclass with a new method (with the same name) in the subclass. No special syntax is needed to do this; the subclass's newly created method is automatically called instead of the superclass's method, as shown in the following code:

```python
class Friend(Contact):
    def __init__(self, name: str, email: str, phone: str) -> None:
        self.name = name
        self.email = email
        self.phone = phone
```

Any method can be overridden, not just __init__(). Before we go on, however, we need to address some problems in this example. Our Contact and Friend classes have duplicate code to set up the name and email properties; this can make code maintenance complicated, as we have to update the code in two or more places. More alarmingly, our Friend class is neglecting to add itself to the all_contacts list we have created on the Contact class. Finally, looking forward, if we add a feature to the Contact class, we'd like it to also be part of the Friend class.

What we really need is a way to execute the original __init__() method on the Contact class from inside our new class. This is what the super() function does; it returns the object as if it was actually an instance of the parent class, allowing us to call the parent method directly:

```python
class Friend(Contact):
    def __init__(self, name: str, email: str, phone: str) -> None:
        super().__init__(name, email)
        self.phone = phone
```

This example first binds the instance to the parent class using super() and calls __init__() on that object, passing in the expected arguments. It then does its own initialization, namely, setting the phone attribute, which is unique to the Friend class.

The Contact class provided a definition for the __repr__() method to produce a string representation. Our class did not override the __repr__() method inherited from the superclass. Here's the consequence of that:

```
>>> f = Friend("Dusty", "Dusty@private.com", "555-1212")
>>> Contact.all_contacts
[Friend('Dusty', 'Dusty@private.com')]
```

The details shown for a Friend instance don't include the new attribute. It's easy to overlook the special method definitions when thinking about class design.

A super() call can be made inside any method. Therefore, all methods can be modified via overriding and calls to super(). The call to super() can also be made at any point in the method; we don't have to make the call as the first line. For example, we may need to manipulate or validate incoming parameters before forwarding them to the superclass.

Multiple inheritance

Multiple inheritance is a touchy subject. In principle, it's simple: a subclass that inherits from more than one parent class can access functionality from both of them. In practice, it requires some care to be sure any method overrides are fully understood.

 As a humorous rule of thumb, if you think you need multiple inheritance, you're probably wrong, but if you know you need it, you might be right.

The simplest and most useful form of multiple inheritance follows a design pattern called the **mixin**. A mixin class definition is not intended to exist on its own, but is meant to be inherited by some other class to provide extra functionality. For example, let's say we wanted to add functionality to our Contact class that allows sending an email to self.email.

Sending email is a common task that we might want to use on many other classes. So, we can write a simple mixin class to do the emailing for us:

```python
class Emailable(Protocol):
    email: str


class MailSender(Emailable):
    def send_mail(self, message: str) -> None:
        print(f"Sending mail to {self.email=}")
        # Add e-mail logic here
```

The `MailSender` class doesn't do anything special (in fact, it can barely function as a standalone class, since it assumes an attribute it doesn't set). We have two classes because we're describing two things: aspects of the host class for a mixin, and new aspects the mixin provides to the host. We needed to create a hint, `Emailable`, to describe the kinds of classes our `MailSender` mixin expects to work with.

This kind of type hint is called a **protocol**; protocols generally have methods, and can also have class-level attribute names with type hints, but not full assignment statements. A protocol definition is a kind of incomplete class; think of it like a contract for features of a class. A protocol tells *mypy* that any class (or subclass) of `Emailable` objects must support an `email` attribute, and it must be a string.

Note that we're relying on Python's name resolution rules. The name `self.email` can be resolved as either an instance variable, or a class-level variable, `Emailable.email`, or a property. The *mypy* tool will check all the classes mixed in with `MailSender` for instance- or class-level definitions. We only need to provide the name of the attribute at the class level, with a type hint to make it clear to *mypy* that the mixin does not define the attribute – the class into which it's mixed will provide the `email` attribute.

Because of Python's duck typing rules, we can use the `MailSender` mixin with any class that has an `email` attribute defined. A class with which `MailSender` is mixed doesn't have to be a formal subclass of `Emailable`; it only has to provide the required attribute.

For brevity, we didn't include the actual email logic here; if you're interested in studying how it's done, see the `smtplib` module in the Python standard library.

The `MailSender` class does allow us to define a new class that describes both a `Contact` and a `MailSender`, using multiple inheritance:

```
class EmailableContact(Contact, MailSender):
    pass
```

The syntax for multiple inheritance looks like a parameter list in the class definition. Instead of including one base class inside the parentheses, we include two (or more), separated by a comma. When it's done well, it's common for the resulting class to have no unique features of its own. It's a combination of mixins, and the body of the class definition is often nothing more than the `pass` placeholder.

We can test this new hybrid to see the mixin at work:

```
>>> e = EmailableContact("John B", "johnb@sloop.net")
>>> Contact.all_contacts
[EmailableContact('John B', 'johnb@sloop.net')]
>>> e.send_mail("Hello, test e-mail here")
Sending mail to self.email='johnb@sloop.net'
```

The `Contact` initializer is still adding the new contact to the `all_contacts` list, and the mixin is able to send mail to `self.email`, so we know that everything is working.

This wasn't so hard, and you're probably wondering what our dire warnings about multiple inheritance were for. We'll get into the complexities in a minute, but let's consider some other options we had for this example, rather than using a mixin:

- We could have used single inheritance and added the `send_mail` function to a subclass of `Contact`. The disadvantage here is that the email functionality then has to be duplicated for any unrelated classes that need an email. For example, if we had email information in the payments part of our application, unrelated to these contacts, and we wanted a `send_mail()` method, we'd have to duplicate the code.

- We can create a standalone Python function for sending an email, and just call that function with the correct email address supplied as a parameter when the email needs to be sent (this is a very common choice). Because the function is not part of a class, it's harder to be sure that proper encapsulation is being used.

- We could explore a few ways of using composition instead of inheritance. For example, `EmailableContact` could have a `MailSender` object as a property instead of inheriting from it. This leads to a more complex `MailSender` class because it now has to stand alone. It also leads to a more complex `EmailableContact` class because it has to associate a `MailSender` instance with each `Contact`.

- We could try to monkey patch (we'll briefly cover monkey patching in *Chapter 13, Testing Object-Oriented Programs*) the Contact class to have a send_mail method after the class has been created. This is done by defining a function that accepts the self argument, and setting it as an attribute on an existing class. This is fine for creating a unit test fixture, but terrible for the application itself.

Multiple inheritance works alright when we're mixing methods from different classes, but it can be messy when we have to call methods on the superclass. When there are multiple superclasses, how do we know which one's methods to call? What is the rule for selecting the appropriate superclass method?

Let's explore these questions by adding a home address to our Friend class. There are a few approaches we might take:

- An address is a collection of strings representing the street, city, country, and other related details of the contact. We could pass each of these strings as a parameter into the Friend class's __init__() method. We could also store these strings in a generic tuple or dictionary. These options work well when the address information doesn't need new methods.

- Another option would be to create our own Address class to hold those strings together, and then pass an instance of this class into the __init__() method in our Friend class. The advantage of this solution is that we can add behavior (say, a method to give directions or to print a map) to the data instead of just storing it statically. This is an example of composition, as we discussed in *Chapter 1, Object-Oriented Design*. The "has-a" relationship of composition is a perfectly viable solution to this problem and allows us to reuse Address classes in other entities, such as buildings, businesses, or organizations. (This is an opportunity to use a dataclass. We'll discuss dataclasses in *Chapter 7, Python Data Structures*.)

- A third course of action is a cooperative multiple inheritance design. While this can be made to work, it doesn't pass muster with *mypy*. The reason, we'll see, is some potential ambiguity that's difficult to describe with the available type hints.

The objective here is to add a new class to hold an address. We'll call this new class AddressHolder instead of Address because inheritance defines an "is-a" relationship. It is not correct to say a Friend class is an Address class, but since a friend can have an Address class, we can argue that a Friend class is an AddressHolder class. Later, we could create other entities (companies, buildings) that also hold addresses. (Convoluted naming and nuanced questions about "is-a" serve as decent indications we should be sticking with composition, rather than inheritance.)

Here's a naïve `AddressHolder` class. We're calling it naïve because it doesn't account for multiple inheritance well:

```
class AddressHolder:
    def __init__(self, street: str, city: str, state: str, code: str)
-> None:
        self.street = street
        self.city = city
        self.state = state
        self.code = code
```

We take all the data and toss the argument values into instance variables upon initialization. We'll look at the consequences of this, and then show a better design.

The diamond problem

We can use multiple inheritance to add this new class as a parent of our existing `Friend` class. The tricky part is that we now have two parent `__init__()` methods, both of which need to be called. And they need to be called with different arguments. How do we do this? Well, we could start with a naïve approach for the `Friend` class, also:

```
class Friend(Contact, AddressHolder):
    def __init__(
        self,
        name: str,
        email: str,
        phone: str,
        street: str,
        city: str,
        state: str,
        code: str,
    ) -> None:
        Contact.__init__(self, name, email)
        AddressHolder.__init__(self, street, city, state, code)
        self.phone = phone
```

In this example, we directly call the `__init__()` function on each of the superclasses and explicitly pass the `self` argument. This example technically works; we can access the different variables directly on the class. But there are a few problems.

First, it is possible for a superclass to remain uninitialized if we neglect to explicitly call the initializer. That wouldn't break this example, but it could cause hard-to-debug program crashes in common scenarios. We would get a lot of strange-looking AttributeError exceptions in classes where there's clearly an __init__() method. It's rarely obvious the __init__() method wasn't actually used.

A more insidious possibility is a superclass being called multiple times because of the organization of the class hierarchy. Look at this inheritance diagram:

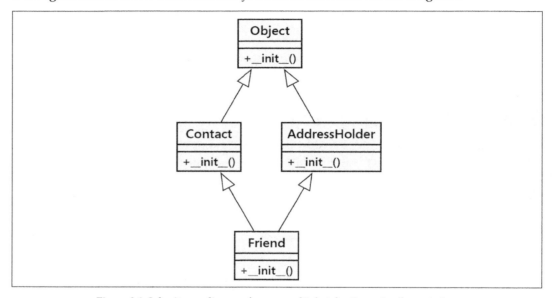

Figure 3.1: Inheritance diagram for our multiple inheritance implementation

The __init__() method from the Friend class first calls __init__() on the Contact class, which implicitly initializes the object superclass (remember, all classes derive from object). The Friend class then calls __init__() on AddressHolder, which implicitly initializes the object superclass *again*. This means the parent class has been set up twice. With the object class, that's relatively harmless, but in some situations, it could spell disaster. Imagine trying to connect to a database twice for every request!

The base class should only be called once. Once, yes, but when? Do we call Friend, then Contact, then Object, and then AddressHolder? Or Friend, then Contact, then AddressHolder, and then Object?

Let's contrive an example to illustrate this problem more clearly. Here, we have a base class, BaseClass, that has a method named call_me(). Two subclasses, LeftSubclass and RightSubclass, extend the BaseClass class, and each overrides the call_me() method with different implementations.

Then, *another* subclass extends both of these using multiple inheritance with a fourth, distinct implementation of the call_me() method. This is called **diamond inheritance** because of the diamond shape of the class diagram:

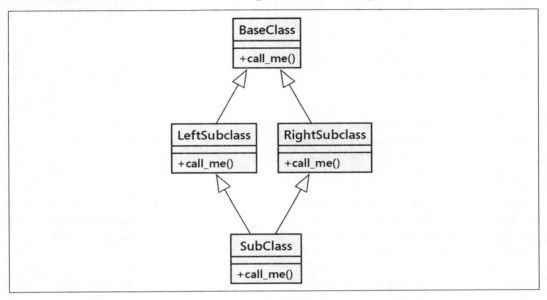

Figure 3.2: Diamond inheritance

Let's convert this diagram into code. This example shows when the methods are called:

```python
class BaseClass:
    num_base_calls = 0

    def call_me(self) -> None:
        print("Calling method on BaseClass")
        self.num_base_calls += 1

class LeftSubclass(BaseClass):
    num_left_calls = 0

    def call_me(self) -> None:
        BaseClass.call_me(self)
        print("Calling method on LeftSubclass")
        self.num_left_calls += 1

class RightSubclass(BaseClass):
    num_right_calls = 0
```

```python
    def call_me(self) -> None:
        BaseClass.call_me(self)
        print("Calling method on RightSubclass")
        self.num_right_calls += 1

class Subclass(LeftSubclass, RightSubclass):
    num_sub_calls = 0

    def call_me(self) -> None:
        LeftSubclass.call_me(self)
        RightSubclass.call_me(self)
        print("Calling method on Subclass")
        self.num_sub_calls += 1
```

This example ensures that each overridden `call_me()` method directly calls the parent method with the same name. It lets us know each time a method is called by printing the information to the screen. It also creates a distinct instance variable to show how many times it has been called.

The `self.num_base_calls += 1` line requires a little sidebar explanation.

This is effectively `self.num_base_calls = self.num_base_calls + 1`. When Python resolves `self.num_base_calls` on the right side of the =, it will first look for an instance variable, then look for the class variable; we've provided a class variable with a default value of zero. After the +1 computation, the assignment statement will create a new instance variable; it will not update the class-level variable.

Each time after the first call, the instance variable will be found. It's pretty cool for the class to provide default values for instance variables.

If we instantiate one `Subclass` object and call the `call_me()` method on it once, we get the following output:

```
>>> s = Subclass()
>>> s.call_me()
Calling method on BaseClass
Calling method on LeftSubclass
Calling method on BaseClass
```

```
Calling method on RightSubclass
Calling method on Subclass
>>> print(
... s.num_sub_calls,
... s.num_left_calls,
... s.num_right_calls,
... s.num_base_calls)
1 1 1 2
```

Thus, we can see the base class's call_me() method being called twice. This could lead to some pernicious bugs if that method is doing actual work, such as depositing into a bank account, twice.

Python's **Method Resolution Order (MRO)** algorithm transforms the diamond into a flat, linear tuple. We can see the results of this in the __mro__ attribute of a class. The linear version of this diamond is the sequence Subclass, LeftSubclass, RightSubClass, BaseClass, object. What's important here is that Subclass lists LeftSubclass before RightSubClass, imposing an ordering on the classes in the diamond.

The thing to keep in mind with multiple inheritance is that we often want to call the next method in the MRO sequence, not necessarily a method of the parent class. The super() function locates the name in the MRO sequence. Indeed, super() was originally developed to make complicated forms of multiple inheritance possible.

Here is the same code written using super(). We've renamed some of the classes, adding an _S to make it clear this is the version using super():

```python
class BaseClass:
    num_base_calls = 0

    def call_me(self):
        print("Calling method on Base Class")
        self.num_base_calls += 1

class LeftSubclass_S(BaseClass):
    num_left_calls = 0

    def call_me(self) -> None:
        super().call_me()
        print("Calling method on LeftSubclass_S")
        self.num_left_calls += 1

class RightSubclass_S(BaseClass):
```

```
        num_right_calls = 0

    def call_me(self) -> None:
        super().call_me()
        print("Calling method on RightSubclass_S")
        self.num_right_calls += 1

class Subclass_S(LeftSubclass_S, RightSubclass_S):
    num_sub_calls = 0

    def call_me(self) -> None:
        super().call_me()
        print("Calling method on Subclass_S")
        self.num_sub_calls += 1
```

The change is pretty minor; we only replaced the naive direct calls with calls to super(). The Subclass_S class, at the bottom of the diamond, only calls super() once rather than having to make the calls for both the left and right. The change is easy enough, but look at the difference when we execute it:

```
>>> ss = Subclass_S()
>>> ss.call_me()
Calling method on BaseClass
Calling method on RightSubclass_S
Calling method on LeftSubclass_S
Calling method on Subclass_S
>>> print(
...     ss.num_sub_calls,
...     ss.num_left_calls,
...     ss.num_right_calls,
...     ss.num_base_calls)
1 1 1 1
```

This output looks good: our base method is only being called once. We can see how this works by looking at the __mro__ attribute of the class:

```
>>> from pprint import pprint
>>> pprint(Subclass_S.__mro__)
(<class 'commerce_naive.Subclass_S'>,
 <class 'commerce_naive.LeftSubclass_S'>,
 <class 'commerce_naive.RightSubclass_S'>,
 <class 'commerce_naive.BaseClass'>,
 <class 'object'>)
```

The order of the classes shows what order super() will use. The last class in the tuple is generally the built-in object class. As noted earlier in this chapter, it's the implicit superclass of all classes.

This shows what super() is actually doing. Since the print statements are executed after the super calls, the printed output is in the order each method is actually executed. Let's look at the output from back to front to see who is calling what:

1. We start with the Subclass_S.call_me() method. This evaluates super().call_me(). The MRO shows LeftSubclass_S as next.

2. We begin evaluation of the LeftSubclass_S.call_me() method. This evaluates super().call_me(). The MRO puts RightSubclass_S as next. This is not a superclass; it's adjacent in the class diamond.

3. The evaluation of the RightSubclass_S.call_me() method, super().call_me(). This leads to BaseClass.

4. The BaseClass.call_me() method finishes its processing: printing a message and setting an instance variable, self.num_base_calls, to BaseClass.num_base_calls + 1.

5. Then, the RightSubclass_S.call_me() method can finish, printing a message and setting an instance variable, self.num_right_calls.

6. Then, the LeftSubclass_S.call_me() method will finish by printing a message and setting an instance variable, self.num_left_calls.

7. This serves to set the stage for Subclass_S to finish its call_me() method processing. It writes a message, sets an instance variable, and rests, happy and successful.

Pay particular attention to this: The super call is *not* calling the method on the superclass of LeftSubclass_S (which is BaseClass). Rather, it is calling RightSubclass_S, even though it is not a direct parent of LeftSubclass_S! This is the *next* class in the MRO, not the parent method. RightSubclass_S then calls BaseClass and the super() calls have ensured each method in the class hierarchy is executed once.

Different sets of arguments

This is going to make things complicated as we return to our Friend cooperative multiple inheritance example. In the __init__() method for the Friend class, we were originally delegating initialization to the __init__() methods of both parent classes, *with different sets of arguments*:

```
Contact.__init__(self, name, email)
AddressHolder.__init__(self, street, city, state, code)
```

How can we manage different sets of arguments when using super()? We only really have access to the next class in the MRO sequence. Because of this, we need a way to pass the *extra* arguments through the constructors so that subsequent calls to super(), from other mixin classes, receive the right arguments.

It works like this. The first call to super() provides arguments to the first class of the MRO, passing the name and email arguments to Contact.__init__(). Then, when Contact.__init__() calls super(), it needs to be able to pass the address-related arguments to the method of the next class in the MRO, which is AddressHolder.__init__().

This problem often manifests itself anytime we want to call superclass methods with the same name, but with different sets of arguments. Collisions often arise around the special method names. Of these, the most common example is having a different set of arguments to various __init__() methods, as we're doing here.

There's no magical Python feature to handle cooperation among classes with divergent __init__() parameters. Consequently, this requires some care to design our class parameter lists. The cooperative multiple inheritance approach is to accept keyword arguments for any parameters that are not required by every subclass implementation. A method must pass the unexpected arguments on to its super() call, in case they are necessary to later methods in the MRO sequence of classes.

While this works and works well, it's difficult to describe with type hints. Instead, we have to silence *mypy* in a few key places.

Python's function parameter syntax provides a tool we can use to do this, but it makes the overall code look cumbersome. Have a look at a version of the Friend multiple inheritance code:

```python
class Contact:
    all_contacts = ContactList()

    def __init__(self, /, name: str = "", email: str = "", **kwargs:
Any) -> None:
        super().__init__(**kwargs)  # type: ignore [call-arg]
        self.name = name
        self.email = email
        self.all_contacts.append(self)

    def __repr__(self) -> str:
        return f"{self.__class__.__name__}(" f"{self.name!r},
{self.email!r}" f")"
```

```python
class AddressHolder:
    def __init__(
        self,
        /,
        street: str = "",
        city: str = "",
        state: str = "",
        code: str = "",
        **kwargs: Any,
    ) -> None:
        super().__init__(**kwargs)  # type: ignore [call-arg]
        self.street = street
        self.city = city
        self.state = state
        self.code = code

class Friend(Contact, AddressHolder):
    def __init__(self, /, phone: str = "", **kwargs: Any) -> None:
        super().__init__(**kwargs)
        self.phone = phone
```

We've added the **kwargs parameter, which collects all additional keyword
argument values into a dictionary. When called with Contact(name="this",
email="that", street="something"), the street argument is put into the
kwargs dictionary; these extra parameters are passed up to the next class with
the super() call. The special parameter / separates parameters that could be
provided by position in the call from parameters that require a keyword to associate
them with an argument value. We've given all string parameters an empty string as a
default value, also.

 If you aren't familiar with the **kwargs syntax, it basically collects
any keyword arguments passed into the method that were not
explicitly listed in the parameter list. These arguments are stored
in a dictionary named kwargs (we can call the variable whatever
we like, but convention suggests kw or kwargs). When we call a
method, for example, super().__init__(), with **kwargs as an
argument value, it unpacks the dictionary and passes the results
to the method as keyword arguments. We'll look at this in more
depth in *Chapter 8, The Intersection of Object-Oriented and Functional
Programming*.

We've introduced two comments that are addressed to *mypy* (and any person scrutinizing the code). The `# type: ignore` comments provide a specific error code, `call-arg`, on a specific line to be ignored. In this case, we need to ignore the `super().__init__(**kwargs)` calls because it isn't obvious to *mypy* what the MRO really will be at runtime. As someone reading the code, we can look at the `Friend` class and see the order: `Contact` and `AddressHolder`. This order means that inside the `Contact` class, the `super()` function will locate the next class, `AddressHolder`.

The *mypy* tool, however, doesn't look this deeply; it goes by the explicit list of parent classes in the `class` statement. Since there's no parent class named, *mypy* is convinced the `object` class will be located by `super()`. Since `object.__init__()` cannot take any arguments, the `super().__init__(**kwargs)` in both `Contact` and `AddressHolder` appears incorrect to *mypy*. Practically, the chain of classes in the MRO will consume all of the various parameters and there will be nothing left over for the `AddressHolder` class's `__init__()` method.

For more information on type hint annotations for cooperative multiple inheritance, see https://github.com/python/mypy/issues/8769. The longevity of this issue suggests how hard the solution can be.

The previous example does what it is supposed to do. But it's supremely difficult to answer the question: *What arguments do we need to pass into* `Friend.__init__()`? This is the foremost question for anyone planning to use the class, so a docstring should be added to the method to explain the entire list of parameters from all the parent classes.

The error message in the event of a misspelled or extraneous parameter can be confusing, also. The message `TypeError: object.__init__() takes exactly one argument (the instance to initialize)` isn't too informative on how an extra parameter came to be provided to `object.__init__()`.

We have covered many of the caveats involved with cooperative multiple inheritance in Python. When we need to account for all possible situations, we have to plan for them, and our code can get messy.

Multiple inheritance following the mixin pattern often works out very nicely. The idea is to have additional methods defined in mixin classes, but to keep all of the attributes centralized in a host class hierarchy. This can avoid the complexity of cooperative initialization.

Design using composition also often works better than complex multiple inheritance. Many of the design patterns we'll be covering in *Chapter 11, Common Design Patterns,* and *Chapter 12, Advanced Design Patterns,* are examples of composition-based design.

The inheritance paradigm depends on a clear "is-a" relationship between classes. Multiple inheritance folds in other relationships that aren't as clear. We can say that an "Email is a kind of Contact," for example. But it doesn't seem as clear that we can say "A Customer is an Email." We might say "A Customer has an Email address" or "A Customer is contacted via Email," using "has an" or "is contacted by" instead of a direct "is-a" relationship.

Polymorphism

We were introduced to polymorphism in *Chapter 1, Object-Oriented Design*. It is a showy name describing a simple concept: different behaviors happen depending on which subclass is being used, without having to explicitly know what the subclass actually is. It is also sometimes called the Liskov Substitution Principle, honoring Barbara Liskov's contributions to object-oriented programming. We should be able to substitute any subclass for its superclass.

As an example, imagine a program that plays audio files. A media player might need to load an AudioFile object and then play it. We can put a play() method on the object, which is responsible for decompressing or extracting the audio and routing it to the sound card and speakers. The act of playing an AudioFile could feasibly be as simple as:

```
audio_file.play()
```

However, the process of decompressing and extracting an audio file is very different for different types of files. While .wav files are stored uncompressed, .mp3, .wma, and .ogg files all utilize totally different compression algorithms.

We can use inheritance with polymorphism to simplify the design. Each type of file can be represented by a different subclass of AudioFile, for example, WavFile and MP3File. Each of these would have a play() method that would be implemented differently for each file to ensure that the correct extraction procedure is followed. The media player object would never need to know which subclass of AudioFile it is referring to; it just calls play() and polymorphically lets the object take care of the actual details of playing. Let's look at a quick skeleton showing how this might work:

```
from pathlib import Path

class AudioFile:
    ext: str
```

```python
    def __init__(self, filepath: Path) -> None:
        if not filepath.suffix == self.ext:
            raise ValueError("Invalid file format")
        self.filepath = filepath

class MP3File(AudioFile):
    ext = ".mp3"

    def play(self) -> None:
        print(f"playing {self.filepath} as mp3")

class WavFile(AudioFile):
    ext = ".wav"

    def play(self) -> None:
        print(f"playing {self.filepath} as wav")

class OggFile(AudioFile):
    ext = ".ogg"

    def play(self) -> None:
        print(f"playing {self.filepath} as ogg")
```

All audio files check to ensure that a valid extension was given upon initialization. If the filename doesn't end with the correct name, it raises an exception (exceptions will be covered in detail in *Chapter 4, Expecting the Unexpected*).

But did you notice how the __init__() method in the parent class is able to access the ext class variable from different subclasses? That's polymorphism at work. The AudioFile parent class merely has a type hint explaining to *mypy* that there will be an attribute named ext. It doesn't actually store a reference to the ext attribute. When the inherited method is used by a subclass, then the subclass' definition of the ext attribute is used. The type hint can help *mypy* spot a class missing the attribute assignment.

In addition, each subclass of AudioFile implements play() in a different way (this example doesn't actually play the music; audio compression algorithms really deserve a separate book!). This is also polymorphism in action. The media player can use the exact same code to play a file, no matter what type it is; it doesn't care what subclass of AudioFile it is looking at. The details of decompressing the audio file are *encapsulated*. If we test this example, it works as we would hope:

```
>>> p_1 = MP3File(Path("Heart of the Sunrise.mp3"))
>>> p_1.play()
playing Heart of the Sunrise.mp3 as mp3
>>> p_2 = WavFile(Path("Roundabout.wav"))
>>> p_2.play()
playing Roundabout.wav as wav
>>> p_3 = OggFile(Path("Heart of the Sunrise.ogg"))
>>> p_3.play()
playing Heart of the Sunrise.ogg as ogg
>>> p_4 = MP3File(Path("The Fish.mov"))
Traceback (most recent call last):
...
ValueError: Invalid file format
```

See how `AudioFile.__init__()` can check the file type without actually knowing which subclass it is referring to?

Polymorphism is actually one of the coolest things about object-oriented programming, and it makes some programming designs obvious that weren't possible in earlier paradigms. However, Python makes polymorphism seem less awesome because of duck typing. Duck typing in Python allows us to use *any* object that provides the required behavior without forcing it to be a subclass. The dynamic nature of Python makes this trivial. The following example does not extend `AudioFile`, but it can be interacted with in Python using the exact same interface:

```python
class FlacFile:
    def __init__(self, filepath: Path) -> None:
        if not filepath.suffix == ".flac":
            raise ValueError("Not a .flac file")
        self.filepath = filepath

    def play(self) -> None:
        print(f"playing {self.filepath} as flac")
```

Our media player can play objects of the `FlacFile` class just as easily as objects of classes that extend `AudioFile`.

Polymorphism is one of the most important reasons to use inheritance in many object-oriented contexts. Because any objects that supply the correct interface can be used interchangeably in Python, it reduces the need for polymorphic common superclasses. Inheritance can still be useful for sharing code, but if all that is being shared is the public interface, duck typing is all that is required.

This reduced need for inheritance also reduces the need for multiple inheritance; often, when multiple inheritance appears to be a valid solution, we can just use duck typing to mimic one of the multiple superclasses.

In some cases, we can formalize this kind of duck typing using a `typing.Protocol` hint. To make *mypy* aware of the expectations, we'll often define a number of functions or attributes (or a mixture) as a formal `Protocol` type. This can help clarify how classes are related. We might, for example, have this kind of definition to define the common features between the `FlacFile` class and the `AudioFile` class hierarchy:

```
class Playable(Protocol):
    def play(self) -> None:
        ...
```

Of course, just because an object satisfies a particular protocol (by providing required methods or attributes) does not mean it will simply work in all situations. It has to fulfill that interface in a way that makes sense in the overall system. Just because an object provides a `play()` method does not mean it will automatically work with a media player. The methods must also have the same meaning, or semantics, in addition to having the same syntax.

Another useful feature of duck typing is that the duck-typed object only needs to provide those methods and attributes that are actually being accessed. For example, if we needed to create a fake file object to read data from, we can create a new object that has a `read()` method; we don't have to override the `write()` method if the code that is going to interact with the fake object will not be calling it. More succinctly, duck typing doesn't need to provide the entire interface of an object that is available; it only needs to fulfill the protocol that is actually used.

Case study

This section expands on the object-oriented design of our example, iris classification. We've been building on this in the previous chapters, and we'll continue building on it in later chapters. In this chapter, we'll review the diagrams created using the **Unified Modeling Language** (**UML**) to help depict and summarize the software we're going to build. We'll move on from the previous chapter to add features for the various ways of computing "nearest" for the *k*-nearest neighbors algorithm. There are a number of variations for this, and it demonstrates how class hierarchies work.

There are several design principles that we'll be exploring as this design becomes more and more complete. One popular set of principles is the **SOLID** principles, which are:

- **S**. Single Responsibility Principle. A class should have one responsibility. This can mean one reason to change when the application's requirements change.
- **O**. Open/Closed. A class should be open to extension but closed to modification.
- **L**. Liskov Substitution. (Named after Barbara Liskov, who created one of the first object-oriented programming languages, CLU.) Any subclass can be substituted for its superclass. This tends to focus a class hierarchy on classes that have very similar interfaces, leading to *polymorphism* among the objects. This the essence of inheritance.
- **I**. Interface Segregation. A class should have the smallest interface possible. This is, perhaps, the most important of these principles. Classes should be relatively small and isolated.
- **D**. Dependency Inversion. This has a peculiar name. We need to know what a bad dependency relationship is so we know how to invert it to have a good relationship. Pragmatically, we'd like classes to be independent, so a Liskov Substitution doesn't involve a lot of code changes. In Python, this often means referring to superclasses in type hints to be sure we have the flexibility to make changes. In some cases, it also means providing parameters so that we can make global class changes without revising any of the code.

We won't look at all of these principles in this chapter. Because we're looking at inheritance, our design will tend to follow the Liskov Substitution design principle. Other chapters will touch on other design principles.

Logical view

Here's the overview of some of the classes shown in the previous chapter's case study. An important omission from those definitions was the `classify` algorithm of the `Hyperparameter` class:

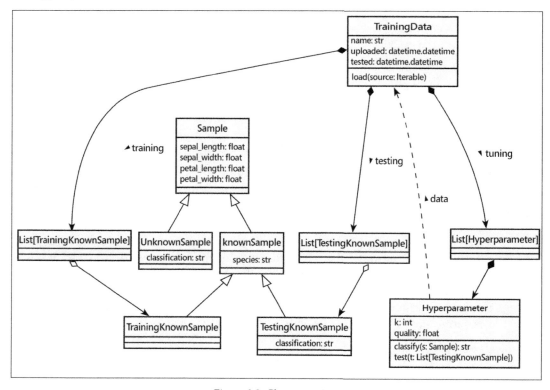

Figure 3.3: Class overview

In the previous chapter, we avoided delving into the classification algorithm. This reflects a common design strategy, sometimes called *"Hard Part, Do Later,"* also called *"Do The Easy Part First."* This strategy encourages following common design patterns where possible to isolate the hard part. In effect, the easy parts define a number of fences that enclose and constrain the novel and unknown parts.

The classification we're doing is based on the *k*-nearest neighbors algorithm, *k*-NN. Given a set of known samples, and an unknown sample, we want to find neighbors near the unknown sample; the majority of the neighbors tells us how to classify the newcomer. This means *k* is usually an odd number, so the majority is easy to compute. We've been avoiding the question, "What do we mean by nearest?"

In a conventional, two-dimensional geometric sense, we can use the "Euclidean" distance between samples. Given an Unknown sample located at (u_x, u_y) and a Training sample at (t_x, t_y), the Euclidean distance between these samples, $ED2(t, u)$, is:

$$ED2(t, u) = \sqrt{(t_x - u_x)^2 + (t_y - u_y)^2}$$

We can visualize it like this:

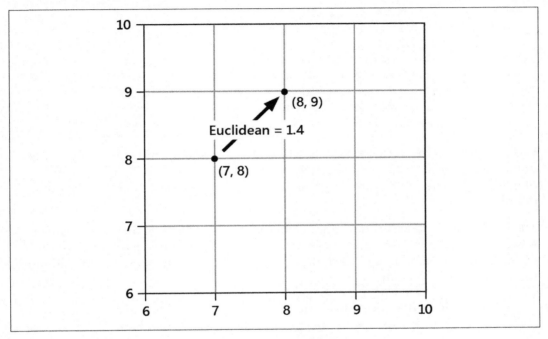

Figure 3.4: Euclidean distance

We've called this ED2 because it's only two-dimensional. In our case study data, we actually have four dimensions: sepal length, sepal width, petal length, and petal width. This is really difficult to visualize, but the math isn't too complex. Even when it's hard to imagine, we can still write it out fully, like so:

$$ED4(t, u) = \sqrt{(t_{sl} - u_{sl})^2 + (t_{sw} - u_{sw})^2 + (t_{pl} - u_{pl})^2 + (t_{pw} - u_{pw})^2}$$

All of the two-dimensional examples expand to four dimensions, in spite of how hard it is to imagine. We'll stick with the easier to visualize *x-y* distance for the diagrams in this section. But we really mean the full four-dimensional computation that includes all of the available measurements.

We can capture this computation as a class definition. An instance of this `ED` class is usable by the `Hyperparameter` class:

```python
class ED(Distance):
    def distance(self, s1: Sample, s2: Sample) -> float:
        return hypot(
            s1.sepal_length - s2.sepal_length,
            s1.sepal_width - s2.sepal_width,
            s1.petal_length - s2.petal_length,
            s1.petal_width - s2.petal_width,
        )
```

We've leveraged the `math.hypot()` function to do the square and square root parts of the distance computation. We've used a superclass, `Distance`, that we haven't defined yet. We're pretty sure it's going to be needed, but we'll hold off a bit on defining it.

The Euclidean distance is one of many alternative definitions of distance between a known and unknown sample. There are two relatively simple ways to compute a distance that are similar, and they often produce consistently good results without the complexity of a square root:

- **Manhattan distance**: This is the distance you would walk in a city with square blocks (somewhat like parts of the city of Manhattan.)

- **Chebyshev distance**: This counts a diagonal step as 1. A Manhattan computation would rank this as 2. The Euclidean distance would be $\sqrt{2} \approx 1.41$, as depicted in *Figure 3.4*.

With a number of alternatives, we're going to need to create distinct subclasses. That means we'll need a base class to define the general idea of distances. Looking over the definitions at hand, it seems like the base class can be the following:

```python
class Distance:
    """Definition of a distance computation"""
    def distance(self, s1: Sample, s2: Sample) -> float:
        pass
```

This seems to capture the essence of the distance computations we've seen. Let's implement a few more subclasses of this to be sure the abstraction really works.

The Manhattan distance is the total number of steps along the x-axis, plus the total number of steps along the y-axis. The formula uses the absolute values of the distances, written as $|t_x - u_x|$, and looks like this:

$$MD(t, u) = |t_x - u_x| + |t_y - u_y|$$

This can be as much as 41% larger than the direct Euclidean distance. However, it will still parallel the direct distance in a way that can yield a good k-NN result, but with a faster computation because it avoids squaring numbers and computing a square root.

Here's a view of the Manhattan distance:

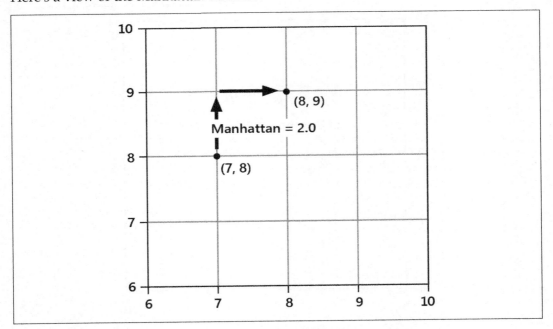

Figure 3.5: Manhattan distance

Here's a subclass of Distance that computes this variation:

```
class MD(Distance):
    def distance(self, s1: Sample, s2: Sample) -> float:
        return sum(
            [
```

```
            abs(s1.sepal_length - s2.sepal_length),
            abs(s1.sepal_width - s2.sepal_width),
            abs(s1.petal_length - s2.petal_length),
            abs(s1.petal_width - s2.petal_width),
        ]
    )
```

The Chebyshev distance is the largest of the absolute x or y distances. This tends to minimize the effects of multiple dimensions:

$$CD(k, u) = max\left(|k_x - u_x|, |k_y - u_y|\right)$$

Here's a view of the Chebyshev distance; it tends to emphasize neighbors that are closer to each other:

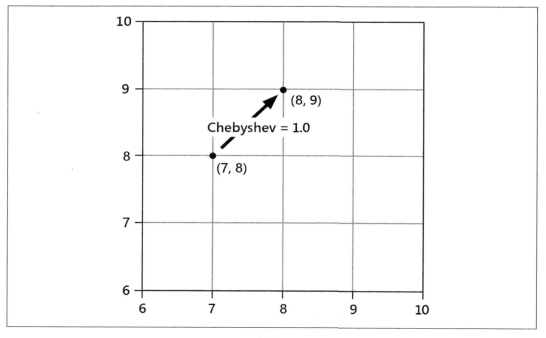

Figure 3.6: Chebyshev distance

Here's a subclass of `Distance` that performs this variant on the distance computation:

```
class CD(Distance())
    def distance(self, s1: Sample, s2: Sample) -> float:
        return sum(
            [
                abs(s1.sepal_length - s2.sepal_length),
                abs(s1.sepal_width - s2.sepal_width),
                abs(s1.petal_length - s2.petal_length),
                abs(s1.petal_width - s2.petal_width),
            ]
        )
```

See *Effects of Distance Measure Choice on KNN Classifier Performance - A Review* (`https://arxiv.org/pdf/1708.04321.pdf`). This paper contains 54 distinct metrics computations. The examples we're looking at are collectively identified as "Minkowski" measures because they're similar and measure each axis equally. Each alternative distance strategy yields different results in the model's ability to classify unknown samples given a set of training data.

This changes the idea behind the `Hyperparameter` class: we now have two distinct hyperparameters. The value of *k*, to decide how many neighbors to examine, and the distance computation, which tells us how to compute "nearest." These are both changeable parts of the algorithm, and we'll need to test various combinations to see which works best for our data.

How can we have all of these different distance computations available? The short answer is we'll need a lot of subclass definitions of a common distance class. The review paper cited above lets us pare down the domain to a few of the more useful distance computations. To be sure we've got a good design, let's look at one more distance.

Another distance

Just to make it clear how easy it is to add subclasses, we'll define a somewhat more complex distance metric. This is the Sorensen distance, also known as Bray-Curtis. If our distance class can handle these kinds of more complex formulas, we can be confident it's capable of handling others:

$$SD(k,u) = \frac{|k_x - u_x| + |k_y - u_y|}{(k_x + u_x) + (k_y + u_y)}$$

We've effectively standardized each component of the Manhattan distance by dividing by the possible range of values.

Here's a diagram to illustrate how the Sorensen distance works:

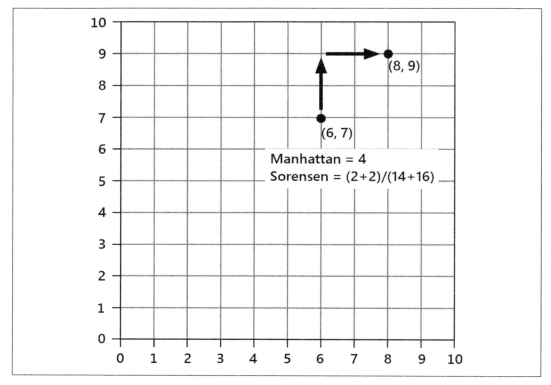

Figure 3.7: Manhattan versus Sorensen distance

The simple Manhattan distance applies no matter how far from the origin we are. The Sorensen distance reduces the importance of measures that are further from the origin so they don't dominate the k-NN by virtue of being large-valued outliers.

We can introduce this into our design by adding a new subclass of Distance. While this is similar, in some ways, to the Manhattan distance, it's often classified separately:

```python
class SD(Distance):
    def distance(self, s1: Sample, s2: Sample) -> float:
        return sum(
            [
```

```
            abs(s1.sepal_length - s2.sepal_length),
            abs(s1.sepal_width - s2.sepal_width),
            abs(s1.petal_length - s2.petal_length),
            abs(s1.petal_width - s2.petal_width),
        ]
    ) / sum(
        [
            s1.sepal_length + s2.sepal_length,
            s1.sepal_width + s2.sepal_width,
            s1.petal_length + s2.petal_length,
            s1.petal_width + s2.petal_width,
        ]
    )
```

This design approach lets us leverage object-oriented inheritance to build a polymorphic family of distance computation functions. We can build on the first few functions to create a wide family of functions and use these as part of hyperparameter tuning to locate the best way to measure distances and perform the required classification.

We'll need to integrate a `Distance` object into the `Hyperparameter` class. This means providing an instance of one of these subclasses. Because they're all implementing the same `distance()` method, we can replace different alternative distance computations to find which performs best with our unique collection of data and attributes.

For now, we can reference a specific distance subclass in our `Hyperparameter` class definition. In *Chapter 11, Common Design Patterns*, we'll look at how we can flexibly plug in any possible distance computation from the hierarchy of `Distance` class definitions.

Recall

Some key points in this chapter:

- A central object-oriented design principle is inheritance: a subclass can inherit aspects of a superclass, saving copy-and-paste programming. A subclass can extend the superclass to add features or specialize the superclass in other ways.

- Multiple inheritance is a feature of Python. The most common form is a host class with mixin class definitions. We can combine multiple classes leveraging the method resolution order to handle common features like initialization.

- Polymorphism lets us create multiple classes that provide alternative implementations for fulfilling a contract. Because of Python's duck typing rules, any classes that have the right methods can substitute for each other.

Exercises

Look around you at some of the physical objects in your workspace and see if you can describe them in an inheritance hierarchy. Humans have been dividing the world into taxonomies like this for centuries, so it shouldn't be difficult. Are there any non-obvious inheritance relationships between classes of objects? If you were to model these objects in a computer application, what properties and methods would they share? Which ones would have to be polymorphically overridden? What properties would be completely different between them?

Now write some code. No, not for the physical hierarchy; that's boring. Physical items have more properties than methods. Just think about a pet programming project you've wanted to tackle in the past year, but never gotten around to. For whatever problem you want to solve, try to think of some basic inheritance relationships and then implement them. Make sure that you also pay attention to the sorts of relationships that you actually don't need to use inheritance for. Are there any places where you might want to use multiple inheritance? Are you sure? Can you see any place where you would want to use a mixin? Try to knock together a quick prototype. It doesn't have to be useful or even partially working. You've seen how you can test code using python -i already; just write some code and test it in the interactive interpreter. If it works, write some more. If it doesn't, fix it!

Now, take a look at the various distance computations in the case study. We need to be able to work with testing data as well as unknown samples provided by a user. What do these two kinds of samples have in common? Can you create a common superclass and use inheritance for these two classes with similar behavior? (We haven't looked closely at the *k*-NN classification yet, but you can provide a "mock" classifier that will provide fake answers.)

When we look at the distance computation, we can see how a Hyperparameter is a composition that includes a distance algorithm plug-in as one of the parameters. Is this a good candidate for a mixin? Why or why not? What limitations does a mixin have that a plug-in does not have?

Summary

We've gone from simple inheritance, one of the most useful tools in the object-oriented programmer's toolbox, all the way through to multiple inheritance – one of the most complicated. Inheritance can be used to add functionality to existing classes and built-in generics. Abstracting similar code into a parent class can help increase maintainability. Methods on parent classes can be called using super, and argument lists must be formatted safely for these calls to work when using multiple inheritance.

In the next chapter, we'll cover the subtle art of handling exceptional circumstances.

4

Expecting the Unexpected

Systems built with software can be fragile. While the software is highly predictable, the runtime context can provide unexpected inputs and situations. Devices fail, networks are unreliable, mere anarchy is loosed on our application. We need to have a way to work around the spectrum of failures that plague computer systems.

There are two broad approaches to dealing with the unforeseen. One approach is to return a recognizable error-signaling value from a function. A value, like None, could be used. Other library functions can then be used by an application to retrieve details of the erroneous condition. A variation on this theme is to pair a return from an OS request with a success or failure indicator. The other approach is to interrupt the normal, sequential execution of statements and divert to statements that handle exceptions. This second approach is what Python does: it eliminates the need to check return values for errors.

In this chapter, we will study **exceptions**, special error objects raised when a normal response is impossible. In particular, we will cover the following:

- How to cause an exception to occur
- How to recover when an exception has occurred
- How to handle different exception types in different ways
- Cleaning up when an exception has occurred
- Creating new types of exception
- Using the exception syntax for flow control

The case study for this chapter will look at data validation. We'll examine a number of ways exceptions can be used to ensure that inputs to our classifier are valid.

We'll start by looking at Python's concept of an Exception, and how exceptions are raised and handled.

Raising exceptions

Python's normal behavior is to execute statements in the order they are found, either in a file or at the >>> prompt interactively. A few statements, specifically if, while, and for, alter the simple top-to-bottom sequence of statement execution. Additionally, an exception can break the sequential flow of execution. Exceptions are raised, and this interrupts the sequential execution of statements.

In Python, the exception that's raised is also an object. There are many different exception classes available, and we can easily define more of our own. The one thing they all have in common is that they inherit from a built-in class called BaseException.

When an exception is raised, everything that was supposed to happen is pre-empted. Instead, exception handling replaces normal processing. Make sense? Don't worry, it will!

The easiest way to cause an exception to occur is to do something silly. Chances are you've done this already and seen the exception output. For example, any time Python encounters a line in your program that it can't understand, it bails with SyntaxError, which is a type of exception. Here's a common one:

```
>>> print "hello world"
  File "<input>", line 1
    print "hello world"
          ^
SyntaxError: Missing parentheses in call to 'print'. Did you mean
print("hello world")?
```

The print() function requires the arguments to be enclosed in parentheses. So, if we type the preceding command into a Python 3 interpreter, we raise a SyntaxError exception.

In addition to SyntaxError, some other common exceptions are shown in the following example:

```
>>> x = 5 / 0
Traceback (most recent call last):
  File "<stdin>", line 1, in <module>
ZeroDivisionError: division by zero

>>> lst = [1,2,3]
>>> print(lst[3])
Traceback (most recent call last):
  File "<stdin>", line 1, in <module>
IndexError: list index out of range

>>> lst + 2
Traceback (most recent call last):
  File "<stdin>", line 1, in <module>
TypeError: can only concatenate list (not "int") to list

>>> lst.add
Traceback (most recent call last):
  File "<stdin>", line 1, in <module>
AttributeError: 'list' object has no attribute 'add'

>>> d = {'a': 'hello'}
>>> d['b']
Traceback (most recent call last):
  File "<stdin>", line 1, in <module>
KeyError: 'b'

>>> print(this_is_not_a_var)
Traceback (most recent call last):
  File "<stdin>", line 1, in <module>
NameError: name 'this_is_not_a_var' is not defined
```

We can partition these exceptions into roughly four categories. Some cases are blurry, but some edges have a bright line separating them:

- Sometimes, these exceptions are indicators of something clearly wrong in our program. Exceptions like SyntaxError and NameError mean we need to find the indicated line number and fix the problem.
- Sometimes, these exceptions are indicators of something wrong in the Python runtime. There's a RuntimeError exception that can get raised. In many cases, this is resolved by downloading and installing a newer Python. (Or, if you're wrestling with a "Release Candidate" version, reporting the bug to the maintainers.)

- Some exceptions are design problems. We may fail to account for an edge case properly and sometimes try to compute an average of an empty list. This will result in a `ZeroDivisionError`. When we find these, again, we'll have to go to the indicated line number. But once we've found the resulting exception, we'll need to work backwards from there to find out what caused the problem that raised the exception. Somewhere there will be an object in an unexpected or not-designed-for state.

- The bulk of the exceptions arise near our program's interfaces. Any user input, or operating system request, including file operations, can encounter problems with the resources outside our program, leading to exceptions. We can subdivide these interface problems further into two sub-groups:

  - External objects in an unusual or unanticipated state. This is common with files that aren't found because the path was spelled incorrectly, or directories that already exist because our application crashed earlier and we restarted it. These will often be some kind of `OSError` with a reasonably clear root cause. It's also common with users entering things incorrectly, or even users maliciously trying to subvert the application. These should be application-specific exceptions to prevent dumb mistakes or intentional abuse.

  - And there's also the (relatively small) category of simple chaos. In the final analysis, a computer system is a lot of interconnected devices and any one of the components could behave badly. These are hard to anticipate and it's harder still to plan a recovery strategy. When working with a small IoT computer, there are few parts, but it may be installed in a challenging physical environment. When working with an enterprise server farm with thousands of components, a 0.1% failure rate means something is always broken.

You may have noticed all of Python's built-in exceptions end with the name `Error`. In Python, the words **error** and **exception** are used almost interchangeably. Errors are sometimes considered more dire than exceptions, but they are dealt with in exactly the same way. Indeed, all the error classes in the preceding example have `Exception` (which extends `BaseException`) as their superclass.

Raising an exception

We'll get to responding to such exceptions in a minute, but first, let's discover what we should do if we're writing a program that needs to inform the user or a calling function that the inputs are invalid. We can use the exact same mechanism that Python uses. Here's a simple class that adds items to a list only if they are even-numbered integers:

```python
from typing import List

class EvenOnly(List[int]):
    def append(self, value: int) -> None:
        if not isinstance(value, int):
            raise TypeError("Only integers can be added")
        if value % 2 != 0:
            raise ValueError("Only even numbers can be added")
        super().append(value)
```

This class extends the built-in list, as we discussed in *Chapter 2, Objects in Python*. We've provided a type hint suggesting we're creating a list of integer objects only. To do this, we've overridden the append method to check two conditions that ensure the item is an even integer. We first check whether the input is an instance of the int type, and then use the modulo operator to ensure it is divisible by two. If either of the two conditions is not met, the raise keyword causes an exception to occur.

The raise keyword is followed by the object being raised as an exception. In the preceding example, two objects are constructed from the built-in TypeError and ValueError classes. The raised object could just as easily be an instance of a new Exception class we create ourselves (we'll see how shortly), an exception that was defined elsewhere, or even an Exception object that has been previously raised and handled.

If we test this class in the Python interpreter, we can see that it is outputting useful error information when exceptions occur, just as before:

```python
>>> e = EvenOnly()
>>> e.append("a string")
Traceback (most recent call last):
  File "<stdin>", line 1, in <module>
  File "even_integers.py", line 7, in add
    raise TypeError("Only integers can be added")
TypeError: Only integers can be added

>>> e.append(3)
Traceback (most recent call last):
  File "<stdin>", line 1, in <module>
  File "even_integers.py", line 9, in add
    raise ValueError("Only even numbers can be added")
ValueError: Only even numbers can be added
>>> e.append(2)
```

While this class is effective for demonstrating exceptions in action, it isn't very good at its job. It is still possible to get other values into the list using index notation or slice notation. These additional behaviors can be avoided by overriding other appropriate methods, some of which are magic double-underscore methods. To be really complete, we'd need to override methods like extend(), insert(), __setitem__ (), and even __init__() to be sure things start off correctly.

The effects of an exception

When an exception is raised, it appears to stop program execution immediately. Any lines that were supposed to run after the exception is raised are not executed, and unless the exception is handled by an except clause, the program will exit with an error message. We'll examine unhandled exceptions first, and then take a close look at handling exceptions.

Take a look at this basic function:

```
from typing import NoReturn

def never_returns() -> NoReturn:
    print("I am about to raise an exception")
    raise Exception("This is always raised")
    print("This line will never execute")
    return "I won't be returned"
```

We've included the NoReturn type hint for this function. This helps ease *mypy*'s worry that there's no way for this function to reach the end and return a string value. The type hint states, formally, the function isn't expected to return a value.

(Note that *mypy* is aware the final return cannot be executed. It does not object to the return type being NoReturn, even though there's a return statement with a string literal. It's clear this cannot be executed.)

If we execute this function, we see that the first print() call is executed and then the exception is raised. The second print() function call is never executed, nor is the return statement. Here's what it looks like:

```
>>> never_returns()
I am about to raise an exception
Traceback (most recent call last):
  File "<input>", line 1, in <module>
  File "<input>", line 6, in never_returns
Exception: This is always raised
```

Furthermore, if we have a function that calls another function that raises an exception, nothing is executed in the first function after the point where the second function's exception was raised. Raising an exception stops all execution right up through the function call stack until it is either handled or forces the interpreter to exit. To demonstrate, let's add a second function that calls the never_returns() function:

```
def call_exceptor() -> None:
    print("call_exceptor starts here...")
    never_returns()
    print("an exception was raised...")
    print("...so these lines don't run")
```

When we call this function, we see that the first print statement executes, as well as the first line in the never_returns() function. But once the exception is raised, nothing else executes:

```
>>> call_exceptor()
call_exceptor starts here...
I am about to raise an exception
Traceback (most recent call last):
  File "<input>", line 1, in <module>
  File "<input>", line 3, in call_exceptor
  File "<input>", line 6, in never_returns
Exception: This is always raised
```

Note that *mypy* didn't recognize what never_returns() does to the processing in call_exceptor(). Based on previous examples, it seems like call_exceptor() is better described as a NoReturn function. When we try this, we get a warning from *mypy*. It turns out the *mypy* focus is rather narrow; it examines function and method definitions in relative isolation; it isn't aware that never_returns() raises an exception.

We can control how exceptions propagate from the initial raise statement. We can react to and deal with the exception inside either of these methods in the call stack.

Look at the output from the unhandled exception above, called a **traceback**. This shows the call stack. The command line ("<module>" is the name used when there's no input file) called call_exceptor(), and call_exceptor() called never_returns(). Inside never_returns(), the exception is initially raised.

The exception propagates up through the call stack. From inside `call_exceptor()`, the pesky `never_returns()` function was called and the exception *bubbled up* to the calling method. From there, it went up one more level to the main interpreter, which, not knowing what else to do with it, gave up and printed the traceback object.

Handling exceptions

Now let's look at the tail side of the exception coin. If we encounter an exception situation, how should our code react to or recover from it? We handle exceptions by wrapping any code that might throw one (whether it is exception code itself, or a call to any function or method that may have an exception raised inside it) inside a `try...except` clause. The most basic syntax looks like this:

```
def handler() -> None:
    try:
        never_returns()
        print("Never executed")
    except Exception as ex:
        print(f"I caught an exception: {ex!r}")
    print("Executed after the exception")
```

If we run this simple script using our existing `never_returns()` function—which, as we know very well, always throws an exception—we get this output:

```
I am about to raise an exception
I caught an exception: Exception('This is always raised')
Executed after the exception
```

The `never_returns()` function happily informs us that it is about to raise an exception and raises it. The `handler()` function's except clause catches the exception. Once caught, we are able to clean up after ourselves (in this case, by outputting that we are handling the situation), and continue on our way. The remainder of the code in the `never_returns()` function remains unexecuted, but the code in the `handler()` function after the `try:` statement is able to recover and continue.

Note the indentation around `try` and `except`. The `try` clause wraps any code that might throw an exception. The `except` clause is then back on the same indentation level as the `try` line. Any code to handle the exception is indented inside the `except` clause. Then normal code resumes at the original indentation level.

The problem with the preceding code is that it uses the `Exception` class to match any type of exception. What if we were writing some code that could raise either `TypeError` or `ZeroDivisionError`? We might need to catch `ZeroDivisionError` because it reflects a known object state, but let any other exceptions propagate to the console because they reflect bugs we need to catch and kill. Can you guess the syntax?

Here's a rather silly function that does just that:

```python
from typing import Union

def funny_division(divisor: float) -> Union[str, float]:
    try:
        return 100 / divisor
    except ZeroDivisionError:
        return "Zero is not a good idea!"
```

This function does a simple computation. We've provided the type hint of `float` for the `divisor` parameter. We can provide an integer, and ordinary Python type coercion will work. The *mypy* tool is aware of the ways integers can be coerced to floats, saving it from having to obsess over the parameter types.

We do, however, have to be very clear about the return types. If we don't raise an exception, we'll compute and return a floating result. If we do raise a `ZeroDivisionError` exception, it will be handled, and we'll return a string result. Any other exceptions? Let's try it and see:

```
>>> print(funny_division(0))
Zero is not a good idea!
>>> print(funny_division(50.0))
2.0
>>> print(funny_division("hello"))
Traceback (most recent call last):
...
TypeError: unsupported operand type(s) for /: 'int' and 'str'
```

The first line of output shows that if we enter 0, we get properly mocked. If we call with a valid number, it operates correctly. Yet if we enter a string (you were wondering how to get a `TypeError`, weren't you?), it fails with an unhandled exception. If we don't specify matching the `ZeroDivisionError` exception class, our handler would also see the `TypeError`, and accuse us of dividing by zero when we sent it a string, which is not a proper behavior at all.

Python also has a bare except syntax. Using `except:` with no exception class to match is widely frowned upon because it will prevent an application from simply crashing when it should. We generally use `except Exception:` to explicitly catch a sensible set of exceptions.

The bare except syntax is actually the same as using `except BaseException:`, which attempts to handle system-level exceptions that are often impossible to recover from. Indeed, this can make it impossible to crash your application when it's misbehaving.

We can even catch two or more different exceptions and handle them with the same code. Here's an example that raises three different types of exceptions. It handles `TypeError` and `ZeroDivisionError` with the same exception handler, but it may also raise a `ValueError` error if you supply the number 13:

```python
def funnier_division(divisor: int) -> Union[str, float]:
    try:
        if divisor == 13:
            raise ValueError("13 is an unlucky number")
        return 100 / divisor
    except (ZeroDivisionError, TypeError):
        return "Enter a number other than zero"
```

We've included multiple exception classes in the `except` clause. This lets us handle a variety of conditions with a common handler. Here's how we can test this with a bunch of different values:

```python
>>> for val in (0, "hello", 50.0, 13):
...     print(f"Testing {val!r}:", end=" ")
...     print(funnier_division(val))
...
Testing 0: Enter a number other than zero
Testing 'hello': Enter a number other than zero
Testing 50.0: 2.0
Testing 13: Traceback (most recent call last):
  File "<input>", line 3, in <module>
  File "<input>", line 4, in funnier_division
ValueError: 13 is an unlucky number
```

The `for` statement iterates over several test inputs and prints the results. If you're wondering about that `end` parameter in the `print` function, it just turns the default trailing newline into a space so that it's joined with the output from the next line.

The number 0 and the string are both caught by the `except` clause, and a suitable error message is printed. The exception from the number 13 is not caught because it is a `ValueError`, which was not included in the types of exceptions being handled. This is all well and good, but what if we want to catch different exceptions and do different things with them? Or maybe we want to do something with an exception and then allow it to continue to bubble up to the parent function, as if it had never been caught?

We don't need any new syntax to deal with these cases. It's possible to stack the `except` clauses, and only the first match will be executed. For the second question, the `raise` keyword, with no arguments, will re-raise the last exception if we're already inside an exception handler. Observe the following code:

```
def funniest_division(divisor: int) -> Union[str, float]:
    try:
        if divider == 13:
            raise ValueError("13 is an unlucky number")
        return 100 / divider
    except ZeroDivisionError:
        return "Enter a number other than zero"
    except TypeError:
        return "Enter a numerical value"
    except ValueError:
        print("No, No, not 13!")
        raise
```

The last line re-raises the `ValueError` error, so after outputting No, No, not 13!, it will raise the exception again; we'll still get the original stack trace on the console.

If we stack exception clauses like we did in the preceding example, only the first matching clause will be run, even if more than one of them fits. How can more than one clause match? Remember that exceptions are objects, and can therefore be subclassed. As we'll see in the next section, most exceptions extend the `Exception` class (which is itself derived from `BaseException`). If we have an `except` clause to match `Exception` before we match `TypeError`, then only the `Exception` handler will be executed, because `TypeError` is an `Exception` by inheritance.

This can come in handy in cases where we want to handle some exceptions specifically, and then handle all remaining exceptions as a more general case. We can list `Exception` in its own clause after catching all the specific exceptions and handle the general case there.

Often, when we catch an exception, we need a reference to the `Exception` object itself. This most often happens when we define our own exceptions with custom arguments, but can also be relevant with standard exceptions. Most exception classes accept a set of arguments in their constructor, and we might want to access those attributes in the exception handler. If we define our own `Exception` class, we can even call custom methods on it when we catch it. The syntax for capturing an exception as a variable uses the as keyword:

```
>>> try:
...       raise ValueError("This is an argument")
... except ValueError as e:
...       print(f"The exception arguments were {e.args}")
...
The exception arguments were ('This is an argument',)
```

When we run this snippet, it prints out the string argument that we passed into `ValueError` upon initialization.

We've seen several variations on the syntax for handling exceptions, but we still don't know how to execute code regardless of whether or not an exception has occurred. We also can't specify code that should be executed **only** if an exception does **not** occur. Two more keywords, `finally` and `else`, provide some additional execution paths. Neither one takes any extra arguments.

We'll show an example with the `finally` clause. For the most part, we often use context managers instead of exception blocks as a cleaner way to implement a finalization that occurs whether or not an exception interrupted processing. The idea is to encapsulate responsibility for finalization in the context manager.

The following example iterates through a number of exception classes, raising an instance of each. Then some not-so-complicated exception handling code runs that illustrates the newly introduced syntax:

```
some_exceptions = [ValueError, TypeError, IndexError, None]

for choice in some_exceptions:
    try:
        print(f"\nRaising {choice}")
        if choice:
            raise choice("An error")
```

```
    else:
        print("no exception raised")
except ValueError:
    print("Caught a ValueError")
except TypeError:
    print("Caught a TypeError")
except Exception as e:
    print(f"Caught some other error: {e.__class__.__name__}")
else:
    print("This code called if there is no exception")
finally:
    print("This cleanup code is always called")
```

If we run this example – which illustrates almost every conceivable exception handling scenario – we'll see the following output:

```
(CaseStudy39) % python ch_04/src/all_exceptions.py

Raising <class 'ValueError'>
Caught a ValueError
This cleanup code is always called

Raising <class 'TypeError'>
Caught a TypeError
This cleanup code is always called

Raising <class 'IndexError'>
Caught some other error: IndexError
This cleanup code is always called

Raising None
no exception raised
This code called if there is no exception
This cleanup code is always called
```

Note how the print statement in the finally clause is executed no matter what happens. This is one way to perform certain tasks after our code has finished running (even if an exception has occurred). Some common examples include the following:

- Cleaning up an open database connection
- Closing an open file
- Sending a closing handshake over the network

All of these are more commonly handled with context managers, one of the topics of *Chapter 8, The Intersection of Object-Oriented and Functional Programming*.

 While obscure, the `finally` clause is executed after the `return` statement inside a `try` clause. While this can be exploited for post-`return` processing, it can also be confusing to folks reading the code.

Also, pay attention to the output when no exception is raised: both the `else` and the `finally` clauses are executed. The `else` clause may seem redundant, as the code that should be executed when no exception is raised could just be placed after the entire `try...except` block. The difference is that the `else` block will not be executed if an exception is caught and handled. We'll see more on this when we discuss using exceptions as flow control later.

Any of the `except`, `else`, and `finally` clauses can be omitted after a `try` block (although `else` by itself is invalid). If you include more than one, the `except` clauses must come first, then the `else` clause, with the `finally` clause at the end. You must be sure the order of the `except` clauses has classes that move from the most specific subclasses to most generic superclasses.

The exception hierarchy

We've already seen several of the most common built-in exceptions, and you'll probably encounter the rest over the course of your regular Python development. As we noticed earlier, most exceptions are subclasses of the `Exception` class. But this is not true of all exceptions. The `Exception` class actually extends a class called `BaseException`. In fact, all exceptions must extend the `BaseException` class or one of its subclasses.

There are two key built-in exception classes, `SystemExit` and `KeyboardInterrupt`, that derive directly from the `BaseException` class instead of the `Exception` class. The `SystemExit` exception is raised whenever the program exits naturally, typically because we called the `sys.exit()` function somewhere in our code (for example, when the user selected an exit menu item, clicked the *Close* button on a window, entered a command to shut down a server, or the OS sent a signal to the application to terminate). This exception is designed to allow us to clean up code before the program ultimately exits.

If we do handle the `SystemExit` exception, we would normally re-raise the exception, since catching it could stop the program from exiting. Imagine a web service with a bug that is holding database locks and can't be stopped without rebooting the server.

We don't want a SystemExit exception to be accidentally caught in generic except Exception: clauses. This is why it derives directly from BaseException.

The KeyboardInterrupt exception is common in command-line programs. It is thrown when the user explicitly interrupts program execution with an OS-dependent key combination (normally, *Ctrl + C*). For Linux and macOS users, the kill -2 <pid> command will also work. This is a standard way for the user to deliberately interrupt a running program and, like the SystemExit exception, it should almost always respond by terminating the program. Also, like SystemExit, it can handle any cleanup tasks inside the finally blocks.

Here is a class diagram that fully illustrates the hierarchy:

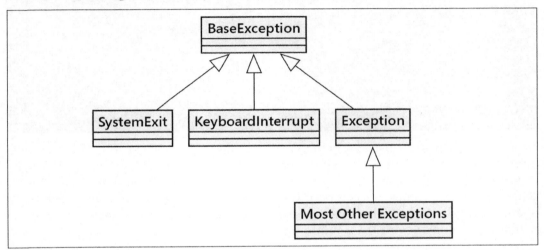

Figure 4.1: Exception hierarchy

When we use the except: clause without specifying any type of exception, it will catch all subclasses of BaseException; which is to say, it will catch all exceptions, including the two special ones. Since we almost always want these to get special treatment, it is unwise to use the except: statement without arguments. If you want to catch all exceptions (other than SystemExit and KeyboardInterrupt), always explicitly catch Exception. Most Python developers assume that except: without a type is an error and will flag it in code review.

Defining our own exceptions

Occasionally, when we want to raise an exception, we find that none of the built-in exceptions are suitable. The distinction is often focused on how applications must handle the exception; when we introduce a new exception it must be because there will be distinct processing in a handler.

There's no good reason to define an exception that's handled exactly like `ValueError`; we can use `ValueError`. Luckily, it's trivial to define new exceptions of our own. The name of the class is usually designed to communicate what went wrong, and we can provide arbitrary arguments in the initializer to include additional information.

All we have to do is inherit from the `Exception` class or one of the existing exceptions that's semantically similar. We don't even have to add any content to the class! We can, of course, extend `BaseException` directly, but this means we're inventing new ways of stopping a running program, a very unusual thing to be creating.

Here's a simple exception we might use in a banking application:

```
>>> class InvalidWithdrawal(ValueError):
...     pass

>>> raise InvalidWithdrawal("You don't have $50 in your account")

Traceback (most recent call last):
  File "<input>", line 1, in <module>
InvalidWithdrawal: You don't have $50 in your account
```

The `raise` statement illustrates how to raise the newly defined exception. We are able to pass an arbitrary number of arguments into the exception. Often a string message is used, but any object that might be useful in a later exception handler can be stored. The `Exception.__init__()` method is designed to accept any arguments and store them as a tuple in an attribute named `args`. This makes exceptions easier to define without needing to override `__init__()`.

Of course, if we do want to customize the initializer, we are free to do so. Here's a revision to the above exception whose initializer accepts the current balance and the amount the user wants to withdraw. In addition, it adds a method to calculate how overdrawn the request is:

```
>>> from decimal import Decimal
>>> class InvalidWithdrawal(ValueError):
...     def __init__(self, balance: Decimal, amount: Decimal) -> None:
...         super().__init__(f"account doesn't have ${amount}")
...         self.amount = amount
...         self.balance = balance
...     def overage(self) -> Decimal:
...         return self.amount - self.balance
```

Since we're working with currency, we've imported the `Decimal` class of numbers. We can't use Python's default `int` or `float` types for money where there are a fixed number of decimal places and exquisitely complex rounding rules that assume exact decimal arithmetic.

(Also note that the account number is not part of the exception. Bankers frown on using account numbers in a way that could expose them in a log or a traceback message.)

Here's an example of creating an instance of this exception:

```
>>> raise InvalidWithdrawal(Decimal('25.00'), Decimal('50.00'))
Traceback (most recent call last):
...
InvalidWithdrawal: account doesn't have $50.00
```

Here's how we would handle an `InvalidWithdrawal` exception if one was raised:

```
>>> try:
...     balance = Decimal('25.00')
...     raise InvalidWithdrawal(balance, Decimal('50.00'))
... except InvalidWithdrawal as ex:
...     print("I'm sorry, but your withdrawal is "
...           "more than your balance by "
...           f"${ex.overage()}")
```

Here we see a valid use of the `as` keyword to save the exception in a local variable, ex. By convention, most Python coders assign the exception a variable like ex, exc, or exception; although, as usual, you are free to call it the_exception_raised_above, or aunt_sally if you prefer.

There are many reasons for defining our own exceptions. It is often useful to add information to the exception or log it in some way. But the utility of custom exceptions truly comes to light when creating a framework, library, or API that is intended for access by other programmers. In that case, be careful to ensure your code is raising exceptions that make sense to the client programmer. Here are some criteria:

- They should clearly describe what went on. The `KeyError` exception, for example, provides the key that could not be found.
- The client programmer should easily see how to fix the error (if it reflects a bug in their code) or handle the exception (if it's a situation they need to be made aware of).

- The handling should be distinct from other exceptions. If the handling is the same as an existing exception, reusing the existing exception is best.

Now that we've looked at raising exceptions and defining new exceptions, we can look at some of the design considerations that surround exceptional data and responding to problems. There are a number of alternative design choices, and we'll start with the idea that exceptions, in Python, can be used for a number of things that aren't – strictly speaking – erroneous.

Exceptions aren't exceptional

Novice programmers tend to think of exceptions as only useful for exceptional circumstances. However, the definition of exceptional circumstances can be vague and subject to interpretation. Consider the following two functions:

```python
def divide_with_exception(dividend: int, divisor: int) -> None:
    try:
        print(f"{dividend / divisor=}")
    except ZeroDivisionError:
        print("You can't divide by zero")

def divide_with_if(dividend: int, divisor: int) -> None:
    if divisor == 0:
        print("You can't divide by zero")
    else:
        print(f"{dividend / divisor=}")
```

These two functions behave identically. If divisor is zero, an error message is printed; otherwise, a message printing the result of the division is displayed. We could avoid ZeroDivisionError ever being thrown by testing for it with an if statement. In this example, the test for a valid division is relatively simple-looking (divisor == 0). In some cases, it can be rather complex. In some cases, it may involve computing intermediate results. In the worst cases, the test for "will this work?" involves using a number of other methods of a class to – in effect – dry-run the operation to see if there would be an error along the way.

Python programmers tend to follow a model summarized by "**It's Easier to Ask Forgiveness Than Permission**," sometimes abbreviated EAFP. The point is to execute code and then deal with anything that goes wrong. The alternative is described as "**Look Before You Leap**," often abbreviated LBYL. This is generally less popular. There are a few reasons for this, but the main one is that it shouldn't be necessary to burn CPU cycles looking for an unusual situation that is not going to arise in the normal path through the code.

Therefore, it is wise to use exceptions for exceptional circumstances, even if those circumstances are only a little bit exceptional. Taking this argument further, exception syntax can be effective for flow control. Like an if statement, exceptions can be used for decision making, branching, and message passing.

Imagine an inventory application for a company that sells widgets and gadgets. When a customer makes a purchase, the item can either be available, in which case the item is removed from inventory and the number of items left is returned, or it might be out of stock. Now, being out of stock is a perfectly normal thing to happen in an inventory application. It is certainly not an exceptional circumstance. But what do we return if it's out of stock? A string saying "out of stock"? A negative number? In both cases, the calling method would have to check whether the return value is a positive integer or something else, to determine if it is out of stock. That seems a bit messy, especially if we forget to do it somewhere in our code.

Instead, we can raise an OutOfStock exception and use the try statement to direct program flow control. Make sense? In addition, we want to make sure we don't sell the same item to two different customers, or sell an item that isn't in stock yet. One way to facilitate this is to lock each type of item to ensure only one person can update it at a time. The user must lock the item, manipulate the item (purchase, add stock, count items left...), and then unlock the item. (This is, in effect, a context manager, one subject of *Chapter 8*.)

Here's an incomplete Inventory example with docstrings that describes what some of the methods should do:

```python
class OutOfStock(Exception):
    pass


class InvalidItemType(Exception):
    pass


class Inventory:
    def __init__(self, stock: list[ItemType]) -> None:
        pass

    def lock(self, item_type: ItemType) -> None:
        """Context Entry.
        Lock the item type so nobody else can manipulate the
        inventory while we're working."""
        pass

    def unlock(self, item_type: ItemType) -> None:
```

```
            """Context Exit.
            Unlock the item type."""
            pass

    def purchase(self, item_type: ItemType) -> int:
        """If the item is not locked, raise a
        ValueError because something went wrong.
        If the item_type does not exist,
          raise InvalidItemType.
        If the item is currently out of stock,
          raise OutOfStock.
        If the item is available,
          subtract one item; return the number of items left.
        """
        # Mocked results.
        if item_type.name == "Widget":
            raise OutOfStock(item_type)
        elif item_type.name == "Gadget":
            return 42
        else:
            raise InvalidItemType(item_type)
```

We could hand this object prototype to a developer and have them implement the methods to do exactly as they say while we work on the code needed to make a purchase. We'll use Python's robust exception handling to consider different branches, depending on how the purchase was made. We can even write a test case to be sure there's no question about how this class should work.

Here's a definition of `ItemType`, just to round out the example:

```
class ItemType:
    def __init__(self, name: str) -> None:
        self.name = name
        self.on_hand = 0
```

Here's an interactive session using this `Inventory` class:

```
>>> widget = ItemType("Widget")
>>> gadget = ItemType("Gadget")
>>> inv = Inventory([widget, gadget])

>>> item_to_buy = widget
>>> inv.lock(item_to_buy)
```

```
>>> try:
...     num_left = inv.purchase(item_to_buy)
... except InvalidItemType:
...     print(f"Sorry, we don't sell {item_to_buy.name}")
... except OutOfStock:
...     print("Sorry, that item is out of stock.")
... else:
...     print(f"Purchase complete. There are {num_left}
{item_to_buy.name}s left")
... finally:
...     inv.unlock(item_to_buy)
...
Sorry, that item is out of stock.
```

All the possible exception handling clauses are used to ensure the correct actions happen at the correct time. Even though OutOfStock is not a terribly exceptional circumstance, we are able to use an exception to handle it suitably. This same code could be written with an if...elif...else structure, but it wouldn't be as easy to read or maintain.

As an aside, one of the exception messages, There are {num_left} {item_to_buy. name}s left, suffers from a goofy English grammar problem. When there's only one item left, it needs a major revision to There is {num_left} {item_to_buy.name} left. In order to support a sensible approach to translation, it's best to avoid fiddling around with grammar details inside the f-string. It's best to deal with it in the else: clause, using something like this to select the message with appropriate grammar:

```
msg = (
    f"there is {num_left} {item_to_buy.name} left"
    if num_left == 1
    else f"there are {num_left} {item_to_buy.name}s left")
print(msg)
```

We can also use exceptions to pass messages between different methods. For example, if we wanted to inform the customer as to what date the item is expected to be in stock again, we could ensure our OutOfStock object requires a back_in_stock parameter when it is constructed. Then, when we handle the exception, we can check that value and provide additional information to the customer. The information attached to the object can be easily passed between two different parts of the program. The exception could even provide a method that instructs the inventory object to reorder or backorder an item.

Using exceptions for flow control can make for some handy program designs. The important thing to take from this discussion is that exceptions are not a bad thing that we should try to avoid. Having an exception occur does not mean that you should have prevented this exceptional circumstance from happening. Rather, it is just a powerful way to communicate information between two sections of code that may not be directly calling each other.

Case study

This chapter's case study will look at some ways that we can find – and help the users fix – potential problems with the data or the application's computations. Both the data and the processing are possible sources of exceptional behavior. They aren't, however, equivalent; we can compare the two as follows:

- Exceptional data is the most common source of problems. The data may not follow the syntax rules and have an invalid physical format. Other, more minor errors may stem from data not having a recognized logical organization, for example wrong spelling of column names. Exceptions can also reflect users attempting to perform an unauthorized operation. We need to alert users and administrators of invalid data or invalid operations.

- Exceptional processing is what is commonly called a **bug**. An application shouldn't try to recover from these problems. While we prefer to find them as part of unit or integration testing (see *Chapter 13, Testing Object-Oriented Programs*), it's possible that a problem escaped our scrutiny and wound up in production, and is exposed to the users of our software. We need to tell the users that something's broken and – as gracefully as possible – stop processing, or "crash." To continue in the presence of a bug is a serious breach of trust.

In our case study, we have three kinds of inputs that need to be examined for potential problems:

1. The known `Sample` instances, provided by a Botanist, and reflecting expert judgement. While this data should be exemplary in its quality, there's no guarantee that someone didn't accidentally rename a file and replace good data with something invalid or otherwise unprocessable.

2. The unknown `Sample` instances, provided by Researchers. These may have all kinds of data quality problems. We'll look at few of them.

3. Actions taken by a Researcher or a Botanist. We'll review the use cases to see what actions should be allowed by each class of user. In some cases, these problems are prevented by offering each class of user a focused menu of actions they can take.

We'll start with a review of the use cases, so we can identify the kinds of exceptions that are required by this application.

Context view

The role of "User" in the Context Diagram from *Chapter 1* is – at this point – less than ideal. It was tolerable as an initial description of the interfaces to the application. As we work through the design, we can see that a more specific term like "Researcher" might be a better description for someone researching a sample and looking for a classification.

Here's an expanded context diagram with a new consideration of users and their authorized actions:

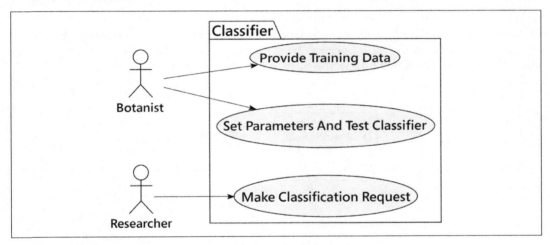

Figure 4.2: Application context diagram

The Botanist is responsible for one kind of data, and has two valid operations. The Researcher is responsible for a different kind of data, and has only one valid operation.

The data and the processing use cases are intimately tied together. When a Botanist provides new training data or sets the parameters and tests the classifier, the application software must be sure their inputs are valid.

Similarly, when a Researcher tries to classify a sample, the software must confirm that the data is valid and can be used. Invalid data must be reported to the Researcher so they can fix their inputs and try again.

We can decompose handling bad data into two parts, each of which is tackled separately:

- Discovering exceptional data. As we've seen in this chapter, this is implemented as raising an exception when invalid data is encountered.

- Responding to exceptional data. This is implemented as a `try:`/`except:` block that provides useful information on the nature of the problem and likely courses of action to resolve it.

We'll start with discovering the exceptional data, first. Raising the right exception is the foundation for handling bad data.

Processing view

While there are a lot of data objects in this application, we're going to narrow our focus to the KnownSample and UnknownSample classes. These two are related to a common superclass, the Sample class. These are created by two other classes. The following diagram shows where the Sample objects are created:

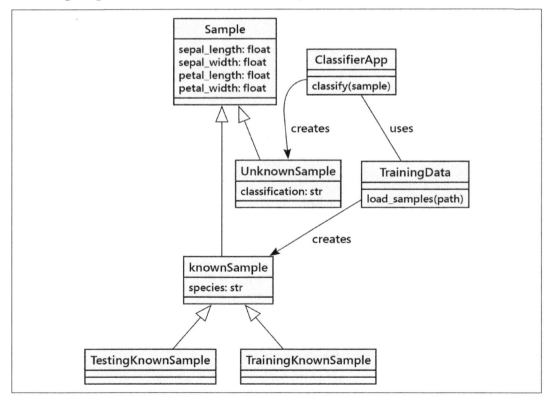

Figure 4.3: Object creation

We've included two classes that will create these two kinds of samples. The `TrainingData` class will load known samples. An overall `ClassifierApp` class will validate an unknown sample, and attempt to classify it.

A `KnownSample` object has five attributes, each of which has a narrowly-defined set of valid values:

- The measurements, `sepal_length`, `sepal_width`, `petal_length`, `petal_width`, are all floating-point numbers. There's a lower-bound of zero for these values.

- The expert-supplied `species` value is a string, with three valid values.

An `UnknownSample` object has only the four measurements. The idea of using a common superclass definition can help us ensure this validation processing is reused.

The rules for valid values listed above only define the valid values for each attribute considered in isolation. In some applications, there may be complex relationships among the attributes, or rules that define relationships among the samples. For our case study, we'll focus on the five attribute validation rules.

What can go wrong?

It helps to consider what can go wrong when loading a `Sample` object, and what – if anything – the user can do about it. Our sample validation rules suggest we may want to raise specialized kinds of `ValueError` exceptions to describe data where the measurements aren't valid float values or the species name isn't one of the known strings.

We can use a class like the following to define the condition of bad data that can't be processed:

```
class InvalidSampleError(ValueError):
    """Source data file has invalid data representation"""
```

This lets us raise an `InvalidSampleError` exception for input data that this application can't process. The intent is to provide a message with the details of what needs to be repaired.

This can help us distinguish between bugs in our code, which may raise a `ValueError` exception, and correct behavior in the presence of bad data, where the `InvalidSampleError` exception will be raised. This means we need to be specific in our `except:` blocks, using the `InvalidSampleError` exception.

If we ever use except `ValueError:`, it will handle both generic exceptions as well as our unique exception. This means we might treat a more serious bug as invalid data. The trick is to be cautious handling generic exceptions; we may be working around a bug.

Bad behavior

Earlier we suggested that a user might attempt an action which is invalid. For example, a Researcher might try to provide classified `KnownSample` objects. The action of loading new training data is reserved for the Botanist; this means an attempt by a Researcher should raise some kind of exception.

Our application works in the context of the overall operating system. For command-line applications, we can partition users into two groups, and use the operating system file ownership and access permissions to limit which group can run which applications. This is an effective and comprehensive solution, and doesn't require any Python code.

For web-based applications, however, we need to authenticate each user to a web application. All of the web application frameworks for Python provide user authentication mechanisms. Many frameworks have handy plug-ins for systems like Open Authentication, OAuth. See `https://oauth.net/2/` for more information.

For web applications, we generally have two tiers of processing:

- **Authentication** of the user. This is where a user identifies themselves. This might involve a single factor like a password, or multiple factors like a physical key or an interaction with a cell phone.

- **Authorization** to perform some action. We'll often define roles for the users, and limit access to various resources based on the user's role. This means raising an exception when the user doesn't have the appropriate role to access a resource.

Many web frameworks will use exceptions as an internal signal that something should not be allowed. This internal exception must then be mapped to external HTTP status codes, like a `401 Authorization Required` response.

This is a deep topic, outside the scope of this book. See, for example, *Building Web Applications with Flask* (`https://www.packtpub.com/product/building-web-applications-with-flask/9781784396152`) for an introduction to web applications.

Creating samples from CSV files

Details of various options for reading samples in different file formats is something we need to defer to *Chapter 9, Strings, Serialization, and File Paths*, where we talk in detail about serialization techniques. For now, we'll skip a number of details and focus on an approach that works very nicely for CSV-formatted data.

CSV – Comma-Separated Values – can be used to define the rows of a spreadsheet. Within each row, the cell values are represented as text, separated by commas. When this data is parsed by Python's csv module, each row can be represented by a dictionary where the keys are the column names and the values are the cell values from a particular row.

For example, a row might look like this:

```
>>> row = {"sepal_length": "5.1", "sepal_width": "3.5",
... "petal_length": "1.4", "petal_width": "0.2",
... "species": "Iris-setosa"}
```

The csv module's DictReader class provides an iterable sequence of dict[str, str] row instances. We need to transform these raw rows into instances of one of the subclasses of Sample, if all of the features have valid string values. If the raw data isn't valid, then we need to raise an exception.

Given rows like the example above, here's a method that will translate from the dictionary to a more useful object. This is part of the KnownSample class:

```
@classmethod
def from_dict(cls, row: dict[str, str]) -> "KnownSample":
    if row["species"] not in {
            "Iris-setosa", "Iris-versicolour", "Iris-virginica"}:
        raise InvalidSampleError(f"invalid species in {row!r}")
    try:
        return cls(
            species=row["species"],
            sepal_length=float(row["sepal_length"]),
            sepal_width=float(row["sepal_width"]),
            petal_length=float(row["petal_length"]),
            petal_width=float(row["petal_width"]),
        )
    except ValueError as ex:
        raise InvalidSampleError(f"invalid {row!r}")
```

The from_dict() method makes a check of the species value, raising an exception if it's not valid. It attempts to create a row, applying the float() function to convert various measurements from string values to float values. If the conversions all work, then the cls parameter – the class to create – will build the expected object.

If any of the float() function evaluations encounters a problem, and raises a ValueError exception; this is used to create our application's unique InvalidSampleError exception.

This style of validation is a mixture of some **Look Before You Leap (LBYL)** and **Easier to Ask Forgiveness than Permission (EAFP)** styles. The most widely-used approach in Python is EAFP. In the case of the species value, however, there's no conversion function similar to float() to raise an exception or bad data. In this example, we've chosen to use LBYL for this attribute value. We'll look at an alternative below.

The from_dict() method is defined with the @classmethod decoration. This means the actual class object becomes the first parameter, cls. When we do this, it means any subclass that inherits this will have the method tailored for that subclass. We can create a new subclass, for example, TrainingKnownSample, using code like this:

```
class TrainingKnownSample(KnownSample):
    pass
```

The TrainingKnownSample.from_dict() method will be given the TrainingKnownSample class as the cls parameter value; without any other code, the from_dict() method of this class will build instances of the TrainingKnownSample class.

While this works nicely, it's not clear to *mypy* that it works. We can use the following definition to provide an explicit type mapping:

```
class TrainingKnownSample(KnownSample):
    @classmethod
    def from_dict(cls, row: dict[str, str]) -> "TrainingKnownSample":
        return cast(TrainingKnownSample, super().from_dict(row))
```

An alternative is to use the simpler class definition and put the cast() operation in the places where from_dict() is actually used, for example, cast(TrainingKnownSample, TrainingKnownSample.from_dict(data)). Since this method is not used in very many places, it's difficult to assert which variation is simpler.

Here's the rest of the KnownSample class, repeated from the previous chapter:

```
class KnownSample(Sample):

    def __init__(
        self,
        species: str,
        sepal_length: float,
        sepal_width: float,
        petal_length: float,
        petal_width: float,
    ) -> None:
        super().__init__(
            sepal_length=sepal_length,
            sepal_width=sepal_width,
            petal_length=petal_length,
            petal_width=petal_width,
        )
        self.species = species

    def __repr__(self) -> str:
        return (
            f"{self.__class__.__name__}("
            f"sepal_length={self.sepal_length}, "
            f"sepal_width={self.sepal_width}, "
            f"petal_length={self.petal_length}, "
            f"petal_width={self.petal_width}, "
            f"species={self.species!r}, "
            f")"
        )
```

Let's see how this works in practice. Here's an example of loading some valid data:

```
>>> from model import TrainingKnownSample
>>> valid = {"sepal_length": "5.1", "sepal_width": "3.5",
...   "petal_length": "1.4", "petal_width": "0.2",
...   "species": "Iris-setosa"}

>>> rks = TrainingKnownSample.from_dict(valid)
>>> rks
TrainingKnownSample(sepal_length=5.1, sepal_width=3.5,
petal_length=1.4, petal_width=0.2, species='Iris-setosa', )
```

We created the dictionary, valid, that a `csv.DictReader` would create from a line of input. Then, we built a `TrainingKnownSample` instance, rks, from this dictionary. The resulting object has proper floating-point values, showing that conversions from strings have been performed as needed.

Here's how the validation behaves. This is an example of the kind of exception raised for bad data:

```
>>> from model import TestingKnownSample, InvalidSampleError
>>> invalid_species = {"sepal_length": "5.1", "sepal_width": "3.5",
...   "petal_length": "1.4", "petal_width": "0.2",
...   "species": "nothing known by this app"}

>>> eks = TestingKnownSample.from_dict(invalid_species)
Traceback (most recent call last):
...
model.InvalidSampleError: invalid species in {'sepal_length': '5.1',
'sepal_width': '3.5', 'petal_length': '1.4', 'petal_width': '0.2',
'species': 'nothing known by this app'}
```

When we tried to create a `TestingKnownSample` instance, the invalid species value raised an exception.

Have we spotted all potential problems? The `csv` module handles the physical format issues, so providing a PDF file, for example, will lead to exceptions being raised by the `csv` module. Invalid species names and float values are checked in the `from_dict()` method.

There are some things we did not check. Here are some additional validations:

- Missing keys. If a key is spelled incorrectly, this code will raise a `KeyError` exception, which would not be restated as an `InvalidSampleError` exception. This change is left as an exercise for the reader.

- Extra keys. If there are unexpected columns, is the data invalid, or do we ignore this? It may be that we're given data from a spreadsheet with extra columns that should be ignored. While it's helpful to be flexible, it's also important to expose potential problems with the input.

- Out-of-range float values. There are likely some sensible upper and lower bounds on the range of measurements. The lower bound of zero, seems clear; negative measurements don't make much sense. The upper bound, however, isn't as clear. There are some statistical techniques for locating outliers, including the **Median Absolute Deviation (MAD)** technique.

See https://www.itl.nist.gov/div898/handbook/eda/section3/eda35h.htm for more information on how to spot data that doesn't seem to fit a normal distribution.

The first of these additional checks can be added to the `from_dict()` method. The second is a decision that must be reached with the users, and then potentially added to the `from_dict()` method.

The outlier detection is more sophisticated. We need to perform this check after all the testing and training samples have been loaded. Because the outlier check doesn't apply to a single row, it needs a different exception. We might define another exception like this:

```
class OutlierError(ValueError):
    """Value lies outside the expected range."""
```

This exception can be used with a simple range check, or the more sophisticated MAD method for outlier detection.

Validating enumerated values

The list of valid species isn't very visible. We've essentially buried it inside the `from_dict()` method, which may become a maintenance problem. When the source data changes, we need to also update this method, something that can be hard to remember and almost as hard to find. If the list of species becomes long, the lines of code could become hard to read.

Using an explicit enum class with the list of valid values is a way to convert this to purely EAFP processing. Consider using the following to validate species. Doing this means redefining a number of classes:

```
>>> from enum import Enum
>>> class Species(Enum):
...     Setosa = "Iris-setosa"
...     Versicolour = "Iris-versicolour"
...     Viginica = "Iris-virginica"

>>> Species("Iris-setosa")
<Species.Setosa: 'Iris-setosa'>

>>> Species("Iris-pinniped")
Traceback (most recent call last):
...
ValueError: 'Iris-pinniped' is not a valid Species
```

When we apply the enum class name, Species, to one of the enumerated literal values, it will raise a ValueError exception to show the string representation of the species is invalid. This parallels the way float() and int() raise ValueError exceptions for a string that's not a valid number.

Switching to enumerated values would also require changes to the class definition for a known sample. The class needs to be modified to use the enumeration, Species, instead of str. For this case study, the list of values is small, and an Enum seems practical. For other problem domains, however, the enumerated list of values could be quite large and an Enum class might be long and uninformative.

Instead of an Enum class, we might continue to use string objects. We can define each unique domain of string values as an extension to a Set[str] class:

```
>>> from typing import Set
>>> class Domain(Set[str]):
...     def validate(self, value: str) -> str:
...         if value in self:
...             return value
...         raise ValueError(f"invalid {value!r}")
>>> species = Domain({"Iris-setosa", "Iris-versicolour",
"Iris-virginica"})
>>> species.validate("Iris-versicolour")
'Iris-versicolour'
>>> species.validate("odobenidae")
Traceback (most recent call last):
...
ValueError: invalid 'odobenidae'
```

We can use the species.validate() function similar to the way we used the float() function. This will validate the string, without coercing it to a different value. Instead, it returns the string. For invalid values, it raises a ValueError exception.

This lets us rewrite the body of the from_dict() method as follows:

```
@classmethod
def from_dict(cls, row: dict[str, str]) -> "KnownSample":
    try:
        return cls(
            species=species.validate(row["species"]),
            sepal_length=float(row["sepal_length"]),
            sepal_width=float(row["sepal_width"]),
```

```
                petal_length=float(row["petal_length"]),
                petal_width=float(row["petal_width"]),
            )
        except ValueError as ex:
            raise InvalidSampleError(f"invalid {row!r}")
```

This variation relies on the global species to be a set of valid species. It also uses a pleasantly consistent EAFP approach to building the required object or raising an exception.

As we mentioned earlier, there are two parts to this design. We've looked at the foundational element, raising an appropriate exception. Now we can look at the context in which we use this from_dict() function, and how errors get reported to users.

Reading CSV files

We'll provide a common template for creating objects from CSV source data. The idea is to leverage the from_dict() methods of the various classes to create the objects our application uses:

```
class TrainingData:

    def __init__(self, name: str) -> None:
        self.name = name
        self.uploaded: datetime.datetime
        self.tested: datetime.datetime
        self.training: list[TrainingKnownSample] = []
        self.testing: list[TestingKnownSample] = []
        self.tuning: list[Hyperparameter] = []

    def load(self, raw_data_iter: Iterable[dict[str, str]]) -> None:
        for n, row in enumerate(raw_data_iter):
            try:
                if n % 5 == 0:
                    test = TestingKnownSample.from_dict(row)
                    self.testing.append(test)
                else:
                    train = TrainingKnownSample.from_dict(row)
                    self.training.append(train)
            except InvalidSampleError as ex:
                print(f"Row {n+1}: {ex}")
```

```
        return
    self.uploaded = datetime.datetime.now(tz=datetime.timezone.utc)
```

The load() method is partitioning the samples into testing and training subsets. It expects an iterable source of dict[str, str] objects, which are produced by a csv.DictReader object.

The user experience implemented here is to report the first failure and return. This might lead to an error message like the following:

```
text Row 2: invalid species in {'sepal_length': 7.9, 'sepal_width':
3.2, 'petal_length': 4.7, 'petal_width': 1.4, 'species': 'Buttercup'}
```

This message has all the required information, but may not be as helpful as desired. We might, for example, want to report *all* failures, instead of the first failure. Here's how we might restructure the load() method:

```python
def load(self, raw_data_iter: Iterable[dict[str, str]]) -> None:
    bad_count = 0
    for n, row in enumerate(raw_data_iter):
        try:
            if n % 5 == 0:
                test = TestingKnownSample.from_dict(row)
                self.testing.append(test)
            else:
                train = TrainingKnownSample.from_dict(row)
                self.training.append(train)
        except InvalidSampleError as ex:
            print(f"Row {n+1}: {ex}")
            bad_count += 1
    if bad_count != 0:
        print(f"{bad_count} invalid rows")
        return
    self.uploaded = datetime.datetime.now(tz=datetime.timezone.utc)
```

This variation would catch each InvalidSampleError error, displaying a message and counting the number of problems. This information might be more helpful because the user could then correct all of the rows which are invalid.

In the case of a very, very large set of data, this may lead to a useless level of detail. If we accidentally used a CSV file with several hundred thousand rows of images of hand-written numbers, for example, instead of Iris data, we'd get several hundred thousand messages telling us each individual row was bad.

Some additional user experience design is required around this loading operation, to make it useful in a wide variety of situations. The foundation, however, is the Python exception that's raised when something's not right. In this case study, we leveraged the `float()` function's `ValueError` and rewrote it to be our application's unique `InvalidSampleError` exception. We also created our own `ValueError` exceptions for unexpected strings.

Don't repeat yourself

The `load()` method of `TrainingData` will create two different subclasses of `KnownSample`. We've put most of the processing into the `KnownSample` superclass; this avoids repeating the validation processing in each subclass.

For an `UnknownSample`, however, we have a tiny problem: there's no species data in an `UnknownSample`. It would be ideal to extract the validation of the four measurements, and keep them separate from validating the species. If we do this, we can't trivially combine building a `Sample` with doing the validation in one simple EAFP kind of method that either creates the desired object or raises an exception that it can't be built.

When a subclass introduces new fields, we have two choices:

- Abandon simple-looking EAFP validation. In this case, we would need to separate validation from object construction. This will lead to the cost of doing `float()` conversions twice: once to validate the data and again to create the target object. Multiple `float()` conversions means we haven't really followed the **Don't Repeat Yourself** (**DRY**) principle.

- Build an intermediate representation that can be used by subclasses. This means the two `KnownSample` subclass of `Sample` would involve three steps. First, build a `Sample` object, validating the four measurements. Then, validate the species. Finally, build the `KnownSample` using the valid fields from the `Sample` object and the valid species value. This creates a temporary object, but avoids repeating any code.

We'll leave the implementation details as an exercise for the reader.

Once the exception is defined, we also need to display the results to the user in a form that guides them to a the right remedial action. This is a separate user experience design consideration that is built on the foundation of the underlying exception.

Recall

Some key points in this chapter:

- Raising an exception happens when something goes wrong. We looked at division by zero as an example. Exceptions can also be raised with the `raise` statement.

- The effects of an exception are to interrupt the normal sequential execution of statements. It saves us from having to write a lot of `if` statements to check to see if things can possibly work or check to see if something actually failed.

- Handling exceptions is done with the `try:` statement, which has an `except:` clause for each kind of exception we want to handle.

- The exception hierarchy follows object-oriented design patterns to define a number of subclasses of the `Exception` class we can work with. Some additional exceptions, `SystemExit` and `KeyboardInterrupt`, are not subclasses of the `Exception` class; handling these introduces risks and doesn't solve very many problems, so we generally ignore them.

- Defining our own exceptions is a matter of extending the `Exception` class. This makes it possible to define exceptions with very specific semantics.

Exercises

If you've never dealt with exceptions before, the first thing you need to do is look at any old Python code you've written and notice if there are places you should have been handling exceptions. How would you handle them? Do you need to handle them at all? Sometimes, letting the exception propagate to the console is the best way to communicate to the user, especially if the user is also the script's coder. Sometimes, you can recover from the error and allow the program to continue. Sometimes, you can only reformat the error into something the user can understand and display it to them.

Some common places to look are file I/O (is it possible your code will try to read a file that doesn't exist?), mathematical expressions (is it possible that a value you are dividing by is zero?), list indices (is the list empty?), and dictionaries (does the key exist?).

Ask yourself whether you should ignore the problem, handle it by checking values first, or handle it with an exception. Pay special attention to areas where you might have used `finally` and `else` to ensure the correct code is executed under all conditions.

Now write some new code, extending the case study to cover any additional validation checks for the input data. For example, we need to check the measurements to be sure they're in a sensible range. This can be an additional subclass of `ValueError`. We can apply the concept to other parts of the case study. For example, we might want to validate `Sample` objects to be sure the values are all positive numbers.

The case study doesn't do any range checking in the `from_dict()` method. Checking the lower bound of zero is easy, and it would be good to add this as the first exercise.

For setting an upper bound on the various measurements, it's important to know the data. First, it's helpful to survey the data and find the actual minimum, maximum, median, and the absolute deviations from the median. Given this summary information, a sensible set of limits can be defined and range checks added.

We haven't addressed creating `UnknownSample` instances, leaving the `from_dict()` method as an exercise for the reader. In the *Don't repeat yourself* section, above, we described an implementation where validating the four measurements in the `from_dict()` processing is refactored into the Sample class. This leads to two design changes:

- In `KnownSample`, use the `Sample.from_dict()` to validate the measurements, validate species, and build the final `KnownSample` object.
- In `UnknownSample`, use the `Sample.from_dict()` to validate the measurements, then build the final `UnknownSample` object.

These changes should lead to a reasonably flexible data validation that doesn't involve copying and pasting the validation rules for measurements or species.

Finally, try to think of places in your code where you can raise exceptions. It can be in code you've written or are working on, or you can write a new project as an exercise. You'll probably have the best luck designing a small framework or API that is meant to be used by other people; exceptions are a terrific communication tool between your code and someone else's. Remember to design and document any self-raised exceptions as part of the API, or they won't know whether or how to handle them!

Summary

In this chapter, we went into the gritty details of raising, handling, defining, and manipulating exceptions. Exceptions are a powerful way to communicate unusual circumstances or error conditions without requiring a calling function to explicitly check return values. There are many built-in exceptions and raising them is trivially easy. There are several different syntaxes for handling different exception events.

In the next chapter, everything we've studied so far will come together as we discuss how object-oriented programming principles and structures should best be applied in Python applications.

5
When to Use Object-Oriented Programming

In previous chapters, we've covered many of the defining features of object-oriented programming. We now know some principles and paradigms of object-oriented design, and we've covered the syntax of object-oriented programming in Python.

Yet, we don't know exactly how and, especially, when to utilize these principles and syntax in practice. In this chapter, we'll discuss some useful applications of the knowledge we've gained, looking at some new topics along the way:

- How to recognize objects
- Data and behaviors, once again
- Wrapping data behaviors using properties
- The Don't Repeat Yourself principle and avoiding repetition

In this chapter, we'll also address some alternative designs for our case study problem. We'll look at ways to partition the sample data into training sets and test sets.

We'll start this chapter with a close look at the nature of objects and their internal state. There are cases when there's no state change, and a class definition isn't desirable.

Treat objects as objects

This may seem obvious; you should generally give separate objects in your problem domain a special class in your code. We've seen examples of this in the case studies in previous chapters: first, we identify objects in the problem, and then model their data and behaviors.

Identifying objects is a very important task in object-oriented analysis and programming. But it isn't always as easy as counting the nouns in short paragraphs that, frankly, the authors have constructed explicitly for that purpose. Remember, objects are things that have both data and behavior. If we are working only with data, we are often better off storing it in a list, set, dictionary, or other Python data structure (which we'll be covering thoroughly in *Chapter 7, Python Data Structures*). On the other hand, if we are working only with behavior, but no stored data, a simple function is more suitable.

An object, however, has both data and behavior. Proficient Python programmers use built-in data structures unless (or until) there is an obvious need to define a class. There is no reason to add an extra level of complexity if it doesn't help organize our code. On the other hand, the need is not always self-evident.

We can often start our Python programs by storing data in a few variables. As the program expands, we will later find that we are passing the same set of related variables to a set of functions. This is the time to think about grouping both variables and functions into a class.

For example, if we are designing a program to model polygons in two-dimensional space, we might start with each polygon represented as a list of points. The points would be modeled as two tuples (x, y) describing where that point is located. This is all data, stored in a set of nested data structures (specifically, a list of tuples). We can (and often do) start hacking at the command prompt:

```
>>> square = [(1,1), (1,2), (2,2), (2,1)]
```

Now, if we want to calculate the distance around the perimeter of the polygon, we need to sum the distances between each point. To do this, we need a function to calculate the distance between two points. Here are two such functions:

```
>>> from math import hypot
>>> def distance(p_1, p_2):
...     return hypot(p_1[0]-p_2[0], p_1[1]-p_2[1])
>>> def perimeter(polygon):
```

```
...        pairs = zip(polygon, polygon[1:]+polygon[:1])
...        return sum(
...            distance(p1, p2) for p1, p2 in pairs
...        )
```

We can exercise the functions to check our work:

```
>>> perimeter(square)
4.0
```

This is a start, but it's not completely descriptive of the problem domain. We can kind of see what a polygon might be. But we need to read the entire batch of code to see how the two functions work together.

We can add type hints to help clarify the intent behind each function. The result looks like this:

```
from __future__ import annotations
from math import hypot
from typing import Tuple, List

Point = Tuple[float, float]

def distance(p_1: Point, p_2: Point) -> float:
    return hypot(p_1[0] - p_2[0], p_1[1] - p_2[1])

Polygon = List[Point]

def perimeter(polygon: Polygon) -> float:
    pairs = zip(polygon, polygon[1:] + polygon[:1])
    return sum(distance(p1, p2) for p1, p2 in pairs)
```

We've added two type definitions, `Point` and `Polygon`, to help clarify our intentions. The definition of `Point` shows how we'll use the built-in tuple class. The definition of `Polygon` shows how the built-in list class builds on the `Point` class.

When writing annotations inside method parameter definitions, we can generally use the type name directly, for example, def method(self, values: list[int]) -> None:. For this to work, we need to use from __future__ import annotations. When defining a new type hint, however, we need to use the names from the typing module. That's why the definition of the new `Point` type uses typing.Tuple in the expression Tuple[float, float].

Now, as object-oriented programmers, we clearly recognize that a polygon class could encapsulate the list of points (data) and the perimeter function (behavior). Further, a Point class, such as we defined in *Chapter 2, Objects in Python*, might encapsulate the x and y coordinates and the distance method. The question is: is it valuable to do this?

For the previous code, maybe yes, maybe no. With our recent experience in object-oriented principles, we can write an object-oriented version in record time. Let's compare them as follows:

```python
from math import hypot
from typing import Tuple, List, Optional, Iterable

class Point:
    def __init__(self, x: float, y: float) -> None:
        self.x = x
        self.y = y

    def distance(self, other: "Point") -> float:
        return hypot(self.x - other.x, self.y - other.y)

class Polygon:
    def __init__(self) -> None:
        self.vertices: List[Point] = []

    def add_point(self, point: Point) -> None:
        self.vertices.append((point))

    def perimeter(self) -> float:
        pairs = zip(
            self.vertices, self.vertices[1:] + self.vertices[:1])
        return sum(p1.distance(p2) for p1, p2 in pairs)
```

There seems to be almost twice as much code here as there was in our earlier version, although we could argue that the add_point method is not strictly necessary. We could also try to insist on using _vertices to discourage the use of the attribute, but the use of leading _ variable names doesn't seem to really solve the problem.

Now, to understand the differences between the two classes a little better, let's compare the two APIs in use. Here's how to calculate the perimeter of a square using the object-oriented code:

```
>>> square = Polygon()
>>> square.add_point(Point(1,1))
>>> square.add_point(Point(1,2))
>>> square.add_point(Point(2,2))
>>> square.add_point(Point(2,1))
>>> square.perimeter()
4.0
```

That's fairly succinct and easy to read, you might think, but let's compare it to the function-based code:

```
>>> square = [(1,1), (1,2), (2,2), (2,1)]
>>> perimeter(square)
4.0
```

Hmm, maybe the object-oriented API isn't so compact! Our first, hacked-in version, without type hints or class definitions, is the shortest. How do we know what the list of tuples is supposed to represent? How do we remember what kind of object we're supposed to pass into the `perimeter` function? We needed some documentation to explain how the first set of functions should be used.

The functions annotated with type hints were quite a bit easier to understand, as were the class definitions. The relationships among the objects are more clearly defined by hints or classes or both.

Code length is not a good indicator of code complexity. Some programmers get hung up on complicated *one-liners* that do an incredible amount of work in one line of code. This can be a fun exercise, but the result is often unreadable, even to the original author the following day. Minimizing the amount of code can often make a program easier to read, but do not blindly assume this is the case.

 No one wins at code golf. Minimizing the volume of code is rarely desirable.

Luckily, this trade-off isn't necessary. We can make the object-oriented `Polygon` API as easy to use as the functional implementation. All we have to do is alter our `Polygon` class so that it can be constructed with multiple points.

Let's give it an initializer that accepts a list of Point objects:

```
class Polygon_2:
    def __init__(self, vertices: Optional[Iterable[Point]] = None) ->
None:
        self.vertices = list(vertices) if vertices else []

    def perimeter(self) -> float:
        pairs = zip(
            self.vertices, self.vertices[1:] + self.vertices[:1])
        return sum(p1.distance(p2) for p1, p2 in pairs)
```

For the perimeter() method, we've used the zip() function to create pairs of vertices, with items drawn from two lists to create a sequence of pairs. One list provided to zip() is the complete sequence of vertices. The other list of vertices starts from vertex 1 (not 0) and ends with the vertex before 1 (that is, vertex 0). For a triangle, this will make three pairs: (v[0], v[1]), (v[1], v[2]), and (v[2], v[0]). We can then compute the distance between the pairs using Point.distance(). Finally, we sum the sequence of distances. This seems to improve things considerably. We can now use this class like the original hacked-in function definitions:

```
>>> square = Polygon_2(
... [Point(1,1), Point(1,2), Point(2,2), Point(2,1)]
... )
>>> square.perimeter()
4.0
```

It's handy to have the details of the individual method definitions. We've built an API that's close to the original, succinct set of definitions. We've added enough formality to be confident the code is likely to work before we even start putting test cases together.

Let's take one more step. Let's allow it to accept tuples too, and we can construct the Point objects ourselves, if needed:

```
Pair = Tuple[float, float]
Point_or_Tuple = Union[Point, Pair]

class Polygon_3:
    def __init__(self, vertices: Optional[Iterable[Point_or_Tuple]] =
None) -> None:
        self.vertices: List[Point] = []
        if vertices:
```

```
        for point_or_tuple in vertices:
            self.vertices.append(self.make_point(point_or_tuple))

    @staticmethod
    def make_point(item: Point_or_Tuple) -> Point:
        return item if isinstance(item, Point) else Point(*item)
```

This initializer goes through the list of items (either `Point` or `Tuple[float, float]`) and ensures that any non-`Point` objects are converted to `Point` instances.

 If you are experimenting with the above code, you should also define these variant class designs by creating subclasses of `Polygon` and overriding the `__init__()` method. Extending a class with dramatically different method signatures can raise error flags from *mypy*.

For an example this small, there's no clear winner between the object-oriented and more data-oriented versions of this code. They all do the same thing. If we have new functions that accept a polygon argument, such as `area(polygon)` or `point_in_polygon(polygon, x, y)`, the benefits of the object-oriented code become increasingly obvious. Likewise, if we add other attributes to the polygon, such as `color` or `texture`, it makes more and more sense to encapsulate that data into a single class.

The distinction is a design decision, but in general, the more important a set of data is, the more likely it is to have multiple functions specific to that data, and the more useful it is to use a class with attributes and methods instead.

When making this decision, it also pays to consider how the class will be used. If we're only trying to calculate the perimeter of one polygon in the context of a much greater problem, using a function will probably be quickest to code and easier to use *one time only*. On the other hand, if our program needs to manipulate numerous polygons in a wide variety of ways (calculating the perimeter, area, and intersection with other polygons, moving or scaling them, and so on), we have almost certainly identified a class of related objects. The class definition becomes more important as the number of instances increases.

Additionally, pay attention to the interaction between objects. Look for inheritance relationships; inheritance is impossible to model elegantly without classes, so make sure to use them. Look for the other types of relationships we discussed in *Chapter 1, Object-Oriented Design*, association and composition.

Composition can, technically, be modeled using only data structures – for example, we can have a list of dictionaries holding tuple values – but it is sometimes less complicated to create a few classes of objects, especially if there is behavior associated with the data.

 One size does not fit all. The built-in, generic collections and functions work well for a large number of simple cases. A class definition works well for a large number of more complex cases. The boundary is hazy at best.

Adding behaviors to class data with properties

Throughout this book, we've focused on the separation of behavior and data. This is very important in object-oriented programming, but we're about to see that, in Python, the distinction is uncannily blurry. Python is very good at blurring distinctions; it doesn't exactly help us to *think outside the box*. Rather, it teaches us to stop thinking about the box.

Before we get into the details, let's discuss some bad object-oriented design principles. Many object-oriented developers teach us to never access attributes directly. They insist that we write attribute access like this:

```
class Color:
    def __init__(self, rgb_value: int, name: str) -> None:
        self._rgb_value = rgb_value
        self._name = name

    def set_name(self, name: str) -> None:
        self._name = name

    def get_name(self) -> str:
        return self._name

    def set_rgb_value(self, rgb_value: int) -> None:
        self._rgb_value = rgb_value

    def get_rgb_value(self) -> int:
        return self._rgb_value
```

The instance variables are prefixed with an underscore to suggest that they are private (other languages would actually force them to be private). Then, the get and set methods provide access to each variable. This class would be used in practice as follows:

```
>>> c = Color(0xff0000, "bright red")
>>> c.get_name()
'bright red'
>>> c.set_name("red")
>>> c.get_name()
'red'
```

The above example is not nearly as readable as the direct access version that Python favors:

```
class Color_Py:
    def __init__(self, rgb_value: int, name: str) -> None:
        self.rgb_value = rgb_value
        self.name = name
```

Here's how this class works. It's slightly simpler:

```
>>> c = Color_Py(0xff0000, "bright red")
>>> c.name
'bright red'
>>> c.name = "red"
>>> c.name
'red'
```

So, why would anyone insist upon the method-based syntax?

The idea of setters and getters seems helpful for encapsulating the class definitions. Some Java-based tools can generate all the getters and setters automagically, making them almost invisible. Automating their creation doesn't make them a great idea. The most important historical reason for having getters and setters was to make the separate compilation of binaries work out in a tidy way. Without a need to link separately compiled binaries, this technique doesn't always apply to Python.

One ongoing justification for getters and setters is that, someday, we may want to add extra code when a value is set or retrieved. For example, we could decide to cache a value to avoid complex computations, or we might want to validate that a given value is a suitable input.

For example, we could decide to change the set_name() method as follows:

```python
class Color_V:
    def __init__(self, rgb_value: int, name: str) -> None:
        self._rgb_value = rgb_value
        if not name:
            raise ValueError(f"Invalid name {name!r}")
        self._name = name

    def set_name(self, name: str) -> None:
        if not name:
            raise ValueError(f"Invalid name {name!r}")
        self._name = name
```

If we had written our original code for direct attribute access, and then later changed it to a method like the preceding one, we'd have a problem: anyone who had written code that accessed the attribute directly would now have to change their code to access a method. If they didn't then change the access style from attribute access to a function call, their code would be broken.

The mantra that we should make all attributes private, accessible through methods, doesn't make much sense in Python. The Python language lacks any real concept of private members! We can see the source; we often say "We're all adults here." What can we do? We can make the syntax distinction between attribute and method less visible.

Python gives us the property function to make methods that *look* like attributes. We can therefore write our code to use direct member access, and if we ever unexpectedly need to alter the implementation to do some calculation when getting or setting that attribute's value, we can do so without changing the interface. Let's see how it looks:

```python
class Color_VP:
    def __init__(self, rgb_value: int, name: str) -> None:
        self._rgb_value = rgb_value
        if not name:
            raise ValueError(f"Invalid name {name!r}")
        self._name = name

    def _set_name(self, name: str) -> None:
        if not name:
            raise ValueError(f"Invalid name {name!r}")
```

```
        self._name = name

    def _get_name(self) -> str:
        return self._name

name = property(_get_name, _set_name)
```

Compared to the earlier class, we first change the name attribute into a (semi-)private _name attribute. Then, we add two more (semi-)private methods to get and set that variable, performing our validation when we set it.

Finally, we have the property construction at the bottom. This is the Python magic. It creates a new attribute on the Color class called name. It sets this attribute to be a **property**. Under the hood, a property attribute delegates the real work to the two methods we just created. When used in an access context (on the right side of the = or :=), the first function gets the value. When used in an update context (on the left side of = or :=), the second function sets the value.

This new version of the Color class can be used in exactly the same way as the earlier version, yet it now performs validation when we set the name attribute:

```
>>> c = Color_VP(0xff0000, "bright red")
>>> c.name
'bright red'
>>> c.name = "red"
>>> c.name
'red'
>>> c.name = ""
Traceback (most recent call last):
  File "<stdin>", line 1, in <module>
  File "setting_name_property.py", line 8, in _set_name
    raise ValueError(f"Invalid name {name!r}")
ValueError: Invalid name ''
```

So, if we'd previously written code to access the name attribute, and then changed it to use our property-based object, the previous code would still work. If it attempts to set an empty property value, this is behavior we wanted to forbid. Success!

Bear in mind that, even with the name property, the previous code is not 100% safe. People can still access the _name attribute directly and set it to an empty string if they want to. But if they access a variable we've explicitly marked with an underscore to suggest it is private, they're the ones that have to deal with the consequences, not us. We established a formal contract, and if they elect to break the contract, they own the consequences.

Properties in detail

Think of the `property` function as returning an object that proxies any requests to get or set the attribute value through the method names we have specified. The `property` built-in is like a constructor for such an object, and that object is set as the public-facing member for the given attribute.

This `property` constructor can actually accept two additional arguments, a `delete` function and a docstring for the property. The `delete` function is rarely supplied in practice, but it can be useful for logging the fact that a value has been deleted, or possibly to veto deleting if we have reason to do so. The docstring is just a string describing what the property does, no different from the docstrings we discussed in *Chapter 2, Objects in Python*. If we do not supply this parameter, the docstring will instead be copied from the docstring for the first argument: the `getter` method.

Here is a silly example that states whenever any of the methods are called:

```python
class NorwegianBlue:
    def __init__(self, name: str) -> None:
        self._name = name
        self._state: str

    def _get_state(self) -> str:
        print(f"Getting {self._name}'s State")
        return self._state

    def _set_state(self, state: str) -> None:
        print(f"Setting {self._name}'s State to {state!r}")
        self._state = state

    def _del_state(self) -> None:
        print(f"{self._name} is pushing up daisies!")
        del self._state

    silly = property(
        _get_state, _set_state, _del_state,
        "This is a silly property")
```

Note that the `state` attribute has a type hint, `str`, but no initial value. It can be deleted, and only exists for part of the life of a `NorwegianBlue`. We need to provide a hint to help *mypy* understand what the type should be. But we don't assign a default value because that's the job of the `setter` method.

If we actually use an instance of this class, it does indeed print out the correct strings when we ask it to:

```
>>> p = NorwegianBlue("Polly")
>>> p.silly = "Pining for the fjords"
Setting Polly's State to 'Pining for the fjords'
>>> p.silly
Getting Polly's State
'Pining for the fjords'
>>> del p.silly
Polly is pushing up daisies!
```

Further, if we look at the help text for the `Silly` class (by issuing `help(Silly)` at the interpreter prompt), it shows us the custom docstring for our `silly` attribute:

```
Help on class NorwegianBlue in module colors:

class NorwegianBlue(builtins.object)
 |  NorwegianBlue(name: str) -> None
 |
 |  Methods defined here:
 |
 |  __init__(self, name: str) -> None
 |      Initialize self.  See help(type(self)) for accurate signature.
 |
 |  ----------------------------------------------------------------------
 |  Data descriptors defined here:
 |
 |  __dict__
 |      dictionary for instance variables (if defined)
 |
 |  __weakref__
 |      list of weak references to the object (if defined)
 |
 |  silly
 |      This is a silly property
```

Once again, everything is working as we planned. In practice, properties are normally only defined with the first two parameters: the `getter` and `setter` functions. If we want to supply a docstring for a property, we can define it on the `getter` function; the property proxy will copy it into its own docstring. The `delete` function is often left empty because object attributes are so rarely deleted.

Decorators – another way to create properties

We can create properties using decorators. This makes the definitions easier to read. Decorators are a ubiquitous feature of Python syntax, with a variety of purposes. For the most part, decorators modify the function definition that they precede. We'll look at the decorator design pattern more broadly in *Chapter 11, Common Design Patterns*.

The property function can be used with the decorator syntax to turn a get method into a property attribute, as follows:

```python
class NorwegianBlue_P:
    def __init__(self, name: str) -> None:
        self._name = name
        self._state: str

    @property
    def silly(self) -> str:
        print(f"Getting {self._name}'s State")
        return self._state
```

This applies the property function as a decorator to the function that follows. It is equivalent to the previous silly = property(_get_state) syntax. The main difference, from a readability perspective, is that we get to mark the silly method as a property at the top of the method, instead of after it is defined, where it can be easily overlooked. It also means we don't have to create private methods with underscore prefixes just to define a property.

Going one step further, we can specify a setter function for the new property as follows:

```python
class NorwegianBlue_P:
    def __init__(self, name: str) -> None:
        self._name = name
        self._state: str

    @property
    def silly(self) -> str:
        """This is a silly property"""
        print(f"Getting {self._name}'s State")
        return self._state

    @silly.setter
    def silly(self, state: str) -> None:
```

```
        print(f"Setting {self._name}'s State to {state!r}")
        self._state = state
```

This syntax, `@silly.setter`, looks odd compared with `@property`, although the intent should be clear. First, we decorate the `silly` method as a getter. Then, we decorate a second method with exactly the same name by applying the `setter` attribute of the originally decorated `silly` method! This works because the `property` function returns an object; this object also has its own `setter` attribute, which can then be applied as a decorator to other methods. Using the same name for the get and set methods helps to group together the multiple methods that access one common attribute.

We can also specify a `delete` function with `@silly.deleter`. Here's what it looks like:

```
@silly.deleter
def silly(self) -> None:
    print(f"{self._name} is pushing up daisies!")
    del self._state
```

We cannot specify a docstring using `property` decorators, so we need to rely on the decorator copying the docstring from the initial getter method. This class operates *exactly* the same as our earlier version, including the help text. You'll see the decorator syntax in widespread use. The function syntax is how it actually works under the hood.

Deciding when to use properties

With the built-in `property` blurring the division between behavior and data, it can be confusing to know when to choose an attribute, or a method, or a property. In the `Color_VP` class example we saw earlier, we added argument value validation to setting an attribute. In the `NorwegianBlue` class example, we wrote detailed log entries when attributes were set and deleted. There are also other factors to take into account when deciding to use a property.

In Python, data, properties, and methods are all attributes of a class. The fact that a method is callable does not distinguish it from other types of attributes; indeed, we'll see in *Chapter 8*, *The Intersection of Object-Oriented and Functional Programming*, that it is possible to create normal objects that can be called like functions. We'll also discover that functions and methods are themselves ordinary objects.

The fact that methods are callable attributes, and properties are also attributes, can help us make this decision. We suggest the following principles:

- Use methods to represent actions; things that can be done to, or performed by, the object. When you call a method, even with only one argument, it should *do* something. Method names are generally verbs.

- Use attributes or properties to represent the state of the object. These are the nouns, adjectives, and prepositions that describe an object.

  - Default to ordinary (non-property) attributes, initialized in the __init__() method. These must be computed eagerly, which is a good starting point for any design.

  - Use properties for attributes in the exceptional case when there's a computation involved with setting or getting (or deleting) an attribute. Examples include data validation, logging, and access controls. We'll look at cache management in a moment. We can also use properties for lazy attributes, where we want to defer the computation because it's costly and rarely needed.

Let's look at a more realistic example. A common need for custom behavior is caching a value that is difficult to calculate or expensive to look up (requiring, for example, a network request or database query). The goal is to store the value locally to avoid repeated calls to the expensive calculation.

We can do this with a custom getter on the property. The first time the value is retrieved, we perform the lookup or calculation. Then, we can locally cache the value as a private attribute on our object (or in dedicated caching software), and the next time the value is requested, we return the stored data. Here's how we might cache a web page:

```python
from urllib.request import urlopen
from typing import Optional, cast

class WebPage:
    def __init__(self, url: str) -> None:
        self.url = url
        self._content: Optional[bytes] = None

    @property
    def content(self) -> bytes:
        if self._content is None:
            print("Retrieving New Page...")
            with urlopen(self.url) as response:
```

```
        self._content = response.read()
    return self._content
```

We'll only read the website content once, when `self._content` has the initial value of `None`. After that, we'll return the value most recently read for the site. We can test this code to see that the page is only retrieved once:

```
import time

webpage = WebPage("http://ccphillips.net/")

now = time.perf_counter()
content1 = webpage.content
first_fetch = time.perf_counter() - now

now = time.perf_counter()
content2 = webpage.content
second_fetch = time.perf_counter() - now

assert content2 == content1, "Problem: Pages were different"
print(f"Initial Request      {first_fetch:.5f}")
print(f"Subsequent Requests {second_fetch:.5f}")
```

The output?

```
% python src/colors.py
Retrieving New Page...
Initial Request      1.38836
Subsequent Requests 0.00001
```

It took about 1.388 seconds to retrieve a page from the `ccphilips.net` web host. The second fetch – from a laptop's RAM – takes 0.01 milliseconds! This is sometimes written as 10 μs, 10 microseconds. Since this is the last digit, we can suspect it's subject to rounding, and the time may be only half that, perhaps as little as 5 μs.

Custom getters are also useful for attributes that need to be calculated on the fly, based on other object attributes. For example, we might want to calculate the average for a list of integers:

```
class AverageList(List[int]):
    @property
    def average(self) -> float:
        return sum(self) / len(self)
```

This small class inherits from `list`, so we get list-like behavior for free. We added a property to the class, and – hey, presto! – our list can have an average as follows:

```
>>> a = AverageList([10, 8, 13, 9, 11, 14, 6, 4, 12, 7, 5])
>>> a.average
9.0
```

Of course, we could have made this a method instead, but if we do, then we ought to call it `calculate_average()`, since methods represent actions. But a property called `average` is more suitable, and is both easier to type and easier to read.

We can imagine a number of similar reductions, including minimum, maximum, standard deviation, median, and mode, all being properties of a collection of numbers. This can simplify a more complex analysis by encapsulating these summaries into the collection of data values.

Custom setters are useful for validation, as we've already seen, but they can also be used to proxy a value to another location. For example, we could add a content setter to the `WebPage` class that automatically logs into our web server and uploads a new page whenever the value is set.

Manager objects

We've been focused on objects and their attributes and methods. Now, we'll take a look at designing higher-level objects; the kind of objects that manage other objects – the objects that tie everything together. These are sometimes called Façade objects because they present a pleasant, easy-to-use façade over some underlying complexity. See *Chapter 12, Advanced Design Patterns*, for an additional look at the Façade design pattern.

Most of the previous examples tend to model concrete ideas. Management objects are more like office managers; they don't do the actual visible work out on the floor, but without them, there would be no communication between departments, and nobody would know what they are supposed to do (although, this can be true anyway if the organization is badly managed!). Analogously, the attributes on a management class tend to refer to other objects that do the visible work; the behaviors on such a class delegate to those other classes at the right time, and pass messages between them.

A manager relies on composite design. We assemble a manager class by knitting other objects together. The overall behavior of the manager emerges from the interaction of objects. To an extent, a manager is also an Adapter among the various interfaces. See *Chapter 12, Advanced Design Patterns*, for an additional look at the Adapter design pattern.

As an example, we'll write a program that does a find-and-replace action for text files stored in a compressed archive file, either a ZIP archive or a TAR archive. We'll need objects to represent the archive file as a whole and each individual text file (luckily, we don't have to write these classes, as they're available in the Python standard library).

An overall manager object will be responsible for ensuring the following three steps occur:

1. Unzipping the compressed file to examine each member
2. Performing the find-and-replace action on text members
3. Zipping up the new files with the untouched as well as changed members

Note that we have to choose between an eager and a lazy approach to the three steps of this process. We can eagerly unzip (or untar) the entire archive, process all the files, and then build a new archive. This tends to use a lot of disk space. An alternative is to lazily extract items one at a time from the archive, perform the find-and-replace, and then build a new compressed archive as we go. The lazy approach doesn't require as much storage.

This design will knit together elements of the `pathlib`, `zipfile`, and the regular expression (`re`) module. The initial design will be focused on the job at hand. Later in this chapter, we'll rethink this design as new requirements surface.

The class is initialized with the archive file's name. We don't do anything else upon creation. We'll define a method with a good, clear verb in its name that does any processing:

```python
from __future__ import annotations
import fnmatch
from pathlib import Path
import re
import zipfile

class ZipReplace:
    def __init__(
            self,
            archive: Path,
            pattern: str,
            find: str,
            replace: str
    ) -> None:
        self.archive_path = archive
```

```
        self.pattern = pattern
        self.find = find
        self.replace = replace
```

Given the archive, the filename pattern to match, and the strings to work with, the object will have everything it needs. We might provide arguments like `ZipReplace(Path("sample.zip"), "*.md", "xyzzy", "xyzzy")`.

The overall manager method for the find-and-replace operation revises a given archive. This method of the `ZipReplace` class (started above) uses two other methods and delegates most of the real work to other objects:

```
def find_and_replace(self) -> None:
    input_path, output_path = self.make_backup()

    with zipfile.ZipFile(output_path, "w") as output:
        with zipfile.ZipFile(input_path) as input:
            self.copy_and_transform(input, output)
```

The `make_backup()` method will use the `pathlib` module to rename the old ZIP file so it's obviously the backup copy, untouched. This backup copy is input to the `copy_and_transform()` method. The original name will be the final output, also. This makes it look like the file was updated "in place." In fact, a new file was created, but the old name will be assigned to the new content.

We create two context managers (a special kind of manager) to control the open files. An open file is entangled with operating system resources. In the case of a ZIP file or TAR archive, there are summaries and checksums that need to be properly written when the file is closed. Using a context manager assures that this additional work is done, and done properly, in spite of any exceptions being raised. All file operations should be wrapped in a `with` statement to leverage Python's context manager and handle proper cleanup. We'll look at this again in *Chapter 9, Strings, Serialization, and File Paths*.

The `copy_and_transform()` method uses methods of the two `ZipFile` instances and the `re` module to transform members of the original file. Since a backup was made of the original file, this will build the output file from the backup file. It examines each member of the archive, performing a number of steps, including expanding the compressed data, doing the transformation with a `transform()` method, and compressing to write to the output file, and then cleaning up the temporary file (and directories).

Obviously, we could do all of these steps in one method of a class, or indeed do the whole thing in one complex script, without ever creating an object. There are several advantages to separating the steps:

- **Readability**: The code for each step is in a self-contained unit that is easy to read and understand. The method name describes what the method does, and less additional documentation is required to understand what is going on.

- **Extensibility**: If a subclass wanted to use compressed TAR files instead of ZIP files, it could override the copy_and_transform() method, reusing all the supporting methods because they apply to any file irrespective of the kind of archive.

- **Partitioning**: An external class could create an instance of this class and use make_backup() or the copy_and_transform() methods directly, bypassing the find_and_replace() manager.

These two methods of the ZipReplace class (started above) make the backup copy and create the new file by reading from the backup and writing new items after they've been modified:

```
def make_backup(self) -> tuple[Path, Path]:
    input_path = self.archive_path.with_suffix(
        f"{self.archive_path.suffix}.old")
    output_path = self.archive_path
    self.archive_path.rename(input_path)
    return input_path, output_path


def copy_and_transform(
    self, input: zipfile.ZipFile, output: zipfile.ZipFile
) -> None:
    for item in input.infolist():
        extracted = Path(input.extract(item))
        if (not item.is_dir()
                and fnmatch.fnmatch(item.filename, self.pattern)):
            print(f"Transform {item}")
            input_text = extracted.read_text()
            output_text = re.sub(self.find, self.replace, input_text)
            extracted.write_text(output_text)
        else:
            print(f"Ignore    {item}")
```

```
        output.write(extracted, item.filename)
        extracted.unlink()
        for parent in extracted.parents:
            if parent == Path.cwd():
                break
            parent.rmdir()
```

The make_backup() method applies a common strategy to avoid damaging a file. The original file is renamed to preserve it, and a new file is created that will have the original file's name. This method is designed to be independent of the file type or other processing details.

The copy_and_transform() function method builds the new archive out of members extracted from the original archive. It performs a number of steps for each member of the archive:

- Extract this file from the original archive.
- If the item is not a directory (this is unlikely, but still possible), and the name matches the wild-card pattern, we want to transform it. This is a three-step process.
    1. Read the file's text.
    2. Transform the file, using the sub() function of the re module.
    3. Write the text, replacing the extracted file. This is where we create a copy of the content.
- Compress the file – either an untouched file or a transformed file – into the new archive.
- We unlink the temporary copy. If there are no links left to the file, it will be deleted by the operating system.
- We clean up any temporary directories created by the extraction process.
- The copy_and_transform() method's operations span the pathlib, zipfile, and re modules. Wrapping these operations up into a manager that uses context managers gives us a tidy package with a small interface.

We can create a main script to use the ZipReplace class:

```
if __name__ == "__main__":
    sample_zip = Path("sample.zip")
    zr = ZipReplace(sample_zip, "*.md", "xyzzy", "plover's egg")
    zr.find_and_replace()
```

We've provided the archive (`sample.zip`), the file matching pattern (`*.md`), the string to replace (`xyzzy`), and the final replacement (`plover's egg`). This will perform a complex series of file operations. A more practical approach is to use the `argparse` module to define the **command-line interface** (**CLI**) for this application.

For brevity, the details are sparsely documented. Our current focus is on object-oriented design; if you are interested in the inner details of the `zipfile` module, refer to the documentation in the standard library, either online or by typing `import zipfile` and `help(zipfile)` into your interactive interpreter.

Of course, an instance of the `ZipReplace` class does not have to be created from the command line; our class could be imported into another module (to perform batch ZIP file processing), or accessed as part of a GUI interface or even a higher-level manager object that knows where to get ZIP files (for example, to retrieve them from an FTP server or back them up to an external disk).

The benefit of the Façade and Adapter design patterns is to encapsulate complexity into a more useful class design. These composite objects tend to be less like physical objects, and enter the realm of conceptual objects. When we step away from objects that have a close parallel with the real world, the methods are actions that change the state of those concepts; care is required because the simple analogies start to disappear in the haze of ideas. It helps when the foundation is a set of concrete data values and well-defined behaviors.

A good example to bear in mind is the World Wide Web. A *web server* provides *content* to *browsers*. The content can include JavaScript that behaves like a desktop application which reaches out to other web servers to present content. These conceptual relationships are implemented by tangible transfers of bytes. It also includes a browser to paint pages of text, images, video, or sound. The foundation is transfers of bytes, a tangible action. In a classroom setting, it's possible to have developers pass sticky notes and rubber balls to each other to represent requests and responses.

This example works nicely. When we're confronted with additional requirements, we need to find a way to build new, related features without duplicating code. We'll talk about this engineering imperative first, then look at the revised design.

Removing duplicate code

Often, the code in management-style classes such as `ZipReplace` is quite generic and can be applied in a variety of ways. It is possible to use either composition or inheritance to help keep this code in one place, thus eliminating duplicate code. Before we look at any examples of this, let's discuss some design principles. Specifically, why is duplicate code a bad thing?

There are several reasons, but they all boil down to readability and maintainability. When we're writing a new piece of code that is similar to an earlier piece, the easiest thing to do is copy and paste the old code and change whatever needs to be changed (variable names, logic, comments) to make it work in the new location. Alternatively, if we're writing new code that seems similar, but not identical, to code elsewhere in the project, it is often easier to write fresh code with similar behavior, rather than figuring out how to extract the overlapping functionality. We sometimes call this copy-pasta programming because the result is a big mass of tangled noodles of code, like a bowl of spaghetti.

But as soon as someone trying to understand the code comes across duplicate (or nearly duplicate) code blocks, they now have an *additional* barrier to understanding. There's an intellectual friction created by a number of side-bar questions. Are they truly identical? If not, how is one section different from the other? What parts are the same? Under what conditions is one section called? When do we call the other? You might argue that you're the only one reading your code, but if you don't touch that code for eight months, it will be as incomprehensible to you as it is to a fresh coder. When we're trying to read two similar pieces of code, we have to understand why they're different, as well as how they're different. This wastes the reader's time; code should always be written to be readable first.

> *[Dusty here, stepping out of formal author mode] I once had to try to understand someone's code that had three identical copies of the same 300 lines of very poorly written code. I had been working with the code for a month before I finally comprehended that the three identical versions were actually performing slightly different tax calculations. Some of the subtle differences were intentional, but there were also obvious areas where someone had updated a calculation in one function without updating the other two. The number of subtle, incomprehensible bugs in the code could not be counted. I eventually replaced all 900 lines with an easy-to-read function of 20 lines or so.*

As the preceding story suggests, keeping two similar pieces of code up to date can be a nightmare. We have to remember to update both sections whenever we update one of them, and we have to remember how multiple sections differ so we can modify our changes when we are editing each of them. If we forget to update all sections, we will end up with extremely annoying bugs that usually manifest themselves as: *"But I fixed that already, why is it still happening?"*

The key factor here is the time spent in troubleshooting, maintenance, and enhancement compared with the time spent initially creating the code. Software that's in use for more than a few weeks will have a lot more eyeballs on it than the time spent creating it. The tiny bit of time we "save" by copying and pasting existing code is more than wasted when we have to maintain it.

One of the author's personal bests was an application that was in use for almost seventeen years. If other developers and users wasted one extra day each year trying to sort out some confusing part of the code, it means the author should have spent at least two more weeks improving the code to head off this future maintenance cost.

 Code is both read and modified many more times and much more often than it is written. Comprehensible code should always be a priority.

This is why programmers, especially Python programmers (who tend to value elegant code more than average developers), follow what is known as the **Don't Repeat Yourself** (**DRY**) principle. Our advice for beginner programmers is to never use the copy-and-paste feature of their editor. To intermediate programmers: think thrice before hitting *Ctrl + C*.

But what should we do instead of code duplication? The simplest solution is often to move the code into a function that accepts parameters to account for whatever parts are different. This isn't a strictly object-oriented solution, but it is frequently optimal.

For example, if we have two pieces of code that unzip a ZIP file into two different directories, we can easily replace it with a function that accepts a parameter for the directory to which it should be unzipped. This may make the function itself slightly longer. The size of a function – measured as lines of code – isn't a good metric for readability. No one wins at code golf.

Good names and docstrings are essential. Each class, method, function, variable, property, attribute, module, and package name should be chosen thoughtfully. When writing docstrings, don't explain how the code works (the code should do that). Be sure to focus on what the code's purpose is, what the preconditions are for using it, and what will be true after the function or method has been used.

The moral of the story is: always make the effort to refactor your code to be easier to read, instead of writing bad code that may seem easier to write. Now we can look at the revised design to the ZipReplace class definition.

In practice

Let's explore two ways we can reuse our existing code. After writing our code to replace strings in a ZIP file full of text files, we are later contracted to scale all the images in a ZIP file to a size suitable for mobile devices. While resolutions vary, 640 x 960 is about the smallest we need. It looks like we could use a very similar paradigm to what we used in ZipReplace.

Our first impulse might be to save a copy of that module and change the find_replace method to scale_image or something similar in the copy.

This processing will rely on the Pillow library to open an image file, scale it, and save it. The Pillow image processing tools can be installed with the following command:

```
% python -m pip install pillow
```

This will provide some great image-processing tools.

As we noted above in the *Removing duplicate code* section of this chapter, this copy-and-paste programming approach is suboptimal. What if someday we want to change the unzip and zip methods to also open TAR files? Or maybe we'll want to use a guaranteed unique directory name for temporary files. In either case, we'd have to change it in two different places!

We'll start by demonstrating an inheritance-based solution to this problem. First, we'll modify our original ZipReplace class into a superclass for processing ZIP files in a variety of ways:

```python
from abc import ABC, abstractmethod

class ZipProcessor(ABC):
    def __init__(self, archive: Path) -> None:
        self.archive_path = archive
        self._pattern: str

    def process_files(self, pattern: str) -> None:
        self._pattern = pattern

        input_path, output_path = self.make_backup()

        with zipfile.ZipFile(output_path, "w") as output:
            with zipfile.ZipFile(input_path) as input:
                self.copy_and_transform(input, output)

    def make_backup(self) -> tuple[Path, Path]:
        input_path = self.archive_path.with_suffix(
            f"{self.archive_path.suffix}.old")
        output_path = self.archive_path
        self.archive_path.rename(input_path)
        return input_path, output_path
```

```
def copy_and_transform(
    self, input: zipfile.ZipFile, output: zipfile.ZipFile
) -> None:
    for item in input.infolist():
        extracted = Path(input.extract(item))
        if self.matches(item):
            print(f"Transform {item}")
            self.transform(extracted)
        else:
            print(f"Ignore    {item}")
        output.write(extracted, item.filename)
        self.remove_under_cwd(extracted)

def matches(self, item: zipfile.ZipInfo) -> bool:
    return (
        not item.is_dir()
        and fnmatch.fnmatch(item.filename, self._pattern))

def remove_under_cwd(self, extracted: Path) -> None:
    extracted.unlink()
    for parent in extracted.parents:
        if parent == Path.cwd():
            break
        parent.rmdir()

@abstractmethod
def transform(self, extracted: Path) -> None:
    ...
```

We dropped the three parameters to __init__(), pattern, find, and replace, that were specific to ZipReplace. Then, we renamed the find_replace() method to process_files(). We decomposed the complex copy_and_transform() method and made it call several other methods to do the real work. This includes a placeholder for a transform() method. These name changes help demonstrate the more generalized nature of our new class.

This new ZipProcessor class is a subclass of ABC, an abstract base class, allowing us to provide placeholders instead of methods. (More on ABCs to come in *Chapter 6, Abstract Base Classes and Operator Overloading*.) This abstract class doesn't actually define a transform() method. If we try to create an instance of the ZipProcessor class, the missing transform() method will raise an exception. The formality of an @abstractmethod decoration makes it clear that there's a piece missing, and the piece must have the expected shape.

Now, before we move on to our image processing application, let's create a version of our original `ZipReplace` class. This will be based on the `ZipProcessor` class to make use of this parent class, as follows:

```python
class TextTweaker(ZipProcessor):
    def __init__(self, archive: Path) -> None:
        super().__init__(archive)
        self.find: str
        self.replace: str

    def find_and_replace(self, find: str, replace: str) -> "TextTweaker":
        self.find = find
        self.replace = replace
        return self

    def transform(self, extracted: Path) -> None:
        input_text = extracted.read_text()
        output_text = re.sub(self.find, self.replace, input_text)
        extracted.write_text(output_text)
```

This code is shorter than the original version, since it inherits its ZIP processing abilities from the parent class. We first import the base class we just wrote and make `TextTweaker` extend that class. Then, we use `super()` to initialize the parent class.

We need two extra parameters, and we've used a technique called a *fluent interface* to provide the two parameters. The `find_and_replace()` method updates the state of the object, then returns the `self` object. This lets us use the class with a line of code like the following:

```python
TextTweaker(zip_data)\
.find_and_replace("xyzzy", "plover's egg")\
.process_files("*.md")
```

We've created an instance of the class, used the `find_and_replace()` method to set some of the attributes, then used the `process_files()` method to start the processing. This is called a "fluent" interface because a number of methods are used to help clarify the parameters and their relationships.

We've done a fair amount of work to recreate a program that is functionally not different from the one we started with! But having done that work, it is now much easier for us to write other classes that operate on files in a ZIP archive, such as the (hypothetically requested) photo scaler.

Further, if we ever want to improve or bug fix the ZIP functionality, we can do it for all subclasses at once by changing only the one `ZipProcessor` base class. Therefore maintenance will be much more effective.

See how simple it is now to create a photo scaling class that takes advantage of the `ZipProcessor` functionality:

```python
from PIL import Image  # type: ignore [import]


class ImgTweaker(ZipProcessor):
    def transform(self, extracted: Path) -> None:
        image = Image.open(extracted)
        scaled = image.resize(size=(640, 960))
        scaled.save(extracted)
```

Look how simple this class is! All that work we did earlier paid off. All we do is open each file, scale it, and save it back. The `ZipProcessor` class takes care of the zipping and unzipping without any extra work on our part. This seems to be a huge win.

Creating reusable code isn't easy. It generally requires more than one use case to make it clear what parts are generic and what parts are specific. Because we need concrete examples, it pays to avoid over-engineering to strive for imagined reuse. This is Python and things can be very flexible. Rewrite as needed to cover the cases as they arrive on the scene.

Case study

In this chapter, we'll continue developing elements of the case study. We want to explore some additional features of object-oriented design in Python. The first is what is sometimes called "syntactic sugar," a handy way to write something that offers a simpler way to express something fairly complex. The second is the concept of a manager for providing a context for resource management.

In *Chapter 4, Expecting the Unexpected*, we built an exception for identifying invalid input data. We used the exception for reporting when the inputs couldn't be used.

Here, we'll start with a class to gather data by reading the file with properly classified training and test data. In this chapter, we'll ignore some of the exception-handling details so we can focus on another aspect of the problem: partitioning samples into testing and training subsets.

Input validation

The `TrainingData` object is loaded from a source file of samples, named `bezdekIris.data`. Currently, we don't make a large effort to validate the contents of this file. Rather than confirm the data contains correctly formatted samples with numeric measurements and a proper species name, we simply create `Sample` instances, and hope nothing goes wrong. A small change to the data could lead to unexpected problems in obscure parts of our application. By validating the input data right away, we can focus on the problems and provide a focused, actionable report back to the user. Something like "Row 42 has an invalid petal_length value of '1b.25'" with the line of data, the column, and the invalid value.

A file with training data is processed in our application via the `load()` method of `TrainingData`. Currently, this method requires an iterable sequence of dictionaries; each individual sample is read as a dictionary with the measurements and the classification. The type hint is `Iterable[dict[str, str]]`. This is one way the `csv` module works, making it very easy to work with. We'll return to additional details of loading the data in *Chapter 8*, *The Intersection of Object-Oriented and Functional Programming*, and *Chapter 9*, *Strings, Serialization, and File Paths*.

Thinking about the possibility of alternative formats suggests the `TrainingData` class should not depend on the `dict[str, str]` row definition suggested by CSV file processing. While expecting a dictionary of values for each row is simple, it pushes some details into the `TrainingData` class that may not belong there. Details of the source document's representation have nothing to do with managing a collection of training and test samples; this seems like a place where object-oriented design will help us disentangle the two ideas.

In order to support multiple sources of data, we will need some common rules for validating the input values. We'll need a class like this:

```python
class SampleReader:
    """
    See iris.names for attribute ordering in bezdekIris.data file
    """

    target_class = Sample
    header = [
        "sepal_length", "sepal_width",
        "petal_length", "petal_width", "class"
    ]

    def __init__(self, source: Path) -> None:
```

```
            self.source = source

    def sample_iter(self) -> Iterator[Sample]:
        target_class = self.target_class
        with self.source.open() as source_file:
            reader = csv.DictReader(source_file, self.header)
            for row in reader:
                try:
                    sample = target_class(
                        sepal_length=float(row["sepal_length"]),
                        sepal_width=float(row["sepal_width"]),
                        petal_length=float(row["petal_length"]),
                        petal_width=float(row["petal_width"]),
                    )
                except ValueError as ex:
                    raise BadSampleRow(f"Invalid {row!r}") from ex
                yield sample
```

This builds an instance of the `Sample` superclass from the input fields read by a
CSV `DictReader` instance. The `sample_iter()` method uses a series of conversion
expressions to translate input data from each column into useful Python objects.
In this example, the conversions are simple, and the implementation is a bunch
of `float()` functions to convert CSV string data into Python objects. We can imagine
more complex conversions might be present for other problem domains.

The `float()` functions – when confronted with bad data – will raise a `ValueError`.
While this is helpful, a bug in a distance formula may also raise a `ValueError`,
leading to possible confusion. It's slightly better for our application to produce
unique exceptions; this makes it easier to identify a root cause for a problem.

The target type, `Sample`, is provided as a class-level variable, `target_class`. This
lets us introduce a new subclass of `Sample` by making one relatively visible change.
This isn't required, but a visible dependency like this provides a way to disentangle
classes from each other.

We'll follow *Chapter 4, Expecting the Unexpected,* and define a unique exception
definition. This is a better way to help disentangle our application's errors from
ordinary bugs in our Python code:

```
class BadSampleRow(ValueError):
    pass
```

To make use of this, we mapped the various float() problems signaled by ValueError exceptions to our application's BadSampleRow exception. This can help someone distinguish between a bad CSV source file and a bad computation due to a bug in a *k*-NN distance computation. While both can raise ValueError exceptions, the CSV processing exception is wrapped into an application-specific exception to disambiguate the context.

We've done the exception transform by wrapping the creation of an instance of the target class in a try: statement. Any ValueError that's raised here will become a BadSampleRow exception. We've used a raise...from... so that the original exception is preserved to help with the debugging.

Once we have valid input, we have to decide whether the object should be used for training or testing. We'll turn to that problem next.

Input partitioning

The SampleReader class we just introduced uses a variable to identify what kind of objects to create. The target_class variable provides a class to use. Note that we need to be a little careful in the ways we refer to SampleReader.target_class or self.target_class.

A simple expression like self.target_class(sepal_length=, ... etc.) looks like a method evaluation. Except, of course, self.target_class is not a method; it's another class. To make sure Python doesn't assume that self.target_class() refers to a method, we've assigned it to a local variable called target_class. Now we can use target_class(sepal_length=, … etc.) and there's no ambiguity.

This is pleasantly Pythonic. We can create subclasses of this reader to create different kinds of samples from the raw data.

This SampleReader class definition exposes a problem. A single source of raw sample data needs to be partitioned into two separate subclasses of KnownSample; it's either a TrainingSample or a TestingSample. There's a tiny difference in behavior between these two classes. A TestingSample is used to confirm the *k*-NN algorithm works, and is used to compare an algorithmic classification against the expert Botanist-assigned species. This is not something a TrainingSample needs to do.

Ideally, a single reader would emit a mixture of the two classes. The design so far only allows for instances of a single class to be created. We have two paths forward to provide the needed functionality:

- A more sophisticated algorithm for deciding what class to create. The algorithm would likely include an `if` statement to create an instance of one object or another.

- A simplified definition of `KnownSample`. This single class can handle immutable training samples separately from mutable testing samples that can be classified (and reclassified) any number of times.

Simplification seems to be a good idea. Less complexity means less code and fewer places for bugs to hide. The second alternative suggests we can separate three distinct aspects of a sample:

- The "raw" data. This is the core collection of measurements. They are immutable. (We'll address this design variation in *Chapter 7, Python Data Structures*.)

- The Botanist-assigned species. This is available for training or testing data, but not part of an unknown sample. The assigned species, like the measurements, is immutable.

- An algorithmically assigned classification. This is applied to the testing and unknown samples. This value can be seen as mutable; each time we classify a sample (or reclassify a test sample), the value changes.

This a profound change to the design created so far. Early in a project, this kind of change can be necessary. Way back in *Chapters 1* and *2*, we decided to create a fairly sophisticated class hierarchy for various kinds of samples. It's time to revisit that design. This won't be the last time we think through this. The essence of good design is to create and dispose of a number of bad designs first.

The sample class hierarchy

We can rethink our earlier designs from several points of view. One alternative is to separate the essential `Sample` class from the additional features. It seems like we can identify four additional behaviors for each `Sample` instance, shown in the following table.

	Known	**Unknown**
Unclassified	Training data	Sample waiting to be classified
Classified	Testing data	Classified sample

We've omitted a detail from the **Classified** row. Each time we do a classification, a specific hyperparameter is associated with the resulting classified sample. It would be more accurate to say it's a sample classified by a specific Hyperparameter object. But this might be too much clutter.

The distinction between the two cells in the **Unknown** column is minute. The distinction is so minor as to be essentially irrelevant to most processing. An **Unknown** sample will be waiting to be classified for – at most – a few lines of code.

If we rethink this, we may be able to create fewer classes and still reflect the object state and behavior changes correctly.

There can be two subclasses of Sample with a separate Classification object. Here's a diagram.

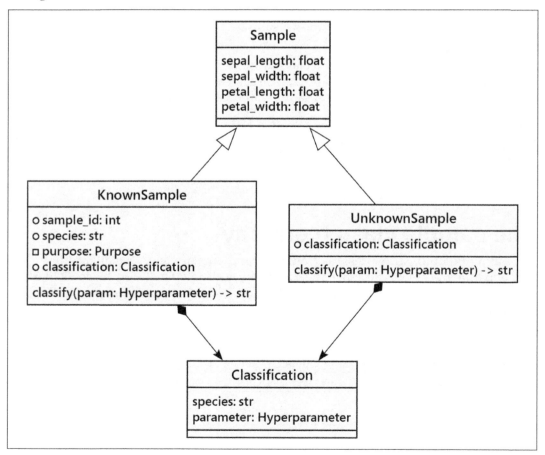

Figure 5.1: Sample class diagram

We've refined the class hierarchy to reflect two essentially different kinds of samples:

- A `KnownSample` instance can be used for testing or training. The difference between other classes is implemented in the method that does classification. We can make this depend on a purpose attribute, shown with a small square (or sometimes a "-") as a prefix. Python doesn't have private variables, but this marker can be helpful as a design note. The public attributes can be shown with a small circle (or a "+" to save space) as a prefix.

  - When the purpose has a value of `Training`, the `classify()` method will raise an exception. The sample cannot be re-classified; that would invalidate the training.

  - When the purpose has a value of `Testing`, the `classify()` method will work normally, applying a given `Hyperparameter` to compute a species.

- An `UnknownSample` instance can be used for user classification. The classification method here does not depend on the value of the purpose attribute, and always performs classification.

Let's look at implementing these behaviors with the @property decorator we learned about in this chapter. We can use @property to fetch computed values as if they were simple attributes. We can also use @property to define attributes that cannot be set.

The purpose enumeration

We'll start by enumerating a domain of purpose values:

```
class Purpose(enum.IntEnum):
    Classification = 0
    Testing = 1
    Training = 2
```

This definition creates a namespace with three objects we can use in our code: `Purpose.Classification`, `Purpose.Testing`, and `Purpose.Training`. For example, we can use `if sample.purpose == Purpose.Testing:` to identify a testing sample.

We can convert to `Purpose` objects from input values using `Purpose(x)` where x is an integer value, 0, 1, or 2. Any other value will raise a `ValueError` exception. We can convert back to numeric values, also. For example, `Purpose.Training.value` is 1. This use of numeric codes can fit well with external software that doesn't deal well with an enumeration of Python objects.

We'll decompose the KnownSample subclass of the Sample class into two parts. Here's the first part. We initialize a sample with the data required by the Sample.__init__() method plus two additional values, the purpose numeric code, and the assigned species:

```python
class KnownSample(Sample):

    def __init__(
        self,
        sepal_length: float,
        sepal_width: float,
        petal_length: float,
        petal_width: float,
        purpose: int,
        species: str,
    ) -> None:
        purpose_enum = Purpose(purpose)
        if purpose_enum not in {Purpose.Training, Purpose.Testing}:
            raise ValueError(
                f"Invalid purpose: {purpose!r}: {purpose_enum}"
            )
        super().__init__(
            sepal_length=sepal_length,
            sepal_width=sepal_width,
            petal_length=petal_length,
            petal_width=petal_width,
        )
        self.purpose = purpose_enum
        self.species = species
        self._classification: Optional[str] = None

    def matches(self) -> bool:
        return self.species == self.classification
```

We validate the purpose parameter's value to be sure it decodes to either Purpose.Training or Purpose.Testing. If the purpose value isn't one of the two allowed values, we'll raise a ValueError exception because the data is unusable.

We've created an instance variable, self._classification, with a leading _ name. This is a convention that suggests the name is not for general use by clients of this class. It's not "private," since there's no notion of privacy in Python. We could call it "concealed" or perhaps "watch out for surprises here."

Instead of a large, opaque wall available in some languages, Python uses a low, decorative floral border that sets this variable apart from the others. You can march right through the floral _ character to look at the value closely, but you probably shouldn't.

Here's the first @property method:

```
@property
def classification(self) -> Optional[str]:
    if self.purpose == Purpose.Testing:
        return self._classification
    else:
        raise AttributeError(f"Training samples have no
classification")
```

This defines a method that will be visible as an attribute name. Here's an example of creating a sample for testing purposes:

```
>>> from model import KnownSample, Purpose
>>> s2 = KnownSample(
...     sepal_length=5.1,
...     sepal_width=3.5,
...     petal_length=1.4,
...     petal_width=0.2,
...     species="Iris-setosa",
...     purpose=Purpose.Testing.value)
>>> s2
KnownSample(sepal_length=5.1, sepal_width=3.5, petal_length=1.4,
petal_width=0.2, purpose=1, species='Iris-setosa')
>>> s2.classification is None
True
```

When we evaluate s2.classification, this will call the method. This function makes sure this is a sample to be used for testing, and returns the value of the "concealed" instance variable self._classification.

If this is a Purpose.Training sample, the property will raise an AttributeError exception because any application that checks the value of the classification for a training sample has a bug in it that needs to be fixed.

Property setters

How do we set the classification? Do we really execute the statement
self._classification = h.classify(self)? The answer is no – we can create
a property that updates the "concealed" instance variable. This is a bit more
complex than the example above:

```
@classification.setter
def classification(self, value: str) -> None:
    if self.purpose == Purpose.Testing:
        self._classification = value
    else:
        raise AttributeError(
            f"Training samples cannot be classified")
```

The initial @property definition for classification is called a "getter." It gets the
value of an attribute. (The implementation uses the __get__() method of a descriptor
object that was created for us.) The @property definition for classification also
creates an additional decorator, @classification.setter. The method decorated by
the setter is used by assignment statements.

Note that the method names for these two properties are both classification. This
is the attribute name to be used.

Now a statement like s2.classification = h.classify(self) will change the
classification from a particular Hyperparameter object. This assignment statement
will use the method to examine the purpose of this sample. If the purpose is testing,
the value will be saved. If the purpose is not Purpose.Testing, then attempting to
set a classification raises an AttributeError exception, and identifies a place where
something's wrong in our application.

Repeated if statements

We have a number of if statements checking for specific Purpose values. This is a
suggestion that this design is not optimal. The variant behavior is not encapsulated
in a single class; instead, multiple behaviors are combined into a class.

The presence of a Purpose enumeration and if statements to check for the
enumerated values is a suggestion that we have multiple classes. The "simplification"
here isn't desirable.

In the *Input partitioning* section of this case study, we suggested there were two paths forward. One was to try and simplify the classes by setting the purpose attribute to separate testing from training data. This seems to have added if statements, without really simplifying the design.

This means we'll have to search for a better partitioning algorithm in a later chapter's case study. For now, we have the capability of creating valid data, but we also have code that's cluttered with if statements. The reader is encouraged to try alternative designs to examine the resulting code to see what seems simpler and easier to read.

Recall

Here are some of the key points in this chapter:

- When we have both data and behavior, this is the sweet spot for object-oriented design. We can leverage Python's generic collections and ordinary functions for many things. When it becomes complex enough that we need to be sure that pieces are all defined together, then we need to start using classes.

- When an attribute value is a reference to another object, the Pythonic approach is to allow direct access to the attribute; we don't write elaborate setter and getter functions. When an attribute value is computed, we have two choices: we can compute it eagerly or lazily. A property lets us be lazy and do the computation just in time.

- We'll often have cooperating objects; the behavior of the application emerges from the cooperation. This can often lead to manager objects that combine behaviors from component class definitions to create an integrated, working whole.

Exercises

We've looked at various ways that objects, data, and methods can interact with each other in an object-oriented Python program. As usual, your first thoughts should be how you can apply these principles to your own work. Do you have any messy scripts lying around that could be rewritten using an object-oriented manager? Look through some of your old code and look for methods that are not actions. If the name isn't a verb, try rewriting it as a property.

Think about code you've written in any language. Does it break the DRY principle? Is there any duplicate code? Did you copy and paste code? Did you write two versions of similar pieces of code because you didn't feel like understanding the original code? Go back over some of your recent code now and see whether you can refactor the duplicate code using inheritance or composition. Try to pick a project you're still interested in maintaining, not code so old that you never want to touch it again. That will help to keep you interested when you do the improvements!

Now, look back over some of the examples we looked at in this chapter. Start with the cached web page example that uses a property to cache the retrieved data. An obvious problem with this example is that the cache is never refreshed. Add a timeout to the property's getter, and only return the cached page if the page has been requested before the timeout has expired. You can use the `time` module (`time.time()` - `an_old_time` returns the number of seconds that have elapsed since `an_old_time`) to determine whether the cache has expired.

Also look at the inheritance-based `ZipProcessor`. It might be reasonable to use composition instead of inheritance here. Instead of extending the class in the `ZipReplace` and `ScaleZip` classes, you could pass instances of those classes into the `ZipProcessor` constructor and call them to do the processing part. Implement this.

Which version do you find easier to use? Which is more elegant? What is easier to read? These are subjective questions; the answer varies for each of us. Knowing the answer, however, is important. If you find you prefer inheritance over composition, you need to pay attention that you don't overuse inheritance in your daily coding. If you prefer composition, make sure you don't miss opportunities to create an elegant inheritance-based solution.

Finally, add some error handlers to the various classes we created in the case study. How should one bad sample be handled? Should the model be inoperable? Or should the row be skipped? There are profound data science and statistical consequences to a seemingly small technical implementation choice. Can we define a class that permits either alternative behavior?

In your daily coding, pay attention to the copy and paste commands. Every time you use them in your editor, consider whether it would be a good idea to improve your program's organization so that you only have one version of the code you are about to copy.

Summary

In this chapter, we focused on identifying objects, especially objects that are not immediately apparent; objects that manage and control. Objects should have both data and behaviors, but properties can be used to blur the distinction between the two. The DRY principle is an important indicator of code quality, and inheritance and composition can be applied to reduce code duplication.

In the next chapter, we'll look at Python's methods for defining abstract base classes. This lets us define a class that's a kind of template; it must be extended with subclasses that add narrowly-defined implementation features. This lets us build families of related classes, confident that they will work together properly.

6
Abstract Base Classes and Operator Overloading

We often need to make a distinction between concrete classes that have a complete set of attributes and methods, and an abstract class that is missing some details. This parallels the philosophical idea of abstraction as a way to summarize complexities. We might say that a sailboat and an airplane have a common, abstract relationship of being vehicles, but the details of how they move are distinct.

In Python, we have two approaches to defining similar things:

- **Duck typing**: When two class definitions have the same attributes and methods, then instances of the two classes have the same protocol and can be used interchangeably. We often say, "When I see a bird that walks like a duck and swims like a duck and quacks like a duck, I call that bird a duck."

- **Inheritance**: When two class definitions have common aspects, a subclass can share common features of a superclass. The implementation details of the two classes may vary, but the classes should be interchangeable when we use the common features defined by the superclass.

We can take inheritance one step further. We can have superclass definitions that are abstract: this means they aren't directly useable by themselves, but can be used through inheritance to create concrete classes.

We have to acknowledge a terminology problem around the terms *base class* and *superclass*. This is confusing because they're synonyms. There are two parallel metaphors here, and we flip back and forth between them. Sometimes, we'll use the "base class is a foundation" metaphor, where another class builds on it via inheritance. Other times, we'll use the "concrete class extends a superclass" metaphor. The "super" class is superior to the concrete class; it's typically drawn above it on a UML class diagram, and it needs to be defined first. For example:

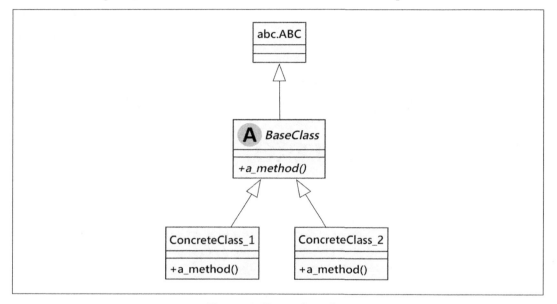

Figure 6.1: Abstract base class

Our base class, named `BaseClass` here, has a special class, `abc.ABC`, as a parent class. This provides some special metaclass features that help make sure the concrete classes have replaced the abstractions. In this diagram, we have added a big "A" circle to mark the class as abstract. This bit of decoration is optional, and often unhelpful, so we won't use it in other diagrams. The slanted font is another hint that the class is abstract.

The diagram shows an abstract method, a_method(), which doesn't have a defined body. A subclass must provide this. Again, a slanted font is used for the method name to provide a hint that it's abstract. The two concrete subclasses provide this missing method.

In this chapter, we'll cover the following topics:

- Creating an abstract base class
- ABCs and type hints

- The `collections.abc` module
- Creating your own abstract base class
- Demystifying the magic – looking under the hood at the implementation of an ABC
- Operator overloading
- Extending built-ins
- Metaclasses

The case study in this chapter will build on the case study material in previous chapters. We'll be able to look closely at different ways to partition data among training sets and testing sets.

We'll start by looking at how we use an abstract class and create a concrete class from it.

Creating an abstract base class

Imagine we are creating a media player with third-party plugins. It is advisable to create an abstract base class (ABC) in this case to document what API the third-party plugins should provide (documentation is one of the stronger use cases for ABCs).

The general design is to have a common feature, like `play()`, that applies to a number of classes. We don't want to pick some particular media format to use as a superclass; it seems somehow wrong to claim that some format is foundational, and all others are derived from it.

We'd prefer to define the media player as an *abstraction*. Each unique kind of media file format can provide a *concrete* implementation of the abstraction.

The `abc` module provides the tools to do this. Here's an abstract class that requires a subclass to provide a concrete method and a concrete property to be useful:

```
class MediaLoader(abc.ABC):
    @abc.abstractmethod
    def play(self) -> None:
        ...

    @property
    @abc.abstractmethod
    def ext(self) -> str:
        ...
```

The abc.ABC class introduces a **metaclass** – a class used to build the concrete class definitions. Python's default metaclass is named type. The default metaclass doesn't check for abstract methods when we try to create an instance. The abc.ABC class includes an extension to the type metaclass to prevent us from creating instances of classes that are not fully defined.

There are two decorators used to describe the placeholders in the abstraction. The example shows @abc.abstractmethod and a combination of @property and @abc.abstractmethod. Python uses decorators widely to make modifications to the general nature of the method or function. In this case, it provides additional details used by the metaclass that was included by the ABC class. Because we marked a method or property as abstract, any subclass of this class must implement that method or property in order to be a useful, concrete implementation.

The bodies of the methods are actually . . . . This three-dot token, the ellipsis, really is valid Python syntax. It's not a placeholder used only in this book; it's the Python code to remind everyone a useful body needs to be written in order to create a working, concrete subclass.

We've used the @property decorator on the ext() method, also. Our intent for the ext property is to provide a simple class-level variable with a string literal value. It's helpful to describe this as an @property to allow the implementation to choose between a simple variable and a method that implements the property. A simple variable in the concrete class will meet the expectations of the abstract class at runtime and will also help *mypy* to check the code for consistent use of types. A method could be used as an alternative to a simple attribute variable in case some more sophisticated computation is required.

One of the consequences of marking these properties is the class now has a new special attribute, __abstractmethods__. This attribute lists all of the names that need to be filled in to create a concrete class:

```
>>> MediaLoader.__abstractmethods__
frozenset({'ext', 'play'})
```

See what happens if you implement a subclass? We'll look at an example that doesn't supply concrete implementations for the abstractions. We'll also look at an example that does supply the required attribute:

```
>>> class Wav(MediaLoader):
...     pass
...
>>> x = Wav()
Traceback (most recent call last):
```

```
    File "<stdin>", line 1, in <module>
TypeError: Can't instantiate abstract class Wav with abstract methods
ext, play

>>> class Ogg(MediaLoader):
...       ext = '.ogg'
...       def play(self):
...           pass
...
>>> o = Ogg()
```

The definition of a Wav subclass fails to implement either of the abstract attributes. When we try to create an instance of the Wav class, an exception is raised. Because this subclass of MediaLoader is still abstract, it is not possible to instantiate the class. The class is still a potentially useful abstract class, but you'd have to subclass it and fill in the abstract placeholders before it can actually do anything.

The Ogg subclass supplies both attributes, so it – at the least – can instantiate cleanly. It's true, the body of the play() method doesn't do very much. What's important is that all of the placeholders were filled, making Ogg a concrete subclass of the abstract MediaLoader class.

 There's a subtle issue with using a class-level variable for the preferred media file extension. Because the ext attribute is a variable, it can be updated. Using o.ext = '.xyz' is not expressly prohibited. Python doesn't have an easy, obvious way to create read-only attributes. We often rely on documentation to explain the consequences of changing the value of the ext attribute.

This has clear advantages when creating a complex application. The use of abstraction like this makes it very easy for *mypy* to conclude that a class does (or does not) have the required methods and attributes.

This also mandates a certain amount of fussy importing to be sure that the module has access to the necessary abstract base classes for an application. One of the advantages of duck typing is the ability to avoid complex imports and still create a useful class that can act polymorphically with peer classes. This advantage is often outweighed by the ability of the abc.ABC class definition to support type checking via *mypy*, and to also do a runtime check for completeness of a subclass definition. The abc.ABC class also provides far more useful error messages when something is wrong.

One important use case for ABCs is the collections module. This module defines the built-in generic collections using a sophisticated set of base classes and mixins.

The ABCs of collections

A really comprehensive use of the abstract base classes in the Python standard library lives in the collections module. The collections we use are extensions of the Collection abstract class. Collection is an extension of an even more fundamental abstraction, Container.

Since the foundation is the Container class, let's inspect it in the Python interpreter to see what methods this class requires:

```
>>> from collections.abc import Container
>>> Container.__abstractmethods__
frozenset({'__contains__'})
```

So, the Container class has exactly one abstract method that needs to be implemented, __contains__(). You can issue help(Container.__contains__) to see what the function signature should look like:

```
>>> help(Container.__contains__)
Help on function __contains__ in module collections.abc:
__contains__(self, x)
```

We can see that __contains__() needs to take a single argument. Unfortunately, the help file doesn't tell us much about what that argument should be, but it's pretty obvious from the name of the ABC and the single method it implements that this argument is the value the user is checking to see whether the container holds.

This __contains__() special method implements the Python in operator. This method is implemented by set, list, str, tuple, and dict. However, we can also define a silly container that tells us whether a given value is in the set of odd integers:

```
from collections.abc import Container

class OddIntegers:
    def __contains__(self, x: int) -> bool:
        return x % 2 != 0
```

We've used the modulo test for oddity. If the remainder of x divided by two is zero, then x was even, otherwise x was odd.

Here's the interesting part: we can instantiate an OddContainer object and determine that, even though we did not extend Container, the class behaves as a Container object:

```
>>> odd = OddIntegers()
>>> isinstance(odd, Container)
True
>>> issubclass(OddIntegers, Container)
True
```

And that is why duck typing is way more awesome than classical polymorphism. We can create is-a relationships without the overhead of writing the code to set up inheritance (or worse, multiple inheritance).

One cool thing about the Container ABC is that any class that implements it gets to use the in keyword for free. In fact, in is just syntax sugar that delegates to the __contains__() method. Any class that has a __contains__() method is a Container and can therefore be queried by the in keyword. For example:

```
>>> odd = OddIntegers()
>>> 1 in odd
True
>>> 2 in odd
False
>>> 3 in odd
True
```

The real value here is the ability to create new kinds of collections that are completely compatible with Python's built-in generic collections. We could, for example, create a dictionary that uses a binary tree structure to retain keys instead of a hashed lookup. We'd start with the Mapping abstract base class definitions, but change the algorithms that support methods like __getitem__(), __setitem__(), and __delitem__().

Python's duck typing works (in part) via the isinstance() and issubclass() built-in functions. These functions are used to determine class relationships. They rely on two internal methods that classes can provide: __instancecheck__() and __subclasscheck__(). An ABC class can provide a __subclasshook__() method, which is used by the __subclasscheck__() method to assert that a given class is a proper subclass of the abstract base class. The details are a bit beyond this book; consider this a signpost pointing out the path that needs to be followed when creating novel classes that need to live side by side with built-in classes.

Abstract base classes and type hints

The concept of an abstract base class is closely tied to the idea of a generic class. An abstract base class is often generic with respect to some detail that is supplied by a concrete implementation.

Most of Python's generic classes – classes like `list`, `dict`, and `set` – can be used as type hints, and these hints can be parameterized to narrow the domain. There's a world of difference between `list[Any]` and `list[int]`; the value `["a", 42, 3.14]` is valid for the first type hint, but invalid for the other. This concept of *parameterizing* the generic type to make it more specific often applies to abstract classes, also.

For this to work, you'll often need to incorporate `from __future__ import annotations` as the very first line of code. This modifies the behavior of Python to permit function and variable annotations to parameterize these standard collections.

Generic classes and abstract base classes are not the same thing. The two concepts overlap, but are distinct:

- Generic classes have an implicit relationship with `Any`. This often needs to be narrowed using type parameters, like `list[int]`. The list class is concrete, and when we want to extend it, we'll need to plug in a class name to replace the `Any` type. The Python interpreter does not use generic class hints in any way; they are only checked by static analysis tools such as *mypy*.

- Abstract classes have placeholders instead of one or more methods. These placeholder methods require a design decision that supplies a concrete implementation. These classes are not completely defined. When we extend it, we'll need to provide a concrete method implementation. This is checked by *mypy*. That's not all. If we don't provide the missing methods, the interpreter will raise a runtime exception when we try to create an instance of an abstract class.

Some classes can be both abstract and generic. As noted above, the type parameter helps *mypy* understand our intention, but isn't required. The concrete implementation is required.

Another concept that's adjacent to abstract classes is the **protocol**. This is the essence of how duck typing works: when two classes have the same batch of methods, they both adhere to a common protocol. Any time we see classes with similar methods, there's a common protocol; this may be formalized with a type hint.

Consider objects that can be hashed. Immutable classes implement the __hash__() method, including strings, integers, and tuples. Generally, mutable classes don't implement the __hash__() method; this includes classes like list, dict, and set. This one method is the Hashable protocol. If we attempt to write a type hint like dict[list[int], list[str]], then *mypy* will object that list[int] can't be used as a key. It can't be a key because the given type, list[int], doesn't implement the Hashable protocol. At runtime, the attempt to create a dictionary item with a mutable key will fail for the same reason: a list doesn't implement the required method.

The essence of creating ABCs is defined in the abc module. We'll look at how this works later. For now, we want to make use of abstract classes, and that means using the definitions in the collections module.

The collections.abc module

One prominent use of abstract base classes is in the collections.abc module. This module provides the abstract base class definitions for Python's built-in collections. This is how list, set, and dict (and a few others) can be built from individual component definitions.

We can use the definitions to build our own unique data structures in ways that overlap with built-in structures. We can also use the definitions when we want to write a type hint for a specific feature of a data structure, without being overly specific about alternative implementations that might also be acceptable.

The definitions in collections.abc don't – trivially – include list, set, or dict. Instead, the module provides definitions like MutableSequence, MutableMapping, and MutableSet, which are – in effect – abstract base classes for which the list, dict, or set classes we use are the concrete implementations. Let's follow the various aspects of the definition of Mapping back to their origins. Python's dict class is a concrete implementation of MutableMapping. The abstraction comes from the idea of mapping a key to a value. The MutableMapping class depends on the Mapping definition, an immutable, frozen dictionary, potentially optimized for lookups. Let's follow the relationships among these abstractions.

Here's the path we want to follow:

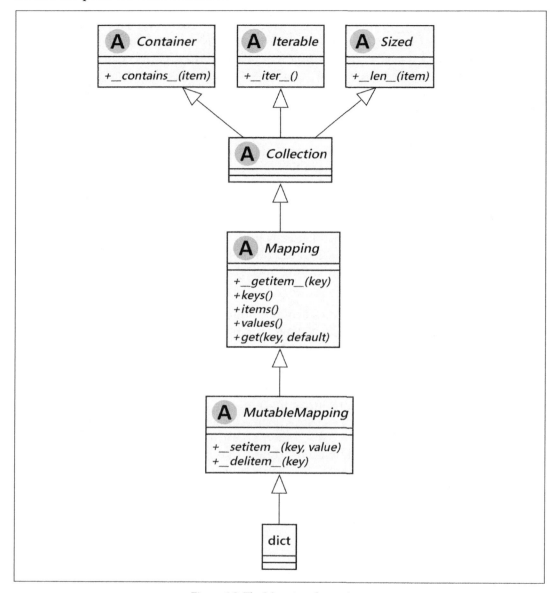

Figure 6.2: The Mapping abstractions

Starting in the middle, we can see the Mapping definition depends on the Collection class definition. The definition of the Collection abstract class, in turn, depends on three other abstract base classes: Sized, Iterable, and Container. Each of these abstractions demands specific methods.

If we're going to create a lookup-only dictionary – a concrete `Mapping` implementation – we'll need to implement at least the following methods:

- The `Sized` abstraction requires an implementation for the `__len__()` method. This lets an instance of our class respond to the `len()` function with a useful answer.

- The `Iterable` abstraction requires an implementation for the `__iter__()` method. This lets an object work with the `for` statement and the `iter()` function. In *Chapter 10, The Iterator Pattern*, we'll revisit this topic.

- The `Container` abstraction requires an implementation for the `__contains__()` method. This permits the `in` and `not in` operators to work.

- The `Collection` abstraction combines `Sized`, `Iterable`, and `Container` without introducing additional abstract methods.

- The `Mapping` abstraction, based on `Collection`, requires, among other things, `__getitem__()`, `__iter__()`, and `__len__()`. It has a default definition for `__contains__()`, based on whatever `__iter__()` method we provide. The `Mapping` definition will provide a few other methods, also.

This list of methods comes directly from the abstract relationships in the base classes. By building our new dictionary-like immutable class from these abstractions, we can be sure that our class will collaborate seamlessly with other Python generic classes.

When we look at the documentation in `https://docs.python.org/3.9/library/collections.abc.html`, we see the page is dominated by a table showing abstract class definitions and the definitions they depend on. There's a lattice of dependencies showing overlap among the class definitions. It's this overlap that allows us to use a `for` statement to iterate through every kind of collection that implements the `Iterable` abstract base class.

Let's define our own immutable `Mapping` object implementation by extending the abstract classes. The goal is to be able to load our dictionary-like mapping once with keys and values, and then use it to map the keys to their values. Since we aren't going to allow any updates, we can apply a variety of algorithms to make it very fast as well as very compact.

The goal is a class with a type hint like the following:

```
BaseMapping = abc.Mapping[Comparable, Any]
```

We're going to create a dictionary-like mapping from some key to – well – an object of any possible type. We've defined the key with the type `Comparable` because we want to be able to compare the keys and sort them into order. Searching through a list in order is often more efficient than searching a list that's not in order.

We'll look at the core of a Lookup class definition first. We'll return to the Comparable class definition after solidifying the essentials of a new kind of mapping from keys to values.

When we look at ways we can construct a dictionary, we see that a dictionary can be built from two different kinds of data structures. Our new mapping has to have this same flexibility. The two structures are exemplified by the following:

```
>>> x = dict({"a": 42, "b": 7, "c": 6})
>>> y = dict([("a", 42), ("b", 7), ("c", 6)])
>>> x == y
True
```

We can build a mapping from an existing mapping, or we can build a mapping from a sequence of two-tuples with keys and values. This means there are two separate definitions for __init__():

* def __init__(self, source: BaseMapping) -> None
* def __init__(self, source: Iterable[tuple[Comparable, Any]]) -> None

These two definitions have distinct type hints. To make it clear to *mypy*, we need to provide **overloaded** method definitions. This is done with a special decoration from the typing module, @overload. We'll provide two method definitions with the two alternatives; after these, we'll provide the real method definition that does the useful work. Because these are type hints, they're not *required*. They're wordy, and they help us be sure we've got a sensible implementation.

Here's the first part of the Lookup class definition. We'll break this into pieces because the __init__() method needs to cover these two cases defined by the alternative overloads:

```
BaseMapping = abc.Mapping[Comparable, Any]
class Lookup(BaseMapping):
    @overload
    def __init__(
            self,
            source: Iterable[tuple[Comparable, Any]]
    ) -> None:
        ...

    @overload
    def __init__(self, source: BaseMapping) -> None:
        ...

    def __init__(
            self,
```

```
        source: Union[Iterable[
            tuple[Comparable, Any]]
            BaseMapping,
            None] = None,
    ) -> None:
        sorted_pairs: Sequence[tuple[Comparable, Any]]
        if isinstance(source, Sequence):
            sorted_pairs = sorted(source)
        elif isinstance(source, abc.Mapping):
            sorted_pairs = sorted(source.items())
        else:
            sorted_pairs = []
        self.key_list = [p[0] for p in sorted_pairs]
        self.value_list = [p[1] for p in sorted_pairs]
```

The __init__() method needs to handle three cases for loading a mapping. This means building the values from a sequence of pairs, or building the values from another mapping object, or creating an empty sequence of values. We need to separate the keys from the values and put them into two parallel lists. A sorted list of keys can be rapidly searched to find a match. The sorted list of values is returned when we get a key's value from the mapping.

Here are the imports needed:

```
from __future__ import annotations
from collections import abc
from typing import Protocol, Any, overload, Union
import bisect
from typing import Iterator, Iterable, Sequence, Mapping
```

Here are the other abstract methods that are defined by the @abstractmethod decorator. We provide the following concrete implementations:

```
    def __len__(self) -> int:
        return len(self.key_list)

    def __iter__(self) -> Iterator[Comparable]:
        return iter(self.key_list)

    def __contains__(self, key: object) -> bool:
        index = bisect.bisect_left(self.key_list, key)
        return key == self.key_list[index]
```

```
    def __getitem__(self, key: Comparable) -> Any:
        index = bisect.bisect_left(self.key_list, key)
        if key == self.key_list[index]:
            return self.value_list[index]
        raise KeyError(key)
```

The __len__(), __iter__(), and __contains__() methods are required by the Sized, Iterable, and Container abstract classes. The Collection abstract class combines the other three without introducing any new abstract methods.

The __getitem__() is required to be a Mapping. Without it, we can't retrieve an individual value for a given key.

The use of the bisect module is one way to find a specific value rapidly in a sorted list of keys. The bisect.bisect_left() function finds the spot where a key belongs in a list. If the key is there, we can return the value to which it maps. If the key is not there, we can raise the KeyError exception.

Note that the __contains__() definition has the object class as the type hint, unlike the other methods. This is required because Python's in operation needs to support any kind of object, even ones that don't obviously support the Comparable protocol.

Here's how it looks when we use our shiny new Lookup class:

```
>>> x = Lookup(
...     [
...         ["z", "Zillah"],
...         ["a", "Amy"],
...         ["c", "Clara"],
...         ["b", "Basil"],
...     ]
... )

>>> x["c"]
'Clara'
```

This collection, generally, behaves a bit like a dictionary. There are a number of dict-like aspects we can't use, though, because we chose an abstract base class that didn't describe the full set of methods for the dict class.

If we try something like this:

```
>>> x["m"] = "Maud"
```

We'll get an exception that spells out the limitation of the class we built:

```
TypeError: 'Lookup' object does not support item assignment
```

This exception is consistent with the rest of our design. An update to this object means inserting an item at the correct position to maintain a sorted order. Shuffling a large list around gets expensive; if we need to update the lookup collection, we should consider other data structures like a Red-Black tree. But, for the pure search operation using the bisect algorithm, this performs nicely.

We skipped over the definition of the Comparable class. This defines the minimum set of features – the protocol – for the keys. It's a way to formalize the comparison rules required to keep the keys for the mapping in order. This helps *mypy* confirm that objects we try to use as keys really can be compared:

```python
from typing import Protocol, Any
class Comparable(Protocol):
    def __eq__(self, other: Any) -> bool: ...
    def __ne__(self, other: Any) -> bool: ...
    def __le__(self, other: Any) -> bool: ...
    def __lt__(self, other: Any) -> bool: ...
    def __ge__(self, other: Any) -> bool: ...
    def __gt__(self, other: Any) -> bool: ...
```

There's no implementation. This definition is used to introduce a new type hint. Because it's a hint, we provide ... as the body for the methods, since the bodies will be provided by existing class definitions like str and int.

Note that we don't rely on items having a hash code. This is an interesting extension to the built-in dict class, which requires the keys be hashable.

The general approach to using abstract classes is this:

1. Find a class that does most of what you need.

2. Identify the methods in the collections.abc definitions that are marked as *abstract*. The documentation often gives a lot of information, but you'll also have to look at the source.

3. Subclass the abstract class, filling in the missing methods.

4. While it can help to make a checklist of the methods, there are tools to help with this. Creating a unit test (we'll cover testing in *Chapter 13, Testing Object-Oriented Programs*) means you need to create an instance of your new class. If you haven't defined all the abstract methods, this will raise an exception. Using *mypy* will also spot abstract methods that aren't properly defined in the concrete subclass.

This is a powerful way to reuse code when we choose the abstractions well; a person can form a mental model of the class without knowing all of the details. It's also a powerful way to create closely related classes that can easily be examined by *mypy*. Beyond those two advantages, the formality of marking a method as abstract gives us a runtime assurance that the concrete subclass really does implement all the required methods.

Now that we've seen how to use an abstract base class, let's look at defining a new abstraction.

Creating your own abstract base class

We have two general paths to creating classes that are similar: we can leverage duck typing or we can define common abstractions. When we leverage duck typing, we can formalize the related types by creating a type hint using a protocol definition to enumerate the common methods, or a Union[] to enumerate the common types.

There are an almost unlimited number of influencing factors that suggest one or the other approach. While duck typing offers the most flexibility, we may sacrifice the ability to use *mypy*. An abstract base class definition can be wordy and potentially confusing.

We'll tackle a small problem. We want to build a simulation of games that involve polyhedral dice. These are the dice including four, six, eight, twelve, and twenty sides. The six-sided dice are conventional cubes. Some sets of dice include 10-sided dice, which are cool, but aren't – technically – a *regular* polyhedron; they're two sets of five "kite-shaped" faces.

One question that comes up is how best to simulate rolls of these different shaped dice. There are three readily available sources of random data in Python: the random module, the os module, and the secrets module. If we turn to third-party modules, we can add in cryptographic libraries like pynacl, which offer yet more random number capabilities.

Rather than bake the choice of random number generator into a class, we can define an abstract class that has the general features of a die. A concrete subclass can supply the missing randomization capability. The random module has a very flexible generator. The os module's capability is limited, but involves using an *entropy collector* to increase randomness. Flexibility and high entropy are generally combined by cryptographic generators.

To create our dice-rolling abstraction, we'll need the abc module. This is distinct from the collections.abc module. The abc module has the foundational definitions for abstract classes:

```python
import abc

class Die(abc.ABC):
    def __init__(self) -> None:
        self.face: int
        self.roll()

    @abc.abstractmethod
    def roll(self) -> None:
        ...

    def __repr__(self) -> str:
        return f"{self.face}"
```

We've defined a class that inherits from the abc.ABC class. Using ABC as the parent class assures us that any attempt to create an instance of the Die class directly will raise a TypeError exception. This is a runtime exception; it's also checked by *mypy*.

We've marked a method, roll(), as abstract with the @abc.abstract decorator. This isn't a very complex method, but any subclass should match this abstract definition. This is only checked by *mypy*. Of course, if we make a mess of the concrete implementation, things are likely to break at runtime. Consider this mess of code:

```python
>>> class Bad(Die):
...     def roll(self, a: int, b: int) -> float:
...         return (a+b)/2
```

This will raise a TypeError exception at runtime. The problem is caused by the base class __init__() not providing the a and b parameters to this strange-looking roll() method. This is valid Python code, but it doesn't make sense in this context. The method will also generate *mypy* errors, providing ample warning the method definition doesn't match the abstraction.

Here's what two proper extensions to the Die class look like:

```python
class D4(Die):
    def roll(self) -> None:
        self.face = random.choice((1, 2, 3, 4))
```

```
class D6(Die):
    def roll(self) -> None:
        self.face = random.randint(1, 6)
```

We've provided methods that provide a suitable definition for the abstract placeholder in the Die class. They use vastly different approaches to selecting a random value. The four-sided die uses random.choice(). The six-sided die – the common cube most people know – uses random.randint().

Let's go a step further and create another abstract class. This one will represent a handful of dice. Again, we have a number of candidate solutions, and we can use an abstract class to defer the final design choices.

The interesting part of this design is the differences in the rules for games with handfuls of dice. In some games, the rules require the player to roll all the dice. The rules for a lot of games with two dice require the player to roll both dice. In other games, the rules allow players to save dice, and re-roll selected dice. In some games, like Yacht, the players are allowed at most two re-rolls. In other games, like Zilch, they are allowed to re-roll until they elect to save their score or roll something invalid and lose all their points, scoring zilch (hence the name).

These are dramatically different rules that apply to a simple list of Die instances. Here's a class that leaves the roll implementation as an abstraction:

```
class Dice(abc.ABC):
    def __init__(self, n: int, die_class: Type[Die]) -> None:
        self.dice = [die_class() for _ in range(n)]

    @abc.abstractmethod
    def roll(self) -> None:
        ...

    @property
    def total(self) -> int:
        return sum(d.face for d in self.dice)
```

The __init__() method expects an integer, n, and the class used to create Die instances, named die_class. The type hint is Type[Die], telling *mypy* to be on the lookout for any subclass of the abstract base class Die. We don't expect an instance of any of the Die subclasses; we expect the class object itself. We'd expect to see SomeDice(6, D6) to create a list of six instances of the D6 class.

We've defined the collection of `Die` instances as a list because that seems simple. Some games will identify dice by their position when saving some dice and rerolling the remainder of the dice, and the integer list indices seem useful for that.

This subclass implements the roll-all-the-dice rule:

```
class SimpleDice(Dice):
    def roll(self) -> None:
        for d in self.dice:
            d.roll()
```

Each time the application evaluates `roll()`, all the dice are updated. It looks like this:

```
>>> sd = SimpleDice(6, D6)
>>> sd.roll()
>>> sd.total
23
```

The object, `sd`, is an instance of the concrete class, `SimpleDice`, built from the abstract class, `Dice`. The instance of `SimpleDice` contains six instances of the `D6` class. This, too, is a concrete class built from the abstract class `Die`.

Here's another subclass that provides a dramatically different set of methods. Some of these fill in the spaces left by abstract methods. Others, however, are unique to the subclass:

```
class YachtDice(Dice):
    def __init__(self) -> None:
        super().__init__(5, D6)
        self.saved: Set[int] = set()

    def saving(self, positions: Iterable[int]) -> "YachtDice":
        if not all(0 <= n < 6 for n in positions):
            raise ValueError("Invalid position")
        self.saved = set(positions)
        return self

    def roll(self) -> None:
        for n, d in enumerate(self.dice):
            if n not in self.saved:
                d.roll()
        self.saved = set()
```

We've created a set of saved positions. This is initially empty. We can use the saving() method to provide an iterable collection of integers as positions to save. It works like this:

```
>>> sd = YachtDice()
>>> sd.roll()
>>> sd.dice
[2, 2, 2, 6, 1]
>>> sd.saving([0, 1, 2]).roll()
>>> sd.dice
[2, 2, 2, 6, 6]
```

We improved the hand from three of a kind to a full house.

In both cases, the Die class and the Dice class, it's not clear that the abc.ABC base class and the presence of an @abc.abstractmethod decoration is dramatically better than providing a concrete base class with a common set of default definitions.

In some languages, the abstraction-based definition is required. In Python, because of duck typing, abstraction is optional. In cases where it clarifies the design intent, use it. In cases where it seems fussy and little more than overhead, set it aside.

Because it's used to define the collections, we'll often use the collection.abc names in type hints to describe the protocols objects must follow. In less common cases, we'll leverage the collections.abc abstractions to create our own unique collections.

Demystifying the magic

We've used abstract base classes and it's clear they're doing a lot of work for us. Let's look inside the class to see some of what's going on:

```
>>> from dice import Die
>>> Die.__abstractmethods__
frozenset({'roll'})
>>> Die.roll.__isabstractmethod__
True
```

The abstract method, roll(), is tracked in a specially named attribute, __abstractmethods__, of the class. This suggests what the @abc.abstractmethod decorator does. This decorator sets __isabstractmethod__ to mark the method. When Python finally builds the class from the various methods and attributes, the list of abstractions is also collected to create a class-level set of methods that must be implemented.

Any subclass that extends Die will also inherit this __abstractmethods__ set. When methods are defined inside the subclass, names are removed from the set as Python builds the class from the definitions. We can only create instances of a class where the set of abstract methods in the class is empty.

Central to this is the way classes are created: a class builds objects. This is the essence of most of object-oriented programming. But what is a class?

1. A class is another object with two very limited jobs: it has the special methods used to create and manage instances of the class, and it also acts as a container for the method definitions for objects of the class. We think of building class objects with the class statement, which leaves open the question of how the class statement builds the class object.

2. The type class is the internal object that builds our application classes. When we enter the code for a class, the details of construction are actually the responsibility of methods of the type class. After type has created our application class, our class then creates the application objects that solve our problem.

The type object is called the **metaclass**, the class used to build classes. This means every class object is an instance of type. Most of the time, we're perfectly happy with letting a class statement be handled by the type class so our application code can run. There's one place, however, where we might want to change how type works.

Because type is itself a class, it can be extended. A class abc.ABCMeta extends the type class to check for methods decorated with @abstractmethod. When we extend abc.ABC, we're creating a new class that uses the ABCMeta metaclass. We can see this in the value of the special __mro__ attribute of the ABCMeta class; this attribute lists the classes used for resolving method names (**MRO** is **Method Resolution Order**). This special attribute lists the following classes to be searched for a given attribute: the abc.ABCMeta class, the type class, and finally the object class.

We can use the ABCMeta metaclass explicitly when we create a new class, if we want:

```
class DieM(metaclass=abc.ABCMeta):
    def __init__(self) -> None:
        self.face: int
        self.roll()

    @abc.abstractmethod
    def roll(self) -> None:
        ...
```

We've used `metaclass` as a keyword parameter when defining the components that make up a class. This means the `abc.ABCMeta` extension to type will be used to create the final class object.

Now that we've seen how classes are built, we can consider other things we can do when creating and extending classes. Python exposes the binding between the syntactic operators, like the `/` operator, and the methods of the implementing class. This allows the `float` and `int` classes to do different things with the `/` operator, but it can also be used for quite different purposes. For example, the `pathlib.Path` class, which we will discuss in *Chapter 9, Strings, Serialization, and File Paths*, also makes use of the `/` operator.

Operator overloading

Python's operators, `+`, `/`, `-`, `*`, and so on, are implemented by special methods on classes. We can apply Python operators more widely than the built-in numbers and collection types. Doing this can be called "overloading" the operators: letting them work with more than the built-in types.

Looking back at the *The collections.abc module* section, earlier in this chapter, we dropped a hint about how Python connects some built-in features with our classes. When we look at the `collections.abc.Collection` class, it is the abstract base class for all `Sized`, `Iterable`, `Containers`; it requires three methods that enable two built-in functions and one built-in operator:

- The `__len__()` method is used by the built-in `len()` function.
- The `__iter__()` method is used by the built-in `iter()` function, which means it's used by the `for` statement.
- The `__contains__()` method is used by the built-in `in` operator. This operator is implemented by methods of built-in classes.

It's not wrong to imagine the built-in `len()` function has this definition:

```
def len(object: Sized) -> int:
    return object.__len__()
```

When we ask for `len(x)`, it's doing the same thing as `x.__len__()`, but is shorter, easier to read, and easier to remember. Similarly, `iter(y)` is effectively `y.__iter__()`. And an expression like `z in S` is evaluated as if it was `S.__contains__(z)`.

And yes, with a few exceptions, all of Python works this way. We write pleasant, easy-to-read expressions that are transformed into special methods. The only exceptions are the logic operations: and, or, not, and if-else. These don't map directly to special method definitions.

Because almost all of Python relies on the special methods, it means we can change their behavior to add features. We can overload the operators with new data types. One prominent example of this is in the pathlib module:

```
>>> from pathlib import Path
>>> home = Path.home()
>>> home / "miniconda3" / "envs"
PosixPath('/Users/slott/miniconda3/envs')
```

Note: Your results will vary, depending on your operating system and your username.

What doesn't vary is that the / operator is used to connect a Path object with string objects to create a new Path object.

The / operator is implemented by the __truediv__() and __rtruediv__() methods. In order to make operations commutative, Python has two places to look for an implementation. Given an expression of A *op* B, where *op* is any of the Python operators like __add__ for +, Python does the following checks for special methods to implement the operator:

1. There's a special case when B is a proper subclass of A. In those rare cases, the order is reversed so B.__*rop*__(A) can be tried before any of the others. This lets the subclass B override an operation from superclass A.

2. Try A.__*op*__(B). If this returns a value that's not the special NotImplemented value, this is the result. For a Path object expression like home / "miniconda3", this is effectively home.__truediv__("miniconda3"). A new Path object is built from the old Path object and the string.

3. Try B.__*rop*__(A). This might be the __radd__() method for the reverse addition implementation. If this method returns a value other than the NotImplemented value, this is the result. Note that the operand ordering is reversed. For commutative operations, like addition and multiplication, this does not matter. For non-commutative operations, like subtraction and division, the change in ordering needs to be reflected in the implementation.

Let's return to our handful of dice example. We can implement a + operator to add a Die instance to a collection of Dice. We'll start with a base definition of a class that contains a heterogenous handful of different kinds of dice. Check the previous Dice class, which assumed homogenous dice. This isn't an abstract class; it has a definition of roll that re-rolls all the dice. We'll start with some basics and then incorporate the __add__() special method:

```python
class DDice:
    def __init__(self, *die_class: Type[Die]) -> None:
        self.dice = [dc() for dc in die_class]
        self.adjust: int = 0

    def plus(self, adjust: int = 0) -> "DDice":
        self.adjust = adjust
        return self

    def roll(self) -> None:
        for d in self.dice:
            d.roll()

    @property
    def total(self) -> int:
        return sum(d.face for d in self.dice) + self.adjust
```

This shouldn't be much of a surprise. It looks a lot like the Dice class defined above. We've added an adjust attribute set by the plus() method so we can use DDice(D6, D6, D6).plus(2). It fits better with some tabletop role-playing games (TTRPGs).

Also, recall that we provide the types of the dice to the DDice class, not instances of the dice. We use the class object, D6, not a Die instance, created by an expression like D6(). The instances of the classes are created by DDice in the __init__() method.

Here's the cool part: we can use the plus operator with DDice objects, Die classes, and integers to define a complex roll of the dice:

```python
def __add__(self, die_class: Any) -> "DDice":
    if isinstance(die_class, type) and issubclass(die_class, Die):
        new_classes = [type(d) for d in self.dice] + [die_class]
        new = DDice(*new_classes).plus(self.adjust)
        return new
    elif isinstance(die_class, int):
        new_classes = [type(d) for d in self.dice]
        new = DDice(*new_classes).plus(die_class)
```

```
            return new
        else:
            return NotImplemented

    def __radd__(self, die_class: Any) -> "DDice":
        if isinstance(die_class, type) and issubclass(die_class, Die):
            new_classes = [die_class] + [type(d) for d in self.dice]
            new = DDice(*new_classes).plus(self.adjust)
            return new
        elif isinstance(die_class, int):
            new_classes = [type(d) for d in self.dice]
            new = DDice(*new_classes).plus(die_class)
            return new
        else:
            return NotImplemented
```

These two methods are similar in many ways. We check for three separate kinds of +
operations:

- If the argument value, die_class, is a type, and it's a subclass of the Die class,
  then we're adding another Die object to a DDice collection. It's an expression
  like DDice(D6) + D6 + D6. The semantics of most operator implementations
  is to create a new object from the previous objects.

- If the argument value is an integer, then we're adding an adjustment to a set
  of dice. This is something like DDice(D6, D6, D6) + 2.

- If the argument value is neither a subclass of Die nor an integer, then
  something else is going on, and this class doesn't have an implementation.
  This may be some kind of bug, or it might be that the other class involved
  in the operation can provide an implementation; returning NotImplemented
  gives the other object a chance at performing the operation.

Because we've provided __radd__() as well as __add__(), these operations
are commutative. We can use expressions like D6 + DDice(D6) + D6 and
2 + DDice(D6, D6).

We need to make specific isinstance() checks because Python operators are
completely generic, and the expected type hint must be Any. We can only narrow
down the applicable types through runtime checks. The *mypy* program is astute
about following the branching logic to confirm that an integer object was properly
used in an integer context.

"But wait," you say. "My favorite game has rules that call for 3d6+2." This is shorthand for rolling three six-sided dice and adding two to the result. In many TTRPGs, this kind of abbreviation is used to summarize the dice.

Can we add multiplication to do this? There's no reason why not. For multiplication, we only need to worry about integers. D6 * D6 isn't used in any of the rules, but 3*D6 matches the text of most TTRPG rules nicely:

```python
def __mul__(self, n: Any) -> "DDice":
    if isinstance(n, int):
        new_classes = [type(d) for d in self.dice for _ in range(n)]
        return DDice(*new_classes).plus(self.adjust)
    else:
        return NotImplemented

def __rmul__(self, n: Any) -> "DDice":
    if isinstance(n, int):
        new_classes = [type(d) for d in self.dice for _ in range(n)]
        return DDice(*new_classes).plus(self.adjust)
    else:
        return NotImplemented
```

These two methods follow a similar design pattern to the __add__() and __radd__() methods. For each existing Die subclass, we'll create several instances of the class. This lets us use 3 * DDice(D6) + 2 as an expression to define a dice-rolling rule. The Python operator precedence rules still apply, so the 3 * DDice(D6) portion is evaluated first.

Python's use of the various *__op__*() and *__rop__*() methods works out extremely well for applying the various operators to objects that are immutable: strings, numbers, and tuples being the primary examples. Our handful of dice presents a bit of a head-scratcher because the state of the individual dice can change. What's important is that we treat the composition of the hand as immutable. Each operation on a DDice object creates a new DDice instance.

What about mutable objects? When we write an assignment statement like some_list += [some_item], we're mutating the value of the some_list object. The += statement does the same thing as the more complex expression some_list.extend([some_item]). Python supports this with operators with names like __iadd__() and __imul__(). These are "in-place" operations, designed to mutate objects.

For example, consider:

```
>>> y = DDice(D6, D6)
>>> y += D6
```

This can be processed one of two ways:

- If DDice implements __iadd__(), this becomes y.__iadd__(D6). The object can mutate itself in place.
- If DDice does not implement __iadd__(), this is y = y.__add__(D6). The object creates a new, immutable object, and that's given the old object's variable name. This lets us do things like string_variable += ".". Under the hood, string_variable is not mutated; it's replaced.

If it makes sense for an object to be mutable, we can support in-place mutation of a DDice object with this method:

```
def __iadd__(self, die_class: Any) -> "DDice":
    if isinstance(die_class, type) and issubclass(die_class, Die):
        self.dice += [die_class()]
        return self
    elif isinstance(die_class, int):
        self.adjust += die_class
        return self
    else:
        return NotImplemented
```

The __iadd__() method appends to the internal collection of dice. It follows rules similar to the __add__() methods: when a class is provided, an instance is created, and it's added to the self.dice list; if an integer is provided, it's added to the self.adjust value.

We can now perform incremental changes to a single dice-rolling rule. We can mutate the state of a single DDice object using assignment statements. Because the object mutates, we aren't creating a lot of copies of the object. The creation of complex dice looks like this:

```
>>> y = DDice(D6, D6)
>>> y += D6
>>> y += 2
```

This builds the 3d6+2 dice roller in incremental pieces.

The use of the internal special method names allows for seamless integration with other Python features. We can build classes using `collections.abc` that fit with existing collections. We can override the methods implementing the Python operators to create easy-to-use syntax.

We can leverage the special method names to add features to Python's built-in generic collections. We'll turn to that topic next.

Extending built-ins

Python has two collections of built-ins that we might want to extend. We can broadly classify these into the following:

- Immutable objects, including numbers, strings, bytes, and tuples. These will often have extended operators defined. In the *Operator overloading* section of this chapter, we looked at how we can provide arithmetic operations for objects of the `Dice` class.

- Mutable collections, including sets, lists, and dictionaries. When we look at the definitions in `collections.abc`, these are sized, iterable containers, three distinct aspects that we might want to focus on. In *The collections.abc module* section of this chapter, we looked at creating an extension to the `Mapping` abstract base class.

There are other built-in types, but these two groupings are generally applicable to a variety of problems. For example, we could create a dictionary that rejects duplicate values.

The built-in dictionary always updates the value associated with a key. This can lead to odd-looking code that works. For example:

```
>>> d = {"a": 42, "a": 3.14}
>>> d
{'a': 3.14}
```

And:

```
>>> {1: "one", True: "true"}
{1: 'true'}
```

These are well-defined behaviors. It may be odd-looking to provide two keys in the expression but have only one key in the result, but the rules for building dictionaries make these inevitable and correct results.

We may, however, not like the behavior of silently ignoring a key. It may make our application needlessly complex to worry about the possibility of duplicates. Let's create a new kind of dictionary that won't update items once they've been loaded.

Studying `collections.abc`, we need to extend a mapping, with a changed definition of __setitem__() to prevent updating an existing key. Working at the interactive Python prompt, we can try this:

```
>>> from typing import Dict, Hashable, Any, Mapping, Iterable
>>> class NoDupDict(Dict[Hashable, Any]):
...     def __setitem__(self, key, value) -> None:
...         if key in self:
...             raise ValueError(f"duplicate {key!r}")
...         super().__setitem__(key, value)
```

And when we put it to use, we see the following:

```
>>> nd = NoDupDict()
>>> nd["a"] = 1
>>> nd["a"] = 2
Traceback (most recent call last):
  ...
  File "<doctest examples.md[10]>", line 1, in <module>
    nd["a"] = 2
  File "<doctest examples.md[7]>", line 4, in __setitem__
    raise ValueError(f"duplicate {key!r}")
ValueError: duplicate 'a'
```

We're not done, but we're off to a good start. This dictionary rejects duplicates under some circumstances.

However, it isn't blocking duplicate keys when we try to construct a dictionary from another dictionary. We don't want this to work:

```
>>> NoDupDict({"a": 42, "a": 3.14})
{'a': 3.14}
```

So we've got some work to do. Some expressions properly raise exceptions, where as other expressions still silently ignore duplicate keys.

The basic problem is that not all methods that set items are using __setitem__(). To alleviate the above problems, we'll need to override __init__() as well.

We'll also need to add type hints to our initial draft. This will let us leverage *mypy* to confirm that our implementation will work in general. Here's a version with __init__() added:

```python
from __future__ import annotations
from typing import cast, Any, Union, Tuple, Dict, Iterable, Mapping
from collections import Hashable

DictInit = Union[
    Iterable[Tuple[Hashable, Any]],
    Mapping[Hashable, Any],
    None]

class NoDupDict(Dict[Hashable, Any]):
    def __setitem__(self, key: Hashable, value: Any) -> None:
        if key in self:
            raise ValueError(f"duplicate {key!r}")
        super().__setitem__(key, value)

    def __init__(self, init: DictInit = None, **kwargs: Any) -> None:
        if isinstance(init, Mapping):
            super().__init__(init, **kwargs)
        elif isinstance(init, Iterable):
            for k, v in cast(Iterable[Tuple[Hashable, Any]], init):
                self[k] = v
        elif init is None:
            super().__init__(**kwargs)
        else:
            super().__init__(init, **kwargs)
```

This version of the NoDupDict class implements an __init__() method that will work with a variety of data types. We enumerated the various types using the DictInit type hint. This includes a sequence of *key-value* pairs, as well as another mapping. In the case of a sequence of key-value pairs, we can use the previously defined __setitem__() to raise an exception in the event of duplicate key values.

This covers the initialization use cases, but – still – doesn't cover every method that can update a mapping. We still have to implement update(), setdefault(), __or__(), and __ior__() to extend all the methods that can mutate a dictionary. While this is a pile of work to create, the work is encapsulated in a dictionary subclass that we can use in our application. This subclass is completely compatible with built-in classes; it implements many methods we didn't write, and it has one extra feature we did write.

We've built a more complex dictionary that extends the core features of a Python dict class. Our version adds a feature to reject duplicates. We've also touched on the use of abc.ABC (and abc.ABCMeta) to create abstract base classes. There are times when we might want to take more direct control of the mechanics of creating a new class. We'll turn next to metaclasses.

Metaclasses

As we noted earlier, creating a new class involves work done by the type class. The job of the type class is to create an empty class object so the various definitions and attributes assignment statements will build the final, usable class we need for our application.

Here's how it works:

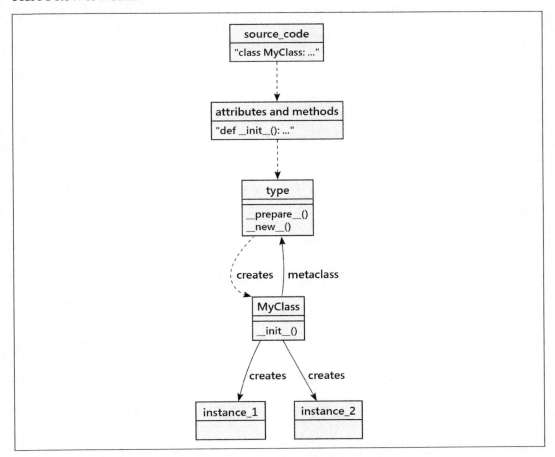

Figure 6.3: How type creates MyClass

The class statement is used to locate the appropriate metaclass; if no special metaclass= is provided, then the type class is used. The type class will prepare a new, empty dictionary, called a namespace, and then the various statements in the class populate this container with attributes and method definitions. Finally, the "new" step completes creation of the class; this is generally where we can make our changes.

Here's a diagram showing how we can use a new class, SpecialMeta, to tap into the way type builds a new class for us:

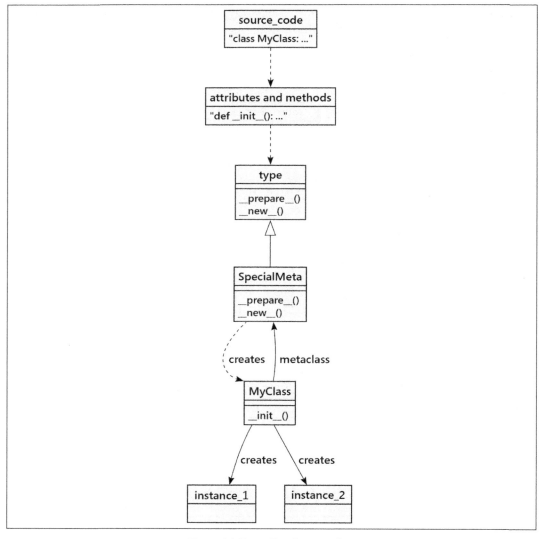

Figure 6.4: Extending the type class

If we use the `metaclass=` option when creating a class, we change the metaclass that's used. In the preceding diagram, `SpecialMeta` is a subclass of the `type` class, and it can do some special processing for our class definitions.

While there are some clever things we can do with this technique, it's important to keep metaclasses in perspective. They change the way class objects are built, with the potential to redefine what it means to be a class. This can drastically shift the foundation of Pythonic object-oriented programming. It can lead to frustration when people reading and maintaining the code can't figure out why something works; it should not be undertaken lightly.

Let's look at a metaclass that builds a few small features into a class definition for us. Let's continue to extend the dice simulation examples from earlier in this chapter. We may have a number of classes of die, each an instance of the abstract base class `Die`. We'd like them all to have an audit log surrounding the `roll()` method supplied by the implementation. We'd like to track each roll separately, perhaps so someone can review them for their statistical validity.

Because we don't want to force the programmers of various kinds of dice to include any extra or new code, we prefer to add logging to the abstract base class for all `Die` classes, and also adjust the concrete implementation of the `roll()` method to create logging output.

This is a tall order. It's made a little more challenging because we're working with abstract classes. This requires some care to disentangle abstract class construction from concrete class construction. We don't want to force programmers to change their concrete `Die` class definitions.

To solve this problem using metaclasses, we need to do three things to each concrete `Die`-related class that gets built:

1. Extend the `ABCMeta` metaclass. We need to support the `@abc.abstractmethod` decoration, so we want all the existing metaclass features from the built-in `type` metaclass.

2. Inject a `logger` attribute into each class. It's common to have the logger name match the class name; this is easy to do in a metaclass. We can create the logger as part of the class, prior to any instances of the class being created.

3. Wrap the concrete `roll()` method into a function that uses the programmer's supplied `roll()` method, but also writes a message to the logger. This is similar to the way a method decorator works.

The metaclass definition needs a __new__() method to make slight adjustments to the way the final class is built. We don't need to extend the __prepare__() method. Our __new__() method will use abc.ABCMeta.__new__() to build the final class object. This ABCMeta class will decide if the object is concrete or remains abstract because roll() was not defined:

```python
import logging
from functools import wraps
from typing import Type, Any

class DieMeta(abc.ABCMeta):
    def __new__(
        metaclass: Type[type],
        name: str,
        bases: tuple[type, ...],
        namespace: dict[str, Any],
        **kwargs: Any,
    ) -> "DieMeta":
        if "roll" in namespace and not getattr(
            namespace["roll"], "__isabstractmethod__", False
        ):
            namespace.setdefault("logger", logging.getLogger(name))

            original_method = namespace["roll"]

            @wraps(original_method)
            def logged_roll(self: "DieLog") -> None:
                original_method(self)
                self.logger.info(f"Rolled {self.face}")

            namespace["roll"] = logged_roll
        new_object = cast(
            "DieMeta", abc.ABCMeta.__new__(
                metaclass, name, bases, namespace)
        )
        return new_object
```

The __new__() method is given a bewildering pile of argument values:

- The metaclass parameter is a reference to the metaclass doing the work. Python doesn't generally create and use instances of metaclasses. Instead, the metaclass itself is passed as a parameter to each method. It's a bit like the self value provided to an object, but it's the class, not an instance of a class.

- The name parameter is the name of the target class, taken from the original class statement.

- The bases parameter is the list of base classes. These are the mixins, sorted into method resolution order. In this example, it will be the superclass we'll define that uses this metaclass, DieLog, shown shortly below.

- The namespace parameter is a dictionary that was started by the __prepare__() method of the built-in type class. The dictionary was updated when the body of the class was executed; def statements and assignment statements will create items in this dictionary. When we get to the __new__() method, the methods (and variables) of the class are staged here, waiting to build the final class object.

- The kwargs parameter will have any keyword arguments provided as part of the class definition. If we used a statement like class D6L(DieLog, otherparam="something") to create a new class, then the otherparam would be one of the kwargs to __new__().

The __new__() method must return the new class definition. Generally, this is the result of using the superclass __new__() method to build the class object. In our case, the superclass method is abc.ABCMeta.__new__().

Within this method, the if statement checks to see if the class being built defined the needed roll() method. If the method is marked with the @abc.abstractmethod decorator, then the method will have an attribute of __isabstractmethod__ and the value of the attribute will be True. For a concrete method – without a decorator – there will be no __isabstractmethod__ attribute value. The condition confirms there's a roll() method and if that roll() method is concrete.

For classes with a concrete roll() method, we'll add "logger" to the namespace that was built, providing a default value of an appropriately named logger. If a logger is already present, we'll leave it in place.

Next, namespace["roll"] picks out the function defined in the concrete class, the roll method. We'll define a replacement method, logged_roll. To be sure the new logged_roll() method looks like the original method, we've used the @wraps decorator. This will copy the original method name and docstring onto the new method, making it look like the definition originally present in the class. This is put back into the namespace so it can be incorporated into the new class.

Finally, we evaluate abc.ABCMeta.__new__() with the metaclass, the class name, the base classes, and the namespace that we modified if there was a concrete implementation of the roll() method. The __new__() operation finalizes the class, doing all the original Python housekeeping.

It can be awkward to use a metaclass; for this reason, it's common to provide a superclass that uses the metaclass. This means our application can extend the superclass without having to fuss around with an extra metaclass= parameter in the class definition:

```
class DieLog(metaclass=DieMeta):
    logger: logging.Logger

    def __init__(self) -> None:
        self.face: int
        self.roll()

    @abc.abstractmethod
    def roll(self) -> None:
        ...

    def __repr__(self) -> str:
        return f"{self.face}"
```

This superclass, DieLog, is built by the metaclass. Any subclass of this class will also be built by the metaclass.

Now, our application can create subclasses of DieLog, without having to worry about the details of the metaclass: we don't have to remember to include metaclass= in the definition. Our final application classes are quite streamlined:

```
class D6L(DieLog):
    def roll(self) -> None:
        """Some documentation on D6L"""
        self.face = random.randrange(1, 7)
```

We've created a dice roller here that logs each roll in a logger named after the class. Here's how it looks logging to the console:

```
>>> import sys
>>> logging.basicConfig(stream=sys.stdout, level=logging.INFO)
>>> d2 = D6L()
INFO:D6L:Rolled 1
>>> d2.face
1
```

The details of the logging aspect of this D6L class are completely divorced from the application-specific processing of this class. We can change the metaclass to change details of the logging, knowing that all of the relevant application classes will be changed when the metaclass changes.

Since a metaclass changes how a class is built, there are no boundaries on the kinds of things a metaclass can do. The common advice is to keep the metaclass features very small because they're obscure. As written, the logged_roll() method of the metaclass will discard any return value from the concrete roll() method in a subclass.

Case study

We'll refine our case study in this chapter. Previously, in *Chapter 2, Objects in Python*, we talked in a vague way about loading the training data and splitting it into two clumps – the training set and the testing set. In *Chapter 5, When to Use Object-Oriented Programming*, we looked at ways to deserialize the source file into Sample instances.

In this chapter, we want to look further at this operation of using the raw data to create a number of TrainingKnownSample instances separate from a number of TestingKnownSample instances. In the previous chapter, we identified four cases for sample objects, shown in the following table:

	Known	Unknown
Unclassified	Training data	Sample waiting to be classified
Classified	Testing data	Classified sample

When looking at the known samples, classified by a Botanist, we need to split the data into two separate classes. We'll use a variety of approaches to do this, including a number of overloaded comparison operations.

Our training data sorting can be approached from two distinct directions:

- We can ingest all the raw data, then distribute it into two collections for later use
- During the process of ingestion, we can make selections among the collections

The net effect is the same. Working with an entire collection can be relatively simple, while using a great deal of memory. Processing items individually can be more complex, without requiring as much memory.

We'll start by building some sophisticated collections. The first will be a list that tracks two sublists.

Extending the list class with two sublists

We can extend the built-in list class to add some features. It's important to note that extending built-in types can be tricky because the type hints for these types are sometimes surprisingly complex.

Python's built-in structures like list have a variety of initialization alternatives:

- We can use list() to create an empty list
- We can use list(x) to create a list from an iterable source of data

To make this clear to *mypy*, we need to use the @overload decorator; this will expose the two distinct ways the list class __init__() method is used:

```python
class SamplePartition(List[SampleDict], abc.ABC):
    @overload
    def __init__(self, *, training_subset: float = 0.80) -> None:
        ...

    @overload
    def __init__(
        self,
        iterable: Optional[Iterable[SampleDict]] = None,
        *,
        training_subset: float = 0.80,
    ) -> None:
        ...

    def __init__(
        self,
        iterable: Optional[Iterable[SampleDict]] = None,
        *,
        training_subset: float = 0.80,
    ) -> None:
        self.training_subset = training_subset
```

```
        if iterable:
            super().__init__(iterable)
        else:
            super().__init__()

    @abc.abstractproperty
    @property
    def training(self) -> List[TrainingKnownSample]:
        ...

    @abc.abstractproperty
    @property
    def testing(self) -> List[TestingKnownSample]:
        ...
```

We've defined two overloads for the __init__() method; these are the formalisms to tell *mypy* what our intent is. The first overload is __init__() with no positional parameters. This should create an empty list of SampleDict objects. The second overload is __init__() with an iterable source of SampleDict objects as the only positional parameter. The lonely * separates parameters where the argument value can be provided positionally from parameters where the argument value must be provided as a keyword. The training_subset parameter will stand out from the ordinary list-like initializer.

The third definition is the actual implementation. This definition of the __init__() method lacks the @overload decorator. The implementation uses the superclass' __init__() method to build a List[SampleDict] object. A subclass might want to extend this method to partition the data when creating a SamplePartition object.

The intent is to be able to subclass this with a class having a name like SomeSamplePartition, and use data = SomeSamplePartition(data, training_subset=0.67) to create an object, data, which is a list with a few extra features.

Since this is a superclass, we haven't provided a definition for the training or testing properties. Each algorithm can have different implementations of the methods that provide values for these attributes.

This depends on the following SampleDict definition:

```
class SampleDict(TypedDict):
    sepal_length: float
    sepal_width: float
    petal_length: float
```

```
        petal_width: float
        species: str
```

This tells *mypy* that we're working with a dictionary that has only the five supplied keys and no others. This can support some validation to check that literal key values match this set.

Let's look at some subclasses that provide different partitioning strategies. We'll start with one that shuffles and cuts, like a deck of cards.

A shuffling strategy for partitioning

One alternative is to shuffle and cut a list – precisely the way a deck of cards is shuffled and cut before a game. We can use `random.shuffle()` to handle the randomized shuffling. The cut is – in a way – a hyperparameter. How large should the training set be compared to the testing set? Suggestions for knowledgeable data scientists include 80% to 20%, 67% to 33%, and an even 50% to 50% split. Because expert opinion varies, we need to provide a way for a scientist to adjust the partition ratio.

We'll make the split a feature of the class. We can create separate subclasses to implement alternative splits. Here's a shuffling implementation:

```
class ShufflingSamplePartition(SamplePartition):
    def __init__(
        self,
        iterable: Optional[Iterable[SampleDict]] = None,
        *,
        training_subset: float = 0.80,
    ) -> None:
        super().__init__(iterable, training_subset=training_subset)
        self.split: Optional[int] = None

    def shuffle(self) -> None:
        if not self.split:
            random.shuffle(self)
            self.split = int(len(self) * self.training_subset)

    @property
    def training(self) -> List[TrainingKnownSample]:
        self.shuffle()
        return [TrainingKnownSample(**sd) for sd in self[: self.split]]
```

```
@property
def testing(self) -> List[TestingKnownSample]:
    self.shuffle()
    return [TestingKnownSample(**sd) for sd in self[self.split :]]
```

Since we're extending the `SamplePartition` superclass, we can leverage the overloaded `__init__()` method definitions. For this subclass, we need to provide a concrete implementation compatible with the superclass.

The two properties, `training` and `testing`, both make use of an internal `shuffle()` method. This method uses the split attribute to make sure it will shuffle the samples exactly one time. In addition to tracking whether or not the data is shuffled, the `self.split` attribute also shows where to split the samples into training and test subsets.

The `training` and `testing` properties also use Python list slicing to subdivide the raw `SampleDict` objects, and build useful `TrainingKnownSample` and `TestingKnownSample` objects from the raw data. These rely on a list comprehension to apply a class constructor, for example `TrainingKnownSample`, to the dictionary of row values in a subset of the list, `self[: self.split]]`. The list comprehension saves us from building a list with a `for` statement and a bunch of `append()` operations. We'll look at even more variations of this in *Chapter 10, The Iterator Pattern*.

Because this depends on the `random` module, the results are difficult to predict, making testing needless complex. Many data scientists want the data shuffled, but they also want reproducible results. By setting `random.seed()` to a fixed value, we can create random, but reproducible, collections of samples.

This works as follows:

```
>>> import random
>>> from model import ShufflingSamplePartition
>>> from pprint import pprint
>>> data = [
...     {
...         "sepal_length": i + 0.1,
...         "sepal_width": i + 0.2,
...         "petal_length": i + 0.3,
...         "petal_width": i + 0.4,
...         "species": f"sample {i}",
...     }
...     for i in range(10)
... ]
```

```
>>> random.seed(42)
>>> ssp = ShufflingSamplePartition(data)
>>> pprint(ssp.testing)
[TestingKnownSample(sepal_length=0.1, sepal_width=0.2,
petal_length=0.3, petal_width=0.4, species='sample 0',
classification=None, ),
 TestingKnownSample(sepal_length=1.1, sepal_width=1.2,
petal_length=1.3, petal_width=1.4, species='sample 1',
classification=None, )]
```

With a random seed of 42, we always get the same two samples in the testing set.

This allows us to build the initial list in a variety of ways. We can, for example, append data items to an empty list, like this:

```
ssp = ShufflingSamplePartition(training_subset=0.67)
for row in data:
    ssp.append(row)
```

The `SamplePartition` subclass of `list` will inherit all the methods of the parent class. This allows us to make changes to the internal state of the list prior to extracting the training and testing subsets. We've added the sizing parameter as a keyword-only parameter to make sure it's clearly separated from the list object used to initialize the list.

An incremental strategy for partitioning

We have an alternative to splitting a single list after it's been built. Instead of extending the `list` class to provide two sub-lists, we can reframe the problem slightly. Let's define a subclass of `SamplePartition` that makes a random choice between testing and training on each `SampleDict` object that is presented via initialization, or the `append()` or `extend()` methods.

Here's an abstraction that summarizes our thinking on this. We'll have three methods for building a list, and two properties that will provide the training and testing sets, as below. We don't inherit from `List` because we're not providing any other list-like features, not even `__len__()`. The class has only five methods, as shown:

```
class DealingPartition(abc.ABC):
    @abc.abstractmethod
    def __init__(
        self,
        items: Optional[Iterable[SampleDict]],
```

```
        *,
        training_subset: Tuple[int, int] = (8, 10),
    ) -> None:
        ...


    @abc.abstractmethod
    def extend(self, items: Iterable[SampleDict]) -> None:
        ...


    @abc.abstractmethod
    def append(self, item: SampleDict) -> None:
        ...


    @property
    @abc.abstractmethod
    def training(self) -> List[TrainingKnownSample]:
        ...


    @property
    @abc.abstractmethod
    def testing(self) -> List[TestingKnownSample]:
        ...
```

This definition has no concrete implementations. It provides five placeholders where methods can be defined to implement the necessary dealing algorithm. We've changed the definition of the training_subset parameter slightly from the previous example. Here, we've defined it as two integers. This lets us count and deal incrementally.

Here's how we can extend this to create a concrete subclass that wraps two internal collections. We'll break this into two parts – first, building the collections, and then building the properties to expose the values of the collections:

```
class CountingDealingPartition(DealingPartition):
    def __init__(
        self,
        items: Optional[Iterable[SampleDict]],
        *,
        training_subset: Tuple[int, int] = (8, 10),
    ) -> None:
        self.training_subset = training_subset
        self.counter = 0
```

```
        self._training: List[TrainingKnownSample] = []
        self._testing: List[TestingKnownSample] = []
        if items:
            self.extend(items)

    def extend(self, items: Iterable[SampleDict]) -> None:
        for item in items:
            self.append(item)

    def append(self, item: SampleDict) -> None:
        n, d = self.training_subset
        if self.counter % d < n:
            self._training.append(TrainingKnownSample(**item))
        else:
            self._testing.append(TestingKnownSample(**item))
        self.counter += 1
```

We've defined an initializer that sets the initial state of two empty collections. Then, it uses the extend() method to build the collections from a source iterable, if it's provided.

The extend() method relies on the append() method to allocate a SampleDict instance to either the testing or training subsets. The append() method actually does all the work. It counts the items and makes a decision based on some modulo arithmetic.

The training subset is defined as a fraction; we've shown it defined as a tuple, (8, 10), with a comment suggesting this means 8/10 or 80% training, the remainder for testing. For a given counter value, c, if $c < 8$ *(mod 10)*, we'll call it training, while if $c \geq 8$ *(mod 10)*, we'll call it testing.

Here are the remaining two methods that are used to expose the values of the two internal list objects:

```
    @property
    def training(self) -> List[TrainingKnownSample]:
        return self._training

    @property
    def testing(self) -> List[TestingKnownSample]:
        return self._testing
```

To an extent, these can be seen as useless. It's common in Python to simply name the two internal collections `self.training` and `self.testing`. If we use attributes, we don't really need these property methods.

We've seen two class designs to partition the source data into testing and training subsets. One version relies on random numbers for shuffling, while the other doesn't rely on a random number generator. There are, of course, other combinations of random-based selection and incremental distribution of items that we've left as exercises for the reader.

Recall

Here are some of the key points in this chapter:

- Using abstract base class definitions is a way to create class definitions with placeholders. This is a handy technique, and can be somewhat clearer than using `raise NotImplementedError` in unimplemented methods.

- ABCs and type hints provide ways to create class definitions. An ABC is a type hint that can help to clarify the essential features we need from an object. It's common, for example, to use `Iterable[X]` to emphasize that we need one aspect of a class implementation.

- The `collections.abc` module defines abstract base classes for Python's built-in collections. When we want to make our own unique collect class that can integrate seamlessly with Python, we need to start with the definitions from this module.

- Creating your own abstract base class leverages the `abc` module. The `abc.ABC` class definition is often a perfect starting point for creating an abstract base class.

- The bulk of the work is done by the `type` class. It's helpful to review this class to understand how classes are created by the methods of `type`.

- Python operators are implemented by special methods in classes. We can – in a way – "overload" an operator by defining appropriate special methods so that the operator works with objects of our unique class.

- Extending built-ins is done via a subclass that modifies the behavior of a built-in type. We'll often use `super()` to leverage the built-in behavior.

- We can implement our own metaclasses to change – in a fundamental way – how Python class objects are built.

Exercises

We've looked at the concept of defining abstract classes to define some – but not all – common features of two objects. Take a quick look around to see how you can apply these principles to your own work. A script can often be restated as a class; each major step of the work a separate method. Do you have similar-looking scripts that – perhaps – share a common abstract definition? Another place to find things that are partially related is in the classes that describe data files. A spreadsheet file often has small variations in layout; this suggests they have a common abstract relationship, but a method needs to be part of an extension to handle the variations in the layouts.

When we think about the DDice class, there's yet another enhancement that would be nice. Right now, the operators are all defined for DDice instances only. In order to create a hand of dice, we need to – somewhere – use a DDice constructor. This leads to 3*DDice(D6)+2, which seems to be needlessly wordy.

It would be nicer to be able to write 3*d6+1. This implies some changes to the design:

1. Since we can't (easily) apply operators to classes, we have to work with instances of classes. We've assumed d6 = D6() was used to create a Die instance that can be an operand.

2. The Die class needs a __mul__() method and an __rmul__() method. When we multiply a Die instance by an integer, this will create a DDice instance populated with the die's type, DDice(type(self)). This is because DDice expects a type and it creates its own instances from the type.

This creates a circular relationship between Die and DDice. It doesn't present any real problems because both definitions are in the same module. We can use strings in the type hints, so having a Die method use a type hint of -> "DDice" works out nicely. The *mypy* program can use strings for forward references to types that haven't been defined yet.

Now, look back over some of the examples we looked at in previous chapters. Can we leverage an abstract class definition to perhaps simplify the various ways in which Sample instances need to behave?

Look at the DieMeta example. As written, the logged_roll() method of the metaclass will discard any return value from the concrete roll() method in a subclass. This may not be appropriate in all cases. What kind of rewrite is required to make the metaclass method wrapper return a value from the wrapped method? Does this change the DieLog superclass definition?

Can we use the superclass to provide a logger? (It seems like the answer is a resounding "yes.")

More importantly, can we use a decorator to provide logging for a concrete `roll()` method? Write this decorator. Then consider whether or not we can trust developers to include this decorator. Should we trust other developers to use the framework correctly? While we can imagine developers forgetting to include the decorator, we can also imagine unit tests to confirm that log entries are written. Which seems better: a visible decorator with a unit test or a metaclass that tweaks code invisibly?

In the case study, we defined the testing and training properties as `Iterable[SampleDict]` instead of `List[SampleDict]`. When we look at `collections.abc`, we see that a `List` is a `Sequence` that is a subclass of the `Iterable` base class. Can you see advantages to distinguishing between these three levels of abstraction? If `Iterable` works in general, should we always use iterables? What aspects distinguish `Sequence` from `Iterable`? Do the different collections of features have any impact on the classes in the case study?

Summary

In this chapter, we focused on identifying objects, especially objects that are not immediately apparent; objects that manage and control. Objects should have both data and behaviors, but properties can be used to blur the distinction between the two. The DRY principle is an important indicator of code quality, and inheritance and composition can be applied to reduce code duplication.

In the next two chapters, we'll cover several of the built-in Python data structures and objects, focusing on their object-oriented properties and how they can be extended or adapted.

7
Python Data Structures

In our examples so far, we've already seen many of the built-in Python data structures in action. You've probably also covered many of them in introductory books or tutorials. In this chapter, we'll discuss the object-oriented features of these data structures, when they should be used instead of a regular class, and when they should not be used. In particular, we'll be covering the following topics:

- Tuples and named tuples
- Dataclasses
- Dictionaries
- Lists and sets
- Three types of queues

This chapter's case study will revisit the data model for the *k*-nearest neighbors classifier. After looking at Python's sophisticated built-in data structure and class definitions, we can simplify some of the application class definitions.

We'll start by looking at some of the foundational constructs. The object class, specifically.

Empty objects

Let's start with the most basic Python built-in, one that we've used implicitly many times already, the one (it turns out) we've extended in every class we have created: the object.

Technically, we can instantiate an `object` without writing a subclass, as follows:

```
>>> o = object()
>>> o.x = 5
    Traceback (most recent call last):
        File "<stdin>", line 1, in <module>
    AttributeError: 'object' object has no attribute 'x'
```

Unfortunately, as you can see, it's not possible to set any attributes on an `object` that was instantiated directly. This isn't because the Python developers wanted to force us to write our own classes, or anything so sinister. They did this to save memory – a lot of memory. When Python allows an object to have arbitrary attributes, it takes a certain amount of system memory to keep track of what attributes each object has, for storing both the attribute name and its value. Even if no attributes are stored, memory is allocated to make it possible to add attributes. Given the dozens, hundreds, or thousands of objects (*every* class extends the `object` class) in a typical Python program, this small amount of memory would quickly become a large amount of memory. So, Python disables arbitrary properties on `object`, and several other built-ins, by default.

 It is possible to restrict arbitrary properties on our own classes using `__slots__`. Slots are part of *Chapter 12, Advanced Design Patterns*. We'll look at them as a way to save memory for objects that occur many, many times.

It is, however, trivial to create an empty object class of our own; we saw it in our earliest example:

```
>>> class MyObject:
...     pass
```

In effect, `class MyObject` is equivalent to `class MyObject(object)`. As we've already seen, it's possible to set attributes on such classes as follows:

```
>>> m = MyObject()
>>> m.x = "hello"
>>> m.x
'hello'
```

If we wanted to group an unknown number of attribute values together, we could store them in an empty object like this. The problem with this approach is the lack of an obvious schema that we can use to understand what attributes should be present and what types of values they'll have.

A focus of this book is the way classes and objects should only be used when you want to specify *both* data and behaviors. Therefore, it is important to decide from the outset whether the data is purely data, or whether it is an object in disguise. Once that design decision is made, the rest of the design can grow from the seed concept.

Tuples and named tuples

Tuples are objects that can store a specific number of other objects in sequence. They are *immutable*, meaning we can't add, remove, or replace objects on the fly. This may seem like a massive restriction, but the truth is, if you need to modify a tuple, you're using the wrong data type (usually, a list would be more suitable). The primary benefit of tuples' immutability is a tuple of immutable objects (like strings and numbers and other tuples) has a hash value, allowing us to use them as keys in dictionaries, and members of a set. (A tuple that contains a mutable structure, like a list, set, or dict, isn't composed of immutable items, and doesn't have a hash value. We'll look closely at this distinction in the next section.)

Instances of Python's built-in generic `tuple` class are used to store data; behavior cannot be associated with a built-in tuple. If we require behavior to manipulate a tuple, we have to pass the tuple into a function (or method on another object) that performs the action. This is the subject of *Chapter 8, The Intersection of Object-Oriented and Functional Programming*.

Tuples overlap with the idea of coordinates or dimensions. A mathematical (x, y) pair or (r, g, b) color are examples of tuples; the order matters, a lot: the color (255, 0, 0) looks nothing like (0, 255, 0). The primary purpose of a tuple is to aggregate different pieces of data together into one container.

We create a tuple by separating values with a comma. Usually, tuples are wrapped in parentheses to make them easy to read and to separate them from other parts of an expression, but this is not always mandatory. The following two assignments are identical (they record a stock, the current price, the 52-week high, and the 52-week low, for a rather profitable company):

```
>>> stock = "AAPL", 123.52, 53.15, 137.98
>>> stock2 = ("AAPL", 123.52, 53.15, 137.98)
```

(When the first edition of this book was printed, this stock was trading around US$ 8 per share; the stock value has almost doubled with each edition of this book!)

If we're grouping a tuple inside of some other object, such as a function call, list comprehension, or generator, the parentheses are required. Otherwise, it would be impossible for the interpreter to know whether it is a tuple or the next function parameter. For example, the following function accepts a tuple and a date, and returns a tuple of the date and the middle value between the stock's high and low value:

```
>>> import datetime
>>> def middle(stock, date):
...     symbol, current, high, low = stock
...     return (((high + low) / 2), date)

>>> middle(("AAPL", 123.52, 53.15, 137.98), datetime.date(2020, 12, 4))
(95.565, datetime.date(2020, 12, 4))
```

In this example, a new four-tuple is created directly inside the function call. The items are separated by commas and the entire tuple is cuddled up inside parentheses. This tuple is then followed by a comma to separate it from the second argument, a `datetime.date` object. When Python displays a tuple, it uses what's called the **canonical** representation; this will always include ( )'s, making the ( )'s a common practice even when they're not – strictly – required. The `return` statement, specifically, has redundant ( )'s around the tuple it creates.

The degenerate cases include a tuple with only one item, written like this `(2.718,)`. The extra comma is required here. An empty tuple is `( )`.

We can sometimes wind up with a statement like this:

```
>>> a = 42,
>>> a
(42,)
```

It's sometimes surprising that the variable a will be a one-tuple. The trailing comma is what creates an expression list with a single item; this is the value of the tuple. The ( )'s are required for two things: (1) to create an empty tuple or (2) to separate a tuple from other expressions. For example, the following creates nested tuples:

```
>>> b = (42, 3.14), (2.718, 2.618),
>>> b
((42, 3.14), (2.718, 2.618))
```

The trailing commas in Python are politely ignored.

The `middle()` function also illustrates **tuple unpacking**. The first line inside the function unpacks the `stock` parameter into four different variables. The tuple has to be exactly the same length as the number of variables, or it will raise an exception.

Unpacking is a very useful feature in Python. A tuple groups related values together to make storing and passing them around simpler; the moment we need to access the pieces, we can unpack them into separate variables. Of course, sometimes we only need access to one of the variables in the tuple. We can use the same syntax that we use for other sequence types (lists and strings, for example) to access an individual value:

```
>>> s = "AAPL", 132.76, 134.80, 130.53
>>> high = s[2]
>>> high
134.8
```

We can even use slice notation to extract larger pieces of tuples, as demonstrated in the following:

```
>>> s[1:3]
(132.76, 134.8)
```

These examples, while illustrating how flexible tuples can be, also demonstrate one of their major disadvantages: readability. How does someone reading this code know what is in position 2 of a specific tuple? They can guess, using the name of the variable we assigned it to, that it is `high` of some sort, but if we had just accessed the tuple value in a calculation without assigning it, there would be no such indication. They would have to paw through the code to find where the tuple was packed or unpacked before they could discover what it does.

Accessing tuple members directly is fine in some circumstances, but don't make a habit of it. The index values become what we might call *magic numbers*: numbers that seem to come out of thin air with no apparent meaning within the code. This opacity is the source of many coding errors and leads to hours of frustrated debugging. Try to use tuples only when you know that all the values are going to be useful at once and it's normally going to be unpacked when it is accessed. Think of (x, y) coordinate pairs and (r, g, b) colors, where the number of items is fixed, the order matters, and the meaning is clear.

One way to provide some useful documentation is to define numerous little helper functions. This can help to clarify the way a tuple is used. Here's an example.

```
>>> def high(stock):
...     symbol, current, high, low = stock
...     return high
>>> high(s)
134.8
```

We need to keep these helper functions collected together into a single namespace. Doing this causes us to suspect that a class is better than a tuple with a lot of helper functions. There are other alternatives to clarifying the contents of tuples, the most important of which is the `typing.NamedTuple` class.

Named tuples via typing.NamedTuple

So, what do we do when we want to group values together but know we're frequently going to need to access them individually? There are actually several options, including these:

- We could use an empty `object` instance, as discussed previously. We can assign arbitrary attributes to this object. But without a good definition of what's allowed and what types are expected, we'll have trouble understanding this. And we'll get a lot of *mypy* errors.

- We could use a dictionary. This can work out nicely, and we can formalize the acceptable list of keys for the dictionary with the `typing.TypedDict` hint. We'll touch on these in the case study for *Chapter 9, Strings, Serialization, and File Paths*.

- We can use a `@dataclass`, the subject of the next section in this chapter.

- We can also provide names to the positions of a tuple. While we're at it, we can also define methods for these named tuples, making them super helpful.

Named tuples are tuples with attitude. They are a great way to create an immutable grouping of data values. When we define a **named tuple** we're creating a subclass of `typing.NamedTuple`, based on a list of names and data types. We don't need to write an __init__() method; it's created for us.

Here's an example:

```
>>> from typing import NamedTuple
>>> class Stock(NamedTuple):
...     symbol: str
...     current: float
...     high: float
...     low: float
```

This new class will have a number of methods, including __init__(), __repr__(), __hash__(), and __eq__(). These will be based on the generic tuple processing with the added benefit of names for the various items. There are more methods, including comparison operations. Here's how we can create a tuple of this class. It looks almost like creating a generic tuple:

```
>>> Stock("AAPL", 123.52, 137.98, 53.15)
```

We can use keyword parameters to make things more clear:

```
>>> s2 = Stock("AAPL", 123.52, high=137.98, low=53.15)
```

The constructor must have exactly the correct number of arguments to create the tuple. Values can be passed in as positional or keyword arguments.

It's important to recognize that the names are provided at the class level, but we are *not* actually creating class-level attributes. The class-level names are used to build the __init__() method; each instance will have the expected names for the positions within the tuple. There's a clever metaclass-level transformation from what we wrote into the somewhat more complex definition of the resulting class with named, positional items. For more information on metaclasses, refer back to *Chapter 6, Abstract Base Classes and Operator Overloading*.

The resulting instance of our NamedTuple subclass, Stock, can then be packed, unpacked, indexed, sliced, and otherwise treated like a normal tuple, but we can also access individual attributes by name as if it were an object:

```
>>> s.high
137.98
>>> s[2]
137.98
>>> symbol, current, high, low = s
>>> current
123.52
```

Named tuples are perfect for many use cases. Like strings, tuples and named tuples are immutable, so we cannot modify an attribute once it has been set. For example, the current value of this company's stock has gone down since we started this discussion, but we can't set the new value, as can be seen in the following:

```
>>> s.current = 122.25
Traceback (most recent call last):
  ...
  File "<doctest examples.md[27]>", line 1, in <module>
    s2.current = 122.25
AttributeError: can't set attribute
```

The immutability refers only to the attributes of the tuple itself. This can seem odd, but it's a consequence of the definitions of an immutable tuple. The tuple can contain mutable elements.

```
>>> t = ("Relayer", ["Gates of Delirium", "Sound Chaser"])
>>> t[1].append("To Be Over")
>>> t
('Relayer', ['Gates of Delirium', 'Sound Chaser', 'To Be Over'])
```

The object, t, is a tuple, which means it's immutable. The tuple object contains two items. The value of t[0] is a string, which is also immutable. The value of t[1], however, is a mutable list. The mutability of the list is not altered by the immutability of the object, t, with which it's associated. A list is mutable, irrespective of context. The tuple, t, is immutable, even if items within it are mutable.

Because the example tuple, t, contains a mutable list, it doesn't have a hash value. This shouldn't be surprising, either. The hash() computation requires the hash from each item within the collection. Since the list value of t[1] can't produce a hash, the tuple t – as a whole – can't produce a hash, either.

Here's what happens when we try:

```
>>> hash(t)
Traceback (most recent call last):
  ...
  File "<doctest examples.md[31]>", line 1, in <module>
    hash(t)
TypeError: unhashable type: 'list'
```

The presence of the unhashable list object means the tuple – as a whole – is also unhashable.

We can create methods to compute derived values of the attributes of a named tuple. We can, for example, redefine our Stock tuple to include the middle computation as a method (or a @property):

```
>>> class Stock(NamedTuple):
...     symbol: str
...     current: float
...     high: float
...     low: float
...     @property
...     def middle(self) -> float:
...         return (self.high + self.low)/2
```

We can't change the state, but we can compute values derived from the current state. This lets us couple computations directly to the tuple holding the source data. Here's an object created with this definition of the Stock class:

```
>>> s = Stock("AAPL", 123.52, 137.98, 53.15)
>>> s.middle
95.565
```

The middle() method is now part of the class definition. The best part? The *mypy* tool can look over our shoulder to be sure the type hints all match up properly throughout our application.

The state of a named tuple is fixed when the tuple is created. If we need to be able to change stored data, a dataclass may be what we need instead. We'll look at those next.

Dataclasses

Since Python 3.7, dataclasses let us define ordinary objects with a clean syntax for specifying attributes. They look – superficially – very similar to named tuples. This is a pleasant approach that makes it easy to understand how they work.

Here's a dataclass version of our Stock example:

```
>>> from dataclasses import dataclass
>>> @dataclass
... class Stock:
...     symbol: str
...     current: float
...     high: float
...     low: float
```

For this case, the definition is nearly identical to the NamedTuple definition.

The dataclass function is applied as a class decorator, using the @ operator. We encountered decorators in *Chapter 6, Abstract Base Classes and Operator Overloading*. We'll dig into them deeply in *Chapter 11, Common Design Patterns*. This class definition syntax isn't much less verbose than an ordinary class with __init__(), but it gives us access to several additional dataclass features.

It's important to recognize that the names are provided at the class level, but are *not* actually creating class-level attributes. The class level names are used to build several methods, including the __init__() method; each instance will have the expected attributes. The decorator transforms what we wrote into the more complex definition of a class with the expected attributes and parameters to __init__().

Because dataclass objects can be stateful, mutable objects, there are a number of extra features available. We'll start with some basics. Here's an example of creating an instance of the Stock dataclass.

```
>>> s = Stock("AAPL", 123.52, 137.98, 53.15)
```

Once instantiated, the Stock object can be used like any ordinary class. You can access and update attributes as follows:

```
>>> s
Stock(symbol='AAPL', current=123.52, high=137.98, low=53.15)
>>> s.current
123.52
>>> s.current = 122.25
>>> s
Stock(symbol='AAPL', current=122.25, high=137.98, low=53.15)
```

As with other objects, we can add attributes beyond those formally declared as part of the dataclass. This isn't always the best idea, but it's supported because this is an ordinary mutable object:

```
>>> s.unexpected_attribute = 'allowed'
>>> s.unexpected_attribute
'allowed'
```

Adding attributes isn't available for frozen dataclasses, which we'll talk about later in this section. At first glance, it seems like dataclasses don't give many benefits over an ordinary class definition with an appropriate constructor. Here's an ordinary class that's similar to the dataclass:

```
>>> class StockOrdinary:
...     def __init__(self, name: str, current: float, high: float, low:
... float) -> None:
...         self.name = name
...         self.current = current
...         self.high = high
...         self.low = low
...
>>> s_ord = StockOrdinary("AAPL", 123.52, 137.98, 53.15)
```

One obvious benefit to a dataclass is we only need to state the attribute names once, saving the repetition in the __init__() parameters and body. But wait, that's not all! The dataclass also provides a much more useful string representation than we get from the implicit superclass, object. By default, dataclasses include an equality comparison, also. This can be turned off in the cases where it doesn't make sense. The following example compares the manually built class to these dataclass features:

```
>>> s_ord
<__main__.StockOrdinary object at 0x7fb833c63f10>

>>> s_ord_2 = StockOrdinary("AAPL", 123.52, 137.98, 53.15)
>>> s_ord == s_ord_2
False
```

The class built manually has an awful default representation, and the lack of an equality test can make life difficult. We'd prefer the behavior of the Stock class defined as a dataclass.

```
>>> stock2 = Stock(symbol='AAPL', current=122.25, high=137.98, low=53.15)
>>> s == stock2
True
```

Class definitions decorated with @dataclass also have many other useful features. For example, you can specify a default value for the attributes of a dataclass. Perhaps the market is currently closed and you don't know what the values for the day are:

```
@dataclass
class StockDefaults:
    name: str
    current: float = 0.0
    high: float = 0.0
    low: float = 0.0
```

You can construct this class with just the stock name; the rest of the values will take on the defaults. But you can still specify values if you prefer, as follows:

```
>>> StockDefaults("GOOG")
StockDefaults(name='GOOG', current=0.0, high=0.0, low=0.0)
>>> StockDefaults("GOOG", 1826.77, 1847.20, 1013.54)
StockDefaults(name='GOOG', current=1826.77, high=1847.2, low=1013.54)
```

We saw earlier that dataclasses support equality comparison by default. If all the attributes compare as equal, then the dataclass objects as a whole also compare as equal. By default, dataclasses do not support other comparisons, such as less than or greater than, and they can't be sorted. However, you can easily add comparisons if you wish, demonstrated as follows:

```
@dataclass(order=True)
class StockOrdered:
    name: str
    current: float = 0.0
    high: float = 0.0
    low: float = 0.0
```

It's okay to ask "Is that all that's needed?" The answer is yes. The order=True parameter to the decorator leads to the creation of all of the comparison special methods. This change gives us the opportunity to sort and compare the instances of this class. It works like this:

```
>>> stock_ordered1 = StockOrdered("GOOG", 1826.77, 1847.20, 1013.54)
>>> stock_ordered2 = StockOrdered("GOOG")
>>> stock_ordered3 = StockOrdered("GOOG", 1728.28, high=1733.18,
low=1666.33)

>>> stock_ordered1 < stock_ordered2
False
>>> stock_ordered1 > stock_ordered2
True
>>> from pprint import pprint
>>> pprint(sorted([stock_ordered1, stock_ordered2, stock_ordered3]))
[StockOrdered(name='GOOG', current=0.0, high=0.0, low=0.0),
 StockOrdered(name='GOOG', current=1728.28, high=1733.18, low=1666.33),
 StockOrdered(name='GOOG', current=1826.77, high=1847.2, low=1013.54)]
```

When the dataclass decorator receives the order=True argument, it will, by default, compare the values based on each of the attributes in the order they were defined. So, in this case, it first compares the name attribute values of the two objects. If those are the same, it compares the current attribute values. If those are also the same, it will move on to high and will even include low if all the other attributes are equal. The rules follow the definition of a tuple: the order of definition is the order of comparison.

Another interesting feature of dataclasses is frozen=True. This creates a class that's similar to a typing.NamedTuple. There are some differences in what we get as features. We'd need to use @dataclass(frozen=True, ordered=True) to create structures. This leads to a question of "Which is better?", which – of course – depends on the details of a given use case. We haven't explored all of the optional features of dataclasses, like initialization-only fields and the __post_init__() method. Some applications don't need all of these features, and a simple NamedTuple may be adequate.

There are a few other approaches. Outside the standard library, packages like attrs, pydantic, and marshmallow provide attribute definition capabilities that are – in some ways – similar to dataclasses. Other packages outside the standard library offer additional features. See https://jackmckew.dev/dataclasses-vs-attrs-vs-pydantic.html for a comparison.

We've looked at two ways to create unique classes with specific attribute values, named tuples and dataclasses. It's often easier to start with dataclasses and add specialized methods. This can save us a bit of programming because some of the basics, like initialization, comparison, and string representations, are handled elegantly for us.

It's time to look at Python's built-in generic collections, dict, list, and set. We'll start by exploring dictionaries.

Dictionaries

Dictionaries are incredibly useful containers that allow us to map objects directly to other objects. Dictionaries are extremely efficient at looking up a **value**, given a specific **key** object that maps to that value. The secret of the speed is using a **hash** of the key to locate the value. Every immutable Python object has a numeric hash code; a relatively simple table is used to map the numeric hashes directly to values. This trick means a dictionary never searches the entire collection for a key; the key is transformed to a hash, which locates the associated value (almost) immediately.

Dictionaries can be created either using the `dict()` constructor or the `{}` syntax shortcut. In practice, the latter format is almost always used. We can prepopulate a dictionary by separating the keys from the values using a colon and separating the key-value pairs using a comma.

We can also create dictionaries using keyword parameters. We can use `dict(current=1235.20, high=1242.54, low=1231.06)` to create the value `{'current': 1235.2, 'high': 1242.54, 'low': 1231.06}`. This `dict()` syntax overlaps with other constructors like dataclasses and named tuples.

For example, in our stock application, we would most often want to look up prices by the stock symbol. We can create a dictionary that uses stock symbols as keys, and tuples (you could also use named tuples or dataclasses as values, of course) of current, high, and low as values, like this:

```
>>> stocks = {
...       "GOOG": (1235.20, 1242.54, 1231.06),
...       "MSFT": (110.41, 110.45, 109.84),
... }
```

As we've seen in previous examples, we can then look up values in the dictionary by requesting a key inside square brackets. If the key is not in the dictionary, it will raise a `KeyError` exception, demonstrated as follows:

```
>>> stocks["GOOG"]
(1235.2, 1242.54, 1231.06)
>>> stocks["RIMM"]
Traceback (most recent call last):
  ...
  File "<doctest examples.md[56]>", line 1, in <module>
    stocks.get("RIMM", "NOT FOUND")
KeyError: 'RIMM'
```

We can, of course, catch the `KeyError` and handle it. But we have other options. Remember, dictionaries are objects, even if their primary purpose is to hold other objects. As such, they have several behaviors associated with them. One of the most useful of these methods is the get method; it accepts a key as the first parameter and an optional default value if the key doesn't exist:

```
>>> print(stocks.get("RIMM"))
None
>>> stocks.get("RIMM", "NOT FOUND")
'NOT FOUND'
```

For even more control, we can use the `setdefault()` method. If the key is in the dictionary, this method behaves just like the `get()` method; it returns the value for that key. Otherwise, if the key is not in the dictionary, it will not only return the default value we supply in the method call (just like the `get()` method does); it will also set the key to that same value. Another way to think of it is that `setdefault()` sets a value in the dictionary only if that value has not previously been set. Then, it returns the value in the dictionary; either the one that was already there or the newly provided default value, as can be seen in the following:

```
>>> stocks.setdefault("GOOG", "INVALID")
(1235.2, 1242.54, 1231.06)
>>> stocks.setdefault("BB", (10.87, 10.76, 10.90))
(10.87, 10.76, 10.9)
>>> stocks["BB"]
(10.87, 10.76, 10.9)
```

The `"GOOG"` stock was already in the dictionary, so when we tried to use `setdefault()` to change it to an invalid value, it just returned the value already in the dictionary. The key `"BB"` was not in the dictionary, so the `setdefault()` method returned the default value and set the new value in the dictionary for us. We then check that the new stock is, indeed, in the dictionary.

The type hints for dictionaries must include the type for the keys and the type for the values. Starting with Python 3.9, and *mypy* release 0.812, we describe this structure with a type hint of `dict[str, tuple[float, float, float]]`; we can avoid importing the `typing` module. Depending on your version of Python, you'll often need to use `from __future__ import annotations` as the first line of code in your module; this includes the necessary language support to treat built-in classes as properly generic type annotations.

Three other useful dictionary methods are `keys()`, `values()`, and `items()`. The first two return iterators over all the keys and all the values in the dictionary. We can use these in `for` loops if we want to process all the keys or values. We'll return to the universality of iterators in *Chapter 10, The Iterator Pattern*. The `items()` method is probably the most useful; it returns an iterator over tuples of (`key`, `value`) pairs for every item in the dictionary. This works great with tuple unpacking in a `for` loop to loop over associated keys and values. The following example does just that to print each stock in the dictionary with its current value:

```
>>> for stock, values in stocks.items():
...     print(f"{stock} last value is {values[0]}")
...
GOOG last value is 1235.2
```

```
MSFT last value is 110.41
BB last value is 10.87
```

Each key/value tuple is unpacked into two variables named `stock` and `values` (we could use any variable names we wanted, but these both seem appropriate) and then printed in a formatted string.

 Notice that the stocks show up in the same order in which they were inserted. This was not true until Python 3.6, and was not a formal part of the language definition until Python 3.7. Before that, the `dict` implementation used a different underlying data structure with a difficult-to-predict ordering. According to PEP 478, Python 3.5's final release was in September 2020, making this older, difficult-to-predict ordering fully obsolete. To preserve the ordering of keys, we used to be forced to use the `OrderedDict` class in the `collections` module, but that's no longer needed.

There are numerous ways to retrieve data from a dictionary once it has been instantiated: we can use square brackets as index syntax, the `get()` method, the `setdefault()` method, or iterate over the `items()` method, among others.

Finally, as you likely already know, we can set a value in a dictionary using the same indexing syntax we use to retrieve a value:

```
>>> stocks["GOOG"] = (1245.21, 1252.64, 1245.18)
>>> stocks['GOOG']
(1245.21, 1252.64, 1245.18)
```

To reflect a change in the GOOG stock, we can update the tuple value in the dictionary. We can use this index syntax to set a value for any key, regardless of whether the key is in the dictionary. If it is in the dictionary, the old value will be replaced with the new one; otherwise, a new key-value pair will be created.

We've been using strings as dictionary keys, so far, but we aren't limited to string keys. It is common to use strings as keys, especially when we're storing data in a dictionary to gather it together (instead of using an object or dataclass with named properties). But we can also use tuples, numbers, or even objects we've defined ourselves as dictionary keys. The essential ingredient is a __hash__() method, which immutable types offer. While we can even use different types of objects as keys in a single dictionary, this is difficult to describe to *mypy*.

Here's an example of a dictionary with a variety of keys and values:

```
>>> random_keys = {}
>>> random_keys["astring"] = "somestring"
>>> random_keys[5] = "aninteger"
>>> random_keys[25.2] = "floats work too"
>>> random_keys[("abc", 123)] = "so do tuples"

>>> class AnObject:
...     def __init__(self, avalue):
...         self.avalue = avalue

>>> my_object = AnObject(14)
>>> random_keys[my_object] = "We can even store objects"
>>> my_object.avalue = 12

>>> random_keys[[1,2,3]] = "we can't use lists as keys"
Traceback (most recent call last):
  ...
  File "<doctest examples.md[72]>", line 1, in <module>
    random_keys[[1,2,3]] = "we can't use lists as keys"
TypeError: unhashable type: 'list'
```

This code shows several different types of keys we can supply to a dictionary. The data structure has a type hint of dict[Union[str, int, float, Tuple[str, int], AnObject], str]. This is clearly terribly complex. Writing type hints for this can be bewildering, suggesting it's not the best approach.

This example also shows one type of object that cannot be used as a key. We've already used lists extensively, and we'll be seeing many more details of them in the next section. Because lists are mutable – they can change at any time (by adding or removing items, for example) – they cannot hash to a single value.

We can use code like the following to examine values in the dictionary. This works because the default behavior of a mapping is to iterate over the keys.

```
>>> for key in random_keys:
...     print(f"{key!r} has value {random_keys[key]!r}")
'astring' has value 'somestring'
5 has value 'aninteger'
25.2 has value 'floats work too'
('abc', 123) has value 'so do tuples'
<__main__.AnObject object at ...> has value 'We can even store objects'
```

To be usable as a dictionary key, an object must be **hashable**, that is, have a __hash__() method to convert the object's state into a unique integer value for rapid lookup in a dictionary or set. The built-in hash() function uses the __hash__() method of the object's class. This hash is used to find values in a dictionary. For example, strings map to integers based on numeric codes for the characters in the string, while tuples combine hashes of the items inside the tuple. Any two objects that are considered equal (such as strings with the same characters or tuples with the same values) *must* also have the same hash value. Note that there is an asymmetry between equality and matching hash values. If two strings have the same hash value, they could still be unequal. Think of hash equality as an approximation for an equality test: if the hashes aren't equal, don't bother looking at the details. If the hashes are equal, invest the time in checking each attribute value or each item of the tuple, or each individual character of the string.

Here's an example of two integers with the same hash value that are not actually equal:

```
>>> x = 2020
>>> y = 2305843009213695971
>>> hash(x) == hash(y)
True
>>> x == y
False
```

When we use these values as keys in a dictionary, a hash collision algorithm will keep them separated. The situation leads to a microscopic slowdown in these rare cases of hash collisions. This is why dictionary lookup isn't **always** immediate: a hash collision might slow down access.

The built-in mutable objects – including lists, dictionaries, and sets – cannot be used as dictionary keys. These mutable collections don't provide hash values. We can, however, create our own class of objects that are both mutable and provide a hash value; this is unsafe because a change to the object's state can make it difficult to find the key in the dictionary.

We can go too far, of course. It is certainly possible to create a class with a mixture of mutable and immutable attributes and confine a customized hash computation to the mutable attributes. Because of the differences in behavior between the mutable and immutable features, this seems like it's really two objects that collaborate, not a single object with mutable and immutable features. We can use the immutable part for dictionary keys and keep the mutable part in the dictionary value.

In contrast, there are no limits on the types of objects that can be used as dictionary values. We can use a string key that maps to a list value, for example, or we can have a nested dictionary as a value in another dictionary.

Dictionary use cases

Dictionaries are extremely versatile and have numerous uses. Here are two major examples:

- We can have dictionaries where all the values are different instances of objects with the same type. For example, our stock dictionary would have a type hint of dict[str, tuple[float, float, float]]. The string key maps to a three-tuple of values. We use the stock symbol as an index to price details. If we had a more complex Stock class, we might have a dictionary with dict[str, Stock] as the type hint for an index into these objects.

- The second design is to have each key represent some aspect or attribute of a single object; the values often have distinct types. We may, for example, represent a stock with {'name': 'GOOG', 'current': 1245.21, 'range': (1252.64, 1245.18)}. This case clearly overlaps with named tuples, dataclasses, and objects in general. Indeed, there's a special type hint for this kind of dictionary, called a TypedDict, that looks like a NamedTuple type hint.

This second example can be confusing; how do we decide how to represent attribute values of an object? We can rank the techniques like this.

1. For a lot of cases, dataclasses offer a number of helpful features with less code writing. They can be immutable, or mutable, giving us a wide range of options.

2. For cases where the data is immutable, a NamedTuple can be slightly more efficient than a frozen dataclass by about 5% – not much. What tips the balance here is an expensive attribute computation. While a NamedTuple can have properties, if the computation is very costly and the results are used frequently, it can help to compute it in advance, something a NamedTuple isn't good at. Check out the documentation for dataclasses and their __post_init__() method as a better choice in the rare case where it's helpful to compute an attribute value in advance.

3. Dictionaries are ideal when the complete set of keys isn't known in advance. When we're starting a design, we may have throwaway prototypes or proofs of concept using dictionaries. When we try to write unit tests and type hints, we may need to ramp up the formality. In some cases, the domain of possible keys is known, and a TypedDict type hint makes sense as a way to characterize the valid keys and value types.

Because of the similar syntax, it's relatively easy to try different designs to see which works better for the problem, which is faster, which is easier to test, and which uses less memory. Sometimes, all three converge and there's one best choice. More often, it's a trade-off.

> Technically, most classes are implemented using dictionaries under the hood. You can see this by loading an object into the interactive interpreter and looking at the __dict__ special attribute, if it's present. When you access an attribute on an object using syntax like obj.attr_name, this is effectively obj.__dict__['attr_name'] under the hood. It's actually a bit more complicated, involving __getattr__() and __getattribute__(), but you get the gist. Even dataclasses have a __dict__ attribute, which just goes to show how widely used dictionaries really are. They aren't universal, but they are common.

Using defaultdict

We've seen how to use the setdefault method to set a default value if a key doesn't exist, but this can get a bit monotonous if we need to set a default value every time we look up a value. For example, if we're writing code that counts the number of times a letter occurs in a given sentence, we could do the following:

```
from __future__ import annotations

def letter_frequency(sentence: str) -> dict[str, int]:
    frequencies: dict[str, int] = {}
    for letter in sentence:
        frequency = frequencies.setdefault(letter, 0)
        frequencies[letter] = frequency + 1
    return frequencies
```

Every time we access the dictionary, we need to check that it has a value already, and if not, set it to zero. When something like this needs to be done every time an empty key is requested, we can create a different version of a dictionary. The defaultdict, defined in the collections module, handles missing keys elegantly:

```
from collections import defaultdict

def letter_frequency_2(sentence: str) -> defaultdict[str, int]:
    frequencies: defaultdict[str, int] = defaultdict(int)
    for letter in sentence:
```

```
        frequencies[letter] += 1
    return frequencies
```

This code looks odd: the `defaultdict()` evaluation accepts a function, `int`, in its constructor. We're not evaluating the `int()` function; we're providing a reference to this function to `defaultdict()`. Whenever a key is accessed that is not already in the dictionary, it calls that function, with no parameters, to create a default value.

Note that the `defaultdict[str, int]` type hint is slightly wordier than the `defaultdict()` evaluation itself. The `defaultdict()` class only needs a function that will create default values. The type of the keys doesn't actually matter at runtime; any object with a __hash__() method will work. When using `defaultdict` as a type hint, though, it needs some additional details before we can be *sure* this will work. We need to provide both the type of the key – `str`, in this example – and the type of object that will be associated with the key – `int`, in this example.

In this example, the `frequencies` object uses the function `int()` to create default values. This is the constructor for an integer object. Normally, integers are created as a literal, by typing an integer number into our code. If we do create an integer using the `int()` constructor, it's often part of a conversion; for example, to convert a string of digits into an integer, like `int("42")`. But if we call `int()` without any arguments, it returns, conveniently, the number zero. In this code, if a letter doesn't exist in the `defaultdict`, the number zero is created by the factory function and returned when we access it. Then, we add one to this number to indicate that we've found an instance of that letter and save the updated value back into the dictionary. The next time we find the same character, the new number will be returned and we can increment the value and save it back into the dictionary.

The `defaultdict()` is useful for creating dictionaries of containers. If we want to create a dictionary of closing stock prices for the past 30 days, we could use a stock symbol as the key and store the prices in a `list`; the first time we access the stock price, we would want to create an empty list. Simply pass the `list` function into the `defaultdict`, like this: `defaultdict(list)`. The `list()` function will be called every time a previously unknown key is accessed. We can do similar things with sets or even empty dictionaries if we want to use a subsidiary dictionary as the value for a key.

Of course, we can also write our own functions and pass them into the `defaultdict`. Suppose we want to create a `defaultdict` where each key maps to a dataclass with information about that key. If we define our dataclass with default values, then our class name will work as a function without arguments.

Consider this dataclass, `Prices`, with all default values:

```
>>> from dataclasses import dataclass
>>> @dataclass
... class Prices:
...     current: float = 0.0
...     high: float = 0.0
...     low: float = 0.0
...
>>> Prices()
Prices(current=0.0, high=0.0, low=0.0)
```

Since the class has default values for all attributes, we can use the class name without argument values and get a useful object. This means our class name will work as the argument to the `defaultdict()` function:

```
>>> portfolio = collections.defaultdict(Prices)
>>> portfolio["GOOG"]
Prices(current=0.0, high=0.0, low=0.0)
>>> portfolio["AAPL"] = Prices(current=122.25, high=137.98, low=53.15)
```

When we print `portfolio`, we see how the default objects were saved in the dictionary:

```
>>> from pprint import pprint
>>> pprint(portfolio)
defaultdict(<class 'dc_stocks.Prices'>,
            {'AAPL': Prices(current=122.25, high=137.98, low=53.15),
             'GOOG': Prices(current=0.0, high=0.0, low=0.0)})
```

This `portfolio` dictionary creates a default `Prices` object for unknown keys. This works because the `Prices` class had default values for all of the attributes.

We can extend this even further. What if we want prices for stocks grouped by month? We want a dictionary with a key of the stock name. Within that we want dictionaries keyed by month. And within that inner dictionary, we want prices. This can be tricky because we want a default function that takes zero arguments and creates a `defaultdict(Prices)` for us. We can define a one-line function:

```
>>> def make_defaultdict():
...     return collections.defaultdict(Prices)
```

We can also use a Python lambda form – a no-name, one expression function for this. A lambda can have parameters, but we don't need any. The single expression is the object we'd like created as a default.

```
>>> by_month = collections.defaultdict(
...         lambda: collections.defaultdict(Prices)
... )
```

Now we can have nested `defaultdict` dictionaries. When a key is missing, a proper default is built.

```
>>> by_month["APPL"]["Jan"] = Prices(current=122.25, high=137.98,
low=53.15)
```

The `by_month` collection's top-level key points to an internal dictionary. The internal dictionary has prices for each month.

Counter

You'd think that algorithms could not get much simpler than using `defaultdict(int)`. The *I want to count specific instances in an iterable* use case is common enough that the Python developers created a specific class for this exact purpose, simplifying things even further. The previous code that counts characters in a string can easily be calculated in a single line:

```
from collections import Counter

def letter_frequency_3(sentence: str) -> Counter[str]:
    return Counter(sentence)
```

The `Counter` object behaves like a beefed-up dictionary where the keys are the items being counted and the values are the quantities of such items. One of the most useful functions is the `most_common()` method. It returns a list of (`key`,`count`) tuples in descending order by the count. You can optionally pass an integer argument into `most_common()` to request a list of only the most common elements. For example, you could write a simple polling application as follows:

```
>>> import collections
>>> responses = [
...         "vanilla",
...         "chocolate",
```

```
...        "vanilla",
...        "vanilla",
...        "caramel",
...        "strawberry",
...        "vanilla"
...    ]

>>> favorites = collections.Counter(responses).most_common(1)
>>> name, frequency = favorites[0]
>>> name
'vanilla'
```

Presumably, you'd get the responses from a database or by using a computer vision algorithm to count the kids who raised their hands. Here, we hardcoded the responses object with literal values so that we can test the most_common() method. This method always returns a list, even when we only asked for one element. The hint is effectively list[tuple[T, int]] where T is the type we're counting. In our example, where we're counting strings, the hint for the most_common() method is list[tuple[str, int]]. We only want the first item from a one-item list, so [0] is required. We can then decompose the two-tuple into the value that was counted and the integer count.

Speaking of lists, it's time to dig a little more deeply into Python's list collection.

Lists

Python's generic list structure is integrated into a number of language features. We don't need to import them and rarely need to use method syntax to access their features. We can visit all the items in a list without explicitly requesting an iterator object, and we can construct a list (as with a dictionary) with very simple-looking syntax. Further, list comprehensions and generator expressions turn them into a veritable Swiss Army knife of computing functionality.

If you don't know how to create or append to a list, how to retrieve items from a list, or what *slice notation* is, we direct you to the official Python tutorial, posthaste. It can be found online at http://docs.python.org/3/tutorial/. In this section, we'll move beyond the basics to cover when lists should be used, and their nature as objects.

In Python, lists should normally be used when we want to store several instances of the *same* type of object; lists of strings or lists of numbers. We'll often use a type hint list[T] to specify the type, T, of object kept in the list, for example, list[int] or list[str].

(Remember that from __future__ import annotations is required for this to work.) Lists must be used when we want to store items in some kind of order. Often, this is the order in which they were inserted, but they can also be sorted by other criteria.

Lists are mutable, so items can be added, replaced, and removed from the list. This can be handy for reflecting the state of some more complex objects.

Like dictionaries, Python lists use an extremely efficient and well-tuned internal data structure so we can worry about what we're storing, rather than how we're storing it. Python expands on lists to provide some specialized data structures for queues and stacks. Python doesn't make a distinction between lists based on arrays or lists that use links. Generally, the built-in list data structure can serve a wide variety of purposes.

Don't use lists for collecting different attributes of individual items. Tuples, named tuples, dictionaries, and objects would all be more suitable for collecting different kinds of attribute values. Our first Stock data examples at the beginning of the chapter stored current price, minimum price, and maximum price, each a different attribute with a distinct meaning in a single sequence. This isn't really ideal, and named tuples or dataclasses were clearly superior.

Here's a rather convoluted counterexample that demonstrates how we could perform the frequency example using a list. It is much more complicated than the dictionary examples and illustrates the effect that choosing the right (or wrong) data structure can have on the readability (and performance) of our code. This is demonstrated as follows:

```python
from __future__ import annotations
import string

CHARACTERS = list(string.ascii_letters) + [" "]

def letter_frequency(sentence: str) -> list[tuple[str, int]]:
    frequencies = [(c, 0) for c in CHARACTERS]
    for letter in sentence:
        index = CHARACTERS.index(letter)
        frequencies[index] = (letter, frequencies[index][1] + 1)
    non_zero = [
        (letter, count)
        for letter, count in frequencies if count > 0
    ]
    return non_zero
```

This code starts with a list of possible characters. The `string.ascii_letters` attribute provides a string of all the letters, lowercase and uppercase, in order. We convert this to a list and then use list concatenation (the + operator causes two lists to be concatenated into one) to add one more character, a space. These are the available characters in our frequency list (the code would break if we tried to add a letter that wasn't in the list).

The first line inside the function uses a list comprehension to turn the `CHARACTERS` list into a list of tuples. Then, we loop over each of the characters in the sentence. We first look up the index of the character in the `CHARACTERS` list, which we know has the same index in our frequencies list, since we created the second list from the first. We then update that index in the frequencies list by creating a new tuple, discarding the original one. Aside from garbage collection and memory waste concerns, this is rather difficult to read!

Finally, we filter the list by examining each tuple and keeping only pairs where the count is greater than zero. This removes the letters we allocated space for but never saw.

Besides being longer, the `CHARACTERS.index(letter)` operation can be very slow. The worst case is to examine each of the characters in the list for a match. On average, it will search half the list. Compare this with a dictionary that does a hash computation and examines one item for a match. (Except in the case of a hash collision where there's a tiny probability of examining more than one and it has to handle hash collision with a second lookup.)

The type hint describes the type of the objects in the list. We summarized it as `list[tuple[str, int]]`. Each of the items in the resulting list will be a two-tuple. This lets *mypy* confirm that the operations respect the structure of the list overall and each tuple within the list.

Like dictionaries, lists are objects, too. They have several methods that can be invoked upon them. Here are some common ones:

- The `append(element)` method adds an element to the end of the list
- The `insert(index, element)` method inserts an item at a specific position
- The `count(element)` method tells us how many times an element appears in the list
- The `index()` method tells us the index of an item in the list, raising an exception if it can't find it

- The find() method does the same thing but returns -1 instead of raising an exception for missing items
- The reverse() method does exactly what it says – turns the list around
- The sort() method has some rather intricate object-oriented behaviors, which we'll cover now

There are a few more that are less commonly used. The complete list of methods is in the *Sequence Types* section of the Python Standard Library documentation: https://docs.python.org/3.9/library/stdtypes.html#sequence-types-list-tuple-range.

Sorting lists

Without any parameters, the sort() method of a list object will generally do as expected. If we have a list[str] object, the sort() method will place the items in alphabetical order. This operation is case sensitive, so all capital letters will be sorted before lowercase letters; that is, Z comes before a. If it's a list of numbers, they will be sorted in numerical order. If a list of tuples is provided, the list is sorted by considering the elements in the tuple in order. If a mixture containing unsortable items is supplied, the sort will raise a TypeError exception.

If we want to place objects of classes we've defined ourselves into a list and make those objects sortable, we have to do a bit more work. The special __lt__() method, which stands for *less than*, must be defined on the class to make instances of that class comparable. The sort method on the list will access this method on each object to determine where it goes in the list. This method should return True if our class is somehow less than the passed parameter, and False otherwise.

Often, when we need comparisons like this, we'll use a dataclass. As discussed in the *Dataclasses* section, the @dataclass(order=True) decorator will assure that all of the comparison methods are built for us. A named tuple also has the ordering operations defined by default.

One tricky situation that arises with sorting is handling a data structure sometimes called a **tagged union**. A union is a description of an object where attributes are not **always** relevant. If an attribute's relevance depends on another attribute's value, this can be seen as a union of distinct subtypes with a tag to distinguish between the two types.

Here's some example data, where a tag value, the **Data Source** column, is required to decide how best to deal with the remaining columns. Some values of **Data Source** tell us to use the timestamp, where as other values tell us to use the creation date.

Data Source	Timestamp	Creation Date	Name, Owner, etc.
Local	1607280522.68012		"Some File", etc.
Remote		"2020-12-06T13:47:52.849153"	"Another File", etc.
Local	1579373292.452993		"This File", etc.
Remote		"2020-01-18T13:48:12.452993"	"That File", etc.

How can we sort these into a single, coherent order? We'd like to have a single, consistent data type in our list, but the source data has two subtypes with a tag.

A simple-seeming if `row.data_source == "Local":` can work to distinguish values, but it can be confusing logic for *mypy* to work with. One or two *ad hoc* if statements aren't too bad, but the design principle of throwing if statements at the problem isn't very scalable.

In this example, we can consider **Timestamp** as the preferred representation. This means we only need to compute timestamps from the creation date string for the items where the data source is "Remote." In this example, either the float value or the string would sort into order properly. This happens to work out well because the string is in the carefully designed ISO format. If it was in American month-day-year format, it would require conversion to a timestamp to be useful.

Converting all of the various input formats to Python's native `datetime.datetime` objects is another choice. This has the advantage of being distinct from any of the input formats. While this is a little more work, it gives us more flexibility because we're not tied to a source data format that may change in the future. The concept is to make every variant input format convert to a single, common `datetime.datetime` instance.

What's central is treating the two subtypes as if they're a single class of objects. This doesn't always work out well. Often this is a design constraint that sneaks up on us when we have additional customers or additional sources of data.

We'll start an implementation with a single type that supports both subtypes of data. This is not ideal, but it matches the source data and is often how we start tackling this kind of data. Here's the essential class definition:

```
from typing import Optional, cast, Any
from dataclasses import dataclass
import datetime

@dataclass(frozen=True)
class MultiItem:
    data_source: str
    timestamp: Optional[float]
    creation_date: Optional[str]
    name: str
    owner_etc: str

    def __lt__(self, other: Any) -> bool:
        if self.data_source == "Local":
            self_datetime = datetime.datetime.fromtimestamp(
                cast(float, self.timestamp)
            )
        else:
            self_datetime = datetime.datetime.fromisoformat(
                cast(str, self.creation_date)
            )
        if other.data_source == "Local":
            other_datetime = datetime.datetime.fromtimestamp(
                cast(float, other.timestamp)
            )
        else:
            other_datetime = datetime.datetime.fromisoformat(
                cast(str, other.creation_date)
            )
        return self_datetime < other_datetime
```

The __lt__() method compares an object of the MultiItem class to another instance of the same class. Because there are two implicit subclasses, we have to check the tag attributes, self.data_source and other.data_source, to see which of the various combinations of fields we're dealing with. We'll do a conversion from a timestamp or a string into a common representation. Then we can compare the two common representations.

The conversion processing is nearly duplicate code. Later in this section, we will look at refactoring this to remove the redundancy. The `cast()` operations are required to make it clear to *mypy* that the item will not be `None`. While we know the rules that match the tag (the **Data Source** column) and the two kinds of values, those rules need to be stated in a way *mypy* can exploit them. The `cast()` is how we tell *mypy* what the data will be at runtime; there's no processing that actually happens.

Note that our application could have incomplete type hints and we could run with a bug and an object that's not an instance of `MultiItem` could be compared with an instance of `MultiItem`. This will likely result in a runtime error. The `cast()` is a claim about the intent and the design, with no runtime impact. Because of Python's duck typing, some unexpected type that has the right attributes can be used and will work. Unit testing is essential even with careful type hints.

The following output illustrates this class in action when it comes to sorting:

```
>>> mi_0 = MultiItem("Local", 1607280522.68012, None, "Some File",
"etc. 0")
>>> mi_1 = MultiItem("Remote", None, "2020-12-06T13:47:52.849153",
"Another File", "etc. 1")
>>> mi_2 = MultiItem("Local", 1579373292.452993, None, "This File",
"etc. 2")
>>> mi_3 = MultiItem("Remote", None, "2020-01-18T13:48:12.452993",
"That File", "etc. 3")
>>> file_list = [mi_0, mi_1, mi_2, mi_3]
>>> file_list.sort()

>>> from pprint import pprint
>>> pprint(file_list)
[MultiItem(data_source='Local', timestamp=1579373292.452993,
creation_date=None, name='This File', owner_etc='etc. 2'),
 MultiItem(data_source='Remote', timestamp=None, creation_date='2020-
01-18T13:48:12.452993', name='That File', owner_etc='etc. 3'),
 MultiItem(data_source='Remote', timestamp=None, creation_date='2020-
12-06T13:47:52.849153', name='Another File', owner_etc='etc. 1'),
 MultiItem(data_source='Local', timestamp=1607280522.68012,
creation_date=None, name='Some File', owner_etc='etc. 0')]
```

The comparison rules were applied among the various subtypes that were conflated into a single class definition. If the rules are more complex, however, this can become unwieldy.

Only the __lt__() method is required to implement to enable sorting. To be complete, the class may also implement the similar __gt__(), __eq__(), __ne__(), __ge__(), and __le__() methods. This ensures all of the <, >, ==, !=, >=, and <= operators also work properly. You can get this for free by implementing __lt__() and __eq__(), and then applying the @total_ordering class decorator to supply the rest:

```python
from functools import total_ordering
from dataclasses import dataclass
from typing import Optional, cast
import datetime


@total_ordering
@dataclass(frozen=True)
class MultiItem:
    data_source: str
    timestamp: Optional[float]
    creation_date: Optional[str]
    name: str
    owner_etc: str

    def __lt__(self, other: "MultiItem") -> bool:
        Exercise: rewrite this to follow the example of __eq__.

    def __eq__(self, other: object) -> bool:
        return self.datetime == cast(MultiItem, other).datetime

    @property
    def datetime(self) -> datetime.datetime:
        if self.data_source == "Local":
            return datetime.datetime.fromtimestamp(
                cast(float, self.timestamp))
        else:
            return datetime.datetime.fromisoformat(
                cast(str, self.creation_date))
```

We didn't repeat the __lt__() method body; we encourage the reader to rewrite it to look more like the __eq__() method. When we provide some combination of < (or >) and =, the @total_order decorator can deduce the remaining logic operator implementations. For example, $a \geq b \equiv \neg(a < b)$. The implementation of __ge__(self, other) is not self < other.

Note that our class method definitions are (very) narrowly focused on comparing `timestamp` and `creation_date` attributes among these objects. The definitions of these methods are – perhaps – less than ideal because they reflect exactly one use case of comparison. We often have two possible designs:

- Define the comparison operations narrowly, focused on a specific use case. In this example, we compare only the timestamps and ignore all other attributes. This is inflexible but can be made very efficient.

- Define the comparison operations broadly, often only supporting `__eq__()` and `__ne__()` because there are too many alternative ordering comparisons that could be used. We extract individual attribute comparison rules outside the class and make them part of the sorting operation.

The second design strategy requires us to localize the comparison as part of evaluating the `sort()` method, instead of making the comparison a general part of the class. The `sort()` method can take an optional key argument. We use this to provide a "key extraction" function to the `sort()` method. This argument to `sort()` is a function that translates each object in a list into an object that can somehow be compared. In our case, we'd like a function to extract either the `timestamp` or the `creation_date` for comparison. It looks like this:

```
@dataclass(frozen=True)
class SimpleMultiItem:
    data_source: str
    timestamp: Optional[float]
    creation_date: Optional[str]
    name: str
    owner_etc: str


def by_timestamp(item: SimpleMultiItem) -> datetime.datetime:
    if item.data_source == "Local":
        return datetime.datetime.fromtimestamp(
            cast(float, item.timestamp))
    elif item.data_source == "Remote":
        return datetime.datetime.fromisoformat(
            cast(str, item.creation_date))
    else:
        raise ValueError(f"Unknown data_source in {item!r}")
```

Here's how we use this `by_timestamp()` function to compare objects using `datetime` objects from each `SimpleMultiItem` object:

```
>>> file_list.sort(key=by_timestamp)
```

We've divorced the sorting rules from the class, leading to a pleasant simplification. We can leverage this kind of design to provide other kinds of sorts. We might, for example, sort by name only. This is slightly simpler because no conversion is required:

```
>>> file_list.sort(key=lambda item: item.name)
```

We've created a lambda object, a tiny no-name function that takes an item as an argument and returns the value of `item.name`. A lambda is a function, but it doesn't have a name, and it can't have any statements. It only has a single expression. If you need statements (for example a try/except clause) you need a conventional function definition outside the `sort()` method arguments.

There are a few sort key operations that are so common that the Python team has supplied them so you don't have to write them yourself. For example, it is common to sort a list of tuples by something other than the first item in the list. The `operator.attrgetter` method can be used as a key to do this:

```
>>> import operator
>>> file_list.sort(key=operator.attrgetter("name"))
```

The `attrgetter()` function fetches a specific attribute from an object. When working with tuples or dictionaries, `itemgetter()` can be used to extract a specific item by name or position. There's even a `methodcaller()`, which returns the result of a method call on the object being sorted. Refer to the `operator` module documentation for more information.

There's rarely one single sort order for data objects. Providing the key function as part of the `sort()` method lets us define a wide variety of sorting rules without creating complex class definitions.

After looking at dictionaries and now lists, we can turn our attention to sets.

Sets

Lists are extremely versatile tools that suit many container object applications. But they are not useful when we want to ensure that objects in a list are unique. For example, a song library may contain many songs by the same artist. If we want to sort through the library and create a list of all the artists, we would have to check the list to see whether we've added the artist already, before we add them again.

This is where sets come in. Sets come from mathematics, where they represent an unordered group of unique items. We can try to add an item to a set five times, but the "is a member of a set" doesn't change after the first time we add it.

In Python, sets can hold any hashable object, not just strings or numbers. Hashable objects implement the __hash__() method; these are the same objects that can be used as keys in dictionaries; so again, mutable lists, sets, and dictionaries are out. Like mathematical sets, they can store only one copy of each object. If we're trying to create a list of song artists, we can create a set of string names and simply add them to the set. This example starts with a list of (song, artist) tuples and creates a set of the artists:

```python
>>> song_library = [
...     ("Phantom Of The Opera", "Sarah Brightman"),
...     ("Knocking On Heaven's Door", "Guns N' Roses"),
...     ("Captain Nemo", "Sarah Brightman"),
...     ("Patterns In The Ivy", "Opeth"),
...     ("November Rain", "Guns N' Roses"),
...     ("Beautiful", "Sarah Brightman"),
...     ("Mal's Song", "Vixy and Tony"),
... ]

>>> artists = set()
>>> for song, artist in song_library:
...     artists.add(artist)
```

There is no built-in syntax for an empty set as there is for lists and dictionaries; we create a set using the set() constructor. However, we can use the curly braces (borrowed from dictionary syntax) to create a set, so long as the set contains values. If we use colons to separate pairs of values, it's a dictionary, as in {'key': 'value', 'key2': 'value2'}. If we just separate values with commas, it's a set, as in {'value', 'value2'}.

Items can be added individually to the set using the add() method, and updated in bulk using the update() method. If we run the script shown above, we see that the set works as advertised:

```python
{'Sarah Brightman', "Guns N' Roses", 'Vixy and Tony', 'Opeth'}
```

If you're paying attention to the output, you'll notice that the items are not printed in the order they were added to the sets. Indeed each time you run this, you may see the items in a different order.

Sets are inherently unordered due to a hash-based data structure used for efficient access to the members. Because of this lack of ordering, sets cannot have items looked up by index. The primary purpose of a set is to divide the world into two groups: *things that are in the set*, and *things that are not in the set*. It is easy to check whether an item is in a set or to loop over the items in a set, but if we want to sort or order them, we have to convert the set to a list. This output shows all three of these activities:

```
>>> "Opeth" in artists
True
>>> alphabetical = list(artists)
>>> alphabetical.sort()
>>> alphabetical
["Guns N' Roses", 'Opeth', 'Sarah Brightman', 'Vixy and Tony']
```

This output is highly variable; any one of the possible orderings could be used, depending on the hash randomization in use.

```
>>> for artist in artists:
...         print(f"{artist} plays good music")
...
Sarah Brightman plays good music
Guns N' Roses plays good music
Vixy and Tony play good music
Opeth plays good music
```

The primary *feature* of a set is uniqueness. Sets are often used to deduplicate data. Sets are also used to create combinations, including unions and differences between collections. Most of the methods on the set type operate on other sets, allowing us to efficiently combine or compare the items in two or more sets.

The union method is the most common and easiest to understand. It takes a second set as a parameter and returns a new set that contains all elements that are in *either* of the two sets; if an element is in both original sets, it will only show up once in the new set. Union is like a logical *or* operation. Indeed, the | operator can be used on two sets to perform the union operation, if you don't like calling methods.

Conversely, the intersection method accepts a second set and returns a new set that contains only those elements that are in *both* sets. It is like a logical and operation, and can also be referenced using the & operator.

Finally, the `symmetric_difference` method tells us what's left; it is the set of objects that are in one set or the other, but not in both. It uses the ^ operator. The following example illustrates these methods by comparing some artists preferred by two different people:

```
>>> dusty_artists = {
...     "Sarah Brightman",
...     "Guns N' Roses",
...     "Opeth",
...     "Vixy and Tony",
... }

>>> steve_artists = {"Yes", "Guns N' Roses", "Genesis"}
```

Here are three examples of union, intersection, and symmetric difference:

```
>>> print(f"All: {dusty_artists | steve_artists}")
All: {'Genesis', "Guns N' Roses", 'Yes', 'Sarah Brightman', 'Opeth',
'Vixy and Tony'}
>>> print(f"Both: {dusty_artists.intersection(steve_artists)}")
Both: {"Guns N' Roses"}
>>> print(
...     f"Either but not both: {dusty_artists ^ steve_artists}"
... )
Either but not both: {'Genesis', 'Sarah Brightman', 'Opeth', 'Yes',
'Vixy and Tony'}
```

The union, intersection, and symmetric difference methods are commutative. We can say dusty_artists.union(steve_artists) or steve_artists.union(dusty_artists) and get the same general result. The order of values will vary because of hash randomization, but the same items will be present in both sets.

There are also methods that return different results depending on who is the caller and who is the argument. These methods include `issubset` and `issuperset`, which are the inverse of each other. Both return a `bool`.

- The `issubset` method returns `True` if all of the items in the calling set are also in the set passed as an argument. We can use the <= operator for this, also.
- The `issuperset` method returns `True` if all of the items in the argument are also in the calling set. Thus, s.issubset(t), s <= t, t.issuperset(s), and t >= s are all identical.

- They will both return True if t contains all the elements in s. (The < and > operators are for proper subsets and proper supersets; there are no named methods for these operations.)

Finally, the difference method returns all the elements that are in the calling set, but not in the set passed as an argument. The difference method can also be represented by the - operator. The following code illustrates these methods in action:

```
>>> artists = {"Guns N' Roses", 'Vixy and Tony', 'Sarah Brightman',
'Opeth'}
>>> bands = {"Opeth", "Guns N' Roses"}

>>> artists.issuperset(bands)
True
>>> artists.issubset(bands)
False
>>> artists - bands
{'Sarah Brightman', 'Vixy and Tony'}

>>> bands.issuperset(artists)
False
>>> bands.issubset(artists)
True
>>> bands.difference(artists)
set()
```

The difference method, in the final expression, returns an empty set, since there are no items in bands that are not in artists. Looked at another way, we start with the value in bands and then remove all the items from artists. It may be helpful to think of as the expression bands - artists.

The union, intersection, and difference methods can all take multiple sets as arguments; they will return, as we might expect, the set that is created when the operation is called on all the parameters.

So, the methods on sets clearly suggest that sets are meant to operate on other sets, and that they are not just containers. If we have data coming in from two different sources and need to quickly combine them in some way, so as to determine where the data overlaps or is different, we can use set operations to efficiently compare them. Or, if we have data incoming that may contain duplicates of data that has already been processed, we can use sets to compare the two and process only the new data.

Finally, it is valuable to know that sets are much more efficient than lists when checking for membership using the in keyword. If you use the `value in container` syntax on a set or a list, it will return `True` if one of the elements in `container` is equal to `value`, and `False` otherwise. However, in a list, it will look at every object in the container until it finds the value, whereas in a set, it simply hashes the value and checks for membership. This means that a set will find the value in the same amount of time no matter how big the container is, but a list will take longer and longer to search for a value as the list contains more and more values.

Three types of queues

We'll look at an application of the list structure to create a queue. A queue is a special kind of buffer, summarized as **First In First Out** (**FIFO**). The idea is to act as a temporary stash so one part of an application can write to the queue while another part consumes items from the queue.

A database might have a queue of data to be written to disk. When our application performs an update, the local cache version of the data is updated so all other applications can see the change. The write to the disk, however, may be placed in a queue for a writer to deal with a few milliseconds later.

When we're looking at files and directories, a queue can be a handy place to stash details of the directories so they can be processed later. We'll often represent a directory as the path from the root of the filesystem to the file of interest. We'll look at `Path` objects in detail in *Chapter 9, Strings, Serialization, and File Paths*. The algorithm works like this:

```
queue starts empty
Add the base directory to the queue
While the queue is not empty:
    Pop the first item from the queue
    If the item is a file:
        Process the item
    Else if the item is a directory:
        For each sub-item in the directory:
            Add this sub-item to the queue
```

We can visualize this list-like structure as growing via an `append()` and shrinking via `pop(0)`. It would look like this:

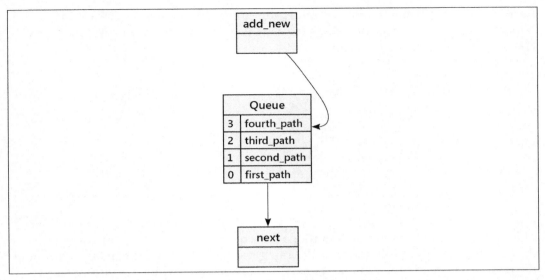

Figure 7.1: Queue concept

The idea is for the queue to grow and shrink: each directory grows the queue and each file shrinks the queue. Eventually, all the files and directories have been processed and the queue is empty. The original order is preserved by the FIFO rule.

We have several ways to implement a queue in Python:

1. List using the pop() and append() methods of a list.
2. The collections.deque structure, which supports popleft() and append() methods. A "deque" is a Double-Ended Queue. This is an elegant queue implementation that's faster than a simple list for the specific operations of appending and popping.
3. The queue module provides a queue often used for multithreading, but it can also be used for our single thread to examine a directory tree. This uses get() and put() methods. Since this structure is designed for concurrency, it locks the data structure to assure that each change is atomic and can't be interrupted by other threads. For a non-concurrent application, the locking overhead is a performance penalty we can avoid. This is the subject of *Chapter 14, Concurrency*.

The heapq module also provides a queue, but it does some extra processing that's irrelevant to this specific example. It keeps items in priority order, not the order they were put into the queue, breaking the FIFO expectation. We'll use this in *Chapter 8*, in the *Functions are objects, too* section.

Each of these implementations is slightly different. This suggests we want to create handy wrapper classes around them to provide a uniform interface. We can create class definitions like the following:

```python
class ListQueue(List[Path]):
    def put(self, item: Path) -> None:
        self.append(item)

    def get(self) -> Path:
        return self.pop(0)

    def empty(self) -> bool:
        return len(self) == 0
```

This shows the three essential operations for a queue. We can put something into the queue, appending it to the end. We can get something from the queue, removing the item at the head of the queue. Finally, we can ask if the queue is empty. We've layered this on a list class by extending it to add three new methods: put(), get(), and empty().

Next is a slightly different implementation. The typing.Deque type hint is the wrapper around the collections.deque class. A recent change to Python changed the underlying collections.deque class, removing the need for a special hint.

```python
from typing import Deque

class DeQueue(Deque[Path]):
    def put(self, item: Path) -> None:
        self.append(item)

    def get(self) -> Path:
        return self.popleft()

    def empty(self) -> bool:
        return len(self) == 0
```

It's hard to see the distinction between this implementation and the generic list implementation. It turns out the popleft() method is a higher-speed version of pop(0) in a conventional list. Otherwise, this looks very similar to the list-based implementation.

Here's a final version that uses the queue module. This queue module's implementation uses locks to prevent the data structure from being damaged by concurrent access across multiple threads. It's generally opaque to us, except as a tiny performance cost.

```python
import queue
from typing import TYPE_CHECKING

if TYPE_CHECKING:
    BaseQueue = queue.Queue[Path]  # for mypy.
else:
    BaseQueue = queue.Queue  # used at runtime.


class ThreadQueue(BaseQueue):
    pass
```

This implementation works because we decided to use the Queue class interface as the template for the other two classes. This meant we didn't have to do any real work to implement this class; this design was the overall target for the other class designs.

The type hints, however, are rather complex-looking. The queue.Queue class definition is also a generic type hint. When the code is being examined by *mypy*, the TYPE_CHECKING variable is True, and we need to provide a parameter to the generic type. When the TYPE_CHECKING variable is False, we're not using *mypy*, and the class name (without any additional parameters) is all that's needed to define a queue at runtime.

These three classes are similar with respect to the three defined methods. We could define an abstract base class for them. Or we could provide the following type hint:

```python
PathQueue = Union[ListQueue, DeQueue, ThreadQueue]
```

This PathQueue type hint summarizes all three types, allowing us to define an object of any of these three classes to use for the final implementation choice.

The question of "which is better" is answered by the standard response of "it depends on what you need to do."

- For single-threaded applications, the collections.deque is ideal; it's designed for this purpose.
- For multi-threaded applications, the queue.Queue is required to provide a data structure that can be read and written by multiple concurrent threads. We'll return to this in *Chapter 14, Concurrency*.

While we can often leverage a built-in structure, like the generic `list` class, for a wide variety of purposes, it may not be ideal. The other two implementations offer advantages over the built-in list. Python's standard library, and the broader ecosystem of external packages available through the Python Package Index (PYPI), can provide improvements over generic structures. What's important is having a specific improvement before searching high and low for a "perfect" package. In our example, the performance difference between the `deque` and the `list` is small. The time is dominated by the OS work required to gather the raw data. For a large file system, perhaps spanning multiple hosts, the difference will add up.

Python's object-orientation gives us the latitude to explore design alternatives. We should feel free to try more than one solution to a problem as a way to better understand the problem, and arrive at an acceptable solution.

Case study

In this chapter's case study, we'll revisit our design, leveraging Python's `@dataclass` definitions. This holds some potential for streamlining our design. We'll be looking at some choices and limitations; this will lead us to explore some difficult engineering trade-offs, where there isn't one obvious best approach.

We'll also look at immutable `NamedTuple` class definitions. These objects have no internal state changes, leading to the possibility of some design simplifications. This will also change our design to make less use of inheritance and more use of composition.

Logical model

Let's review the design we have so far for our `model.py` module. This shows the hierarchy of `Sample` class definitions, used to reflect the various ways samples are used:

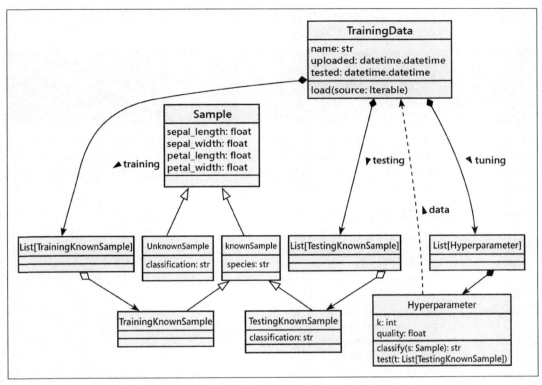

Figure 7.2: Class diagram so far

The various `Sample` classes are a very good fit with the dataclass definition. These objects have a number of attributes, and the methods built automatically seem to fit the behaviors we want. Here's the revised `Sample` class, implemented as a `@dataclass` instead of being built entirely by hand:

```
from dataclasses import dataclass, asdict
from typing import Optional

@dataclass
class Sample:
    sepal_length: float
    sepal_width: float
    petal_length: float
    petal_width: float
```

We've used the @dataclass decorator to create a class from the supplied attribute type hints. We can use the resulting Sample class like this:

```
>>> from model import Sample
>>> x = Sample(1, 2, 3, 4)
>>> x
Sample(sepal_length=1, sepal_width=2, petal_length=3, petal_width=4)
```

This example shows how we create instances of a class defined with the @dataclass decorator. Note that a representation function, __repr__(), was automatically created for us; it displays a useful level of detail, as shown in the example above. This is very pleasant. It almost feels like cheating!

Here are the definitions for some more of the Sample class hierarchy.

```
@dataclass
class KnownSample(Sample):
    species: str

@dataclass
class TestingKnownSample(KnownSample):
    classification: Optional[str] = None

@dataclass
class TrainingKnownSample(KnownSample):
    """Note: no classification instance variable available."""
    pass
```

This seems to cover the user stories described in *Chapter 1, Object-Oriented Design,* and expanded in *Chapter 4, Expecting the Unexpected.* We can provide training data, test the classifier, and handle the classification of unknown samples. We didn't have to write very much code and we get a lot of useful features.

We do have a potential problem, however. While we are permitted to set a classification attribute on a TrainingKnownSample instance, this doesn't seem to be a great idea. Here's an example, where we create a sample to be used for training, and then also set a classification attribute.

```
>>> from model import TrainingKnownSample
>>> s1 = TrainingKnownSample(
...     sepal_length=5.1, sepal_width=3.5, petal_length=1.4,
...     petal_width=0.2, species="Iris-setosa")
```

```
>>> s1
TrainingKnownSample(sepal_length=5.1, sepal_width=3.5,
petal_length=1.4, petal_width=0.2, species='Iris-setosa')

# This is undesirable...
>>> s1.classification = "wrong"
>>> s1
TrainingKnownSample(sepal_length=5.1, sepal_width=3.5,
petal_length=1.4, petal_width=0.2, species='Iris-setosa')
>>> s1.classification
'wrong'
```

Generally, Python doesn't stop us from creating a new attribute, like `classification`, in an object. This behavior could be the source of hidden bugs. (A good unit test will often expose these bugs.) Note the additional attribute is not reflected in the `__repr__()` method processing or `__eq__()` method comparisons for this class. It's not a serious problem. In later sections, we'll address it using frozen dataclasses as well as the `typing.NamedTuple` class.

The remaining classes in our model don't enjoy the same huge benefit from being implemented as dataclasses as the `Sample` classes did. When a class has a lot of attributes, and few methods, then the `@dataclass` definition is a big help.

Another class to benefit the most from the `@dataclass` treatment is the `Hyperparameter` class. Here's the first part of the definition, with the method body omitted:

```
@dataclass
class Hyperparameter:
    """A specific tuning parameter set with k and a distance
algorithm"""

    k: int
    algorithm: Distance
    data: weakref.ReferenceType["TrainingData"]

    def classify(self, sample: Sample) -> str:
        """The k-NN algorithm"""
        ...
```

This reveals an interesting feature that is made available when we use `from __future__ import annotations`. Specifically, the value of `weakref.ReferenceType["TrainingData"]` has two distinct goals:

- The *mypy* tool uses this to check type references. We must provide a qualifier, `weakref.ReferenceType["TrainingData"]`. This uses a string as a forward reference to the yet-undefined `TrainingData` class.
- When evaluated at runtime by the `@dataclass` decorator to build a class definition, the additional type qualifier isn't used.

We've omitted the details of the `classify()` method. We'll examine some alternative implementations in *Chapter 10, The Iterator Pattern*.

We haven't seen all the features of dataclasses. In the next section, we'll freeze them to help spot the kind of bug where a piece of training data is used for testing purposes.

Frozen dataclasses

The general case for dataclasses is to create mutable objects. The state of an object can be changed by assigning new values to the attributes. This isn't always a desirable feature, and we can make a dataclass immutable.

We can describe the UML diagram of the design by adding a stereotype of «Frozen». This notation can help to remind us of the implementation choice of making the object immutable. We must also respect an important rule of frozen dataclasses: an extension via inheritance must also be frozen.

The definition of the frozen `Sample` objects must be kept separate from the mutable objects that are part of processing an unknown or testing sample. This splits our design into two families of classes:

- A small hierarchy of immutable classes, specifically `Sample` and `KnownSample`
- Some associated classes that leverage these frozen classes

The related classes for testing samples, training samples, and unknown samples form a loose collection of classes with nearly identical methods and attributes. We can call this a "paddling" of related classes. This comes from the duck typing rule: "When I see a bird that walks like a duck and quacks like a duck, I call that bird a duck." Objects created from classes with the same attributes and methods are interchangeable, even though they lack a common abstract superclass.

We can describe this revised design with a diagram like this:

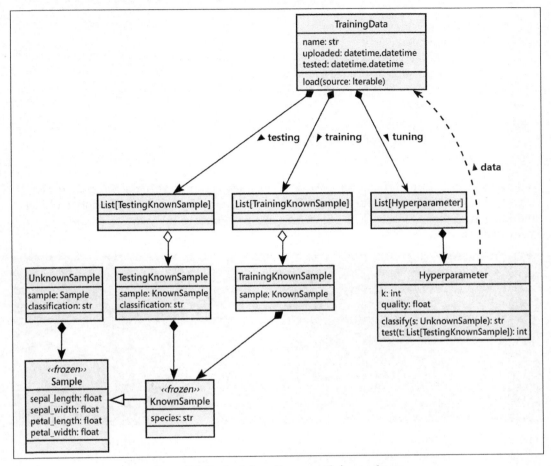

Figure 7.3: Revised class diagram with frozen classes

Here's the change to the Sample class hierarchy. It's relatively minor and easy to overlook the frozen=True in a few places:

```
@dataclass(frozen=True)
class Sample:
    sepal_length: float
    sepal_width: float
    petal_length: float
    petal_width: float


@dataclass(frozen=True)
class KnownSample(Sample):
```

```
        species: str

    @dataclass
    class TestingKnownSample:
        sample: KnownSample
        classification: Optional[str] = None

    @dataclass(frozen=True)
    class TrainingKnownSample:
        """Cannot be classified."""
        sample: KnownSample
```

When we create an instance of a `TrainingKnownSample` or `TestingKnownSample`, we have to respect the composition of these objects: there's a frozen `KnownSample` object inside each of these classes. The following example shows one way to create a composite object.

```
>>> from model_f import TrainingKnownSample, KnownSample
>>> s1 = TrainingKnownSample(
...     sample=KnownSample(
...         sepal_length=5.1, sepal_width=3.5,
...         petal_length=1.4, petal_width=0.2, species="Iris-setosa"
...     )
... )
>>> s1
TrainingKnownSample(sample=KnownSample(sepal_length=5.1, sepal_width=3.5,
petal_length=1.4, petal_width=0.2, species='Iris-setosa'))
```

This nested construction of a `TrainingKnownSample` instance containing a `KnownSample` object is explicit. It exposes the immutable `KnownSample` object.

The frozen design has a very pleasant consequence for detecting subtle bugs. The following example shows the exception raised by improper use of a `TrainingKnownSample`:

```
>>> s1.classification = "wrong"
Traceback (most recent call last):
... details omitted
dataclasses.FrozenInstanceError: cannot assign to field
'classification'
```

We can't accidentally introduce a bug that changes a training instance.

We get one more bonus feature that makes it easier to spot duplicates when allocating instances to the training set. The frozen versions of the Sample (and KnownSample) classes produce a consistent hash() value. This makes it easier to locate duplicate values by examining the subset of items with a common hash value.

Appropriate use of @dataclass and @dataclass(frozen=True) can be a big help in implementing object-oriented Python. These definitions provide a rich set of features with minimal code.

One other technique available to us is similar to the frozen dataclass, the typing.NamedTuple. We'll look at this next.

NamedTuple classes

Using typing.NamedTuple is somewhat similar to using @dataclass(frozen=True). There are some significant differences in the implementation details, however. In particular, the typing.NamedTuple class does not support inheritance in the most obvious way. This leads us to a design based around composition of objects in the Sample class hierarchy. With inheritance, we're often extending a base class to add features. With composition, we're often building multi-part objects of several different classes.

Here's the definition of Sample as NamedTuple. It looks similar to the @dataclass definition. The definition of KnownSample, however, must change dramatically:

```
class Sample(NamedTuple):
    sepal_length: float
    sepal_width: float
    petal_length: float
    petal_width: float


class KnownSample(NamedTuple):
    sample: Sample
    species: str
```

The KnownSample class is a composite, built from a Sample instance, plus the species assigned when the data was loaded initially. Since these are both subclasses of typing.NamedTuple, the values are immutable.

We've shifted from inheritance to composition in our design. Here are the two concepts, side by side:

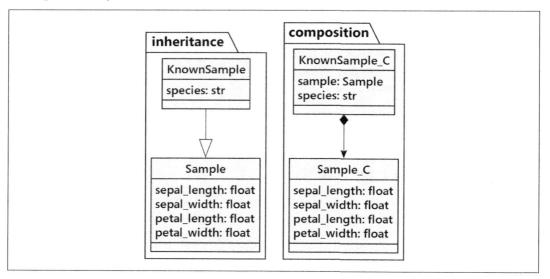

Figure 7.4: Inheritance-based versus composition-based class designs

The differences can be easy to overlook in the diagram:

- Using an **inheritance-focused** design, a KnownSample instance is a Sample instance. It has five attributes: all four attributes inherited from the Sample class plus one attribute unique to the KnownSample subclass.

- Using a **composition-focused** design, a KnownSample_C instance is composed of a Sample instance and a species classification. It has two attributes.

As we've seen, both designs will work. The choice is difficult and often revolves around the number and the complexity of the methods that are inherited from the superclass. In this example, there are no methods of importance to the application defined in the Sample class.

The inheritance versus composition design decision represents a difficult choice with no single, right answer. The decision is often helped by a nuanced understanding of whether a subclass truly is a member of the superclass or not. Metaphorically, we often ask if an Apple is a Fruit to help understand narrower subclasses and generic superclasses. The problem we have is that an Apple can also be a Dessert, confounding what seemed to be a simple decision with additional details.

Don't forget, an Apple (as applesauce) may be part of the Main Course, also. This kind of complication can make an "is-a" question harder to answer. In our case, the "is-a" relationship between samples, known samples, unknown samples, testing, and training samples may not be the best path forward. We seem to have multiple roles (i.e., testing, training, to-be-classified) that are associated with each sample, and there may only be two subclasses of Sample, known and unknown.

The TestingKnownSample and TrainingKnownSample class definitions follow the duck typing rule. They have similar attributes and can be used interchangeably in many cases.

```python
class TestingKnownSample:
    def __init__(
        self, sample: KnownSample, classification: Optional[str] = None
    ) -> None:
        self.sample = sample
        self.classification = classification

    def __repr__(self) -> str:
        return (
            f"{self.__class__.__name__}(sample={self.sample!r},"
            f"classification={self.classification!r})"
        )

class TrainingKnownSample(NamedTuple):
    sample: KnownSample
```

In this case, both TestingKnownSample and TrainingKnownSample are composite objects that contain a KnownSample object. The primary difference is the presence (or absence) of an additional attribute, the classification value.

Here's an example of creating a TrainingKnownSample and trying (erroneously) to set the classification:

```python
>>> from model_t import TrainingKnownSample, KnownSample, Sample
>>> s1 = TrainingKnownSample(
...     sample=KnownSample(
...         sample=Sample(sepal_length=5.1, sepal_width=3.5,
...         petal_length=1.4, petal_width=0.2),
...         species="Iris-setosa"
...     ),
... )
>>> s1
TrainingKnownSample(sample=KnownSample(sample=Sample(sepal_length=5.1,
sepal_width=3.5, petal_length=1.4, petal_width=0.2), species='Iris-
setosa'))
```

```
>>> s1.classification = "wrong"
Traceback (most recent call last):
...
AttributeError: 'TrainingKnownSample' object has no attribute
'classification'
```

The code reflects the composite-of-composite design. A TrainingKnownSample instance contains a KnownSample object, which contains a Sample object. The example shows that we cannot add a new attribute to a TrainingKnownSample instance.

Conclusion

Up to now, we've seen a total of four ways to address object-oriented design and implementation.

- In previous chapters, we've looked at creating objects "from scratch," writing all the method definitions ourselves. We've emphasized inheritance among the classes in the Sample class hierarchy.

- In this chapter, we've seen a stateful class definition using @dataclass. This supports inheritance among the classes in the Sample class hierarchy.

- We've also seen a stateless (or immutable) definition using @dataclass(frozen=True). This tends to discourage some aspects of inheritance and favor composition.

- Finally, we've looked at stateless (or immutable) definitions using NamedTuple. This must be designed using composition. This preliminary overview of these classes makes the design seem quite simple. We'll return to this in *Chapter 8, The Intersection of Object-Oriented and Functional Programming*.

We have a lot of flexibility in Python. It's important to look at the choices from the viewpoint of our future self trying to add or alter features. It helps to follow the SOLID design principles and focus on Single Responsibility and Interface Segregation to isolate and encapsulate our class definitions.

Recall

We've explored a variety of built-in Python data structures in this chapter. Python lets us do a great deal of object-oriented programming without the overheads of numerous, potentially confusing, class definitions. We can rely on a number of built-in classes where they fit our problem.

In this chapter, we looked at the following:

- Tuples and named tuples let us leverage a simple collection of attributes. We can extend the `NamedTuple` definition to add methods when those are necessary.
- Dataclasses provide sophisticated collections of attributes. A variety of methods can be provided for us, simplifying the code we need to write.
- Dictionaries are an essential feature, used widely in Python. There are many places where keys are associated with values. The syntax for using the built-in dictionary class makes it easy to use.
- Lists and sets are also first-class parts of Python; our applications can make use of these.
- We also looked at three types of queues. These are more specialized structures with more focused patterns of access than a generic list object. The idea of specialization and narrowing the domain of features can lead to performance improvements, also, making the concept widely applicable.

Additionally, in the case study, we looked at ways to use these built-in classes to define our data samples used for testing and training.

Exercises

The best way to learn how to choose the correct data structure is to do it wrong a few times (intentionally or accidentally!). Take some code you've recently written, or write some new code that uses a list. Try rewriting it using some different data structures. Which ones make more sense? Which ones don't? Which have the most elegant code?

Try this with a few different pairs of data structures. You can look at examples you've done for previous chapter exercises. Are there objects with methods where you could have used dataclasses, `namedtuple`, or `dict` instead? Attempt both and see. Are there dictionaries that could have been sets because you don't really access the values? Do you have lists that check for duplicates? Would a set suffice? Or maybe several sets? Would one of the queue implementations be more efficient? Is it useful to restrict the API to the top of a stack rather than allowing random access to the list?

Have you written any container objects recently that you could improve by inheriting a built-in and overriding some of the *special* double-underscore methods? You may have to do some research (using `dir` and `help`, or the Python library reference) to find out which methods need overriding.

Are you sure inheritance is the correct tool to apply; could a composition-based solution be more effective? Try both (if it's possible) before you decide. Try to find different situations where each method is better than the other.

If you were familiar with the various Python data structures and their uses before you started this chapter, you may have been bored. But if that is the case, there's a good chance you use data structures too much! Look at some of your old code and rewrite it to use more self-made classes. Carefully consider the alternatives and try them all out; which one makes for the most readable and maintainable system?

The MultiItem example in this section started with a clunky-looking __lt__() method. The second version had a slightly nicer __eq__() method. Rewrite __lt__() to follow the design pattern of __eq__().

The bigger problem with the original class design was trying to handle the variety of subtypes and their optional fields. The presence of an optional attribute is a suggestion that – perhaps – there are distinct classes struggling to separate from each other. What happens if we distinguish between two closely related but distinct classes: LocalItem (which uses timestamp) and RemoteItem (which uses created_date). We can define a common type hint as a Union[LocalItem, RemoteItem]. If each class has a property like creation_datetime that computes a datetime.datetime object, would processing be simpler? Build the two classes; create some test data. How does it look to separate the two subtypes?

Always critically evaluate your code and design decisions. Make a habit of reviewing old code and take note of whether your understanding of *good design* has changed since you wrote it. Software design has a large aesthetic component, and like artists with oil on canvas, we all have to find the style that suits us best.

Summary

We've covered several built-in data structures and attempted to understand how to choose one for specific applications. Sometimes, the best thing we can do is create a new class of objects, but often, one of the built-ins provides exactly what we need. When it doesn't, we can always use inheritance or composition to adapt them to our use cases. We can even override special methods to completely change the behavior of built-in syntaxes.

In the next chapter, we'll discuss how to integrate the object-oriented and not-so-object-oriented aspects of Python. Along the way, we'll discover that it's more object-oriented than it looks at first sight!

8

The Intersection of Object-Oriented and Functional Programming

There are many aspects of Python that appear more reminiscent of structural or functional programming than object-oriented programming. Although object-oriented programming has been the most visible paradigm of the past two decades, the old models have seen a recent resurgence. As with Python's data structures, most of these tools are syntactic sugar over an underlying object-oriented implementation; we can think of them as a further abstraction layer built on top of the (already abstracted) object-oriented paradigm. In this chapter, we'll be covering a grab bag of Python features that are not strictly object-oriented:

- Built-in functions that take care of common tasks in one call
- An alternative to method overloading
- Functions as objects
- File I/O and context managers

The case study in this chapter will revisit some of the essential algorithms of *k*-nearest neighbor classification. We'll look at how we can use functions instead of classes with methods. For parts of the application, separating algorithms from a class definition can provide some flexibility.

We'll start this chapter by looking at some of Python's built-in functions. Some of these are closely related to class definitions, allowing us to use a functional style of programming with the underlying complex objects.

Python built-in functions

There are numerous functions in Python that perform a task or calculate a result on certain types of objects without being methods on the underlying class. They usually abstract common calculations that apply to multiple types of classes. This is duck typing at its best; these functions accept objects that have certain attributes or methods, and are able to perform generic operations using those methods. We've used many of the built-in functions already, but let's quickly go through the important ones and pick up a few neat tricks along the way.

The len() function

One simple example of functions that are related to object methods is the len() function, which returns the number of items in some kind of container object, such as a dictionary or list. You've seen it before, demonstrated as follows:

```
>>> len([1, 2, 3, 4])
4
```

You may wonder why these objects don't have a length property instead of having to call a function on them. Technically, they do. Most objects that len() will apply to have a method called __len__() that returns the same value. So len(myobj) seems to call myobj.__len__().

Why should we use the len() function instead of the __len__() method? Obviously, __len__() is a special double-underscore method, suggesting that we shouldn't call it directly. There must be an explanation for this. The Python developers don't make such design decisions lightly.

The main reason is efficiency. When we call the __len__() method of an object, the object has to look the method up in its namespace, and, if the special __getattribute__() method (which is called every time an attribute or method on an object is accessed) is defined on that object, it has to be called as well. Furthermore, the __getattribute__() method may have been written to do something clever, for example, refusing to give us access to special methods such as __len__()! The len() function doesn't encounter any of this. It actually calls the __len__() method on the underlying class, so len(myobj) maps to MyObj.__len__(myobj).

Another reason is maintainability. In the future, Python developers may want to change len() so that it can calculate the length of objects that don't have __len__(), for example, by counting the number of items returned in an iterator. They'll only have to change one function instead of countless __len__() methods in many objects across the board.

The functional style, len(myobj), is described by some as more readable than the alternative method style, myobj.len(). Some debate the inconsistency of this syntax, but others prefer it for those few common operations that are applied to a wide number of collection types.

Another, sometimes overlooked, reason for len() being an external function is backward compatibility. This is often cited in articles as *for historical reasons*, which can be a mildly dismissive way of saying a mistake was made long ago and we're stuck with it. Strictly speaking, len() isn't a mistake; it's a design decision that has stood the test of time and has some benefits.

The reversed() function

The reversed() function takes any sequence as input and returns a copy of that sequence in reverse order. It is normally used in for statements when we want to iterate over items from back to front.

Similar to the len() function, reversed() calls the __reversed__() method on the class for the parameter. If that method does not exist, reversed builds the reversed sequence itself using calls to __len__() and __getitem__(), which are used to define a sequence. We only need to override __reversed__() if we want to somehow customize or optimize the process, as demonstrated in the following code:

```
>>> class CustomSequence:
...     def __init__(self, args):
...         self._list = args
...     def __len__(self):
...         return 5
...     def __getitem__(self, index):
...         return f"x{index}"

>>> class FunkyBackwards(list):
...     def __reversed__(self):
...         return "BACKWARDS!"
```

Let's exercise this function on three different kinds of lists:

```
>>> generic = [1, 2, 3, 4, 5]
>>> custom = CustomSequence([6, 7, 8, 9, 10])
>>> funkadelic = FunkyBackwards([11, 12, 13, 14, 15])

>>> for sequence in generic, custom, funkadelic:
...     print(f"{sequence.__class__.__name__}: ", end="")
...     for item in reversed(sequence):
...         print(f"{item}, ", end="")
...     print()
list: 5, 4, 3, 2, 1,
CustomSequence: x4, x3, x2, x1, x0,
FunkyBackwards: B, A, C, K, W, A, R, D, S, !,
```

The for statements at the end print reversed versions of a generic list object, and instances of the CustomSequence class and the FunkyBackwards class. The output shows that reversed works on all three of them, but has very different results.

When we reverse CustomSequence, the __getitem__() method is called for each item, which just inserts an x before the index. For FunkyBackwards, the __reversed__() method returns a string, each character of which is output individually in the for loop.

> The CustomSequence class is incomplete. It doesn't define a proper version of __iter__(), so a forward for loop over them will never end. This is the subject of *Chapter 10, The Iterator Pattern*.

The enumerate() function

Sometimes, when we're examining items in a container with a for statement, we want access to the index (the current position in the container) of the current item being processed. The for statement doesn't provide us with indexes, but the enumerate() function gives us something better: it creates a sequence of tuples, where the first object in each tuple is the index and the second is the original item.

This is useful because it assigns an index number. It works well for sets or dictionaries where there isn't an inherent index order to the values. It also works for text files, which have an implied line number. Consider some simple code that outputs each of the lines in a file with the associated line numbers:

```
>>> from pathlib import Path
>>> with Path("docs/sample_data.md").open() as source:
...     for index, line in enumerate(source, start=1):
...         print(f"{index:3d}: {line.rstrip()}")
```

Running this shows the following:

```
1: # Python 3 Object-Oriented Programming
2:
3: Chapter 8. The Intersection of Object-Oriented and Functional
Programming
4:
5: Some sample data to show how the `enumerate()` function works.
```

The enumerate function is an iterable: it returns a sequence of tuples. Our for statement splits each tuple into two values, and the print() function formats them together. We used the optional start=1 on the enumerate function to provide a convention 1-based sequence of line numbers.

We've only touched on a few of the more important Python built-in functions. As you can see, many of them call into object-oriented concepts, while others subscribe to purely functional or procedural paradigms. There are numerous others in the standard library; some of the more interesting ones include the following:

- abs(), str(), repr(), pow(), and divmod() map directly to the special methods __abs__(), __str__(), __repr__(), __pow__(), and __divmod__()
- bytes(), format(), hash(), and bool() also map directly to the special methods __bytes__(), __format__(), __hash__(), and __bool__()

And several more. *Section 3.3, Special Methods Names* of *The Python Language Reference*, provides the details of these mappings. Other interesting built-in functions include the following:

- all() and any(), which accept an iterable object and return True if all, or any, of the items evaluate to true (such as a non-empty string or list, a non-zero number, an object that is not None, or the literal True).
- eval(), exec(), and compile(), which execute string as code inside the interpreter. Be careful with these ones; they are not safe, so don't execute code an unknown user has supplied to you (in general, assume all unknown users are malicious, foolish, or both).
- hasattr(), getattr(), setattr(), and delattr(), which allow attributes on an object to be manipulated by their string names.

- `zip()`, which takes two or more sequences and returns a new sequence of tuples, where each tuple contains a single value from each sequence.

- And many more! See the interpreter help documentation for each of the functions listed in `help("builtins")`.

What's central is avoiding a narrow viewpoint that an object-oriented programming language must always use `object.method()` syntax for everything. Python strives for readability, and a simple `len(collection)` seems more clear than the slightly more consistent *potential* alternative, `collection.len()`.

An alternative to method overloading

One prominent feature of many object-oriented programming languages is a tool called **method overloading**. Method overloading refers to having multiple methods with the same name that accept different sets of parameters. In statically typed languages, this is useful if we want to have a method that accepts either an integer or a string, for example. In non-object-oriented languages, we might need two functions, called add_s and add_i, to accommodate such situations. In statically typed object-oriented languages, we'd need two methods, both called add, one that accepts strings, and one that accepts integers.

In Python, we've already seen that we only need one method, which accepts any type of object. It may have to do some testing on the object type (for example, if it is a string, convert it to an integer), but only one method is required.

The type hints for a parameter that can take on multiple types can become rather complex. We'll often have to use a `typing.Union` hint to show that a parameter can have values from `Union[int, str]`. This definition clarifies the alternatives so *mypy* can confirm that we're using the overloaded function properly.

We have to distinguish between two varieties of overloading here:

- Overloading parameters to allow alternative types using `Union[...]` hints
- Overloading the method by using more complex patterns of parameters

For example, an email message method might come in two versions, one of which accepts a parameter for the *from* email address. The other method might look up a default *from* email address instead. Some languages force us to write multiple methods with the same name and different parameter patterns. Python doesn't permit multiple definitions of methods with the same name, but it does provide a different, equally flexible way to specify variant parameters.

We've seen some of the possible ways to send argument values to methods and functions in previous examples, but now we'll cover all the details. The simplest function accepts no parameters. We probably don't need an example, but here's one for completeness:

```
>>> def no_params():
...     return "Hello, world!"
```

And here's how it's called:

```
>>> no_params()
'Hello, world!'
```

In this case, since we're working interactively, we omitted the type hint. A function that does accept parameters will provide the names of those parameter names in a comma-separated list. Only the name of each parameter needs to be supplied. A type hint, however, is always helpful. The hints follow the names, separated by a colon, :.

When calling the function, the values for the positional parameters must be specified in order, and none can be missed or skipped. This is the most common way in which we've specified parameters in our previous examples:

```
>>> def mandatory_params(x, y, z):
...     return f"{x=}, {y=}, {z=}"
```

To call it, type the following:

```
>>> a_variable = 42
>>> mandatory_params("a string", a_variable, True)
```

Python code is generic with respect to type. This means that any type of object can be passed as an argument value: an object, a container, a primitive, even functions and classes. The preceding call shows a hardcoded string, the value of a variable, and a Boolean passed into the function.

Generally, our applications are not completely generic. That's why we often provide type hints to narrow the domain of possible values. In the rare case when we're writing something truly generic, we can use the typing.Any hint to tell *mypy* that we really mean that any object is usable:

```
>>> from typing import Any
>>> def mandatory_params(x: Any, y: Any, z: Any) -> str:
...     return f"{x=}, {y=}, {z=}"
```

We can use *mypy* to locate code like this using the `--disallow-any-expr` option. This can flag lines that may be in need of some clarity on what types are really important.

Default values for parameters

If we want to make a parameter's value optional, we can specify a default value. Some other languages (Java, for example) require a second method with a different set of parameters. In Python, we define a single method; we can provide a default value for a parameter using an equals sign. If the calling code does not supply an argument value for the parameter, it will be assigned the given default value. This means calling code can still choose to override the default by passing in a different value. If a value of None is used as the default for optional parameter values, the typing module lets us describe this using the Optional type hint.

Here's a function definition with default parameter definitions:

```
def latitude_dms(
    deg: float, min: float, sec: float = 0.0, dir: Optional[str] = None
) -> str:
    if dir is None:
        dir = "N"
    return f"{deg:02.0f}° {min+sec/60:05.3f}{dir}"
```

The first two parameters are mandatory and must be provided. The last two parameters have default argument values and can be omitted.

There are several ways we can call this function. We can supply all argument values in order, as though all the parameters were positional, as can be seen in the following:

```
>>> latitude_dms(36, 51, 2.9, "N")
'36° 51.048N'
```

Alternatively, we can supply just the mandatory argument values in order, allowing one of the keyword parameters (sec) to use a default value, and providing a keyword argument for the dir parameter:

```
>>> latitude_dms(38, 58, dir="N")
'38° 58.000N'
```

We've used equals sign syntax when calling a function to skip default values that we aren't interested in.

Surprisingly, we can even use the equals sign syntax to mix up the order of arguments for the positional parameters, so long as all the parameters are given an argument value:

```
>>> latitude_dms(38, 19, dir="N", sec=7)
'38° 19.117N'
```

You may occasionally find it useful to make a *keyword-only* parameter. To use this, the argument value must be supplied as a keyword argument. You can do that by placing a * before all of the keyword-only parameters:

```
def kw_only(
    x: Any, y: str = "defaultkw", *, a: bool, b: str = "only"
) -> str:
    return f"{x=}, {y=}, {a=}, {b=}"
```

This function has one positional parameter, x, and three keyword parameters, y, a, and b. The x and y parameters are both mandatory, but a can only be passed as a keyword argument. y and b are both optional with default values, but if b is supplied, it can only be a keyword argument.

This function fails if you don't pass a:

```
>>> kw_only('x')
Traceback (most recent call last):
  File "<stdin>", line 1, in <module>
TypeError: kw_only() missing 1 required keyword-only argument: 'a'
```

It also fails if you pass a as a positional argument:

```
>>> kw_only('x', 'y', 'a')
Traceback (most recent call last):
  File "<stdin>", line 1, in <module>
TypeError: kw_only() takes from 1 to 2 positional arguments but 3 were given
```

But you can pass a and b as keyword arguments:

```
>>> kw_only('x', a='a', b='b')
"x='x', y='defaultkw', a='a', b='b'"
```

We can also mark parameters as being supplied only by position. We do this by providing these names before a single / that separates the positional-only parameters from the more flexible parameters that follow.

```python
def pos_only(x: Any, y: str, /, z: Optional[Any] = None) -> str:
    return f"{x=}, {y=}, {z=}"
```

This function requires argument values for the x and y parameters be the first two, and named arguments for x and y are specifically not permitted. Here's what happens if we try:

```python
>>> pos_only(x=2, y="three")
Traceback (most recent call last):
  ...
  File "<doctest hint_examples.__test__.test_pos_only[0]>", line 1, in <module>
    pos_only(x=2, y="three")
TypeError: pos_only() got some positional-only arguments passed as keyword arguments: 'x, y'

>>> pos_only(2, "three")
"x=2, y='three', z=None"

>>> pos_only(2, "three", 3.14159)
"x=2, y='three', z=3.14159"
```

We must provide argument values for the first two parameters, x and y, positionally. The third parameter, z, can be provided positionally, or with a keyword.

We have three separate kinds of parameter possibilities:

- **Positional only**: These are handy in a few cases; see PEP 570 for examples: https://www.python.org/dev/peps/pep-0570.

- **Either positional or keyword**: This is the case for most parameters. The order is designed to be helpful, and keywords can be used for clarification. More than three positional parameters invites confusion, so a long list of positional parameters isn't a great idea.

- **Keyword only**: After the *, the argument values *must* have a keyword supplied. This can be helpful to make rarely used options more visible. It can help to think of keywords as keys to a dictionary.

Choosing how to call the method normally takes care of itself, depending on which values need to be supplied, and which can be left at their defaults. For simple methods with a few argument values, positional parameters are more or less expected. For complex methods with a lot of argument values, using keywords can help to clarify how things work.

Additional details on defaults

One thing to take note of with keyword arguments is that anything we provide as a default argument is evaluated exactly once when the function is first created, not when it is evaluated. This means we can't have dynamically generated default values. For example, the following code won't behave quite as expected:

```
number = 5

def funky_function(x: int = number) -> str:
    return f"{x=}, {number=}"
```

The default value for the x parameter is the current value *when the function is defined*. We can see that behavior when we try to evaluate this with different values for the number variable:

```
>>> funky_function(42)
'x=42, number=5'

>>> number = 7
>>> funky_function()
'x=5, number=5'
```

The first evaluation looks like our expectation; the default value is the original value. This is a coincidence. The second evaluation, after changing the global variable, number, shows that the function definition has a fixed value for the default – the variable is not re-evaluated.

To make this work, we'll often use None as a default value and assign the current value of a global variable within the body of the function:

```
def better_function(x: Optional[int] = None) -> str:
    if x is None:
        x = number
    return f"better: {x=}, {number=}"
```

This `better_function()` does not have a value for the `number` variable bound into the function definition. It uses the current value of a global `number` variable. Yes, this function is implicitly dependent on a global variable, and the docstring should explain that, ideally surrounded by flame emojis to make it clear to anyone reading it how the function's results may not be obviously idempotent.

A slightly more compact way to set a parameter value to an argument or a default looks like this:

```
def better_function_2(x: Optional[int] = None) -> str:
    x = number if x is None else x
    return f"better: {x=}, {number=}"
```

The `number if x is None else x` expression seems to make it clear that x will have the value of the global, `number`, or the argument value provided for x.

The "evaluation at definition time" can trip us up when working with mutable containers such as lists, sets, and dictionaries. It seems like a good design decision to make an empty list (or set or dictionary) as a default value for a parameter. We shouldn't do this because it will create only one instance of the mutable object, when the code is first constructed. This one object will be reused, demonstrated as follows:

```
from typing import List


def bad_default(tag: str, history: list[str] = []) -> list[str]:
    """ A Very Bad Design (VBD™)."""
    history.append(tag)
    return history
```

This is very bad design. We can try to create a history list, h, and append things to it. This seems to work. Spoiler alert: the default object is one specific mutable, `list`, that's shared:

```
>>> h = bad_default("tag1")
>>> h = bad_default("tag2", h)
>>> h
['tag1', 'tag2']

>>> h2 = bad_default("tag21")
>>> h2 = bad_default("tag22", h2)
>>> h2
['tag1', 'tag2', 'tag21', 'tag22']
```

Whoops, that's not quite what we expected! When we tried to create a second history list, h2, it was based on the one and only default value:

```
>>> h
['tag1', 'tag2', 'tag21', 'tag22']
>>> h is h2
True
```

The usual way to get around this is to make the default value None. We've seen this in previous examples, and this is a common approach:

```
def good_default(
        tag: str, history: Optional[list[str]] = None
) -> list[str]:
    history = [] if history is None else history
    history.append(tag)
    return history
```

This will build a fresh, empty list[str] object if no parameter was supplied. This is the best way to work with default values that are also mutable objects.

Variable argument lists

Default values alone do not allow us all the flexibility we might want. One thing that makes Python really slick is the ability to write methods that accept an arbitrary number of positional or keyword arguments without explicitly naming them. We can also pass arbitrary lists and dictionaries into such functions. In other languages, these are sometimes called variadic arguments, **varargs**.

For example, we could write a function to accept a link or list of URLs and download the web pages. The idea is to avoid the confusing-looking overhead of a singleton list when we only want one page downloaded. Instead of accepting a single value with a list of URLs, we can accept an arbitrary number of arguments, where each argument is a URL. We do this by defining one positional parameter to receive all the argument values. This parameter has to be last (among the positional parameters), and we'll decorate it with a * in the function definition, as follows:

```
from urllib.parse import urlparse
from pathlib import Path

def get_pages(*links: str) -> None:
    for link in links:
        url = urlparse(link)
        name = "index.html" if url.path in ("", "/") else url.path
```

```
        target = Path(url.netloc.replace(".", "_")) / name
        print(f"Create {target} from {link!r}")
        # etc.
```

The * in the *`links` parameter says, *I'll accept any number of arguments and put them all in a tuple named* `links`. If we supply only one argument, it will be a list with one element; if we supply no arguments, it will be an empty list. Thus, all these function calls are valid:

```
>>> get_pages()

>>> get_pages('https://www.archlinux.org')
Create www_archlinux_org/index.html from 'https://www.archlinux.org'

>>> get_pages('https://www.archlinux.org',
...         'https://dusty.phillips.codes',
...         'https://itmaybeahack.com'
... )
Create www_archlinux_org/index.html from 'https://www.archlinux.org'
Create dusty_phillips_codes/index.html from 'https://dusty.phillips.
codes'
Create itmaybeahack_com/index.html from 'https://itmaybeahack.com'
```

Note that our type hint suggested that all of the positional argument values are of the same type, `str`, in this example. This is a widespread expectation: the variable parameters feature is little more than syntactic sugar, saving us from writing a dumb-looking list. The alternative to one type for the variable parameter tuple is potentially confusing: why write a function expecting a complex collection of distinct types, but – somehow – not state this in the parameter definitions? Don't write that function.

We can also accept arbitrary keyword arguments. These arrive in the function as a dictionary. They are specified with two asterisks (as in **`kwargs`) in the function declaration. This tool is commonly used in configuration setups. The following class allows us to specify a set of options with default values:

```
from __future__ import annotations
from typing import Dict, Any

class Options(Dict[str, Any]):
    default_options: dict[str, Any] = {
        "port": 21,
        "host": "localhost",
```

```
        "username": None,
        "password": None,
        "debug": False,
    }

    def __init__(self, **kwargs: Any) -> None:
        super().__init__(self.default_options)
        self.update(kwargs)
```

This class leverages a feature of the __init__() method. We have a dictionary of default options, with the boring name of default_options, defined as part of the class. The __init__() method starts initializing this instance with the values from the class-level dictionary of defaults. We do that instead of modifying the dictionary directly, in case we instantiate two separate sets of options. (Remember, class-level variables are shared among all instances of the class.)

After having seeded the instance from the class-level source data, __init__() uses the update() method inherited from the superclass to change any non-default values to those supplied as keyword arguments. Because the value of kwargs is also a dictionary, the update() method handles the merge of default values with override values.

Here's a session demonstrating the class in action:

```
>>> options = Options(username="dusty", password="Hunter2",
...     debug=True)
>>> options['debug']
True
>>> options['port']
21
>>> options['username']
'dusty'
```

We're able to access our options instance using dictionary indexing syntax. The Options dictionary includes both default values and the ones we set using keyword arguments.

Note that the parent class is typing.Dict[str, Any], the class for a generic dictionary limited to strings for keys. When we initialize the default_options object, we can rely on the from __future__ import annotations statement and use dict[str, Any] to tell the *mypy* tool what to expect for this variable. The distinction is important: the class relies on typing.Dict as a superclass.

The variable needs a type hint, and we can use either the `typing.Dict` class or we can use the built-in `dict` class. We suggest using the `typing` module only when absolutely required, and using the built-in classes as much as possible.

In the preceding example, it's possible to pass arbitrary keyword arguments to the `Options` initializer to represent options that don't exist in the default dictionary. This can be handy when adding new features to an application. This can be bad when debugging a spelling mistake. Providing the "Port" option instead of the "port" option will lead to two similar-looking options where only one should have existed.

One way to limit the risk of spelling mistakes is to write an `update()` method that only replaces existing keys. This can prevent misspellings from creating problems. The solution is interesting and we'll leave it as an exercise for the reader.

Keyword arguments are also very useful when we need to accept arbitrary arguments to pass to a second function, but we don't know what those arguments will be. We saw this in action in *Chapter 3, When Objects Are Alike*, when we were building support for multiple inheritance.

We can, of course, combine the variable argument and variable keyword argument syntax in one function call, and we can use normal positional and default arguments as well. The following example is somewhat contrived, but demonstrates the four types of parameters in action:

```python
from __future__ import annotations
import contextlib
import os
import subprocess
import sys
from typing import TextIO
from pathlib import Path


def doctest_everything(
        output: TextIO,
        *directories: Path,
        verbose: bool = False,
        **stems: str
) -> None:
    def log(*args: Any, **kwargs: Any) -> None:
        if verbose:
            print(*args, **kwargs)

    with contextlib.redirect_stdout(output):
        for directory in directories:
```

```
            log(f"Searching {directory}")
            for path in directory.glob("**/*.md"):
                if any(
                        parent.stem == ".tox"
                        for parent in path.parents
                ):
                    continue
                log(
                    f"File {path.relative_to(directory)}, "
                    f"{path.stem=}"
                )
                if stems.get(path.stem, "").upper() == "SKIP":
                    log("Skipped")
                    continue
                options = []
                if stems.get(path.stem, "").upper() == "ELLIPSIS":
                    options += ["ELLIPSIS"]
                search_path = directory / "src"
                print(
                    f"cd '{Path.cwd()}'; "
                    f"PYTHONPATH='{search_path}' doctest '{path}' -v"
                )
                option_args = (
                    ["-o", ",".join(options)] if options else []
                )
                subprocess.run(
                    ["python3", "-m", "doctest", "-v"]
                        + option_args + [str(path)],
                    cwd=directory,
                    env={"PYTHONPATH": str(search_path)},
                )
```

This example processes an arbitrary list of directory paths to run the **doctest** tool on markdown files in those directories. Let's look at each parameter definition in detail:

- The first parameter, output, is an open file to which output will be written.
- The directories parameter will be given all non-keyword arguments. These should all be Path() objects.
- The keyword-only parameter, verbose, tells us whether to print information on each file processed.

- • Finally, we can supply any other keyword as the name of a file to process specially. Four names – output, directories, verbose, and stems – are effectively special filenames that can't be given special processing. Any other keyword argument will be collected into the stems dictionary, and these names will be singled out for special processing. Specifically, if a file stem is listed with a value of "SKIP", the file won't be tested. If there's a value of "ellipsis", then a special option flag will be provided to doctest.

We create an inner helper function, log(), which will print messages only if the verbose parameter has been set. This function keeps code readable by encapsulating this functionality in a single location.

The outermost with statement redirects all output normally sent to sys.stdout to the desired file. This lets us collect a single log from print() functions. The for statement examines all the positional argument values collected into the directories parameter. Each directory is examined with the glob() method to locate all *.md files in any subdirectory.

A file's *stem* is the name without its path or suffix. So ch_03/docs/examples.md has a stem of examples. If the stem was used as a keyword argument, the value of that argument provides additional details of what to do for files with that specific stem. For example, if we provide the keyword argument examples='SKIP', this will populate the **stems dictionary, and any file with a stem of examples will be skipped.

We use subprocess.run() because of the way doctest works out the local directory. When we want to run doctest in a number of different directories, it seems easiest to be sure that the current working directory (cwd) is set first, before we run doctest.

In common cases, this function could be called as follows:

```
doctest_everything(
    sys.stdout,
    Path.cwd() / "ch_02",
    Path.cwd() / "ch_03",
)
```

This command would locate all the *.md files in these two directories and run doctest. The output would appear on the console because we redirected sys.stdout back to sys.stdout. Very little output would be produced because the verbose parameter would have a default value of False.

If we want to collect detailed output, we can call it with the help of the following command:

```
doctest_log = Path("doctest.log")
with doctest_log.open('w') as log:
    doctest_everything(
        log,
        Path.cwd() / "ch_04",
        Path.cwd() / "ch_05",
        verbose=True
    )
```

This tests files in two directories and tells us what it's doing. Notice that it is impossible to specify verbose as a positional argument in this example; we must pass this as a keyword argument. Otherwise, Python would think it was another Path in the *directories list.

If we want to change the processing for a selected set of files in the list, we can pass additional keyword arguments, as follows:

```
doctest_everything(
    sys.stdout,
    Path.cwd() / "ch_02",
    Path.cwd() / "ch_03",
    examples="ELLIPSIS",
    examples_38="SKIP",
    case_study_2="SKIP",
    case_study_3="SKIP",
)
```

This will test two directories, but won't display any output, since we didn't specify verbose. This will apply the doctest --ellipsis option to any file with a step of examples. Similarly, any file with a stem of examples_38, case_study_2, or case_study_3, are skipped.

Because we can provide any name we choose, and they will all be collected into the value of the stems parameter, we can make use of this flexibility to match names of files in the directory structures. There are, of course, a number of limitations on Python identifiers that don't match operating system filenames, making this less than perfect. It does, however, show the amazing flexibility of Python function arguments.

Unpacking arguments

There's one more nifty trick involving positional and keyword parameters. We've used it in some of our previous examples, but it's never too late for an explanation. Given a list or dictionary of values, we can pass a sequence of values into a function as if they were normal positional or keyword arguments. Have a look at this code:

```
>>> def show_args(arg1, arg2, arg3="THREE"):
...     return f"{arg1=}, {arg2=}, {arg3=}"
```

The function accepts three parameters, one of which has a default value. But when we have a list of three argument values, we can use the * operator inside a function call to unpack it into the three arguments.

Here's what it looks like when we run it with *some_args to provide a three-element iterable:

```
>>> some_args = range(3)
>>> show_args(*some_args)
'arg1=0, arg2=1, arg3=2'
```

The value of *some_args has to match the positional parameter definition. Because there's a default value for arg3, making it optional, we can provide two or three values.

If we have a dictionary of arguments, we can use the ** syntax to unpack a dictionary to supply argument values for keyword parameters. It looks like this:

```
>>> more_args = {
...         "arg1": "ONE",
...         "arg2": "TWO"}
>>> show_args(**more_args)
"arg1='ONE', arg2='TWO', arg3='THREE'"
```

This is often useful when mapping information that has been collected from user input or from an outside source (for example, an internet page or a text file) and needs to be provided to a function or method call. Rather than decompose an external source of data into individual keyword parameters, we simply provide the keyword parameters from the dictionary keys. An expression like show_args(arg1=more_args['arg1'], arg2=more_args['arg2']) seems an error-prone way to match a parameter name with the dictionary key.

This unpacking syntax can be used in some areas outside of function calls, too. The Options class shown in the *Variable argument lists* section, earlier in this chapter, had an __init__() method that looked like this:

```
def __init__(self, **kwargs: Any) -> None:
    super().__init__(self.default_options)
    self.update(kwargs)
```

An even more succinct way to do this would be to unpack the two dictionaries like this:

```
def __init__(self, **kwargs: Any) -> None:
    super().__init__({**self.default_options, **kwargs})
```

The expression {**self.default_options, **kwargs} merges dictionaries by unpacking each dictionary into keyword arguments and then assembling a final dictionary from them. Because the dictionaries are unpacked in order from left to right, the resulting dictionary will contain all the default options, with any of the kwarg options replacing some of the keys. Here's an example:

```
>>> x = {'a': 1, 'b': 2}
>>> y = {'b': 11, 'c': 3}
>>> z = {**x, **y}
>>> z
{'a': 1, 'b': 11, 'c': 3}
```

This dictionary unpacking is a handy consequence of the way the ** operator transforms a dictionary into named parameters for a function call.

After looking at sophisticated ways we can provide argument values to functions, we need to look at functions a little more broadly. Python considers functions as one kind of "callable" object. This means functions are objects, and higher-order functions can accept functions as argument values and return functions as results.

Functions are objects, too

There are numerous situations where we'd like to pass around a small object that is simply called to perform an action. In essence, we'd like an object that is a callable function. This is most frequently done in event-driven programming, such as graphical toolkits or asynchronous servers; we'll see some design patterns that use it in *Chapter 11, Common Design Patterns*, and *Chapter 12, Advanced Design Patterns*.

In Python, we don't need to wrap such methods in a class definition because functions are already objects! We can set attributes on functions (though this isn't a common activity), and we can pass them around to be called at a later date. They even have a few special properties that can be accessed directly.

Here's yet another contrived example, sometimes used as an interview question:

```
>>> def fizz(x: int) -> bool:
...     return x % 3 == 0
>>> def buzz(x: int) -> bool:
...     return x % 5 == 0
>>> def name_or_number(
...         number: int, *tests: Callable[[int], bool]) -> None:
...     for t in tests:
...         if t(number):
...             return t.__name__
...     return str(number)
>>> for i in range(1, 11):
...     print(name_or_number(i, fizz, buzz))
```

The fizz() and buzz() functions check to see whether their parameter, x, is an exact multiple of another number. This relies on the definition of the modulo operator: if x is a multiple of 3, then 3 divides x with no remainder. Sometimes they say $x \equiv 0 \ (mod \ 3)$ in the math books. In Python, we say x % 3 == 0.

The name_or_number() function uses any number of test functions, provided as the tests parameter value. The for statement assigns each function in the tests collection to a variable, t, then evaluates the variable with the number parameter's value. If the function's value is true, then the result is the function's name.

Here's how this function looks when we apply it to a number and another function:

```
>>> name_or_number(1, fizz)
'1'
>>> name_or_number(3, fizz)
'fizz'
>>> name_or_number(5, fizz)
'5'
```

In each case, the value of the tests parameter is (fizz,) a tuple that contains only the fizz function. The name_or_number() function evaluates t(number), where t is the fizz() function. When fizz(number) is true, the value returned is the value of the function's __name__ attribute – the 'fizz' string. Function names are available at runtime as an attribute of the function.

What if we provide multiple functions? Each is applied to the number until one is true:

```
>>> name_or_number(5, fizz, buzz)
'buzz'
```

This is, by the way, not completely correct. What should happen for a number like 15? Is it fizz or buzz or both? Because it's both, some work needs to be done in the name_or_number() function to collect **all** the names of all the true functions. That sounds like it would make a good exercise.

We can add to our list of special functions. We might define bazz() to be true for multiples of seven. This, too, sounds like a good exercise.

If we run this code, we can see that we were able to pass two different functions into our name_or_number() function, and get different output for each one:

```
>>> for i in range(1, 11):
...     print(name_or_number(i, fizz, buzz))
1
2
fizz
4
buzz
fizz
7
8
fizz
buzz
```

We could apply our functions to an argument value using t(number). We were able to get the value of the function's __name__ attribute using t.__name__.

Function objects and callbacks

The fact that functions are top-level objects is most often used to pass them around to be executed at a later date, for example, when a certain condition has been satisfied. Callbacks are common as part of building a user interface: when the user clicks on something, the framework can call a function so the application code can create a visual response. For very long-running tasks, like file transfers, it is often helpful for the transfer library to call back to the application with status on the number of bytes transferred so far – this makes it possible to display status thermometers to show status.

Let's build an event-driven timer using callbacks so that things will happen at scheduled intervals. This can be handy for an **IoT** (**Internet of Things**) application built on a small CircuitPython or MicroPython device. We'll break this down into two parts: a task, and a scheduler that executes the function object stored in the task:

```python
from __future__ import annotations
import heapq
import time
from typing import Callable, Any, List, Optional
from dataclasses import dataclass, field


Callback = Callable[[int], None]


@dataclass(frozen=True, order=True)
class Task:
    scheduled: int
    callback: Callback = field(compare=False)
    delay: int = field(default=0, compare=False)
    limit: int = field(default=1, compare=False)

    def repeat(self, current_time: int) -> Optional["Task"]:
        if self.delay > 0 and self.limit > 2:
            return Task(
                current_time + self.delay,
                cast(Callback, self.callback),  # type: ignore [misc]
                self.delay,
                self.limit - 1,
            )
        elif self.delay > 0 and self.limit == 2:
            return Task(
                current_time + self.delay,
                cast(Callback, self.callback),  # type: ignore [misc]
            )
        else:
            return None
```

The Task class definition has two mandatory fields and two optional fields. The mandatory fields, scheduled and callback, provide a scheduled time to do something and a callback function, the thing to be done at the scheduled time. The scheduled time has an int type hint; the time module can use floating-point time, for super-accurate operations. We're going to ignore these details. Also, the *mypy* tool is well aware that integers can be coerced to floating-point numbers, so we don't have to be super-fussy-precise about numeric types.

The callback has a hint of `Callable[[int], None]`. This summarizes what the function definition should look like. A callback function definition should look like `def some_name(an_arg: int) -> None:`. If it doesn't match, *mypy* will alert us to the potential mismatch between our callback function definition and the contract specified by the type hint.

The `repeat()` method can return a task for those tasks that might repeat. It computes a new time for the task, provides the reference to the original function object, and may provide a subsequent delay and a changed limit. The changed limit will count the number of repetitions toward zero, giving us a defined upper limit on processing; it's always nice to be sure that iteration will terminate.

The `# type: ignore [misc]` comments are there because there's a feature here that's confusing to *mypy*. When we use code like `self.callback` or `someTask.callback()`, it looks like an ordinary method. The code in the `Scheduler` class is not going to use it as an ordinary method; it will be used as a reference to a separate function defined entirely outside of the class. The assumption wired into Python is this: a `Callable` attribute must be a method, and that means the method must have a `"self"` variable. In this case, the callable object is a separate function. The easiest way to refute the assumption is by silencing *mypy*'s checking of this line of code. An alternative is to assign `self.callback` to another non-`self` variable to make it look like it's an external function.

Here's the overall `Scheduler` class that uses these `Task` objects and their associated callback functions:

```
class Scheduler:
    def __init__(self) -> None:
        self.tasks: List[Task] = []

    def enter(
        self,
        after: int,
        task: Callback,
        delay: int = 0,
        limit: int = 1,
    ) -> None:
        new_task = Task(after, task, delay, limit)
        heapq.heappush(self.tasks, new_task)

    def run(self) -> None:
        current_time = 0
        while self.tasks:
```

```
        next_task = heapq.heappop(self.tasks)
        if (delay := next_task.scheduled - current_time) > 0:
            time.sleep(next_task.scheduled - current_time)
        current_time = next_task.scheduled
        next_task.callback(current_time)  # type: ignore [misc]
        if again := next_task.repeat(current_time):
            heapq.heappush(self.tasks, again)
```

The central feature of the Scheduler class is a heap queue, a List of Task objects kept in a specific order. We mentioned the heap queue in the *Three types of queues* section of *Chapter 7, Python Data Structures*, noting that the priority ordering made it inappropriate for that use case. Here, however, the heap data structure makes use of the flexibility of a list to keep items in order without the overhead of a complete sort of the entire list. In this case, we want to keep items in order by the time they're required to be executed: "first things first" order. When we push something to a heap queue, it's inserted so the time order will be maintained. When we pop the next thing from the queue, the heap may be adjusted to keep the first things at the front of the queue.

The Scheduler class provides an enter() method to add a new task to the queue. This method accepts a delay parameter representing the interval to wait before executing the callback task, and the task function itself, a function to be executed at the correct time. This task function should fit the type hint of Callback, defined above.

There are no runtime checks to ensure the callback function really does meet the type hint. It's only checked by *mypy*. More importantly, the after, delay, and limit parameters should have some validation checks. For example, a negative value of after or delay should raise a ValueError exception. There's a special method name, __post_init__(), that a dataclass can use for validation. This is invoked after __init__() and can be used for other initialization, pre-computing derived values, or validating that the combination of values is sensible.

The run() method removes items from the queue in order by the time they're supposed to be performed. If we're at (or past) the required time, then the value computed for delay will be zero or negative, and we don't need to wait; we can perform the callback immediately. If we're before the required time, then we need to sleep until the time arrives.

At the appointed time, we'll update our current time in the current_time variable. We'll call the callback function provided in the Task object. And then we'll see if the Task object's repeat() method will provide another repeat task into the queue.

The important things to note here are the lines that touch callback functions. The function is passed around like any other object and the Scheduler and Task classes never know or care what the original name of the function is or where it was defined. When it's time to call the function, the Scheduler simply evaluates the function with new_task.callback(current_time).

Here's a set of callback functions that test the Scheduler class:

```
import datetime

def format_time(message: str) -> None:
    now = datetime.datetime.now()
    print(f"{now:%I:%M:%S}: {message}")

def one(timer: float) -> None:
    format_time("Called One")

def two(timer: float) -> None:
    format_time("Called Two")

def three(timer: float) -> None:
    format_time("Called Three")

class Repeater:
    def __init__(self) -> None:
        self.count = 0

    def four(self, timer: float) -> None:
        self.count += 1
        format_time(f"Called Four: {self.count}")
```

These functions all meet the definition of the Callback type hint, so they'll work nicely. The Repeater class definition has a method, four(), that meets the definition. That means an instance of Repeater can also be used.

We've defined a handy utility function, format_time(), to write common messages. It uses the format string syntax to add the current time to the message. The three small callback functions output the current time and a short message telling us which of the callbacks has been fired.

Here's an example of creating a scheduler and loading it up with callback functions:

```
s = Scheduler()
s.enter(1, one)
s.enter(2, one)
s.enter(2, two)
s.enter(4, two)
s.enter(3, three)
s.enter(6, three)
repeater = Repeater()
s.enter(5, repeater.four, delay=1, limit=5)
s.run()
```

This example allows us to see how multiple callbacks interact with the timer.

The Repeater class demonstrates that methods can be used as callbacks too, since they are really functions that happen to be bound to an object. Using a method of an instance of the Repeater class is a function like any other.

The output shows that events are run in the expected order:

```
01:44:35: Called One
01:44:36: Called Two
01:44:36: Called One
01:44:37: Called Three
01:44:38: Called Two
01:44:39: Called Four: 1
01:44:40: Called Three
01:44:40: Called Four: 2
01:44:41: Called Four: 3
01:44:42: Called Four: 4
01:44:43: Called Four: 5
```

Note that some events have the same scheduled run time. Scheduled after 2 seconds, for example, both callback functions one() and two() are defined. They both ran at 01:44:36. There's no rule to decide how to resolve the tie between these two functions. The scheduler's algorithm is to pop an item from the heap queue, execute the callback function, then pop another item from the heap queue; if it has the same execution time, then evaluate the next callback function. Which of the two callbacks is performed first and which is done second is an implementation detail of the heap queue. If order matters to your application, you'll need an additional attribute to distinguish among items scheduled at the same time; a priority number is often used for this.

Because Python is a dynamic language, the contents of a class are not fixed. There are some more advanced programming techniques available to us. In the next section, we'll look at changing the methods of a class.

Using functions to patch a class

One of the things we noted in the previous example was that *mypy* assumed that the Callable attribute, callback, was a method of the Task class. This leads to a potentially confusing *mypy* error message, Invalid self argument "Task" to attribute function "callback" with type "Callable[[int], None]". In the previous example, the callable attribute was emphatically not a method.

The presence of the confusion means that a callable attribute can be treated as a method of a class. Since we can generally supply extra methods to a class, it means we can patch in additional methods at runtime.

Does it mean we *should* do this? It's perhaps a bad idea, except in a very special situation.

It is possible to add or change a function to an instantiated object, demonstrated as follows. First we'll define a class, A, with a method, show_something():

```
>>> class A:
...     def show_something(self):
...         print("My class is A")

>>> a_object = A()
>>> a_object.show_something()
My class is A
```

This looks like what we'd expect. We invoke the method on an instance of the class and see the results of the print() function. Now, let's patch this object, replacing the show_something() method:

```
>>> def patched_show_something():
...     print("My class is NOT A")

>>> a_object.show_something = patched_show_something
>>> a_object.show_something()
My class is NOT A
```

We've patched the object introducing an attribute that's a callable function. When we use a_object.show_something(), the rule is to look in local attributes first, then look in class attributes. Because of this, we've used a callable attribute to create a localized patch to this instance of the A class.

We can create another instance of the class, unpatched, and see that it's still using the class-level method:

```
>>> b_object = A()
>>> b_object.show_something()
My class is A
```

If we can patch an object, you'd think we can also patch the class. We can. It is possible to replace methods on classes instead of objects. If we change the class, we have to account for the self argument that will be implicitly provided to methods defined in the class.

It's very important to note that patching a class will change the method for all instances of that object, even ones that have already been instantiated. Obviously, replacing methods like this can be both dangerous and confusing to maintain. Somebody reading the code will see that a method has been called and look up that method on the original class. But the method on the original class is not the one that was called. Figuring out what really happened can become a tricky, frustrating debugging session.

There's a cardinal assumption that needs to underpin everything we write. It's a kind of contract that is essential to understanding how software works:

> The code people see in a module file must be the code that is running.

Breaking this assumption will really confuse people. Our previous example showed an instance of class A that had a method named show_something() with behavior clearly different to the definition for class A. That's going to be lead people to distrust your application software.

This technique does have its uses though. Often, replacing or adding methods at runtime (called **monkey patching**) is used in automated testing. If testing a client-server application, we may not want to actually connect to the server while testing the client; this may result in accidental transfers of funds or embarrassing test emails being sent to real people.

Instead, we can set up our test code to replace some of the key methods on the object that sends requests to the server so that it only records that the methods have been called. We'll cover this in detail in *Chapter 13, Testing Object-Oriented Programs*. Outside the narrow realm of testing, monkey patching is generally a sign of bad design.

This is sometimes justified as part of a bug fix for imported components. If this is done, the patch needs to be clearly flagged so anyone looking at the code knows what bug is being worked around and when the fix can be removed. We call this kind of code *tech debt*, because the complication of using a monkey patch is a liability.

In the case of our class in this example, a subclass of A with a distinct implementation of show_something() would make things much more clear than a patched method.

We can use class definitions to create objects that are usable as if they were functions. This gives us another path toward using small, separate functions to build applications.

Callable objects

Just as functions are objects that can have attributes set on them, it is possible to create an object that can be called as though it were a function. Any object can be made callable by giving it a __call__() method that accepts the required arguments. Let's make our Repeater class, from the timer example, a little easier to use by making it a callable, as follows:

```
class Repeater_2:
    def __init__(self) -> None:
        self.count = 0

    def __call__(self, timer: float) -> None:
        self.count += 1
        format_time(f"Called Four: {self.count}")
```

This example isn't much different from the earlier class; all we did was change the name of the repeater function to __call__ and pass the object itself as a callable. How does this work? We can do the following interactively to see an example:

```
class Repeater_2:
    def __init__(self) -> None:
        self.count = 0

    def __call__(self, timer: float) -> None:
```

```
        self.count += 1
        format_time(f"Called Four: {self.count}")

rpt = Repeater_2()
```

At this point, we've created a callable object, rpt(). When we evaluate something like rpt(1), Python will evaluate rpt.__call__(1) for us because there's a __call__() method defined. It looks like this:

```
>>> rpt(1)
04:50:32: Called Four: 1
>>> rpt(2)
04:50:35: Called Four: 2
>>> rpt(3)
04:50:39: Called Four: 3
```

Here's an example of using this variation on the Repeater_2 class definition with a Scheduler object:

```
s2 = Scheduler()
s2.enter(5, Repeater_2(), delay=1, limit=5)
s2.run()
```

Note that, when we make the enter() call, we pass as an argument the value Repeater_2(). Those two parentheses are creating a new instance of the class. The instance that is created has the __call__() method, which can be used by the Scheduler. When working with callable objects, it's essential to create an instance of a class; it's the object that's callable, not the class.

At this point, we've seen two different kinds of callable objects:

1. Python's functions, built with the def statement.
2. Callable objects. These are instances of a class with the __call__() method defined.

Generally, the simple def statement is all we need. Callable objects, however, can do something an ordinary function can't do. Our Repeater_2 class counts the number of times it was used. An ordinary function is stateless. A callable object can be stateful. This needs to be used with some care, but some algorithms can have a dramatic performance improvement from saving results in a cache, and a callable object is a great way to save results from a function so they don't need to be recomputed.

File I/O

Our examples so far that have touched the filesystem have operated entirely on text files without much thought as to what is going on under the hood. Operating systems represent files as a sequence of bytes, not text. We'll take a deep dive into the relationship between bytes and text in *Chapter 9, Strings, Serialization, and File Paths.* For now, be aware that reading textual data from a file is a fairly involved process, but Python takes care of most of the work for us behind the scenes.

The concept of files has been around since long before anyone coined the term *object-oriented programming.* However, Python has wrapped the interface that operating systems provide in a sweet abstraction that allows us to work with file (or file-like, vis-à-vis duck typing) objects.

The confusion arises because the operating system file and the Python file object are both, commonly, called "files." It's difficult to be ultra-cautious and wrap each reference to the term *file* with appropriate context to distinguish bytes on a disk from the OS libraries for accessing those bytes from the Python file object that wraps the OS libraries.

Python's open() built-in function is used to open the OS file and return a Python file object. For reading text from a file, we only need to pass the name of the file into the function. The OS file will be opened for reading, and the bytes will be converted to text using the platform's default encoding.

A file "name" can be a name relative to the current working directory. It can also be an absolute name, beginning from the root of the directory tree. A file's name is the tail end of a path to the file from the root of the filesystem. The root in a Linux-based filesystem is "/". In Windows, there's a filesystem on each device, so we use a more complex name like "C:\". While Windows uses \ for separating elements of the file path, Python's pathlib uses "/" consistently, converting the string to the OS-specific names when needed.

Of course, we don't always want to *read* files; often we want to *write* data to them! To open a file for writing, we need to pass a mode argument as the second positional argument to open(), with a value of "w":

```
>>> contents = "Some file contents\n"
>>> file = open("filename.txt", "w")
>>> file.write(contents)
>>> file.close()
```

We could also supply the value "a" as a mode argument, to *append* to the end of the file, rather than completely overwriting existing file content.

These files with built-in wrappers for converting bytes to text are great, but it'd be awfully inconvenient if the file we wanted to open was an image, executable, or other binary file, wouldn't it?

To open a binary file, we modify the mode string to append "b". So, "wb" would open a file for writing bytes, while "rb" allows us to read them. They will behave like text files, but without the automatic encoding of text to bytes. When we read such a file, it will return bytes objects instead of str, and when we write to it, it will fail if we try to pass a text object.

 These mode strings for controlling how files are opened are rather cryptic and are neither Pythonic nor object-oriented. However, they are consistent with virtually every other programming language out there because they are based on the venerable standard I/O library. File I/O is one of the fundamental jobs an operating system has to handle, and all programming languages have to talk to the operating system using the same system calls.

Since all files are actually bytes, it's important to be aware that reading text means that the bytes are converted to text characters. Most operating systems use an encoding called UTF-8 to represent the Unicode characters Python uses as bytes. In some cases, other encodings might be used, and we may have to provide an encoding='cp1252' argument value when opening a text file that uses an uncommon encoding.

Once a file is opened for reading, we can call any of the read(), readline(), or readlines() methods to get the contents of the file. The read() method returns the entire contents of the file as a str or bytes object, depending on whether there is "b" in the mode. Be careful not to use this method without arguments on huge files. You don't want to find out what happens if you try to load that much data into memory!

It is also possible to read a fixed number of bytes from a file; we pass an integer argument to the read() method, describing how many bytes we want to read. The next call to read() will load the next sequence of bytes, and so on. We can do this inside a while statement to read the entire file in manageable chunks.

Some file formats define neatly bounded chunks for us. The logging module can transmit log objects as bytes. A process reading those bytes must first read four bytes to determine the size of the log message. The size value defines how many more bytes must be read to gather a single, complete message.

The `readline()` method returns a single line from the file (where each line ends in a newline, a carriage return, or both, depending on the operating system on which the file was created). We can call it repeatedly to get additional lines. The plural `readlines()` method returns a list of all the lines in the file. Like the `read()` method, it's not safe to use on very large files. These two methods even work when the file is open in bytes mode, but it only makes sense if we are parsing text-like data that has newlines at reasonable positions. An image or audio file, for example, will not have newline characters in it (unless the newline byte happened to represent a certain pixel or sound), so applying `readline()` wouldn't make sense.

For readability, and to avoid reading a large file into memory at once, it is often better to use a `for` statement to consume lines from a file object. For text files, it will read each line, one at a time, and we can process it inside the `for` statement. For binary files, this will also work, but it's often unlikely that the binary file adheres to text file rules. For binary files, it's better to read fixed-sized chunks of data using the `read()` method, passing a parameter for the maximum number of bytes to read.

Reading a file might look like this:

```python
with open("big_number.txt") as input:
    for line in input:
        print(line)
```

Writing to a file is just as easy; the `write()` method on file objects writes a string (or bytes, for binary data) object to the file. It can be called repeatedly to write multiple strings, one after the other. The `writelines()` method accepts a sequence of strings and writes each of the iterated values to the file. The `writelines()` method does *not* append a new line after each item in the sequence. It is basically a poorly named convenience function to write the contents of a sequence of strings without having to explicitly iterate over it using a `for` statement.

Writing to a file might look like this:

```python
results = str(2**2048)
with open("big_number.txt", "w") as output:
    output.write("# A big number\n")
    output.writelines(
        [
            f"{len(results)}\n",
            f"{results}\n"
        ]
    )
```

The explicit newline characters, \n, are required to create line breaks in the file. Only the print() function adds newlines automatically. Because the open() function is built-in, there are no imports required for simple file input and output operations.

Lastly, and we do mean lastly, we come to the close() method. This method should be called when we are finished reading or writing the file, to ensure any buffered writes are written to the disk, that the file has been properly cleaned up, and that all resources associated with the file are released back to the operating system. It's very important to be explicit and clean up after ourselves, especially in long-running processes like web servers.

Each open file is a context manager, usable by the with statement. If we use files like this, the close() happens automatically at the end of the context. We'll look closely at using context managers to control the OS resources in the next section.

Placing it in context

The need to close files when we are finished with them can make our code quite ugly. Because an exception may occur at any time during file I/O, we ought to wrap all calls to a file in a try...finally clause. The file should be closed in the finally clause, regardless of whether I/O was successful. This isn't very Pythonic. Of course, there is a more elegant way to do it.

Python's file objects are also **context managers**. By using the with statement, the context management methods ensure that the file is closed, even if an exception is raised. By using the with statement, we no longer have to explicitly manage the closing of the file.

Here is what a file-oriented with statement looks like in practice:

```
>>> source_path = Path("requirements.txt")
>>> with source_path.open() as source_file:
...     for line in source_file:
...         print(line, end='')
```

The open method of a Path object returns a file object, which has __enter__() and __exit__() methods. The returned object is assigned to the variable named source_file by the as clause. We know the file will be closed when the code returns to the outer indentation level, and that this will happen even if an exception is raised. (We'll look at Path objects in more detail in *Chapter 9, Strings, Serialization, and File Paths*. For now, we'll use them to open our files.)

The `with` statement is used widely, often where startup and cleanup code need to be connected in spite of anything that might go wrong. For example, the `urlopen` call returns a context object that can be used in a `with` statement to clean up the socket when we're done. Locks in the `threading` module can automatically release the lock after the body of the `with` statement has been executed.

Most interestingly, because any object that has the appropriate special methods can be a context manager, used by the `with` statement, we can use it in our own frameworks. For example, remember that strings are immutable, but sometimes you need to build a string from multiple parts. For efficiency, this is usually done by storing the component strings in a list and joining them at the end. Let's extend the list class to create a simple context manager that allows us to construct a sequence of characters and automatically convert it to a string upon exit:

```
>>> class StringJoiner(list):
...     def __enter__(self):
...         return self
...     def __exit__(self, exc_type, exc_val, exc_tb):
...         self.result = "".join(self)
```

This code adds the two special methods required of a context manager to the `list` class it inherits from. The __enter__() method performs any required setup code (in this case, there isn't any) and then returns the object that will be assigned to the variable after as in the `with` statement. Often, as we've done here, this is the context manager object itself. The __exit__() method accepts three arguments. In a normal situation, these are all given a value of `None`. However, if an exception occurs inside the `with` block, they will be set to values related to the type, value, and traceback for the exception. This allows the __exit__() method to perform any cleanup code that may be required, even if an exception occurred. In our example, we create a result string by joining the characters in the string, regardless of whether an exception was thrown. In some cases, it may be necessary to do more sophisticated cleanup to respond to the exceptional condition.

Formally, the type hints look like this:

```
from typing import List, Optional, Type, Literal
from types import TracebackType


class StringJoiner(List[str]):
    def __enter__(self) -> "StringJoiner":
        return self

    def __exit__(
```

```
        self,
        exc_type: Optional[Type[BaseException]],
        exc_val: Optional[BaseException],
        exc_tb: Optional[TracebackType],
    ) -> Literal[False]:
        self.result = "".join(self)
        return False
```

Note that we've defined __exit__() to always return False. A return value of False makes sure any exception that is raised in the context will be seen. This is the typical behavior. We can, however, silence the exceptions raised by returning True. This means changing the type hint from Literal[False] to bool and – of course – examining the exception details to see if it should be silenced. We might, for example, check exc_type to see if it is StopIteration, like this:

```
    return exc_type == StopIteration
```

This will silence only StopIteration exceptions, and allow all others to propagate outside the context. For a refresher on exceptions, refer back to *Chapter 4, Expecting the Unexpected*.

While this is one of the simplest context managers we could write, and its usefulness is dubious, it does work with a with statement. Have a look at it in action:

```
>>> with StringJoiner("Hello") as sj:
...        sj.append(", ")
...        sj.extend("world")
...        sj.append("!")
>>> sj.result
'Hello, world!'
```

This code constructs a string by appending and extending an initial list of characters. When the with statement finishes the indented statements of the context, the __exit__() method is called, and the result attribute becomes available on the StringJoiner object, sj. We then print this value to see the resulting string. Note that the __exit__() is always executed, even if there's an exception. The following example raises an exception inside the context, and the final result is still built:

```
>>> with StringJoiner("Partial") as sj:
...        sj.append(" ")
...        sj.extend("Results")
...        sj.append(str(2 / 0))
...        sj.extend("Even If There's an Exception")
```

```
Traceback (most recent call last):
    ...
  File "<doctest examples.md[60]>", line 3, in <module>
    sj.append(str(2 / 0))
ZeroDivisionError: division by zero
>>> sj.result
'Partial Results'
```

The division by zero raised an exception. The statement appending this to the sj
variable failed, and the remaining statements within the context aren't executed. The
context's __exit__() method is executed, with details of the exception. The __exit__()
method computed the result attribute, and allowed the exception to propagate. The sj
variable has the partial result.

We can also build a context manager from a simple function. This relies on a feature
of an iterator, something we'll look at deeply in *Chapter 10, The Iterator Pattern*.
For now, it's enough to know that the yield statement produces the first result of
a sequence of results. Because of the way iterators work in Python, we can write
a function that has the __enter__() processing and the __exit__() processing
separated by a single yield statement.

The example of a string joiner is a stateful context manager, and using a function can
cleanly separate the state-changing object from the context manager that makes the
state change.

Here's a revised "string joiner" object that implements part of the work. It contains
the strings and also the final result attribute:

```
class StringJoiner2(List[str]):
    def __init__(self, *args: str) -> None:
        super().__init__(*args)
        self.result = "".join(self)
```

Separate from this is a context manager that has some steps for entering the context
and exiting it:

```
from contextlib import contextmanager
from typing import List, Any, Iterator


@contextmanager
def joiner(*args: Any) -> Iterator[StringJoiner2]:
    string_list = StringJoiner2(*args)
    try:
```

```
        yield string_list
    finally:
        string_list.result = "".join(string_list)
```

The steps prior to the `yield` are performed on entry into the context. The expression in the `yield` statement is assigned to the `as` variable in the `with` statement. When the context finishes normally, the code after the `yield` is processed. The `try:` statement's `finally:` clause will make sure that the final result attribute is always set, irrespective of the presence of an exception. Since the `try:` statement doesn't explicitly match any exceptions, it doesn't silence anything, and the exception will be visible outside the enclosing `with` statement. This behaves identically to the `StringJoiner` examples above; the only change is to replace `StringJoiner` – a class that is a context manager – with `joiner`.

The `@contextmanager` decorator is used to add some features around this function to make it work like a context manager class definition. This saves us from the overhead of a class that defines both `__enter__()` and `__exit__()` methods. In this case, the context management involves so few lines of code that a decorated function seems more appropriate than a longer and more complex-looking class.

Context managers can do many things. The reason why we cover them adjacent to simple file operations is because one of the important places we can use context managers is when opening files, databases, or network connections. Any place where external, operating system-managed resources are involved, we need a context manager to be sure that the external resources are properly released no matter what goes wrong in our application programming.

 Any time we're working with a file, always wrap the processing in a `with` statement.

Case study

While object-oriented programming is helpful for encapsulating features, it's not the only way to create flexible, expressive, and succinct application programs. Functional programming emphasizes functional design and function composition over object-oriented design.

In Python, functional design often involves using a few object-oriented techniques. This is one of the beauties of Python: being able to choose an appropriate set of design tools to address the problem effectively.

We often depict object-oriented designs with the classes and their various associations. For functional design, we're interested in functions to transform objects. A functional design can follow mathematical practices closely.

In this part of the case study, we'll revisit a number of features of the classifier as functions mixed with class definitions. We'll step away from a pure object-oriented view and adopt a hybrid view. In particular, we'll look closely at segregating data into a training set and a testing set.

Processing overview

The initial analysis from *Chapter 1, Object-Oriented Design*, identified three distinct processes for gathering training data, testing the classifier, and actually doing classification. The context diagram looked like this:

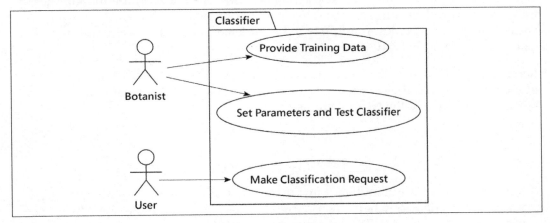

Figure 8.1: Context diagram

We can think of these as separate functions to build some collections of sample data:

1. A function based on the "Provide Training Data" use case would transform source data into two collections of samples, a training set and a testing set. We'd like to avoid placing items in the testing set that are exact matches for items in the training set, creating some constraints on this process. We can think of this as a mapping from a KnownSample to a TestingKnownSample or a TrainingKnownSample.

2. A function based on the "Set Parameters and Test Classifier" use case would transform a Hyperparameter (the *k* value and the distance algorithm) and the testing set of samples into a quality score. We can think of this as a mapping from TestingKnownSample to a correct or incorrect classification, and a reduction to a single value showing the number correct out of the number of tests.

3. A function based on the "Make Classification Request" use case would transform a Hyperparameter (the k value and the distance algorithm) and a single sample into a classification result.

We'll look at each of these functions separately. We can build an alternative model for our application using these processing steps to define a functional approach.

Splitting the data

In effect, splitting the data into two subsets can be defined around some filter functions. We'll avoid Python for a moment and focus on the conceptual math to make sure we have the logic completely correct before diving into code. Conceptually, we have a pair of functions, $e(s_i)$ and $r(s_i)$, that decide if a sample, s_i, is for testing, e, or training, r. These functions are used to partition the samples into two subsets. (If testing and training didn't both begin with t, we'd have an easier time finding names. It might help to think about $e(s_i)$ for evaluation and testing, and $r(s_i)$ for running a real classification.)

It's simpler if these two functions are exclusive, $e(s_i) = \neg r(s_i)$. (We'll use $\neg$ instead of the longer not.) If they are proper inverses of each other, this means we only need to define one of the two functions:

$$R = \{s_i \mid s_i \in S \wedge r(s_i)\}$$

$$E = \{s_i \mid s_i \in S \wedge \neg r(s_i)\}$$

If the above syntax is unfamiliar, it just means that the training set is all items, s_i, from the source data, S, where $r(s_i)$ is true. The testing set is all the items from the source where $r(s_i)$ is false. This mathematical formalism can help make sure all the cases are properly covered.

This concept is a kind of "comprehension" or "builder" for a set of samples. We can translate the mathematical comprehension into a Python list comprehension in a fairly direct way. We'll implement our conceptual function $r(s_i)$ as a Python function, `training()`. We'll also expose the index value, i, as a separate parameter to this function:

```
def training(s: Sample, i: int) -> bool:
    pass

training_samples = [
    TrainingKnownSample(s)
    for i, s in enumerate(samples)
```

```
        if training(s, i)]

test_samples = [
    TestingKnownSample(s)
    for i, s in enumerate(samples)
    if not training(s, i)]
```

In *Chapter 10, The Iterator Pattern*, we'll dive into this deeply. For now, it's enough to see that the comprehensions have three parts: an expression, a for clause, and an if condition. The for clause provides the values, in effect the $s_i \in S$ portion of the formal statement. The if condition filters the values, in effect the $r(s_i)$ clause. The final expression, s, determines what is accumulated into the resulting list object.

We've composed a TrainingKnownSample object as a wrapper around the source KnownSample instances. This leverages the composition-based design from *Chapter 7, Python Data Structures*.

We can use the index value to partition the data. The remainder after division, the modulo, can be used to break data into subsets. The value of i % 5, for example, is a value from 0 to 4. If we use i % 5 == 0 as test data, 20% of the values will be selected. When i % 5 != 0, this is the remaining 80% of the data that will be used for training.

The following is a list comprehension without the [] wrapper. We've used the list() function to consume items from the generator and build a list:

```
test_samples = list(
    TestingKnownSample(s)
    for i, s in enumerate(samples)
    if not training(s, i))
```

The processing with [] or list() is the same. Some folks like the clarity of list(), even though it's wordier than []. If we create our own extension to the list class, it's slightly simpler to find list(...) than to find all the places where [...] is used and separate out the list builders from other uses of [].

Rethinking classification

In *Chapter 2, Objects in Python*, we wrestled with a number of ways of handling the state change that goes with classification. There are two similar processes, one for KnownSample objects that will be used for testing, and one for UnknownSample objects being classified by users. The process diagrams are simple-looking but conceal an important question.

Here's the user's classification of an unknown sample:

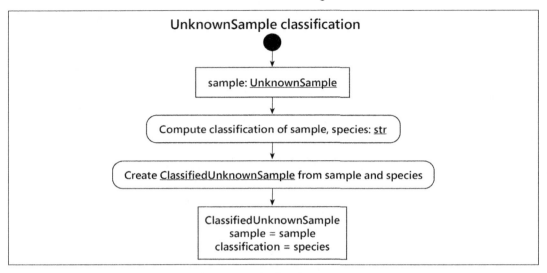

Figure 8.2: UnknownSample classification process diagram

We can borrow this (with a few tiny class changes) and use it for testing. Here's an approach to handling classification for test purposes that parallels the unknown sample process:

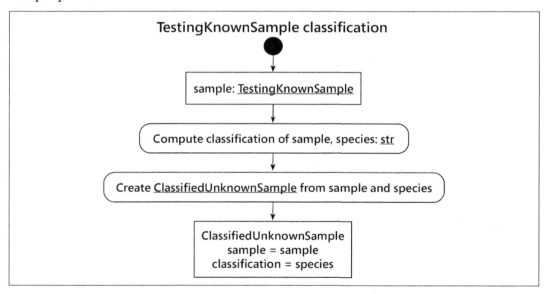

Figure 8.3: TestingKnownSample classification process diagram

Ideally, the same code can be used in both cases, reducing the overall complexity of the application.

As we consider the different alternatives to the process view, this leads to changes in the logical view. Here's a revised view, thinking of these classes as immutable compositions. We've included notes to suggest when these objects are created during application processing. We've highlighted two classes requiring careful consideration:

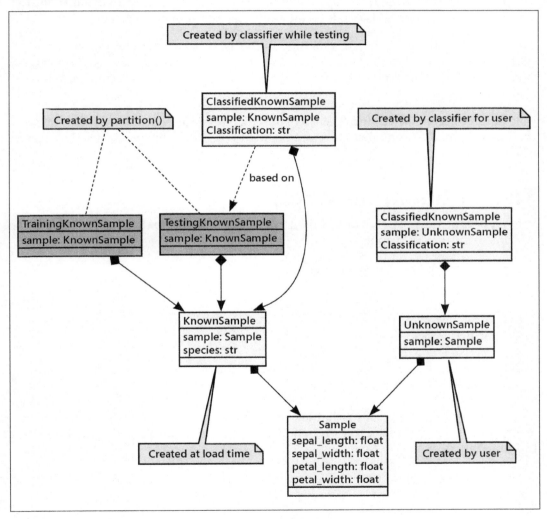

Figure 8.4: Revised logical view

The `TestingKnownSample` and the `TrainingKnownSample` classes have very minor differences. They don't introduce new attributes or methods. Here are the differences:

- `TrainingKnownSample` instances are never used for classification.
- `TestingKnownSample` and `UnknownSample` instances are used for classification and testing. We'll create a `ClassifiedKnownSample` object from a `TestingKnownSample` object by repackaging the `KnownSample` instance into a new container. This creates a more consistent set of definitions.

The idea is that the `classifier()` method of the `Hyperparameter` class should work with objects of two classes, summarized by the type hint `Union[TestingKnownSample, UnknownSample]`. This kind of hint can help us spot application code that uses the classes incorrectly.

This diagram seems to capture the ways in which these objects are used. Having these details available can lead to more detailed type hints that can be used to clarify our intent.

The partition() function

We can define multiple versions of the `training()` function to divide our data into an 80/20, 75/25, or 67/33 split:

```
def training_80(s: KnownSample, i: int) -> bool:
    return i % 5 != 0

def training_75(s: KnownSample, i: int) -> bool:
    return i % 4 != 0

def training_67(s: KnownSample, i: int) -> bool:
    return i % 3 != 0
```

Here's a function, `partition()`, that takes one of the `training_xx()` functions as an argument. The `training_xx()` function is applied to a sample to decide if it's training data or not:

```
TrainingList = List[TrainingKnownSample]
TestingList = List[TestingKnownSample]

def partition(
```

```
    samples: Iterable[KnownSample],
    rule: Callable[[KnownSample, int], bool]
) -> Tuple[TrainingList, TestingList]:

    training_samples = [
        TrainingKnownSample(s)
        for i, s in enumerate(samples) if rule(s, i)
    ]

    test_samples = [
        TestingKnownSample(s)
        for i, s in enumerate(samples) if not rule(s, i)
    ]

    return training_samples, test_samples
```

We've built a "higher-order" function that takes another function as an argument value. This is a very cool feature of functional programming that is an integral part of Python.

This `partition()` function builds two lists from a source of data and a function. This covers the simple case, where we don't care about introducing values into the `testing` list that are duplicates of values in the `training` list.

While this is pleasantly succinct and expressive, it has a hidden cost. We'd like to avoid examining the data twice. For the small set of known samples in this particular problem, the processing is not particularly costly. But we may have a generator expression creating the raw data in the first place. Since we can only consume a generator once, we'd like to avoid creating multiple copies of a large set of data.

Also, we'd like to avoid assigning test values that happen to be exact matches for training values. This turns into a more complex problem. We'll defer this until *Chapter 10, The Iterator Pattern*.

One-pass partitioning

We can create multiple pools of samples in one pass through the data. There are several approaches; we'll show one that has simpler type hints. Again, this is a function, not a full class definition. The individual sample instances have distinct classes, but this process yields objects of distinct classes, and is a better fit for a functional style.

The idea is to create two empty list objects, one for training, the other for testing. We can then assign specific type hints to each list, and leverage *mypy* to be sure we are using the lists appropriately:

```python
def partition_1(
        samples: Iterable[KnownSample],
        rule: Callable[[KnownSample, int], bool]
) -> Tuple[TrainingList, TestingList]:

    training: TrainingList = []
    testing: TestingList = []

    for i, s in enumerate(samples):
        training_use = rule(s, i)
        if training_use:
            training.append(TrainingKnownSample(s))
        else:
            testing.append(TestingKnownSample(s))

    return training, testing
```

In this `partition_1()` function, we've used the `rule` function to determine if the data will be used for training. We expect one of the `training_xx()` functions defined earlier in this case study to be provided as the argument for the `rule` parameter.

Based on this output, we can create an appropriate class for each sample instance, and then assign the sample to an appropriate list.

This example doesn't check for duplicates between testing samples and training samples. Some data scientists suggest we don't want any test samples that are exact matches for training samples; it biases the testing. We can see where that needed decision can be inserted between when the `training_use` variable is assigned and when the final appends are done to either list. If `training_use` is `False` and the item already exists in the training set, this item, too, must be used for training.

We can refactor this algorithm slightly by performing the type conversions later in the process. This lets us create a dictionary of various "pools" of `KnownSample` objects based on the intended usage. So far, we only have two pools – training, where a `training_xx()` rule is `True`, and testing:

```python
from collections import defaultdict, Counter

def partition_1p(
```

```
    samples: Iterable[KnownSample],
    rule: Callable[[KnownSample, int], bool]
) -> tuple[TrainingList, TestingList]:

    pools: defaultdict[bool, list[KnownSample]] = defaultdict(list)
    partition = ((rule(s, i), s) for i, s in enumerate(samples))
    for usage_pool, sample in partition:
        pools[usage_pool].append(sample)

    training = [TrainingKnownSample(s) for s in pools[True]]
    testing = [TestingKnownSample(s) for s in pools[False]]
    return training, testing
```

The `defaultdict` object, `pools`, will map Boolean values to `List[KnownSample]` objects. We provided the `list` function to set a default value when a key is accessed that did not previously exist. We only anticipate two keys, and this could also have been written as `pools: dict[bool, list[KnownSample]] = {True: [], False: []}`.

The partitioning starts by creating a generator function to apply the given `rule` function to each sample. The result is a two-tuple; we could write an explicit type hint of `tuple[bool, KnownSample]`. This generator expression assigned to the partition `variable` is lazy, and doesn't compute anything until the values are consumed by the `for` statement.

The `for` statement consumes values from the generator, appending each sample to the appropriate pool. When values are consumed, the generator function is evaluated, producing a stream of two-tuples with the pool, a Boolean value, and the `KnownSample` instance.

Once the `KnownSample` objects have been partitioned, we can wrap them up as instances of the `TrainingKnownSample` class or the `TestingKnownSample` class. The type hints seem simpler in this example than in the previous version.

This doesn't actually create two copies of the data. References to the `KnownSample` objects are collected into a dictionary. From these, the two lists of `TrainingKnownSample` and `TestingKnownSample` objects are created. Each of the derived objects contains a reference to the original `KnownSample` object. The structure of the temporary dictionary represents some memory overhead, but overall, we've avoided duplicating data, reducing the memory required by this application.

This example suffers from a complication. It's not perfectly clear how to prevent creating test samples that are exact matches for training samples. An additional `if` statement inside the `for` statement could check for an item with `usage_pool` of `False` (in other words, a testing item) that also existed in `pools[True]` (in other words, the training items). This is quite a bit of extra complexity.

Rather than add the additional steps here, we'll wait for *Chapter 10, The Iterator Pattern*, and revise the algorithm to handle duplicate removal that avoids too many special cases or extra `if` statements.

In the case study for *Chapter 5, When to Use Object-Oriented Programming*, we used `with` statements and the `csv` module to load the raw sample data. In that chapter, we defined a `SampleReader` class. It's important to review the older definition with these newer partitioning functions to create an integrated whole that can properly read and partition the source of sample data.

Recall

We've touched on a number of ways that object-oriented and functional programming techniques are part of Python:

- Python built-in functions provide access to special methods that can be implemented by a wide variety of classes. Almost all classes, most of them utterly unrelated, provide an implementation for `__str__( )` and `__repr__()` methods, which can be used by the built-in `str()` and `repr()` functions. There are many functions like this where a function is provided to access implementations that cut across class boundaries.

- Some object-oriented languages rely on "method overloading" – a single name can have multiple implementations with different combinations of parameters. Python provides an alternative, where one method name can have optional, mandatory, position-only, and keyword-only parameters. This provides tremendous flexibility.

- Functions are objects and can be used in ways that other objects are used. We can provide them as argument values; we can return them from functions. A function has attributes, also.

- File I/O leads us to look closely at how we interact with external objects. Files are always composed of bytes. Python will convert the bytes to text for us. The most common encoding, UTF-8, is the default, but we can specify other encodings.

- Context managers are a way to be sure that the operating system entanglements are correctly cleaned up even when there's an exception raised. The use goes beyond simply handling files and network connections, however. Anywhere we have a clear context where we want consistent processing on entry or exit, we have a place where a context manager can be useful.

Exercises

If you haven't encountered with statements and context managers before, I encourage you, as usual, to go through your old code, find all the places where you were opening files, and make sure they are safely closed using the with statement. Look for places to write your own context managers as well. Ugly or repetitive try...finally clauses are a good place to start, but you may find them useful any time you need to do before and/or after tasks in context.

You've probably used many of the basic built-in functions before now. We covered several of them, but didn't go into a great deal of detail. Play with enumerate, zip, reversed, any, and all until you know you'll remember to use them when they are the right tool for the job. The enumerate function is especially important because not using it results in some pretty ugly while loops.

Also explore some applications that pass functions around as callable objects, as well as using the __call__() method to make your own objects callable. You can get the same effect by attaching attributes to functions or by creating a __call__() method on an object. In which case would you use one syntax, and when would it be more suitable to use the other?

The relationship between arguments, keyword arguments, variable arguments, and variable keyword arguments can be a bit confusing. We saw how painfully they can interact when we covered multiple inheritance. Devise some other examples to see how they can work well together, as well as to understand when they don't.

The Options example for using **kwargs has a potential problem. The update() method inherited from the dict class will add or replace keys. What if we only want to replace key values? We'd have to write our own version of update() that will update existing keys and raise a ValueError exception when a new key is provided

The name_or_number() function example has a blatant bug. It is not completely correct. For a number 15, it will not report both "fizz" and "buzz". Fix the name_or_number() function to collect all the names of all the true functions. A good exercise.

The name_or_number() function example has two test functions, fizz(), and buzz(). We need an additional function, bazz(), to be true for multiples of seven. Write the function and be sure it works with the name_or_number() function. Be sure that the number 105 is handled correctly.

It's helpful to review the previous case studies and combine them into a more complete application. The chapter case studies tend to focus on details, avoiding the overall integration of a more complete application. We've left the integration as work for the reader to allow them to dig more deeply into the design.

Summary

We covered a grab bag of topics in this chapter. Each represented an important non-object-oriented feature that is popular in Python. Just because we can use object-oriented principles does not always mean we should!

However, we also saw that Python typically implements such features by providing a syntax shortcut to traditional object-oriented syntax. Knowing the object-oriented principles underlying these tools allows us to use them more effectively in our own classes.

We discussed a series of built-in functions and file I/O operations. There are a whole bunch of different syntaxes available to us when calling functions with arguments, keyword arguments, and variable argument lists. Context managers are useful for the common pattern of sandwiching a piece of code between two method calls. Even functions are objects, and, conversely, any normal object can be made callable.

In the next chapter, we'll learn more about string and file manipulation, and even spend some time with one of the least object-oriented topics in the standard library: regular expressions.

9
Strings, Serialization, and File Paths

Before we get involved with higher-level design patterns, let's take a deep dive into one of Python's most common objects: the string. We'll see that there is a lot more to the string than meets the eye, and we'll also cover searching strings for patterns, and serializing data for storage or transmission.

All of these topics are elements of making objects persistent. Our application can create objects in files for use at a later time. We often take persistence – the ability to write data to a file and retrieve it at an arbitrary later date – for granted. Because persistence happens via files, at the byte level, via OS writes and reads, it leads to two transformations: data we have stored must be decoded into a nice, useful object collection of objects in memory; objects from memory need to be encoded to some kind of clunky text or bytes format for storage, transfer over the network, or remote invocation on a distant server.

In this chapter, we'll look at the following topics:

- The complexities of strings, bytes, and byte arrays
- The ins and outs of string formatting
- The mysterious regular expression
- How to use the `pathlib` module to manage the filesystem
- A few ways to serialize data, including Pickle and JSON

This chapter will extend the case study to examine how best to work with collections of data files. We'll look at another serialization format, CSV, in the case study. This will help us explore alternative representations for the training and testing data.

We'll start by looking Python strings. They do so much and it's easy to overlook the wealth of available features.

Strings

Strings are a basic primitive in Python; we've used them in nearly every example we've discussed so far. All they do is represent an immutable sequence of characters. However, though you may not have considered it before, *character* is a bit of an ambiguous word; can Python strings represent sequences of accented characters? Chinese characters? What about Greek, Cyrillic, or Farsi?

In Python 3, the answer is yes. Python strings are all represented in Unicode, a character definition standard that can represent virtually any character in any language on the planet (and some made-up languages and random characters as well). This is done seamlessly. So, let's think of Python 3 strings as an immutable sequence of Unicode characters. We've touched on many of the ways strings can be manipulated in previous examples, but let's quickly cover it all in one place: a crash course in string theory!

It's very important to step away from the older encodings we used to know and love. The ASCII encoding, for example, was limited to one byte per character. Unicode has several ways to encode a character into bytes. The most popular, called UTF-8, tends to parallel the old ASCII encoding for some punctuation and letters. It's approximately one byte per character. But, if you need one of the thousands of other Unicode characters, there may be multiple bytes involved.

The important rule is this: we *encode* our characters to create bytes; we *decode* bytes to recover the characters. The two are separated by a high fence with a gate labeled encode on one side and decode on the other. We can visualize it like this:

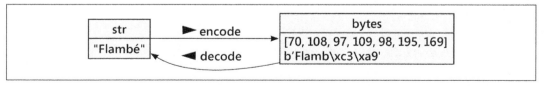

Figure 9.1: Strings and bytes

There's a potential source of confusion that arises from the canonical display of a bytes value. Python will show a bytes value as b'Flamb\xc3\xa9'. In a bytes value, the letters are shorthand for numbers and use the older ASCII encoding scheme.

For most letters, the UTF-8 and ASCII encoding are the same. The `b'` prefix tells us these are bytes, and the letters are really only ASCII codes, not proper Unicode characters. We can see this because the Unicode é – encoded in UTF-8 – takes two bytes, and there's no ASCII shorthand for either of those bytes.

String manipulation

As you know, strings can be created in Python by wrapping a sequence of characters in single or double quotes. Multiline strings can easily be created using three quote characters, and multiple hardcoded strings can be concatenated together by placing them side by side. Here are some examples:

```
>>> a = "hello"
>>> b = 'world'
>>> c = '''a multiple
... line string'''
>>> d = """More
... multiple"""
>>> e = ("Three " "Strings "
...         "Together")
```

That last string is automatically composed into a single string by the interpreter. It is also possible to concatenate strings using the + operator (as in `"hello " + "world"`). Of course, strings don't have to be hardcoded. They can also come from various outside sources, such as text files and user input, or can be transmitted on the network.

Watch for missing operators

The automatic concatenation of adjacent strings can make for some hilarious bugs when a comma is missed. It is, however, extremely useful when a long string needs to be placed inside a function call without exceeding the 79-character line-length limit suggested by PEP-8, the Python style guide.

Like other sequences, strings can be iterated over (character by character), indexed, sliced, or concatenated. The syntax is the same as for lists and tuples.

The `str` class has numerous methods on it to make manipulating strings easier. The `dir()` and `help()` functions can tell us how to use all of them; we'll consider some of the more common ones directly.

Several Boolean convenience methods help us identify whether or not the characters in a string match a certain pattern. Most of these, such as `isalpha()`, `isupper()`, `islower()`, `startswith()`, and `endswith()`, have reasonably easy-to-understand interpretations. The `isspace()` method is also fairly obvious, but remember that all whitespace characters (including tab and newline) are considered, not just the space character. When in doubt, the `help()` function is useful:

```
>>> help(str.isalpha)
Help on method_descriptor:
isalpha(...)
    S.isalpha() -> bool

    Return True if all characters in S are alphabetic and there is at
    least one character in S, False otherwise.

    A string is alphabetic if all characters in the string are
    alphabetic and there is at least one character in the string.
```

The `istitle()` method returns `True` if the first character of each word is capitalized and all other characters are lowercase. Note that it does not strictly enforce the English grammatical definition of title formatting. For example, Leigh Hunt's poem *The Glove and the Lions* follows common style guides for a title, but doesn't fit the narrow rule of Python's method. Similarly, Robert Service's *The Cremation of Sam McGee* follows the usual English rules for a valid title, even though there is an uppercase letter in the middle of the last word; Python's `istitle()` method will return `False`, unaware of the rules for capitalizing a name like McGee or words like *and the* in a title.

Be careful with the `isdigit()`, `isdecimal()`, and `isnumeric()` methods, as they are more nuanced than we would expect. Many Unicode characters are considered numbers besides the 10 digits we are used to. Worse, the period character that we use to construct floats from strings is not considered a decimal character, so `'45.2'.isdecimal()` returns `False`. The real decimal character is represented by the Unicode value 0660, as in 45.2 (or `45\u06602`). Further, these methods do not verify whether the strings are valid numbers; `127.0.0.1` returns `True` for all three methods. We might think we should use that decimal character instead of a period for all numeric quantities, but passing that character into the `float()` or `int()` constructor converts that decimal character to a zero:

```
>>> float('45\u06602')
4502.0
```

The result of all these inconsistencies is that the Boolean numeric checks must be used carefully, knowing the details of the rules. We'll often need to write a regular expression (discussed later in this chapter) to confirm whether the string matches a specific numeric pattern. We call this LBYL-style programming: "Look Before You Leap." One very common approach is to use a try/except block wrapped around an int() or float() conversion attempt. We call this EAFP-style programming: "It's Easier to Ask Forgiveness than to Ask Permission." The EAFP style fits naturally with Python.

Other methods useful for pattern-matching do not return Booleans. The count() method tells us how many times a given substring shows up in the string, while find(), index(), rfind(), and rindex() tell us the position of a given substring within the original string. Most operations start at the zero index and work from left to right. The two r (for *right* or *reverse*) methods start searching from the highest index end of the string and work from right to left. The find() methods return -1 if the substring can't be found, while index() raises a ValueError exception in this situation. Have a look at some of these methods in action:

```
>>> s = "hello world"
>>> s.count('l')
3
>>> s.find('l')
2
>>> s.rindex('m')
Traceback (most recent call last):
...
File "<doctest examples.md[11]>", line 1, in <module>
s.rindex('m')
ValueError: substring not found
```

Most of the remaining string methods return transformations of the string. The upper(), lower(), capitalize(), and title() methods create new strings with all alphabetical characters following the given format rules. The translate() method can use a dictionary to map arbitrary input characters to specified output characters.

For all of these methods, note that the input string remains unmodified; a brand new str instance is created. If we need to manipulate the resultant string, we should assign it to a new variable, as in new_value = value.capitalize(). Often, once we've performed the transformation, we don't need the old value anymore, so a common idiom is to assign it to the same variable, as in value = value.title().

Finally, a couple of string methods return or operate on lists. The `split()` method accepts a substring and splits the string into a list of strings breaking wherever that substring occurs. You can pass a number as a second parameter to limit the number of resultant strings. The `rsplit()` method behaves identically to `split()` if you don't limit the number of strings, but if you do supply a limit, it starts splitting from the end of the string. The `partition()` and `rpartition()` methods split the string at only the first or last occurrence of the substring, and return a tuple of three values: characters before the substring, the substring itself, and the characters after the substring.

As the inverse of `split()`, the `join()` method accepts a list of strings, and returns all of those strings combined together by placing the original string between them. The `replace()` method accepts two arguments, and returns a string where each instance of the first argument has been replaced with the second. Here are some of these methods in action:

```
>>> s = "hello world, how are you"
>>> s2 = s.split(' ')
>>> s2
['hello', 'world,', 'how', 'are', 'you']
>>> '#'.join(s2)
'hello#world,#how#are#you'
>>> s.replace(' ', '**')
'hello**world,**how**are**you'
>>> s.partition(' ')
('hello', ' ', 'world, how are you')
```

There you have it, a whirlwind tour of the most common methods on the `str` class! Now, let's look at Python 3's approach to composing strings and values from variables and other expressions to create new strings.

String formatting

Python 3 has powerful string formatting and templating mechanisms that allow us to construct strings comprised of template text and interspersed representations of objects usually from variables, but also from expressions. We've used it in many previous examples, but it is much more versatile than the simple formatting specifiers we've used.

A format string (also called an **f-string**) has a prefix on the opening quotation mark of f, as in `f"hello world"`. If such a string contains the special characters { and }, expressions, including variables from the surrounding scope, are evaluated and then interpolated into the string. Here's an example:

```
>>> name = "Dusty"
>>> activity = "reviewing"
>>> message = f"Hello {name}, you are currently {activity}."
>>> print(message)
```

If we run these statements, it replaces the braces with variables, in order:

```
Hello Dusty, you are currently reviewing.
```

Escaping braces

Brace characters are often useful in strings, aside from formatting. We need a way to escape them in situations where we want them to be displayed as themselves, rather than being replaced. This can be done by doubling the braces. For example, we can use Python to format a basic Java program:

```
>>> classname = "MyClass"
>>> python_code = "print('hello world')"
>>> template = f"""
... public class {classname} {{
...     public static void main(String[] args) {{
...         System.out.println("{python_code}");
...     }}
... }}
... """
```

Where we see the {{ and }} sequence in the template – that is, the braces enclosing the Java class and method definition – we know the f-string will replace them with single braces, rather than some argument in the surrounding methods. Here's the output:

```
>>> print(template)

public class MyClass {
    public static void main(String[] args) {
        System.out.println("print('hello world')");
    }
}
```

The class name and contents of the output have been replaced with two parameters, while the double braces have been replaced with single braces, giving us a valid Java file. Turns out, this is about the simplest possible Python program to print the simplest possible Java program that can print the simplest possible Python program.

f-strings can contain Python code

We aren't restricted to interpolating the values of simple string variables into an f-string template. Any primitives, such as integers or floats, can be formatted. More interestingly, complex objects, including lists, tuples, dictionaries, and arbitrary objects, can be used, and we can access indexes and variables or call functions on those objects from within the format string.

For example, if our email message had grouped the From and To email addresses into a tuple and placed the subject and message in a dictionary, for some reason (perhaps because that's the input required for an existing send_mail function we want to use), we can format it like this:

```
>>> emails = ("steve@example.com", "dusty@example.com")
>>> message = {
...     "subject": "Next Chapter",
...     "message": "Here's the next chapter to review!",
... }

>>> formatted = f"""
... From: <{emails[0]}>
... To: <{emails[1]}>
... Subject: {message['subject']}
...
... {message['message']}
... """
```

The variables inside the braces in the template string look a little weird, so let's look at what they're doing. The two email addresses are looked up by the expression emails[x], where x is either 0 or 1. This is an ordinary tuple indexing operation, so emails[0] refers to the first item in the emails tuple. Similarly, the expression message['subject'] gets an item from a dictionary.

This works out particularly well when we have a more complex object to display. We can extract object attributes and properties and even call methods inside the f-string. Let's change our email message data once again, this time to a class:

```
>>> class Notification:
...     def __init__(
...             self,
...             from_addr: str,
...             to_addr: str,
...             subject: str,
...             message: str
...     ) -> None:
...         self.from_addr = from_addr
...         self.to_addr = to_addr
...         self.subject = subject
...         self._message = message
...     def message(self):
...         return self._message
```

Here's an instance of the `Notification` class:

```
>>> email = Notification(
...     "dusty@example.com",
...     "steve@example.com",
...     "Comments on the Chapter",
...     "Can we emphasize Python 3.9 type hints?",
... )
```

We can use this email instance to fill in an f-string as follows:

```
>>> formatted = f"""
... From: <{email.from_addr}>
... To: <{email.to_addr}>
... Subject: {email.subject}
...
... {email.message()}
... """
```

Pretty much any Python code that you would expect to return a string (or a value that can convert to a string with the `str()` function) can be executed inside an f-string. As an example of how powerful it can get, you can even use a list comprehension or ternary operator in a format string parameter:

```
>>> f"{[2*a+1 for a in range(5)]}"
'[1, 3, 5, 7, 9]'
>>> for n in range(1, 5):
...     print(f"{'fizz' if n % 3 == 0 else n}")
```

```
1
2
fizz
4
```

In some cases, we'll want to include a label on the value. This is great for debugging; we can add an = suffix to the expression. It looks like this:

```
>>> a = 5
>>> b = 7
>>> f"{a=}, {b=}, {31*a//42*b + b=}"
'a=5, b=7, 31*a//42*b + b=28'
```

This technique creates a label and a value for us. It can be very helpful. Of course, there are a number of more sophisticated formatting options available to us.

Making it look right

It's nice to be able to include variables in template strings, but sometimes the variables need a bit of coercion to make them look the way we want them to in the output. We're planning a sailing trip around the Chesapeake Bay. Starting from Annapolis, we want to visit Saint Michaels, Oxford, and Cambridge. To do this, we'll need to know the distances among these sailing ports. Here's a useful distance computation for relatively short distances. First, the formal math, because that can help explain the code:

$$d = \sqrt{(R \times \Delta\phi)^2 + (R \times cos(\phi_1) \times \Delta\lambda)^2}$$

This follows the same pattern as the hypotenuse of a triangle computation.

$$h = \sqrt{(x_2 - x_1)^2 + (y_2 - y_1)^2}$$

There are some differences, which are important:

- We wrote $\Delta\phi$ for the differences in the north-south latitudes, converted to radians from degrees. This seemed simpler than $r(y_2) - r(y_1)$.

- We wrote $\Delta\lambda$ for the differences in the east-west longitudes, converted to radians from degrees. This is simpler than $r(x_2) - r(x_1)$ mod 2π. In some parts of the world, the longitudes will be a mix of positive and negative numbers, and we'll need to sort out the minimum positive-valued distance rather than compute a trip all the way around the world.

- The value of R converts radians to nautical miles (about 1.85 km, 1.15 statute miles, exactly 1/60th of a degree of latitude).

- The cosine computation reflects the way longitude distances compress toward zero at the pole. At the north pole, we can walk in a tiny circle and cover all 360°. At the equator, we have to walk (or walk and sail) 40,000 km to cover the same 360°.

Otherwise, this is similar to the math.hypot() function we used in the *Chapter 3* case study, which means it involves square roots and awkwardly too-precise floating-point numbers.

Here's the code:

```
def distance(
        lat1: float, lon1: float, lat2: float, lon2: float
) -> float:

    d_lat = radians(lat2) - radians(lat1)
    d_lon = min(
        (radians(lon2) - radians(lon1)) % (2 * pi),
        (radians(lon1) - radians(lon2)) % (2 * pi),
    )
    R = 60 * 180 / pi
    d = hypot(R * d_lat, R * cos(radians(lat1)) * d_lon)
    return d
```

Here's our test case:

```
>>> annapolis = (38.9784, 76.4922)
>>> saint_michaels = (38.7854, 76.2233)
>>> round(distance(*annapolis, *saint_michaels), 9)
17.070608794
```

That sounds like fun. A 17.070608794 nautical mile trip in a sailboat going about 6 knots will take 2.845101465666667 hours to cross the bay. If the wind is lighter, maybe we'll only go 5 knots, and the trip will take 3.4141217588000004 hours.

This is too many decimal places to be really useful. The boat is 42 feet (12.8m) long; that's 0.007 nautical miles; so, anything after the third decimal place is noise, not a useful result. We'll need to adjust these distances to provide useful information. Also, we have multiple legs, and we don't want to treat each leg as a special case. We need to provide better organization and better display of the data.

Here's how we'd like to plan this trip. First, we'll define our four waypoints for the places we want to go. Then we'll combine the waypoints into legs.

```
>>> annapolis = (38.9784, 76.4922)
>>> saint_michaels = (38.7854, 76.2233)
>>> oxford = (38.6865, 76.1716)
```

```
>>> cambridge = (38.5632, 76.0788)

>>> legs = [
...     ("to st.michaels", annapolis, saint_michaels),
...     ("to oxford", saint_michaels, oxford),
...     ("to cambridge", oxford, cambridge),
...     ("return", cambridge, annapolis),
... ]
```

We can then use the distance computation to figure out how far it is to each destination. We can figure the speed to cover the distance, and we can even compute the fuel required if we can't sail and have to motor:

```
>>> speed = 5
>>> fuel_per_hr = 2.2
>>> for name, start, end in legs:
...     d = distance(*start, *end)
...     print(name, d, d/speed, d/speed*fuel_per_hr)
    to st.michaels 17.070608794397305 3.4141217588794612
    7.511067869534815
    to oxford 6.407736547720565 1.281547309544113 2.8194040809970486
    to cambridge 8.580230239760064 1.716046047952013 3.7753013054944287
    return 31.571582240989173 6.314316448197834 13.891496186035237
```

While we've structured the whole journey, we still have too many digits. Distances only need two decimal places at most. A tenth of an hour is six minutes; we don't need too many digits there. And fuel, similarly, can be computed to the nearest tenth of a gallon. (A tenth of a gallon is 0.4 liters.)

The f-string substitution rules include formatting that can help us. After the expression (a variable is a very simple expression), we can use : followed by a detailed description of the layout of the numbers. We'll return to the details after an example. Here's an improved plan with more useful print formatting:

```
>>> speed = 5
>>> fuel_per_hr = 2.2
>>> print(f"{'leg':16s} {'dist':5s} {'time':4s} {'fuel':4s}")
leg              dist  time fuel
>>> for name, start, end in legs:
...     d = distance(*start, *end)
...     print(
...         f"{name:16s} {d:5.2f} {d/speed:4.1f} "
...         f"{d/speed*fuel_per_hr:4.0f}"
```

```
...        )
to st.michaels   17.07  3.4    8
to oxford         6.41  1.3    3
to cambridge      8.58  1.7    4
return           31.57  6.3   14
```

As an example, the `:5.2f` format specifier says the following, from left to right:

- 5: take up at most five spaces – this guarantees column alignment when using a fixed-width font
- `.`: show the decimal point
- 2: show two places after the decimal
- f: format the input value as a floating-point numeric value

Nifty! The location is formatted as 16s. This follows the same pattern as the float format:

- 16 means it should take up 16 characters. By default, with strings, if the string is shorter than the specified number of characters, it appends spaces to the right-hand side of the string to make it long enough (beware, however: if the original string is too long, it won't be truncated!).
- s means it is a string value.

When we wrote the headings, we used an odd-looking f-string:

```
f"{'leg':16s} {'dist':5s} {'time':4s} {'fuel':4s}")
```

This has string literals like `'leg'` with a format of 16s, and `'dist'` with a format of 5s. The sizes are copied from the detail lines to make sure the headers fit over their respective columns. Making sure the sizes match makes it easy to be sure the heading and the details align.

All these format specifiers have the same pattern; the details are optional:

- A filler character (space if nothing is provided) that's used to pad out the number to fill in the specified size.
- The alignment rule. By default, numbers are right-aligned and strings are left-aligned. Characters like <, ^, and > can force left, centered, or right alignment.
- How to handle the sign (default is – for negative, nothing for positive.) You can use + to show all signs. Also, " " (a space) leaves a space for positive numbers and - for negative numbers to assure proper alignment.

- A 0 if you want leading zeroes to fill in the front of the number.

- The overall size of the field. This should include signs, decimal places, commas, and the period itself for floating-point numbers.

- A , if you want 1,000 groups separated by ",". Use _ to separate groups with an "_". If you have a locale where grouping is done with ".", and the decimal separator is ",", you'll want to use the n format to use all of the locale settings. The f format is biased toward locales that use "," for grouping.

- The . if it's a float (f) or general (g) number, followed by the number of digits to the right of the decimal point.

- The type. Common types are s for strings, d for decimal integers, and f for floating-point. The default is s for string. Most of the other format specifiers are alternative versions of these; for example, o represents octal format and X represents hexadecimal format for integers. The n type specifier can be useful for formatting any kind of number in the current locale's format. For floating-point numbers, the % type will multiply by 100 and format a float as a percentage.

This is a very sophisticated way to display numbers. It can simplify otherwise confusing output, by reducing clutter and aligning data into columns when the information is related.

Faulty Navigation Advice

These waypoints are a little misleading. The route from St. Michaels to Oxford is only 6.41 miles if you're a bird. There's a big peninsula in the way, and it's actually a delightfully longer trip outside Poplar and Tilghman Islands and up the Choptank River. A superficial analysis of distances needs to be backed up with actually looking at the nautical chart and inserting a number of additional waypoints. Our algorithm permits this, and updating the list of legs is easy.

Custom formatters

While these standard formatters apply to most built-in objects, it is also possible for other objects to define nonstandard specifiers. For example, if we pass a datetime object into format, we can use the specifiers used in the datetime.strftime() function, as follows:

```
>>> import datetime
>>> important = datetime.datetime(2019, 10, 26, 13, 14)
>>> f"{important:%Y-%m-%d %I:%M%p}"
'2019-10-26 01:14PM'
```

It is even possible to write custom formatters for objects we create ourselves, but that is beyond the scope of this book. Look into overriding the __format__() special method if you need to do this in your code.

The Python formatting syntax is quite flexible, but it is a difficult mini-language to remember. It's helpful to bookmark the page in the Python standard library to help look up details. While good for many things, this formatting capability isn't powerful enough for larger-scale templating needs, such as generating web pages. There are several third-party templating libraries you can look into if you need to do more than basic formatting of a few strings.

The format() method

F-strings were introduced in Python 3.6. Since Python 3.5's support ended in 2020 (see PEP-478 for details), we no longer need to worry about old Python runtimes without f-strings. There's a slightly more general tool for plugging values into a string template: the format() method of a string. It uses the same formatting specifiers as f-strings. The values come from parameter values to the format() method. Here's an example:

```
>>> from decimal import Decimal
>>> subtotal = Decimal('2.95') * Decimal('1.0625')
>>> template = "{label}: {number:*^{size}.2f}"
>>> template.format(label="Amount", size=10, number=subtotal)
'Amount: ***3.13***'

>>> grand_total = subtotal + Decimal('12.34')
>>> template.format(label="Total", size=12, number=grand_total)
'Total: ***15.47****'
```

The format() method behaves similarly to an f-string with one important distinction: you can access values provided as the arguments to the format() method only. This permits us to provide message templates as configuration items in a complex application.

We have three ways to refer to the arguments that will be inserted into the template string:

- **By name**: The example has {label} and {number} in the template and provides the label= and number= named arguments to the format() method.
- **By position**: We can use {0} in the template, and this will use the first positional argument to format(), like this: "Hello {0}!".format("world").

- **By implied position**: We can use {} in the template, and this will use the positional arguments in order from the template, like this: `"{} {}!".format("Hello", "world")`.

Between f-strings and the `format()` method of a template, we can create complex string values by interpolating expressions or values into a template. In most cases, the f-string is what we need. In rare cases where a format string might be a configuration parameter for a complex application, the `format()` method is helpful.

Strings are Unicode

At the beginning of this section, we defined strings as immutable collections of Unicode characters. This actually makes things very complicated at times, because Unicode isn't a storage format. If you get a string of bytes from a file or a socket, for example, they won't be in Unicode. They will, in fact, be the built-in type `bytes`. Bytes are immutable sequences of...well, bytes. Bytes are the basic storage format in computing. They represent 8 bits, usually described as an integer between 0 and 255, or a hexadecimal equivalent between `0x00` and `0xFF`. Bytes don't represent anything specific; a sequence of bytes may store characters of an encoded string, or pixels in an image, or represent an integer, or part of a floating-point value.

If we print a `bytes` object, Python uses a canonical display that's reasonably compact. Any of the individual byte values that map to ASCII characters are displayed as characters, while non-character ASCII bytes are printed as escapes, either a one-character escape like \n or a hex code like \x1b. You may find it odd that a byte, represented as an integer, can map to an ASCII character. But the old ASCII code defined Latin letters for many different byte values. In ASCII the character a is represented by the same byte as the integer 97, which is the hexadecimal number `0x61`. All of these are an interpretation of the binary pattern `0b1100001`.

```
>>> list(map(hex, b'abc'))
['0x61', '0x62', '0x63']
>>> list(map(bin, b'abc'))
['0b1100001', '0b1100010', '0b1100011']
```

Here's how the canonical display bytes might look when they have a mixture of values that have ASCII character representations and values that don't have a simple character:

```
>>> bytes([137, 80, 78, 71, 13, 10, 26, 10])
b'\x89PNG\r\n\x1a\n'
```

The first byte used a hexadecimal escape, \x89. The next three bytes had ASCII characters, P, N, and G. The next two characters had one-character escapes, \r and \n. The seventh byte also had a hexadecimal escape, \x1a, because there was no other encoding. The final byte is another one-character escape, \n. The eight bytes were expanded into 17 printable characters, not counting the prefix b' and the final '.

Many I/O operations only know how to deal with bytes, even if the bytes object is the encoding of textual data. It is therefore vital to know how to convert between bytes values and Unicode str values.

The problem is that there are many encodings that map bytes to Unicode text. Several are true international standards, but many others are parts of commercial offerings, making them really popular, but not – exactly – standardized. The Python codecs module provides many of these code-decode rules for decoding bytes into a string and encoding a string into bytes.

The important consequence of multiple encodings is that the same sequence of bytes represents completely different text characters when mapped using different encodings! So, bytes must be decoded using the same character set with which they were encoded. It's not possible to get text from bytes without knowing how the bytes should be decoded. If we receive unknown bytes without a specified encoding, the best we can do is guess what format they are encoded in, and we are likely to be wrong.

Decoding bytes to text

If we have an array of bytes from somewhere, we can convert it to Unicode using the .decode() method on the bytes class. This method accepts a string for the name of the character encoding. There are many such encodings; common ones include ASCII, UTF-8, latin-1, and cp-1252. Of these, UTF-8 is one of the most commonly used.

The sequence of bytes (in hex), 63 6c 69 63 68 c3 a9, actually represents the characters of the word cliche in UTF-8 encoding:

```
>>> characters = b'\x63\x6c\x69\x63\x68\xc3\xa9'
>>> characters
b'clich\xc3\xa9'
```

The first line creates a bytes literal as a b'' string. The b character immediately before the string tells us that we are defining a bytes object instead of a normal Unicode text string. Within the string, each byte is specified using – in this case – a hexadecimal number. The \x character escapes within the byte string, and each says *the next two characters represent a byte using hexadecimal digits*.

The final line is the output, showing us Python's canonical representation of a `bytes` object. The first five of the seven bytes had an ASCII character that could be used. The final two bytes, however, don't have ASCII characters, and `\xc3\xa9` had to be used.

Provided we are using a shell that understands UTF-8 encoding, we can decode the bytes to Unicode and see the following:

```
>>> characters.decode("utf-8")
'cliché'
```

The `decode` method returns a text (Unicode) `str` object, with the correct characters. Note that the `\xc3\xa9` sequence of bytes maps to a single Unicode character.

In some cases, the Python terminal may not have the correct encodings defined so the operating system can pick the right characters from the OS font. Yes, there's a very complex mapping from bytes to text to displayed characters, part of which is a Python problem, and part of which is an OS problem. Ideally, your computer is using UTF-8 encodings and has fonts with the full Unicode character set. If not, you may need to research the `PYTHONIOENCODING` environment variable. See `https://docs.python.org/3.9/using/cmdline.html#envvar-PYTHONIOENCODING`.

However, if we had decoded this same string using the Cyrillic `iso8859-5` encoding, we'd have ended up with this:

```
>>> characters.decode("iso8859-5")
'clichУ╓'
```

This is because the `\xc3\xa9` bytes map to different characters in the other encoding. Over the years a lot of different encodings have been invented, and not all of them are in wide use.

```
>>> characters.decode("cp037")
'Ä%ÑÄÇZ'
```

This is why we need to know the encoding used. Generally, UTF-8 should be the encoding of choice. This is a common default, but it isn't universal.

Encoding text to bytes

The flip side of converting bytes to Unicode is situations where we convert outgoing Unicode into byte sequences. This is done with the `encode()` method on the `str` class, which, like the `decode()` method, requires an encoding name. The following code creates a Unicode string and encodes it in different character sets:

```
>>> characters = "cliché"
>>> characters.encode("UTF-8")
b'clich\xc3\xa9'

>>> characters.encode("latin-1")
b'clich\xe9'

>>> characters.encode("cp1252")
b'clich\xe9'

>>> characters.encode("CP437")
b'clich\x82'

>>> characters.encode("ascii")
Traceback (most recent call last):
...
File "<doctest examples.md[73]>", line 1, in <module>
characters.encode("ascii")
UnicodeEncodeError: 'ascii' codec can't encode character '\xe9' in
position 5: ordinal not in range(128)
```

Now you should understand the importance of encodings! The accented character is represented as a different byte by most of these encodings; if we use the wrong one when we are decoding bytes to text, we get the wrong character.

The exception in the last case is not always the desired behavior; there may be cases where we want the unknown characters to be handled in a different way. The encode method takes an optional string argument named errors that can define how such characters should be handled. This string can be one of the following:

- "strict"
- "replace"
- "ignore"
- "xmlcharrefreplace"

The strict replacement strategy is the default we just saw. When a byte sequence is encountered that does not have a valid representation in the requested encoding, an exception is raised. When the replace strategy is used, the character is replaced with a different character. In ASCII, it is a question mark; other encodings may use different symbols, such as an empty box.

The `ignore` strategy simply discards any bytes it doesn't understand, while the `xmlcharrefreplace` strategy creates an `xml` entity representing the Unicode character. This can be useful when converting unknown strings for use in an XML document.

Here's how each of the strategies affects our sample word:

```
>>> characters = "cliché"
>>> characters.encode("ascii", "replace")
b'clich?'

>>> characters.encode("ascii", "ignore")
b'clich'

>>> characters.encode("ascii", "xmlcharrefreplace")
b'clich&#233;'
```

It is possible to call the `str.encode()` and `bytes.decode()` methods without passing an encoding name. The encoding will be set to the default encoding for the current platform. This will depend on the current operating system and locale or regional settings; you can look it up using the `sys.getdefaultencoding()` function. It is usually a good idea to specify the encoding explicitly, though, since the default encoding for a platform may change, or the program may one day be extended to work on text from a wider variety of sources.

If you are encoding text and don't know which encoding to use, it is best to use UTF-8 encoding. UTF-8 is able to represent any Unicode character. In modern software, it is a widely used, standard encoding to ensure documents in any language — or even multiple languages — can be exchanged. The various other possible encodings are useful for legacy documents or in software that uses different character encodings by default.

The UTF-8 encoding uses one byte to represent ASCII and other common characters, and up to four bytes for other characters. UTF-8 is special because it is (mostly) backward-compatible with ASCII; an ASCII document encoded using UTF-8 will be almost identical to the original ASCII document.

Encode vs. Decode

It's hard to remember whether to use encode or decode to convert from binary bytes to Unicode text. The problem is that the letters "code" in Uni*code* can be confusing. I suggest ignoring them. If we think of bytes as code, we encode plain text to bytes and decode bytes back to plain text.

Mutable byte strings

The bytes type, like str, is immutable. We can use index and slice notation on a bytes object and search for a particular sequence of bytes, but we can't extend or modify them. This can be inconvenient when dealing with I/O, as it is often necessary to buffer incoming or outgoing bytes until they are ready to be sent. For example, if we are receiving data from a socket, we may have to accumulate the results of several recv calls before we have received an entire message.

This is where the bytearray built-in comes in. This type behaves something like a list, except it only holds bytes. The constructor for the class can accept a bytes object to initialize it. The extend method can be used to append another bytes object to the existing array (for example, when more data comes from a socket or other I/O channel).

Slice notation can be used on bytearray to modify the item in place, without the overhead of creating a new object. For example, this code constructs a bytearray from a bytes object and then replaces two bytes:

```
>>> ba = bytearray(b"abcdefgh")
>>> ba[4:6] = b"\x15\xa3"
>>> ba
bytearray(b'abcd\x15\xa3gh')
```

We used slice notation to replace bytes in the [4:6] slice with two replacement bytes, b"\x15\xa3".

If we want to manipulate a single element in bytearray, the value must be an integer between 0 and 255 (inclusive), which is a specific bytes pattern. If we try to pass a character or bytes object, it will raise an exception.

A single byte character can be converted to an integer using the ord() (short for *ordinal*) function. This function returns the integer representation of a single character:

```
>>> ba = bytearray(b"abcdefgh")
>>> ba[3] = ord(b'g')
>>> ba[4] = 68
>>> ba
bytearray(b'abcgDfgh')
```

After constructing the array, we replace the character at index 3 (the fourth character, as indexing starts at 0, as with lists) with byte 103. This integer was returned by the ord() function and is the ASCII character for the lowercase g.

For illustration, we also replaced the next character up with byte number 68, which maps to the ASCII character for the uppercase D.

The bytearray type has methods that allow it to behave like a list (we can append integer bytes to it, for example). It can also behave like a bytes object (we can use methods such as count() and find()). The difference is that bytearray is a mutable type, which can be useful for building up complex sequences of bytes from a specific input source. We may, for example, have to read a four byte header with length information before reading the payload bytes. It's handy to be able to perform the reads directly into a mutable bytearray to save creating lots of small objects in memory.

Regular expressions

You know what's really hard to do using object-oriented principles? Parsing strings to match arbitrary patterns, that's what. There have been a fair number of academic papers written in which object-oriented design is used to set up string-parsing, but the results seem too verbose and hard to read, and they are not widely used in practice.

In the real world, string-parsing in most programming languages is handled by regular expressions. These are not verbose, but, wow, are they ever hard to read, at least until you learn the syntax. Even though regular expressions are not object-oriented, the Python regular expression library provides a few classes and objects that you can use to construct and run regular expressions.

While we use regular expressions to "match" a string, this is only a partial description of what a regular expression really is. It can help to think of a regular expression as a mathematical rule that could generate a (potentially infinite) collection of strings. When we "match" a regular expression, it's similar to asking if a given string is in the set generated by the expression. What's tricky is rewriting some fancy math using the paltry collection of punctuation marks available in the original ASCII character set. To help explain the syntax of regular expressions, we'll take a little side-tour through some of these typographic problems that make regular expressions a challenge to read.

Here's an idealized mathematical regular expression for a small set of strings: *world*. We want to match these five characters. The set has one string, "world", that matches. This doesn't seem too complex; the expression amounts to w AND o AND r AND l AND d with "AND" being implied. This parallels the way $d = rt$ means d = r *times* t; the multiplication is implied.

Here's a regular expression for a pattern with repeats: hel^2o. We want to match five characters, but one of them must occur twice. This set has one string, `"hello"`, that matches. This emphasizes the parallel between regular expressions, multiplication, and exponents. It also points out the use of exponents to distinguish between matching the 2 character and matching the previous regular expression two times.

Sometimes, we want some flexibility, and we want to match any digit. Mathematical typesetting lets us use a new font for this: we can say $\mathbb{D}^4$. This fancy-looking D means any digit, or $\mathbb{D} = \{0,1,2,3,4,5,6,7,8,9\}$, and the raised 4 means four copies. This describes a set that has 10,000 possible matching strings from `"0000"` to `"9999"`. Why use the fancy math typesetting? We can use different fonts and letter arrangements to distinguish the concept of "any digit" and "four copies" from the letter D and the digit 4. Code – as we'll see – lacks the fancy fonts, forcing designers to work around the distinction between letters meaning themselves, like D, and letters having other useful meanings, like $\mathbb{D}$.

And yes, a regular expression looks a lot like a long multiplication. There's a very strong parallel with "must have these" and multiplication. Is there a parallel with addition? Yes, it's the idea of optional or alternative constructs; in effect an "or" instead of the default "and."

What if we want to describe years in a date where there could be two digits or four digits? Mathematically, we might say $\mathbb{D}^2|\mathbb{D}^4$. What if we're not sure how many digits? We have a special "to any power," the Kleene star. We can say $\mathbb{D}^*$ to mean any number of repeats of a character in the $\mathbb{D}$ set.

All of this math typesetting has to be implemented in the regular expression language. This can make it difficult to sort out precisely what a regular expression means.

Regular expressions are used to solve a common problem: given a string, determine whether that string matches a given pattern and, optionally, collect substrings that contain relevant information. They can be used to answer questions such as the following:

- Is this string a valid URL?
- What is the date and time of all warning messages in a log file?
- Which users in `/etc/passwd` are in a given group?
- What username and document were requested by the URL a visitor typed?

There are many similar scenarios where regular expressions are the correct answer. In this section, we'll gain enough knowledge of regular expressions to compare strings against relatively common patterns.

There are important limitations here. Regular expressions don't describe languages with recursive structures. When we look at XML or HTML, for example, a <p> tag can contain inline <span> tags, like this: <p><span>hello</span><span>world</span></p>. This recursive nesting of tag-within-tag is generally not a great thing to try and process with a regular expression. We can recognize the individual elements of the XML language, but higher-level constructs like a paragraph tag with other tags inside it require more powerful tools than regular expressions. The XML parsers in the Python standard library can handle these more complex constructs.

Matching patterns

Regular expressions are a complicated mini-language. We need to be able to describe individual characters as well as classes of characters, as well as operators that group and combine characters, all using a few ASCII-compatible characters. Let's start with literal characters, such as letters, numbers, and the space character, which always match themselves. Let's see a basic example:

```
>>> import re

>>> search_string = "hello world"
>>> pattern = r"hello world"

>>> if match := re.match(pattern, search_string):
...     print("regex matches")
...     print(match)
regex matches
<re.Match object; span=(0, 11), match='hello world'>
```

The Python Standard Library module for regular expressions is called re. We import it and set up a search string and pattern to search for; in this case, they are the same string. Since the search string matches the given pattern, the conditional passes and the print statement executes.

A successful match returns a re.Match object describing what – exactly – matched. A failing match returns None, which is equivalent to False in the Boolean context of an if-statement.

We've used the "walrus" operator (:=) to compute the results of re.match() and save those results in a variable all as part of an if-statement. This is one of the most common ways to use the walrus operator to compute a result and then test the result to see if it's truthy. This is a little optimization that can help clarify how the results of the matching operation will be used if they are not None.

We'll almost always use "raw" strings with the r prefix for regular expressions. Raw strings do not have the backslash escapes processed by Python into other letters. In an ordinary string, for example, \b is transformed to a single backspace character. In a raw string, it's two characters, \ and b. In this example, the r-string wasn't really needed because the pattern didn't involve any special \d or \w kinds of regular expression symbols. Using r-strings is a good habit, and we'll try to do it consistently.

Bear in mind that the match function matches the pattern anchored at the beginning of the string. Thus, if the pattern were r"ello world", no match would be found because the search_string value starts with "h" not "e". With confusing asymmetry, the parser stops searching as soon as it finds a match, so the pattern r"hello wo" matches the search_string value successfully, with a few characters left over. Let's build a small example program to demonstrate these differences and help us learn other regular expression syntax:

```python
import re
from typing import Pattern, Match


def matchy(pattern: Pattern[str], text: str) -> None:
    if match := re.match(pattern, text):
        print(f"{pattern=!r} matches at {match=!r}")
    else:
        print(f"{pattern=!r} not found in {text=!r}")
```

The matchy() function expands on the earlier example; it accepts the pattern and search string as parameters. We can see how the start of the pattern must match, but a value is returned as soon as a match is found.

Here are some examples of using this function:

```
>>> matchy(pattern=r"hello wo", text="hello world")
pattern='hello wo' matches at match=<re.Match object; span=(0, 8),
match='hello wo'>
>>> matchy(pattern=r"ello world", text="hello world")
pattern='ello world' not found in text='hello world'
```

We'll be using this function throughout the next few sections. A sequence of test cases is a common way to develop a regular expression – from a bunch of examples of text we want to match and text we don't want to match, we test to make sure our expression works as expected.

If you need control over whether items happen at the beginning or end of a line (or if there are no newlines in the string, or at the beginning and end of the string), you can use the ^ and $ characters to represent the start and end of the string respectively.

If you want a pattern to match an entire string, it's a good idea to include both of these:

```
>>> matchy(pattern=r"^hello world$", text="hello world")
pattern='^hello world$' matches at match=<re.Match object; span=(0, 11),
match='hello world'>
>>> matchy(pattern=r"^hello world$", text="hello worl")
pattern='^hello world$' not found in text='hello worl'
```

We call the ^ and $ characters "anchors." They anchor the match to the beginning or end of the string. What's important is that they don't literally match themselves; they're also called meta-characters. If we were doing fancy math typesetting, we'd use a different font to distinguish between ^ meaning anchored at the beginning and ^ meaning the actual "^" character. Since we don't have fancy math typesetting in Python code, we use \ to distinguish between meta-character and ordinary character. In this case, ^ is a meta-character, and \^ is the ordinary character.

```
>>> matchy(pattern=r"\^hello world\$", text="hello worl")
pattern='\\^hello world\\$' not found in text='hello worl'

>>> matchy(pattern=r"\^hello world\$", text="^hello world$")
pattern='\\^hello world\\$' matches at match=<re.Match object; span=(0,
13), match='^hello world$'>
```

Because we used \^, we need to match the ^ character in the string; this is not the meta-character acting as an anchor. Note that we used r"\^hello..." to create a raw string. Python's canonical display came back as '\\^hello...'. The canonical version – with double \\ – can be awkward to type. While raw strings are easier to work with, they don't display the way we entered them.

Matching a selection of characters

Let's start with matching an arbitrary character. The period character, when used in a regular expression pattern, is a meta-character that stands for a set containing all characters. This will match any single character. Using a period in the string means you don't care what the character is, just that there is a character there. Here is some example output from the matchy() function:

```
pattern='hel.o world' matches at match=<re.Match object; span=(0, 11),
match='hello world'>

pattern='hel.o world' matches at match=<re.Match object; span=(0, 11),
match='helpo world'>
```

```
pattern='hel.o world' matches at match=<re.Match object; span=(0, 11),
match='hel o world'>

pattern='hel.o world' not found in text='helo world'
```

Notice how the last example does not match because there is no character at the period's position in the pattern. We can't match "nothing" without some extra features. We'll get to the idea of optional characters later in this section.

That's all well and good, but what if we only want a smaller set of characters to match? We can put a set of characters inside square brackets to match any one of those characters. So, if we encounter the string [abc] in a regular expression pattern, this defines a set of alternatives to match one character in the string being searched; this one character will be in the set of characters. Note that the [] around the set are meta-characters; they enclose the set and don't match themselves. Let's see a few examples:

```
pattern='hel[lp]o world' matches at match=<re.Match object; span=(0, 11),
match='hello world'>

pattern='hel[lp]o world' matches at match=<re.Match object; span=(0, 11),
match='helpo world'>

pattern='hel[lp]o world' not found in text='helPo world'
```

As with ^ and $, the characters ., [and] are meta-characters. Meta-characters define a more complex feature of a regular expression. If we want to actually match a [character, we'd use \[to escape the meta-meaning and understand this to match [instead of starting the definition of a class of characters.

These square bracket sets could be named *character sets*, but they are more often referred to as **character classes**. Often, we want to include a large range of characters inside these sets, and typing them all out can be monotonous and error-prone. Fortunately, the regular expression designers thought of this and gave us a shortcut. The dash character, in a character set, will create a range. This is especially useful if you want to match *all lowercase letters*, *all letters*, or *all numbers,* as follows:

```
'hello  world' does not match pattern='hello [a-z] world'
'hello b world' matches pattern='hello [a-z] world'
'hello B world' matches pattern='hello [a-zA-Z] world'
'hello 2 world' matches pattern='hello [a-zA-Z0-9] world'
```

There are some character classes that are so common they have their own abbreviations. \d is digits, \s is whitespace, and \w is "word" characters. Instead of [0-9], use \d. Instead of trying to enumerate all the Unicode whitespace characters, use \s. Instead of [a-z0-9_], use \w. Here's an example:

```
>>> matchy(r'\d\d\s\w\w\w\s\d\d\d\d', '26 Oct 2019')
pattern='\\d\\d\\s\\w\\w\\w\\s\\d\\d\\d\\d' matches at match=<re.Match
object; span=(0, 11), match='26 Oct 2019'>
```

Without the defined sets, this pattern would start out as [0-9][0-9][\t\n\r\f\v] [A-Za-z0-9_][A-Za-z0-9_][A-Za-z0-9_]. It gets quite long as we repeat the [\t\n\r\f\v] class and the [0-9] class four more times.

When defining a class with []'s, the – becomes a meta-character. What if we want to match [A-Z] and -, too? We can do this by including the – at the very beginning or the very end; [A-Z-] means any character between A and Z, and the -, also.

Escaping characters

As we've noted above, a lot of characters have special meanings. For example, putting a period character in a pattern matches any arbitrary character. How do we match just a period in a string? We'll use backslashes to escape the special meaning and change the character from a meta-character (like a class definition, or an anchor or the start of a class) and understand it as an ordinary character. This means we'll often have a bunch of \ characters in a regular expression, making r-strings really helpful.

Here's a regular expression to match two-digit decimal numbers between 0.00 and 0.99:

```
pattern='0\\.[0-9][0-9]' matches at match=<re.Match object; span=(0, 4),
match='0.05'>
pattern='0\\.[0-9][0-9]' not found in text='005'
pattern='0\\.[0-9][0-9]' not found in text='0,05'
```

For this pattern, the two characters \. match the single . character. If the period character is missing or is a different character, it will not match.

This backslash escape sequence is used for a variety of special characters in regular expressions. You can use \[to insert a square bracket without starting a character class, and \(to insert a parenthesis, which we'll later see is also a meta-character.

More interestingly, we can also use the escape symbol followed by a character to represent special characters such as newlines (\n) and tabs (\t). As we saw earlier, some character classes can be represented more succinctly using escape strings.

To make the raw strings and backslashes more clear, we'll include the function calls again to show the code we wrote separate from Python's canonical display of the raw strings.

```
>>> matchy(r'\(abc\]', "(abc]")
pattern='\\(abc\\]' matches at match=<re.Match object; span=(0, 5),
match='(abc]'>

>>> matchy(r'\s\d\w', " 1a")
pattern='\\s\\d\\w' matches at match=<re.Match object; span=(0, 3),
match=' 1a'>

>>> matchy(r'\s\d\w', "\t5n")
pattern='\\s\\d\\w' matches at match=<re.Match object; span=(0, 3),
match='\t5n'>

>>> matchy(r'\s\d\w', " 5n")
pattern='\\s\\d\\w' matches at match=<re.Match object; span=(0, 3),
match=' 5n'>
```

To summarize, this use of a backslash has two distinct meanings:

- For meta-characters, a backslash escapes the meta-meaning. For example, . is a class of characters, whereas \. is a single character; similarly, ^ is an anchor at the start of a string, but \^ is the hat character.

- For a few ordinary characters, a backslash is used to name a character class. There aren't many examples of this; the most commonly used are \s, \d, \w, \S, \D, and \W. The uppercase variants, \S, \D, and \W, are the inverses of the lower case. For example, \d is any digit, and \D is any non-digit.

This odd distinction can be confusing at first. What's often helpful is to remember \ in front of a letter creates a special case, whereas \ in front of punctuation removes a meta-character meaning.

Repeating patterns of characters

With this information, we can match most strings of a known length, but most of the time, we don't know how many characters to match inside a pattern. Regular expressions can take care of this, too. We can modify a pattern with a suffix character. When we think of a regular expression as a product, a repeating sequence is like raising to a power. This follows the pattern of a*a*a*a == a**4.

The asterisk (*) character says that the previous pattern can be matched zero or more times. This probably sounds silly, but it's one of the most useful repetition characters. Before we explore why, consider some silly examples to make sure we understand what it does:

```
>>> matchy(r'hel*o', 'hello')
pattern='hel*o' matches at match=<re.Match object; span=(0, 5),
match='hello'>

>>> matchy(r'hel*o', 'heo')
pattern='hel*o' matches at match=<re.Match object; span=(0, 3),
match='heo'>

>>> matchy(r'hel*o', 'helllllo')
pattern='hel*o' matches at match=<re.Match object; span=(0, 8),
match='helllllo'>
```

So, the * character in the pattern says that the previous pattern (the l character) is optional, and if present, can be repeated as many times as possible to match the pattern. The rest of the characters (h, e, and o) have to appear exactly once.

This gets more interesting if we combine the asterisk with patterns that match multiple characters. So, .*, for example, will match any string, whereas [a-z]* matches any collection of lowercase letters, including the empty string. Here are a few examples:

```
>>> matchy(r'[A-Z][a-z]* [a-z]*\.', "A string.")
pattern='[A-Z][a-z]* [a-z]*\\.' matches at match=<re.Match object;
span=(0, 9), match='A string.'>
>>> matchy(r'[A-Z][a-z]* [a-z]*\.', "No .")
pattern='[A-Z][a-z]* [a-z]*\\.' matches at match=<re.Match object;
span=(0, 4), match='No .'>
>>> matchy(r'[a-z]*.*', "")
pattern='[a-z]*.*' matches at match=<re.Match object; span=(0, 0),
match=''>
```

The plus (+) sign in a pattern behaves similarly to an asterisk; it states that the previous pattern can be repeated one or more times; this means the expression is not optional. The question mark (?) ensures a pattern shows up exactly zero or one times, but not more. Let's explore some of these by playing with numbers (remember that \d matches the same character class as [0-9]):

```
>>> matchy(r'\d+\.\d+', "0.4")
pattern='\\d+\\.\\d+' matches at match=<re.Match object; span=(0, 3),
match='0.4'>
>>> matchy(r'\d+\.\d+', "1.002")
pattern='\\d+\\.\\d+' matches at match=<re.Match object; span=(0, 5),
match='1.002'>
>>> matchy(r'\d+\.\d+', "1.")
pattern='\\d+\\.\\d+' not found in text='1.'

>>> matchy(r'\d?\d%', "1%")
pattern='\\d?\\d%' matches at match=<re.Match object; span=(0, 2),
match='1%'>
>>> matchy(r'\d?\d%', "99%")
pattern='\\d?\\d%' matches at match=<re.Match object; span=(0, 3),
match='99%'>
>>> matchy(r'\d?\d%', "100%")
pattern='\\d?\\d%' not found in text='100%'
```

These examples illustrate the two different uses of \, also. For the . character, \. changes it from a meta-character that matches anything to a literal period. For the d character, \d changes it from a literal d to a class of characters, [0-9]. Don't forget that *, +, and ? are meta-characters, and matching them literally means using *, \+, or \?.

Grouping patterns together

So far, we've seen how we can repeat a pattern multiple times, but we are restricted in what patterns we can repeat. If we want to repeat individual characters, we're covered, but what if we want a repeating sequence of characters? Enclosing any set of patterns in parentheses allows them to be treated as a single pattern when applying repetition operations. Compare these patterns:

```
pattern='abc{3}' matches at match=<re.Match object; span=(0, 5),
match='abccc'>
pattern='(abc){3}' not found in text='abccc'
pattern='(abc){3}' matches at match=<re.Match object; span=(0, 9),
match='abcabcabc'>
```

This follows from the core mathematics behind regular expressions. The formulas abc^3 and $(abc)^3$ have dramatically different meanings.

Combined with complex patterns, this grouping feature greatly expands our pattern-matching repertoire. Here's a regular expression that matches simple English sentences:

```
>>> matchy(r'[A-Z][a-z]*( [a-z]+)*\.$', "Eat.")
pattern='[A-Z][a-z]*( [a-z]+)*\\.$' matches at match=<re.Match object;
span=(0, 4), match='Eat.'>

>>> matchy(r'[A-Z][a-z]*( [a-z]+)*\.$', "Eat more good food.")
pattern='[A-Z][a-z]*( [a-z]+)*\\.$' matches at match=<re.Match object;
span=(0, 19), match='Eat more good food.'>

>>> matchy(r'[A-Z][a-z]*( [a-z]+)*\.$', "A good meal.")
pattern='[A-Z][a-z]*( [a-z]+)*\\.$' matches at match=<re.Match object;
span=(0, 12), match='A good meal.'>
```

The first word starts with a capital, followed by zero or more lowercase letters, [A-Z][a-z]*. Then, we enter a parenthetical that matches a single space followed by a word of one or more lowercase letters, [a-z]+. This entire parenthetical is repeated zero or more times, ([a-z]+)*. The pattern is terminated with a period. There cannot be any other characters after the period, as indicated by the $ anchor at the end of the pattern.

We've seen many of the most basic patterns, but the regular expression language supports many more. It is worth bookmarking Python's documentation for the re module and reviewing it frequently. There are very few things that regular expressions cannot match, and they should be the first tool you reach for when parsing strings that don't involve complex recursive definitions.

Parsing information with regular expressions

Let's now focus on the Python side of things. The regular expression syntax is the furthest thing from object-oriented programming. However, Python's re module provides an object-oriented interface to enter the regular expression engine.

We've been checking whether the re.match() function returns a valid object or not. If a pattern does not match, that function returns None. If it does match, however, it returns a useful object that we can inspect for information about the pattern.

So far, our regular expressions have answered questions such as *does this string match this pattern?* Matching patterns is useful, but in many cases, a more interesting question is *if this string matches this pattern, what is the value of a relevant substring?* If you use groups to identify parts of the pattern that you want to reference later, you can get them out of the match return value, as illustrated in the next example:

```
def email_domain(text: str) -> Optional[str]:
    email_pattern = r"[a-z0-9._%+-]+@([a-z0-9.-]+\.[a-z]{2,})"
    if match := re.match(email_pattern, text, re.IGNORECASE):
        return match.group(1)
    else:
        return None
```

The full specification describing all valid email addresses is extremely complicated, and the regular expression that accurately matches all possibilities is obscenely long. So, we cheated and made a smaller regular expression that matches many common email addresses; the point is that we want to access the domain name (after the @ sign) so we can connect to that address. This is done easily by wrapping that part of the pattern in parentheses and calling the group() method on the object returned by match().

We've used an additional argument value, re.IGNORECASE, to mark this pattern as case-independent. This saves us from having to use [a-zA-Z...] in three places in the pattern. It is a handy simplification when case doesn't matter.

There are three ways to collect the groups that match. We've used the group() method, which provides one matching group. Since there's only one pair of ()'s, this seems prudent. The more general groups() method returns a tuple of all the () groups matched inside the pattern, which we can index to access a specific value. The groups are ordered from left to right. However, bear in mind that groups can be nested, meaning you can have one or more groups inside another group. In this case, the groups are returned in the order of their leftmost ('s, so the outermost group will be returned before its inner matching groups.

We can also provide names for groups. The syntax is very complex-looking. We have to use (?P<name>...) instead of (...) to collect the matched text as a group. The ?P<name> is how we provide a group name of name inside the ()'s. This lets us use the groupdict() method to extract names and their contents.

Here's an alternative to the email domain parser; this one uses named groups:

```
def email_domain_2(text: str) -> Optional[str]:
    email_pattern = r"(?P<name>[a-z0-9._%+-]+)@(?P<domain>[a-z0-9.-]+\.
[a-z]{2,})"
    if match := re.match(email_pattern, text, re.IGNORECASE):
        return match.groupdict()["domain"]
    else:
        return None
```

We've changed the pattern to add ?P<name> and ?<domain> inside the ()'s to provide names to these capture groups. This part of the regular expression doesn't change what is matched, it provides names to the capture groups.

Other features of the re module

In addition to the match() function, the re module provides a couple of other useful functions, search() and findall(). The search() function finds the first instance of a matching pattern, relaxing the restriction that the pattern should be implicitly anchored to the first letter of the string. Note that you can get a similar effect by using match() and putting a .* character at the front of the pattern to match any characters between the start of the string and the pattern you are looking for.

The findall() function behaves similarly to search(), except that it finds all non-overlapping instances of the matching pattern, not just the first one. Think of it searching for the first match, then continuing the search after the end of the first matching to find the next one.

Instead of returning a list of re.Match objects, as you would expect, it returns a list of matching strings, or tuples. Sometimes it's strings, sometimes it's tuples. It's not a very good API at all! As with all bad APIs, you'll have to memorize the differences and not rely on intuition. The type of the return value depends on the number of bracketed groups inside the regular expression:

- If there are no groups in the pattern, re.findall() will return a list of strings, where each value is a complete substring from the source string that matches the pattern
- If there is exactly one group in the pattern, re.findall() will return a list of strings where each value is the contents of that group
- If there are multiple groups in the pattern, re.findall() will return a list of tuples where each tuple contains a value from a matching group, in order

Consistency Helps

When you are designing function calls in your own Python libraries, try to make the function always return a consistent data structure. It is often good to design functions that can take arbitrary inputs and process them, but the return value should not switch from a single value to a list, or a list of values to a list of tuples depending on the input. Let re.findall() be a lesson!

The examples in the following interactive session will hopefully clarify the differences:

```
>>> import re
>>> re.findall(r"\d+[hms]", "3h 2m   45s")
['3h', '2m', '45s']
>>> re.findall(r"(\d+)[hms]", "3h:2m:45s")
['3', '2', '45']
>>> re.findall(r"(\d+)([hms])", "3h, 2m, 45s")
[('3', 'h'), ('2', 'm'), ('45', 's')]
>>> re.findall(r"((\d+)([hms]))", "3h - 2m - 45s")
[('3h', '3', 'h'), ('2m', '2', 'm'), ('45s', '45', 's')]
```

It seems like it's always a good practice to decompose the data elements to the extent possible. In this case, we separated the numeric value from the units, hours, minutes, or seconds, making it easier to convert a complex string into a time interval.

Making regular expressions efficient

Whenever you call one of the regular expression methods, the re module has to convert the pattern string into an internal structure that makes searching strings fast. This conversion takes a non-trivial amount of time. If a regular expression pattern is going to be reused multiple times (for example, inside a for or while statement), it would be better if this conversion step could be done only once.

This is possible with the re.compile() method. It returns an object-oriented version of the regular expression that has been compiled down and has the methods we've explored (match(), search(), and findall()), among others. The changes to what we've seen are minor. Here's what we've been using:

```
>>> re.findall(r"\d+[hms]", "3h 2m   45s")
```

We can create a two-step operation, where a single pattern is reused for a number of strings.

```
>>> duration_pattern = re.compile(r"\d+[hms]")
>>> duration_pattern.findall("3h 2m   45s")
['3h', '2m', '45s']
>>> duration_pattern.findall("3h:2m:45s")
['3h', '2m', '45s']
```

Compiling the patterns in advance of using them is a handy optimization. It makes the application slightly simpler and a bit more efficient.

This has definitely been a condensed introduction to regular expressions. At this point, we have a good feel for the basics and will recognize when we need to do further research. If we have a string pattern-matching problem, regular expressions will almost certainly be able to solve them for us. However, we may need to look up new syntax in a more comprehensive coverage of the topic. But now we know what to look for! Some tools, like Pythex at `https://pythex.org`, can help develop and debug regular expressions. Let's move on to a completely different topic: filesystem paths.

Filesystem paths

Most operating systems provide a *filesystem*, a way of mapping a logical abstraction of *directories* (often depicted as *folders*) and *files* to the bits and bytes stored on a hard drive or another storage device. As humans, we typically interact with the filesystem using a drag-and-drop interface with images of folders and files of different types. Or we can use command-line programs such as `cp`, `mv`, and `mkdir`.

As programmers, we have to interact with the filesystem with a series of system calls. You can think of these as library functions supplied by the operating system so that programs can call them. They have a clunky interface with integer file handles and buffered reads and writes, and that interface is different depending on which operating system you are using. The Python `os` module exposes some of these underlying calls.

Inside the `os` module is the `os.path` module. While it works, it's not very intuitive. It requires a lot of string concatenation and you have to be conscious of OS differences. For example, there is an `os.sep` attribute representing the path separator; that's a `"/"` on POSIX-compliant OSes and `"\"` for Windows. Using it can lead to code that looks like this:

```
>>> import os.path
>>> path = os.path.abspath(
...     os.sep.join(
...         ["", "Users", "dusty", "subdir", "subsubdir", "file.ext"]))
>>> print(path)
/Users/dusty/subdir/subsubdir/file.ext
```

The `os.path` module conceals some of the platform-specific details. But this still forces us to work with paths as strings.

Working with filesystem paths in the form of strings is often irritating. Paths that are easy to type on the command line become illegible in Python code. When working with multiple paths (for example, when processing images in a data pipeline for a machine learning computer vision problem), just managing those directories becomes a bit of an ordeal.

So, the Python language designers included a module called `pathlib` in the standard library. It's an object-oriented representation of paths and files that is much more pleasant to work with. The preceding path, using `pathlib`, would look like this:

```
>>> from pathlib import Path
>>> path = Path("/Users") / "dusty" / "subdir" / "subsubdir" / "file.ext"
>>> print(path)
/Users/dusty/subdir/subsubdir/file.ext
```

As you can see, it's quite a bit easier to see what's going on. Notice the unique use of the division operator as a path separator so you don't have to do anything with `os.sep`. This is an elegant use of overloading Python's `__truediv__()` method to provide this feature for `Path` object.

In a more real-world example, consider some code that counts the number of lines of code – excluding whitespace and comments – in all Python files in a given directory and subdirectories:

```python
from pathlib import Path
from typing import Callable


def scan_python_1(path: Path) -> int:
    sloc = 0
    with path.open() as source:
        for line in source:
            line = line.strip()
            if line and not line.startswith("#"):
                sloc += 1
    return sloc


def count_sloc(path: Path, scanner: Callable[[Path], int]) -> int:
    if path.name.startswith("."):
        return 0
    elif path.is_file():
```

```
        if path.suffix != ".py":
            return 0
        with path.open() as source:
            return scanner(path)
    elif path.is_dir():
        count = sum(
            count_sloc(name, scanner) for name in path.iterdir())
        return count
    else:
        return 0
```

In typical `pathlib` usage, we rarely have to construct many `Path` objects. In this example, the base `Path` is provided as a parameter. The bulk of the `Path` manipulation is locating other files or directories relative to a given `Path`. The rest of the `Path`-related processing is asking for attributes of a specific `Path`.

The `count_sloc()` function looks at the name of the path, skipping names beginning with ".". This avoids the "." and ".." directories, but it also skips directories like `.tox`, `.coverage`, or `.git` that are created by our tools.

There are three general cases:

- Actual files that might have Python source. We make sure the suffix of the file name is `.py` to be sure we want to open the file. We'll call the given `scanner()` function to open and read each Python file. There are several approaches to counting source code; we've shown one here, in the `scan_python_1()` function that should be provided as an argument value.
- Directories. In this case, we iterate through the directory's content, calling `count_sloc()` on the items we find inside this directory.
- Other filesystem objects like device mount names, symbolic links, devices, FIFO queues, and sockets. We ignore these.

The `Path.open` method takes similar arguments to the `open` built-in function, but it uses a more object-oriented syntax. We can use `Path('./README.md').open()` to open the file for reading, if the path already exists.

The `scan_python_1()` function iterates over each line in the file and adds it to the count. We skip whitespace and comment lines, since these don't represent actual source code. The total count is returned to the calling function.

Here's how we invoke this function to count lines of code in one directory.

```
>>> base = Path.cwd().parent
>>> chapter =  base / "ch_02"
>>> count = count_sloc(chapter, scan_python_1)
>>> print(
...     f"{chapter.relative_to(base)}: {count} lines of code"
... )
ch_02: 542 lines of code
```

This shows the one-and-only Path() constructor in this fairly complex example. We leap up to the parent directory from the **current working directory (CWD)**. From there we can descend into the ch_02 subdirectory and rummage around, looking at directories and Python files.

This also shows how we provide the scan_python_1() function as the argument value for the scanner parameter. For more insight into using functions as parameters to other functions, see *Chapter 8, The Intersection of Object-Oriented and Functional Programming*.

The Path class in the pathlib module has a method or property to cover pretty much everything you might want to do with a path. In addition to those we covered in the example, here are a few more methods and attributes of a Path object:

- .absolute() returns the full path from the root of the filesystem. This helps show where relative paths came from.
- .parent returns a path to the parent directory.
- .exists() checks whether the file or directory exists.
- .mkdir() creates a directory at the current path. It takes Boolean parents and exist_ok arguments to indicate that it should recursively create the directories if necessary and that it shouldn't raise an exception if the directory already exists.

Refer to the standard library documentation at https://docs.python.org/3/library/pathlib.html for even more uses. The authors are proud to have contributed to this library.

Almost all of the standard library modules that accept a string path can also accept a pathlib.Path object. An os.PathLike type hint is used to describe parameters that accept a Path. For example, you can open a ZIP file by passing a path into it:

```
>>> zipfile.ZipFile(Path('nothing.zip'), 'w').writestr('filename',
'contents')
```

Some external packages may not work with `Path` objects. In those cases, you'll have to cast the path to a string using `str(pathname)`.

Statements vs. Lines of Code

The `scan_python_1()` function counts each line of a triple-quoted, multi-line strings as if they're lines of code. If we're sure each *physical* line matters, then a long docstring might be relevant, even when it's not really code. On the other hand, we might decide that we want to count meaningful *statements* instead of physical lines; in this case, we'll need a smarter function that uses the `ast` module. It's far, far better to work with the **Abstract Syntax Trees (ASTs)** than it is to try and work with the source text. Using the `ast` module doesn't change the `Path` processing. It's a little more complex than reading the text, and outside the scope of this book. If we count statements (not lines that could be statements or could be triple-quoted comments) there are 257 statements, in 542 lines of code.

We've looked at working strings, bytes, and filesystem paths. The next concept we need to cover is how to save our application's objects to files and recovering objects from the bytes of a file. We call this process serialization.

Serializing objects

We've been working with bytes and file paths as foundations that support working with persistent objects. To make an object persistent, we need to create a series of bytes that represent the state of the object, and write those bytes to a file. The missing piece of persistence, then, is this process of encoding objects as a series of bytes. We also want to decode objects and their relationships from a series of bytes. This encoding and decoding is also described as **serializing** and **deserializing**.

When we look at web services, we'll often see a service described as RESTful. The "REST" concept is REpresentational State Transfer; the server and client will exchange representations of object states. The distinction here can be helpful: the two pieces of software don't exchange objects. The applications have their own internal objects; they exchange a representation of object state.

There are several ways to serialize objects. We'll start with a simple and general approach using the `pickle` module. Later, we'll look at the `json` package as an alternative.

The Python `pickle` module is an object-oriented way to store object state directly in a special storage format. It essentially converts an object's state (and all the state of all the objects it holds as attributes) into a series of bytes that can be stored or transported however we see fit.

For basic tasks, the `pickle` module has an extremely simple interface. It comprises four basic functions for storing and loading data: two for manipulating file-like objects, and two for manipulating `bytes` objects so we can work with pickled objects without necessarily having an open file.

The `dump()` method accepts an object to be written and a file-like object to write the serialized bytes to. A file-like object must have a `write()` method, and that method must know how to handle a `bytes` argument. This means a file opened for text output wouldn't work; we need to open the file with a mode value of `wb`.

The `load()` method does exactly the opposite; it reads a serialized object's state from a file-like object. This object must have the proper file-like `read()` and `readline()` methods, each of which must, of course, return `bytes`. The `pickle` module will read the bytes and the `load()` method will return the fully reconstructed object. Here's an example that stores and then loads some data in a list object:

```python
>>> import pickle
>>> some_data = [
...    "a list", "containing", 5, "items",
...    {"including": ["str", "int", "dict"]}
...    ]

>>> with open("pickled_list", 'wb') as file:
...     pickle.dump(some_data, file)

>>> with open("pickled_list", 'rb') as file:
...     loaded_data = pickle.load(file)

>>> print(loaded_data)
['a list', 'containing', 5, 'items', {'including': ['str', 'int',
'dict']}]

>>> assert loaded_data == some_data
```

This code serializes the object referred to by `some_list`. This includes the associated strings, and dictionaries, and even an integer. This is stored in the file and then loaded from the same file. In each case, we open the file using a `with` statement so that it is automatically closed. We've been careful to use modes of `wb` and `rb` to be sure the file is in bytes mode instead of text mode.

The `assert` statement at the end would raise an error if the newly loaded object was not equal to the original object. Equality does not imply that they are the same object. Indeed, if we were to print the `id()` of both objects, we would discover they are distinct objects with distinct internal identifiers. However, because they are both lists whose contents are equal, the two lists are also considered equal.

The `dumps()` and `loads()` functions behave much like their file-like counterparts, except they return or accept `bytes` instead of file-like objects. The `dumps` function requires only one argument, the object to be stored, and it returns a serialized `bytes` object. The `loads()` function requires a `bytes` object and returns the restored object. The `'s'` character in the method names is short for string; it's a legacy name from ancient versions of Python, where `str` objects were used instead of `bytes`.

It is possible to call `dump()` or `load()` on a single open file more than once. Each call to `dump` will store a single object (plus any objects it is composed of or contains), while a call to `load()` will load and return just one object. So, for a single file, each separate call to `dump()` when storing the object should have an associated call to `load()` when restoring at a later date.

It's important to be aware that the representation of the state of an object is highly focused on a specific major release of Python. A pickle file created in Python 3.7, for example, may not be usable by Python 3.8. This suggests that pickle files are good for temporary persistence, but not suitable for long-term storage or sharing among Python applications that might not all have a common version.

The process of recovering the state of an object from a pickled representation can – under some circumstances – result in evaluating arbitrary code buried in the pickle file. This means a pickle file can be a vector for malicious code. This leads to a prominent warning in the documentation for the pickle module:

Warning

The pickle module is not secure. Only unpickle data you trust.

This advice generally leads us to avoid accepting pickle-format files without trusting the sender and having assurance no person in the middle has tampered with the file. An application that uses a pickle for a temporary cache has nothing to worry about.

Customizing pickles

With most common Python objects, pickling *just works*. Basic primitive types such as integers, floats, and strings can be pickled, as can any container objects, such as lists or dictionaries, provided the contents of those containers are also picklable. Further, and importantly, any object can be pickled, so long as all of its attributes are also picklable.

So, what makes an attribute unpicklable? Usually, it has something to do with dynamic attribute values subject to change. For example, if we have an open network socket, open file, running thread, subprocess, processing pool, or database connection stored as an attribute on an object, it will not make sense to pickle these objects. Device and operating system state will be meaningless when we attempt to reload the object later. We can't just pretend the original thread or socket connection exists when we reload! No, we need to somehow customize how such transient and dynamic data is dumped and loaded.

Here's a class that loads the contents of a web page every hour to ensure that they stay up to date. It uses the `threading.Timer` class to schedule the next update:

```python
from threading import Timer
import datetime
from urllib.request import urlopen

class URLPolling:
    def __init__(self, url: str) -> None:
        self.url = url
        self.contents = ""
        self.last_updated: datetime.datetime
        self.timer: Timer
        self.update()

    def update(self) -> None:
        self.contents = urlopen(self.url).read()
        self.last_updated = datetime.datetime.now()
        self.schedule()

    def schedule(self) -> None:
        self.timer = Timer(3600, self.update)
        self.timer.setDaemon(True)
        self.timer.start()
```

Objects like `url`, `contents`, and `last_updated` are all picklable, but if we try to pickle an instance of this class, things go a little nutty on the `self.timer` instance:

```
>>> import pickle
>>> poll = URLPolling("http://dusty.phillips.codes")
>>> pickle.dumps(poll)
Traceback (most recent call last):
  ...
  File "<doctest url_poll.__test__.test_broken[2]>", line 1, in
<module>
pickle.dumps(poll)
TypeError: cannot pickle '_thread.lock' object
```

That's not a very useful error, but it looks like we're trying to pickle something we shouldn't be pickling. That would be the `Timer` instance; we're storing a reference to `self.timer` in the `schedule()` method, and that attribute cannot be serialized.

When `pickle` tries to serialize an object, it simply tries to store the state, the value of the object's `__dict__` attribute; `__dict__` is a dictionary mapping all the attribute names on the object to their values. Luckily, before checking `__dict__`, `pickle` checks to see whether a `__getstate__()` method exists. If it does, it will store the return value of that method instead of the `__dict__` object.

Let's add a `__getstate__()` method to our `URLPolling` class that simply returns a copy of the `__dict__` without the unpicklable timer object:

```
def __getstate__(self) -> dict[str, Any]:
    pickleable_state = self.__dict__.copy()
        if "timer" in pickleable_state:
            del pickleable_state["timer"]
        return pickleable_state
```

If we pickle an instance of this expanded version of `URLPolling`, it will no longer fail. And we can even successfully restore that object using `loads()`. However, the restored object doesn't have a `self.timer` attribute, so it will not be refreshing the content like it is designed to do. We need to somehow create a new timer (to replace the missing one) when the object is unpickled.

As we might expect, there is a complementary `__setstate__()` method that can be implemented to customize unpickling. This method accepts a single argument, which is the object returned by `__getstate__`. If we implement both methods, `__getstate__()` is not required to return a dictionary, since `__setstate__()` will know what to do with whatever object `__getstate__()` chooses to return. In our case, we simply want to restore the `__dict__`, and then create a new timer:

```
def __setstate__(self, pickleable_state: dict[str, Any]) -> None:
    self.__dict__ = pickleable_state
    self.schedule()
```

The parallels between __init__() and __setstate__() are important. Both involve a call to self.schedule() to create (or recreate) the internal timer object. This is a common pattern for working with pickled objects that have dynamic state that must be recovered.

The pickle module is very flexible and provides other tools to further customize the pickling process if you need them. However, these are beyond the scope of this book. The tools we've covered are sufficient for many basic pickling tasks. Objects to be pickled are normally relatively simple data objects. Some of the popular machine learning frameworks, like scikit-learn, use pickle to preserve the model that was created. This lets a data scientist use the model for predictions or for further testing.

Because of the security limitation, we need an alternative format for exchanging data. A text-based format can be helpful because it's often easier to inspect a text file to be sure it isn't malicious. We'll look at JSON as a popular text-based serialization format.

Serializing objects using JSON

There are many formats that have been used for text-based data exchange over the years. **Extensible Markup Language (XML)** is popular, but the files tend to be large. **Yet Another Markup Language (YAML)** is another format that you may see referenced occasionally. Tabular data is frequently exchanged in the **Comma-Separated Value (CSV)** format. Many of these are fading into obscurity and there are many more that you will encounter over time. Python has solid standard or third-party libraries for all of them.

Before using such libraries on untrusted data, make sure to investigate security concerns with each of them. XML and YAML, for example, both have obscure features that, used maliciously, can allow arbitrary commands to be executed on the host machine. These features may not be turned off by default. Do your research. Even something as simple-seeming as a ZIP file or a JPEG image can be hacked to create a data structure that can crash a web server.

JavaScript Object Notation (JSON) is a human-readable format for exchanging data. JSON is a standard format that can be interpreted by a wide array of heterogeneous client systems. This means JSON is extremely useful for transmitting data between completely decoupled systems. The JSON format does not have any support for executable code; because only data can be serialized, it is more difficult to inject malicious content.

Because JSON can be easily interpreted by JavaScript engines, it is often used for transmitting data from a web server to a JavaScript-capable web browser. If the web application serving the data is written in Python, the server needs a way to convert internal data into the JSON format.

There is a module to do this, predictably named `json`. This module provides a similar interface to the `pickle` module, with `dump()`, `load()`, `dumps()`, and `loads()` functions. The default calls to these functions are nearly identical to those in `pickle`, so let's not repeat the details. There are a couple of differences: obviously, the output of these calls is valid JSON notation, rather than a pickled object. In addition, the `json` functions operate on `str` objects, rather than `bytes`. Therefore, when dumping to or loading from a file, we need to create text files rather than binary ones.

The JSON serializer is not as robust as the `pickle` module; it can only serialize basic types such as integers, floats, and strings, and simple containers such as dictionaries and lists. Each of these has a direct mapping to a JSON representation, but JSON is unable to represent objects unique to Python like class or function definitions.

Generally, the `json` module's functions try to serialize the object's state using the value of the object's __dict__ attribute. A better approach is to supply custom code to serialize an object's state into a JSON-friendly dictionary. We also want to go the other way: deserializing a JSON dictionary to recover a Python object's state.

In the `json` module, both the object encoding and decoding functions accept optional arguments to customize the behavior. The `dump()` and `dumps()` functions accept a poorly named `cls` keyword argument. (It's short for "class", which we have to spell funny because `class` is a reserved keyword.) If this argument value is provided to the function, it should be a subclass of the `JSONEncoder` class, with the `default()` method overridden. This overridden `default()` method accepts an arbitrary Python object and converts it to a dictionary that `json` can serialize. If it doesn't know how to process the object, we should call the `super()` method, so that it can take care of serializing basic types in the normal way.

The `load()` and `loads()` methods also accept such a `cls` argument that can be a subclass of the inverse class, `JSONDecoder`. However, it is normally sufficient to pass a function into these methods using the `object_hook` keyword argument. This function accepts a dictionary and returns an object; if it doesn't know what to do with the input dictionary, it can return it unmodified.

Let's look at an example. Imagine we have the following simple contact class that we want to serialize:

```
class Contact:
    def __init__(self, first, last):
        self.first = first
        self.last = last

    @property
    def full_name(self):
        return("{} {}".format(self.first, self.last))
```

We can try to serialize the __dict__ attribute:

```
>>> import json
>>> c = Contact("Noriko", "Hannah")
>>> json.dumps(c.__dict__)
'{"first": "Noriko", "last": "Hannah"}'
```

But accessing the special __dict__ attribute in this fashion is kind of crude. This can lead to problems when an attribute has a value that's not already serialized by the json module; datetime objects are a common problem. Also, what if the receiving code (perhaps some JavaScript on a web page) wanted that full_name property to be supplied? Of course, we could construct the dictionary by hand, but let's create a custom encoder instead:

```
import json

class ContactEncoder(json.JSONEncoder):
    def default(self, obj: Any) -> Any:
        if isinstance(obj, Contact):
            return {
                "__class__": "Contact",
                "first": obj.first,
                "last": obj.last,
                "full_name": obj.full_name,
            }
        return super().default(obj)
```

The default method needs to check to see what kind of object we're trying to serialize. If it's a Contact, we convert it to a dictionary manually. Otherwise, we let the parent class handle serialization (by assuming that it is a basic type, which json knows how to handle). Notice that we pass an extra attribute to identify this object as a contact, since there would be no way to tell upon loading it.

In some cases, we may want to provide a more complete, fully qualified name, including the package and module. Remember that the format of the dictionary depends on the code at the receiving end; there has to be an agreement as to how the data is going to be specified.

We can use this class to encode a contact by passing the class (not an instantiated object) to the dump or dumps function:

```
>>> c = Contact("Noriko", "Hannah")
>>> text = json.dumps(c, cls=ContactEncoder)
>>> text
'{"__class__": "Contact", "first": "Noriko", "last": "Hannah",
"full_name": "Noriko Hannah"}'
```

For decoding, we can write a function that accepts a dictionary and checks the existence of the __class__ attribute to decide whether to convert it to a Contact instance or leave it as a default dictionary:

```
def decode_contact(json_object: Any) -> Any:
    if json_object.get("__class__") == "Contact":
        return Contact(json_object["first"], json_object["last"])
    else:
        return json_object
```

We can pass this function to the load() or loads() function using the object_hook keyword argument:

```
>>> some_text = (
...     '{"__class__": "Contact", "first": "Milli", "last": "Dale", '
...     '"full_name": "Milli Dale"}'
... )
>>> c2 = json.loads(some_text, object_hook=decode_contact)
>>> c2.full_name
'Milli Dale'
```

These examples show how we can use JSON to exchange objects that encode a number of common Python objects. For uncommon Python objects, there are straightforward ways to add an encoder or a decoder to handle more complex cases. In larger applications, we might include a special to_json() method to produce a useful serialization of an object.

Case study

In the previous chapters of the case study, we've been skirting an issue that arises frequently when working with complex data. Files have both a logical layout and a physical format. We've been laboring under a tacit assumption that our files are in CSV format, with a layout defined by the first line of the file. In *Chapter 2*, we touched on file loading. In *Chapter 6*, we revisited loading data and partitioning it into training and testing sets.

In both previous chapters, we trusted that the data would be in a CSV format. This isn't a great assumption to make. We need to look at the alternatives and elevate our assumptions into a design choice. We also need to build in the flexibility to make changes as the context for using our application evolves.

It's common to map complex objects to dictionaries, which have a tidy JSON representation. For this reason, the `Classifier` web application makes use of dictionaries. We can also parse CSV data into dictionaries. The idea of working with dictionaries provides a kind of grand unification of CSV, Python, and JSON. We'll start by looking at the CSV format before moving on to some alternatives for serialization, like JSON.

CSV format designs

We can make use of the `csv` module to read and write files. **CSV** stands for **Comma-Separated Values**, designed (originally) to export and import data from a spreadsheet.

The CSV format describes a sequence of rows. Each row is a sequence of strings. That's all there is, and it can be a bit of a limitation.

The "comma" in CSV is a role, not a specific character. The purpose of this character is to separate the columns of data. For the most part, the role of the comma is played by the literal ",". But other actors can fill this role. It's common to see the tab character, written as "\t" or "\x09", fill the role of the comma.

The end-of-line is often the CRLF sequence, written as "\r\n" or \x0d\x0a. On macOS X and Linux, it's also possible to use a single newline character, \n, at the end of each row. Again, this is a role, and other characters could be used.

In order to contain the comma character within a column's data, the data can be quoted. This is often done by surrounding a column's value with the " character. It's possible to specify a different quote character when describing a CSV dialect.

Because CSV data is simply a sequence of strings, any other interpretation of the data requires processing by our application. For example, within the TrainingSample class, the load() method includes processing like the following:

```
test = TestingKnownSample(
    species=row["species"],
    sepal_length=float(row["sepal_length"]),
    sepal_width=float(row["sepal_width"]),
    petal_length=float(row["petal_length"]),
    petal_width=float(row["petal_width"]),
)
```

This load() method extracts specific column values from each row, applies a conversion function to build a Python object from the text, and uses all of the attribute values to build a resulting object.

There are two ways to consume (and produce) CSV-formatted data. We can work with each row as a dictionary, or we can process each row as a simple list of strings. We'll look at both alternatives to see how well they apply to the data in our case study.

CSV dictionary reader

We can read CSV files as a sequence of strings, or as a dictionary. When we read the file as a sequence of strings, there are no special provisions for column headers. We're forced to manage the details of which column has a particular attribute. This is unpleasantly complex, but sometimes necessary.

We can also read a CSV file so each row becomes a dictionary. We can provide a sequence of keys, or the first line of the file can provide the keys. This is relatively common, and it saves a little bit of confusion when the column headers are part of the data.

We've been looking at the Bezdek Iris data for our case study. There's a copy of the data in the Kaggle repository, https://www.kaggle.com/uciml/iris. The data is also available at https://archive.ics.uci.edu/ml/datasets/iris. The UCI Machine Learning Repository file, bezdekIris.data, does not have column titles; these are provided separately in a file named iris.names.

The iris.names file has a great deal of information in it, including this in section 7 of the document:

```
7. Attribute Information:
   1. sepal length in cm
   2. sepal width in cm
   3. petal length in cm
   4. petal width in cm
   5. class:
      -- Iris Setosa
      -- Iris Versicolour
      -- Iris Virginica
```

This defines the five columns of data. This separation between the metadata and the sample data isn't ideal, but we can copy and paste this information into code to make something useful from it.

We'll use it to define an Iris reader class as follows:

```python
class CSVIrisReader:
    """
    Attribute Information:
        1. sepal length in cm
        2. sepal width in cm
        3. petal length in cm
        4. petal width in cm
        5. class:
            -- Iris Setosa
            -- Iris Versicolour
            -- Iris Virginica
    """

    header = [
        "sepal_length",  # in cm
        "sepal_width",   # in cm
        "petal_length",  # in cm
        "petal_width",   # in cm
        "species",  # Iris-setosa, Iris-versicolour, Iris-virginica
    ]

    def __init__(self, source: Path) -> None:
        self.source = source

    def data_iter(self) -> Iterator[dict[str, str]]:
```

```
        with self.source.open() as source_file:
            reader = csv.DictReader(source_file, self.header)
            yield from reader
```

We transformed the documentation into a sequence of column names. The transformation isn't arbitrary. We matched the resulting KnownSample class attribute names.

In relatively simple applications, there's a single source of data, so the attribute names for classes and column names for CSV files are easy to keep aligned. This isn't always the case. In some problem domains, the data may have several variant names and formats. We may choose attribute names that seem good, but may not simply match any of the input files.

The data_iter() method has a name suggesting it is an iterator over multiple data items. The type hint (Iterator[Dict[str, str]]) confirms this. The function uses yield from to provide rows from the CSV DictReader object as they're demanded by a client process.

This is a "lazy" way to read lines from the CSV as they're required by another object. The iterator is like a factory using kanban techniques – it prepares data in response to demand. This doesn't slurp in the entire file, creating a gigantic list of dictionaries. Instead, the iterator produces one dictionary at a time, as they're requested.

One way to request data from an iterator is to use the built-in list() function. We can use this class as follows:

```python
>>> from model import CSVIrisReader
>>> from pathlib import Path
>>> test_data = Path.cwd().parent/"bezdekIris.data"
>>> rdr = CSVIrisReader(test_data)
>>> samples = list(rdr.data_iter())
>>> len(samples)
150
>>> samples[0]
{'sepal_length': '5.1', 'sepal_width': '3.5', 'petal_length': '1.4',
'petal_width': '0.2', 'species': 'Iris-setosa'}
```

The CSV DictReader produces a dictionary. We provided the keys for this dictionary with the self.header value; an alternative is to use the first row of the file as the keys. In this case, the file doesn't have column headers in the first row, so we provided column headers.

The `data_iter()` method produces rows for a consuming class or function. In this example, the `list()` function consumes the available rows. As expected, the dataset has 150 rows. We've shown the first row.

Note that the attribute values are strings. This is always true when reading CSV files: all of the input values are strings. Our application must convert the strings to `float` values to be able to create `KnownSample` objects.

Another way to consume values is with a `for` statement. This how the `load()` method of the `TrainingData` class works. It uses code that looks like this:

```
def load(self, raw_data_iter: Iterator[Dict[str, str]]) -> None:
    for n, row in enumerate(raw_data_iter):
        ... more processing here
```

We combine an `IrisReader` object with this object to load the samples. It looks like this:

```
>>> training_data = TrainingData("besdekIris")
>>> rdr = CSVIrisReader(test_data)
>>> training_data.load(rdr.data_iter())
```

The `load()` method will consume values produced by the `data_iter()` method. The loading of the data is a cooperative process from the two objects.

Working with CSV data as dictionaries seems to be very handy. To show an alternative, we'll turn to reading data using a non-dictionary CSV reader.

CSV list reader

The non-dictionary CSV reader produces a list of strings from each row. This is not what our `TrainingData` collection's `load()` method expects, however.

We have two choices to meet the interface requirement for the `load()` method:

1. Convert the list of column values to a dictionary.
2. Change `load()` to use a list of values in a fixed order. This would have the unfortunate consequence of forcing the `load()` method of the `TrainingData` class to match a specific file layout. Alternatively, we'd have to re-order input values to match the requirements of `load()`; doing this is about as complex as building a dictionary.

Building a dictionary seems relatively easy; this allows the load() method to work with data where the column layout varies from our initial expectation.

Here's a CSVIrisReader_2 class that uses csv.reader() to read a file, and builds dictionaries based on the attribute information published in the iris.names file.

```
class CSVIrisReader_2:
    """
    Attribute Information:
        1. sepal length in cm
        2. sepal width in cm
        3. petal length in cm
        4. petal width in cm
        5. class:
            -- Iris Setosa
            -- Iris Versicolour
            -- Iris Virginica
    """

    def __init__(self, source: Path) -> None:
        self.source = source

    def data_iter(self) -> Iterator[dict[str, str]]:
        with self.source.open() as source_file:
            reader = csv.reader(source_file)
            for row in reader:
                yield dict(
                    sepal_length=row[0],  # in cm
                    sepal_width=row[1],   # in cm
                    petal_length=row[2],  # in cm
                    petal_width=row[3],   # in cm
                    species=row[4]  # class string
                )
```

The data_iter() method yields individual dictionary objects. This for-with-yield summarizes what a yield from does. When we write yield from X, that is effectively the same as the longer

```
for item in X:
    yield item
```

For this application, the non-dictionary processing works by creating a dictionary from the input row. This doesn't seem to have any advantage over the `csv.DictReader` class.

The other big alternative is JSON serialization. We'll look at ways to apply the techniques shown in this chapter to our case study data.

JSON serialization

The JSON format can serialize a number of commonly used Python object classes, including:

- None
- Boolean
- Float and integer
- String
- Lists of compatible objects
- Dictionaries with string keys and compatible objects as values

The "compatible objects" can include nested structures. This dictionary-within-list and dictionary-within-dictionary recursion can allow JSON to represent very complex things.

We might consider a theoretical (but invalid) type hint like the following:

```
JSON = Union[
    None, bool, int, float, str, List['JSON'], Dict[str, 'JSON']
]
```

This hint isn't directly supported by *mypy*, because it involves explicit recursion: the JSON type is defined based on the JSON type. This hint can be a helpful conceptual framework for understanding what we can represent in JSON notation. As a practical matter, we often use `Dict[str, Any]` to describe JSON objects, ignoring the details of other structures that might be present. We can be a little more specific, though, when we know the expected keys for the dictionary; we'll expand on this below.

In JSON notation, our data will look like this:

```
[
  {
    "sepal_length": 5.1,
    "sepal_width": 3.5,
    "petal_length": 1.4,
    "petal_width": 0.2,
    "species": "Iris-setosa"
  },
  {
    "sepal_length": 4.9,
    "sepal_width": 3.0,
    "petal_length": 1.4,
    "petal_width": 0.2,
    "species": "Iris-setosa"
  },
```

Note that the numeric values don't have quotation marks, and they will be converted to float values if they have a . character or converted to an integer if they lack the . character.

The json.org standards require a single JSON object in a file. This encourages us to create a "list-of-dict" structure. Pragmatically, the structure of the file can be summarized by this type hint:

```
JSON_Samples = List[Dict[str, Union[float, str]]]
```

The document – as a whole – is a list. It contains a number of dictionaries that map string keys to either float or string values.

Above, we noted that we can be more specific about the keys expected. In this case, we want to limit our application to working with specific dictionary keys. We can be a bit more precise, by using the typing.TypedDict hint:

```
class SampleDict(TypedDict):
    sepal_length: float
    sepal_width: float
    petal_length: float
    petal_width: float
    species: str
```

This can be helpful to *mypy* (and other people reading our code) by showing what the expected structure *should* be. We can even add `total=True` to assert that the definition shows the entire domain of valid keys.

This `TypedDict` hint doesn't really confirm the contents of the JSON document are valid or sensible, however. Remember, *mypy* is only a static check on the code, and has no runtime impact. To check the JSON document's structure, we'll need something more sophisticated than a Python type hint.

Here's our JSON reader class definition:

```
class JSONIrisReader:
    def __init__(self, source: Path) -> None:
        self.source = source

    def data_iter(self) -> Iterator[SampleDict]:
        with self.source.open() as source_file:
            sample_list = json.load(source_file)
        yield from iter(sample_list)
```

We've opened the source file and loaded the list-of-dict objects. We can then yield the individual sample dictionaries by iterating over the list.

This has a hidden cost. We'll look at how newline-delimited JSON – a modification to the standard – can help reduce the memory used.

Newline-delimited JSON

For large collections of objects, reading a single, massive list into memory first isn't ideal. The "newline-delimited" JSON format, described by `ndjson.org`, provides a way to put a large number of separate JSON documents into a single file.

The file would look like this:

```
{"sepal_length": 5.0, "sepal_width": 3.3, "petal_length": 1.4, "petal_
width": 0.2, "species": "Iris-setosa"}
{"sepal_length": 7.0, "sepal_width": 3.2, "petal_length": 4.7, "petal_
width": 1.4, "species": "Iris-versicolor"}
```

There's no overall [ ] to create a list. Each individual sample *must* be complete on one physical line of the file.

This leads to a slight difference in the way we process the sequence of documents:

```
class NDJSONIrisReader:
    def __init__(self, source: Path) -> None:
        self.source = source

    def data_iter(self) -> Iterator[SampleDict]:
        with self.source.open() as source_file:
            for line in source_file:
                sample = json.loads(line)
                yield sample
```

We've read each line of the file and used `json.loads()` to parse the single string into a sample dictionary. The interface is the same: an `Iterator[SampleDict]`. The technique for producing that iterator is unique to newline-delimited JSON.

JSON validation

We noted that our *mypy* type hint doesn't really guarantee the JSON document is – in any way – what we expected. There is a package in the Python Package Index that can be used for this. The `jsonschema` package lets us provide a specification for a JSON document, and then confirm whether or not the document meets the specification.

We'll need to install an additional library to do the validation:

```
python -m pip install jsonschema
```

The JSON Schema validation is a runtime check, unlike the *mypy* type hint. This means using validation will make our program slower. It can also help to diagnose subtly incorrect JSON documents. For details, see `https://json-schema.org`. This is evolving toward standardization, and there are several versions of compliance checking available.

We'll focus on newline-delimited JSON. This means we need a schema for each sample document within the larger collection of documents. This kind of additional validation might be relevant when receiving a batch of unknown samples to classify. Before doing anything, we'd like to be sure the sample document has the right attributes.

A JSON Schema document is also written in JSON. It includes some metadata to help clarify the purpose and meaning of the document. It's often a little easier to create a Python dictionary with the JSON Schema definition.

Here's a candidate definition for the Iris schema for an individual sample:

```
IRIS_SCHEMA = {
    "$schema": "https://json-schema.org/draft/2019-09/hyper-schema",
    "title": "Iris Data Schema",
    "description": "Schema of Bezdek Iris data",
    "type": "object",
    "properties": {
        "sepal_length": {
            "type": "number", "description": "Sepal Length in cm"},
        "sepal_width": {
            "type": "number", "description": "Sepal Width in cm"},
        "petal_length": {
            "type": "number", "description": "Petal Length in cm"},
        "petal_width": {
            "type": "number", "description": "Petal Width in cm"},
        "species": {
            "type": "string",
            "description": "class",
            "enum": [
                "Iris-setosa", "Iris-versicolor", "Iris-virginica"],
        },
    },
    "required": [
"sepal_length", "sepal_width", "petal_length", "petal_width"],
}
```

Each sample is an `object`, the JSON Schema term for a dictionary with keys and values. The `properties` of an object are the dictionary keys. Each one of these is described with a type of data, `number` in this case. We can provide additional details, like ranges of values. We provided a description, taken from the `iris.names` file.

In the case of the `species` property, we've provided an enumeration of the valid string values. This can be handy for confirming that the data meets our overall expectations.

We use this schema information by creating a `jsonschema` validator and applying the validator to check each sample we read. An extended class might look like this:

```
class ValidatingNDJSONIrisReader:
    def __init__(self, source: Path, schema: dict[str, Any]) -> None:
        self.source = source
        self.validator = jsonschema.Draft7Validator(schema)
```

```
def data_iter(self) -> Iterator[SampleDict]:
    with self.source.open() as source_file:
        for line in source_file:
            sample = json.loads(line)
            if self.validator.is_valid(sample):
                yield sample
            else:
                print(f"Invalid: {sample}")
```

We've accepted an additional parameter in the __init__() method with the schema definition. We use this to create the Validator instance that will be applied to each document.

The data_iter() method uses the is_valid() method of validator to process only samples that pass the JSON Schema validation. The others will be reported and ignored. We've printed the output using the print() function. It would be smarter to use the file=sys.stderr keyword parameter to direct the output to the error output. It would be even better to use the logging package to write error messages to a log.

Note that we now have two separate, but similar definitions for the raw data that builds a Sample instance:

1. A type hint, SampleDict, describing the expected Python intermediate data structure. This can be applied to CSV as well as JSON data, and helps summarize the relationship between the load() method of the TrainingData class, and the various readers.

2. A JSON Schema that *also* describes an expected external data structure. This doesn't describe a Python object, it describes the JSON serialization of a Python object.

For very simple cases, these two descriptions of the data seem redundant. In more complex situations, however, these two will diverge, and fairly complex conversions between external schema, intermediate results, and the final class definition is a common feature of Python applications. This occurs because there are a variety of ways to serialize Python objects. We need to be flexible enough to work with a useful variety of representations.

Recall

In this chapter, we've looked at the following topics:

- The ways to encode strings into bytes and decode bytes into strings. While some older character encodings (like ASCII) treat bytes and characters alike, this leads to confusion. Python text can be any Unicode character and Python bytes are numbers in the range 0 to 255.

- String formatting lets us prepare string objects that have template pieces and dynamic pieces. This works for a lot of situations in Python. One is to create readable output for people, but we can use f-strings and the string format() method everywhere we're creating a complex string from pieces.

- We use regular expressions to decompose complex strings. In effect, a regular expression is the opposite of a fancy string formatter. Regular expressions struggle to separate the characters we're matching from "meta-characters" that provide additional matching rules, like repetition or alternative choices.

- We've looked at a few ways to serialize data, including Pickle, CSV, and JSON. There are other formats, including YAML, that are similar enough to JSON and Pickle that we didn't need to cover them in detail. Other serializations like XML and HTML are quite a bit more complex, and we've avoided them.

Exercises

We've covered a wide variety of topics in this chapter, from strings to regular expressions, to object serialization, and back again. Now it's time to consider how these ideas can be applied to your own code.

Python strings are very flexible, and Python is an extremely powerful tool for string-based manipulations. If you don't do a lot of string processing in your daily work, try designing a tool that is exclusively intended for manipulating strings. Try to come up with something innovative, but if you're stuck, consider writing a web log analyzer (how many requests per hour? How many people visit more than five pages?) or a template tool that replaces certain variable names with the contents of other files.

Spend a lot of time toying with the string formatting operators until you've got the syntax memorized. Write a bunch of template strings and objects to pass into the format function, and see what kind of output you get. Try the exotic formatting operators, such as percentage or hexadecimal notation. Try out the fill and alignment operators, and see how they behave differently for integers, strings, and floats. Consider writing a class of your own that has a __format__ method; we didn't discuss this in detail, but explore just how much you can customize formatting.

Make sure you understand the difference between bytes and str objects. The way that Python's canonical display of bytes looks like a string can be confusing. The only tricky part is knowing how and when to convert between the two. For practice, try writing text data to a file opened for writing bytes (you'll have to encode the text yourself), and then reading from the same file.

Do some experimenting with bytearray. See how it can act both like a bytes object and a list or container object at the same time. Try writing to a buffer that holds data in the bytes array until it is a certain length before returning it. You can simulate the code that puts data into the buffer by using time.sleep calls to ensure data doesn't arrive too quickly.

Study regular expressions online. Study them some more. Especially learn about named groups, greedy versus lazy matching, and regex flags, three features that we didn't cover in this chapter. Make conscious decisions about when not to use them. Many people have very strong opinions about regular expressions and either overuse them or refuse to use them at all. Try to convince yourself to use them only when appropriate, and figure out when that is.

If you've ever written an adapter to load small amounts of data from a file or database and convert it to an object, consider using a pickle instead. Pickles are not efficient for storing massive amounts of data, but they can be useful for loading configuration or other simple objects. Try coding it multiple ways: using a pickle, a text file, or a small database. Which do you find easiest to work with?

Try experimenting with pickling data, then modifying the class that holds the data, and loading the pickle into the new class. What works? What doesn't? Is there a way to make drastic changes to a class, such as renaming an attribute or splitting it into two new attributes and still get the data out of an older pickle? (Hint: try placing a private pickle version number on each object and update it each time you change the class; you can then put a migration path in __setstate__.)

If you do any web development at all, the JSON serializer will be central. It can simplify things to stick with standard JSON serializable objects, rather than writing custom encoders or object_hooks, but the design depends on the complexity of the objects and the state representations being transferred.

In the case study, we applied the JSON Schema validation to a JSON file. It can also be applied to the rows read from a file in CSV format. This is a powerful combination of tools to work with data in two common formats; it helps to apply rigorous validation rules to assure that the rows meet the application's expectations. To see how this works, modify the `CSVIrisReader` class to include JSON Schema validation of the rows of data.

Summary

We've covered string manipulation, regular expressions, and object serialization in this chapter. Hardcoded strings and program variables can be combined into outputtable strings using the powerful string formatting system. It is important to distinguish between binary and textual data, and bytes and `str` have specific purposes that must be understood. Both are immutable, but the `bytearray` type can be used when manipulating bytes.

Regular expressions are a complex topic, and we only scratched the surface. There are many ways to serialize Python data; pickles and JSON are two of the most popular.

In the next chapter, we'll look at a design pattern that is so fundamental to Python programming that it has been given special syntax support: the iterator pattern.

10

The Iterator Pattern

We've discussed how many of Python's built-ins and idioms seem, at first blush, to fly in the face of object-oriented principles, but are actually providing access to real objects under the hood. In this chapter, we'll discuss how the for loop, which seems so structured, is actually a lightweight wrapper around a set of object-oriented principles. We'll also see a variety of extensions to this syntax that automatically create even more types of object. We will cover the following topics:

- What design patterns are
- The iterator protocol – one of the most powerful design patterns
- List, set, and dictionary comprehensions
- Generator functions, and how they build on other patterns

The case study for this chapter will revisit the algorithms for partitioning sample data into testing and training subsets to see how the iterator design pattern applies to this part of the problem.

We'll start with an overview of what design patterns are and why they're so important.

Design patterns in brief

When engineers and architects decide to build a bridge, or a tower, or a building, they follow certain principles to ensure structural integrity. There are various possible designs for bridges (suspension and cantilever, for example), but if the engineer doesn't use one of the standard designs, and doesn't have a brilliant new design, it is likely the bridge they design will collapse.

Design patterns are an attempt to bring this same formal definition for correctly designed structures to software engineering. There are many different design patterns to solve different general problems. Design patterns are applied to solve a common problem faced by developers in some specific situation. The design pattern is a suggestion as to the ideal solution for that problem, in terms of object-oriented design. What's central to a pattern is that it is reused often in unique contexts. One clever solution is a good idea. Two similar solutions might be a coincidence. Three or more reuses of an idea and it starts to look like a repeating pattern.

Knowing design patterns and choosing to use them in our software does not, however, guarantee that we are creating a *correct* solution. In 1907, the Québec Bridge (to this day, the longest cantilever bridge in the world, just short of a kilometer long) collapsed before construction was completed, because the engineers who designed it grossly underestimated the weight of the steel used to construct it. Similarly, in software development, we may incorrectly choose or apply a design pattern, and create software that *collapses* under normal operating situations or when stressed beyond its original design limits.

Any one design pattern proposes a set of objects interacting in a specific way to solve a general problem. The job of the programmer is to recognize when they are facing a specific version of such a problem, then to choose and adapt the general pattern to their precise needs.

In this chapter, we'll look deeply at the iterator design pattern. This pattern is so powerful and pervasive that the Python developers have provided multiple syntaxes to access the object-oriented principles underlying the pattern. We will be covering other design patterns in the next two chapters. Some of them have language support and some don't, but none of them are so intrinsically a part of the Python coder's daily life as the iterator pattern.

Iterators

In typical design pattern parlance, an **iterator** is an object with a next() method and a done() method; the latter returns True if there are no items left in the sequence. In a programming language without built-in support for iterators, the iterator would be used like this:

```
while not iterator.done():
    item = iterator.next()
    # do something with the item
```

In Python, iteration is available across many language features, so the method gets a special name, __next__. This method can be accessed using the next(iterator) built-in. Rather than a done() method, Python's iterator protocol raises the StopIteration exception to notify the client that the iterator has completed. Finally, we have the much more readable for item in iterator: syntax to actually access items in an iterator instead of messing around with a while statement. Let's look at each these in more detail.

The iterator protocol

The Iterator abstract base class, in the collections.abc module, defines the *iterator* protocol in Python. This definition is also referenced by the typing module to provide suitable type hints. At the foundation, any Collection class definition must be Iterable. To be Iterable means implementing an __iter__() method; this method creates an Iterator object.

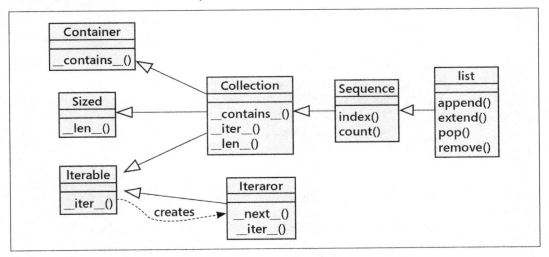

Figure 10.1: The abstractions for Iterable

As mentioned, an Iterator class must define a __next__() method that the for statement (and other features that support iteration) can call to get a new element from the sequence. In addition, every Iterator class must also fulfill the Iterable interface. This means an Iterator will also provide an __iter__() method.

This might sound a bit confusing, so have a look at the following example. Note that this is a very verbose way to solve this problem. It explains iteration and the two protocols in question, but we'll be looking at several more readable ways to get this effect later in this chapter:

```python
from typing import Iterable, Iterator

class CapitalIterable(Iterable[str]):
    def __init__(self, string: str) -> None:
        self.string = string

    def __iter__(self) -> Iterator[str]:
        return CapitalIterator(self.string)

class CapitalIterator(Iterator[str]):
    def __init__(self, string: str) -> None:
        self.words = [w.capitalize() for w in string.split()]
        self.index = 0

    def __next__(self) -> str:
        if self.index == len(self.words):
            raise StopIteration()

        word = self.words[self.index]
        self.index += 1
        return word
```

This example defines a `CapitalIterable` class whose job is to loop over each of the words in a string and output them with the first letter capitalized. We formalized this by using the `Iterable[str]` type hint as a superclass to make it clear what our intention was. Most of the work of this iterable class is delegated to the `CapitalIterator` implementation. One way to interact with this iterator is as follows:

```python
>>> iterable = CapitalIterable('the quick brown fox jumps over the lazy
dog')
>>> iterator = iter(iterable)
>>> while True:
...     try:
...         print(next(iterator))
...     except StopIteration:
...         break
...
The
```

```
Quick
Brown
Fox
Jumps
Over
The
Lazy
Dog
```

This example first constructs an iterable, assigning it to a variable with the boringly obvious name of `iterable`. It then retrieves a `CapitalIterator` instance from the `iterable` object. The distinction may need explanation; the iterable is an object with elements that can be iterated over. Normally, these elements can be looped over multiple times, maybe even at the same time or in overlapping code. The iterator, on the other hand, represents a specific location in that iterable; some of the items have been consumed and some have not. Two different iterators might be at different places in the list of words, but any one iterator can mark only one place.

Each time `next()` is called on the iterator, it returns another token from the iterable, in order, and updates its internal state to point to the next item. Eventually, the iterator will be exhausted (won't have any more elements to return), in which case a `StopIteration` exception is raised, and we break out of the `while` statement.

Python has a simpler syntax for constructing an iterator from an iterable:

```
>>> for i in iterable:
...     print(i)
...
The
Quick
Brown
Fox
Jumps
Over
The
Lazy
Dog
```

As you can see, the `for` statement, in spite of not looking remotely object-oriented, is actually a shortcut to some fundamentally object-oriented design principles. Keep this in mind as we discuss comprehensions, as they, too, appear to be the polar opposite of an object-oriented tool. Yet, they use the same iteration protocol as `for` statements and are another kind of shortcut.

The number of iterable classes in Python is large. We're not surprised when strings, tuples, and lists are iterable. A set, clearly, must be iterable, even if the order of elements may be difficult to predict. A mapping will iterate over the keys by default; other iterators are available. A file iterates over the available lines. A regular expression has a method, `finditer()`, that is an iterator over each instance of a matching substring that it can find. The `Path.glob()` method will iterate over matching items in a directory. The `range()` object is also an iterator. You get the idea: anything even vaguely collection-like will support some kind of iterator.

Comprehensions

Comprehensions are simple, but powerful, syntaxes that allow us to transform or filter an iterable object in as little as one line of code. The resultant object can be a perfectly normal list, set, or dictionary, or it can be a *generator expression* that can be efficiently consumed while keeping just one element in memory at a time.

List comprehensions

List comprehensions are one of the most powerful tools in Python, so people tend to think of them as advanced. They're not. Indeed, we've taken the liberty of littering previous examples with comprehensions, assuming you would understand them. While it's true that advanced programmers use comprehensions a lot, it's not because they're advanced. It's because a comprehension is so fundamental to Python, it can handle many of the most common operations in application software.

Let's have a look at one of those common operations; namely, converting a list of items into a list of related items. Specifically, let's assume we just read a list of strings from a file, and now we want to convert it to a list of integers. We know every item in the list is an integer, and we want to do some activity (say, calculate an average) on those numbers. Here's one simple way to approach it:

```
>>> input_strings = ["1", "5", "28", "131", "3"]

>>> output_integers = []
>>> for num in input_strings:
...     output_integers.append(int(num))
```

This works fine and it's only three lines of code. If you aren't used to comprehensions, you may not even think it looks ugly! Now, look at the same code using a list comprehension:

```
>>> output_integers = [int(num) for num in input_strings]
```

We're down to one line and, importantly for performance, we've dropped an append method call for each item in the list. Overall, it's pretty easy to tell what's going on, even if you're not used to comprehension syntax.

The square brackets indicate, as always, that we're creating a list. Inside this list is a `for` clause that iterates over each item in the input sequence. The only thing that may be confusing is what's happening between the list's opening brace and the start of the `for` statement. Whatever expression is provided here is applied to *each* of the items in the input list. The item in question is referenced by the `num` variable from the `for` clause. So, this expression applies the `int` function to each element and stores the resulting integer in the new list.

Terminology-wise, we call this a **mapping**. We are applying the result expression, `int(num)` in this example, to map values from the source iterable to create a resulting iterable list.

That's all there is to a basic list comprehension. Comprehensions are highly optimized, making them far faster than `for` statements when processing a large number of items. When used wisely, they're also more readable. These are two compelling reasons to use them widely.

Converting one list of items into a related list isn't the only thing we can do with a list comprehension. We can also choose to exclude certain values by adding an `if` statement inside the comprehension. We call this a **filter**. Have a look:

```
>>> output_integers = [int(num) for num in input_strings if len(num) < 3]
>>> output_integers
[1, 5, 28, 3]
```

The essential difference between this example and the previous one is the `if len(num) < 3` clause. This extra code excludes any strings with more than two characters. The `if` clause is applied to each element **before** the final `int()` function, so it's testing the length of a string. Since our input strings are all integers at heart, it excludes any number over 99.

A list comprehension can be used to map input values to output values, applying a filter along the way to include or exclude any values that meet a specific condition. A great many algorithms involve mapping and filtering operations.

Any iterable can be the input to a list comprehension. In other words, anything we can wrap in a `for` statement can also be used as the source for a comprehension.

For example, text files are iterable; each call to __next__() on the file's iterator will return one line of the file. We can examine the lines of a text file by naming the open file in the `for` clause of a list comprehension. We can then use the `if` clause to extract interesting lines of text. This example finds a subset of lines in a test file:

```
>>> from pathlib import Path
>>> source_path = Path('src') / 'iterator_protocol.py'
>>> with source_path.open() as source:
...     examples = [line.rstrip()
...         for line in source
...         if ">>>" in line]
```

In this example, we've added some whitespace to make the comprehension more readable (list comprehensions don't *have* to fit on one physical line even though they're one logical line). This example creates a list of lines that have the ">>>" prompt in them. The presence of ">>>" suggests there might be a doctest example in this file. The list of lines has rstrip() applied to remove trailing whitespace, like the \n that ends each line of text returned by the iterator. The resulting list object, examples, suggests some of the test cases that can be found within the code. (This isn't as clever as doctest's own parser.)

Let's extend this example to capture the line numbers for each example with a ">>>" prompt in it. This is a common requirement, and the built-in enumerate() function helps us pair a number with each item provided by the iterator:

```
>>> with source_path.open() as source:
...     examples = [(number, line.rstrip())
...         for number, line in enumerate(source, start=1)
...         if ">>>" in line]
```

The enumerate() function consumes an iterable, providing an iterable sequence of two-tuples of a number and the original item. If the line passes our ">>>" test, we'll create a two-tuple of the number and the cleaned-up text. We've done some sophisticated processing in – effectively – one line of code. Essentially, though, it's a filter and a mapping. First it extracts tuples from the source, then it filters the lines that match the given `if` clause, then it evaluates the (number, line.rstrip()) expression to create resulting tuples, and finally, collects it all into a list object. The ubiquity of this iterate-filter-map-collect pattern drives the idea behind a list comprehension.

Set and dictionary comprehensions

Comprehensions aren't restricted to lists. We can use a similar syntax with braces to create sets and dictionaries as well. Let's start with sets. One way to create a set is to wrap a list comprehension in the set() constructor, which converts it to a set. But why waste memory on an intermediate list that gets discarded, when we can create a set directly?

Here's an example that uses a named tuple to model author/title/genre triples, and then retrieves a set of all the authors that write in a specific genre:

```
>>> from typing import NamedTuple
>>> class Book(NamedTuple):
...     author: str
...     title: str
...     genre: str

>>> books = [
...     Book("Pratchett", "Nightwatch", "fantasy"),
...     Book("Pratchett", "Thief Of Time", "fantasy"),
...     Book("Le Guin", "The Dispossessed", "scifi"),
...     Book("Le Guin", "A Wizard Of Earthsea", "fantasy"),
...     Book("Jemisin", "The Broken Earth", "fantasy"),
...     Book("Turner", "The Thief", "fantasy"),
...     Book("Phillips", "Preston Diamond", "western"),
...     Book("Phillips", "Twice Upon A Time", "scifi"),
... ]
```

We've defined a small library of instances of the Book class. We can create a set from each of these objects by using a set comprehension. It looks a lot like a list comprehension, but uses {} instead of []:

```
>>> fantasy_authors = {b.author for b in books if b.genre == "fantasy"}
```

The highlighted set comprehension sure is short in comparison to the demo-data setup! If we were to use a list comprehension, of course, Terry Pratchett would have been listed twice. As it is, the nature of sets removes the duplicates, and we end up with the following:

```
>>> fantasy_authors
{'Pratchett', 'Le Guin', 'Turner', 'Jemisin'}
```

Note that sets don't have a defined ordering, so your output may differ from this example. For testing purposes, we'll sometimes set the `PYTHONHASHSEED` environment variable to impose an order. This introduces a tiny security vulnerability, so it's only suitable for testing.

Still using braces, we can introduce a colon to make `key:value` pairs required to create a dictionary comprehension. For example, it may be useful to quickly look up the author or genre in a dictionary if we know the title. We can use a dictionary comprehension to map titles to `books` objects:

```
fantasy_titles = {b.title: b for b in books if b.genre == "fantasy"}
```

Now, we have a dictionary, and can look up books by title using the normal syntax, `fantasy_titles['Nightwatch']`. We've created a high-performance index from a lower-performance sequence.

In summary, comprehensions are not advanced Python, nor are they features that subvert object-oriented programming. They are a more concise syntax for creating a list, set, or dictionary from an existing iterable source of data.

Generator expressions

Sometimes we want to process a new sequence without pulling a new list, set, or dictionary into system memory. If we're iterating over items one at a time, and don't actually care about having a complete container (such as a list or dictionary) created, a container is a waste of memory. When processing one item at a time, we only need the current object available in memory at any one moment. But when we create a container, all the objects have to be stored in that container before we start processing them.

For example, consider a program that processes log files. A very simple log might contain information in this format:

```
Apr 05, 2021 20:03:29 DEBUG This is a debugging message.
Apr 05, 2021 20:03:41 INFO This is an information method.
Apr 05, 2021 20:03:53 WARNING This is a warning. It could be serious.
Apr 05, 2021 20:03:59 WARNING Another warning sent.
Apr 05, 2021 20:04:05 INFO Here's some information.
Apr 05, 2021 20:04:17 DEBUG Debug messages are only useful if you want
to figure something out.
Apr 05, 2021 20:04:29 INFO Information is usually harmless, but
helpful.
Apr 05, 2021 20:04:35 WARNING Warnings should be heeded.
Apr 05, 2021 20:04:41 WARNING Watch for warnings.
```

Log files for popular web servers, databases, or email servers can contain many gigabytes of data (one of the authors once had to clean nearly two terabytes of logs off a misbehaving system). If we want to process each line in the log, we can't use a list comprehension; it would create a list containing every line in the file. This probably wouldn't fit in RAM and could bring the computer to its knees, depending on the operating system.

If we used a `for` statement on the log file, we could process one line at a time before reading the next one into memory. Wouldn't be nice if we could use comprehension syntax to get the same effect?

This is where generator expressions come in. They use the same syntax as comprehensions, but they don't create a final container object. We call them **lazy**; they reluctantly produce values on demand. To create a generator expression, wrap the comprehension in `()` instead of `[]` or `{}`.

The following code parses a log file in the previously presented format and outputs a new log file that contains only the WARNING lines:

```python
>>> from pathlib import Path

>>> full_log_path = Path.cwd() / "data" / "sample.log"
>>> warning_log_path = Path.cwd() / "data" / "warnings.log"

>>> with full_log_path.open() as source:
...     warning_lines = (line for line in source if "WARN" in line)
...     with warning_log_path.open('w') as target:
...         for line in warning_lines:
...             target.write(line)
```

We've opened the `sample.log` file, a file perhaps too large to fit in memory. A generator expression will filter out the warnings (in this case, it uses the `if` syntax and leaves the line unmodified). This is lazy, and doesn't really do anything until we consume its output. We can open another file as a subset. The final `for` statement consumes each individual line from the `warning_lines` generator. At no time is the full log file read into memory; the processing happens one line at a time.

If we run it on our sample file, the resulting `warnings.log` file looks like this:

```
Apr 05, 2021 20:03:53 WARNING This is a warning. It could be serious.
Apr 05, 2021 20:03:59 WARNING Another warning sent.
Apr 05, 2021 20:04:35 WARNING Warnings should be heeded.
Apr 05, 2021 20:04:41 WARNING Watch for warnings.
```

Of course, with a short input file, we could have safely used a list comprehension, doing all the processing in memory. When the file is millions of lines long, the generator expression will have a huge impact on both memory and speed.

> The core of a comprehension is the generator expression. Wrapping a generator in [ ] creates a list. Wrapping a generator in { } creates a set. Using { } and : to separate keys and values creates a dictionary. Wrapping a generator in ( ) is still a generator expression, not a tuple.

Generator expressions are frequently most useful inside function calls. For example, we can call sum, min, or max on a generator expression instead of a list, since these functions process one object at a time. We're only interested in the aggregate result, not any intermediate container.

In general, of the four options, a generator expression should be used whenever possible. If we don't actually need a list, set, or dictionary, but simply need to filter or apply a mapping to items in a sequence, a generator expression will be most efficient. If we need to know the length of a list, or sort the result, remove duplicates, or create a dictionary, we'll have to use the comprehension syntax and create a resulting collection.

Generator functions

Generator functions embody the essential features of a generator expression, which is the generalization of a comprehension. The generator function syntax looks even less object-oriented than anything we've seen, but we'll discover that once again, it is a syntax shortcut to create a kind of iterator object. It helps us build processing following the standard iterator-filter-mapping pattern.

Let's take the log file example a little further. If we want to decompose the log into columns, we'll have to do a more significant transformation as part of the mapping step. This will involve a regular expression to find the timestamp, the severity word, and the message as a whole. We'll look at a number of solutions to this problem to show how generators and generator functions can be applied to create the objects we want.

Here's a version, avoiding generator expressions entirely:

```
import csv
import re
from pathlib import Path
```

```
from typing import Match, cast

def extract_and_parse_1(
        full_log_path: Path, warning_log_path: Path
)-> None:
    with warning_log_path.open("w") as target:
        writer = csv.writer(target, delimiter="\t")
        pattern = re.compile(
            r"(\w\w\w \d\d, \d\d\d\d \d\d:\d\d:\d\d) (\w+) (.*)")
        with full_log_path.open() as source:
            for line in source:
                if "WARN" in line:
                    line_groups = cast(
                        Match[str], pattern.match(line)).groups()
                    writer.writerow(line_groups)
```

We've defined a regular expression to match three groups:

- The complex date string, (\w\w\w \d\d, \d\d\d\d \d\d:\d\d:\d\d), which is a generalization of strings like "Apr 05, 2021 20:04:41".

- The severity level, (\w+), which matches a run of letters, digits, or underscores. This will match words like INFO and DEBUG.

- An optional message, (.*), which will collect all characters to the end of the line.

This pattern is assigned to the pattern variable. As an alternative, we could also use split(' ') to break the line into space-separated words; the first four words are the date, the next word is the severity, and all the remaining words are the message. This isn't as flexible as defining a regular expression.

The decomposition of the line into groups involves two steps. First, we apply pattern.match() to the line of text to create a Match object. Then we interrogate the Match object for the sequence of groups that matched. We have a cast(Match[str], pattern.match(line)) to tell *mypy* that every line will create a Match object. The type hint for re.match() is Optional[Match] because it returns a None when there's no Match. We're using cast() to make the claim that every line will match, and if it doesn't match, we want this function to raise an exception.

This deeply nested function seems maintainable, but so many levels of indent in so few lines is kind of ugly. More alarmingly, if there is some irregularity in the file, and we want to handle the case where the pattern.match(line) returns None, we'd have to include another if statement, leading to even deeper levels of nesting. Deeply nested conditional processing leads to statements where the conditions under which they are executed can be obscure.

The reader has to mentally integrate all of the preceding `if` statements to work out the condition. This can be a problem with this kind of solution.

Now let's consider a truly object-oriented solution, without any shortcuts:

```python
import csv
import re
from pathlib import Path
from typing import Match, cast, Iterator, Tuple, TextIO

class WarningReformat(Iterator[Tuple[str, ...]]):
    pattern = re.compile(
        r"(\w\w\w \d\d, \d\d\d\d \d\d:\d\d:\d\d) (\w+) (.*)")

    def __init__(self, source: TextIO) -> None:
        self.insequence = source

    def __iter__(self) -> Iterator[tuple[str, ...]]:
        return self

    def __next__(self) -> tuple[str, ...]:
        line = self.insequence.readline()
        while line and "WARN" not in line:
            line = self.insequence.readline()
        if not line:
            raise StopIteration
        else:
            return tuple(
                cast(Match[str],
                    self.pattern.match(line)
                ).groups()
            )

def extract_and_parse_2(
        full_log_path: Path, warning_log_path: Path
) -> None:
    with warning_log_path.open("w") as target:
        writer = csv.writer(target, delimiter="\t")
        with full_log_path.open() as source:
            filter_reformat = WarningReformat(source)
            for line_groups in filter_reformat:
                writer.writerow(line_groups)
```

We've defined a formal `WarningReformat` iterator that emits the three-tuple of the date, warning, and message. We've used a type hint of `tuple[str, ...]` because it matches the output from the `self.pattern.match(line).groups()` expression: it's a sequence of strings, with no constraint on how many will be present. The iterator is initialized with a `TextIO` object, something file-like that has a `readline()` method.

This `__next__()` method reads lines from the file, discarding any lines that are not `WARNING` lines. When we encounter a `WARNING` line, we parse it and return the three-tuple of strings.

The `extract_and_parse_2()` function uses an instance of the `WarningReformat` class in a `for` statement; this will evaluate the `__next__()` method repeatedly to process the subsequent `WARNING` line. When we run out of lines, the `WarningReformat` class raises a `StopIteration` exception to tell the function statement we're finished iterating. It's pretty ugly compared to the other examples, but it's also powerful; now that we have a class in our hands, we can do whatever we want with it.

With that background behind us, we finally get to see true generators in action. This next example does *exactly* the same thing as the previous one: it creates an object with a `__next__()` method that raises `StopIteration` when it's out of inputs:

```python
from __future__ import annotations
import csv
import re
from pathlib import Path
from typing import Match, cast, Iterator, Iterable


def warnings_filter(
        source: Iterable[str]
) -> Iterator[tuple[str, ...]]:
    pattern = re.compile(
        r"(\w\w\w \d\d, \d\d\d\d \d\d:\d\d:\d\d) (\w+) (.*)")
    for line in source:
        if "WARN" in line:
            yield tuple(
                cast(Match[str], pattern.match(line)).groups())


def extract_and_parse_3(
        full_log_path: Path, warning_log_path: Path
) -> None:
    with warning_log_path.open("w") as target:
        writer = csv.writer(target, delimiter="\t")
        with full_log_path.open() as infile:
```

```
        filter = warnings_filter(infile)
        for line_groups in filter:
            writer.writerow(line_groups)
```

The `yield` statement in the `warning_filters()` function is the key to generators. When Python sees `yield` in a function, it takes that function and wraps it up in an object that follows the `Iterator` protocol, not unlike the class defined in our previous example. Think of the `yield` statement as similar to the `return` statement; it returns a line. Unlike `return`, however, the function is only suspended. When it is called again (via `next()`), it will start where it left off – on the line after the `yield` statement – instead of at the beginning of the function. In this example, there is no line *after* the `yield` statement, so it jumps to the next iteration of the `for` statement. Since the `yield` statement is inside an `if` statement, it only yields lines that contain WARNING.

While it looks like this is just a function looping over the lines, it is actually creating a special type of object, a generator object:

```
>>> print(warnings_filter([]))
<generator object warnings_filter at 0xb728c6bc>
```

All the function does is create and return a generator object. In this example, an empty list was provided, and a generator was built. The generator object has `__iter__()` and `__next__()` methods on it, just like the one we created from a class definition in the previous example. (Using the `dir()` built-in function on it will reveal what else is part of a generator.) Whenever the `__next__()` method is called, the generator runs the function until it finds a `yield` statement. It then suspends execution, retaining the current state, and returning the value from `yield`. The next time the `__next__()` method is called, it restores the state and picks up execution where it left off.

This generator function is nearly identical to this generator expression:

```
warnings_filter = (
    tuple(cast(Match[str], pattern.match(line)).groups())
    for line in source
    if "WARN" in line
)
```

We can see how these various patterns align. The generator expression has all the elements of the statements, slightly compressed, and in a different order:

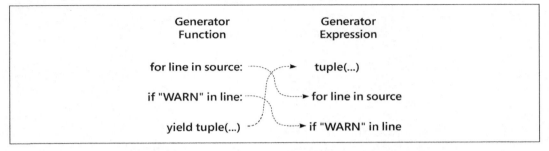

Figure 10.2: Generator functions compared with generator expressions

A comprehension, then, is a generator wrapped in [] or {} to create a concrete object. In some cases, it can make sense to use list(), set(), or dict() as a wrapper around a generator. This is helpful when we're considering replacing the generic collection with a customized collection of our own. Changing list() into MySpecialContainer() seems to make the change more apparent.

The generator expression has the advantage of being short and appearing right where it's needed. The generator function has a name and parameters, meaning it can be reused. More importantly, a generator function can have multiple statements and more complex processing logic in the cases where statements are needed. One common reason for switching from a generator expression to a function is to add exception handling.

Yield items from another iterable

Often, when we build a generator function, we end up in a situation where we want to yield data from another iterable object, possibly a list comprehension or generator expression we constructed inside the generator, or perhaps some external items that were passed into the function. We'll look at how to do this with the yield from statement.

Let's adapt the generator example a bit so that instead of accepting an input file, it accepts the name of a directory. The idea is to keep our existing warnings filter generator in place, but tweak the structure of the functions that use it. We'll operate on iterators as both input and result; this way the same function could be used regardless of whether the log lines came from a file, memory, the web, or another iterator.

This version of the code illustrates a new `file_extract()` generator. This does some basic setup before yielding information from the `warnings_filter()` generator:

```python
def file_extract(
        path_iter: Iterable[Path]
) -> Iterator[tuple[str, ...]]:
    for path in path_iter:
        with path.open() as infile:
            yield from warnings_filter(infile)


def extract_and_parse_d(
        directory: Path, warning_log_path: Path) -> None:
    with warning_log_path.open("w") as target:
        writer = csv.writer(target, delimiter="\t")
        log_files = list(directory.glob("sample*.log"))
        for line_groups in file_extract(log_files):
            writer.writerow(line_groups)
```

Our top-level function `extract_and_parse_d()` has a slight change to use the `file_extract()` function instead of opening a file and applying the `warnings_filter()` to one file. The `file_extract()` generator will yield all of the WARNING lines from *all* of the files provided in the argument value.

The `yield from` syntax is a useful shortcut when writing chained generators.

What's central in this example is the laziness of each of the generators involved. Consider what happens when the `extract_and_parse_d()` function, the client, makes a demand:

1. The client evaluates `file_extract(log_files)`. Since this is in a `for` statement, there's an `__iter__()` method evaluation.

2. The `file_extract()` generator gets an iterator from the `path_iter` iterable, and uses this to get the next `Path` instance. The `Path` object is used to create a file object that's provided to the `warnings_filter()` generator.

3. The `warnings_filter()` generator uses the file's iterator over lines to read until it finds a WARNING line, which it parses, yielding exactly one tuple. The fewest number of lines were read to find this line.

4. The `file_extract()` generator is yielding from the `warnings_filter()` generator, so the single tuple is provided to the ultimate client, the `extract_and_parse_d()` function.

5. The `extract_and_parse_d()` function writes the single tuple to the open CSV file, and then demands another tuple. This request goes to `file_extract()`, which pushes the demand down to `warnings_filter()`, which pushes the demand to an open file to provide lines until a WARNING line is found.

Each generator is lazy and provides one response, doing the least amount of work it can get away with to produce the result. This means that a directory with a huge number of giant log files is processed by having one open log file, and one current line being parsed and processed. It won't fill memory no matter how large the files are.

We've seen how generator functions can provide data to other generator functions. We can do this with ordinary generator expressions, also. We'll make some small changes to the `warnings_filter()` function to show how we can create a stack of generator expressions.

Generator stacks

The generator function (and the generator expression) for `warnings_filter` makes an unpleasant assumption. The use of `cast()` makes a claim to *mypy* that's – perhaps – a bad claim to make. Here's the example:

```
warnings_filter = (
    tuple(cast(Match[str], pattern.match(line)).groups())
    for line in source
    if "WARN" in line
)
```

The use of `cast()` is a way of claiming the `pattern.match()` will always yield a `Match[str]` object. This isn't a great assumption to make. Someone may change the format of the log file to include a multiple-line message, and our WARNING filter would crash every time we encountered a multi-line message.

Here's a message that would cause problems followed by a message that's easy to process:

```
Jan 26, 2015 11:26:01 INFO This is a multi-line information
message, with misleading content including WARNING
and it spans lines of the log file WARNING used in a confusing way
Jan 26, 2015 11:26:13 DEBUG Debug messages are only useful if you want
to figure something out.
```

The first line has the word WARN in a multi-line message that will break our assumption about lines that contain the word WARN. We need to handle this with a little more care.

We can rewrite this generator expression to create a generator function, and add an assignment statement (to save the Match object) and an if statement to further decompose the filtering. We can use the walrus operator := to save the Match object, also.

We could reframe the generator expression as the following generator function:

```
def warnings_filter(source: Iterable[str]
) -> Iterator[Sequence[str]]:
    pattern = re.compile
        (r"(\w\w\w \d\d, \d\d\d\d \d\d:\d\d:\d\d) (\w+) (.*)")
    for line in source:
        if match := pattern.match(line):
            if "WARN" in match.group(2):
                yield match.groups()
```

As we noted above, this complex filtering tends toward deeply nested if statements, which can create logic that's difficult to summarize. In this case, the two conditions aren't terribly complex. An alternative is to change this into a series of map and filter stages, each of which does a separate, small transformation on the input. We can decompose the matching and filtering into the following:

- Map the source line to an Optional[Match[str]] object using the pattern.match() method.
- Filter to reject any None objects, passing only good Match objects and applying the groups() method to create a List[str].
- Filter the strings to reject the non-WARN lines, and pass the WARN lines.

Each of these stages is a generator expression following the standard pattern. We can expand the warnings_filter expression into a stack of three expressions:

```
possible_match_iter = (pattern.match(line) for line in source)
group_iter = (
    match.groups() for match in possible_match_iter if match)
warnings_filter = (
    group for group in group_iter if "WARN" in group[1])
```

These expressions are, of course, utterly lazy. The final `warnings_filter` uses the iterable, `group_iter`. This iterable gets matches from another generator, `possible_match_iter`, which gets source text lines from the `source` object, an iterable source of lines. Since each of these generators is getting items from another lazy iterator, there's only one line of data being processed through the `if` clause and the final expression clause at each stage of this process.

Note that we can exploit the surrounding `()` to break each expression into multiple lines. This can help show the map or filter operation that's embodied in each expression.

We can inject additional processing as long as it fits this essential mapping-and-filtering design pattern. Before moving on, we're going to switch to a slightly more friendly regular expression for locating lines in our log file:

```
pattern = re.compile(
    r"(?P<dt>\w\w\w \d\d, \d\d\d\d \d\d:\d\d:\d\d)"
    r"\s+(?P<level>\w+)"
    r"\s+(?P<msg>.*)"
)
```

This regular expression is broken into three adjacent strings; Python will automatically concatenate string literals. The expression uses three named groups. The date-time stamp, for example, is group number one, a hard-to-remember bit of trivia. The `?P<dt>` inside the `()` means the `groupdict()` method of a `Match` object will have the key `dt` in the resulting dictionary. As we introduce more processing steps, we'll need to be much more clear about the intermediate results.

Here's an image of the regular expression that can sometimes be helpful:

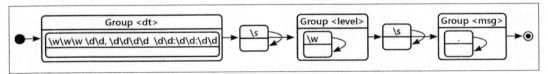

Figure 10.3: Log line regular expression diagram

Let's expand this example to transform the date-time stamp to another format. This involves injecting a transformation from the input format to the desired output format. We can do this in one big gulp, or we can do it in a series of small sips.

This sequence of steps makes it easier to add or change one individual step without breaking the entire pipeline of processing:

```python
possible_match_iter = (
    pattern.match(line) for line in source)
group_iter = (
    match.groupdict() for match in possible_match_iter if match)
warnings_iter = (
    group for group in group_iter if "WARN" in group["level"])
dt_iter = (
    (
        datetime.datetime.strptime(g["dt"], "%b %d, %Y %H:%M:%S"),
        g["level"],
        g["msg"],
    )
    for g in warnings_iter
)
warnings_filter = (
    (g[0].isoformat(), g[1], g[2]) for g in dt_iter)
```

We've created two additional stages. One parses the input time to create a Python datetime object; the second stage formats the datetime object as an ISO. Breaking the transformation down into small steps lets us treat each mapping operation and each filtering operating as discrete, separate steps. We can add, change, and delete with a little more flexibility when we create these smaller, easier-to-understand steps. The idea is to isolate each transformation into a separate object, described by a generator expression.

The result of the dt_iter expression is an iterable over anonymous tuples. This is a place where a NamedTuple can add clarity. See *Chapter 7, Python Data Structures*, for more information on NamedTuple.

We have an additional way to look at these transformational steps, using the built-in map() and filter() functions. These functions provide features similar to generator expressions, using another, slightly different syntax:

```python
possible_match_iter = map(pattern.match, source)
good_match_iter = filter(None, possible_match_iter)
group_iter = map(lambda m: m.groupdict(), good_match_iter)
warnings_iter = filter(lambda g: "WARN" in g["level"], group_iter)
```

```
dt_iter = map(
    lambda g: (
        datetime.datetime.strptime(g["dt"], "%b %d, %Y %H:%M:%S"),
        g["level"],
        g["msg"],
    ),
    warnings_iter,
)
warnings_filter = map(
    lambda g: (g[0].isoformat(), g[1], g[2]), dt_iter)
```

The lambda objects are anonymous functions. Each lambda is a callable object with parameters and a single expression that is evaluated and returned. There's no name and no statements in the body of a lambda. Each stage in this pipeline is a discrete mapping or filtering operation. While we can combine mapping and filtering into a single map(lambda ..., filter(lambda ..., source)), this can be too confusing to be helpful.

The possible_match_iter applies the pattern.match() to each line. The good_match_iter uses the special filter(None, source) that passes non-None objects, and rejects None objects. The group_iter uses a lambda to evaluate m.groups() for each object, m, in good_match_iter. The warnings_iter will filter the group_iter results, keeping only the WARN lines, and rejecting all others. The dt_iter and the final warnings_filter expressions perform a conversion from the source datetime format to a generic datetime object, followed by formatting the datetime object in a different string format.

We've seen a number of ways of approaching a complex map-filter problem. We can write nested for and if statements. We can create explicit Iterator subclass definitions. We can create iterator-based objects using function definitions that include the yield statement. This provides us the formal interface of the Iterator class without the lengthy boilerplate required to define __iter__() and __next__() methods. Additionally, we can use generator expressions and even comprehensions to apply the iterator design pattern in a number of common contexts.

The iterator pattern is a foundational aspect of Python programming. Every time we work with a collection, we'll be iterating through the items, and we'll be using an iterator. Because iteration is so central, there are a variety of ways of tackling the problem. We can use for statements, generator functions, generator expressions, and we can build our own iterator classes.

Case study

Python makes extensive use of iterators and iterable collections. This underlying aspect appears in many places. Each for statement makes implicit use of this. When we use functional programming techniques, such as generator expressions, and the map(), filter(), and reduce() functions, we're exploiting iterators.

Python has an itertools module full of additional iterator-based design patterns. This is worthy of study because it provides many examples of common operations that are readily available using built-in constructs.

We can apply these concepts in a number of places in our case study:

- Partitioning all the original samples into testing and training subsets.
- Testing a particular k and distance hyperparameter set by classifying all the test cases.
- The k-nearest neighbors (k-NN) algorithm itself and how it locates the k nearest neighbors from all the training samples.

The common aspect of these three processing examples is the "for all" aspect of each one. We'll take a little side-trip into the math behind comprehensions and generator functions. The math isn't terribly complex, but the following section can be thought of as deep background. After this digression, we'll dive into partitioning data into training and testing subsets using the iterator concepts.

The Set Builder background

Formally, we can summarize operations like partitioning, testing, and even locating nearest neighbors with a logic expression. Some developers like the formality of it because it can help describe the processing without forcing a specific Python implementation.

Here's the essential rule for partitioning, for example. This involves a "for all" condition that describes the elements of a set of samples, S:

$$\forall s \in S \mid s \in R \lor s \in E$$

In other words, for all s in the universe of available samples, S, the value of s is either in the training set, R, or the testing set, E. This summarizes the result of a successful partition of the data. It doesn't describe an algorithm, directly, but having this rule can help us be sure we haven't missed something important.

We can also summarize a performance metric for testing. The recall metric has a "for all" implied by the $\sum$ construct:

$$q = \sum_{e \in E} 1 \textbf{ if } knn(e) = s(e) \textbf{ else } 0$$

The quality score, q, is the sum for all e in the testing set, E, of 1 where the `knn()` classifier applied to e matches the species for e, `s(e)`, otherwise 0. This can map nicely to a Python generator expression.

The k-NN algorithm involves a bit more complexity in its definition. We can think of it as a partitioning problem. We need to start with a collection of ordered pairs. Each pair is the distance from an unknown, u, to a training sample, r, summarized as $d(u, r)$. As we saw in *Chapter 3*, there are a number of ways to compute this distance. This has to be done for all training samples, r, in the universe of training samples, R:

$$\forall r \in R \mid \langle d(u, r), r \rangle$$

Then we need to partition these distances into two subsets, N, and F (near and far) such that all distances in N are less than or equal to all distances in F:

$$\forall n \in N \wedge f \in F \mid d(u, n) \le d(u, f)$$

We also need to be sure the number of elements in the near set, N, is equal to the desired number of neighbors, k.

This final formalism exposes an interesting nuance to the computation. What if there are more than k neighbors with the same distance metric? Should *all* of the equidistant training samples be included in voting? Or should we arbitrarily slice exactly k of the equidistant samples? If we "arbitrarily" slice, what's the exact rule that gets used for choosing among the equidistant training samples? Does the selection rule even matter? These could be significant issues, and they're outside the scope of this book.

The example later in the chapter uses the `sorted()` function, which tends to preserve the original order. Can this lead to a bias to our classifier when confronted with equidistant choices? This, too, may be a significant issue, and it's also outside the scope of this book.

Given a little bit of set theory, we can tackle the ideas of partitioning the data, and computing the k nearest neighbors, making use of the common iterator features. We'll start with the partitioning algorithm's implementation in Python.

Multiple partitions

Our goal is to separate testing and training data. There's a tiny bump in the road, however, called **deduplication**. The statistical measures of overall quality rely on the training and testing sets being independent; this means we need to avoid duplicate samples being split between testing and training sets. Before we can create testing and training partitions, we need to find any duplicates.

We can't – easily – compare each sample with all of the other samples. For a large set of samples, this may take a very long time. A pool of ten thousand samples would lead to 100 million checks for duplication. This isn't practical. Instead, we can partition our data into subgroups where the values for all the measured features are *likely* to be equal. Then, from those subgroups, we can choose testing and training samples. This lets us avoid comparing every sample with all of the other samples to look for duplicates.

If we use Python's internal hash values, we can create buckets containing samples that may have equal values. In Python, if items are equal, they must have the same integer hash value. The inverse is not true: items may coincidentally have the same hash value, but may not actually be equal.

Formally, we can say this:

$$a = b \Rightarrow h(a) = h(b)$$

That is, if two objects in Python, a and b, are equal, they must also have the same hash value $h(x)$. The reverse is not true because equality is more than a simple hash value check; it's possible that $h(a) = h(b) \land a \neq b$; the hash values may be the same, but the underlying objects aren't actually equal. We call this a "hash collision" of two unequal values.

Continuing this thought, the following is a matter of definition for modulo:

$$h(a) = h(b) \Rightarrow h(a) = h(b) \pmod{m}$$

If two values are equal, they are also equal to any modulo of those values. When we want to know if a == b, we can ask if a % 2 == b % 2; if both numbers are odd or both numbers are even, then there's a chance a and b could be equal. If one number is even and the other is odd, there's no way they can be equal.

For complex objects, we can use hash(a) % m == hash(b) % m. If the two hash values, modulo m, are the same, then the hash values could be the same, and the two objects, a and b, could also be equal. We know it's possible for several objects to have the same hash value, and even more objects to have the same hash value modulo m.

While this doesn't tell us if two items are equal, this technique limits the domain of objects required for exact equality comparison to very small pools of a few items instead of the entire set of all samples. We can avoid duplicates if we avoid splitting up one of these subgroups.

Here's a view of seven samples broken into three subgroups based on their hash codes modulo 3. Most of the subgroups have items that are potentially equal, but actually aren't equal. One of the groups has an actual duplicate sample:

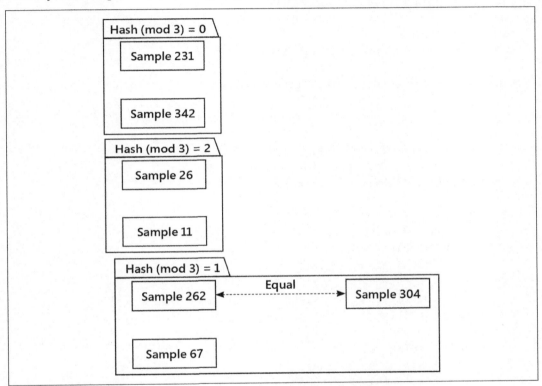

Figure 10.4: Partitioning sample data to locate duplicates

To find the duplicate sample, we don't need to compare each sample against the other six. We can look within each subgroup and compare a few samples to see if they happen to be duplicates.

The idea behind this deduplication approach is to separate the entire suite of samples into sixty buckets where the samples have equal hash values, modulo sixty. Samples in the same bucket *could* be equal, and as a simple expedient, we can treat them as equal. Samples in separate buckets have different hash values and cannot possibly be equal.

We can avoid having duplicate samples in both testing and training by using an entire bucket's set of samples together. That way, the duplicates are either all testing or all training, but never split.

Here's a partition function that first creates 60 separate buckets for samples. Then, some fraction of the buckets are allocated for testing, the rest for training. Specifically, 12, 15, or 20 buckets out of 60 are about 20%, 25%, or 33% of the population. Here's an implementation that deduplicates as it partitions into testing and training subsets:

```python
import itertools
from typing import DefaultDict, Iterator

ModuloDict = DefaultDict[int, List[KnownSample]]


def partition_2(
    samples: Iterable[KnownSample],
    training_rule: Callable[[int], bool]
) -> tuple[TrainingList, TestingList]:

    rule_multiple = 60
    partitions: ModuloDict = collections.defaultdict(list)
    for s in samples:
        partitions[hash(s) % rule_multiple].append(s)

    training_partitions: list[Iterator[TrainingKnownSample]] = []
    testing_partitions: list[Iterator[TestingKnownSample]] = []
    for i, p in enumerate(partitions.values()):
        if training_rule(i):
            training_partitions.append(
                TrainingKnownSample(s) for s in p)
        else:
            testing_partitions.append(
                TestingKnownSample(s) for s in p)

    training = list(itertools.chain(*training_partitions))
    testing = list(itertools.chain(*testing_partitions))
    return training, testing
```

There are three steps in this partitioning:

1. We create sixty separate lists of samples that – because the hashes are equal – may have duplicates. We keep these batches together to avoid splitting duplicates so they're in both testing and training subsets.

2. We build two lists of iterators. Each list has an iterator over a subset of the buckets. The `training_rule()` function is used to make sure we get 12/60, 15/60, or 20/60 buckets in testing, and the rest in training. Since each of these iterators is lazy, these lists of iterators can be used to accumulate samples.

3. Finally, we use the `itertools.chain` to consume values from a sequence of generators. A chain of iterators will consume the items from each of the various individual bucket-level iterators to create the two final partitions of samples.

Note that the type hint for `ModuloDict` defines a subtype of the generic `DefaultDict`. It provides a key of `int` and the value will be a `list[KnownSample]` instances. We've provided this named type to avoid repeating the long definition of the dictionaries we'll be working with.

The `itertools.chain()` is a pretty clever kind of iterator. It consumes data from other iterators. Here's an example:

```
>>> p1 = range(1, 10, 2)
>>> p2 = range(2, 10, 2)
>>> itertools.chain(p1, p2)
<itertools.chain object at ...>

>>> list(itertools.chain(p1, p2))
[1, 3, 5, 7, 9, 2, 4, 6, 8]
```

We created two `range()` objects, `p1`, and `p2`. A chain object will be an iterator, and we used the `list()` function to consume all the values.

The steps above can create a large mapping as an intermediate data structure. It also creates sixty generators, but these don't require very much memory. The final two lists contain references to the same `Sample` objects as the partitioning dictionary. The good news is the mapping is temporary and only exists during this function.

This function also depends on a `training_rule()` function. This function has a type hint of `Callable[[int], bool]`. Given the index value for a partition (a value from 0 to 59, inclusive), we can assign it to a testing or training partition.

We can use different implementations to get to 80%, 75%, or 66% testing data. For example:

```
lambda i: i % 4 != 0
```

The above lambda object will perform a 75% training and 25% testing split.

Once we've partitioned the data, we can use iterators for classifying samples as well as testing the quality of our classification process.

Testing

The testing process can also be defined as a higher-order function, a function that accepts a function as a parameter value. We can summarize the testing effort as a map-reduce problem. Given a Hyperparameter with a k value and a distance algorithm, we need to use an iterator for the following two steps:

- A function classifies all test samples, mapping each test sample to 1 if the classification was correct or 0 for an incorrect classification. This is the map part of map-reduce.
- A function computes a summary with the count of correct values from the long sequence of actual classified samples. This is the reduce part of map-reduce.

Python provides high-level functions for these map and reduce operations. This allows us to focus on the details of the mapping and ignore the boilerplate part of iterating over the data items.

Looking forward to the next section, we'll want to refactor the Hyperparameter class to split the classifier algorithm into a separate, standalone function. We'll make the classifier function a **Strategy** that we provide when we create an instance of the Hyperparameter class. Doing this means we can more easily experiment with some alternatives. We'll look at three different ways to approach refactoring a class.

Here's one definition that relies on an external classifier function:

```
Classifier = Callable[
    [int, DistanceFunc, TrainingList, AnySample], str]

class Hyperparameter(NamedTuple):
    k: int
    distance_function: DistanceFunc
    training_data: TrainingList
```

```
    classifier: Classifier

    def classify(self, unknown: AnySample) -> str:
        classifier = self.classifier
        return classifier(
            self.k, self.distance_function,
            self.training_data,
            unknown
        )

    def test(self, testing: TestingList) -> int:
        classifier = self.classifier
        test_results = (
            ClassifiedKnownSample(
                t.sample,
                classifier(
                    self.k, self.distance_function,
                    self.training_data, t.sample
                ),
            )
            for t in testing
        )
        pass_fail = map(
            lambda t: (
                1 if t.sample.species == t.classification else 0),
            test_results
        )
        return sum(pass_fail)
```

The test() method uses two mapping operations and a reduce operation. First, we define a generator that will map each testing sample to a ClassifiedKnownSample object. This object has the original sample and the results of the classification.

Second, we define a generator that will map each ClassifiedKnownSample object to a 1 (for a test that matched the expected species) or a 0 (for a test that failed). This generator depends on the first generator to provide values.

The actual work is the summation: this consumes values from the second generator. The second generator consumes objects from the first generator. This technique can minimize the volume of data in memory at any one time. It also decomposes a complex algorithm into two separate steps, allowing us to make changes as necessary.

There's an optimization available here, also. The value of t.classification in the second generator is self.classify(t.sample.sample). It's possible to reduce this to a single generator and eliminate creating intermediate ClassifiedKnownSample objects.

Here's how the test operation looks. We can build a Hyperparameter instance using a function for distance, manhattan(), and a classifier function, k_nn_1():

```
h = Hyperparameter(1, manhattan, training_data, k_nn_1)
h.test(testing_data)
```

We'll look at the implementations of various classifiers in the next two sections. We'll start with the base definition, k_nn_1(), and then look at one based on the bisect module next.

The essential k-NN algorithm

We can summarize the *k*-NN algorithm as having the following steps:

1. Create a list of all (distance, training sample) pairs.
2. Sort these in ascending order.
3. Pick to the first *k*, which will be the *k* nearest neighbors.
4. Chose the mode (the highest frequency) label for the *k* nearest neighbors.

The implementation would look like this:

```
class Measured(NamedTuple):
    distance: float
    sample: TrainingKnownSample

def k_nn_1(
    k: int, dist: DistanceFunc, training_data: TrainingList,
    unknown: AnySample
) -> str:
    distances = sorted(
        map(
            lambda t: Measured(dist(t, unknown), t), training_data
        )
    )
    k_nearest = distances[:k]
    k_frequencies: Counter[str] = collections.Counter(
        s.sample.sample.species for s in k_nearest
    )
```

```
    mode, fq = k_frequencies.most_common(1)[0]
    return mode
```

While clear, this does accumulate a large number of distance values in the `distances` list object, when only *k* are actually needed. The `sorted()` function consumes the source generator and creates a (potentially large) list of intermediate values.

One of the high-cost parts of this specific *k*-NN algorithm is sorting the entire set of training data after the distances have been computed. We summarize the complexity with the description as an *O(n log n)* operation. A way to avoid cost is to avoid sorting the entire set of distance computations.

Steps 1 to *3* can be optimized to keep only the *k* smallest distance values. We can do this by using the `bisect` module to locate the position in a sorted list where a new value can be inserted. If we only keep values that are smaller than the *k* values in the list, we can avoid a lengthy sort.

k-NN using the bisect module

Here's an alternative implementation of *k*-NN that tries to avoid sorting all of the distance computations:

1. For each training sample:
    a. Compute the distance from this training sample to the unknown sample.
    b. If it's greater than the last of the *k* nearest neighbors seen so far, discard the new distance.
    c. Otherwise, find a spot among the *k* values; insert the new item; truncate the list to length *k*.

2. Find the frequencies of result values among the *k* nearest neighbors.

3. Choose the mode (the highest frequency) among the *k* nearest neighbors.

If we seed the list of *k* nearest neighbors with floating point infinity values, ∞ to mathematicians, `float("inf")` in Python, then the first few computed distances, *d*, will be kept because $d < \infty$. After the first *k* distances have been computed, the remaining distances must be smaller than one of the *k* neighbor's distances to be relevant:

```
def k_nn_b(
    k: int, dist: DistanceFunc, training_data: TrainingList,
    unknown: AnySample
```

```
    ) -> str:
        k_nearest = [
            Measured(float("inf"), cast(TrainingKnownSample, None))
            for _ in range(k)
        ]
        for t in training_data:
            t_dist = dist(t, unknown)
            if t_dist > k_nearest[-1].distance:
                continue
            new = Measured(t_dist, t)
            k_nearest.insert(bisect.bisect_left(k_nearest, new), new)
            k_nearest.pop(-1)
        k_frequencies: Counter[str] = collections.Counter(
            s.sample.sample.species for s in k_nearest
        )
        mode, fq = k_frequencies.most_common(1)[0]
        return mode
```

Instead of sorting all distances into a big list, we're inserting (and removing) one distance from a much smaller list. After the first *k* distances are computed, this algorithm involves two kinds of state change: a new item is inserted into the *k* nearest neighbors, and the most distant of the *k+1* neighbors is removed. While this doesn't change the overall complexity in a dramatic way, these are relatively inexpensive operations when performed on a very small list of only *k* items.

k-NN using the heapq module

We have yet another trick up our sleeve. We can use the heapq module to maintain a sorted list of items. This lets us implement the sorting operation as each item is placed into the overall list. This doesn't reduce the general complexity of the processing, but it replaces two inexpensive insert and pop operations with *potentially* less expensive insert operations.

The idea is to start with an empty list and insert items into the list, ensuring that (a) the items are kept in order, and (b) the item at the head of the list always has the least distance. The heap queue algorithm can maintain an upper bound on the size of the queue. Keeping only *k* items should also reduce the volume of data required in memory.

We can then pop *k* items from the heap to retrieve the nearest neighbors.

```
def k_nn_q(
    k: int, dist: DistanceFunc, training_data: TrainingList,
    unknown: AnySample
) -> str:
    measured_iter = (
        Measured(dist(t, unknown), t) for t in training_data)
    k_nearest = heapq.nsmallest(k, measured_iter)
    k_frequencies: Counter[str] = collections.Counter(
        s.sample.sample.species for s in k_nearest
    )
    mode, fq = k_frequencies.most_common(1)[0]
    return mode
```

This is elegantly simple. It's not, however, remarkably fast. It turns out that the cost of computing the distances outweighs the cost savings from using a more advanced heap queue to reduce the number of items being sorted.

Conclusion

We can compare these distinct *k*-NN algorithms by providing a consistent set of training and test data. We'll use a function like the following:

```
def test_classifier(
        training_data: List[TrainingKnownSample],
        testing_data: List[TestingKnownSample],
        classifier: Classifier) -> None:
    h = Hyperparameter(
        k=5,
        distance_function=manhattan,
        training_data=training_data,
        classifier=classifier)
    start = time.perf_counter()
    q = h.test(testing_data)
    end = time.perf_counter()
    print(
        f'| {classifier.__name__:10s} '
        f'| q={q:5}/{len(testing_data):5} '
        f'| {end-start:6.3f}s |')
```

We've created a consistent `Hyperparameter` instance. Each instance has a common value of *k* and a common distance function; they have a distinct classifier algorithm. We can execute the `test()` method and display the time required.

A `main()` function can use this to examine the various classifiers:

```python
def main() -> None:
    test, train = a_lot_of_data(5_000)
    print("| algorithm  | test quality  | time    |")
    print("|------------|---------------|---------|")
    test_classifier(test, train, k_nn_1)
    test_classifier(test, train, k_nn_b)
    test_classifier(test, train, k_nn_q)
```

We've applied each of the classifiers to a consistent set of data. We haven't shown the `a_lot_of_data()` function. This creates two lists of `TrainingKnownSample` and `TestingKnownSample` instances. We've left this as an exercise for the reader.

Here are the performance results comparing these alterative *k*-NN algorithms:

algorithm	test quality	time
k_nn_1	q= 241/ 1000	6.553s
k_nn_b	q= 241/ 1000	3.992s
k_nn_q	q= 241/ 1000	5.294s

The test quality is the number of correct test cases. The number is low because the data is completely random, and a correct classification rate of about 25% is what's expected if our random data uses four different species names.

The original algorithm, `k_nn_1`, is the slowest, something we suspected. This provides the necessary evidence that optimization of this may be necessary. The `bisect` based processing, row `k_nn_b` in the table, suggests that working with a small list outweighs the costs of performing the bisect operation many times. The `heapq` processing time, row `k_nn_h`, was better than the original algorithm, but only by about 20%.

It's important to do both a theoretical analysis of the algorithm's complexity as well as a benchmark with actual data. Before spending time and effort on performance improvement, we need to start with benchmark analysis to identify where we might be able to do things more efficiently. It's also important to confirm that the processing is correct before trying to optimize performance.

In some cases, we'll need detailed analysis of specific functions or even Python operators. The `timeit` module can be helpful here. We might need to do something like the following:

```
>>> import timeit

>>> m = timeit.timeit(
...     "manhattan(d1, d2)",
...     """
... from model import Sample, KnownSample, TrainingKnownSample,
TestingKnownSample
... from model import manhattan, euclidean
... d1 = TrainingKnownSample(KnownSample(Sample(1, 2, 3, 4), "x"))
... d2 = KnownSample(Sample(2, 3, 4, 5), "y")
... """)
```

The value computed for `m` can help us make a concrete comparison between distance computations. The `timeit` module will execute the given statement, `manhattan(d1, d2)`, after performing the one-time setup of some imports and creation of sample data.

Iterators are both a performance boost and a potential way to clarify the overall design. They can be helpful with our case study because so much of the processing iterates over large collections of data.

Recall

This chapter looked at a design pattern that seems ubiquitous in Python, the iterator. The Python iterator concept is a foundation of the language and is used widely. In this chapter we examined a number of aspects:

- Design patterns are good ideas we see repeated in software implementations, designs, and architectures. A good design pattern has a name, and a context where it's usable. Because it's only a pattern, not reusable code, the implementation details will vary each time the pattern is followed.

- The `Iterator` protocol is one of the most powerful design patterns because it provides a consistent way to work with data collections. We can view strings, tuples, lists, sets, and even files as iterable collections. A mapping contains a number of iterable collections including the keys, the values, and the items (key and value pairs.)

- List, set, and dictionary comprehensions are short, pithy summaries of how to create a new collection from an existing collection. They involve a source iterable, an optional filter, and a final expression to define the objects in the new collection.
- Generator functions build on other patterns. They let us define iterable objects that have map and filter capabilities.

Exercises

If you don't use comprehensions in your daily coding very often, the first thing you should do is search through some existing code and find some for loops. See whether any of them can be trivially converted to a generator expression or a list, set, or dictionary comprehension.

Test the claim that list comprehensions are faster than for loops. This can be done with the built-in timeit module. Use the help documentation for the timeit.timeit function to find out how to use it. Basically, write two functions that do the same thing, one using a list comprehension, and one using a for loop to iterate over several thousand items. Pass each function into timeit.timeit, and compare the results. If you're feeling adventurous, compare generators and generator expressions as well. Testing code using timeit can become addictive, so bear in mind that code does not need to be hyperfast unless it's being executed an immense number of times, such as on a huge input list or file.

Play around with generator functions. Start with basic iterators that require multiple values (mathematical sequences are canonical examples; the Fibonacci sequence is overused if you can't think of anything better). Try some more advanced generators that do things such as take multiple input lists and somehow yield values that merge them. Generators can also be used on files; can you write a simple generator that shows lines that are identical in two files?

Extend the log processing exercise to replace the WARNING filter with a time range filter; all the messages between Jan 26, 2015 11:25:46 and Jan 26, 2015 11:26:15, for example.

Once you can find WARNING lines or lines within a specific time, combine the two filters to select only the warnings within the given time. You can use an and condition within a single generator, or combine multiple generators, in effect building an and condition. Which seems more adaptable to changing requirements?

When we presented the class WarningReformat(Iterator[Tuple[str, ...]]): example of an iterator, we made a questionable design decision. The __init__() method accepted an open file as an argument value and the __next__() method used readline() on that file. What if we change this slightly and create an explicit iterator object that we use inside another iterator?

```
def __init__(self, source: TextIO) -> None:
    self.insequence = iter(source)
```

If we make this change, then __next__() can use line = next(self.insequence) instead of line = self.insequence.readline(). Switching from object.readline() to next(object) is an interesting generalization. Does it change anything about the extract_and_parse_2() function? Does it permit us to use generator expressions along with the WarningReformat iterator?

Take this one further step. Refactor the WarningReformat class into two separate classes, one to filter for WARN and a separate class to parse and reformat each line of the input log. Rewrite the extract_and_parse_2() function using instances of these two classes. Which is "better"? What metric did you use to evaluate "better"?

The case study summarized the *k*-NN algorithm as a kind of comprehension to compute distance values, sort and pick the *k* nearest. The case study didn't talk much about the partitioning algorithm to separate training data from test data. This, too, seems like it might work out as a pair of list comprehensions. There's an interesting problem here, though. We'd like to create two lists, reading the source exactly once. This isn't easily done with list comprehensions. However, look at the itertools module for some possible designs. Specifically, the itertools.tee() function will provide multiple iterables from a single source.

Look at the recipes section of the itertools module. How can the itertools. partition() function be used to partition data?

Summary

In this chapter, we learned that design patterns are useful abstractions that provide best-practice solutions for common programming problems. We covered our first design pattern, the iterator, as well as numerous ways that Python uses and abuses this pattern for its own nefarious purposes. The original iterator pattern is extremely object-oriented, but it is also rather ugly and verbose to code around. However, Python's built-in syntax abstracts the ugliness away, leaving us with a clean interface to these object-oriented constructs.

Comprehensions and generator expressions can combine container construction with iteration in a single line. Generator functions can be constructed using the yield syntax.

We'll cover several more design patterns in the next two chapters.

11

Common Design Patterns

In the previous chapter, we were briefly introduced to design patterns, and covered the iterator pattern, a pattern so useful and common that it has been abstracted into the core of the programming language itself. In this chapter, we'll be reviewing other common patterns and how they are implemented in Python. As with iteration, Python often provides an alternative syntax to make working with such problems simpler. We will cover both the *traditional* design, and the Python version for these patterns.

In this chapter, we'll see:

- The Decorator pattern
- The Observer pattern
- The Strategy pattern
- The Command pattern
- The State pattern
- The Singleton pattern

This chapter's case study will emphasize how the distance calculation is an example of the Strategy design pattern, and how we can leverage abstract base classes to design a variety of distance computations that can be compared to see which produces the most useful results.

Consistent with the practice in *Design Patterns: Elements of Reusable Object-Oriented Software*, we'll capitalize the pattern names. This can help them stand out from ordinary English usage.

We'll start with the Decorator pattern. This is used to combine different kinds of functionality into a single resulting object.

The Decorator pattern

The Decorator pattern allows us to *wrap* an object that provides core functionality with other objects that alter this functionality. Any object that uses the decorated object will interact with it in exactly the same way as if it were undecorated (that is, the interface of the decorated object is identical to that of the core object).

There are two primary uses of the Decorator pattern:

- Enhancing the response of a component as it sends data to a second component
- Supporting multiple optional behaviors

The second option is often a suitable alternative to multiple inheritance. We can construct a core object, and then create a decorator wrapping that core. Since the decorator object has the same interface as the core object, we can even wrap the new object in other decorators. Here's how it looks in a UML diagram:

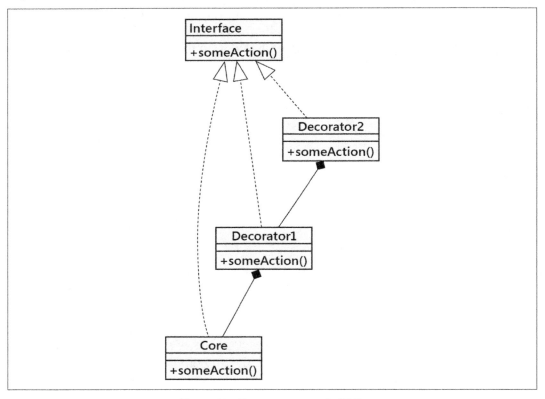

Figure 11.1: Decorator pattern in UML

Here, **Core** and all the decorators implement a specific **Interface**. The dashed lines show "implements" or "realizes." The decorators maintain a reference to the core instance of that **Interface** via composition. When called, the decorator does some added processing before or after calling its wrapped interface. The wrapped object may be another decorator, or the core functionality. While multiple decorators may wrap each other, the object at the end of the chain of all those decorators provides the core functionality.

It's essential that each of these is providing an implementation of a common feature. The intent is to provide a composition of processing steps from the various decorators, applied to the core. Often decorators are small, typically a function definition without any state.

In Python, because of duck typing, we don't need to formalize these relationships with an official abstract interface definition. It's sufficient to make sure the classes have matching methods. In some cases, we may define a `typing.Protocol` as a type hint to help *mypy* reason about the relationships.

A Decorator example

Let's look at an example from network programming. We want to build a small server that provides some data and a client that interacts with that server. The server will be simulating rolling complex handfuls of dice. The client will request a handful and wait for an answer that contains some random numbers.

This example has two processes interacting via a TCP socket, a way to transmit bytes among computer systems. Sockets are created by a server that listens for connections. When a client attempts to connect to the socket, the server must accept the new connection, and the two processes can then pass bytes back and forth; for this example, there will be a request from client to server and a response from server to client. The TCP socket is part of the foundation for HTTP, around which the world wide web is built.

The client and server processes will use the `socket.send()` method to transmit a string of bytes through the socket. They'll also use `socket.recv()` to receive bytes. We'll start with an interactive server that waits for a connection from a client and then responds to the request. We'll call this module `socket_server.py`. Here's the general outline:

```
import contextlib
import socket

def main_1() -> None:
    server = socket.socket(socket.AF_INET, socket.SOCK_STREAM)
```

```
            server.bind(("localhost", 2401))
            server.listen(1)
            with contextlib.closing(server):
                while True:
                    client, addr = server.accept()
                    dice_response(client)
                    client.close()
```

The server is bound to the "public" socket, using a more or less arbitrary port number of 2401. This is where the server is listening for connection requests. When a client tries to connect to this socket, a child socket is created so the client and server can talk, leaving the public socket ready for more connections. A web server will often use multiple threads to allow a large number of concurrent sessions. We're not using threads, and a second client has to wait until the server is done with the first client. It's a coffee shop queue with exactly one barista making espressos.

(Note that TCP/IP sockets have both a host address and a port number. The port number must be above 1023. Port numbers 1023 and below are reserved and require special OS privileges. We chose port 2401 because it doesn't seem to be used for anything else.)

The dice_response() function does all the real work of our service. It accepts a socket parameter so it can respond to the client. It reads bytes with a client request, creates a response, then sends it. In order to handle exceptions gracefully, the dice_response() function looks like this:

```
    def dice_response(client: socket.socket) -> None:
        request = client.recv(1024)
        try:
            response = dice.dice_roller(request)
        except (ValueError, KeyError) as ex:
            response = repr(ex).encode("utf-8")
        client.send(response)
```

We've wrapped another function, dice_roller(), in an exception handler. This is a common pattern to separate error-handling and other overheads from the real work of computing a dice roll and responding to the client with useful numbers for their role-playing game:

```
    import random

    def dice_roller(request: bytes) -> bytes:
        request_text = request.decode("utf-8")
```

```
    numbers = [random.randint(1, 6) for _ in range(6)]
    response = f"{request_text} = {numbers}"
    return response.encode("utf-8")
```

This isn't too sophisticated. We'll expand on this in the section on *The Command pattern* later in this chapter. For now, however, it will provide a sequence of random numbers.

Note that we're not really doing anything with the request object that came from the client. For the first few examples, we'll be reading these bytes and ignoring them. The request is a placeholder for a more complex request describing how many dice to roll and how many times to roll them.

We can leverage the Decorator design pattern to add features. The decorator will be wrapping the core dice_response() function, which is given a socket object that it can read and write. To make use of the design pattern, it's important to exploit the way this function relies on the socket.send() and socket.recv() methods when we add features. We need to preserve the interface definition as we add decorations.

To test the server, we can write a very simple client that connects to the same port and outputs the response before exiting:

```
import socket

def main() -> None:
    server = socket.socket(socket.AF_INET, socket.SOCK_STREAM)
    server.connect(("localhost", 2401))
    count = input("How many rolls: ") or "1"
    pattern = input("Dice pattern nd6[dk+-]a: ") or "d6"
    command = f"Dice {count} {pattern}"
    server.send(command.encode("utf8"))
    response = server.recv(1024)
    print(response.decode("utf-8"))
    server.close()

if __name__ == "__main__":
    main()
```

This client asks two questions and creates a fairly complex-looking string, command, that contains a count and dice-rolling pattern. Right now, the server doesn't use this command. This is a teaser for a more sophisticated dice roller.

To use these two separate applications, follow these steps:

1. Open two terminal windows, side by side. (It can help to change the window titles to "client" and "server". Users of macOS Terminal can use the **change title** item in the **shell** menu. Windows users can use the `title` command.)

2. In the server window, start the server application:

   ```
   python src/socket_server.py
   ```

3. In the client window, start the client application:

   ```
   python src/socket_client.py
   ```

4. Enter your responses to the prompts in the client window. For example:

   ```
   How many rolls: 2

   Dice pattern nd6[dk+-]a: d6
   ```

5. The client will send the command, read the response, print it to the console, and exit. Run the client as many times as you want to get a sequence of dice rolls.

The result will look something like this:

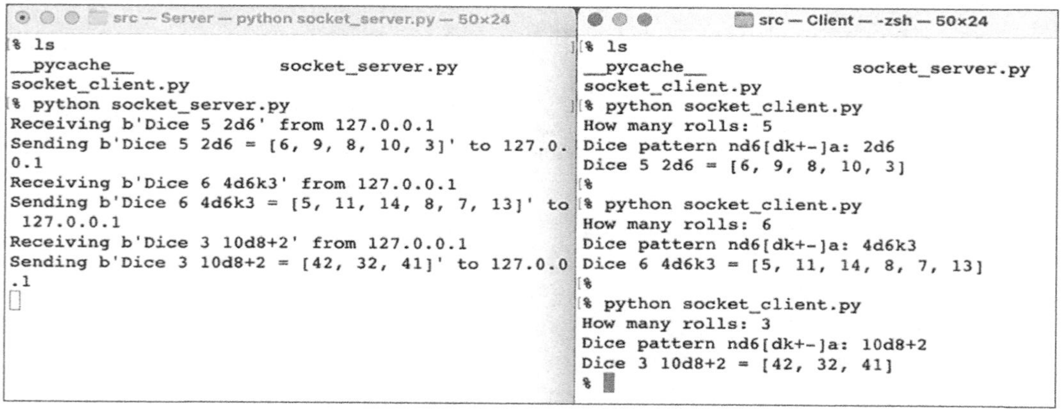

Figure 11.2: Server and client

On the left side is the server. We started the application, and it started listening on port 2401 for clients. On the right side is the client. Each time we run the client, it connects to the public socket; the connection operation creates a child socket that can be used for the rest of the interaction. The client sends a command the server responds to that command, and the client prints it.

Now, looking back at our server code, we see two sections. The `dice_response()` function reads data and sends data back to the client via a `socket` object. The remaining script is responsible for creating that `socket` object. We'll create a pair of decorators that customize the socket behavior without having to extend or modify the socket itself.

Let's start with a *logging* decorator. This object outputs any data being sent to the server's console before it sends it to the client:

```python
class LogSocket:
    def __init__(self, socket: socket.socket) -> None:
        self.socket = socket

    def recv(self, count: int = 0) -> bytes:
        data = self.socket.recv(count)
        print(
            f"Receiving {data!r} from {self.socket.getpeername()[0]}"
        )
        return data

    def send(self, data: bytes) -> None:
        print(f"Sending {data!r} to {self.socket.getpeername()[0]}")
        self.socket.send(data)

    def close(self) -> None:
        self.socket.close()
```

This class decorates a `socket` object and presents the `send()`, `recv()`, and `close()` interface to clients using it. A better decorator could properly implement all of the arguments to send, (which actually accepts an optional flags argument), but let's keep our example simple. Whenever `send()` is called on an instance of the `LogSocket` class, it logs the output to the screen before sending data to the client using the original socket. Similarly, for `recv()`, it reads and logs the data it received.

We only have to change one line in our original code to use this decorator. Instead of calling the `dice_response()` function with the original client socket, we call it with a decorated socket:

```python
def main_2() -> None:
    server = socket.socket(socket.AF_INET, socket.SOCK_STREAM)
    server.bind(("localhost", 2401))
    server.listen(1)
    with contextlib.closing(server):
```

```
        while True:
            client, addr = server.accept()
            logging_socket = cast(socket.socket, LogSocket(client))
            dice_response(logging_socket)
            client.close()
```

We've decorated the core socket with a LogSocket. The LogSocket will print to the console as well as invoking methods of the socket it decorates. The essential processing in the dice_response() function doesn't change, because the LogSocket instance behaves like the underlying socket object.

Note that we needed to use an explicit cast() to tell *mypy* the LogSocket instance would provide a similar interface to an ordinary socket. For a simple case like this, we have to ask ourselves why we didn't just extend the socket class and override the send method. A subclass could call super().send() and super().recv() to do the actual sending, after we logged it. Decoration offers an advantage over inheritance: a decoration can be reused among various classes in various class hierarchies. In this specific little example, there aren't too many socket-like objects, so the possibilities of reuse are limited.

If we switch our focus to something more generic than a socket, we can create potentially reusable decorators. Processing strings or bytes seems more common than processing a socket. Changing the structure can give us some desirable flexibility in addition to reuse potential. Originally, we broke the processing into a dice_response() function that handled the socket reading and writing, separate from a dice_roller() function that works with bytes. Because the dice_roller() function consumes the request bytes and produces response bytes, it can be a little simpler to expand and add features to it.

We can have a family of related decorators. We can decorate already decorated objects. The idea is to give ourselves flexibility through composition. Let's rework the logging decorator to focus on the bytes request and response instead of the socket object. The following should look similar to the earlier example but with some code shifted around to reside in a single __call__() method:

```
Address = Tuple[str, int]


class LogRoller:
    def __init__(
            self,
            dice: Callable[[bytes], bytes],
            remote_addr: Address
    ) -> None:
        self.dice_roller = dice
```

```
        self.remote_addr = remote_addr

    def __call__(self, request: bytes) -> bytes:
        print(f"Receiving {request!r} from {self.remote_addr}")
        dice_roller = self.dice_roller
        response = dice_roller(request)
        print(f"Sending {response!r} to {self.remote_addr}")
        return response
```

Here's a second decorator that compresses data using gzip compression on the resulting bytes:

```
import gzip
import io


class ZipRoller:
    def __init__(self, dice: Callable[[bytes], bytes]) -> None:
        self.dice_roller = dice

    def __call__(self, request: bytes) -> bytes:
        dice_roller = self.dice_roller
        response = dice_roller(request)
        buffer = io.BytesIO()
        with gzip.GzipFile(fileobj=buffer, mode="w") as zipfile:
            zipfile.write(response)
        return buffer.getvalue()
```

This decorator compresses the incoming data before sending it on to the client. It decorates an underlying `dice_roller` object that computes a response to a request.

Now that we have these two decorators, we can write code that piles one decoration on top of another:

```
def dice_response(client: socket.socket) -> None:
    request = client.recv(1024)
    try:
        remote_addr = client.getpeername()
        roller_1 = ZipRoller(dice.dice_roller)
        roller_2 = LogRoller(roller_1, remote_addr=remote_addr)
        response = roller_2(request)
    except (ValueError, KeyError) as ex:
        response = repr(ex).encode("utf-8")
    client.send(response)
```

The intent here is to separate three aspects of this application:

- Zipping the resulting document
- Writing a log
- Doing the underlying computation

We can apply the zip or logging to any similar application that works with receiving and sending bytes. We can, if we want, make the zipping operation a dynamic choice, also. We might have a separate configuration file to enable or disable the GZip feature. This means something like the following:

```
if config.zip_feature:
    roller_1 = ZipRoller(dice.dice_roller)
else:
    roller_1 = dice.dice_roller
```

We have a dynamic set of decorations. Try writing this using a multiple inheritance mixin and see how confused it becomes!

Decorators in Python

The Decorator pattern is useful in Python, but there are additional options. For example, we can use monkey-patching – changing the class definition at runtime – to get a similar effect. For example, `socket.socket.send = log_send` will change the way the built-in socket works. There are sometimes surprising implementation details that can make this unpleasantly complex. Single inheritance, where the *optional* calculations are done in one large method with a bunch of `if` statements, could be an option. Multiple inheritance should not be written off just because it's not suitable for the specific example seen previously.

In Python, it is very common to use this pattern on functions. As we saw in a previous chapter, functions are objects too. In fact, function decoration is so common that Python provides a special syntax to make it easy to apply such decorators to functions.

For example, we can look at the logging example in a more general way. Instead of logging only send calls on sockets, we may find it helpful to log all calls to certain functions or methods. The following example implements a decorator that does just this:

```
from functools import wraps

def log_args(function: Callable[..., Any]) -> Callable[..., Any]:
```

```
@wraps(function)
def wrapped_function(*args: Any, **kwargs: Any) -> Any:
    print(f"Calling {function.__name__}(*{args}, **{kwargs})")
    result = function(*args, **kwargs)
    return result

return wrapped_function
```

This decorator function is very similar to the example we explored earlier; in the earlier examples, the decorator took a socket-like object and created a socket-like object. This time, our decorator takes a function object and returns a new function object. We've provided a type hint of `Callable[..., Any]` to state that any function will work here. This code comprises three separate tasks:

- A function, `log_args()`, that accepts another function, `function`, as a parameter value.
- This function defines (internally) a new function, named `wrapped_function`, that does some extra work before calling the original function and returning the results from the original function.
- The new inner function, `wrapped_function()`, is returned from the decorator function.

Because we're using `@wraps(function)`, the new function will have a copy of the original function's name and the original function's docstring. This avoids having all of the functions we decorate wind up named `wrapped_function`.

Here's a sample function to demonstrate the decorator in use:

```
def test1(a: int, b: int, c: int) -> float:
    return sum(range(a, b + 1)) / c
test1 = log_args(test1)
```

This function can be decorated and used like this:

```
>>> test1(1, 9, 2)
Calling test1(*(1, 9, 2), **{})
22.5
```

This syntax allows us to build decorated function objects dynamically, just as we did with the socket example. If we don't use assignment to assign the new object to the old name, we can even keep the decorated and the non-decorated versions for different situations. We could use a statement like `test1_log = log_args(test1)` to create a second, decorated version of the `test1()` function, named `test1_log()`.

Typically, these decorators are general modifications that are applied permanently to different functions. In this situation, Python supports a special syntax to apply the decorator at the time the function is defined. We've already seen this syntax in a few places; now, let's understand how it works.

Instead of applying the decorator function after the method definition, we can use the @decorator syntax to do it all at once:

```
@log_args
def test1(a: int, b: int, c: int) -> float:
    return sum(range(a, b + 1)) / c
```

The primary benefit of this syntax is that we can easily see that the function has been decorated whenever we read the function definition. If the decorator is applied later, someone reading the code may miss that the function has been altered at all. Answering a question like *Why is my program logging function calls to the console?* can become much more difficult! However, the syntax can only be applied to functions we define, since we don't have access to the source code of other modules. If we need to decorate functions that are part of somebody else's third-party library, we have to use the earlier syntax.

Python's decorators permit parameters, also. One of the most useful decorators in the standard library is functools.lru_cache. The idea of a cache is to save computed results of a function to avoid recomputing them. Rather than save all of the parameters and results, we can keep the cache small by discarding the **least recently used (LRU)** values. For example, here's a function that involves a potentially expensive computation:

```
>>> from math import factorial
>>> def binom(n: int, k: int) -> int:
...        return factorial(n) // (factorial(k) * factorial(n-k))

>>> f"6-card deals: {binom(52, 6):,d}"
'6-card deals: 20,358,520'
```

We can use the lru_cache decorator to avoid doing this computation once the answer is known. Here's the small change required:

```
>>> from math import factorial
>>> from functools import lru_cache

>>> @lru_cache(64)
... def binom(n: int, k: int) -> int:
...        return factorial(n) // (factorial(k) * factorial(n-k))
```

The parameterized decorator, `@lru_cache(64)`, used to create this second version of the `binom()` function means it will save the most recent 64 results to avoid recomputing values when they've already been computed once. No change is needed elsewhere in the application. Sometimes, the speedup from this small change can be dramatic. We can, of course, fine-tune the size of the cache based on the data and the number of computations that are being performed.

Parameterized decorators like this involve a two-step dance. First, we customize the decorator with the parameter, then we apply that customized decorator to a function definition. These two separate steps parallel the way callable objects are initialized with the __init__() method, and can be called, like a function, via their __call__() method.

Here's an example of a configurable logging decorator, `NamedLogger`:

```python
class NamedLogger:
    def __init__(self, logger_name: str) -> None:
        self.logger = logging.getLogger(logger_name)

    def __call__(
            self,
            function: Callable[..., Any]
    ) -> Callable[..., Any]:
        @wraps(function)
        def wrapped_function(*args: Any, **kwargs: Any) -> Any:
            start = time.perf_counter()
            try:
                result = function(*args, **kwargs)
                µs = (time.perf_counter() - start) * 1_000_000
                self.logger.info(
                    f"{function.__name__}, { µs:.1f}µs")
                return result
            except Exception as ex:
                µs = (time.perf_counter() - start) * 1_000_000
                self.logger.error(
                    f"{ex}, {function.__name__}, { µs:.1f}µs")
                raise

        return wrapped_function
```

The __init__() method makes sure we can use code like `NamedLogger("log4")` to create a decorator; this decorator will make sure the function that follows uses a specific logger.

The __call__() method follows the pattern shown above. We define a new function, wrapped_function(), that does the work, and return that newly minted function. We can use it like this:

```
>>> @NamedLogger("log4")
... def test4(median: float, sample: float) -> float:
...     return abs(sample-median)
```

We've created an instance of the NamedLogger class. Then we applied this instance to the test4() function definition. The __call__() method is invoked, and will create a new function, the decorated version of the test4() function.

There are a few more use cases for the decorator syntax. For example, when a decorator is a method of a class, it can also save information about the decorated function, creating a registry of decorated functions. Further, classes can also be decorated; in that case, the decorator returns a new class instead of a new function. In all of these more advanced cases, we're using ordinary object-oriented design with the simpler-looking syntax of @decorator.

The Observer pattern

The Observer pattern is useful for state monitoring and event handling situations. This pattern allows a given object to be monitored by an unknown and dynamic group of *observer* objects. The core object being observed needs to implement an interface that makes it *observable*.

Whenever a value on the core object changes, it lets all the observer objects know that a change has occurred, by calling a method announcing there's been a change of state. This is used widely in GUIs to make sure that any state change in the underlying model is reflected in the views of the model. It's common to have detail and summary views; a change to the details must also update the widgets that display the details and update any summaries that are displayed, also. Sometimes a large change in mode may lead to a number of items being changed. For instance, clicking a "lock" icon may alter a number of displayed items to reflect their status as locked. This can be implemented as a number of observers attached to the observable display widget.

In Python, the observer can be notified via the __call__() method, making each observer behave like a function or other callable object. Each observer may be responsible for different tasks whenever the core object changes; the core object doesn't know or care what those tasks are, and the observers don't typically know or care what other observers are doing.

This allows tremendous flexibility by decoupling the response to a state change from the change itself.

Here is a depiction of the Observer design pattern in UML:

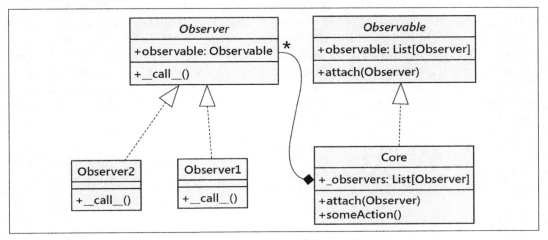

Figure 11.3: Observer pattern in UML

We've shown the Core object as containing a list of observer objects. To be observable, the Core class must adhere to a common understanding of observability; specifically, it must provide a list of observers and a way to attach new observers.

We've shown the Observer subclasses as having a __call__() method. This will be used by the observable to notify each observer of a state change. As with the Decorator pattern, we don't need to formalize the relationships with formally defined abstract superclasses. In most cases, we can rely on duck typing rules; as long as the observers have the right interface, they can be used in the defined role in this pattern. If they lack the proper interface, *mypy* may catch the conflict, and a unit test should catch the problem.

An Observer example

Outside a GUI, the Observer pattern is useful for saving intermediate states of objects. Using observer objects can be handy in systems where a rigorous audit of changes is required. It's also handy in a system where chaos reigns and components are unreliable.

Complex, cloud-based applications can suffer from chaos issues due to unreliable connections. We can use observers to record state changes, making recovery and restart easier.

For this example, we'll define a core object to maintain a collection of important values, and then have one or more observers create serialized copies of that object. These copies might be stored in a database, on a remote host, or in a local file, for example. Because we can have a number of observers, it's easy to modify the design to use different data caches. For this example, we're thinking of a dice game called Zonk or Zilch or Ten Thousand, where a player will roll six dice, score some points for triples and runs, and possibly roll again, leading to a sequence of dice. (The rules are a bit more complex than this glib summary.)

We'll start with a few overheads to help make our intention clear:

```python
from __future__ import annotations
from typing import Protocol


class Observer(Protocol):
    def __call__(self) -> None:
        ...


class Observable:
    def __init__(self) -> None:
        self._observers: list[Observer] = []

    def attach(self, observer: Observer) -> None:
        self._observers.append(observer)

    def detach(self, observer: Observer) -> None:
        self._observers.remove(observer)

    def _notify_observers(self) -> None:
        for observer in self._observers:
            observer()
```

The Observer class is a protocol, an abstract superclass for our observers. We didn't formalize it as an abc.ABC abstract class; we're not relying on the runtime error offered by the abc module. When defining a Protocol, we're relying on *mypy* to confirm that all observers actually implement the required method.

The Observable class defines the _observers instance variable and three methods that are purely part of this protocol definition. An observable object can append an observer, remove an observer, and – most important – notify all the observers of a state change. The only thing the core class needs to do that's special or different is to make calls to the _notify_observers() method when there's a state change. Appropriate notification is an important piece of the design for an observable object.

Here's part of the Zonk game we care about. This class keeps a player's hands:

```
from typing import List
Hand = List[int]

class ZonkHandHistory(Observable):
    def __init__(self, player: str, dice_set: Dice) -> None:
        super().__init__()
        self.player = player
        self.dice_set = dice_set
        self.rolls: list[Hand]

    def start(self) -> Hand:
        self.dice_set.roll()
        self.rolls = [self.dice_set.dice]
        self._notify_observers()   # State change
        return self.dice_set.dice

    def roll(self) -> Hand:
        self.dice_set.roll()
        self.rolls.append(self.dice_set.dice)
        self._notify_observers()   # State change
        return self.dice_set.dice
```

This class makes calls to self._notify_observers() on important state changes. This will notify all the observer instances. The observers might cache copies of the hand, send details over a network, update widgets on a GUI – any number of things. The _notify_observers() method inherited from Observable iterates over any registered observers and lets each know that the state of the hand has changed.

Now let's implement a simple observer object; this one will print out some state to the console:

```
class SaveZonkHand(Observer):
    def __init__(self, hand: ZonkHandHistory) -> None:
        self.hand = hand
```

```
        self.count = 0

    def __call__(self) -> None:
        self.count += 1
        message = {
            "player": self.hand.player,
            "sequence": self.count,
            "hands": json.dumps(self.hand.rolls),
            "time": time.time(),
        }
        print(f"SaveZonkHand {message}")
```

There's nothing terribly exciting here; the observed object is set up in the initializer, and when the observer is called, we do *something*, in this example, printing a line. Note that the superclass, Observer, isn't actually needed here. The context in which this class is used is sufficient for *mypy* to confirm this class matches the required Observer protocol. While we don't need to state that it's an Observer, it can help readers to see that this class implements the Observer protocol.

We can test the SaveZonkHand observer in an interactive console:

```
>>> d = Dice.from_text("6d6")
>>> player = ZonkHandHistory("Bo", d)

>>> save_history = SaveZonkHand(player)
>>> player.attach(save_history)
>>> r1 = player.start()
SaveZonkHand {'player': 'Bo', 'sequence': 1, 'hands': '[[1, 1, 2, 3, 6,
6]]', 'time': 1609619907.52109}
>>> r1
[1, 1, 2, 3, 6, 6]
>>> r2 = player.roll()
SaveZonkHand {'player': 'Bo', 'sequence': 2, 'hands': '[[1, 1, 2, 3, 6,
6], [1, 2, 2, 6, 6, 6]]', 'time': ...}
```

After attaching the observer to the Inventory object, whenever we change one of the two observed properties, the observer is called and its action is invoked. Note that our observer tracks a sequence number and includes a timestamp. These are outside the game definition, and are kept separate from the essential game processing by being part of the SaveZonkHand observer class.

We can add multiple observers of a variety of classes. Let's add a second observer that has a limited job to check for three pairs and announce it:

```
class ThreePairZonkHand:
    """Observer of ZonkHandHistory"""
    def __init__(self, hand: ZonkHandHistory) -> None:
        self.hand = hand
        self.zonked = False

    def __call__(self) -> None:
        last_roll = self.hand.rolls[-1]
        distinct_values = set(last_roll)
        self.zonked = len(distinct_values) == 3 and all(
            last_roll.count(v) == 2 for v in distinct_values
        )
        if self.zonked:
            print("3 Pair Zonk!")
```

For this example, we omitted naming `Observer` as a superclass. We can trust the *mypy* tool to note how this class is used and what protocols it must implement. Introducing this new `ThreePairZonkHand` observer means that when we change the state of the hand, there may be two sets of output, one for each observer. The key idea here is that we can easily add totally different types of observers to do different kinds of things, in this case, copying the data as well as checking for a special case in the data.

The Observer pattern detaches the code being observed from the code doing the observing. If we were not using this pattern, we would have had to put code in the `ZonkHandHistory` class to handle the different cases that might come up: logging to the console, updating a database or file, checking for special cases, and so on. The code for each of these tasks would all be mixed in with the core class definition. Maintaining it would be a nightmare and adding new monitoring functionality at a later date would be painful.

The Strategy pattern

The Strategy pattern is a common demonstration of abstraction in object-oriented programming. The pattern implements different solutions to a single problem, each in a different object. The core class can then choose the most appropriate implementation dynamically at runtime.

Typically, different algorithms have different trade-offs; one might be faster than another, but uses a lot more memory, while a third algorithm may be most suitable when multiple CPUs are present or a distributed system is provided.

Here is the Strategy pattern in UML:

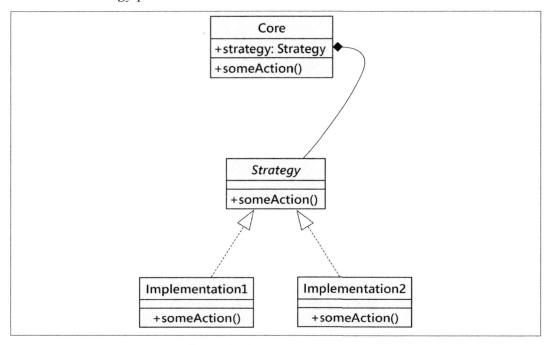

Figure 11.4: Strategy pattern in UML

The **Core** code connecting to the **Strategy** abstraction simply needs to know that it is dealing with some kind of class that fits the Strategy interface for this particular action. Each of the implementations should perform the same task, but in different ways. The implementation interfaces need to be identical, and it's often helpful to leverage an abstract base class to make sure the implementations match.

This idea of a plug-in strategy is also an aspect of the Observer pattern. Indeed, the idea of strategy objects is an important aspect of many of the patterns covered in this chapter. The common idea is to use a separate object to isolate conditional or replaceable processing and delegate the work to the separate object. This works for observables, decorations, and – as we'll see – commands and states, also.

A Strategy example

One common example of the Strategy pattern is sort routines; over the years, numerous algorithms have been invented for sorting a collection of objects. Quick sort, merge sort, and heap sort are all algorithms with different features, each useful in its own right, depending on the size and type of inputs, how out of order they are, and the requirements of the system.

If we have client code that needs to sort a collection, we could pass it to an object with a sort() method. This object may be a QuickSorter or MergeSorter object, but the result will be the same in either case: a sorted list. The strategy used to do the sorting is abstracted from the calling code, making it modular and replaceable.

Of course, in Python, we typically just call the sorted() function or list.sort() method and trust that it will do the sorting quickly enough that the details of the TimSort algorithm don't really matter. For details on how amazingly fast TimSort is, see https://bugs.python.org/file4451/timsort.txt. While sorting is a helpful concept, it's not the most practical example, so let's look at something different.

As a simpler example of the Strategy design pattern, consider a desktop wallpaper manager. When an image is displayed on a desktop background, it can be adjusted to the screen size in different ways. For example, assuming the image is smaller than the screen, it can be tiled across the screen, centered on it, or scaled to fit. There are other, more complicated strategies that can be used as well, such as scaling to the maximum height or width, combining it with a solid, semi-transparent, or gradient background color, or other manipulations. While we may want to add these strategies later, let's start with a few basic ones.

You'll need to install the pillow module. If you're using **conda** to manage your virtual environments, use conda install pillow to install the Pillow project's PIL implementation. If you're not using **conda**, use python -m pip install pillow.

Our Strategy objects need to take two inputs: the image to be displayed, and a tuple of the width and height of the screen. They each return a new image the size of the screen, with the image manipulated to fit according to the given strategy.

Here are some preliminary definitions, including an abstract superclass for all of the strategy variants:

```
import abc
from pathlib import Path
from PIL import Image  # type: ignore [import]
from typing import Tuple

Size = Tuple[int, int]

class FillAlgorithm(abc.ABC):
    @abc.abstractmethod
    def make_background(
            self,
            img_file: Path,
            desktop_size: Size
    ) -> Image:
        pass
```

Is this abstraction necessary? This sits right on the fence between too simple to require an abstraction and complex enough that the superclass helps. The function signature is kind of complex, with a special type hint to describe the size tuple. For this reason, the abstraction can help check each implementation to be sure all the types match.

Note that we need to include the special # type: ignore [import] comment to make sure *mypy* isn't confused by the lack of annotations in the PIL modules.

Here's our first concrete strategy; this is a fill algorithm that tiles the images:

```
class TiledStrategy(FillAlgorithm):
    def make_background(
            self,
            img_file: Path,
            desktop_size: Size
    ) -> Image:
        in_img = Image.open(img_file)
        out_img = Image.new("RGB", desktop_size)
        num_tiles = [
            o // i + 1 for o, i in zip(out_img.size, in_img.size)]
        for x in range(num_tiles[0]):
            for y in range(num_tiles[1]):
                out_img.paste(
                    in_img,
                    (
                        in_img.size[0] * x,
                        in_img.size[1] * y,
                        in_img.size[0] * (x + 1),
                        in_img.size[1] * (y + 1),
```

```
        ),
    )
    return out_img
```

This works by dividing the output height and width by the input image height and width. The num_tiles sequence is a way of doing the same computation to widths and heights. It's a two-tuple computed via a list comprehension to be sure both width and height are processed the same way.

Here's a fill algorithm that centers the image without re-scaling it:

```
class CenteredStrategy(FillAlgorithm):
    def make_background(
            self,
            img_file: Path,
            desktop_size: Size
    ) -> Image:
        in_img = Image.open(img_file)
        out_img = Image.new("RGB", desktop_size)
        left = (out_img.size[0] - in_img.size[0]) // 2
        top = (out_img.size[1] - in_img.size[1]) // 2
        out_img.paste(
            in_img,
            (left, top, left + in_img.size[0], top + in_img.size[1]),
        )
        return out_img
```

Finally, here's a fill algorithm that scales the image up to fill the entire screen:

```
class ScaledStrategy(FillAlgorithm):
    def make_background(
            self,
            img_file: Path,
            desktop_size: Size
    ) -> Image:
        in_img = Image.open(img_file)
        out_img = in_img.resize(desktop_size)
        return out_img
```

Here we have three strategy subclasses, each using PIL.Image to perform their task. All the strategy implementations have a make_background() method that accepts the same set of parameters. Once selected, the appropriate Strategy object can be called to create a correctly sized version of the desktop image. TiledStrategy computes the number of input image tiles that would fit in the width and height of the display screen and copies the image into each tile location, repeatedly, without rescaling, so it may not fill the entire space. CenteredStrategy figures out how much space needs to be left on the four edges of the image to center it. ScaledStrategy forces the image to the output size, without preserving the original aspect ratio.

Here's an overall object that does resizing, using one of these Strategy classes. The `algorithm` instance variable is filled in when a `Resizer` instance is created:

```python
class Resizer:
    def __init__(self, algorithm: FillAlgorithm) -> None:
        self.algorithm = algorithm

    def resize(self, image_file: Path, size: Size) -> Image:
        result = self.algorithm.make_background(image_file, size)
        return result
```

And here's a `main` function that builds an instance of the `Resizer` class and applies one of the available Strategy classes:

```python
def main() -> None:
    image_file = Path.cwd() / "boat.png"
    tiled_desktop = Resizer(TiledStrategy())
    tiled_image = tiled_desktop.resize(image_file, (1920, 1080))
    tiled_image.show()
```

What's important is the binding of the Strategy instance happens as late as possible in the processing. The decision can be made (and unmade) at any point in the processing because any of the available strategy objects can be plugged into a `Resizer` object at any time.

Consider how switching between these options would be implemented without the Strategy pattern. We'd need to put all the code inside one great big method and use an awkward `if` statement to select the expected one. Every time we wanted to add a new strategy, we'd have to make the method even more ungainly.

Strategy in Python

The preceding canonical implementation of the Strategy pattern, while very common in most object-oriented libraries, isn't ideal in Python. It involves some overheads that aren't really necessary.

These strategy classes each define objects that do nothing but provide a single method. We could just as easily call that function `__call__` and make the object callable directly. Since there is no other data associated with the object, we need do no more than create a set of top-level functions and pass them around as our strategies instead.

Instead of the overheads of an abstract class, we could summarize these strategies with a type hint of:

```
FillAlgorithm = Callable[[Image, Size], Image]
```

When we do this, we can eliminate all of the references to `FillAlgorithm` in class definitions; we'd change `class CenteredStrategy(FillAlgorithm):` to `class CenteredStrategy:`.

Because we have a choice between an abstract class and a type hint, the Strategy design pattern seems superfluous. This leads to an odd conversation, starting with *"Because Python has first-class functions, the Strategy pattern is unnecessary."* In truth, Python's first-class functions allow us to implement the Strategy pattern in a more straightforward way, without the overhead of class definitions. The pattern is more than the implementation details. Knowing the pattern can help us choose a good design for our program, and implement it using the most readable syntax. The Strategy pattern, whether a class or a top-level function, should be used when we need to allow client code or the end user to select from multiple implementations of the same interface at runtime.

There's a bright line separating mixin class definitions from plug-in strategy objects. As we saw in *Chapter 6, Abstract Base Classes and Operator Overloading*, mixin class definitions are created in the source code, and cannot easily be tweaked at runtime. A plug-in strategy object, however, is filled in at runtime, allowing late binding of the strategy. The code tends to be very similar between them, and it helps to have clear docstrings on each class to explain how the various classes fit together.

The Command pattern

When we think about class responsibilities, we can sometimes distinguish "passive" classes that hold objects and maintain an internal state, but don't initiate very much, and "active" classes that reach out into other objects to take action and do things. This is not a very crisp distinction, but it can help separate the relatively passive Observer and the more active Command design patterns. An Observer is notified that something changed. A Commander, on the other hand, will be active, making state changes in other objects. We can combine the two aspects, and that's one of the beauties of talking about a software architecture by describing the various patterns that apply to a class or a relationship among classes.

The Command pattern generally involves a hierarchy of classes that each do something. A Core class can create a command (or a sequence of commands) to carry out actions.

In a way, it's a kind of meta-programming: by creating Command objects that contain a bunch of statements, the design has a higher-level "language" of Command objects.

Here's a UML diagram showing a **Core** object and a collection of **Commands**:

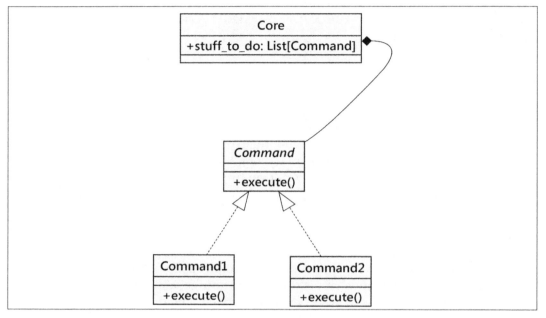

Figure 11.5: Command pattern in UML

This looks similar to the diagrams for the Strategy and Observer patterns because all these patterns rely on delegating work from a **Core** object to a plug-in object. In this case, a sequence of individual plug-in objects that represent a sequence of commands to perform.

A Command example

As an example, we'll look at the fancy dice rolling that was omitted from the Decorator pattern example earlier in this chapter. In the earlier example, we had a function, dice_roller(), that computed a sequence of random numbers:

```python
def dice_roller(request: bytes) -> bytes:
    request_text = request.decode("utf-8")
    numbers = [random.randint(1, 6) for _ in range(6)]
    response = f"{request_text} = {numbers}"
    return response.encode("utf-8")
```

This isn't very clever; we'd rather handle something a little more sophisticated. We want to be able to write strings like 3d6 to mean three six-sided dice, 3d6+2 to mean three six-sided dice plus a bonus of two more, and something a little more obscure like 4d6d1 to mean "roll four six-sided dice and drop one of the lowest dice." We might want to combine things and write 4d6d1+2, also, to combine dropping the lowest and adding two to the result.

These d1 and +2 options at the end can be viewed as a series of commands. There are four common varieties: "drop," "keep," "add," and "subtract." There can be a lot more, of course, to reflect a wide variety of game mechanics and desired statistical distributions, but we'll look at four commands that modify a batch of dice.

Here's the regular expression we're going to implement:

```
dice_pattern = re.compile(r"(?P<n>\d*)d(?P<d>\d+)(?P<a>[dk+-]\d+)*")
```

This regular expression can be a little daunting. Some people find the railroad diagrams at https://www.debuggex.com to be helpful. Here's a depiction as a UML state diagram:

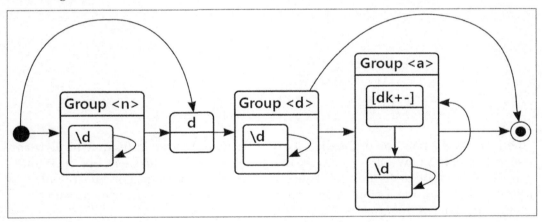

Figure 11.6: Dice-parsing regular expression

This pattern has four parts:

1. The first grouping, (?P<n>\d*), captures a batch of digits for the number of dice, saving this as a group named n. This is optional, allowing us to write d6 instead of 1d6.

2. The letter "d", which must be present, but isn't captured.

3. The next grouping, (?P<d>\d+), captures the digits for the number of faces on each die, saving this as a group named d. If we were very fussy, we might try to limit this to (4|6|8|10|12|20|100) to define an acceptable list of regular polyhedral dice (and two common irregular polyhedrons). We didn't provide this short list; instead, we'll accept any sequence of digits.

4. The final grouping, (?P<a>[dk+-]\d+)*, defines a repeating series of adjustments. Each one has a prefix and a sequence of digits, for example, d1 or k3 or +1 or -2. We'll capture the whole sequence of adjustments as group a, and decompose the parts separately. Each of these parts will become a command, following the Command design pattern.

We can think of each part of dice rolling as a distinct command. One command rolls the dice, and then subsequent commands adjust the value of the dice. For example, 3d6+2 means roll three dice (for example, ⊡, ⊡, ⊡) and add 2 to get 13 in total. The class, overall, looks like this:

```python
class Dice:
    def __init__(self, n: int, d: int, *adj: Adjustment) -> None:
        self.adjustments = [cast(Adjustment, Roll(n, d))] + list(adj)
        self.dice: list[int]
        self.modifier: int

    def roll(self) -> int:
        for a in self.adjustments:
            a.apply(self)
        return sum(self.dice) + self.modifier
```

When we want a new roll of the dice, a Dice object applies the individual Adjustment objects to create a new roll. We can see one of the kinds of Adjustment objects in the __init__() method: a Roll object. This is put first into a sequence of adjustments; after that any additional adjustments are processed in order. Each adjustment is another kind of command.

Here are the various kinds of adjustment commands that change the state of a Dice object:

```python
class Adjustment(abc.ABC):
    def __init__(self, amount: int) -> None:
        self.amount = amount

    @abc.abstractmethod
    def apply(self, dice: "Dice") -> None:
        ...
```

```
class Roll(Adjustment):
    def __init__(self, n: int, d: int) -> None:
        self.n = n
        self.d = d

    def apply(self, dice: "Dice") -> None:
        dice.dice = sorted(
            random.randint(1, self.d) for _ in range(self.n))
        dice.modifier = 0

class Drop(Adjustment):
    def apply(self, dice: "Dice") -> None:
        dice.dice = dice.dice[self.amount :]

class Keep(Adjustment):
    def apply(self, dice: "Dice") -> None:
        dice.dice = dice.dice[: self.amount]

class Plus(Adjustment):
    def apply(self, dice: "Dice") -> None:
        dice.modifier += self.amount

class Minus(Adjustment):
    def apply(self, dice: "Dice") -> None:
        dice.modifier -= self.amount
```

An instance of the Roll() class sets the values of the dice and the modifier attribute of a Dice instance. The other Adjustment objects either remove some dice or change the modifier. The operations depend on the dice being sorted. That makes it easy to drop the worst or keep the best via slice operations. Because each adjustment is a kind of command, they make adjustments to the overall state of the dice that were rolled.

The missing piece is translating the string dice expression into a sequence of Adjustment objects. We've made this a @classmethod of the Dice class. This lets us use Dice.from_text() to create a new Dice instance. It also provides the subclass as the first parameter value, cls, making sure that each subclass creates proper instances of itself, not this parent class. Here's the definition of this method:

```
@classmethod
def from_text(cls, dice_text: str) -> "Dice":
    dice_pattern = re.compile(
```

```
          r"(?P<n>\d*)d(?P<d>\d+)(?P<a>[dk+-]\d+)*")
adjustment_pattern = re.compile(r"([dk+-])(\d+)")
adj_class: dict[str, Type[Adjustment]] = {
    "d": Drop,
    "k": Keep,
    "+": Plus,
    "-": Minus,
}

if (dice_match := dice_pattern.match(dice_text)) is None:
    raise ValueError(f"Error in {dice_text!r}")

n = int(dice_match.group("n")) if dice_match.group("n") else 1
d = int(dice_match.group("d"))
adjustment_matches = adjustment_pattern.finditer(
    dice_match.group("a") or "")
adjustments = [
    adj_class[a.group(1)](int(a.group(2)))
    for a in adjustment_matches
]
return cls(n, d, *adjustments)
```

The overall `dice_pattern` is applied first and the result is assigned to the `dice_match` variable. If the result is a `None` object, the pattern didn't match, and we can't do much more than raise a `ValueError` exception and give up. The `adjustment_pattern` is used to decompose the string of adjustments in the suffix of the dice expression. A list comprehension is used to create a list of objects from the `Adjustment` class definitions.

Each adjustment class is a separate command. The `Dice` class will inject a special command, `Roll`, that starts the processing by simulating a roll of the dice. Then the adjust commands can apply their individual changes to the initial roll.

This design allows us to manually create an instance like this:

```
dice.Dice(4, dice.D6, dice.Keep(3))
```

The first two parameters define the special `Roll` command. The remaining parameters can include any number of further adjustments. In this case, there's only one, a `Keep(3)` command. The alternative is to parse text, like this: `dice.Dice.from_text("4d6k3")`. This will build the `Roll` command and the other `Adjustment` commands. Each time we want a new roll of the dice, the sequence of commands is executed, rolling the dice and then adjusting that roll to give a final outcome.

The State pattern

The State pattern is structurally similar to the Strategy pattern, but its intent and purpose are very different. The goal of the State pattern is to represent state transition systems: systems where an object's behavior is constrained by the state it's in, and there are narrowly defined transitions to other states.

To make this work, we need a manager or context class that provides an interface for switching states. Internally, this class contains a pointer to the current state. Each state knows what other states it is allowed to be in and will transition to those states depending on the actions invoked upon it.

Here's how it looks in UML:

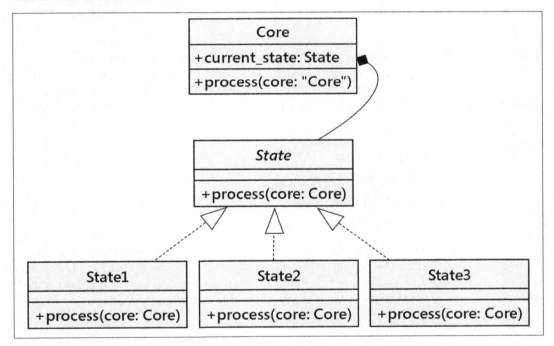

Figure 11.7: State pattern in UML

The State pattern decomposes the problem into two types of classes: the **Core** class and multiple **State** classes. The **Core** class maintains the current state, and forwards actions to a current state object. The **State** objects are typically hidden from any other objects that are calling the **Core** object; it acts like a black box that happens to perform state management internally.

A State example

One of the most compelling state-specific processing examples is parsing text. When we write a regular expression, we're detailing a series of alternative state changes used to match a pattern against a sample piece of text. At a higher level, parsing the text of a programming language or a markup language is also highly stateful work. Markup languages like XML, HTML, YAML, TOML, or even reStructuredText and Markdown all have stateful rules for what is allowed next and what is not allowed next.

We'll look at a relatively simple language that crops up when solving **Internet of Things (IoT)** problems. The data stream from a GPS receiver is an interesting problem. Parsing statements in this language is an example of the State design pattern. The language is the NMEA 0183 language from the National Marine Electronics Association.

The output from a GPS antenna is a stream of bytes that form a sequence of "sentences." Each sentence starts with $, includes printable characters in the ASCII encoding, and ends with a carriage return and a newline character. A GPS device's output includes a number of different kinds of sentences, including the following:

- GPRMC – recommended minimum data
- GPGGA – global position
- GPGLL – latitude and longitude
- GPGSV – satellites in view
- GPGSA – active satellites

There are many, many more messages available, and they come out of the antenna device at a pace that can be bewildering. They all have a common format, however, making them easy to validate and filter so we can use the good ones, and ignore the ones that aren't providing useful information for our specific application.

A typical message looks like this:

```
$GPGLL,3723.2475,N,12158.3416,W,161229.487,A,A*41
```

This sentence has the following structure:

$	Starts the sentence
GPGLL	The "talker," GP, and the type of message, GLL
3723.2475	Latitude, 37°23.2475
N	North of the equator
12158.3416	Longitude, 121°58.3416
W	West of the 0° meridian
161229.487	The timestamp in UTC: 16:12:29.487
A	Status, A=valid, V=not valid
A	Mode, A=Autonomous, D=DGPS, E=DR
*	Ends the sentence, starts the checksum
41	Hexadecimal checksum of the text (excluding the $ and * characters)

With a few exceptions, all the messages from a GPS will have a similar pattern. The exceptional messages will start with !, and our design will safely ignore them.

When building IoT devices, we need to be aware of two complicating factors:

1. Things aren't very reliable, meaning our software must be prepared for broken or incomplete messages.
2. The devices are tiny and some common Python techniques that work on a large, general-purpose laptop computer won't work well in a tiny Circuit Playground Express chip with only 32K of memory.

What we need to do, then, is to read and validate the message as the bytes arrive. This saves time (and memory) when ingesting data. Because there's a defined upper bound of 82 bytes for these GPS messages, we can use Python bytearray structures as a place to process the bytes of a message.

The process for reading a message has a number of distinct states. The following state transition diagram shows the available state changes:

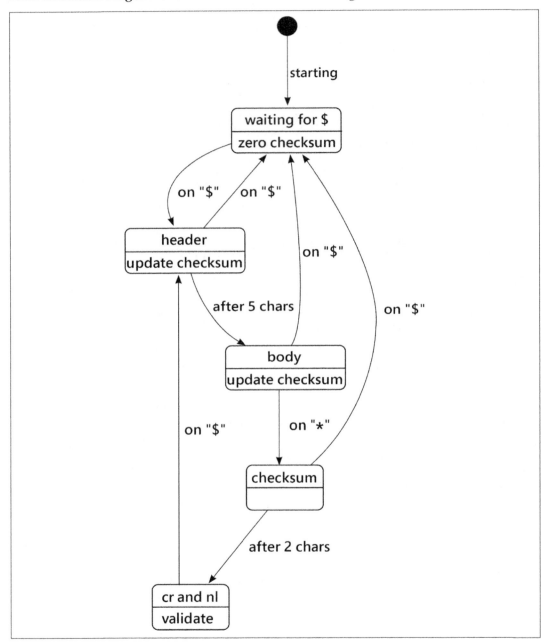

Figure 11.8: State transitions to parse NMEA sentences

We start in a state of waiting for the next $. We'll assume that IoT devices have loose wires and power problems. (Some people can solder really well, so unreliability may not be as common for them as it is for the authors.)

Once we've received the $, we'll transition to a state of reading the five-character header. If, at any time, we get another $, it means we lost some bytes somewhere, and we need to start over again. Once we have all five characters with the message name, we can transition to reading the message body. This will have up to 73 more bytes. When we receive a *, it tells us we're at the end of the body. Again, if we see a $ along the way, it means something's wrong and we should restart.

The final two bytes (after the *) represent a hexadecimal value that should equal the computed checksum of the preceding message (header and body). If the checksum is good, the message can be used by the application. There will be one or more "whitespace" characters – usually carriage return and newline characters – at the end of the message.

We can imagine each of these states as an extension of the following class:

```
class NMEA_State:
    def __init__(self, message: "Message") -> None:
        self.message = message

    def feed_byte(self, input: int) -> "NMEA_State":
        return self

    def valid(self) -> bool:
        return False

    def __repr__(self) -> str:
        return f"{self.__class__.__name__}({self.message})"
```

We've defined each state to work with a Message object. Some reader object will feed a byte to the current state, which will do something with the byte (usually save it) and return the next state. The exact behavior depends on the byte received; for example, most states will reset the message buffer to empty and transition to the Header state when they receive a $. Most states will return False for the valid() function. One state, however, will validate a complete message, and possibly return True for the valid() function, if the checksum is correct.

For the purists, the class name doesn't strictly follow PEP-8. It's challenging to include abbreviations or acronyms and keep a properly camel-cased name. It seems like `NmeaState` isn't as clear. While a compromise class name might be `NMEAState`, the clash between abbreviations and class name seems confusing. We prefer to cite "*A foolish consistency is the hobgoblin of little minds...*" in this specific case. Keeping the class hierarchy internally consistent is more important than the full PEP-8 level of consistency.

The `Message` object is a wrapper around two `bytearray` structures where we accumulate the content of the message:

```python
class Message:
    def __init__(self) -> None:
        self.body = bytearray(80)
        self.checksum_source = bytearray(2)
        self.body_len = 0
        self.checksum_len = 0
        self.checksum_computed = 0

    def reset(self) -> None:
        self.body_len = 0
        self.checksum_len = 0
        self.checksum_computed = 0

    def body_append(self, input: int) -> int:
        self.body[self.body_len] = input
        self.body_len += 1
        self.checksum_computed ^= input
        return self.body_len

    def checksum_append(self, input: int) -> int:
        self.checksum_source[self.checksum_len] = input
        self.checksum_len += 1
        return self.checksum_len

    @property
    def valid(self) -> bool:
        return (
            self.checksum_len == 2
            and int(self.checksum_source, 16) == self.checksum_computed
        )
```

This definition of the Message class encapsulates much of what's important about each sentence that comes from the GPS device. We defined a method, body_append(), for accumulating bytes in the body, and accumulating a checksum of those bytes. In this case, the ^ operator is used to compute the checksum. This is a real Python operator; it's the bit-wise exclusive OR. An exclusive OR means "one or the other but not both." You can see it in action with an expression like bin(ord(b'a') ^ ord(b'z')). The bits in b'a' are 0b1100001. The bits in b'z' are 0b1111010. Applying "one or the other but not both" to the bits, the exclusive OR is 0b0011011.

Here's the reader that builds valid Message objects by undergoing a number of state changes as bytes are received:

```
class Reader:
    def __init__(self) -> None:
        self.buffer = Message()
        self.state: NMEA_State = Waiting(self.buffer)

    def read(self, source: Iterable[bytes]) -> Iterator[Message]:
        for byte in source:
            self.state = self.state.feed_byte(cast(int, byte))
            if self.buffer.valid:
                yield self.buffer
                self.buffer = Message()
                self.state = Waiting(self.buffer)
```

The initial state is an instance of the Waiting class, a subclass of NMEA_State. The read() method consumes one byte from the input, and then hands it to the current NMEA_State object for processing. The state object may save the byte or may discard it, the state object may transition to another state, or it may return the current state. If the state's valid() method is True, the message is complete, and we can yield it for further processing by our application.

Note that we're reusing a Message object's byte arrays until it's complete and valid. This avoids allocating and freeing a lot of objects while ignoring incomplete messages on a noisy line. This is not typical for Python programs on large computers. In some applications, we don't need to save the original message, but only need to save the values of a few fields, further reducing the amount of memory used.

To reuse the buffers in the Message object, we need to make sure it's not part of any specific State object. We've made the current Message object part of the overall Reader, and provided the working Message object to each State as an argument value.

Now that we've seen the context, here are the classes to implement the various states for an incomplete message. We'll start with the state of waiting for the initial $ to begin a message. When a $ is seen, the parser transitions to a new state, Header:

```python
class Waiting(NMEA_State):
    def feed_byte(self, input: int) -> NMEA_State:
        if input == ord(b"$"):
            return Header(self.message)
        return self
```

When we're in the Header state, we've seen the $, and we're waiting for the five characters that identify the talker ("GP") and the sentence type (for example, "GLL"). We'll accumulate bytes until we get five of them, and then transition to the Body state:

```python
class Header(NMEA_State):
    def __init__(self, message: "Message") -> None:
        self.message = message
        self.message.reset()

    def feed_byte(self, input: int) -> NMEA_State:
        if input == ord(b"$"):
            return Header(self.message)
        size = self.message.body_append(input)
        if size == 5:
            return Body(self.message)
        return self
```

The Body state is where we accumulate the bulk of the message. For some applications, we may want to apply additional processing on the header and transition back to waiting for headers when we receive a message type we don't want. This can shave off a little bit of processing time when dealing with devices that produce a lot of data.

When the * arrives, the body is complete, and the next two bytes must be part of the checksum. This means transitioning to a Checksum state:

```python
class Body(NMEA_State):
    def feed_byte(self, input: int) -> NMEA_State:
        if input == ord(b"$"):
            return Header(self.message)
        if input == ord(b"*"):
            return Checksum(self.message)
        self.message.body_append(input)
        return self
```

The Checksum state is similar to accumulating bytes in the Header state: we're waiting for a specific number of input bytes. After the checksum, most messages are followed by ASCII \r and \n characters. If we receive either of these, we transition to an End state where we can gracefully ignore these excess characters:

```
class Checksum(NMEA_State):
    def feed_byte(self, input: int) -> NMEA_State:
        if input == ord(b"$"):
            return Header(self.message)
        if input in {ord(b"\n"), ord(b"\r")}:
            # Incomplete checksum... Will be invalid.
            return End(self.message)
        size = self.message.checksum_append(input)
        if size == 2:
            return End(self.message)
        return self
```

The End state has an additional feature: it overrides the default valid() method. For all other states, the valid() method is False. Once we've received a complete message, this state's class definition changes the validity rule: we now depend on the Message class to compare the computed checksum with the final checksum bytes to tell us if the message is valid:

```
class End(NMEA_State):
    def feed_byte(self, input: int) -> NMEA_State:
        if input == ord(b"$"):
            return Header(self.message)
        elif input not in {ord(b"\n"), ord(b"\r")}:
            return Waiting(self.message)
        return self

    def valid(self) -> bool:
        return self.message.valid
```

This state-oriented change in behavior is one of the best reasons for using this design pattern. Instead of a complex set of if conditions to decide if we have a complete message and it has all the right parts and punctuation marks, we've refactored the complexity into a number of individual states and the rules for transition from state to state. This leads us to only checking validity when we've received $, five characters, a body, *, two more characters, and confirmed the checksum is correct.

Here's a test case to show how this works:

```
>>> message = b'''
... $GPGGA,161229.487,3723.2475,N,12158.3416,W,1,07,1.0,9.0,M,,,,0000*18
... $GPGLL,3723.2475,N,12158.3416,W,161229.487,A,A*41
... '''
>>> rdr = Reader()
>>> result = list(rdr.read(message))
[Message(bytearray(b'GPGGA,161229.487,3723.2475,N,12158.3416,W,1,07,1
.0,9.0,M,,,,0000'), bytearray(b'18'), computed=18), Message(bytearray
(b'GPGLL,3723.2475,N,12158.3416,W,161229.487,A,A'), bytearray(b'41'),
computed=41)]
```

We've copied two example messages from the SiRF NMEA Reference Manual, revision 1.3, to be sure our parsing was correct. See https://www.sparkfun.com/ products/13750 for more information on GPS IoT devices. See http://aprs.gids.nl/ nmea/ for additional examples and details.

It's often helpful to use state transitions when parsing complex messages because we can refactor the validation into individual state definitions and state transition rules.

State versus Strategy

The State pattern looks very similar to the Strategy pattern; indeed, the UML diagrams for the two are identical. The implementation, too, is identical. We could even have written our states as first-class functions instead of wrapping them in objects, as was suggested in the section on the Strategy pattern earlier in this chapter.

These two patterns are similar because they both delegate work to other objects. This decomposes a complex problem into several closely related but simpler problems.

The Strategy pattern is used to choose an algorithm at runtime; generally, only one of those algorithms is going to be chosen for a particular use case. The idea here is to provide an implementation choice at runtime, as late in the design process as possible. Strategy class definitions are rarely aware of other implementations; each Strategy generally stands alone.

The State pattern, on the other hand, is designed to allow switching between different states dynamically, as some process evolves. In our example, the state changed as bytes were consumed and an evolving set of validity conditions satisfied. State definitions are generally defined as a group with an ability to switch among the various state objects.

To an extent, the End state used to parse an NMEA message has both State pattern features and Strategy pattern features. Because the implementation of the valid() method is different from other states, this reflects a different strategy for determining the validity of a sentence.

The Singleton pattern

The Singleton pattern is a source of some controversy; many have accused it of being an *anti-pattern*, a pattern that should be avoided, not promoted. In Python, if someone is using the Singleton pattern, they're almost certainly doing something wrong, probably because they're coming from a more restrictive programming language.

So, why discuss it at all? Singleton is useful in overly object-oriented languages and is a vital part of traditional object-oriented programming. More relevantly, the idea behind singleton is useful, even if we implement the concept in a totally different way in Python.

The basic idea behind the Singleton pattern is to allow exactly one instance of a certain object to exist. Typically, this object is a sort of manager class like those we discussed in *Chapter 5, When to Use Object-Oriented Programming*. Such manager objects often need to be referenced by a wide variety of other objects; passing references to the manager object around to the methods and constructors that need them can make code hard to read.

Instead, when a singleton is used, the separate objects request the single instance of the manager object from the class. The UML diagram doesn't fully describe it, but here it is for completeness:

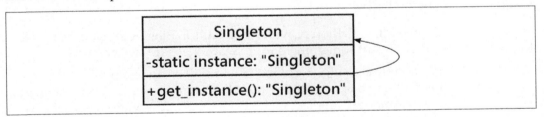

Figure 11.9: Singleton pattern in UML

In most programming environments, singletons are enforced by making the constructor private (so no one can create additional instances of it), and then providing a static method to retrieve the single instance. This method creates a new instance the first time it is called, and then returns that same instance for all subsequent calls.

Singleton implementation

Python doesn't have private constructors, but for this purpose, we can use the __new__() class method to ensure that only one instance is ever created:

```
>>> class OneOnly:
...     _singleton = None
...     def __new__(cls, *args, **kwargs):
...         if not cls._singleton:
...             cls._singleton = super().__new__(cls, *args, **kwargs)
...         return cls._singleton
```

When __new__() is called, it normally constructs a new instance of the requested class. When we override it, we first check whether our singleton instance has been created; if not, we create it using a super call. Thus, whenever we call the constructor on OneOnly, we always get the exact same instance:

```
>>> o1 = OneOnly()
>>> o2 = OneOnly()
>>> o1 == o2
True
>>> id(o1) == id(o2)
True
>>> o1
<__main__.OneOnly object at 0x7fd9c49ef2b0>
>>> o2
<__main__.OneOnly object at 0x7fd9c49ef2b0>
```

The two objects are equal and located at the same address; thus, they are the same object. This particular implementation isn't very transparent, since it's not obvious that the special method is being used to create a singleton object.

We don't actually need this. Python provides two built-in Singleton patterns we can leverage. Rather than invent something hard to read, there are two choices:

- A Python module *is* a singleton. One import will create a module. All subsequent attempts to import the module return the one-and-only singleton instance of the module. In places where an application-wide configuration file or cache is required, make this part of a distinct module. Library modules like logging, random, and even re have module-level singleton caches. We'll look at using module-level variables below.

- A Python class definition can also be pressed into service as a singleton. A class can only be created once in a given namespace. Consider using a class with class-level attributes as a singleton object. This means defining methods with the @staticmethod decorator because there will never be an instance created, and there's no self variable.

To use module-level variables instead of a complex Singleton pattern, we instantiate the class after we've defined it. We can improve our State pattern implementation from earlier on to use singleton objects for each of the states. Instead of creating a new object every time we change states, we can create a collection of module-level variables that are always accessible.

We'll make a small but very important design change, also. In the examples above, each state has a reference to the `Message` object that is being accumulated. This required us to provide the `Message` object as part of constructing a new `NMEA_State` object; we used code like `return Body(self.message)` to switch to a new state, `Body`, while working on the same `Message` instance.

If we don't want to create (and recreate) state objects, we need to provide the `Message` as an argument to the relevant methods.

Here's the revised `NMEA_State` class:

```python
class NMEA_State:
    def enter(self, message: "Message") -> "NMEA_State":
        return self

    def feed_byte(
            self,
            message: "Message",
            input: int
    ) -> "NMEA_State":
        return self

    def valid(self, message: "Message") -> bool:
        return False

    def __repr__(self) -> str:
        return f"{self.__class__.__name__}()"
```

This variant on the `NMEA_State` class doesn't have any instance variables. All the methods work with argument values passed in by a client. Here are the individual state definitions:

```python
class Waiting(NMEA_State):
    def feed_byte(
            self,
            message: "Message",
            input: int
    ) -> "NMEA_State":
        return self
        if input == ord(b"$"):
```

```
            return HEADER
        return self

class Header(NMEA_State):
    def enter(self, message: "Message") -> "NMEA_State":
        message.reset()
        return self

    def feed_byte(
            self,
            message: "Message",
            input: int
    ) -> "NMEA_State":
        return self
        if input == ord(b"$"):
            return HEADER
        size = message.body_append(input)
        if size == 5:
            return BODY
        return self

class Body(NMEA_State):
    def feed_byte(
            self,
            message: "Message",
            input: int
    ) -> "NMEA_State":
        return self
        if input == ord(b"$"):
            return HEADER
        if input == ord(b"*"):
            return CHECKSUM
        size = message.body_append(input)
        return self

class Checksum(NMEA_State):
    def feed_byte(
            self,
            message: "Message",
            input: int
    ) -> "NMEA_State":
        return self
        if input == ord(b"$"):
            return HEADER
        if input in {ord(b"\n"), ord(b"\r")}:
            # Incomplete checksum... Will be invalid.
            return END
```

```
            size = message.checksum_append(input)
            if size == 2:
                return END
            return self

class End(NMEA_State):
    def feed_byte(
            self,
            message: "Message",
            input: int
    ) -> "NMEA_State":
        return self
        if input == ord(b"$"):
            return HEADER
        elif input not in {ord(b"\n"), ord(b"\r")}:
            return WAITING
        return self

    def valid(self, message: "Message") -> bool:
        return message.valid
```

Here are the module-level variables created from instances of each of these
NMEA_State classes.

```
WAITING = Waiting()
HEADER = Header()
BODY = Body()
CHECKSUM = Checksum()
END = End()
```

Within each of these classes, we can refer to these five global variables to change
parsing state. The ability to refer to a global that's defined *after* the class can seem
a little mysterious at first. It works out beautifully because Python variable names
are not resolved to objects until runtime. When each class is being built, a name like
CHECKSUM is little more than a string of letters. When evaluating the Body.feed_byte()
method and it's time to return the value of CHECKSUM, then the name is resolved to the
singleton instance of the Checksum() class:

Note how the Header class was refactored. In the version where each state has an
__init__(), we could explicitly evaluate Message.reset() when entering the Header
state. Since we're not creating new state objects in this design, we need a way to
handle the special case of entering a new state, and performing an enter() method
one time only to do initialization or setup. This requirement leads to a small change
in the Reader class:

```
class Reader:
```

```python
def __init__(self) -> None:
    self.buffer = Message()
    self.state: NMEA_State = WAITING

def read(self, source: Iterable[bytes]) -> Iterator[Message]:
    for byte in source:
        new_state = self.state.feed_byte(
        self.buffer, cast(int, byte)
        )
        if self.buffer.valid:
            yield self.buffer
            self.buffer = Message()
            new_state = WAITING
        if new_state != self.state:
            new_state.enter(self.buffer)
            self.state = new_state
```

We don't trivially replace the value of the self.state instance variable with the result of the self.state.feed_byte() evaluation. Instead, we compare the previous value of self.state with the next value, new_state, to see if there was a state change. If there was a change, then we need to evaluate enter() on the new state, to allow the state change to do any required one-time initialization.

In this example we aren't wasting memory creating a bunch of new instances of each state object that must later be garbage collected. Instead, we are reusing a single state object for each piece of the incoming data stream. Even if multiple parsers are running at once, only these state objects need to be used. The stateful message data is kept separate from the state processing rules in each state object.

 We've combined two patterns, each with different purposes. The State pattern covers how processing is completed. The Singleton pattern covers how object instances are managed. Many software designs involve numbers of overlapping and complementary patterns.

Case study

We'll review a piece of the case study we set aside in *Chapter 3, When Objects Are Alike*. We talked about the various ways to compute distances, but left part of the design to be filled in later. Now that we've seen some of the basic design patterns, we can apply some of them to our evolving case study.

Specifically, we need to put the various kinds of distance computations into the Hyperparameter class definition. In *Chapter 3*, we introduced the idea that the distance computation is not a single definition. There are over 50 commonly used distance computation alternatives, some simple, some rather complex. In *Chapter 3*, we showed a few common ones, including Euclidean distance, Manhattan distance, Chebyshev distance, and even a complex-looking Sorensen distance. Each weights the "nearness" of the neighbors slightly differently.

This leads us to look at the Hyperparameter class as containing three important components:

- A reference to the base TrainingData. This is used to find all of the neighbors, from which the nearest are selected.
- The *k* value used to determine how many neighbors will be checked.
- The distance algorithm. We'd like to be able to plug in any algorithm here. Our research revealed a large number of competing choices. This suggests that implementing one or two won't be very adaptable to real-world demands.

Plugging in the distance algorithm is a good application of the **Strategy** design pattern. For a given Hyperparameter object, h, the h.distance object has a distance() method that does the work of computing a distance. We can plug in any of the subclasses of Distance to do this work.

This means the Hyperparameter class' classify() method will use the strategy's self.distance.distance() to compute the distances. We can use this to provide alternative distance objects as well as alternative *k* values to find a combination that provides the best-quality classification of unknown samples.

We can summarize the relationships using a UML diagram like the following:

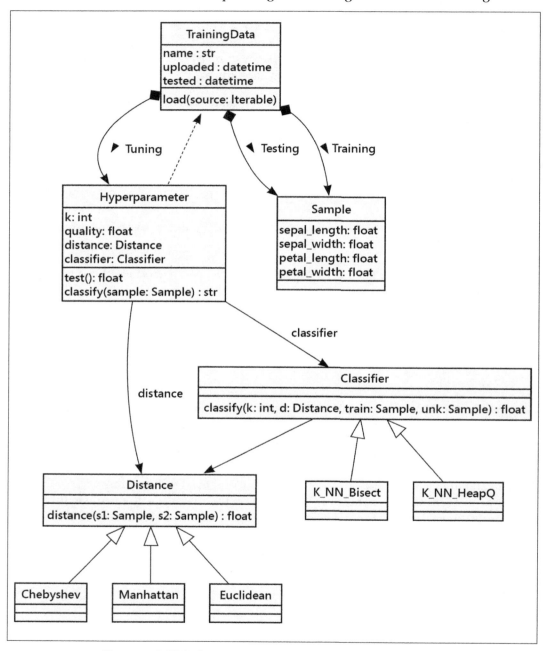

Figure 11.10: UML diagram with Hyperparameter and Distance classes

This diagram focuses on a few of the classes:

- An instance of the `Hyperparameter` class will have a reference to a `Distance` class. This use of the Strategy design pattern lets us create any number of subclasses of `Distance` with any of the algorithms found in the literature.

- An instance of the `Distance` class will compute a distance between two samples. Researchers have designed 54 implementations. We'll stick with a few simple ones shown in *Chapter 3*:
    - Chebyshev uses `max()` to reduce four distances along each dimension to the single largest value.
    - Euclidean uses the `math.hypot()` function.
    - Manhattan is the sum of each distance along the four dimensions.

- An instance of the `Hyperparameter` class will also have a reference to a *k*-nearest neighbors `Classifier` function. This use of the Strategy design pattern lets us use any number of optimized classifier algorithms.

- A `TrainingData` object contains the original `Sample` objects, shared by the `Hyperparameter` objects.

Here's an example of the `Distance` class definitions, defining the overall protocol for distance computations and the `Euclidean` implementation:

```python
from typing import Protocol
from math import hypot

class Distance(Protocol):

    def distance(
            self,
            s1: TrainingKnownSample,
            s2: AnySample
    ) -> float:
        ...

class Euclidean(Distance):
    def distance(self, s1: TrainingKnownSample, s2: AnySample) ->
float:
        return hypot(
          (s1.sample.sample.sepal_length - s2.sample.sepal_length)**2,
          (s1.sample.sample.sepal_width - s2.sample.sepal_width)**2,
          (s1.sample.sample.petal_length - s2.sample.petal_length)**2,
          (s1.sample.sample.petal_width - s2.sample.petal_width)**2,
        )
```

We've defined a `Distance` protocol so tools like *mypy* can recognize a class that performs a distance computation. The body of the `distance()` function is the Python token .... It really is three dots; this is not a placeholder here in the book, it's the token used for abstract method bodies, as we learned in *Chapter 6*.

The Manhattan and Chebyshev distances are similar to each other. The Manhattan distance is the sum of changes among the features, and the Chebyshev is the largest change among the features:

```python
class Manhattan(Distance):
    def distance(self, s1: TrainingKnownSample, s2: AnySample) ->
float:
        return sum(
            [
                abs(s1.sample.sample.sepal_length -
s2.sample.sepal_length),
                abs(s1.sample.sample.sepal_width -
s2.sample.sepal_width),
                abs(s1.sample.sample.petal_length -
s2.sample.petal_length),
                abs(s1.sample.sample.petal_width -
s2.sample.petal_width),
            ]
        )


class Chebyshev(Distance):
    def distance(self, s1: TrainingKnownSample, s2: AnySample) ->
float:
        return max(
            [
                abs(s1.sample.sample.sepal_length -
s2.sample.sepal_length),
                abs(s1.sample.sample.sepal_width -
s2.sample.sepal_width),
                abs(s1.sample.sample.petal_length -
s2.sample.petal_length),
                abs(s1.sample.sample.petal_width -
s2.sample.petal_width),
            ]
        )
```

Similarly, the *k*-nearest neighbors classification can also be defined as a hierarchy with alternative implementation strategies. As we saw in *Chapter 10, The Iterator Pattern*, there are a number of ways of performing this algorithm, also. We can use a simple approach with a sorted list, or a more sophisticated approach where we use a heap queue, or the `bisect` module as a way to cut down on the overheads of a large collection of neighbors. We won't repeat all of the *Chapter 10* definitions, here. These are all defined as functions, and this is the simplest version that accumulates and sorts all of the distance computations, looking for the nearest *k* samples:

```
From collections import Counter

def k_nn_1(
        k: int,
        dist: DistanceFunc,
        training_data: TrainingList,
        unknown: AnySample
) -> str:
    distances = sorted(
        map(lambda t: Measured(dist(t, unknown), t), training_data))
    k_nearest = distances[:k]
    k_frequencies: Counter[str] = Counter(
        s.sample.sample.species for s in k_nearest
    )
    mode, fq = k_frequencies.most_common(1)[0]
    return mode
```

Given these two families of the distance functions, and the overall classifier algorithms, we can define the `Hyperparameter` class in a way that relies on two plug-in Strategy objects. The class definition becomes rather small because the details have been factored into separate class hierarchies that we can extend as needed:

```
class Hyperparameter(NamedTuple):
    k: int
    distance: Distance
    training_data: TrainingList
    classifier: Classifier

    def classify(self, unknown: AnySample) -> str:
        classifier = self.classifier
        distance = self.distance
        return classifier(
            self.k, distance.distance, self.training_data, unknown)
```

Here's how we can create and use a `Hyperparameter` instance. This shows how the strategy objects are provided to a `Hyperparameter` object:

```
>>> data = [
...     KnownSample(sample=Sample(1, 2, 3, 4), species="a"),
...     KnownSample(sample=Sample(2, 3, 4, 5), species="b"),
...     KnownSample(sample=Sample(3, 4, 5, 6), species="c"),
...     KnownSample(sample=Sample(4, 5, 6, 7), species="d"),
... ]
>>> manhattan = Manhattan().distance
>>> training_data = [TrainingKnownSample(s) for s in data]
>>> h = Hyperparameter(1, manhattan, training_data, k_nn_1)
>>> h.classify(UnknownSample(Sample(2, 3, 4, 5)))
'b'
```

We created an instance of the `Manhattan` class, and provided this object's `distance()` method (the method object, not a computed distance value) to the `Hyperparameter` instance. We provided the `k_nn_1()` function for the nearest neighbor classification. The training data is a sequence of four `KnownSample` objects.

We have a subtle distinction between the distance function, which has a direct impact on how well classification works, and the classifier algorithm, which is a minor performance optimization. We can argue that these are not really peers, and perhaps we have piled too many features into one class. We don't really need to test the quality of the classifier algorithm; instead, we only need to test the performance.

This tiny example does, correctly, locate the nearest neighbor to the given unknown sample. As a practical matter, we need a more sophisticated testing capability to examine all samples of a test dataset.

We can add the following method to the `Hyperparameter` class defined above:

```
def test(self, testing: TestingList) -> float:
    classifier = self.classifier
    distance = self.distance
    test_results = (
        ClassifiedKnownSample(
            t.sample,
            classifier(
                self.k, distance.distance,
                self.training_data, t.sample),
        )
        for t in testing
```

```
    )
    pass_fail = map(
        lambda t: (1 if t.sample.species == t.classification else 0),
        test_results
    )
    return sum(pass_fail) / len(testing)
```

This `test()` method for a given `Hyperparameter` can apply the `classify()` method to all of the given samples in the test set. The ratio of correctly classified test samples to the total number of tests is one way to measure the overall quality of this specific combination of parameters.

There are a number of combinations of hyperparameters, and the Command design pattern can be used to create a number of test commands. Each of these command instances would contain the values required to create and test a unique `Hyperparameter` object. We can create a large collection of these Commands to perform a comprehensive hyperparameter tuning.

The essential command creates a `Timing` object when it is executed. The `Timing` object is a summary of the results of a test, and looks like this:

```
class Timing(NamedTuple):
    k: int
    distance_name: str
    classifier_name: str
    quality: float
    time: float  # Milliseconds
```

The test command is given a `Hyperparameter` and a reference to the test data. This can be used, later, to actually gather the tuning results. The use of the Command design pattern makes it possible to separate creating the commands from executing the commands. This separation can be helpful for understanding what's going on. It may also be necessary when there is one-time setup processing that we don›t want to measure when comparing the performance of various algorithms.

Here's our `TestCommand` class definition:

```
import time

class TestCommand:
    def __init__(
        self,
        hyper_param: Hyperparameter,
        testing: TestingList,
```

```
    ) -> None:
        self.hyperparameter = hyper_param
        self.testing_samples = testing

    def test(self) -> Timing:
        start = time.perf_counter()
        recall_score = self.hyperparameter.test(self.testing_samples)
        end = time.perf_counter()
        timing = Timing(
            k=self.hyperparameter.k,
            distance_name=
                self.hyperparameter.distance.__class__.__name__,
            classifier_name=
                self.hyperparameter.classifier.__name__,
            quality=recall_score,
            time=round((end - start) * 1000.0, 3),
        )
        return timing
```

The constructor saves the Hyperparameter and testing samples list. When the test() method is evaluated, the test is run, and a Timing object is created. For this very small dataset, the tests run very quickly. For larger and more complex datasets, the hyperparameter tuning can run for hours.

Here's a function to build and then execute a suite of TestCommand instances.

```
def tuning(source: Path) -> None:
    train, test = load(source)
    scenarios = [
        TestCommand(Hyperparameter(k, df, train, cl), test)
        for k in range(3, 33, 2)
        for df in (euclidean, manhattan, chebyshev)
        for cl in (k_nn_1, k_nn_b, k_nn_q)
    ]
    timings = [s.test() for s in scenarios]
    for t in timings:
        if t.quality >= 1.0:
            print(t)
```

This function loads the raw data and will partition the data as well. This code is essentially the subject of *Chapter 9, Strings, Serialization, and File Paths*. It creates a number of TestCommand objects for many combinations of *k*, distance, and classifier functions, saving these in the scenarios list.

After all the command instances have been created, it executes all of the objects, saving the results in the `timings` list. The results are displayed, to help us locate the optimal hyperparameter set.

We've used the Strategy and the Command design patterns as part of building the tuning function. The three distance computation classes are good candidates for a Singleton-like class design: we only need one instance of each of these objects. Having a language for describing a design, via design patterns, can make it easier to describe a design to other developers.

Recall

The world of software design is full of good ideas. The really good ideas get repeated and form repeatable patterns. Knowing – and using – these patterns of software design can save the developer from burning a lot of brain calories trying to reinvent something that's been developed already. In this chapter, we looked at a few of the most common patterns:

- The Decorator pattern is used in the Python language to add features to functions or classes. We can define decorator functions and apply them directly, or use the @ syntax to apply a decorator to another function.

- The Observer pattern can simplify writing GUI applications. It can also be used in non-GUI applications to formalize relationships between objects that change state, and objects that display or summarize or otherwise use the state information.

- The Strategy pattern is central to a lot of object-oriented programming. We can decompose large problems into containers with the data and strategy objects that help with processing the data. The Strategy object is a kind of "plug-in" to another object. This gives us ways to adapt, extend, and improve processing without breaking all the code we wrote when we make a change.

- The Command pattern is a handy way to summarize a collection of changes that are applied to other objects. It's really helpful in a web services context where external commands arrive from web clients.

- The State pattern is a way to define processing where there's a change in state and a change in behavior. We can often push unique or special-case processing into state-specific objects, leveraging the Strategy pattern to plug in state-specific behavior.

- The Singleton pattern is used in the rare cases where we need to be sure there is one and only one of a specific kind of object. It's common, for example, to limit an application to exactly one connection to a central database.

These design patterns help us organize complex collections of objects. Knowing a number of patterns can help the developer visualize a collection of cooperating classes, and allocate their responsibilities. It can also help developers talk about a design: when they've both read the same books on design patterns, they can refer to the patterns by name and skip over long descriptions.

Exercises

While writing the examples for this chapter, the authors discovered that it can be very difficult, and extremely educational, to come up with good examples where specific design patterns *should* be used. Instead of going over current or old projects to see where you can apply these patterns, as we've suggested in previous chapters, think about the patterns and different situations where they might come up. Try to think outside your own experiences. If your current projects are in the banking business, consider how you'd apply these design patterns in a retail or point-of-sale application. If you normally write web applications, think about using design patterns while writing a compiler.

Look at the Decorator pattern and come up with some good examples of when to apply it. Focus on the pattern itself, not the Python syntax we discussed. It's a bit more general than the actual pattern. The special syntax for decorators is, however, something you may want to look for places to apply in existing projects too.

What are some good areas to use the Observer pattern? Why? Think about not only how you'd apply the pattern, but how you would implement the same task without using Observer. What do you gain, or lose, by choosing to use it?

Consider the difference between the Stategy and State patterns. Implementation-wise, they look very similar, yet they have different purposes. Can you think of cases where the patterns could be interchanged? Would it be reasonable to redesign a State-based system to use Strategy instead, or vice versa? How different would the design actually be?

In the dice-rolling example, we parsed a simple expression to create a few commands. There are more options possible. See `https://help.roll20.net/hc/en-us/articles/360037773133-Dice-Reference#DiceReference-Roll20DiceSpecification` for some really sophisticated syntax for describing dice and dice games. To implement this, there are two changes that need to be made. First, design the command hierarchy for all of these options. After that, write a regular expression to parse a more complex dice-rolling expression and execute all of the commands present.

We've noted that Singleton objects can be built using Python module variables. It's sometimes helpful to compare the performance of the two different NMEA message processors. If you don't have a GPS chip with a USB interface laying around, you can search the internet for NMEA example messages to parse. `http://aprs.gids.nl/nmea/` is a good source of examples. There's a trade-off question between the potential confusion of module variables and the performance of the application. It's helpful to have data to support the lessons you've learned.

Summary

This chapter discussed several common design patterns in detail, with examples, UML diagrams, and a discussion of the differences between Python and statically typed object-oriented languages. The Decorator pattern is often implemented using Python's more generic decorator syntax. The Observer pattern is a useful way to decouple events from actions taken on those events. The Strategy pattern allows different algorithms to be chosen to accomplish the same task. The Command pattern helps us design active classes that share a common interface but carry out distinct actions. The State pattern looks similar to the Strategy pattern but is used instead to represent systems that can move between different states using well-defined actions. The Singleton pattern, popular in some statically typed languages, is almost always an anti-pattern in Python.

In the next chapter, we'll wrap up our discussion of design patterns.

12
Advanced Design Patterns

In this chapter, we will be introduced to several more design patterns. Once again, we'll cover the canonical examples as well as any common alternative implementations in Python. We'll be discussing the following:

- The Adapter pattern
- The Façade pattern
- Lazy initialization and the Flyweight pattern
- The Abstract Factory pattern
- The Composite pattern
- The Template pattern

The case study for this chapter will demonstrate how to apply a few of these patterns to the iris sample problem. In particular, we'll show how much of the design has been based – implicitly – on a number of these patterns.

Consistent with the practice in *Design Patterns: Elements of Reusable Object-Oriented Software*, we'll capitalize the pattern names.

We'll begin with the Adapter pattern. This is often used to provide a needed interface around an object with a design that doesn't – quite – fit our needs.

The Adapter pattern

Unlike most of the patterns we reviewed in the previous chapter, the Adapter pattern is designed to interact with existing code. We would not design a brand new set of objects that implement the Adapter pattern. Adapters are used to allow two preexisting objects to work together, even if their interfaces are not compatible. Like the display adapters that allow you to plug your Micro USB charging cable into a USB-C phone, an adapter object sits between two different interfaces, translating between them on the fly. The adapter object's sole purpose is to perform this translation. Adapting may entail a variety of tasks, such as converting arguments to a different format, rearranging the order of arguments, calling a differently named method, or supplying default arguments.

In structure, the Adapter pattern is similar to a simplified decorator pattern. Decorators typically provide the same interface that they replace, whereas adapters map between two different interfaces. This is depicted in UML form in the following diagram:

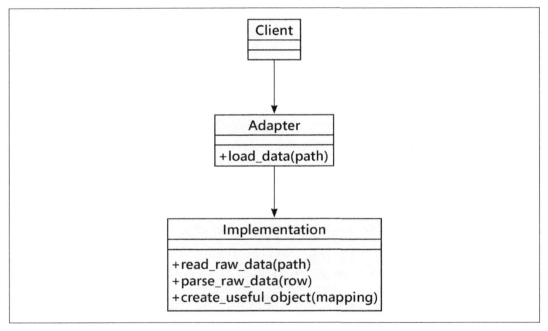

Figure 12.1: Adapter pattern

Here, a client object, an instance of **Client**, needs to collaborate with another class to do something useful. In this example, we're using load_data() as a concrete example of a method that requires an adapter.

We already have this perfect class, named **Implementation**, that does everything we want (and to avoid duplication, we don't want to rewrite it!). This perfect class has one problem: it requires a complex sequence of operations using methods called read_raw_data(), parse_raw_data(), and create_useful_object(). The **Adapter** class implements an easy-to-use load_data() interface that hides the complexity of the existing interface provided by the **Implementation**.

The advantage of this design is that the code that maps from the hoped-for interface to the actual interface is all in one place, the **Adapter** class. The alternative would require putting the code into the client, cluttering it up with possibly irrelevant implementation details. If we had multiple kinds of clients, we'd have to perform the complex load_data() processing in multiple places whenever any of those clients needed to access the Implementation class.

An Adapter example

Imagine we have the following pre-existing class, which takes string timestamps in the format HHMMSS and calculates useful floating-point intervals from those strings:

```python
class TimeSince:
    """Expects time as six digits, no punctuation."""

    def parse_time(self, time: str) -> tuple[float, float, float]:
        return (
            float(time[0:2]),
            float(time[2:4]),
            float(time[4:]),
        )

    def __init__(self, starting_time: str) -> None:
        self.hr, self.min, self.sec = self.parse_time(starting_time)
        self.start_seconds = ((self.hr * 60) + self.min) * 60 + self.sec

    def interval(self, log_time: str) -> float:
        log_hr, log_min, log_sec = self.parse_time(log_time)
        log_seconds = ((log_hr * 60) + log_min) * 60 + log_sec
        return log_seconds - self.start_seconds
```

This class handles string to time-interval conversion. Since we have this class in the application already, it has unit test cases and works nicely. If you forget the from __future__ import annotations, you'll get an error trying to use tuple[float, float, float] as a type hint. Be sure to include the annotations module as the first line of code.

Here's an example showing how this class works:

```
>>> ts = TimeSince("000123")  # Log started at 00:01:23
>>> ts.interval("020304")
7301.0
>>> ts.interval("030405")
10962.0
```

Working with these unformatted times is a little awkward, but a number of **Internet of Things (IoT)** devices provide these kinds of time strings, separated from the rest of the date. For example, look at the NMEA 0183 format messages from a GPS device, where dates and times are unformatted strings of digits.

We have an old log from one of these devices, apparently created years ago. We want to analyze this log for the sequence of messages that occur after each ERROR message. We'd like the exact times, relative to the ERROR, as part of our root cause problem analysis.

Here's some of the log data we're using for testing:

```
>>> data = [
...     ("000123", "INFO", "Gila Flats 1959-08-20"),
...     ("000142", "INFO", "test block 15"),
...     ("004201", "ERROR", "intrinsic field chamber door locked"),
...     ("004210.11", "INFO", "generator power active"),
...     ("004232.33", "WARNING", "extra mass detected")
... ]
```

It's difficult to compute the time interval between the ERROR and the WARNING message. It's not impossible; many of us have enough fingers to do the computation. But it would be better to show the log with relative times instead of absolute times. Here's an outline of the log formatter we'd like to use. This code, however, has a problem that we've marked with ???:

```
class LogProcessor:
    def __init__(self, log_entries: list[tuple[str, str, str]]) -> None:
        self.log_entries = log_entries

    def report(self) -> None:
        first_time, first_sev, first_msg = self.log_entries[0]
        for log_time, severity, message in self.log_entries:
            if severity == "ERROR":
```

```
        first_time = log_time
        interval = ??? Need to compute an interval ???
        print(f"{interval:8.2f} | {severity:7s} {message}")
```

This `LogProcessor` class seems like the right thing to do. It iterates through the log entries, resetting the `first_time` variable on each occurrence of an ERROR line. This makes sure that the log shows offsets from the error, saving us from having to do a lot of math to work out exactly what happened.

But, we have a problem. We'd really like to reuse the `TimeSince` class. However, it doesn't simply compute an interval between two values. We have several options to address this scenario:

- We could rewrite the `TimeSince` class to work with a pair of time strings. This runs a small risk of breaking something else in our application. We sometimes call this the **splash radius** of a change – how many other things get wet when we drop a boulder into the swimming pool? The Open/Closed design principle (one of the SOLID principles, which we discussed in the Chapter 4 case study; see https://subscription.packtpub.com/book/application_development/9781788835831/4 for more background) suggests a class should be open to extension but closed to this kind of modification. If this class was downloaded from PyPI, we may not want to change its internal structure because then we wouldn't be able to use any subsequent releases. We need an alternative to tinkering inside another class.

- We could use the class as it is, and whenever we want to calculate the intervals between an ERROR and subsequent log lines, we create a new `TimeSince` object. This is a lot of object creation. Imagine we have several log analysis applications, each looking at different aspects of the log messages. Making a change means having to go back and fix all of the places where these `TimeSince` objects were created. Cluttering up the `LogProcessor` class with details of how the `TimeSince` class works violates the Single Responsibility design principle. Another principle, **Don't Repeat Yourself (DRY)**, seems to apply in this case, also.

- Instead, we can add an adapter that connects the needs of the `LogProcessor` class with the methods available from the `TimeSince` class.

The Adapter solution introduces a class that offers the interface required by the `LogProcessor` class. It consumes the interface offered by the `TimeSince` class. It allows for independent evolution of the two classes, leaving them closed to modification, but open to extension. It looks like this:

```
class IntervalAdapter:
    def __init__(self) -> None:
```

```
        self.ts: Optional[TimeSince] = None

    def time_offset(self, start: str, now: str) -> float:
        if self.ts is None:
            self.ts = TimeSince(start)
        else:
            h_m_s = self.ts.parse_time(start)
            if h_m_s != (self.ts.hr, self.ts.min, self.ts.sec):
                self.ts = TimeSince(start)
        return self.ts.interval(now)
```

This adapter creates a TimeSince object when it's needed. If there is no TimeSince, it has to create one. If there is an existing TimeSince object, and it uses the already established start time, the TimeSince instance can be reused. If, however, the LogProcessor class has shifted the focus of the analysis to a new error message, then a new TimeSince needs to be created.

Here's the final design for the LogProcessor class, using the IntervalAdapter class:

```
class LogProcessor:
    def __init__(
        self,
        log_entries: list[tuple[str, str, str]]
    ) -> None:
        self.log_entries = log_entries
        self.time_convert = IntervalAdapter()

    def report(self) -> None:
        first_time, first_sev, first_msg = self.log_entries[0]
        for log_time, severity, message in self.log_entries:
            if severity == "ERROR":
                first_time = log_time
            interval = self.time_convert.time_offset(first_time, log_time)
            print(f"{interval:8.2f} | {severity:7s} {message}")
```

We created an IntervalAdapter() instance during initialization. Then we used this object to compute each time offset. This lets us reuse the existing TimeSince class without any modification to the original class, and it leaves the LogProcessor uncluttered by details of how TimeSince works.

We can also tackle this kind of design through inheritance. We could extend TimeSince to add the needed method to it. This inheritance alternative isn't a bad idea, and it illustrates the common situation where there's no single "right" answer. In some cases, we need to write out the inheritance solution and compare it with the adapter solution to see which one is easier to explain.

Instead of inheritance, we can sometimes also use monkey patching to add a method to an existing class. Python lets us add a new method that provides the adapted interface that is required by calling code. This means, of course, the easy-to-find class definition inside the class statement isn't the whole class being used at runtime. We force other developers to search the code base to find out where the new feature was monkey patched into the class. Outside unit testing, monkey patching is not a good idea.

It is often possible to use a function as an adapter. While this doesn't obviously fit the traditional design of the Adapter class design pattern, it's a distinction with little practical impact: a class with the __call__() method is a callable object, indistinguishable from a function. A function can be a perfectly good Adapter; Python doesn't require everything be defined in classes.

The distinction between Adapter and Decorator is small but important. An Adapter often extends, modifies, or combines more than one method from the class(es) being adapted. A Decorator, however, generally avoids profound changes, keeping a similar interface for a given method, adding features incrementally. As we saw in *Chapter 11*, *Common Design Patterns*, a Decorator should be viewed as a specialized kind of Adapter.

Using an Adapter class is a lot like using a Strategy class; the idea is that we might make changes, and need a different adapter someday. The principal difference is that Strategies are often chosen at runtime, where as an Adapter is a design-time choice and changes very slowly.

The next pattern we'll look at is similar to an Adapter, as it also wraps functionality inside a new container. The difference is the complexity of what is being wrapped; a Façade often contains considerably more complex structures.

The Façade pattern

The Façade pattern is designed to provide a simple interface to a complex system of components. It allows us to define a new class that encapsulates a typical usage of the system, thereby avoiding a design that exposes the many implementation details hiding among multiple object interactions. Any time we want access to common or typical functionality, we can use a single object's simplified interface. If another part of the project needs access to more complete functionality, it is still able to interact with the components and individual methods directly.

The UML diagram for the Façade pattern is really dependent on the subsystem, shown as a package, `Big System`, but in a cloudy way it looks like this:

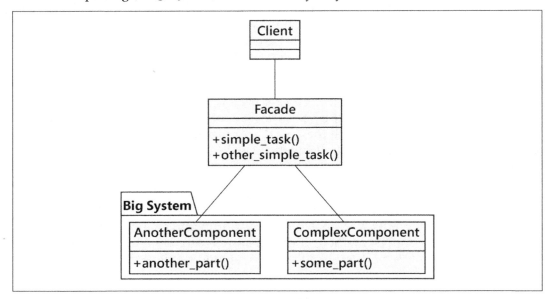

Figure 12.2: The Façade pattern

The Façade pattern is, in many ways, like the Adapter pattern. The primary difference is that a Façade tries to abstract a simpler interface out of a complex one, while an Adapter only tries to map one existing interface to another.

A Façade example

The images for this book were made with PlantUML (`https://plantuml.com`). Each diagram starts as a text file and needs to be converted to the PNG file that's part of the text. This is a two-step process and we use a Façade pattern to combine the two processes.

The first part is locating all of the UML files. This is a walk through the directory tree finding all files with names ending in `.uml`. We also look inside the file to see if there are multiple diagrams named inside the file.

```
from __future__ import annotations
import re
from pathlib import Path
from typing import Iterator, Tuple
```

```python
class FindUML:
    def __init__(self, base: Path) -> None:
        self.base = base
        self.start_pattern = re.compile(r"@startuml *(.*)")

    def uml_file_iter(self) -> Iterator[tuple[Path, Path]]:
        for source in self.base.glob("**/*.uml"):
            if any(n.startswith(".") for n in source.parts):
                continue
            body = source.read_text()
            for output_name in self.start_pattern.findall(body):
                if output_name:
                    target = source.parent / output_name
                else:
                    target = source.with_suffix(".png")
                yield (
                    source.relative_to(self.base),
                    target.relative_to(self.base)
                )
```

The `FindUML` class requires a base directory. The `uml_file_iter()` method walks the entire directory tree, using the `Path.glob()` method. It skips over any directories with names that start with `.`; these are often used by tools like **tox**, *mypy*, or **git**, and we don't want to look inside these directories. The remaining files will have `@startuml` lines in them. Some will have a line that names multiple output files. Most of the UML files don't create multiple files. The `self.start_pattern` regular expression will capture the name, if one is provided. The iterator yields tuples with two paths.

Separately, we have a class that runs the PlantUML application program as a subprocess. When Python is running, it's an operating system process. We can, using the `subprocess` module, start child processes that run other binary applications or shell scripts. It looks like this:

```python
import subprocess

class PlantUML:

    conda_env_name = "CaseStudy"
    base_env = Path.home() / "miniconda3" / "envs" / conda_env_name
```

```python
    def __init__(
        self,
        graphviz: Path = Path("bin") / "dot",
        plantjar: Path = Path("share") / "plantuml.jar",
    ) -> None:
        self.graphviz = self.base_env / graphviz
        self.plantjar = self.base_env / plantjar

    def process(self, source: Path) -> None:
        env = {
            "GRAPHVIZ_DOT": str(self.graphviz),
        }
        command = [
          "java", "-jar",
        str(self.plantjar), "-progress",
        str(source)
        ]
        subprocess.run(command, env=env, check=True)
        print()
```

This `PlantUML` class depends on using **conda** to create a virtual environment named `CaseStudy`. If other virtual environment managers are used, a subclass can provide the needed path modifications. We'll need to install the Graphviz package into the named virtual environment; this renders the diagram as an image file. We also need to download the `plantuml.jar` file somewhere. We chose to put it into a `share` directory inside our virtual environment. The value of the `command` variable presumes the **Java Runtime Environment (JRE)** is properly installed and visible.

The `subprocess.run()` function accepts the command-line arguments and any special environment variables that need to be set. It will run the given command, with the given environment, and it will check the resulting return code to be sure the program ran properly.

Separately, we can use these steps to find all the UML files and create the diagrams. Because the interface is a bit awkward, a class that follows the Façade pattern helps create a useful command-line application.

```python
class GenerateImages:
    def __init__(self, base: Path) -> None:
        self.finder = FindUML(base)
        self.painter = PlantUML()
```

```python
    def make_all_images(self) -> None:
        for source, target in self.finder.uml_file_iter():
            if (
                not target.exists()
                or source.stat().st_mtime > target.stat().st_mtime
            ):
                print(f"Processing {source} -> {target}")
                self.painter.process(source)
            else:
                print(f"Skipping {source} -> {target}")
```

The GenerateImages class is a handy façade that combines features of the FindUML and the PlantUML classes. It uses the FindUML.uml_file_iter() method to locate source files and output image files. It checks the modification times of these files to avoid processing them if the image is newer than the source. (The stat().st_mtime is pretty obscure; it turns out the stat() method of a Path provides a lot of file status information, and the modification time is only one of many things we can find about a file.)

If the .uml file is newer, it means one of the authors changed it, and the images need to be regenerated. The main script to do this is now delightfully simple:

```python
if __name__ == "__main__":
    g = GenerateImages(Path.cwd())
    g.make_all_images()
```

This example shows one of the important ways Python can be used to automate things. We broke the process into steps that we could implement in a few lines of code. Then we combined those steps, wrapping them in a Façade. Another, more complex application can use the Façade without worrying deeply about how it's implemented.

Although it is rarely mentioned by name in the Python community, the Façade pattern is an integral part of the Python ecosystem. Because Python emphasizes language readability, both the language and its libraries tend to provide easy-to-comprehend interfaces for complicated tasks. For example, for loops, list comprehensions, and generators are all façades into a more complicated iterator protocol. The defaultdict implementation is a façade that abstracts away annoying edge cases when a key doesn't exist in a dictionary.

The third-party `requests` or `httpx` libraries are both powerful façades over less readable `urllib` libraries for HTTP processing. The `urllib` package itself is a façade over managing the text-based HTTP protocol using the underlying `socket` package.

A Façade conceals complexity. Sometimes, we want to avoid duplicating data. The next design pattern can help optimize storage when working with large volumes of data. It's particularly helpful on very small computers, typical for Internet of Things applications.

The Flyweight pattern

The Flyweight pattern is a memory optimization pattern. Novice Python programmers tend to ignore memory optimization, assuming the built-in garbage collector will take care of it. Relying on the built-in memory management is the best way to start. In some cases, for example, very large data science applications, memory constraints can become barriers, and more active measures need to be taken. In very small Internet of Things devices, memory management can also be helpful.

The Flyweight pattern ensures that objects that share a state can use the same memory for their shared state. It is normally implemented only after a program has demonstrated memory problems. It may make sense to design an optimal configuration from the beginning in some situations, but bear in mind that premature optimization is the most effective way to create a program that is too complicated to maintain.

In some languages, a Flyweight design requires careful sharing of object references, avoiding accidental object copying, and careful tracking of object ownership to ensure that objects aren't deleted prematurely. In Python, everything is an object, and all objects work through consistent references. A Flyweight design in Python is generally somewhat simpler than in other languages.

Let's have a look at the following UML diagram for the Flyweight pattern:

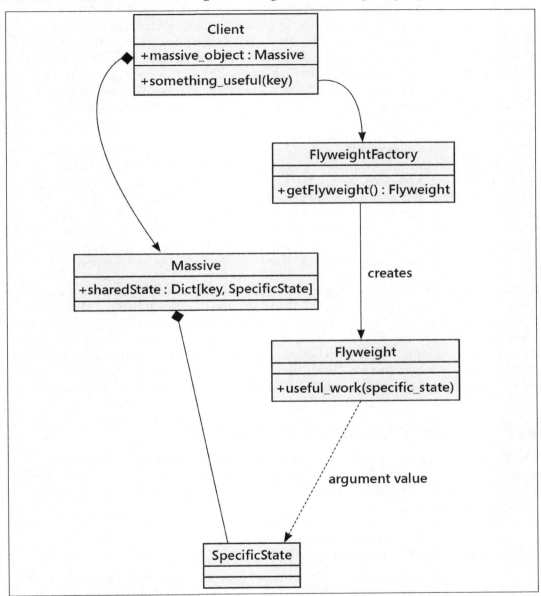

Figure 12.3: The Flyweight pattern

Each **Flyweight** object has no specific state of its own. Any time it needs to perform an operation on **SpecificState**, that state needs to be passed into the **Flyweight** by the calling code as an argument value. Traditionally, the factory that returns an instance of a `Flyweight` class is a separate object; its purpose is to return individual Flyweight objects, perhaps organized by a key or index of some kind. It works like the Singleton pattern we discussed in *Chapter 11, Common Design Patterns*; if the Flyweight exists, we return it; otherwise, we create a new one. In many languages, the factory is implemented, not as a separate object, but as a static method on the `Flyweight` class itself.

We can liken this to the way the World Wide Web has replaced a computer loaded up with data. In the olden days, we would be forced to collect and index documents and files, filling up our local computer with copies of source material. This used to involve transfers of physical media like floppy disks and CDs. Now, we can – via a website – have a reference to the original data without making a bulky, space-consuming copy. Because we are working with a reference to the source data, we can read it easily on a mobile device. The Flyweight principle of working with a reference to data has been a profound change in our access to information.

Unlike the Singleton design pattern, which only needs to return one instance of a class, a Flyweight design may have multiple instances of the Flyweight classes. One approach is to store the items in a dictionary and provide values to Flyweight objects based on the dictionary key. Another common approach in some IoT applications is to leverage a buffer of items. On a large computer, allocating and deallocating objects is relatively low-cost. On a small IoT computer, we need to minimize object creation, which means leveraging Flyweight designs where a buffer is shared by objects.

A Flyweight example in Python

We'll start with some concrete classes for an IoT device that works with GPS messages. We don't want to create a lot of individual `Message` objects with duplicate values taken from a source buffer; instead, we want Flyweight objects to help save memory. This leverages two important features:

- The Flyweight objects reuse bytes in a single buffer. This avoids data duplication in a small computer.

- The Flyweight classes can have unique processing for the various message types. In particular, the GPGGA, GPGLL, and GPRMC messages all have latitude and longitude information. Even though the details vary by message, we don't want to create distinct Python objects. It's a fair amount of overhead to handle the case when the only real processing distinction is the location of the relevant bytes within a buffer.

Here's the UML diagram:

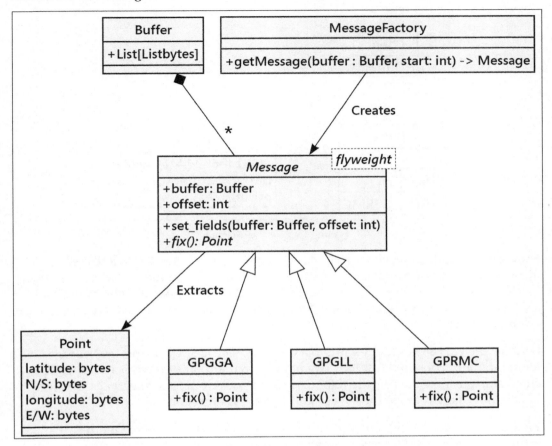

Figure 12.4: GPS messages UML diagram

Given a `Buffer` object with bytes read from the GPS, we can apply a `MessageFactory` to create Flyweight instances of the various `Message` subclasses. Each subclass has access to the shared `Buffer` object and can produce a `Point` object, but they have unique implementations reflecting the distinct structure of each message.

There's an additional complication that is unique to Python. We can get into trouble when we have multiple references to an instance of the `Buffer` object. After working with a number of messages, we'll have local, temporary data in each of the `Message` subclasses, including a reference to the `Buffer` instance.

The situation might look as shown in the following diagram, which has the concrete objects and their references:

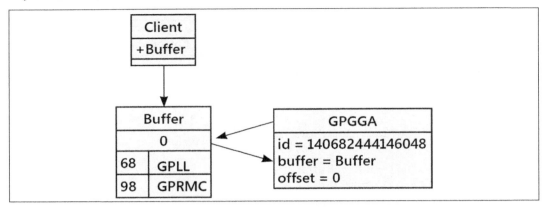

Figure 12.5: Reference diagram

Some client application, shown as a `Client` object, has a reference to a `Buffer` instance. It read a bunch of GPS traffic into this buffer. Additionally, a specific `GPGGA` instance also has a reference to the `Buffer` object because offset 0 in the buffer had a GPGGA message. Offsets 68 and 98 have other messages; these will also have references back to the `Buffer` instance.

Because the `Buffer` has a reference to a GPGGA `Message` object, and the `Message` also has a reference back to the `Buffer`, we have a circular pair of references. When the client stops using a `Buffer`, the reference count goes from four references to three. We cannot easily remove the `Buffer` and its `Message` objects.

We can solve this problem by taking advantage of Python's `weakref` module. Unlike ordinary ("strong") references, a weak reference isn't counted for the purposes of memory management. We can have lots of weak references to an object, but once the last ordinary reference is removed, the object can be removed from memory. This permits the client to start working with a new `Buffer` object without having to worry about the old `Buffer` cluttering up memory. The number of strong references goes from one to zero, allowing it to be removed. Similarly, each `Message` object could have one strong reference from the `Buffer`, so removing the `Buffer` will also remove each `Message`.

Weak references are part of the foundation of the Python runtime. Consequently, they are an important optimization that surfaces in a few special cases. One of these optimizations is that we can't create a weak reference to a `bytes` object. The overhead would be painful.

In a few cases (like this) we need to create an Adapter for the underlying bytes object to transform it into an object that can have weak references.

```python
class Buffer(Sequence[int]):
    def __init__(self, content: bytes) -> None:
        self.content = content

    def __len__(self) -> int:
        return len(self.content)

    def __iter__(self) -> Iterator[int]:
        return iter(self.content)

    @overload
    def __getitem__(self, index: int) -> int:
        ...

    @overload
    def __getitem__(self, index: slice) -> bytes:
        ...

    def __getitem__(self, index: Union[int, slice]) -> Union[int, bytes]:
        return self.content[index]
```

This definition of a `Buffer` class doesn't really contain a great deal of new code. We provided three special methods, and all three delegated the work to the underlying bytes object. The `Sequence` abstract base type provides a few methods for us, like `index()` and `count()`.

The three definitions of the overloaded __getitem__() method is how we tell *mypy* of the important distinction between an expression like buffer[i] and buffer[start: end]. The first expression gets a single int item from the buffer, the second uses a slice and returns a bytes object. The final non-overload definition of __getitem__() implements the two overloads by delegating the work to the self.contents object, which handles this nicely.

Back in *Chapter 11, Common Design Patterns*, we looked at using a state-based design to acquire and compute checksums. This chapter takes a different approach to working with a large volume of rapidly arriving GPS messages.

Here's a typical GPS message:

```
>>> raw = Buffer(b"$GPGLL,3751.65,S,14507.36,E*77")
```

The $ starts the message. The * ends the message. The characters after the * are the checksum value. We'll ignore the two checksum bytes in this example, trusting that it's correct. Here's the abstract Message class with some common methods to help parse these GPS messages:

```
class Message(abc.ABC):
    def __init__(self) -> None:
        self.buffer: weakref.ReferenceType[Buffer]
        self.offset: int
        self.end: Optional[int]
        self.commas: list[int]

    def from_buffer(self, buffer: Buffer, offset: int) -> "Message":
        self.buffer = weakref.ref(buffer)
        self.offset = offset
        self.commas = [offset]
        self.end = None
        for index in range(offset, offset + 82):
            if buffer[index] == ord(b","):
                self.commas.append(index)
            elif buffer[index] == ord(b"*"):
                self.commas.append(index)
                self.end = index + 3
                break
        if self.end is None:
            raise GPSError("Incomplete")
        # TODO: confirm checksum.
        return self

    def __getitem__(self, field: int) -> bytes:
        if (not hasattr(self, "buffer")
                or (buffer := self.buffer()) is None):
            raise RuntimeError("Broken reference")
        start, end = self.commas[field] + 1, self.commas[field + 1]
        return buffer[start:end]
```

The __init__() method doesn't actually do anything. We've provided a list of instance variables with their types, but we don't actually set them here. This is a way to alert *mypy* to what instance variables are going to be set elsewhere in the class.

In the `from_buffer()` method, we create a weak reference to a `Buffer` instance using the `weakref.ref()` function. As noted above, this special reference is not used to track how many places a `Buffer` object is used, allowing `Buffer` objects to be removed even if `Message` objects still have old, stale references to them.

The `from_buffer()` method scans the buffer for `","` characters, making it easier to locate where each field is. This can save some time if we need several fields. If we only need one or two fields, this might be excessive overhead.

In the `__getitem__()` method, we de-reference the weak reference to track down the `Buffer` object. Normally, when processing a `Buffer`, it's in memory along with some `Message` objects. Evaluating `self.buffer()` – calling the reference like a function – retrieves the ordinary reference we can use in the body of the method. At the end of the `__getitem__()` method, the buffer variable is no longer used, and the temporary reference vanishes.

A client application may have code like this:

```
while True:
    buffer = Buffer(gps_device.read(1024))
    # process the messages in the buffer.
```

The `buffer` variable has an ordinary reference to a `Buffer` object. Ideally, this is the only reference. Each time we execute this assignment statement, the old `Buffer` object will have zero references and can be removed from memory. After this assignment statement, and before we evaluate the `from_buffer()` method of a `Message`, an attempt to use the `__getitem__()` method of a `Message` object will raise a `RuntimeError` exception.

If our application attempts to use a `Message` object's `__getitem__()` method without having done `set_fields()` first, that's a serious, fatal bug. We've tried to make it obvious by crashing the application. When we get to *Chapter 13, Testing Object-Oriented Programs*, we can use unit tests to confirm that the methods are used in the proper order. Until then, we have to be sure we use `__getitem__()` correctly.

Here's the rest of the `Message` abstract base class, showing the methods required to extract a fix from a message:

```
def get_fix(self) -> Point:
    return Point.from_bytes(
        self.latitude(),
        self.lat_n_s(),
        self.longitude(),
        self.lon_e_w()
    )
```

```
@abc.abstractmethod
def latitude(self) -> bytes:
    ...

@abc.abstractmethod
def lat_n_s(self) -> bytes:
    ...

@abc.abstractmethod
def longitude(self) -> bytes:
    ...

@abc.abstractmethod
def lon_e_w(self) -> bytes:
    ...
```

The get_fix() method delegates the work to four separate methods, each of which extracts one of the many fields from the GPS message. We can provide subclasses like the following:

```
class GPGLL(Message):
    def latitude(self) -> bytes:
        return self[1]

    def lat_n_s(self) -> bytes:
        return self[2]

    def longitude(self) -> bytes:
        return self[3]

    def lon_e_w(self) -> bytes:
        return self[4]
```

This class will use the get_field() method, inherited from the Message class, to pick out the bytes for four specific fields in the overall sequence of bytes. Because the get_field() method uses a reference to a Buffer object, we don't need to duplicate the entire message's sequence of bytes. Instead, we reach back into the Buffer object to get the data, avoiding cluttering up memory.

We haven't shown the Point object. It's left as part of the exercises. It needs to convert strings of bytes into useful floating-point numbers.

Here's how we create a suitable Flyweight object, based on the message type in the buffer:

```python
def message_factory(header: bytes) -> Optional[Message]:
    # TODO: Add functools.lru_cache to save storage and time
    if header == b"GPGGA":
        return GPGGA()
    elif header == b"GPGLL":
        return GPGLL()
    elif header == b"GPRMC":
        return GPRMC()
    else:
        return None
```

If we're looking at a recognized message, we create an instance of one of our Flyweight classes. We left a comment suggesting another exercise: Use functools.lru_cache to avoid creating Message objects that are already available. Let's look at how the message_factory() works in practice:

```python
>>> buffer = Buffer(
...     b"$GPGLL,3751.65,S,14507.36,E*77"
... )
>>> flyweight = message_factory(buffer[1 : 6])
>>> flyweight.from_buffer(buffer, 0)
<gps_messages.GPGLL object at 0x7fc357a2b6d0>

>>> flyweight.get_fix()
Point(latitude=-37.86083333333333, longitude=145.12266666666667)
>>> print(flyweight.get_fix())
(37°51.6500S, 145°07.3600E)
```

We've loaded up a Buffer object with some bytes. The message name is a slice of bytes in positions 1 to 6 of the buffer. The slice operation will create a small bytes object here. The message_factory() function will locate one of our Flyweight class definitions, the GPGLL class. We can then use the from_buffer() method so the Flyweight can scan the Buffer, starting from offset zero, looking for "," bytes to locate the starting point and ending point for the various fields.

When we evaluate get_fix(), the GPGLL flyweight will extract four fields, convert the values to useful degrees and return a Point object with two floating-point values. If we want to correlate this with other devices, we might want to show a value that has degrees and minutes separated from each other. It can be more helpful to see 37°51.6500S than 37.86083333333333.

Multiple messages in a buffer

Let's stretch this out a bit, to look at a buffer with a sequence of messages in it. We'll put two GPGLL messages into a sequence of bytes. We'll include explicit end-of-line whitespace characters that some GPS devices include in the data stream.

```
>>> buffer_2 = Buffer(
...     b"$GPGLL,3751.65,S,14507.36,E*77\\r\\n"
...     b"$GPGLL,3723.2475,N,12158.3416,W,161229.487,A,A*41\\r\\n"
... )
>>> start = 0
>>> flyweight = message_factory(buffer_2[start+1 : start+6])
>>> p_1 = flyweight.from_buffer(buffer_2, start).get_fix()
>>> p_1
Point(latitude=-37.86083333333333, longitude=145.12266666666667)
>>> print(p_1)
(37°51.6500S, 145°07.3600E)
```

We've found the first GPGLL message, created a GPGLL object, and extracted the fix from the message. The next message begins where the previous message ends. This lets us start at a new offset in the buffer and examine a different region of bytes.

```
>>> flyweight.end
30
>>> next_start = buffer_2.index(ord(b"$"), flyweight.end)
>>> next_start
32
>>>
>>> flyweight = message_factory(buffer_2[next_start+1 : next_start+6])
>>> p_2 = flyweight.from_buffer(buffer_2, next_start).get_fix()
>>> p_2
Point(latitude=37.387458333333335, longitude=-121.97236)
>>> print(p_2)
(37°23.2475N, 121°58.3416W)
```

We've used the message_factory() function to create a new GPGLL object. Since the data from the message isn't in the object, we can reuse the previous GPGLL object. We can take out the flyweight = line of code, and the results are the same. When we use the from_buffer() method, we'll locate a new batch of "," characters. When we use the get_fix() method, we'll get values from a new place in the overall collection of bytes.

This implementation creates a few short strings of bytes to create a cacheable object for use by `message_factory()`. It creates new float values when it creates a `Point`. It avoids slinging around large blocks of bytes, however, by making the message processing objects reuse a single `Buffer` instance.

Generally, using the Flyweight pattern in Python is a matter of making sure we have references to the original data. Generally, Python avoids making implicit copies of objects; almost all object creation is obvious, using a class name or perhaps comprehension syntax. One case where object creation is not obvious is taking a slice from a sequence, like a buffer of bytes: when we use `bytes[start: end]`, this makes a copy of the bytes. Too many of these and our IoT device is out of usable memory. A Flyweight design avoids creating new objects, and – in particular – avoids slicing strings and bytes to create copies of the data.

Our example also introduced `weakref`. This isn't essential for a Flyweight design, but it can be helpful to identify objects that can be removed from memory. While the two are often seen together, they're not closely related.

The Flyweight pattern can have an enormous impact on memory consumption. It is common for programming solutions that optimize CPU, memory, or disk space to result in more complicated code than their unoptimized brethren. It is therefore important to weigh up the trade-offs when deciding between code maintainability and optimization. When choosing optimization, try to use patterns such as Flyweight to ensure that the complexity introduced by optimization is confined to a single (well-documented) section of the code.

Before we look at the Abstract Factory pattern, we'll digress a bit, to look at another memory optimization technique, unique to Python. This is the __slots__ magic attribute name.

Memory optimization via Python's __slots__

If you have a lot of Python objects in one program, another way to save memory is through the use of __slots__. This is a sidebar, since it's not a common design pattern outside the Python language. It is a helpful Python design pattern because it can shave a few bytes off an object that's used widely. Instead of a Flyweight design – where storage is intentionally shared – a slots design creates objects with their own private data, but avoids Python's built-in dictionary. Instead, there is direct mapping from attribute name to a sequence of values, avoiding the rather large hash table that is a part of every Python `dict` object.

Looking back at our previous example in this chapter, we avoided describing the Point object that was created as part of the get_fix() method of each subclass of Message. Here's one possible definition of the Point class:

```python
class Point:
    __slots__ = ("latitude", "longitude")

    def __init__(self, latitude: float, longitude: float) -> None:
        self.latitude = latitude
        self.longitude = longitude

    def __repr__(self) -> str:
        return (
            f"Point(latitude={self.latitude}, "
            f"longitude={self.longitude})"
        )
```

Each instance of a Point can have exactly two attributes with the names latitude and longitude. The __init__() method sets these values and provides useful type hints for tools like *mypy*.

In most other respects, this class is the same as a class without __slots__. The most notable difference is we cannot add attributes. Here's an example, showing what exception is raised:

```python
>>> p2 = Point(latitude=49.274, longitude=-123.185)
>>> p2.extra_attribute = 42
Traceback (most recent call last):
...
AttributeError: 'Point' object has no attribute 'extra_attribute'
```

The extra housekeeping of defining the names of the slots can be helpful when our application creates vast numbers of these objects. In many cases, however, our application is built on one or a very small number of instances of a class, and the memory-saving from introducing __slots__ is negligible.

In some cases, using a NamedTuple can be as effective at saving memory as using __slots__. We looked at these in *Chapter 7, Python Data Structures*.

We've seen how to manage complexity by wrapping objects in a Façade. We've seen how to manage memory use by using Flyweight objects that have little (or no) internal state. Next, we'll look at how we can create a variety of different kinds of objects using a *factory*.

The Abstract Factory pattern

The Abstract Factory pattern is appropriate when we have multiple possible implementations of a system that depend on some configuration or platform detail. The calling code requests an object from the Abstract Factory, not knowing exactly what class of object will be returned. The underlying implementation returned may depend on a variety of factors, such as the current locale, operating system, or local configuration.

Common examples of the Abstract Factory pattern include code for operating-system-independent toolkits, database backends, and country-specific formatters or calculators. An operating-system-independent GUI toolkit might use an Abstract Factory pattern that returns a set of WinForm widgets under Windows, Cocoa widgets under Mac, GTK widgets under Gnome, and QT widgets under KDE. Django provides an abstract factory that returns a set of object-relational classes for interacting with a specific database backend (MySQL, PostgreSQL, SQLite, and others) depending on a configuration setting for the current site. If the application needs to be deployed in multiple places, each one can use a different database backend by changing only one configuration variable. Different countries have different systems for calculating taxes, subtotals, and totals on retail merchandise; an Abstract Factory can return a particular tax calculation object.

There are two central features of an Abstract Factory:

- We need to have multiple implementation choices. Each implementation has a factory class to create objects. A single Abstract Factory defines the interface to the implementation factories.

- We have a number of closely related objects, and the relationships are implemented via multiple methods of each factory.

The following UML class diagram seems like a clutter of relationships:

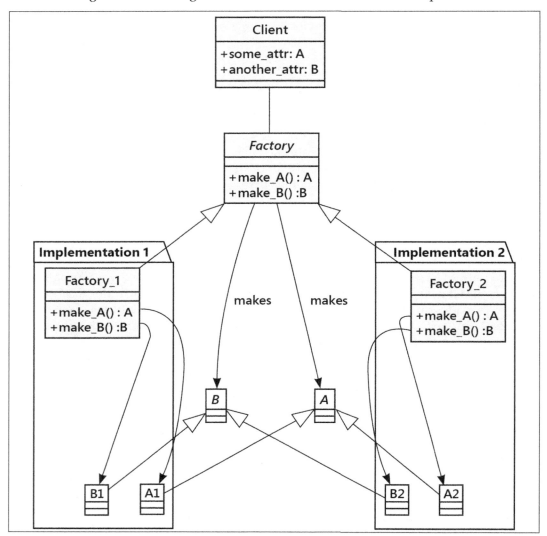

Figure 12.6: Abstract Factory pattern

There's an essential symmetry here that's very important. The client needs instances of class A and class B. To the client, these are abstract class definitions. The Factory class is an abstract base class that requires an implementation. Each of the implementation packages, implementation_1 and implementation_2, provides concrete Factory subclasses that will build the necessary A and B instances for the client.

An Abstract Factory example

The UML class diagram for the Abstract Factory pattern is hard to understand without a specific example, so let's turn things around and create a concrete example first. Let's look at two card games, Poker and Cribbage. Don't panic, you don't need to know all the rules, only that they're similar in a few fundamental ways but different in the details. This is depicted in the following diagram:

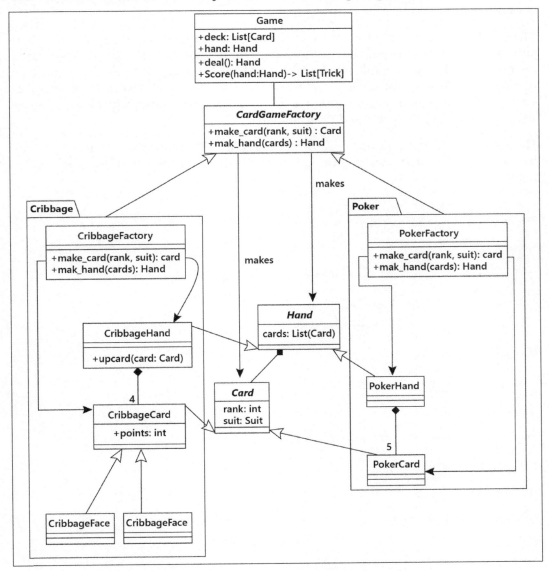

Figure 12.7: Abstract Factory pattern for Cribbage and Poker

The Game class requires Card objects and Hand objects (among several others). We've shown that the abstract Card objects are contained within the abstract Hand collection. Each implementation provides some unique features. For the most part, the PokerCard matches the generic Card definition. The PokerHand class, however, extends the Hand abstract base class with all the unique rules for defining the rank of the hand. Poker players know that there are a very, very large number of Poker game variants. We've shown a hand containing five cards because this seems to be a common feature of many games.

The Cribbage implementation introduces a number of types of CribbageCard subclasses, each of which has an additional attribute, points. The CribbageFace cards are all worth 10 points, while for the other kinds of CribbageCard classes the number of points matches the rank. The CribbageHand class extends the abstract base class of Hand with the unique rules for finding all the scoring combinations in a hand. We can use an Abstract Factory to build Card and Hand objects.

Here are the core definitions of Hand and Card. We didn't make these official abstract base classes. Python doesn't require this, and the extra complexity didn't seem helpful.

```python
from enum import Enum, auto
from typing import NamedTuple, List

class Suit(str, Enum):
    Clubs = "\N{Black Club Suit}"
    Diamonds = "\N{Black Diamond Suit}"
    Hearts = "\N{Black Heart Suit}"
    Spades = "\N{Black Spade Suit}"

class Card(NamedTuple):
    rank: int
    suit: Suit

    def __str__(self) -> str:
        return f"{self.rank}{self.suit}"

class Trick(int, Enum):
    pass

class Hand(List[Card]):
    def __init__(self, *cards: Card) -> None:
```

```
        super().__init__(cards)

    def scoring(self) -> List[Trick]:
        pass
```

These seem to capture the essence of "card" and "hand of cards." We'll need to extend these with subclasses that pertain to each game. We'll also need an Abstract Factory that creates cards and hands for us:

```
import abc

class CardGameFactory(abc.ABC):
    @abc.abstractmethod
    def make_card(self, rank: int, suit: Suit) -> "Card":
        ...

    @abc.abstractmethod
    def make_hand(self, *cards: Card) -> "Hand":
        ...
```

We've made the factory an actual abstract base class. Each individual game needs to provide extensions for the game's unique features of Hand and Card. The game will also provide an implementation of the CardGameFactory class that can build the expected classes.

We can define the cards for cribbage like this:

```
class CribbageCard(Card):
    @property
    def points(self) -> int:
        return self.rank

class CribbageAce(Card):
    @property
    def points(self) -> int:
        return 1

class CribbageFace(Card):
    @property
    def points(self) -> int:
        return 10
```

These extensions to the base `Card` class all have an additional points property. In Cribbage, one of the kinds of tricks is any combination of cards worth 15 points. Most cards have points equal to the rank, but the Jack, Queen, and King are all worth 10 points. This also means the Cribbage extension to `Hand` has a rather complex method for scoring, which we'll omit for now.

```python
class CribbageHand(Hand):
    starter: Card

    def upcard(self, starter: Card) -> "Hand":
        self.starter = starter
        return self

    def scoring(self) -> list[Trick]:
        """15's. Pairs. Runs. Right Jack."""
        ... details omitted ...
        return tricks
```

To provide some uniformity between the games, we've designated the scoring combinations in Cribbage and the rank of the hand in Poker as a subclass of "Trick." In Cribbage, there's a fairly large number of point-scoring tricks. In Poker, on the other hand, there's a single Trick that represents the hand as a whole. Tricks don't seem to be a place where an Abstract Factory is useful.

The computation of the various scoring combinations in Cribbage is a rather sophisticated problem. It involves looking at all possible combinations of cards that total to 15 points, among other things. These details are unrelated to the Abstract Factory design pattern.

The Poker variant has its own unique complication: Aces are a higher rank than the King:

```python
class PokerCard(Card):
    def __str__(self) -> str:
        if self.rank == 14:
            return f"A{self.suit}"
        return f"{self.rank}{self.suit}"


class PokerHand(Hand):
    def scoring(self) -> list[Trick]:
        """Return a single 'Trick'"""
        ... details omitted ...
        return [rank]
```

Ranking the various hands in poker is also a rather sophisticated problem, but outside the Abstract Factory realm. Here's the concrete factory that builds hands and cards for Poker:

```
class PokerFactory(CardGameFactory):
    def make_card(self, rank: int, suit: Suit) -> "Card":
        if rank == 1:
            # Aces above kings
            rank = 14
        return PokerCard(rank, suit)

    def make_hand(self, *cards: Card) -> "Hand":
        return PokerHand(*cards)
```

Note the way the make_card() method reflects the way Aces work in Poker. Having the Ace outrank the King reflects a common complication in a number of card games; we need to reflect the various ways Aces work.

Here's a test case for how Cribbage works:

```
>>> factory = CribbageFactory()
>>> cards = [
...     factory.make_card(6, Suit.Clubs),
...     factory.make_card(7, Suit.Diamonds),
...     factory.make_card(8, Suit.Hearts),
...     factory.make_card(9, Suit.Spades),
... ]
>>> starter = factory.make_card(5, Suit.Spades)
>>> hand = factory.make_hand(*cards)
>>> score = sorted(hand.upcard(starter).scoring())
>>> [t.name for t in score]
['Fifteen', 'Fifteen', 'Run_5']
```

We've created an instance of the CribbageFactory class, a concrete implementation of the abstract CardGameFactory class. We can use the factory to create some cards, and we can also use the factory to create a hand of cards. When playing Cribbage, an additional card is flipped, called the "starter." In this case, our hand is four cards in sequence, and the starter happens to fit with that sequence. We can score the hand and see that there are three scoring combinations: there are two ways to make 15 points, plus a run of five cards.

This design provides some hints toward what needs to be done when we want to add support for more games. Introducing new rules means creating the new Hand and Card subclasses and extending the Abstract Factory class definition, also. Of course, inheritance leads to the opportunity for reuse, something we can capitalize on to create families of games with similar rules.

Abstract Factories in Python

The previous example highlights an interesting consequence of the way Python's duck typing works. Do we really need the abstract base class, CardGameFactory? It provides a framework used for type checking, but otherwise doesn't have any useful features. Since we don't really need it, we can think of this design as having three parallel modules:

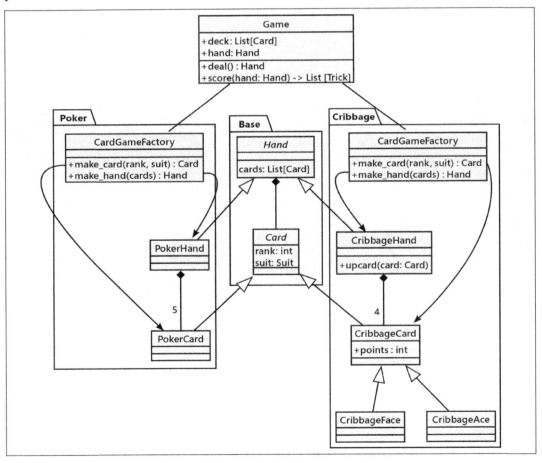

Figure 12.8: Abstract Factory without abstract base classes

Both of the defined games implement a class, CardGameFactory, that defines the unique features of the game. Because these are in separate modules, we can use the same name for each class. This lets us write a Cribbage application that uses `from cribbage import CardGameFactory`. This skips past the overhead of a common abstract base class and lets us provide extensions as separate modules sharing some common base class definitions. Each alternative implementation also provides a common module-level interface: they expose a standard class name that handles the remaining details of creating unique objects.

In this case, the Abstract Factory becomes a concept, and is not implemented as an actual abstract base class. We'll need to provide adequate documentation in the docstrings for all classes that purport to be CardGameFactory implementations. We can clarify our intentions by defining a protocol using typing.Protocol. It could look like this:

```
class CardGameFactoryProtocol(Protocol):
    def make_card(self, rank: int, suit: Suit) -> "Card":
        ...

    def make_hand(self, *cards: Card) -> "Hand":
        ...
```

This definition allows *mypy* to confirm that a Game class can refer to either a poker.CardGameFactory or a cribbage.CardGameFactory because both implement the same protocol. Unlike the abstract base class definition, this is not a runtime check. A protocol definition is only used by *mypy* to confirm that the code is likely to pass its unit test suite.

The Abstract Factory pattern helps us define related families of objects, for instance, playing cards and hands. A single factory can produce two separate classes of objects that are closely related. In some cases, the relationships aren't a simple collection and item. Sometimes there are sub-collections in addition to items. These kinds of structures can be handled using the Composite design pattern.

The Composite pattern

The Composite pattern allows complex tree structures to be built from simple components, often called **nodes**. A node with children will behave like a container; a node without children will behave like a single object. A composite object is – generally – a container object, where the content may be another composite object.

Traditionally, each node in a composite object must be either a **leaf** node (that cannot contain other objects) or a **composite** node. The key is that both composite and leaf nodes can have the same interface. The following UML diagram shows this elegant parallelism as a some_action() method:

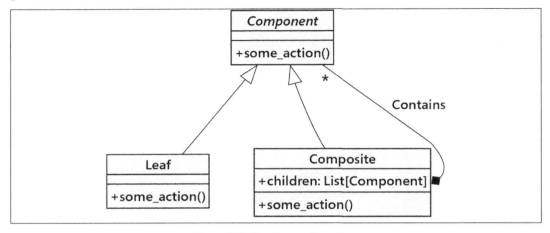

Figure 12.9: The Composite pattern

This simple pattern, however, allows us to create complex arrangements of elements, all of which satisfy the interface of the component object. The following diagram depicts a concrete instance of such a complicated arrangement:

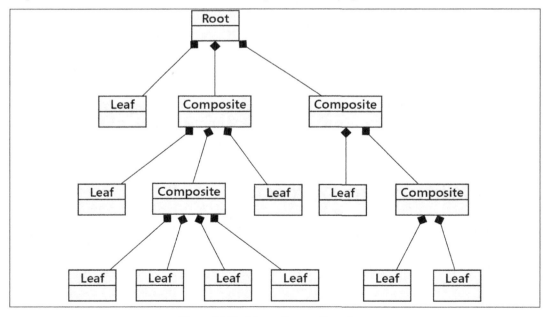

Figure 12.10: A large Composite pattern

The Composite pattern applies to language processing. Both natural languages and artificial languages (like Python) tend to follow rules that are hierarchical and fit nicely with the Composite design pattern. Markup languages, like HTML, XML, RST, and Markdown, tend to reflect some common composite concepts like lists of lists, and headers with sub-headings.

A programming language involves recursive tree structures. The Python standard library includes the ast module, which provides the classes that define the structure of Python code. We can use this module to examine Python code without resorting to regular expressions or other hard-to-get-correct text processing.

A Composite example

The Composite pattern needs to be applied to tree structures like the files and folders of a file system. Regardless of whether a node in the tree is an ordinary data file or a folder, it is still subject to operations such as moving, copying, or deleting the node. We can create a component interface that supports these operations, and then use a composite object to represent folders, and leaf nodes to represent data files.

Of course, in Python, once again, we can take advantage of duck typing to implicitly provide the interface, so we only need to write two classes. Let's define these interfaces first in the following code:

```python
class Folder:
    def __init__(
            self,
            name: str,
            children: Optional[dict[str, "Node"]] = None
    ) -> None:
        self.name = name
        self.children = children or {}
        self.parent: Optional["Folder"] = None

    def __repr__(self) -> str:
        return f"Folder({self.name!r}, {self.children!r})"

    def add_child(self, node: "Node") -> "Node":
        node.parent = self
        return self.children.setdefault(node.name, node)

    def move(self, new_folder: "Folder") -> None:
        pass
```

```
        def copy(self, new_folder: "Folder") -> None:
            pass

        def remove(self) -> None:
            pass


class File:
    def __init__(self, name: str) -> None:
        self.name = name
        self.parent: Optional[Folder] = None

    def __repr__(self) -> str:
        return f"File({self.name!r})"

    def move(self, new_path):
        pass

    def copy(self, new_path):
        pass

    def remove(self):
        pass
```

For each `Folder`, a composite object, we maintain a dictionary of children. The children may be a mixture of `Folder` and `File` instances. For many composite implementations, a list is sufficient, but in this case, a dictionary will be useful for looking up children by name.

Thinking about the methods involved, there are several patterns:

- For doing a move, relocating the `Folder` will carry along all the children. Relocating a `File` will turn out to be precisely the same code because we don't need to consider the children.

- For doing a copy, we'll need to copy all of the children. Since there's no data outside the `File` nodes of the composite object, we don't need to do anything more.

- For a delete, we should follow the Linux pattern of clearing out the children before trying to remove a parent.

This design lets us create subclasses with distinct operation implementations. Each subclass implementation could make external requests, or perhaps make OS requests on the local machine.

To take advantage of the similar operations, we can extract the common methods into a parent class. Let's refactor this to create a base class, Node, with the following code:

```
class Node(abc.ABC):
    def __init__(
        self,
        name: str,
    ) -> None:
        self.name = name
        self.parent: Optional["Folder"] = None

    def move(self, new_place: "Folder") -> None:
        previous = self.parent
        new_place.add_child(self)
        if previous:
            del previous.children[self.name]

    @abc.abstractmethod
    def copy(self, new_folder: "Folder") -> None:
        ...

    @abc.abstractmethod
    def remove(self) -> None:
        ...
```

This abstract Node class defines that each node has a string with a reference to a parent. Keeping the parent information around lets us look "up" the tree toward the root node. This makes it possible to move and remove files by making a change to the parent's collection of children.

We've created the move() method on the Node class. This works by reassigning a Folder or a File object to a new location. It follows up by removing the object from its previous location. For the move() method, the target should be an existing folder, or we'll get an error because a File instance doesn't have an add_child() method. As in many examples in technical books, error handling is woefully absent, to help focus on the principles under consideration. A common practice is to handle the AttributeError exception by raising a new TypeError exception. See *Chapter 4, Expecting the Unexpected*.

We can then extend this class to provide the unique features of a `Folder` that has children, and a `File`, which is the leaf node of the tree and has no children:

```python
class Folder(Node):
    def __init__(
            self,
            name: str,
            children: Optional[dict[str, "Node"]] = None
    ) -> None:
        super().__init__(name)
        self.children = children or {}

    def __repr__(self) -> str:
        return f"Folder({self.name!r}, {self.children!r})"

    def add_child(self, node: "Node") -> "Node":
        node.parent = self
        return self.children.setdefault(node.name, node)

    def copy(self, new_folder: "Folder") -> None:
        target = new_folder.add_child(Folder(self.name))
        for c in self.children:
            self.children[c].copy(target)

    def remove(self) -> None:
        names = list(self.children)
        for c in names:
            self.children[c].remove()
        if self.parent:
            del self.parent.children[self.name]

class File(Node):
    def __repr__(self) -> str:
        return f"File({self.name!r})"

    def copy(self, new_folder: "Folder") -> None:
        new_folder.add_child(File(self.name))

    def remove(self) -> None:
```

```
                if self.parent:
                    del self.parent.children[self.name]
```

When we add a child to a Folder, we'll do two things. First, we tell the child who their new parent is. This makes sure that each Node (except the root Folder instance) has a parent. Second, we'll drop the new Node into the folder's collection of children, if it doesn't already exist.

When we copy Folder objects around, we need to make sure all the children are copied. Each child could, in turn, be another Folder, with children. This recursive walk involves delegating the copy() operation to each sub-Folder within a Folder instance. The implementation for a File object, on the other hand, is simpler.

The recursive design for removal is similar to the recursive copy. A Folder instance must first remove all of the children; this may involve removing sub-Folder instances. A File object, on the other hand, can be directly removed.

Well, that was easy enough. Let's see if our composite file hierarchy is working properly with the following code snippet:

```
>>> tree = Folder("Tree")
>>> tree.add_child(Folder("src"))
Folder('src', {})
>>> tree.children["src"].add_child(File("ex1.py"))
File('ex1.py')
>>> tree.add_child(Folder("src"))
Folder('src', {'ex1.py': File('ex1.py')})
>>> tree.children["src"].add_child(File("test1.py"))
File('test1.py')
>>> tree
Folder('Tree', {'src': Folder('src', {'ex1.py': File('ex1.py'), 'test1.
py': File('test1.py')})})
```

The value of tree can be a little difficult to visualize. Here's a variation on the display that can help.

```
+-- Tree
    +-- src
        +-- ex1.py
        +-- test1.py
```

We didn't cover the algorithm for producing this nested visualization. It's not too difficult to add to the class definitions. We can see that the parent folder, Tree, has a sub-folder, src, with two files inside it. We can describe a filesystem operation like this:

```
>>> test1 = tree.children["src"].children["test1.py"]
>>> test1
File('test1.py')
>>> tree.add_child(Folder("tests"))
Folder('tests', {})
>>> test1.move(tree.children["tests"])
>>> tree
Folder('Tree',
    {'src': Folder('src',
        {'ex1.py': File('ex1.py')}),
     'tests': Folder('tests',
        {'test1.py': File('test1.py')})})
```

We've created a new folder, tests, and moved the file. Here's another view of the resulting composite objects:

```
+-- Tree
    +-- src
        +-- ex1.py
    +-- tests
        +-- test1.py
```

The Composite pattern is extremely useful for a variety of tree-like structures, including GUI widget hierarchies, file hierarchies, tree sets, graphs, and HTML DOM. Sometimes, if only a shallow tree is being created, we can get away with a list of lists or a dictionary of dictionaries, and do not need to implement custom component, leaf, and composite classes. Indeed, JSON, YAML, and TOML documents often follow the dict-of-dict pattern. While we often use abstract base classes for this, it isn't required; Python's duck typing can make it easy to add other objects to a composite hierarchy, as long as they have the correct interface.

One of the important aspects of the Composite pattern is a common interface for the various subtypes of a node. We needed two implementation variants for Folder and File classes. In some cases, these operations are similar, and it can help to offer a template implementation of a complex method.

The Template pattern

The Template pattern (sometimes called the Template method) is useful
for removing duplicate code; it's intended to support the **Don't Repeat
Yourself** principle we discussed in *Chapter 5, When to Use Object-Oriented
Programming*. It is designed for situations where we have several different tasks to
accomplish that have some, but not all, steps in common. The common steps are
implemented in a base class, and the distinct steps are overridden in subclasses to
provide custom behavior. In some ways, it's like the Strategy pattern, except similar
sections of the algorithms are shared using a base class. Here it is in the UML format:

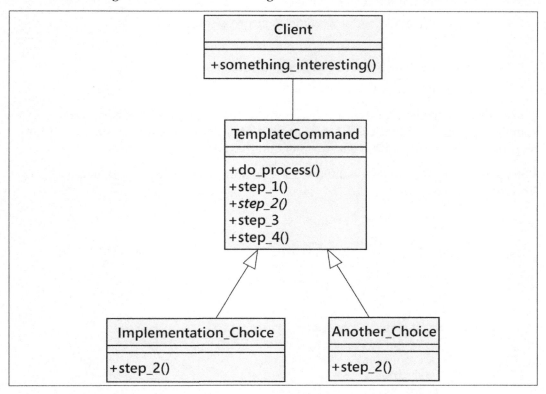

Figure 12.11: The Template pattern

A Template example

Let's create a car sales reporter as an example. We can store records of sales in an
SQLite database table. SQLite is the built-in database engine that allows us to store
records using SQL syntax. Python includes SQLite in its standard library, so there are
no extra modules to install.

We have two common tasks we need to perform:

- Select all sales of new vehicles and output them to the screen in a comma-delimited format
- Output a comma-delimited list of all salespeople with their gross sales and save it to a file that can be imported to a spreadsheet

These seem like quite different tasks, but they have some common features. In both cases, we need to perform the following steps:

1. Connect to the database
2. Construct a query for new vehicles or gross sales
3. Issue the query
4. Format the results into a comma-delimited string
5. Output the data to a file or email

The query construction and output steps are different for the two tasks, but the remaining steps are identical. We can use the Template pattern to put the common steps in a base class, and the varying steps in two subclasses.

Before we start, let's create a database and put some sample data in it, using a few lines of SQL:

```python
import sqlite3

def test_setup(db_name: str = "sales.db") -> sqlite3.Connection:
    conn = sqlite3.connect(db_name)

    conn.execute(
        """
        CREATE TABLE IF NOT EXISTS Sales (
            salesperson text,
            amt currency,
            year integer,
            model text,
            new boolean
        )
        """
    )

    conn.execute(
        """
        DELETE FROM Sales
        """
```

```
    )

    conn.execute(
        """
        INSERT INTO Sales
        VALUES('Tim', 16000, 2010, 'Honda Fit', 'true')
        """
    )
    conn.execute(
        """
        INSERT INTO Sales
        VALUES('Tim', 9000, 2006, 'Ford Focus', 'false')
        """
    )
    conn.execute(
        """
        INSERT INTO Sales
        VALUES('Hannah', 8000, 2004, 'Dodge Neon', 'false')
        """
    )
    conn.execute(
        """
        INSERT INTO Sales
        VALUES('Hannah', 28000, 2009, 'Ford Mustang', 'true')
        """
    )
    conn.execute(
        """
        INSERT INTO Sales
        VALUES('Hannah', 50000, 2010, 'Lincoln Navigator', 'true')
        """
    )
    conn.execute(
        """
        INSERT INTO Sales
        VALUES('Jason', 20000, 2008, 'Toyota Prius', 'false')
        """
    )
    conn.commit()
    return conn
```

Hopefully, you can see what's going on here even if you don't know SQL; we've created a table named Sales to hold the data, and used six insert statements to add sales records. The data is stored in a file named sales.db. Now we have a sample database with a table we can work with in developing our Template pattern.

Since we've already outlined the steps that the template has to perform, we can start by defining the base class that contains the steps. Each step gets its own method (to make it easy to selectively override any one step), and we have one more managerial method that calls the steps in turn. Without any method content, here's how the class might look as a first step toward completion:

```python
class QueryTemplate:
    def __init__(self, db_name: str = "sales.db") -> None:

    def connect(self) -> None:
        pass

    def construct_query(self) -> None:
        pass

    def do_query(self) -> None:
        pass

    def output_context(self) -> ContextManager[TextIO]:
        pass

    def output_results(self) -> None:
        pass

    def process_format(self) -> None:
        self.connect()
        self.construct_query()
        self.do_query()
        self.format_results()
        self.output_results()
```

The process_format() method is the primary method to be called by an outside client. It ensures each step is executed in order, but it does not care whether that step is implemented in this class or in a subclass. For our examples, we expect the construct_query() and the output_context() methods are likely to change.

In Python, we can formalize our expectation by using an abstract base class. An alternative is to raise a NotImplementedError exception for the missing method in the template. This will provide a runtime check if we subclass the QueryTemplate and – perhaps – misspell the name of our attempted override of the construct_query() method.

The remaining methods are going to be identical between our two classes:

```
class QueryTemplate:
    def __init__(self, db_name: str = "sales.db") -> None:
        self.db_name = db_name
        self.conn: sqlite3.Connection
        self.results: list[tuple[str, ...]]
        self.query: str
        self.header: list[str]

    def connect(self) -> None:
        self.conn = sqlite3.connect(self.db_name)

    def construct_query(self) -> None:
        raise NotImplementedError("construct_query not implemented")

    def do_query(self) -> None:
        results = self.conn.execute(self.query)
        self.results = results.fetchall()

    def output_context(self) -> ContextManager[TextIO]:
        self.target_file = sys.stdout
        return cast(ContextManager[TextIO], contextlib.nullcontext())

    def output_results(self) -> None:
        writer = csv.writer(self.target_file)
        writer.writerow(self.header)
        writer.writerows(self.results)

    def process_format(self) -> None:
        self.connect()
        self.construct_query()
        self.do_query()
        with self.output_context():
            self.output_results()
```

This is a kind of abstract class. It doesn't use a formal abstract base class; instead, the two methods we expect to update show two distinct approaches to providing an abstract definition:

- The construct_query() method must be overridden. The method definition base class raises the NotImplementedError exception. This is an alternative for creating an abstract interface in Python. Raising NotImplementedError helps the programmer understand that the class is meant to be subclassed and these methods overridden. It can be described as "smuggling in an abstract base class without being explicit" in the class definition and without using @abc.abstracmethod decorators.

- The output_context() method may be overridden. There's a default implementation provided that sets the self.target_file instance variable and also returns a context value. The default uses sys.stdout as the output file and a null context manager.

Now we have a template class that takes care of the boring details, but is flexible enough to allow the execution and formatting of a wide variety of queries. The best part is, if we ever want to change our database engine from SQLite to another database engine (such as py-postgresql), we only have to do it here, in this template class, and we don't have to touch the two (or two hundred) subclasses we might have written.

Let's have a look at the concrete classes now:

```python
import datetime

class NewVehiclesQuery(QueryTemplate):
    def construct_query(self) -> None:
        self.query = "select * from Sales where new='true'"
        self.header = ["salesperson", "amt", "year", "model", "new"]

class SalesGrossQuery(QueryTemplate):
    def construct_query(self) -> None:
        self.query = (
            "select salesperson, sum(amt) "
            " from Sales group by salesperson"
        )
        self.header = ["salesperson", "total sales"]

    def output_context(self) -> ContextManager[TextIO]:
        today = datetime.date.today()
        filepath = Path(f"gross_sales_{today:%Y%m%d}.csv")
        self.target_file = filepath.open("w")
        return self.target_file
```

These two classes are actually pretty short, considering what they're doing: connecting to a database, executing a query, formatting the results, and outputting them. The superclass takes care of the repetitive work, but lets us easily specify those steps that vary between tasks. Further, we can also easily change steps that are provided in the base class. For example, if we wanted to output something other than a comma-delimited string (for example, an HTML report to be uploaded to a website), we can still override the output_results() method.

Case study

The previous chapters of the case study have contained a number of design patterns. We'll pick a variation on the model and walk through some of the patterns from this chapter and how they were applied.

Here's an overview of several parts of the application's classes. This is from the case study in *Chapter 7, Python Data Structures*:

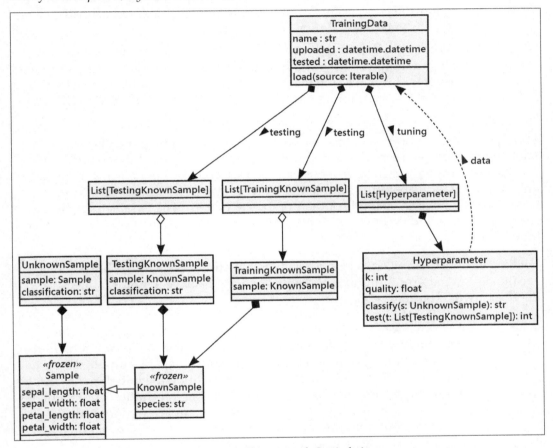

Figure 12.12: The case study Logical view

This involves a number of patterns we've seen in this chapter. We'll start with the Hyperparameter class, which is a Façade that includes two separate complex components, the classifier algorithm and the training data.

First, we'll look at the classifier algorithm. In *Chapter 10, The Iterator Pattern*, we saw how the classifier is itself a complex structure. We looked at three alternatives: k_nn_1(), which had a naïve sort, k_nn_b(), which used bisection, and k_nn_q(), which used a heap queue. This exploration relied on several design patterns from this chapter:

- The classifier depends on the Strategy design pattern to incorporate one of the many distance computations. We defined a class, Distance, and made sure each distance computation was a subclass. The classifier algorithm was given the distance computation as a parameter.

- The classifier is a Façade that provides a uniform interface for testing and evaluating a sample. Each variation on the classifier used a slightly different data structure for managing the collection of nearest neighbors. We don't want to sort a large training set; we only want to track the subset of nearest neighbors.

Throughout the previous chapters, we've made sure the training data leverages the Flyweight design pattern to avoid keeping multiple copies of the training data. The idea of wrapping each Sample object with a separate frozen dataclass to include known information about the sample is a kind of Flyweight design, also. More fundamentally, it is an example of the Composite pattern. The useable sample is a composite and avoids keeping multiple copies of the underlying KnownSample objects in memory.

Looking at the TrainingData class, we can see how this design also follows the Façade design pattern. A number of distinct operations have a uniform interface. There are two important parts:

- Loading raw Sample instances to partition them into training and testing subsets. The various data formats described in *Chapter 9, Strings, Serialization, and File Paths*, can be seen as complex algorithms that are simplified by a uniform Façade. The choice of algorithm to partition the initial set of samples into a training set and a testing set is, similarly, an application of the Strategy design pattern. This lets us change the ratio of samples used for training and testing using a different implementation from a strategy class hierarchy.

- Keeping the testing and training sets to be used for hyperparameter tuning is done by partitioning the raw data into two disjoint lists.

The idea of creating TrainingKnownSample or TestingKnownSample instances is an example of the Abstract Factory pattern. The partitioning algorithm can be described by an Abstract Factory class definition. Each partitioning algorithm becomes a concrete factory that creates different mixtures of training and testing objects.

In *Chapter 11, Common Design Patterns*, we looked closely at the hyperparameter tuning process. The *k*-nearest neighbors algorithm depends on two parameters, called hyperparameters:

- The algorithm used to compute the distances between samples.
- The number of samples, *k*, used. The most common of the *k* nearest neighbors becomes the label assigned to the unknown sample. If the value for *k* is odd, we can avoid an even split between two choices, ensuring there's always a winner.

In *Chapter 11*, the tuning algorithm shown is not particularly speedy but is patiently thorough: the grid search algorithm. In that chapter, we used the Command design pattern to enumerate various combinations of *k* and distance computations. Each combination was a command that – when executed – provided quality and timing information.

There were three major phases of work involved in the application, as a whole. These were presented in *Chapter 1, Object-Oriented Design*, as the various use cases:

1. A Botanist provides training data
2. A Botanist uses hyperparameter tuning to locate an optimal model
3. Users make use of this to classify their unknown samples

This pattern of work suggests the Template design pattern may be required to ensure that classes like the `TrainingData` class and the overall application work consistently. Currently, it doesn't seem like a carefully designed class hierarchy is needed. When we review *Chapter 1*, however, the initial intent was to use this example to learn more about classifiers, and eventually extend this from the simple example of classifying iris species to more complex real-world problems. This follows what's called "the telescope rule":

> *Thomson's Rule for First-Time Telescope Makers: "It is faster to make a four-inch mirror then a six-inch mirror than to make a six-inch mirror."*
>
> *-- Programming Pearls, Communications of the ACM, September 1985*

The intent behind the problem is to build something workable, using a variety of design patterns. The various components can then be replaced, revised, and expanded to tackle larger and more complex problems. The telescope maker will learn a lot about telescopes from making their first mirror, and those lessons can be applied to making their next, more useful telescope. A similar pattern of learning applies to software and object-oriented design. If the various components are designed well and follow established patterns, then the changes to improve and expand are not damaging or disruptive.

Recall

Often, we'll spot really good ideas that are repeated; the repetition can form a recognizable pattern. Exploiting a pattern-based approach to software design can save the developer from wasting time trying to reinvent something already well understood. In this chapter, we looked at a few more advanced design patterns:

- An Adapter class is a way to insert an intermediary so a client can make use of an existing class even when the class is not a perfect match. The software adapter parallels the idea of USB hardware adapters between various kinds of devices with various USB interface connectors.

- The Façade pattern is a way to create a unified interface over a number of objects. The idea parallels the façade of a building that unifies separate floors, rooms, and halls into a single space.

- We can leverage the Flyweight pattern to implement a kind of lazy initialization. Instead of copying objects, we can design Flyweight classes that share a common pool of data, minimizing or avoiding initialization entirely.

- When we have closely related classes of objects, the Abstract Factory pattern can be used to build a class that can emit instances that will work together.

- The Composition pattern is widely used for complex document types. It covers programming languages, natural languages, and markup languages, including XML and HTML. Even something like the filesystem with a hierarchy of directories and files fits this design pattern.

- When we have a number of similar, complex classes, it seems appropriate to create a class following the Template pattern. We can leave gaps or openings in the template into which we can inject any unique features.

These patterns can help a designer focus on accepted, good design practices. Each problem is, of course, unique, so the patterns must be adapted. It's often better to make an adaptation to a known pattern and avoid trying to invent something completely new.

Exercises

Before diving into exercises for each design pattern, take a moment to add the os and pathlib calls to implement the methods for the File and Folder objects in the section on *The Composite pattern*. The copy() method on File will need to read and write the bytes of a file. The copy() method on Folder is quite a bit more complicated, as you first have to duplicate the folder, and then recursively copy each of its children to the new location. The examples we provided update the internal data structure, but don't apply changes to the operating system. Be careful about testing this in isolated directories. You don't want to accidentally destroy important files.

Now, as in the previous chapter, look at the patterns we've discussed and consider ideal places where you might implement them. You may want to apply the Adapter pattern to existing code, as it is usually applicable when interfacing with existing libraries, rather than new code. How can you use an Adapter to force two interfaces to interact with each other correctly?

Can you think of a system complex enough to justify using the Façade pattern? Consider how façades are used in real-life situations, such as the driver-facing interface of a car, or the control panel in a factory. It is similar in software, except the users of the façade interface are other programmers, rather than people trained to use it. Are there complex systems in your latest project that could benefit from the Façade pattern?

It's possible you don't have any huge, memory-consuming code that would benefit from the Flyweight pattern, but can you think of situations where it might be useful? Anywhere that large amounts of overlapping data need to be processed, a Flyweight is waiting to be used. Would it be useful in the banking industry? In web applications? At what point does adopting the Flyweight pattern make sense? When is it overkill?

The Abstract Factory pattern, or the somewhat more Pythonic derivatives we discussed, can be very useful for creating one-touch-configurable systems. Can you think of places where such systems are useful?

The Composite pattern applies in a number of places. There are tree-like structures all around us in programming. Some of them, like our file hierarchy example, are blatant; others are fairly subtle. What situations might arise where the Composite pattern would be useful? Can you think of places where you can use it in your own code? What if you adapted the pattern slightly; for example, to contain different types of leaf or composite nodes for different types of objects?

The `ast` module provides a composite tree structure for Python code. A particularly useful thing is to use the `ast` module to locate all of the import statements in some code. This can help confirm that a project's list of required modules, often in a `requirements.txt` file, is complete and consistent.

A Template method is helpful when decomposing a complex operation so it is open to extension. It appears that the *k*-nearest neighbors algorithm might be a good candidate for a Template method. In *Chapter 10*, *The Iterator Pattern*, we rewrote the *k*-nearest neighbors algorithm as three completely separate functions. Was this necessary? Could we have rewritten it into a method that decomposes the problem into three steps: computing distances, finding the *k*-nearest, and then finding the mode? Compare this design with doing it as separate functions; which do you find more expressive?

Summary

In this chapter, we went into detail on several more design patterns, covering their canonical descriptions as well as alternatives for implementing them in Python, which is often more flexible and versatile than traditional object-oriented languages. The Adapter pattern is useful for matching interfaces, while the Façade pattern is suited to simplifying them. Flyweight is a complicated pattern and only useful if memory optimization is required. Abstract Factories allow the runtime separation of implementations depending on configuration or system information. The Composite pattern is used universally for tree-like structures. A Template method can be helpful for breaking complex operations into steps to avoid repeating the common features.

This is the last of the truly object-oriented design chapters in this book. In the next two chapters, we'll discuss how important it is to test Python programs, and how to do it, focusing on object-oriented principles. Then we'll look at the concurrency features of Python and how to exploit them to get work done more quickly.

13

Testing Object-Oriented Programs

Skilled Python programmers agree that testing is one of the most important aspects of software development. Even though this chapter is placed near the end of the book, it is not an afterthought; everything we have studied so far will help us when writing tests. In this chapter, we'll look at the following topics:

- The importance of unit testing and test-driven development
- The standard library unittest module
- The pytest tool
- The mock module
- Code coverage

In the case study for this chapter, we'll focus – no surprise – on writing some tests for the case study examples.

We'll start with some of the fundamental reasons why automated software testing is so important.

Why test?

Many programmers already know how important it is to test their code. If you're among them, feel free to skim this section. You'll find the next section – where we actually see how to create tests in Python – much more scintillating.

If you're not convinced of the importance of testing, we remind you that without any tests, code will be broken, and no one has any way to know it. Read on!

Some people argue that testing is more important in Python code because of its dynamic nature; compiled languages such as Java and C++ are occasionally thought to be somehow *safer* because they enforce type checking at compile time. However, Python tests rarely check types. They check values. They make sure that the right attributes have been set at the right time or that the sequence has the right length, order, and values. These higher-level concepts need to be tested in any language. The real reason Python programmers test more than programmers of other languages is that it is so easy to test in Python!

But why test? Do we really need to test? What if we didn't test? To answer those questions, reflect on the last time you wrote any code. Did it run correctly the first time? Free of syntax errors? Free of logic problems? It's possible, in principle, to type in code that's perfect once in a while. As a practical matter, the number of obvious syntax errors that had to be corrected is an indicator that perhaps there are more subtle logic errors that also had to be corrected.

We don't need a formal, separate test to make sure our code works. Running the program, as we generally do, and fixing the errors is a crude form of testing. Python's interactive interpreter and near-zero compile times makes it easy to write a few lines of code and run the program to make sure those lines are doing what is expected. While acceptable at the beginning of a project, this turns into a liability that grows over time. Attempting to change a few lines of code can affect parts of the program that we haven't realized will be influenced by the changes, and without tests, we don't know what we broke. Attempts at redesigns or even small optimization rewrites can be plagued with problems. Furthermore, as a program grows, the number of paths that the interpreter can take through that code also grows, and it quickly becomes impossible or a crude manual test to exercise all of them.

To assure ourselves and others that our software works, we write automated tests. These are programs that automatically run certain inputs through other programs or parts of programs. We can run these test programs in seconds and cover far more potential input situations than one programmer would think to test every time they change something.

> *Software features that can't be demonstrated by automated tests simply don't exist.*

> *- Extreme Programming Explained, Kent Beck*

There are four main reasons to write tests:

- To ensure that code is working the way the developer thinks it should
- To ensure that code continues working when we make changes
- To ensure that the developer understood the requirements
- To ensure that the code we are writing has a maintainable interface

When we have automated tests, we can run them every time we change code, whether it is during initial development or maintenance releases. Testing can confirm that we didn't inadvertently break anything when adding or extending features.

The last two of the preceding points have interesting consequences. When we write tests, it helps us design the API, interface, or pattern that code takes. Thus, if we misunderstood the requirements, writing a test can help highlight the misunderstanding. From the other side, if we're not certain how we want to design a class, we can write a test that interacts with that class so we have an idea of the most natural way to confirm that the interface works. In fact, it is often beneficial to write the tests before we write the code we are testing.

There are some other interesting consequences of focusing on software testing. We'll look at three of these consequences:

- Using tests to drive development
- Managing different objectives for testing
- Having a consistent pattern for test scenarios

Let's start with using tests to drive the development effort.

Test-driven development

Write tests first is the mantra of test-driven development. Test-driven development takes the *untested code is broken code* concept one step further and suggests that only unwritten code should be untested. We don't write any code until after we have written the tests that will prove it works. The first time we run a test, it should fail, since the code hasn't been written. Then, we write the code that ensures the test passes, and then write another test for the next segment of code.

Test-driven development can be fun; it allows us to build little puzzles to solve. Then, we implement the code to solve those puzzles. After that, we make a more complicated puzzle, and we write code that solves the new puzzle without unsolving the previous one.

There are two goals of the test-driven methodology. The first is to ensure that tests really get written.

Secondly, writing tests first forces us to consider exactly how the code will be used. It tells us what methods objects need to have and how attributes will be accessed. It helps us break up the initial problem into smaller, testable problems, and then recombine the tested solutions into larger, also tested, solutions. Writing tests can thus become a part of the design process. Often, when we're writing a test for a new object, we discover anomalies in the design that force us to consider new aspects of the software.

Testing makes software better. Writing tests before we release the software makes it better before the final code is written.

All of the code examined in the book has been run through an automated test suite. It's the only way to be absolutely sure the examples are rock-solid, working code.

Testing objectives

We have a number of distinct objectives for running tests. These are often called types of testing, but the word "type" is heavily overused in the software industry. In this chapter, we'll look at only two of these testing goals:

- **Unit tests** confirm that software components work in isolation. We'll focus on this first, since Fowler's Test Pyramid seems to suggest unit testing creates the most value. If the various classes and functions each adhere to their interfaces and produce the expected results, then integrating them is also going to work nicely and have relatively few surprises. It's common to use the **coverage** tool to be sure all the lines of code are exercised as part of the unit test suite.

- **Integration tests** – unsurprisingly – confirm software components work when integrated. Integration tests are sometimes called system tests, functional tests, and acceptance tests, among others. When an integration test fails, it often means an interface wasn't defined properly, or a unit test didn't include some edge case that's exposed through the integration with other components. Integration testing seems to depend on having good unit testing, making it secondary in importance.

We note that "unit" isn't formally defined by the Python language. This is an intentional choice. A unit of code is often a single function or a single class. It can be a single module, also. The definition gives us a little flexibility to identify isolated, individual units of code.

While there are many distinct objectives for tests, the techniques used tend to be similar. For additional material, see `https://www.softwaretestinghelp.com/types-of-software-testing/` for a list of over 40 different types of testing objectives; this is overwhelming, which is why we will only focus on unit tests and integration tests. All tests have a common pattern to them, and we'll look at a general pattern of testing next.

Testing patterns

Writing code is often challenging. We need to figure out what the internal state of the object is, what state changes it undergoes, and determine the other objects it collaborates with. Throughout the book, we've provided a number of common patterns for designing classes.

Tests, in a way, are simpler than class definitions, and all have essentially the same pattern:

```
GIVEN some precondition(s) for a scenario
WHEN we exercise some method of a class
THEN some state change(s) or side effect(s) will occur that we can
confirm
```

In some cases, the preconditions can be complex or perhaps the state changes or side effects are complex. They might be so complex that we have to break them into multiple steps. What's important about this three-part pattern is how it disentangles the setup, execution, and expected results from each other. This model applies to a wide variety of tests. If we want to make sure the water's hot enough to make another cup of tea, we'll follow a similar set of steps:

- GIVEN a kettle of water on the stove
- AND the burner is off
- WHEN we flip open the lid on the kettle
- THEN we see steam escaping

This pattern is quite handy for making sure we have a clear setup and an observable result.

Let's say we need to write a function to compute an average of a list of numbers, excluding None values that might be in the sequence. We might start out like this:

```
def average(data: list[Optional[int]]) -> float:
    """

    GIVEN a list, data = [1, 2, None, 3, 4]
    WHEN we compute m = average(data)
    THEN the result, m, is 2.5
    """

    pass
```

We've roughed out a definition of the function, with a summary of how we think it should behave. The GIVEN step defines some data for our test case. The WHEN step defines precisely what we're going to be doing. Finally, the THEN step describes the expected results. The automated test tool can compare actual results against the stated expectation and report back if the test fails. We can then refine this into a separate test class or function using our preferred test framework. The ways unittest and pytest implement the concept differ slightly, but the core concept remains in both frameworks. Once that's done, the test should fail and we can start implementing the real code, given this test as a clear goal line we want to cross.

Some techniques that can help design test cases are **equivalence partitioning** and **boundary value analysis**. These help us decompose the domain of all possible inputs to a method or function into partitions. A common example is locating two partitions, "valid data" and "invalid data." Given the partitions, the values at the boundaries of the partitions become interesting values to use in test cases. See https://www.softwaretestinghelp.com/what-is-boundary-value-analysis-and-equivalence-partitioning/ for more information.

We'll start by looking at the built-in testing framework, unittest. It has a disadvantage of being a bit wordy and complicated looking. It has the advantage of being built-in and usable immediately; no further installs are required.

Unit testing with unittest

Let's start our exploration with Python's built-in test library. This library provides a common object-oriented interface for *unit tests*. The Python library for this is called, unsurprisingly, unittest. It provides several tools for creating and running unit tests, the most important being the TestCase class. (The names follow a Java naming style, so many of the method names don't look very Pythonic.) The TestCase class provides a set of methods that allow us to compare values, set up tests, and clean up when they have finished.

When we want to write a set of unit tests for a specific task, we create a subclass of TestCase and write individual methods to do the actual testing. These methods must all start with the name test. When this convention is followed, the tests automatically run as part of the test process. For simple examples, we can bundle the GIVEN, WHEN, and THEN concepts into the test method. Here's a very simple example:

```python
import unittest

class CheckNumbers(unittest.TestCase):
    def test_int_float(self) -> None:
        self.assertEqual(1, 1.0)

if __name__ == "__main__":
    unittest.main()
```

This code subclasses the TestCase class and adds a method that calls the TestCase.assertEqual() method. The GIVEN step is a pair of values, 1 and 1.0. The WHEN step is a kind of degenerate example because there's no new object created and no state change happening. The THEN step is the assertion that the two values will test as equal.

When we run the test case, this method will either succeed silently or it will raise an exception, depending on whether the two parameters are equal. If we run this code, the main function from unittest will give us the following output:

```
.
-----------------------------------------------------------
Ran 1 test in 0.000s

OK
```

Did you know that floats and integers can be compared as equal?

Let's add a failing test, as follows:

```python
    def test_str_float(self) -> None:
        self.assertEqual(1, "1")
```

The output of this code is more sinister, as integers and strings are not considered equal:

```
.F
===========================================================
FAIL: test_str_float (__main__.CheckNumbers)
-----------------------------------------------------------
```

```
Traceback (most recent call last):
  File "first_unittest.py", line 9, in test_str_float
    self.assertEqual(1, "1")
AssertionError: 1 != '1'


----------------------------------------------------------------

Ran 2 tests in 0.001s

FAILED (failures=1)
```

The dot on the first line indicates that the first test (the one we wrote before) passed successfully; the letter F after it shows that the second test failed. Then, at the end, it gives us some informative summary telling us how and where the test failed, along with a count of the number of failures.

Even the OS-level return code provides a useful summary. The return code is zero if all tests pass and non-zero if any tests fail. This helps when building continuous integration tools: if the unittest run fails, the proposed change shouldn't be permitted.

We can have as many test methods on one TestCase class as we like. As long as the method name begins with test, the test runner will execute each one as a separate, isolated test.

Each test should be completely independent of other tests.

Results or calculations from a test should have no impact on any other test.

In order to keep tests isolated from each other, we may have several tests with a common GIVEN, implemented by a common setUp() method. This suggests that we'll often have classes that are similar, and we'll need to use inheritance to design the tests so they can share features and still remain completely independent.

The key to writing good unit tests is keeping each test method as short as possible, testing a small unit of code with each test case. If our code does not seem to naturally break up into small, testable units, it's probably a sign that the code needs to be redesigned. The *Imitating objects using Mocks* section, later in this chapter, provides a way to isolate objects for testing purposes.

The unittest module imposes a requirement to structure tests as a class definition. This is – in some ways – a bit of overhead. The pytest package has slightly more clever test discovery and a slightly more flexible way to construct tests as functions instead of methods of a class. We'll look at pytest next.

Unit testing with pytest

We can create unit tests using a library that provides a common framework for the test scenarios, along with a test runner to execute the tests and log results. Unit tests focus on testing the least amount of code possible in any one test. The standard library includes the `unittest` package. While widely used, this package tends to force us to create a fair amount of boilerplate code for each test case.

One of the more popular alternatives to the standard library `unittest` is `pytest`. This has the advantage of letting us write smaller, and more clear, test cases. The lack of overheads makes this a desirable alternative.

Since `pytest` is not part of the standard library, you'll need to download and install it yourself. You can get it from the `pytest` home page at `https://docs.pytest.org/en/stable/`. You can install it with any of the installers.

In a Terminal window, activate the virtual environment you're working in. (If you're using venv, for example, you might use `python -m venv c:\path\to\myenv`.) Then, use an OS command like the following:

```
% python -m  pip install pytest
```

The Windows command should be the same as the command on macOS and Linux.

The `pytest` tool can use a substantially different test layout from the `unittest` module. It doesn't require test cases to be subclasses of `unittest.TestCase`. Instead, it takes advantage of the fact that Python functions are first-class objects and allows any properly named function to behave like a test. Rather than providing a bunch of custom methods for asserting equality, it uses the `assert` statement to verify results. This makes tests simpler, more readable, and, consequently, easier to maintain.

When we run `pytest`, it starts in the current folder and searches for any modules or sub packages with names beginning with the characters `test_`. (Including the `_` character.) If any functions in this module also start with `test` (no `_` required), they will be executed as individual tests. Furthermore, if there are any classes in the module whose name starts with `Test`, any methods on that class that start with `test_` will also be executed in the test environment.

It also searches in a folder named – unsurprisingly – `tests`. Because of this, it's common to have code broken up into two folders: the `src/` directory contains the working module, library, or application, while the `tests/` directory contains all the test cases.

Using the following code, let's port the simple `unittest` example we wrote earlier to pytest:

```
def test_int_float() -> None:
    assert 1 == 1.0
```

For the same test, we've written two lines of more readable code, in comparison to the six lines required in our first `unittest` example.

However, we are not forbidden from writing class-based tests. Classes can be useful for grouping related tests together or for tests that need to access related attributes or methods on the class. The following example shows an extended class with a passing and a failing test; we'll see that the error output is more comprehensive than that provided by the `unittest` module:

```
class TestNumbers:
    def test_int_float(self) -> None:
        assert 1 == 1.0

    def test_int_str(self) -> None:
        assert 1 == "1"
```

Notice that the class doesn't have to extend any special objects to be discovered as a test case (although pytest will run standard `unittest` `TestCases` just fine). If we run `python -m pytest tests/<filename>`, the output looks as follows:

```
% python -m pytest tests/test_with_pytest.py
========================= test session starts =========================
platform darwin -- Python 3.9.0, pytest-6.2.2, py-1.10.0, pluggy-0.13.1
rootdir: /path/to/ch_13
collected 2 items

tests/test_with_pytest.py .F                                    [100%]

============================== FAILURES ===============================
_____ TestNumbers.test_int_str _____

self = <test_with_pytest.TestNumbers object at 0x7fb557f1a370>

    def test_int_str(self) -> None:
>       assert 1 == "1"
E       AssertionError: assert 1 == "1"

tests/test_with_pytest.py:15: AssertionError
```

```
===================== short test summary info =====================
FAILED tests/test_with_pytest.py::TestNumbers::test_int_str - Asse...
===================== 1 failed, 1 passed in 0.07s =====================
```

The output starts with some useful information about the platform and interpreter. This can be useful for sharing or discussing bugs across disparate systems. The third line tells us the name of the file being tested (if there are multiple test modules picked up, they will all be displayed), followed by the familiar .F we saw in the unittest module; the . character indicates a passing test, while the letter F demonstrates a failure.

After all tests have run, the error output for each of them is displayed. It presents a summary of local variables (there is only one in this example: the self parameter passed into the function), the source code where the error occurred, and a summary of the error message. In addition, if an exception other than an AssertionError is raised, pytest will present us with a complete traceback, including source code references.

By default, pytest suppresses output from print() if the test is successful. This is useful for test debugging; when a test is failing, we can add print() statements to the test to check the values of specific variables and attributes as the test runs. If the test fails, these values are output to help with diagnosis. However, once the test is successful, the print() output is not displayed, and they are easily ignored. We don't have to clean up the test output by removing print(). If the tests ever fail again, due to future changes, the debugging output will be immediately available.

Interestingly, this use of the assert statement exposes a potential problem to *mypy*. When we use the assert statement, *mypy* can examine the types, and will alert us to a potential problem with assert 1 == "1". This code is unlikely to be right, and it will not only fail as a unit test, but will also fail a *mypy* inspection.

We've looked at how pytest supports the WHEN and THEN steps of a test using a function and the assert statement. Now, we need to look more closely at how to handle GIVEN steps. There are two ways to establish the GIVEN precondition for a test; we'll start with one that works for simple cases.

pytest's setup and teardown functions

pytest supports setup and teardown capabilities, similar to the methods used in unittest, but it provides even more flexibility. We'll discuss these general functions briefly; pytest provides us with a powerful fixtures capability, which we'll discuss in the next section.

If we are writing class-based tests, we can use two methods called `setup_method()` and `teardown_method()`. They are called before and after each test method in the class to perform setup and cleanup duties, respectively.

In addition, `pytest` provides other setup and teardown functions to give us more control over when preparation and cleanup code is executed. The `setup_class()` and `teardown_class()` methods are expected to be class methods; they accept a single argument representing the class in question (there is no `self` argument because there's no instance; instead, the class is provided). These methods are run by `pytest` when the class is initiated rather than on each test run.

Finally, we have the `setup_module()` and `teardown_module()` functions, which are run by `pytest` immediately before and after all tests (in functions or classes) in that module. These can be useful for *one-time* setup, such as creating a socket or database connection that will be used by all tests in the module. Be careful with this one, as it can accidentally introduce dependencies between tests if some object state isn't correctly cleaned up between tests.

That short description doesn't do a great job of explaining exactly when these methods are called, so let's look at an example that illustrates exactly when it happens:

```python
from __future__ import annotations
from typing import Any, Callable

def setup_module(module: Any) -> None:
    print(f"setting up MODULE {module.__name__}")

def teardown_module(module: Any) -> None:
    print(f"tearing down MODULE {module.__name__}")

def test_a_function() -> None:
    print("RUNNING TEST FUNCTION")

class BaseTest:
    @classmethod
    def setup_class(cls: type["BaseTest"]) -> None:
        print(f"setting up CLASS {cls.__name__}")

    @classmethod
    def teardown_class(cls: type["BaseTest"]) -> None:
        print(f"tearing down CLASS {cls.__name__}\n")
```

```
    def setup_method(self, method: Callable[[], None]) -> None:
        print(f"setting up METHOD {method.__name__}")

    def teardown_method(self, method: Callable[[], None]) -> None:
        print(f"tearing down METHOD {method.__name__}")

class TestClass1(BaseTest):
    def test_method_1(self) -> None:
        print("RUNNING METHOD 1-1")

    def test_method_2(self) -> None:
        print("RUNNING METHOD 1-2")

class TestClass2(BaseTest):
    def test_method_1(self) -> None:
        print("RUNNING METHOD 2-1")

    def test_method_2(self) -> None:
        print("RUNNING METHOD 2-2")
```

The sole purpose of the `BaseTest` class is to extract four methods that are otherwise identical to the two test classes, and use inheritance to reduce the amount of duplicate code. So, from the point of view of `pytest`, the two subclasses have not only two test methods each, but also two setup and two teardown methods (one at the class level, one at the method level).

If we run these tests using `pytest` with the `print()` function output suppression disabled (by passing the `-s` or `--capture=no` flag), they show us when the various functions are called in relation to the tests themselves:

```
% python -m pytest --capture=no tests/test_setup_teardown.py
=========================== test session starts
===========================
platform darwin -- Python 3.9.0, pytest-6.2.2, py-1.10.0, pluggy-0.13.1
rootdir: /.../ch_13
collected 5 items

tests/test_setup_teardown.py setting up MODULE test_setup_teardown
RUNNING TEST FUNCTION
.setting up CLASS TestClass1
setting up METHOD test_method_1
RUNNING METHOD 1-1
```

```
.tearing down METHOD test_method_1
setting up METHOD test_method_2
RUNNING METHOD 1-2
.tearing down METHOD test_method_2
tearing down CLASS TestClass1

setting up CLASS TestClass2
setting up METHOD test_method_1
RUNNING METHOD 2-1
.tearing down METHOD test_method_1
setting up METHOD test_method_2
RUNNING METHOD 2-2
.tearing down METHOD test_method_2
tearing down CLASS TestClass2

tearing down MODULE test_setup_teardown

=========================== 5 passed in 0.01s
===========================
```

The setup and teardown methods for the module as a whole are executed at the beginning and end of the session. Then, the lone module-level test function is run. Next, the setup method for the first class is executed, followed by the two tests for that class. These tests are each individually wrapped in separate `setup_method()` and `teardown_method()` calls. After the tests have executed, the teardown method on the class is called. The same sequence happens for the second class, before the `teardown_module()` method is finally called, exactly once.

While these function names provide a lot of options for testing, we'll often have setup conditions that are shared across multiple test scenarios. These can be reused via a composition-based design; pytest calls these designs "fixtures." We'll look at fixtures next.

pytest fixtures for setup and teardown

One of the most common uses for the various setup functions is to ensure the GIVEN step of a test is prepared. This often involves creating objects and making sure certain class or module variables have known values before a test method is run.

In addition to a set of special method names for a test class, pytest offers a completely different way of doing this, using what are known as **fixtures**. Fixtures are functions to build the GIVEN condition, prior to a test's WHEN step.

The pytest tool has a number of built-in fixtures, we can define fixtures in a configuration file and reuse them, and we can define unique fixtures as part of our tests. This allows us to separate configuration from the execution of tests, allowing fixtures to be used across multiple classes and modules.

Let's look at a class that does a few computations that we need to test:

```python
from typing import List, Optional

class StatsList(List[Optional[float]]):
    """Stats with None objects rejected"""

    def mean(self) -> float:
        clean = list(filter(None, self))
        return sum(clean) / len(clean)

    def median(self) -> float:
        clean = list(filter(None, self))
        if len(clean) % 2:
            return clean[len(clean) // 2]
        else:
            idx = len(clean) // 2
            return (clean[idx] + clean[idx - 1]) / 2

    def mode(self) -> list[float]:
        freqs: DefaultDict[float, int] = collections.defaultdict(int)
        for item in filter(None, self):
            freqs[item] += 1
        mode_freq = max(freqs.values())
        modes = [item
            for item, value in freqs.items()
            if value == mode_freq]
        return modes
```

This class extends the built-in list class to add three statistical summary methods, mean(), median(), and mode(). For each method, we need to have some set of data we can use; this configuration of a StatsList with known data is the fixture we'll be testing.

To use a fixture to create the GIVEN precondition, we add the fixture name as a parameter to our test function. When a test runs, the names of a test function's parameters will be located in the collection of fixtures, and those fixture-creating functions will be executed for us automatically.

For example, to test the StatsList class, we will want to repeatedly provide a list of valid integers. We can write our tests as follows:

```python
import pytest
from stats import StatsList


@pytest.fixture
def valid_stats() -> StatsList:
    return StatsList([1, 2, 2, 3, 3, 4])


def test_mean(valid_stats: StatsList) -> None:
    assert valid_stats.mean() == 2.5


def test_median(valid_stats: StatsList) -> None:
    assert valid_stats.median() == 2.5
    valid_stats.append(4)
    assert valid_stats.median() == 3


def test_mode(valid_stats: StatsList) -> None:
    assert valid_stats.mode() == [2, 3]
    valid_stats.remove(2)
    assert valid_stats.mode() == [3]
```

Each of the three test functions accepts a parameter named valid_stats; this parameter is created by pytest automatically calling the valid_stats function for us. The function was decorated with @pytest.fixture so it could be used in this special way by pytest.

And yes, the names must match. The **pytest** runtime looks for functions with the @fixture decorator that match the parameter name.

Fixtures can do a lot more than return simple objects. A request object can be passed into the fixture factory to provide extremely useful methods and attributes to modify the fixture's behavior. The module, cls, and function attributes of the request object allow us to see exactly which test is requesting the fixture. The config attribute of the request object allows us to check command-line arguments and a great deal of other configuration data.

If we implement the fixture as a generator, it can also run cleanup code after each test is run. This provides the equivalent of a teardown method on a per-fixture basis. We can use it to clean up files, close connections, empty lists, or reset queues. For unit tests, where items are isolated, a mock object is a better idea than performing a teardown on a stateful object. See the *Imitating objects using Mocks* section, later in this chapter, for a simpler approach that's ideal for unit testing.

For integration tests, we might want to test some code that creates, deletes, or updates files. We'll often use the pytest tmp_path fixture to write these to directories that can be deleted later, saving us from having to do a teardown in a test. While rarely needed for unit testing, a teardown is helpful for stopping subprocesses or removing database changes that are part of an integration test. We'll see this a little later in this section. First, let's look at a small example of a fixture with setup and teardown capabilities.

To get started on the concept of a fixture that does both setup and teardown, here's a little bit of code that makes a backup copy of a file and writes a new file with a checksum of an existing file:

```
import tarfile
from pathlib import Path
import hashlib

def checksum(source: Path, checksum_path: Path) -> None:
    if checksum_path.exists():
        backup = checksum_path.with_stem(f"(old) {checksum_path.stem}")
        backup.write_text(checksum_path.read_text())
    checksum = hashlib.sha256(source.read_bytes())
    checksum_path.write_text(f"{source.name} {checksum.hexdigest()}\n")
```

There are two scenarios:

- The source file exists; a new checksum is added to the directory
- The source file and a checksum file both exist; in this case, the old checksum is copied to a backup location and a new checksum is written

We won't test both scenarios, but we will show how a fixture can create – and then delete – the files required for a test sequence. We'll focus on the second scenario because it's more complex. We'll break the testing into two parts, starting with the fixture:

```
from __future__ import annotations
import checksum_writer
import pytest
from pathlib import Path
from typing import Iterator
import sys

@pytest.fixture
def working_directory(tmp_path: Path) -> Iterator[tuple[Path, Path]]:
    working = tmp_path / "some_directory"
```

```
        working.mkdir()
        source = working / "data.txt"
        source.write_bytes(b"Hello, world!\n")
        checksum = working / "checksum.txt"
        checksum.write_text("data.txt Old_Checksum")

    yield source, checksum

        checksum.unlink()
        source.unlink()
```

The `yield` statement is the secret for making this work. Our fixture is really a generator that produces one result and then waits for the next request of a value. The first result that's created follows a number of steps: a working directory is created, a source file is created in the working directory, and then an old checksum file is created. The `yield` statement provides two paths to the test and waits for the next request. This work completes the GIVEN condition setup for the test.

When the test function finishes, `pytest` will try to get one final item from this fixture. This lets the function unlink the files, removing them. There's no return value, which signals the end of the iteration. In addition to leveraging the generator protocol, the `working_directory` fixture relies on the `tmp_path` fixture of `pytest` to create a temporary working location for this test.

Here's the test that uses this `working_directory` fixture:

```
@pytest.mark.skipif(
    sys.version_info < (3, 9), reason="requires python3.9 feature")
def test_checksum(working_directory: tuple[Path, Path]) -> None:
    source_path, old_checksum_path = working_directory
    checksum_writer.checksum(source_path, old_checksum_path)
    backup = old_checksum_path.with_stem(
        f"(old) {old_checksum_path.stem}")
    assert backup.exists()
    assert old_checksum_path.exists()
    name, checksum = old_checksum_path.read_text().rstrip().split()
    assert name == source_path.name
    assert (
        checksum == "d9014c4624844aa5bac314773d6b689a"
        "d467fa4e1d1a50a1b8a99d5a95f72ff5"
    )
```

The test is marked with a `skipif` condition because this test won't work in Python 3.8; the `with_stem()` method of a `Path` isn't part of the older `pathlib` implementation. This assures us that the test is counted but noted as inappropriate for a specific Python release. We'll return to this in the *Skipping tests with pytest* section, later in this chapter.

The reference to the `working_directory` fixture forces `pytest` to execute the fixture function, providing the test scenario with two paths to be used as part of the GIVEN condition prior to testing. The WHEN step evaluates the `checksum_writer.checksum()` function with these two paths. The THEN steps are a sequence of `assert` statements to make sure the files are created with the expected values. After the test is run, `pytest` will use `next()` to get another item from the fixture; this action executes the code after the `yield`, resulting in a teardown after the test.

When testing components in isolation, we won't often need to use the teardown feature of a fixture. For integration tests, however, where a number of components are used in concert, it may be necessary to stop processes or remove files. In the next section, we'll look at a more sophisticated fixture. This kind of fixture can be used for more than a single test scenario.

More sophisticated fixtures

We can pass a `scope` parameter to create a fixture that lasts longer than one test. This is useful when setting up an expensive operation that can be reused by multiple tests, as long as the resource reuse doesn't break the atomic or unit nature of the test: one unit test should not rely on, and should not be impacted by, any other unit test.

As an example, we'll define a server that's part of a client-server application. We want multiple web servers to send their log messages to a single, centralized log. In addition to isolated unit tests, we need to have an integration test. This test makes sure the web server and the log collector properly integrate with each other. The integration test will need to start and stop this log collection server.

There are at least three levels to the testing pyramid. Unit tests are the foundation, exercising each component in isolation. Integration tests are the middle of the pyramid, making sure the components integrate properly with each other. A system test or acceptance test is the top of the pyramid, making sure the entire suite of software does what it claims.

We'll look at a log collection server that accepts messages and writes them to a single, central file. These messages are defined by the `logging` module's `SocketHandler`. We can depict each message as a block of bytes with a header and a payload. In the following table, we've shown the structure using slices of the block of bytes.

Here's how a message is defined:

Slice start	Slice stop	Meaning	Python module and function for parsing
0	4	payload_size	`struct.unpack(">L", bytes)`
4	payload_size+4	payload	`pickle.loads(bytes)`

The size of the header is shown as a four-byte slice, but the size shown here can be misleading. The header is formally and officially defined by a format string used by the `struct` module, `">L"`. The `struct` module has a function, `calcsize()`, to compute the actual length from the format string. Instead of using a literal 4, which is derived from the size of the `">L"` format, our code will derive the size, `size_bytes`, from the size format string, `size_format`. Using one proper source, `size_format`, for both pieces of information follows the design principle of Don't Repeat Yourself.

Here's an example buffer with a message from the `logging` module embedded in it. The first line is the header with the payload size, a four-byte value. The next lines are the pickled data for a log message:

```
b'\x00\x00\x02d' b'}q\x00(X\x04\x00\x00\x00nameq\x01X\x03\x00\x00\
x00appq\x02X\x03\x00\x00\x00msgq\x03X\x0b\x00\x00\x00Factorial
...
\x19X\n\x00\x00\x00MainThreadq\x1aX\x0b\x00\x00\x00processNameq\x1bX\
x0b\x00\x00\x00MainProcessq\x1cX\x07\x00\x00\x00processq\x1dMcQu.'
```

To read these messages, we'll need to collect the payload size bytes first. Then, we can consume the payload that follows. Here's the socket server that reads the headers and the payloads and writes them to a file:

```
from __future__ import annotations
import json
from pathlib import Path
import socketserver
from typing import TextIO
import pickle
import struct

class LogDataCatcher(socketserver.BaseRequestHandler):
    log_file: TextIO
    count: int = 0
    size_format = ">L"
    size_bytes = struct.calcsize(size_format)
```

```
    def handle(self) -> None:
        size_header_bytes = self.request.recv(LogDataCatcher.size_bytes)
        while size_header_bytes:
            payload_size = struct.unpack(
                LogDataCatcher.size_format, size_header_bytes)
            payload_bytes = self.request.recv(payload_size[0])
            payload = pickle.loads(payload_bytes)
            LogDataCatcher.count += 1
            self.log_file.write(json.dumps(payload) + "\n")
            try:
                size_header = self.request.recv(
                    LogDataCatcher.size_bytes)
            except (ConnectionResetError, BrokenPipeError):
                break

def main(host: str, port: int, target: Path) -> None:
    with target.open("w") as unified_log:
        LogDataCatcher.log_file = unified_log
        with socketserver.TCPServer(
                (host, port), LogDataCatcher) as server:
            server.serve_forever()
```

The socketserver.TCPServer object will listen for connection requests from a client. When a client connects, it will create an instance of the LogDataCatcher class and evaluate the handle() method of that object to gather data from that client. The handle() method decodes the size and payload with a two-step dance. First, it reads a few bytes to find the size of the payload. It uses struct.unpack() to decode those bytes into a useful number, payload_size, and then reads the given number of bytes to get the payload. The pickle.loads() will load a Python object from the payload bytes. This is serialized into JSON notation using json.dumps() and written to the open file. Once a message has been handled, we can try to read the next few bytes to see if there's more data waiting. This server will absorb messages from the client until the connection is dropped, leading to an error in the read and an exit from the while statement.

This log collection server can absorb logging messages from an application anywhere in a network. This example implementation is single-threaded, meaning it only handles one client at a time. We can use additional mixins to create a multithreaded server that will accept messages from multiple sources. In this example, we want to focus on testing a single application that depends on this server.

For completeness, here's the main script that starts the server running:

```
if __name__ == "__main__":
    HOST, PORT = "localhost", 18842
    main(HOST, PORT, Path("one.log"))
```

We provide a host IP address, a port number, and the file to which we want all the messages written. As a practical matter, we might consider using the argparse module and the os.environ dictionary to provide these values to the application. For now, we've hardcoded them.

Here's the remote_logging_app.py application, which transmits log records to the log-catching server:

```
from __future__ import annotations
import logging
import logging.handlers
import time
import sys
from math import factorial

logger = logging.getLogger("app")

def work(i: int) -> int:
    logger.info("Factorial %d", i)
    f = factorial(i)
    logger.info("Factorial(%d) = %d", i, f)
    return f

if __name__ == "__main__":
    HOST, PORT = "localhost", 18842
    socket_handler = logging.handlers.SocketHandler(HOST, PORT)
    stream_handler = logging.StreamHandler(sys.stderr)
    logging.basicConfig(
        handlers=[socket_handler, stream_handler],
        level=logging.INFO)

    for i in range(10):
        work(i)

    logging.shutdown()
```

This application creates two logging handlers. The `SocketHandler` instance will open a socket on the given server and port number, and start writing bytes. The bytes will include headers and payloads. The `StreamHandler` instance will write to the terminal window; this is the default log handler that we would get if we didn't create any special handlers. We configure our logger with both handlers so each log message goes both to our console and to the stream server collecting the messages. The actual work? A little bit of math to compute the factorial of a number. Each time we run this application, it should blast out 20 log messages.

To test the integrated client and server, we need to start the server in a separate process. We don't want to start and stop it many times (that takes a while), so we will start it once and use it in multiple tests. We'll break this into two sections, starting with the two fixtures:

```python
from __future__ import annotations
import subprocess
import signal
import time
import pytest
import logging
import sys
import remote_logging_app
from typing import Iterator, Any


@pytest.fixture(scope="session")
def log_catcher() -> Iterator[None]:
    print("loading server")
    p = subprocess.Popen(
        ["python3", "src/log_catcher.py"],
        stdout=subprocess.PIPE,
        stderr=subprocess.STDOUT,
        text=True,
    )
    time.sleep(0.25)

    yield

    p.terminate()
    p.wait()
    if p.stdout:
        print(p.stdout.read())
    assert (
        p.returncode == -signal.SIGTERM.value
```

```
    ), f"Error in watcher, returncode={p.returncode}"

@pytest.fixture
def logging_config() -> Iterator[None]:
    HOST, PORT = "localhost", 18842
    socket_handler = logging.handlers.SocketHandler(HOST, PORT)
    remote_logging_app.logger.addHandler(socket_handler)
    yield
    socket_handler.close()
    remote_logging_app.logger.removeHandler(socket_handler)
```

The `log_catcher` fixture will start the `log_catcher.py` server as a subprocess. This has a scope set to `"session"` in the `@fixture` decorator, which means it's done once for the whole testing session. The scope can be one of the strings `"function"`, `"class"`, `"module"`, `"package"`, or `"session"`, providing distinct places where the fixture is created and reused. The startup involves a tiny pause (250 ms) to make sure the other process has started properly. When this fixture reaches the `yield` statement, this part of the GIVEN test setup is done.

The `logging_config` fixture will tweak the log configuration for the `remote_logging_app` module that's being tested. When we look at the `work()` function in the `remote_logging_app.py` module, we can see that it expects a module-level `logger` object. This test fixture creates a `SocketHandler` object, adds this to the `logger`, and then executes the `yield` statement.

Once both of these fixtures have contributed to the GIVEN condition, we can define test cases that contain the WHEN steps. Here are two examples for two similar scenarios:

```
def test_1(log_catcher: None, logging_config: None) -> None:
    for i in range(10):
        r = remote_logging_app.work(i)

def test_2(log_catcher: None, logging_config: None) -> None:
    for i in range(1, 10):
        r = remote_logging_app.work(52 * i)
```

These two scenarios both require the two fixtures. The `log_catcher` fixture, with a session scope, is prepared once and used for both tests. The `logging_config` fixture, however, has default scope, which means it's prepared for each test function.

The type hint of None follows the definition of the fixture as Iterator[None]. There's no value returned in the yield statement. For these tests, the setup operation is preparing the overall runtime environment by starting a process.

When a test function finishes, the logging_config fixture resumes after the yield statement. (This fixture is an iterator, and the next() function is used to try to get a second value from it.) This closes and removes the handler, cleanly breaking the network connection with the log catcher process.

When testing finishes overall, the log_catcher fixture can then terminate the child process. To help with debugging, we print any output. To be sure the test worked, we check the OS return code. Because the process was terminated (via p.terminate()), the return code should be the signal.SIGTERM value. Other return code values, particularly a return code of one, mean the log catcher crashed and the test failed.

We've omitted a detailed THEN check, but it would also be part of the log_catcher fixture. The existing assert statement makes sure the log catcher terminated with the expected return code. Once the catcher in the sky has finished absorbing log messages, this fixture should also read the log file to be sure it contains the expected entries for the two scenarios.

Fixtures can also be parameterized. We can use a decorator like @pytest. fixture(params=[some, list, of, values]) to create multiple copies of a fixture, which will lead to multiple tests with each of the parameter values.

The sophistication of pytest fixtures makes them very handy for a wide variety of test setup and teardown requirements. Earlier in this section, we hinted at ways to mark tests as inappropriate for a particular version of Python. In the next section, we'll look at how we can mark tests to be skipped.

Skipping tests with pytest

It is sometimes necessary to skip tests in pytest, for a similar variety of reasons: the code being tested hasn't been written yet, the test only runs on certain interpreters or operating systems, or the test is time-consuming and should only be run under certain circumstances. In the previous section, one of our tests would not work in Python 3.8, and needed to be skipped.

One way to skip tests is by using the pytest.skip() function. It accepts a single argument: a string describing why it has been skipped. This function can be called anywhere. If we call it inside a test function, the test will be skipped. If we call it at the module level, all the tests in that module will be skipped. If we call it inside a fixture, all tests that reference the fixture will be skipped.

Of course, in all these locations, it is often only desirable to skip tests if certain conditions have or have not been met. Since we can execute the `skip()` function at any place in Python code, we can execute it inside an `if` statement. We may write a test that looks as follows:

```python
import sys
import pytest


def test_simple_skip() -> None:
    if sys.platform != "ios":
        pytest.skip("Test works only on Pythonista for ios")

    import location  # type: ignore [import]

    img = location.render_map_snapshot(36.8508, -76.2859)
    assert img is not None
```

This test will skip on most operating systems. It should run on the Pythonista port of Python for iOS. It shows how we can skip a scenario conditionally, and since the `if` statement can check any valid conditional, we have a lot of power over when tests are skipped. Often, we check `sys.version_info` to check the Python interpreter version, `sys.platform` to check the operating system, or `some_library.__version__` to check whether we have a recent enough version of a given module.

Since skipping an individual test method or function based on a condition is one of the most common uses of test skipping, `pytest` provides a convenient decorator that allows us to do this in one line. The decorator accepts a single string, which can contain any executable Python code that evaluates to a Boolean value. For example, the following test will only run on Python 3.9 or higher:

```python
import pytest
import sys


@pytest.mark.skipif(
    sys.version_info < (3, 9),
    reason="requires 3.9, Path.removeprefix()"
)
def test_feature_python39() -> None:
    file_name = "(old) myfile.dat"
    assert file_name.removeprefix("(old) ") == "myfile.dat"
```

The `pytest.mark.xfail` decorator marks a test as expected to fail. If the test is successful, it will be recorded as a failure (it failed to fail!). If it fails, it will be reported as expected behavior. In the case of `xfail`, the conditional argument is optional. If it is not supplied, the test will be marked as expected to fail under all conditions.

The `pytest` framework has a ton of other features besides those described here, and the developers are constantly adding innovative new ways to make your testing experience more enjoyable. They have thorough documentation on their website at `https://docs.pytest.org/`.

 The `pytest` tool can find and run tests defined using the standard `unittest` library, in addition to its own testing infrastructure. This means that if you want to migrate from `unittest` to `pytest`, you don't have to rewrite all your old tests.

We've looked at using a fixture to set up and tear down a complex environment for testing. This is helpful for some integration tests, but a better approach may be to imitate an expensive object or a risky operation. Additionally, any kind of teardown operation is inappropriate for unit tests. A unit test isolates each software component as a separate unit to be tested. This means we'll often replace all of the interface objects with imitations, called "mocks," to isolate the unit being tested. Next, we'll turn to creating mock objects to isolate units and imitate expensive resources.

Imitating objects using Mocks

Isolated problems are easier to diagnose and solve. Figuring out why a gasoline car won't start can be tricky because there are so many interrelated parts. If a test fails, uncovering all the interrelationships makes diagnosis of the problem difficult. We often want to isolate items by providing simplified imitations. It turns out there are two reasons to replace perfectly good code with imitation (or "mock") objects:

- The most common case is to isolate a unit under test. We want to create collaborating classes and functions so we can test one unknown component in an environment of known, trusted test fixtures.
- Sometimes, we want to test code that requires an object that is either expensive or risky to use. Things like shared databases, filesystems, and cloud infrastructures can be very expensive to set up and tear down for testing.

In some cases, this may lead to designing an API to have a testable interface. Designing for testability often means designing a more usable interface, too. In particular, we have to expose assumptions about collaborating classes so we can inject a mock object instead of an instance of an actual application class.

For example, imagine we have some code that keeps track of flight statuses in an external key-value store (such as redis or memcache), such that we can store the timestamp and the most recent status. The implementation will require the redis client; it's not needed to write unit tests. The client can be installed with the python -m pip install redis command like this:

```
% python -m pip install redis
Collecting redis
  Downloading redis-3.5.3-py2.py3-none-any.whl (72 kB)
     |████████████████████████████████| 72 kB 1.1 MB/s
Installing collected packages: redis
Successfully installed redis-3.5.3
```

If you want to run this with a real redis server, you'll also need to download and install redis. This can be done as follows:

1. Download the Docker desktop to help manage this application. See https:// www.docker.com/products/docker-desktop.

2. Use the docker pull redis command from a Terminal window to download a redis server image. This image can be used to build a running Docker container.

3. You can then start the server with docker run -p 6379:6379 redis. This will start a container running the redis image. Then you can use this for integration testing.

An alternative that avoids **docker** involves a number of platform-specific steps. See https://redislabs.com/ebook/appendix-a/ for a number of installation scenarios. The examples that follow will assume **docker** is being used; the minor changes that are required to switch to a native installation of redis are left as an exercise for the reader.

Here's some code that saves status in a redis cache server:

```
from __future__ import annotations
import datetime
from enum import Enum
import redis
```

```python
class Status(str, Enum):
    CANCELLED = "CANCELLED"
    DELAYED = "DELAYED"
    ON_TIME = "ON TIME"

class FlightStatusTracker:
    def __init__(self) -> None:
        self.redis = redis.Redis(host="127.0.0.1", port=6379, db=0)

    def change_status(self, flight: str, status: Status) -> None:
        if not isinstance(status, Status):
            raise ValueError(f"{status!r} is not a valid Status")
        key = f"flightno:{flight}"
        now = datetime.datetime.now(tz=datetime.timezone.utc)
        value = f"{now.isoformat()}|{status.value}"
        self.redis.set(key, value)

    def get_status(self, flight: str) -> tuple[datetime.datetime, Status]:
        key = f"flightno:{flight}"
        value = self.redis.get(key).decode("utf-8")
        text_timestamp, text_status = value.split("|")
        timestamp = datetime.datetime.fromisoformat(text_timestamp)
        status = Status(text_status)
        return timestamp, status
```

The Status class defines an enumeration of four string values. We've provided symbolic names like Status.CANCELLED so that we can have a finite, bounded domain of valid status values. The actual values stored in the database will be strings like "CANCELLED" that – for now – happen to match the symbols we'll be using in the application. In the future, the domain of values may expand or change, but we'd like to keep our application's symbolic names separate from the strings that appear in the database. It's common to use numeric codes with Enum, but they can be difficult to remember.

There are a lot of things we ought to test for in the change_status() method. We check to be sure the status argument value really is a valid instance of the Status enumeration, but we could do more. We should check that it raises the appropriate error if the flight argument value isn't sensible. More importantly, we need a test to prove that the key and value have the correct formatting when the set() method is called on the redis object.

One thing we don't have to check in our unit tests, however, is that the redis object is storing the data properly. This is something that absolutely should be tested in integration or application testing, but at the unit test level, we can assume that the py-redis developers have tested their code and that this method does what we want it to. As a rule, unit tests should be self-contained; the unit under test should be isolated from outside resources, such as a running Redis instance.

Instead of integrating with a Redis server, we only need to test that the set() method was called the appropriate number of times and with the appropriate arguments. We can use Mock() objects in our tests to replace the troublesome method with an object we can introspect. The following example illustrates the use of Mock:

```python
import datetime
import flight_status_redis
from unittest.mock import Mock, patch, call
import pytest


@pytest.fixture
def mock_redis() -> Mock:
    mock_redis_instance = Mock(set=Mock(return_value=True))
    return mock_redis_instance


@pytest.fixture
def tracker(
    monkeypatch: pytest.MonkeyPatch, mock_redis: Mock
) -> flight_status_redis.FlightStatusTracker:
    fst = flight_status_redis.FlightStatusTracker()
    monkeypatch.setattr(fst, "redis", mock_redis)
    return fst



def test_monkeypatch_class(
    tracker: flight_status_redis.FlightStatusTracker, mock_redis: Mock
) -> None:
    with pytest.raises(ValueError) as ex:
        tracker.change_status("AC101", "lost")
    assert ex.value.args[0] == "'lost' is not a valid Status"
    assert mock_redis.set.call_count == 0
```

This test uses the raises() context manager to make sure the correct exception is raised when an inappropriate argument is passed in. In addition, it creates a Mock object for the redis instance that the FlightStatusTracker will use.

The mock object contains an attribute, `set`, which is a mock method that will always return `True`. The test, however, makes sure the `redis.set()` method is never called. If it is, it means there is a bug in our exception handling code.

Note the navigation into the mock object. We use `mock_redis.set` to examine the mocked `set()` method of a `Mock` object created by the `mock_redis` fixture. The `call_count` is an attribute that all `Mock` objects maintain.

While we can use code like `flt.redis = mock_redis` to replace a real object with a `Mock` object during a test, there is potential for problems. Simply replacing a value or even replacing a class method can only work for objects that are destroyed and created for each test function. If we need to patch items at the module level, the module isn't going to be reimported. A much more general solution is to use a patcher to inject a `Mock` object temporarily. In this example, we used the `monkeypatch` fixture of `pytest` to make a temporary change to the `FlightStatusTracker` object. A `monkeypatch` has its own automatic teardown at the end of a test, allowing us to use monkeypatched modules and classes without breaking other tests.

This test case will be flagged by *mypy*. The *mypy* tool will object to using a string argument value for the status parameter of the `change_status()` function; this clearly must be an instance of the `Status` enumeration. A special comment can be added to silence the *mypy* argument type check, `# type: ignore [arg-type]`.

Additional patching techniques

In some cases, we only need to inject a special function or method for the duration of a single test. We may not really be creating a sophisticated `Mock` object that's used in multiple tests. We may only need a small `Mock` for a single test. In this case, we may not need to use all the features of the `monkeypatch` fixture, either. For example, if we want to test the timestamp formatting in the `Mock` method, we need to know exactly what `datetime.datetime.now()` is going to return. However, this value changes from run to run. We need some way to pin it to a specific datetime value so we can test it deterministically.

Temporarily setting a library function to a specific value is one place where patching is essential. In addition to the `monkeypatch` fixture, the `unittest.mock` library provides a `patch` context manager. This context manager allows us to replace attributes on existing libraries with mock objects. When the context manager exits, the original attribute is automatically restored so as not to impact other test cases. Here's an example:

```
def test_patch_class(
    tracker: flight_status_redis.FlightStatusTracker, mock_redis: Mock
) -> None:
```

```
fake_now = datetime.datetime(2020, 10, 26, 23, 24, 25)
utc = datetime.timezone.utc
with patch("flight_status_redis.datetime") as mock_datetime:
    mock_datetime.datetime = Mock(now=Mock(return_value=fake_now))
    mock_datetime.timezone = Mock(utc=utc)
    tracker.change_status(
    "AC101", flight_status_redis.Status.ON_TIME)
mock_datetime.datetime.now.assert_called_once_with(tz=utc)
expected = f"2020-10-26T23:24:25|ON TIME"
mock_redis.set.assert_called_once_with("flightno:AC101", expected)
```

We don't want our test results to depend on the computer's clock, so we built the fake_now object with a specific date and time we can expect to see in our test results. This kind of replacement is very common in unit tests.

The patch() context manager returns a Mock object that was used to replace some other object. In this case, the object being replaced is the entire datetime module inside the flight_status_redis module. When we assigned mock_datetime.datetime, we replaced the datetime class inside the mocked datetime module with our own Mock object; this new Mock defines one attribute, now. Because the utcnow attribute is a Mock that returns a value, it behaves like a method and returns a fixed, known value, fake_now. When the interpreter exits the patch context manager, the original datetime functionality is restored.

After calling our change_status() method with known values, we use the assert_called_once_with() method of the Mock object to ensure that the now() function was indeed called exactly once with the expected arguments (no arguments, in this case). We also use the assert_called_once_with() method on the Mock redis.set method to make sure it called with arguments that were formatted as we expected them to be. In addition to the "called once with," we can also check the exact list of mock calls that were made. This sequence is available in the mock_calls attribute of a Mock object.

Mocking dates so you can have deterministic test results is a common patching scenario. The technique applies to any stateful object, but is particularly important for external resources (like the clock) that exist outside our application.

For the special case of datetime and time, packages like freezegun can simplify the monkeypatching required so that a known, fixed date is available.

The patches we made in this example are intentionally sweeping. We replaced the entire `datetime` module with a `Mock` object. This will tend to expose unexpected uses of datetime features; if any method not specifically mocked (like the `now()` method was mocked) gets used, it will return `Mock` objects that are likely to crash code under test.

The previous example also shows how testability needs to guide our API design. The `tracker` fixture has an interesting problem: it creates a `FlightStatusTracker` object, which constructs a Redis connection. After the Redis connection is built, we replace it. When we run tests for this code, however, we will discover that each test will create an unused Redis connection. Some tests may fail if there is no Redis server running. Because this test requires external resources, it's not a proper unit test. There are two possible layers of failure: the code doesn't work, or the unit tests don't work because of some hidden external dependency. This can become a nightmare to sort out.

We could solve this problem by mocking the `redis.Redis` class. A `Mock` for this class can return a mock instance in a `setUp` method. A better idea, however, might be to rethink our implementation more fundamentally. Instead of constructing the `redis` instance inside `__init__`, we should allow the user to pass one in, as in the following example:

```
def __init__(
        self,
        redis_instance: Optional[redis.Connection] = None
) -> None:
    self.redis = (
        redis_instance
        if redis_instance
        else redis.Redis(host="127.0.0.1", port=6379, db=0)
    )
```

This allows us to pass a connection in when we are testing so that the `Redis` method never gets constructed. Additionally, it allows any client code that talks to `FlightStatusTracker` to pass in their own `redis` instance. There are a variety of reasons they might want to do this: they may have already constructed one for other parts of their code; they may have created an optimized implementation of the `redis` API; perhaps they have one that logs metrics to their internal monitoring systems. By writing a unit test, we've uncovered a use case that makes our API more flexible from the start, rather than waiting for clients to demand we support their exotic needs.

This has been a brief introduction to the wonders of mocking code. Mock objects have been part of the standard unittest library since Python 3.3. As you see from these examples, they can also be used with pytest and other test frameworks. Mock objects have other, more advanced features that you may need to take advantage of as your code becomes more complicated. For example, you can use the spec argument to invite a mock to imitate an existing class, so that it raises an error if code tries to access an attribute that does not exist on the imitated class. You can also construct mock methods that return different arguments each time they are called by passing a list as the side_effect argument. The side_effect parameter is quite versatile; you can also use it to execute arbitrary functions when the mock is called or to raise an exception.

The point of unit testing is to be sure that each "unit" works in isolation. Often, a unit is an individual class, and we'll need to mock the collaborators. In some cases, there's a composition of classes or a Façade for which a number of application classes can be tested together as a "unit." There's a clear boundary, however, when applying mocks inappropriately. If we need to look inside some external module or class (one we didn't write) to see how to mock its dependencies, we've taken a step too far.

Don't examine the implementation details of classes outside your application to see how to mock their collaborators; instead, mock the entire class you depend on.

This generally leads to providing a mock for an entire database or external API.

We can extend this idea of imitating objects one step further. There's a specialized fixture we use when we want to ensure data has been left untouched. We'll look at this next.

The sentinel object

In many designs, we'll have a class with attribute values that can be provided as parameters to other objects, without really doing any processing on those objects. For example, we may provide a Path object to a class, and the class then provides this Path object to an OS function; the class we designed doesn't do anything more than save the object. From a unit testing perspective, the object is "opaque" to the class we're testing – the class we're writing doesn't look inside the object at state or methods.

The unittest.mock module provides a handy object, the sentinel, that can be used to create opaque objects that we can use in test cases to be sure that the application stored and forwarded the object untouched.

Here's a class, `FileChecksum`, that saves an object computed by the `sha256()` function of the `hashlib` module:

```
class FileChecksum:
    def __init__(self, source: Path) -> None:
        self.source = source
        self.checksum = hashlib.sha256(source.read_bytes())
```

We can isolate this code from the other modules for unit testing purposes. We'll create a `Mock` for the `hashlib` module, and we'll use a `sentinel` for the result:

```
from unittest.mock import Mock, sentinel


@pytest.fixture
def mock_hashlib(monkeypatch) -> Mock:
    mocked_hashlib = Mock(sha256=Mock(return_value=sentinel.checksum))
    monkeypatch.setattr(checksum_writer, "hashlib", mocked_hashlib)
    return mocked_hashlib


def test_file_checksum(mock_hashlib, tmp_path) -> None:
    source_file = tmp_path / "some_file"
    source_file.write_text("")
    cw = checksum_writer.FileChecksum(source_file)
    assert cw.source == source_file
    assert cw.checksum == sentinel.checksum
```

Our `mocked_hashlib` object provides a method, `sha256`, that returns the unique `sentinel.checksum` object. This is an object, created by the `sentinel` object, with very few methods or attributes. Any attribute name can be created as a unique object; we've chosen "checksum" here. The resulting object is designed for equality checks and nothing else. A `sentinel` in a test case is a way to be sure the `FileChecksum` class doesn't do anything wrong or unexpected with the objects it was given.

The test case creates a `FileChecksum` object. The test confirms that the file was the provided argument value, `source_file`. The test also confirms that the checksum matched the original `sentinel` object. This confirms that the `FileChecksum` instance stored the checksum results properly and presented the result as the value of the `checksum` attribute.

If we change the implementation of the `FileChecksum` class to – for example – use properties instead of direct access to the attribute, the test will confirm the checksum was treated as an opaque object that came from the `hashlib.sha256()` function and was not processed in any other way.

We've looked at two unit testing frameworks: the built-in `unittest` package and the external `pytest` package. They both provide ways for us to write clear, simple tests that can confirm that our application works. It's important to have a clear objective defining the required amount of testing. Python has an easy-to-use coverage package that gives us one objective measure of test quality.

How much testing is enough?

We've already established that untested code is broken code. But how can we tell how well our code is tested? How do we know how much of our code is actually being tested and how much is broken? The first question is the more important one, but it's hard to answer. Even if we know we have tested every line of code in our application, we do not know that we have tested it properly. For example, if we write a `stats` test that only checks what happens when we provide a list of integers, it may still fail spectacularly if used on a list of floats, strings, or self-made objects. The onus of designing complete test suites still lies with the programmer.

The second question – how much of our code is actually being tested – is easy to verify. **Code coverage** is a count of the number of lines of code that are executed by a program. From the number of lines that are in the program as a whole, we know what percentage of the code was really tested or covered. If we additionally have an indicator that tells us which lines were not tested, we can more easily write new tests to ensure those lines are less likely to harbor problems.

The most popular tool for testing code coverage is called, memorably enough, `coverage.py`. It can be installed like most other third-party libraries, using the `python -m pip install coverage` command.

We don't have space to cover all the details of the coverage API, so we'll just look at a few typical examples. If we have a Python script that runs all our unit tests for us (this could be using `unittest.main`, `unittest discover`, or `pytest`), we can use the following command to perform coverage analysis for a specific unit test file:

```
% export PYTHONPATH=$(pwd)/src:$PYTHONPATH
% coverage run -m pytest tests/test_coverage.py
```

This command will create a file named `.coverage`, which holds the data from the run.

Windows Powershell users can do the following:

```
> $ENV:PYTHONPATH = "$pwd\src" + ";" + $PYTHONPATH
> coverage run -m pytest tests/test_coverage.py
```

We can now use the `coverage report` command to get an analysis of the code coverage:

```
% coverage report
```

The resulting output should be as follows:

```
Name                       Stmts   Miss  Cover
--------------------------------------------
src/stats.py                  19     11    42%
tests/test_coverage.py         7      0   100%
--------------------------------------------
TOTAL                         26     11    58%
```

This report lists the files that were executed (our unit test and the module it imported), the number of lines of code in each file, and the number of lines of code that were executed by the test. The two numbers are then combined to show the amount of code coverage. Not surprisingly, the entire test was executed, but only a fraction of the `stats` module was exercised.

If we pass the `-m` option to the `report` command, it will add a column that identifies the lines that are missing from the test execution. The output looks as follows:

```
Name                       Stmts   Miss  Cover   Missing
--------------------------------------------------------
src/stats.py                  19     11    42%   18-23, 26-31
tests/test_coverage.py         7      0   100%
--------------------------------------------------------
TOTAL                         26     11    58%
```

The ranges of lines listed here identify the lines in the `stats` module that were not executed during the test run.

The example code uses the same `stats` module we created earlier in this chapter. However, it deliberately uses a single test that fails to test a lot of code in the file. Here's the test:

```python
import pytest
from stats import StatsList


@pytest.fixture
def valid_stats() -> StatsList:
    return StatsList([1, 2, 2, 3, 3, 4])


def test_mean(valid_stats: StatsList) -> None:
    assert valid_stats.mean() == 2.5
```

This test doesn't test the median or mode functions, which correspond to the line numbers that the coverage output told us were missing.

The textual report provides sufficient information, but if we use the `coverage html` command, we can get an even more useful interactive HTML report, which we can view in a web browser. The interactive report has a number of useful filters we can enable. The web page even highlights which lines in the source code were and were not tested.

Here's how it looks:

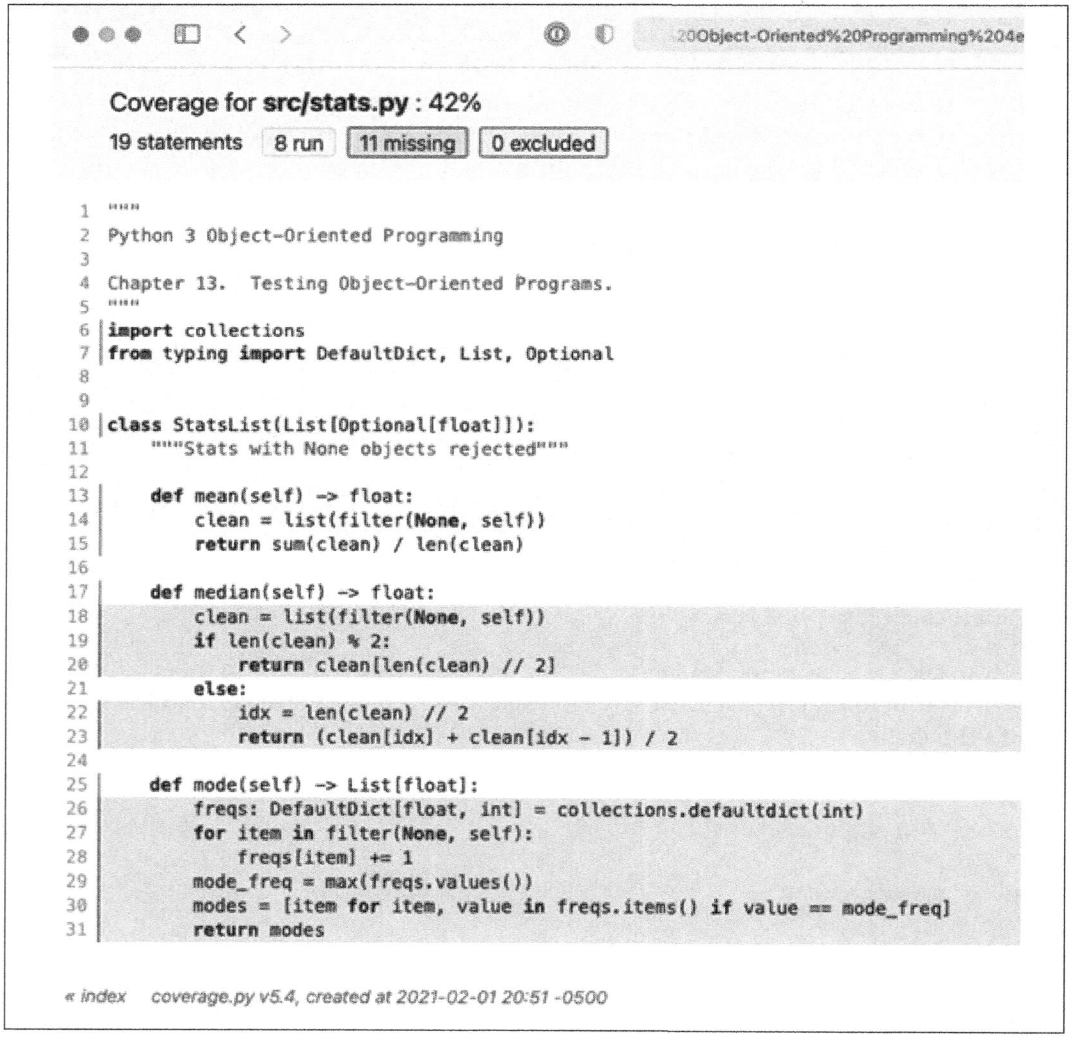

Figure 13.1: Interactive HTML coverage report

We created the HTML report using the `coverage` module with `pytest`. To do this, we previously installed the `pytest` plugin for code coverage, using `python -m pip install pytest-cov`. The plugin adds several command-line options to `pytest`, the most useful being `--cover-report`, which can be set to `html`, `report`, or `annotate` (the latter actually modifies the original source code to highlight any lines that were not covered).

It can be helpful to include more than the `src` directory tree in coverage analysis. A large project may have a complex tests directory, including additional tools and supporting libraries. As the project evolves, there may be some test or support code that's obsolete, but hasn't been cleaned up yet.

Unfortunately, if we could somehow run a coverage report on this section of the chapter, we'd find that we have not covered most of what there is to know about code coverage! It is possible to use the coverage API to manage code coverage from within our own programs (or test suites), and `coverage.py` accepts numerous configuration options that we haven't touched on. We also haven't discussed the difference between statement coverage and branch coverage (the latter is much more useful and is the default in recent versions of `coverage.py`), or other styles of code coverage.

Bear in mind that while 100 percent code coverage is a goal that we should all strive for, 100 percent coverage is not enough! Just because a statement was tested does not mean that it was tested properly for all possible inputs. The boundary value analysis technique includes looking at five values to bracket the edge cases: a value below the minimum, the minimum, in the middle somewhere, the maximum, and a value above the maximum. For non-numeric types, there may not be a tidy range, but the advice can be adapted to other data structures. For lists and mappings, for example, this advice often suggests testing with empty lists or mapping with unexpected keys. The Hypothesis package (`https://pypi.org/project/hypothesis/`) can help with more sophisticated test cases.

It's difficult to emphasize how important testing is. The test-driven development approach encourages us to describe our software via visible, testable objectives. We have to decompose complex problems into discrete, testable solutions. It's not uncommon to have more lines of test code than actual application code. A short but confusing algorithm is sometimes best explained through examples, and each example should be a test case.

Testing and development

One of the many ways these unit tests can help is when debugging application problems. When each unit seems to work in isolation, any remaining problems will often be the result of an improperly used interface between components. When searching for the root cause of a problem, a suite of passing tests acts as a set of signposts, directing the developer into the wilderness of untested features in the borderlands between components.

When a problem is found, the cause is often one of the following:

- Someone writing a new class failed to understand an interface with an existing class and used it incorrectly. This indicates a need for a new unit test to reflect the right way to use the interface. This new test should cause the new code to fail its expanded test suite. An integration test is also helpful, but not as important as the new unit test focused on interface details.

- The interface was not spelled out in enough detail, and both parties using the interface need to reach an agreement on how the interface should be used. In this case, both sides of the interface will need additional unit tests to show what the interface should be. Both classes should fail these new unit tests; they can then be fixed. Additionally, an integration test can be used to confirm that the two classes agree.

The idea here is to use test cases to drive the development process. A "bug" or an "incident" needs to be translated into a test case that fails. Once we have a concrete expression of a problem in the form of a test case, we can create or revise software until all the tests pass.

If bugs do occur, we'll often follow a test-driven plan, as follows:

1. Write a test (or multiple tests) that duplicates or proves the bug in question is occurring. This test will, of course, fail. In more complex applications, it may be difficult to find the exact steps to recreate a bug in an isolated unit of code; finding this is valuable work, since it requires knowledge of the software, and captures the knowledge as a test scenario.

2. Then, write the code to make the tests stop failing. If the tests were comprehensive, the bug will be fixed, and we will know we didn't break something new while attempting to fix something.

Another benefit of test-driven development is the value of the test cases for further enhancement. Once the tests have been written, we can improve our code as much as we like and be confident that our changes didn't break anything we have been testing for. Furthermore, we know exactly when our refactor is finished: when the tests all pass.

Of course, our tests may not comprehensively test everything we need them to; maintenance or code refactoring can still cause undiagnosed bugs that don't show up in testing. Automated tests are not foolproof. As E. W. Dijkstra said, "Program testing can be used to show the presence of bugs, but never to show their absence!" We need to have good reasons why our algorithm is correct, as well as test cases to show that it doesn't have any problems.

Case study

We'll return to some material from an earlier chapter and apply some careful testing to be sure we've got a good, workable implementation. Back in *Chapter 3*, *When Objects Are Alike*, we looked at the distance computations that are part of the *k*-nearest neighbors classifier. In that chapter, we looked at several computations that produced slightly different results:

- **Euclidean distance**: This is the direct line from one sample to another.
- **Manhattan distance**: This follows streets-and-avenues around a grid (like the city of Manhattan), adding up the steps required along a series of straight-line paths.
- **Chebyshev distance**: This is the largest of the streets-and-avenues distances.
- **Sorensen distance**: This is a variation of the Manhattan distance that weights nearby steps more heavily than distant steps. It tends to magnify small distances, making more subtle discriminations.

These algorithms all produce distinct results from the same inputs; they all involve complex-looking math, and they all need to be tested in isolation to ensure we have implemented them correctly. We'll start with unit tests of the distances.

Unit testing the distance classes

We need to create some test cases for each distance computation algorithm. When we look at the various equations, we can see that there are four pairs of relevant values from two samples: the sepal length and width, and the petal length and width. To be extremely thorough, we could create at least 16 distinct cases for each algorithm:

- **Case 0**: All four values are the same; the distance should be zero.
- **Cases 1-4**: One of the four values is different between the two samples. For example, a test sample might have measurements of ("sepal_length": 5.1, "sepal_width": 3.5, "petal_length": 1.4, "petal_width": 0.2), where as a training sample might have measurements of ("sepal_length": 5.2, "sepal_width": 3.5, "petal_length": 1.4, "petal_width": 0.2); only one of these values is distinct.

- **Cases 5-10**: A pair of values is different.
- **Cases 11-14**: Three values are different between the two samples.
- **Case 15**: All four values are different.

In addition, the concepts of equivalence partitioning and boundary value analysis suggest that we also need to locate values where there is a profound state change. For example, invalid values will raise exceptions, something that should also be tested. This can create a number of sub-cases within each of the cases enumerated above.

We won't create all 16 cases for each of the four algorithms in this part of the case study. Instead, we'll take a close look at whether or not all 16 cases are really required. To get started, we'll limit ourselves to one case for each distance algorithm. This will be an example of case 15, where all four values of the two samples are different.

With mathematical results, we need to compute the expected answers outside the software we're building. We can, of course, try to compute the expected answers with pencil and paper or a spreadsheet.

One trick that can be helpful when working with more advanced math is to use the sympy package as a way to check the math more carefully.

For example, the Euclidean distance between a known sample, k, and an unknown sample, u, has the following formal definition:

$$ED(k, u) = \sqrt{(k_{sl} - u_{sl})^2 + (k_{pl} - u_{pl})^2 + (k_{sw} - u_{sw})^2 + (k_{pw} - u_{pw})^2}$$

This computes the distance among all four measurements. For example, the known sepal length is k_{sl}. The other attributes have similar names.

While sympy can do a great many things, we want to use it for two specific purposes:

1. To confirm that our Python version of the formula really is correct
2. To compute the expected results using specific variable substitutions

We do this by using sympy to perform the operations symbolically. Instead of plugging in specific floating-point values, we want to transform the Python expression into conventional mathematical notation.

This is a test case that's applied to the design, not the implementation. It confirms the code's design is very likely to match the original intent. We've translated the nicely typeset names like k_{sl} for "known sepal length" into a Pythonic (but not as easy to read) k_sl. Here's our interaction with sympy:

```
>>> from sympy import *

>>> ED, k_sl, k_pl, k_sw, k_pw, u_sl, u_pl, u_sw, u_pw = symbols(
...      "ED, k_sl, k_pl, k_sw, k_pw, u_sl, u_pl, u_sw, u_pw")

>>> ED = sqrt( (k_sl-u_sl)**2 + (k_pl-u_pl)**2 + (k_sw-u_sw)**2 +
(k_pw-u_pw)**2 )
>>> ED
sqrt((k_pl - u_pl)**2 + (k_pw - u_pw)**2 + (k_sl - u_sl)**2 +
(k_sw - u_sw)**2)

>>> print(pretty(ED, use_unicode=False))
   _____
  /                2                2               2               2
\/   (k_pl - u_pl)  + (k_pw - u_pw)  + (k_sl - u_sl)  + (k_sw - u_sw)
```

We imported `sympy` and defined the batch of symbols that match the original formula. We need to define these objects so `sympy` will work with them as mathematical symbols, not ordinary Python objects. Then, we did our best to translate the Euclidean distance formula from math into Python. It seems right, but we'd like to be sure.

Note that when we asked for the value of `ED`, we didn't see the results of a Python computation. Because we've defined the variables as symbols, `sympy` builds a representation of the equation that we can work with.

When we used the `pretty()` function from `sympy`, it displayed an ASCII art version of our expression, which looks a lot like the original. We used the `use_unicode=False` option because that looked best in this book. When printed with an appropriate font, the `use_unicode=True` version may be easier to read.

The formula is something we can share with experts to be sure our test cases really do properly describe the behavior of this particular class. Because the formula looks right, we can evaluate it with concrete values:

```
>>> e = ED.subs(dict(
...      k_sl=5.1, k_sw=3.5, k_pl=1.4, k_pw=0.2,
...      u_sl=7.9, u_sw=3.2, u_pl=4.7, u_pw=1.4,
... ))
>>> e.evalf(9)
4.50111097
```

The subs() method substitutes values for the symbols in the formula. We then use the evalf() method to evaluate the result as a floating-point number. We can use this to create a unit test case for the class.

Before we look at the test case, here's an implementation of the Euclidean distance class. As an optimization, this uses math.hypot():

```python
class ED(Distance):
    def distance(self, s1: Sample, s2: Sample) -> float:
        return hypot(
            s1.sepal_length - s2.sepal_length,
            s1.sepal_width - s2.sepal_width,
            s1.petal_length - s2.petal_length,
            s1.petal_width - s2.petal_width,
        )
```

It seems like this implementation matches the math. The best way to check is to create an automated test. Recall that tests often have a GIVEN-WHEN-THEN outline. We can expand this to the following conceptual scenario:

```
Scenario: Euclidean Distance Computation

    Given an unknown sample, U, and a known sample, K
    When we compute the Euclidean Distance between them
    Then we get the distance, ED.
```

We can provide the values used in the symbolic computation for U, K, and the expected distance. We'll start with a test fixture that supports the GIVEN step:

```python
@pytest.fixture
def known_unknown_example_15() -> Known_Unknown:
    known_row: Row = {
        "species": "Iris-setosa",
        "sepal_length": 5.1,
        "sepal_width": 3.5,
        "petal_length": 1.4,
        "petal_width": 0.2,
    }
    k = TrainingKnownSample(**known_row)
    unknown_row = {
        "sepal_length": 7.9,
        "sepal_width": 3.2,
```

```
        "petal_length": 4.7,
        "petal_width": 1.4,
    }
    u = UnknownSample(**unknown_row)
    return k, u
```

We've created a `TrainingKnownSample` and an `UnknownSample` object that we can use in subsequent tests. This fixture definition depends on a number of important type hints and definitions:

```
From __future__ import annotations
import pytest
from model import TrainingKnownSample, UnknownSample
from model import CD, ED, MD, SD
from typing import Tuple, TypedDict

Known_Unknown = Tuple[TrainingKnownSample, UnknownSample]
class Row(TypedDict):
    species: str
    sepal_length: float
    sepal_width: float
    petal_length: float
    petal_width: float
```

We can provide the distance computation as a WHEN step, and a final THEN comparison in an `assert` statement. We need to use an `approx` object for comparison because we're working with floating-point values, and exact comparisons rarely work out well.

For this application, the number of decimal places in the test case seems excessive. We've left all the digits so the values will fit with the defaults used by `approx`, which is a relative error of 1×10^{-6}, or `1e-6` in Python notation. Here's the rest of the test case:

```
def test_ed(known_unknown_example_15: Known_Unknown) -> None:
    k, u = known_unknown_example_15
    assert ED().distance(k, u) == pytest.approx(4.50111097)
```

This is pleasantly short and to the point. Given two samples, the distance result should match what we computed by hand, or computed using `sympy`.

Each of the distance classes needs a test case. Here are two other distance computations. The expected results come from validating the formula and providing concrete values, as we did previously:

```python
def test_cd(known_unknown_example_15: Known_Unknown) -> None:
    k, u = known_unknown_example_15
    assert CD().distance(k, u) == pytest.approx(3.3)

def test_md(known_unknown_example_15: Known_Unknown) -> None:
    k, u = known_unknown_example_15
    assert MD().distance(k, u) == pytest.approx(7.6)
```

For the Chebyshev and Manhattan distances, we're adding the individual steps for each of the four attributes and computing the sum or finding the largest individual distance. We can work these out by hand and be confident that our expected answer is right.

The Sorensen distance, however, is a little more complex and can benefit from a comparison with the symbolic results. Here's the formal definition:

$$SD(k, u) = \frac{|k_{pl} - u_{pl}| + |k_{pw} - u_{pw}| + |k_{sl} - u_{sl}| + |k_{sw} - u_{sw}|}{k_{pl} + k_{pw} + k_{sl} + k_{sw} + u_{pl} + u_{pw} + u_{sl} + u_{sw}}$$

Here's the symbolic definition that we can use to compare our implementation against the definition. The equation displayed looks a lot like the formal definition, giving us the confidence to use it to compute expected values. Here's a definition extracted from the code that we'd like to check:

```python
>>> SD = sum(
...     [abs(k_sl - u_sl), abs(k_sw - u_sw), abs(k_pl - u_pl),
abs(k_pw - u_pw)]
... ) / sum(
...     [k_sl + u_sl, k_sw + u_sw, k_pl + u_pl, k_pw + u_pw])
>>> print(pretty(SD, use_unicode=False))
|k_pl - u_pl| + |k_pw - u_pw| + |k_sl - u_sl| + |k_sw - u_sw|
-------------------------------------------------------------
   k_pl + k_pw + k_sl + k_sw + u_pl + u_pw + u_sl + u_sw
```

The ASCII-art version of the formula looks a lot like the formal definition, giving us a lot of confidence that we can use sympy to compute expected answers. We'll substitute specific example values to see what the expected results should be:

```
>>> e = SD.subs(dict(
...        k_sl=5.1, k_sw=3.5, k_pl=1.4, k_pw=0.2,
...        u_sl=7.9, u_sw=3.2, u_pl=4.7, u_pw=1.4,
... ))
>>> e.evalf(9)
0.277372263
```

Now that we're sure we have valid expected results, we can plug this expectation into a unit test case. Here's how the test case looks:

```
def test_sd(known_unknown_example_15: Known_Unknown) -> None:
    k, u = known_unknown_example_15
    assert SD().distance(k, u) == pytest.approx(0.277372263)
```

We've used sympy as a design aid to help us create unit test cases. It's not run as a regular part of the testing process. We only want to use it for the obscure cases where we aren't sure we can trust ourselves to compute an expected answer with paper and pencil.

As we noted at the beginning of this chapter's case study, there are 16 different combinations of values where the known and the unknown sample attributes are different. We've provided only one of the 16 combinations.

Using the coverage tool, we can see that all of the relevant code is tested with this one case. Do we really need the other 15 cases? There are two viewpoints:

- From a "black box" point of view, we don't know what's in the code, and we need to test all the combinations. This kind of black box testing relies on the assumption that the values could have some complex interdependency that can only be found through patient examination of all cases.

- From a "white box" point of view, we can look at the various distance function implementations and see that all four attributes are treated uniformly. An examination of the code tells us a single case is sufficient.

For Python applications, we suggest following white box testing unless there's a compelling reason to avoid looking at the code. We can use the coverage report to confirm that one case really has tested the relevant code.

Instead of creating 16 different test cases for the various distance algorithms, we can focus our efforts on making sure the application is reliable and uses minimal computing resources. We can also focus on testing other parts of the application. We'll look at the Hyperparameter class next, because it depends on the Distance computation class hierarchy.

Unit testing the Hyperparameter class

The Hyperparameter class relies on a distance computation. We have two strategies for testing a complex class like this:

- An integration test that uses the distance computations already tested
- A unit test that isolates the Hyperparameter class from any of the distance computations to be sure the class works

As a general rule of thumb, every line of code needs to be exercised by at least one unit test. After that, integration tests can also be used to ensure that the interface definitions are honored by all of the modules, classes, and functions. The spirit of "test everything" is more important than "make the number come out right"; counting lines is one way to ensure that we've tested everything.

We'll look at testing the classify() method of the Hyperparameter class using Mock objects to isolate the Hyperparameter class from any of the distance computations. We'll also mock the TrainingData object to further isolate an instance of this class.

Here's the relevant code we'll be testing:

```
class Hyperparameter:

    def __init__(
            self,
            k: int,
            algorithm: "Distance",
            training: "TrainingData"
    ) -> None:
        self.k = k
        self.algorithm = algorithm
        self.data: weakref.ReferenceType["TrainingData"] = \
            weakref.ref(training)
        self.quality: float

    def classify(
            self,
            sample: Union[UnknownSample, TestingKnownSample]) -> str:
        """The k-NN algorithm"""
        training_data = self.data()
        if not training_data:
            raise RuntimeError("No TrainingData object")
        distances: list[tuple[float, TrainingKnownSample]] = sorted(
```

```
            (self.algorithm.distance(sample, known), known)
            for known in training_data.training
    )
    k_nearest = (known.species for d, known in distances[: self.k])
    frequency: Counter[str] = collections.Counter(k_nearest)
    best_fit, *others = frequency.most_common()
    species, votes = best_fit
    return species
```

The `algorithm` attribute of the `Hyperparameter` class is a reference to an instance of one of the distance computation objects. When we replace this, the `Mock` object must be callable and must return an appropriate sortable number.

The `data` attribute is a reference to a `TrainingData` object. The `Mock` to replace the data object must provide a `training` attribute that is a list of mocked samples. Since these values are provided to another mock without any intermediate processing, we can use a `sentinel` object to confirm that the training data was provided to the mocked distance function.

The idea can be summarized as watching the `classify()` method "go through the motions." We provide mocks and sentinels to confirm that requests are made and the results of those requests are captured.

For the more complex test, we'll need some mock sample data. This will rely on `sentinel` objects. The objects will be passed through to a mocked distance computation. Here's the definition of some mocked sample objects we'll use:

```
from __future__ import annotations
from model import Hyperparameter
from unittest.mock import Mock, sentinel, call


@pytest.fixture
def sample_data() -> list[Mock]:
    return [
        Mock(name="Sample1", species=sentinel.Species3),
        Mock(name="Sample2", species=sentinel.Species1),
        Mock(name="Sample3", species=sentinel.Species1),
        Mock(name="Sample4", species=sentinel.Species1),
        Mock(name="Sample5", species=sentinel.Species3),
    ]
```

This fixture is a list of mocks for KnownSamples. We've provided a unique name for each sample to help with debugging. We've provided a species attribute, since that's the attribute used by the classify() method. We didn't provide any other attributes, because they aren't used by the unit under test. We will use this sample_data fixture to create a Hyperparameter instance that will have a mock distance computation and this mock collection of data. Here's the test fixture we'll use:

```
@pytest.fixture
def hyperparameter(sample_data: list[Mock]) -> Hyperparameter:
    mocked_distance = Mock(distance=Mock(side_effect=[11, 1, 2, 3, 13]))
    mocked_training_data = Mock(training=sample_data)
    mocked_weakref = Mock(
        return_value=mocked_training_data)
    fixture = Hyperparameter(
        k=3, algorithm=mocked_distance, training=sentinel.Unused)
    fixture.data = mocked_weakref
    return fixture
```

The mocked_distance object will provide a sequence of results that look like the results of distance computations. The distance computations are tested separately, and we've isolated the classify() method from the specific distance computations with this Mock. We've provided the list of mocked KnownSample instances via a Mock object that will behave like a weak reference; the training attribute of this mock object will be the given sample data.

To be sure the Hyperparameter instance makes the right requests, we evaluate the classify() method. Here's the entire scenario, including these two final THEN steps:

- GIVEN a sample data fixture with five instances reflecting two species
- WHEN we apply the *k*-NN algorithm
- THEN the result is the species with the closest three distances
- AND the mock distance computation was invoked with all of the training data

Here's the final test, using the above fixtures:

```
def test_hyperparameter(sample_data: list[Mock], hyperparameter: Mock)
-> None:
    s = hyperparameter.classify(sentinel.Unknown)
    assert s == sentinel.Species1
    assert hyperparameter.algorithm.distance.mock_calls == [
```

```
        call(sentinel.Unknown, sample_data[0]),
        call(sentinel.Unknown, sample_data[1]),
        call(sentinel.Unknown, sample_data[2]),
        call(sentinel.Unknown, sample_data[3]),
        call(sentinel.Unknown, sample_data[4]),
    ]
```

This test case checks the distance algorithm to make sure the entire training set of data was used. It also confirms that the nearest neighbors were used to locate the resulting species for the unknown sample.

Since we tested the distance computations separately, we have a great deal of confidence in running an integration test that combines these various classes into a single, working application. For debugging purposes, it is very helpful to isolate each component into a separately tested unit.

Recall

In this chapter, we've looked at a number of topics related to testing applications written in Python. These topics include the following:

- We described the importance of unit testing and test-driven development as a way to be sure our software does what is expected.

- We started by using the unittest module because it's part of the standard library and readily available. It seems a little wordy, but otherwise works well for confirming that our software works.

- The pytest tool requires a separate installation, but it seems to produce tests that are slightly simpler than those written with the unittest module. More importantly, the sophistication of the fixture concept lets us create tests for a wide variety of scenarios.

- The mock module, part of the unittest package, lets us create mock objects to better isolate the unit of code being tested. By isolating each piece of code, we can narrow our focus on being sure it works and has the right interface. This makes it easier to combine components.

- Code coverage is a helpful metric to ensure that our testing is adequate. Simply adhering to a numeric goal is no substitute for thinking, but it can help to confirm that efforts were made to be thorough and careful when creating test scenarios.

We've been looking at several kinds of tests with a variety of tools:

- Unit tests with the `unittest` package or the `pytest` package, often using `Mock` objects to isolate the fixture or unit being tested.

- Integration tests, also with `unittest` and `pytest`, where more complete integrated collections of components are tested.

- Static analysis can use *mypy* to examine the data types to be sure they're used properly. This is a kind of test to ensure the software is acceptable. There are other kinds of static tests, and tools like `flake8`, `pylint`, and `pyflakes` can be used for these additional analyses.

Some research will turn up scores of additional types of tests. Each distinct type of test has a distinct objective or approach to confirming the software works. A performance test, for example, seeks to establish the software is fast enough and uses an acceptable number of resources.

We can't emphasize enough how important testing is. Without automated tests, software can't be considered complete, or even usable. Starting from test cases lets us define the expected behavior in a way that's specific, measurable, achievable, results-based, and trackable: SMART.

Exercises

Practice test-driven development. That is your first exercise. It's easier to do this if you're starting a new project, but if you have existing code you need to work on, you can start by writing tests for each new feature you implement. This can become frustrating as you become more enamored with automated tests. The old, untested code will start to feel rigid and tightly coupled, and will become uncomfortable to maintain; you'll start feeling like changes you make are breaking the code and you have no way of knowing, for lack of tests. But if you start small, adding tests to the code base improves it over time. It's not unusual for there to be more test code than application code!

So, to get your feet wet with test-driven development, start a fresh project. Once you've started to appreciate the benefits (you will) and realize that the time spent writing tests is quickly regained in terms of more maintainable code, you'll want to start writing tests for existing code. This is when you should start doing it, not before. Writing tests for code that we *know* works is boring. It is hard to get interested in the project until we realize just how broken the code we thought was working really is.

Try writing the same set of tests using both the built-in `unittest` module and `pytest`. Which do you prefer? `unittest` is more similar to test frameworks in other languages, while `pytest` is arguably more Pythonic. Both allow us to write object-oriented tests and test object-oriented programs with ease.

We used `pytest` in our case study, but we didn't touch on any features that wouldn't have been easily testable using `unittest`. Try adapting the tests to use test skipping or fixtures. Try the various setup and teardown methods. Which feels more natural to you?

Try running a coverage report on the tests you've written. Did you miss testing any lines of code? Even if you have 100 percent coverage, have you tested all the possible inputs? If you're doing test-driven development, 100 percent coverage should follow quite naturally, as you will write a test before the code that satisfies that test. However, if you're writing tests for existing code, it is more likely that there will be edge conditions that go untested.

Getting the case study code to 100 percent coverage can be tricky, since we've been skipping around and implementing some aspects of the case study in several different ways. It may be necessary to write several similar tests for alternative implementations of case study classes. It can help to make reusable fixtures so that we can provide consistent testing among the alternative implementations.

When creating test cases, it can help to think carefully about the values that are somehow different, such as the following, for example:

- Empty lists when you expect full ones
- Negative numbers, zero, one, or infinity compared to positive integers
- Floats that don't round to an exact decimal place
- Strings when you expected numerals
- Unicode strings when you expected ASCII
- The ubiquitous `None` value when you expected something meaningful

If your tests cover such edge cases, your code will be in good shape.

The numeric methods for distance computations are something that might be better tested using the Hypothesis project. Check out the documentation here: `https://hypothesis.readthedocs.io/en/latest/`. We can use Hypothesis to easily confirm that the order of operands in a distance computation doesn't matter; that is, `distance(s1, s2) == distance(s2, s1)`, given any two samples. It's often helpful to include Hypothesis testing to confirm that the essential *k*-nearest neighbors classifier algorithm works for randomly shuffled data; this will ensure there's no bias for the first or last item in the training set.

Summary

We have finally covered the most important topic in Python programming: automated testing. Test-driven development is considered a best practice. The standard library unittest module provides a great out-of-the-box solution for testing, while the pytest framework has some more Pythonic syntaxes. Mocks can be used to emulate complex classes in our tests. Code coverage gives us an estimate of how much of our code is being run by our tests, but it does not tell us that we have tested the right things.

In the next chapter, we'll jump into a completely different topic: concurrency.

14
Concurrency

Concurrency is the art of making a computer do (or appear to do) multiple things at once. Historically, this meant inviting the processor to switch between different tasks many times per second. In modern systems, it can also literally mean doing two or more things simultaneously on separate processor cores.

Concurrency is not inherently an object-oriented topic, but Python's concurrent systems provide object-oriented interfaces, as we've covered throughout the book. This chapter will introduce you to the following topics:

- Threads
- Multiprocessing
- Futures
- AsyncIO
- The dining philosophers benchmark

The case study for this chapter will address ways we can speed up model testing and hyperparameter tuning. We can't make the computation go away, but we can leverage a modern, multi-core computer to get it done in less time.

Concurrent processes can become complicated. The basic concepts are fairly simple, but the bugs that can occur are notoriously difficult to track down when the sequence of state changes is unpredictable. However, for many projects, concurrency is the only way to get the performance we need. Imagine if a web server couldn't respond to a user's request until another user's request had been completed! We'll see how to implement concurrency in Python, and some common pitfalls to avoid.

The Python language explicitly executes statements in order. To consider concurrent execution of statements, we'll need to take a step away from Python.

Background on concurrent processing

Conceptually, it can help to think of concurrent processing by imagining a group of people who can't see each other and are trying to collaborate on a task. Perhaps their vision is impaired or blocked by screens, or their workspace has awkward doorways they can't quite see through. These people can, however, pass tokens, notes, and work-in-process to each other.

Imagine a small delicatessen in an old seaside resort city (on the Atlantic coast of the US) with an awkward countertop layout. The two sandwich chefs can't see or hear each other. While the owner can afford to pay two fine chefs, the owner can't afford more than one serving tray. Due to the awkward complications of the ancient building, the chefs can't really see the tray, either. They're forced to reach down below their counter to be sure the serving tray is in place. Then, assured the tray is there, they carefully place their work of art – complete with pickles and a few potato chips – onto the tray. (They can't see the tray, but they're spectacular chefs who can place a sandwich, pickles, and chips flawlessly.)

The owner, however, can see the chefs. Indeed, passers-by can watch the chefs work. It's a great show. The owner typically deals the order tickets out to each chef in strict alternation. And ordinarily, the one and only serving tray can be placed so the sandwich arrives, and is presented at the table with a flourish. The chefs, as we said, have to wait to feel the tray before their next creation warms someone's palate.

Then one day, one of the chefs (we'll call him Michael, but his friends call him Mo) is nearly done with an order, but has to run to the cooler for more of those dill pickles everyone loves. This delays Mo's prep time, and the owner sees that the other chef, Constantine, looks like he'll finish just a fraction of a second before Mo. Even though Mo has returned with the pickles, and is ready with the sandwich, the owner does something embarrassing. The rule is clear: check first, then place the sandwich. Everyone in the shop knows this. When the owner moves the tray from the opening below Mo's station to the opening below Constantine's, then Mo placed their creation – what would have been a delightful Reuben sandwich with extra sauerkraut – into the empty space where a tray should have been, where it splashes onto the delicatessen floor, embarrassing everyone.

How could the foolproof method of checking for the tray, then depositing the sandwich have failed to work? It had survived the test of many busy lunch hours, and yet, a small disruption in the regular sequence of events, and a mess ensues. The separation in time between testing for the tray and depositing the sandwich is an opportunity for the owner to make a state change.

There's a race between owner and chefs. Preventing unexpected state changes is the essential design problem for concurrent programming.

One solution could be to use a semaphore – a flag – to prevent unexpected changes to the tray. This is a kind of shared lock. Each chef is forced to seize the flag before plating; and once they have the flag, they can be confident the owner won't move the tray until they return the flag to the little flag-stand between the chef stations.

Concurrent work requires some method for synchronizing access to shared resources. One essential power of large, modern computers is managing concurrency through operating system features, collectively called the kernel.

Older and smaller computers, with a single core in a single CPU, had to interleave everything. The clever coordination made things appear to be working at the same time. Newer multi-core computers (and large multi-processor computers) can actually perform operations concurrently, making the scheduling of work a bit more involved.

We have several ways to achieve concurrent processing:

- The operating system lets us run more than one program at a time. The Python subprocess module gives us ready access to these capabilities. The multiprocessing module provides a number of convenient ways to work. This is relatively easy to start, but each program is carefully sequestered from all other programs. How can they share data?

- Some clever software libraries allow a single program to have multiple concurrent threads of operation. The Python threading module gives us access to multi-threading. This is more complex to get started, and each thread has complete access to the data in all other threads. How can we coordinate updates to shared data structures?

Additionally, concurrent.futures and asyncio provide easier-to-use wrappers around the underlying libraries. We'll start this chapter by looking at Python's use of the threading library to allow many things to happen concurrently in a single OS process. This is simple, but has some challenges when working with shared data structures.

Threads

A thread is a sequence of Python byte-code instructions that may be interrupted and resumed. The idea is to create separate, concurrent threads to allow computation to proceed while the program is waiting for I/O to happen.

For example, a server can start processing a new network request while it waits for data from a previous request to arrive. Or an interactive program might render an animation or perform a calculation while waiting for the user to press a key. Bear in mind that while a person can type more than 500 characters per minute, a computer can perform billions of instructions per second. Thus, a ton of processing can happen between individual key presses, even when typing quickly.

It's theoretically possible to manage all this switching between activities within your program, but it would be virtually impossible to get right. Instead, we can rely on Python and the operating system to take care of the tricky switching part, while we create objects that appear to be running independently but simultaneously. These objects are called **threads**. Let's take a look at a basic example. We'll start with the essential definition of the thread's processing, as shown in the following class:

```python
class Chef(Thread):
    def __init__(self, name: str) -> None:
        super().__init__(name=name)
        self.total = 0

    def get_order(self) -> None:
        self.order = THE_ORDERS.pop(0)

    def prepare(self) -> None:
        """Simulate doing a lot of work with a BIG computation"""
        start = time.monotonic()
        target = start + 1 + random.random()
        for i in range(1_000_000_000):
            self.total += math.factorial(i)
            if time.monotonic() >= target:
                break
        print(
            f"{time.monotonic():.3f} {self.name} made {self.order}")

    def run(self) -> None:
        while True:
            try:
                self.get_order()
                self.prepare()
            except IndexError:
                break   # No more orders
```

A thread in our running application must extend the `Thread` class and implement the `run` method. Any code executed by the `run` method is a separate thread of processing, scheduled independently. Our thread is relying on a global variable, `THE_ORDERS`, which is a shared object:

```python
import math
import random
from threading import Thread, Lock
import time

THE_ORDERS = [
    "Reuben",
    "Ham and Cheese",
    "Monte Cristo",
    "Tuna Melt",
    "Cuban",
    "Grilled Cheese",
    "French Dip",
    "BLT",
]
```

In this case, we've defined the orders as a simple, fixed list of values. In a larger application, we might be reading these from a socket or a queue object. Here's the top-level program that starts things running:

```python
Mo = Chef("Michael")
Constantine = Chef("Constantine")

if __name__ == "__main__":
    random.seed(42)
    Mo.start()
    Constantine.start()
```

This will create two threads. The new threads don't start running until we call the `start()` method on the object. When the two threads have started, they both pop a value from the list of orders and then commence to perform a large computation and – eventually – report their status.

The output looks like this:

```
1.076 Constantine made Ham and Cheese
1.676 Michael made Reuben
2.351 Constantine made Monte Cristo
```

```
2.899 Michael made Tuna Melt
4.094 Constantine made Cuban
4.576 Michael made Grilled Cheese
5.664 Michael made BLT
5.987 Constantine made French Dip
```

Note that the sandwiches aren't completed in the exact order that they were presented in the THE_ORDERS list. Each chef works at their own (randomized) pace. Changing the seed will change the times, and may adjust the order slightly.

What's important about this example is the threads are sharing data structures, and the concurrency is an illusion created by clever scheduling of the threads to interleave work from the two chef threads.

The only update to a shared data structure in this small example is to pop from a list. If we were to create our own class and implement more complex state changes, we could uncover a number of interesting and confusing issues with using threads.

The many problems with threads

Threads can be useful if appropriate care is taken to manage shared memory, but modern Python programmers tend to avoid them for several reasons. As we'll see, there are other ways to code concurrent programming that are receiving more attention from the Python community. Let's discuss some of the pitfalls before moving on to alternatives to multithreaded applications.

Shared memory

The main problem with threads is also their primary advantage. Threads have access to all the process memory and thus all the variables. A disregard for the shared state can too easily cause inconsistencies.

Have you ever encountered a room where a single light has two switches and two different people turn them on at the same time? Each person (thread) expects their action to turn the lamp (a variable) on, but the resulting value (the lamp) is off, which is inconsistent with those expectations. Now imagine if those two threads were transferring funds between bank accounts or managing the cruise control for a vehicle.

The solution to this problem in threaded programming is to *synchronize* access to any code that reads or (especially) writes a shared variable. Python's threading library offers the Lock class, which can be used via the with statement to create a context where a single thread has access to update shared objects.

The synchronization solution works in general, but it is way too easy to forget to apply it to shared data in a specific application. Worse, bugs due to inappropriate use of synchronization are really hard to track down because the order in which threads perform operations is inconsistent. We can't easily reproduce the error. Usually, it is safest to force communication between threads to happen using a lightweight data structure that already uses locks appropriately. Python offers the queue.Queue class to do this; a number of threads can write to a queue, where a single thread consumes the results. This gives us a tidy, reusable, proven technique for having multiple threads sharing a data structure. The multiprocessing.Queue class is nearly identical; we will discuss this in the *Multiprocessing* section of this chapter.

In some cases, these disadvantages might be outweighed by the one advantage of allowing shared memory: it's fast. If multiple threads need access to a huge data structure, shared memory can provide that access quickly. However, this advantage is usually nullified by the fact that, in Python, it is impossible for two threads running on different CPU cores to be performing calculations at exactly the same time. This brings us to our second problem with threads.

The global interpreter lock

In order to efficiently manage memory, garbage collection, and calls to machine code in native libraries, Python has a **global interpreter lock**, or **GIL**. It's impossible to turn off, and it means that thread scheduling is constrained by the GIL preventing any two threads from doing computations at the exact same time; the work is interleaved artificially. When a thread makes an OS request – for example, to access the disk or network – the GIL is released as soon as the thread starts waiting for the OS request to complete.

The GIL is disparaged, mostly by people who don't understand what it is or the benefits it brings to Python. While it can interfere with multithreaded compute-intensive programming, the impact for other kinds of workloads is often minimal. When confronted with a compute-intensive algorithm, it may help to switch to using the dask package to manage the processing. See https://dask.org for more information on this alternative. The book *Scalable Data Analysis in Python with Dask* can be informative, also.

 While the GIL can be a problem in the reference implementation of Python that most people use, it can be selectively disabled in IronPython. See *The IronPython Cookbook* for details on how to release the GIL for compute-intensive processing in IronPython.

Thread overhead

One additional limitation of threads, as compared to other asynchronous approaches we will be discussing later, is the cost of maintaining each thread. Each thread takes up a certain amount of memory (both in the Python process and the operating system kernel) to record the state of that thread. Switching between the threads also uses a (small) amount of CPU time. This work happens seamlessly without any extra coding (we just have to call start() and the rest is taken care of), but the work still has to happen somewhere.

These costs can be amortized over a larger workload by reusing threads to perform multiple jobs. Python provides a ThreadPool feature to handle this. It behaves identically to ProcessPool, which we will discuss shortly, so let's defer that discussion until later in this chapter.

In the next section, we'll look at the principal alternative to multi-threading. The multiprocessing module lets us work with OS-level subprocesses.

Multiprocessing

Threads exist within a single OS process; that's why they can share access to common objects. We can do concurrent computing at the process level, also. Unlike threads, separate processes cannot directly access variables set up by other processes. This independence is helpful because each process has its own GIL and its own private pool of resources. On a modern multi-core processor, a process may have its own core, permitting concurrent work with other cores.

The multiprocessing API was originally designed to mimic the threading API. However, the multiprocessing interface has evolved, and in recent versions of Python, it supports more features more robustly. The multiprocessing library is designed for when CPU-intensive jobs need to happen in parallel and multiple cores are available. Multiprocessing is not as useful when the processes spend a majority of their time waiting on I/O (for example, network, disk, database, or keyboard), but it is the way to go for parallel computation.

The multiprocessing module spins up new operating system processes to do the work. This means there is an entirely separate copy of the Python interpreter running for each process. Let's try to parallelize a compute-heavy operation using similar constructs to those provided by the threading API, as follows:

```
from multiprocessing import Process, cpu_count
import time
import os
```

```
class MuchCPU(Process):
    def run(self) -> None:
        print(f"OS PID {os.getpid()}")

        s = sum(
            2*i+1 for i in range(100_000_000)
        )


if __name__ == "__main__":
    workers = [MuchCPU() for f in range(cpu_count())]
    t = time.perf_counter()
    for p in workers:
        p.start()
    for p in workers:
        p.join()
    print(f"work took {time.perf_counter() - t:.3f} seconds")
```

This example just ties up the CPU computing the sum of 100 million odd numbers.
You may not consider this to be useful work, but it can warm up your laptop on a
chilly day!

The API should be familiar; we implement a subclass of Process (instead of Thread)
and implement a run method. This method prints out the OS **process ID (PID)**, a
unique number assigned to each process on the machine, before doing some intense
(if misguided) work.

Pay special attention to the if __name__ == "__main__": guard around the
module-level code that prevents it from running if the module is being imported,
rather than run as a program. This is good practice in general, but when using the
multiprocessing module, it is essential. Behind the scenes, the multiprocessing
module may have to reimport our application module inside each of the new
processes in order to create the class and execute the run() method. If we allowed
the entire module to execute at that point, it would start creating new processes
recursively until the operating system ran out of resources, crashing your computer.

This demo constructs one process for each processor core on our machine, then starts
and joins each of those processes. On a 2020-era MacBook Pro with a 2 GHz Quad-
Core Intel Core i5, the output looks as follows:

```
% python src/processes_1.py
OS PID 15492
OS PID 15493
OS PID 15494
```

```
OS PID 15495
OS PID 15497
OS PID 15496
OS PID 15498
OS PID 15499
work took 20.711 seconds
```

The first eight lines are the process ID that was printed inside each MuchCPU instance. The last line shows that the 100 million summations can run in about 20 seconds. During those 20 seconds, all eight cores were running at 100 percent, and the fans were buzzing away trying to dissipate the heat.

If we subclass threading.Thread instead of multiprocessing.Process in MuchCPU, the output looks as follows:

```
% python src/processes_1.py
OS PID 15772
OS PID 15772
OS PID 15772
OS PID 15772
OS PID 15772
OS PID 15772
OS PID 15772
OS PID 15772
work took 69.316 seconds
```

This time, the threads are running inside the same OS process and take over three times as long to run. The display showed that no core was particularly busy, suggesting the work was being shunted around among the various cores. The general slowdown is the cost of the GIL interleaving compute-intensive work.

We might expect the single process version to be at least eight times as long as the eight-process version. The lack of a simple multiplier suggests there are a number of factors involved in how the low-level instructions are processed by Python, the OS schedulers, and even the hardware itself. This suggests that predictions are difficult, and it's best to plan on running multiple performance tests with multiple software architectures.

Starting and stopping individual Process instances involves a lot of overhead. The most common use case is to have a pool of workers and assign tasks to them. We'll look at this next.

Multiprocessing pools

Because each process is kept meticulously separate by the operating system, interprocess communication becomes an important consideration. We need to pass data between these separate processes. One really common example is having one process write a file that another process can read. When the two processes are reading and writing a file, and running concurrently, we have to be sure the reader is waiting for the writer to produce data. The operating system *pipe* structure can accomplish this. Within the shell, we can write ps -ef | grep python and pass output from the ps command to the grep command. The two commands run concurrently. For Windows PowerShell users, there are similar kinds of pipeline processing, using different command names. (See https://docs.microsoft.com/en-us/powershell/scripting/learn/ps101/04-pipelines?view=powershell-7.1 for examples.)

The multiprocessing package provides some additional ways to implement interprocess communication. Pools can seamlessly hide the way data is moved between processes. Using a pool looks much like a function call: you pass data into a function, it is executed in another process or processes, and when the work is done, a value is returned. It is important to understand how much work is being done to support this: objects in one process are pickled and passed into an operating system process pipe. Then, another process retrieves data from the pipe and unpickles it. The requested work is done in the subprocess and a result is produced. The result is pickled and passed back through the pipe. Eventually, the original process unpickles and returns it. Collectively, we call this pickling, transferring, and unpickling *serializing* the data. For more information, see *Chapter 9, Strings, Serialization, and File Paths*.

The serialization to communicate between processes takes time and memory. We want to get as much useful computation done with the smallest serialization cost. The ideal mix depends on the size and complexity of the objects being exchanged, meaning that different data structure designs will have different performance levels.

 Performance predictions are difficult to make. It's essential to profile the application to ensure the concurrency design is effective.

Armed with this knowledge, the code to make all this machinery work is surprisingly simple. Let's look at the problem of calculating all the prime factors of a list of random numbers. This is a common part of a variety of cryptography algorithms (not to mention attacks on those algorithms!).

It requires months, possibly years of processing power to factor the 232-digit numbers used by some encryption algorithms. The following implementation, while readable, is not at all efficient; it would take years to factor even a 100-digit number. That's okay because we want to see it using lots of CPU time factoring 9-digit numbers:

```python
from __future__ import annotations
from math import sqrt, ceil
import random
from multiprocessing.pool import Pool

def prime_factors(value: int) -> list[int]:
    if value in {2, 3}:
        return [value]
    factors: list[int] = []
    for divisor in range(2, ceil(sqrt(value)) + 1):
        quotient, remainder = divmod(value, divisor)
        if not remainder:
            factors.extend(prime_factors(divisor))
            factors.extend(prime_factors(quotient))
            break
    else:
        factors = [value]
    return factors

if __name__ == "__main__":
    to_factor = [
        random.randint(100_000_000, 1_000_000_000)
        for i in range(40_960)
    ]
    with Pool() as pool:
        results = pool.map(prime_factors, to_factor)
    primes = [
        value
        for value, factor_list in zip(to_factor, results)
            if len(factor_list) == 1
    ]
    print(f"9-digit primes {primes}")
```

Let's focus on the parallel processing aspects, as the brute force recursive algorithm for calculating factors is pretty clear. We create the to_factor list of 40,960 individual numbers. Then we construct a multiprocessing pool instance.

By default, this pool creates a separate process for each of the CPU cores in the machine it is running on.

The map() method of the pool accepts a function and an iterable. The pool pickles each of the values in the iterable and passes it to an available worker process in the pool, which executes the function on it. When that process is finished doing its work, it pickles the resulting list of factors and passes it back to the pool. Then, if the pool has more work available, the worker takes on the next job.

Once all the workers in the pool are finished processing (which could take some time), the results list is passed back to the original process, which has been waiting patiently for all this work to complete. The results of map() will be in the same order as the requests. This makes it sensible to use zip() to match up the original value with the computed prime factors.

It is often more useful to use the similar map_async() method, which returns immediately even though the processes are still working. In that case, the results variable would not be a list of values, but a contract (or a deal or an obligation) to return a list of values in the future when the client calls results.get(). This future object also has methods such as ready() and wait(), which allow us to check whether all the results are in yet. This is suitable for processing where the completion time is highly variable.

Alternatively, if we don't know all the values we want to get results for in advance, we can use the apply_async() method to queue up a single job. If the pool has a process that isn't already working, it will start immediately; otherwise, it will hold onto the task until there is a free worker process available.

Pools can also be closed; they refuse to take any further tasks, but continue to process everything currently in the queue. They can also be terminated, which goes one step further and refuses to start any jobs still in the queue, although any jobs currently running are still permitted to complete.

There are a number of constraints on how many workers make sense, including the following:

- Only cpu_count() processes can be computing simultaneously; any number can be waiting. If the workload is CPU-intensive, a larger pool of workers won't compute any faster. If the workload involves a lot of input/output, however, a large pool might improve the rate at which work is completed.

- For very large data structures, the number of workers in the pool may need to be reduced to make sure memory is used effectively.

- Communication between processes is expensive; easily serialized data is the best policy.

- Creating new processes takes a non-zero amount of time; a pool of a fixed size helps minimize the impact of this cost.

The multiprocessing pool gives us a tremendous amount of computing power with relatively little work on our part. We need to define a function that can perform the parallelized computation, and we need to map arguments to that function using an instance of the `multiprocessing.Pool` class.

In many applications, we need to do more than a mapping from a parameter value to a complex result. For these applications, the simple `poll.map()` may not be enough. For more complicated data flows, we can make use of explicit queues of pending work and computed results. We'll look at creating a network of queues next.

Queues

If we need more control over communication between processes, the `queue.Queue` data structure is useful. There are several variants offering ways to send messages from one process to one or more other processes. Any picklable object can be sent into a `Queue`, but remember that pickling can be a costly operation, so keep such objects small. To illustrate queues, let's build a little search engine for text content that stores all relevant entries in memory.

This particular search engine scans all files in the current directory in parallel. A process is constructed for each core on the CPU. Each of these is instructed to load some of the files into memory. Let's look at the function that does the loading and searching:

```
from __future__ import annotations
from pathlib import Path
from typing import List, Iterator, Optional, Union, TYPE_CHECKING

if TYPE_CHECKING:
    Query_Q = Queue[Union[str, None]]
    Result_Q = Queue[List[str]]

def search(
        paths: list[Path],
        query_q: Query_Q,
        results_q: Result_Q,
) -> None:
    print(f"PID: {os.getpid()}, paths {len(paths)}")
    lines: List[str] = []
    for path in paths:
        lines.extend(
```

```
            l.rstrip() for l in path.read_text().splitlines()

    while True:
        if (query_text := query_q.get()) is None:
            break
        results = [l for l in lines if query_text in l]
        results_q.put(results)
```

Remember, the search() function is run in a separate process (in fact, it is run in cpu_count() separate processes) from the main process that created the queues. Each of these processes is started with a list of pathlib.Path objects, and two multiprocessing.Queue objects; one for incoming queries and one to send outgoing results. These queues automatically pickle the data in the queue and pass it into the subprocess over a pipe. These two queues are set up in the main process and passed through the pipes into the search function inside the child processes.

The type hints reflect the way *mypy* wants details about the structure of data in each queue. When TYPE_CHECKING is True, it means *mypy* is running, and needs enough details to be sure the objects in the application match the descriptions of the objects in each of the queues. When TYPE_CHECKING is False, this is the ordinary runtime for the application, and the structural details of the queued messages can't be provided.

The search() function does two separate things:

1. When it starts, it opens and reads all the supplied files in the list of Path objects. Each line of text in those files is accumulated into the lines list. This preparation is relatively expensive, but it's done exactly once.

2. The while statement is the main event processing loop for search. It uses query_q.get() to get a request from its queue. It searches lines. It uses results_q.put() to put a response into the results queue.

The while statement has the characteristic design pattern for queue-based processing. The process will get a value from a queue of some work to perform, perform the work, and then put the result into another queue. We can decompose very large and complex problems into processing steps and queues so that the work is done concurrently, producing more results in less time. This technique also lets us tailor the processing steps and the number of workers to make best use of a processor.

The main part of the application builds this pool of workers and their queues. We'll follow the **Façade** design pattern (refer back to *Chapter 12, Advanced Design Patterns* for more information). The idea here is to define a class, DirectorySearch, to wrap the queues and the pool of worker processes into a single object.

This object can set up the queues and the workers, and an application can then interact with them by posting a query and consuming the replies.

```python
from __future__ import annotations
from fnmatch import fnmatch
import os

class DirectorySearch:
    def __init__(self) -> None:
        self.query_queues: List[Query_Q]
        self.results_queue: Result_Q
        self.search_workers: List[Process]

    def setup_search(
        self, paths: List[Path], cpus: Optional[int] = None) -> None:
        if cpus is None:
            cpus = cpu_count()
        worker_paths = [paths[i::cpus] for i in range(cpus)]
        self.query_queues = [Queue() for p in range(cpus)]
        self.results_queue = Queue()

        self.search_workers = [
            Process(
                target=search, args=(paths, q, self.results_queue))
            for paths, q in zip(worker_paths, self.query_queues)
        ]
        for proc in self.search_workers:
            proc.start()

    def teardown_search(self) -> None:
        # Signal process termination
        for q in self.query_queues:
            q.put(None)

        for proc in self.search_workers:
            proc.join()

    def search(self, target: str) -> Iterator[str]:
        for q in self.query_queues:
            q.put(target)

        for i in range(len(self.query_queues)):
```

```
        for match in self.results_queue.get():
            yield match
```

The `setup_search()` method prepares the worker subprocesses. The `[i::cpus]` slice operation lets us break this list into a number of equally-sized parts. If the number of CPUs is 8, the step size will be 8, and we'll use 8 different offset values from 0 to 7. We also construct a list of `Queue` objects to send data into each worker process. Finally, we construct a **single** results queue. This is passed into all of the worker subprocesses. Each of them can put data into the queue and it will be aggregated in the main process.

Once the queues are created and the workers started, the `search()` method provides the target to all the workers at one time. They can then all commence examining their separate collections of data to emit answers.

Since we're searching a fairly large number of directories, we use a generator function, `all_source()`, to locate all the `*.py` `Path` objects under the given base directory. Here's the function to find all the source files:

```
def all_source(path: Path, pattern: str) -> Iterator[Path]:
    for root, dirs, files in os.walk(path):
        for skip in {".tox", ".mypy_cache", "__pycache__", ".idea"}:
            if skip in dirs:
                dirs.remove(skip)
        yield from (
            Path(root) / f for f in files if fnmatch(f, pattern))
```

The `all_source()` function uses the `os.walk()` function to examine a directory tree, rejecting file directories that are filled with files we don't want to look at. This function uses the `fnmatch` module to match a file name against the kind of wild-card patterns the Linux shell uses. We can use a pattern parameter of `'*.py'`, for example, to find all files with names ending in `.py`. This seeds the `setup_search()` method of the `DirectorySearch` class.

The `teardown_search()` method of the `DirectorySearch` class puts a special termination value into each queue. Remember, each worker is a separate process, executing the `while` statement inside the `search()` function and reading from a queue of requests. When it reads a `None` object, it will break out of the `while` statement and exit the function. We can then use the `join()` to collect all the child processes, cleaning up politely. (If we don't do the `join()`, some Linux distros can leave "zombie processes" – children not properly rejoined with their parent because the parent crashed; these consume system resources and often require a reboot.)

Now let's look at the code that makes a search actually happen:

```python
if __name__ == "__main__":
    ds = DirectorySearch()
    base = Path.cwd().parent
    all_paths = list(all_source(base, "*.py"))
    ds.setup_search(all_paths)
    for target in ("import", "class", "def"):
        start = time.perf_counter()
        count = 0
        for line in ds.search(target):
            # print(line)
            count += 1
        milliseconds = 1000*(time.perf_counter()-start)
        print(
            f"Found {count} {target!r} in {len(all_paths)} files "
            f"in {milliseconds:.3f}ms"
        )
    ds.teardown_search()
```

This code creates a `DirectorySearch` object, `ds`, and provides all of the source paths starting from the parent of the current working directory, via `base = Path.cwd().parent`. Once the workers are prepared, the `ds` object performs searches for a few common strings, `"import"`, `"class"`, and `"def"`. Note that we've commented out the `print(line)` statement that shows the useful results. For now, we're interested in performance. The initial file reads take a fraction of a second to get started. Once all the files are read, however, the time to do the search is dramatic. On a MacBook Pro with 134 files of source code, the output looks like this:

```
python src/directory_search.py
PID: 36566, paths 17
PID: 36567, paths 17
PID: 36570, paths 17
PID: 36571, paths 17
PID: 36569, paths 17
PID: 36568, paths 17
PID: 36572, paths 16
PID: 36573, paths 16
Found 579 'import' in 134 files in 111.561ms
Found 838 'class' in 134 files in 1.010ms
Found 1138 'def' in 134 files in 1.224ms
```

The search for `"import"` took about 111 milliseconds (0.111 seconds.) Why was this so slow compared with the other two searches? It's because the `search()` function was still reading the files when the first request was put in the queue. The first request's performance reflects the one-time startup cost of loading the file content into memory. The next two requests run in about 1 millisecond each. That's amazing! Almost 1,000 searches per second on a laptop with only a few lines of Python code.

This example of queues to feed data among workers is a single-host version of what could become a distributed system. Imagine the searches were being sent out to multiple host computers and then recombined. Now imagine you had access to the fleet of computers in Google's data centers and you might understand why they can return search results so quickly!

We won't discuss it here, but the `multiprocessing` module includes a manager class that can take a lot of the boilerplate out of the preceding code. There is even a version of `multiprocessing.Manager` that can manage subprocesses on remote systems to construct a rudimentary distributed application. Check the Python `multiprocessing` documentation if you are interested in pursuing this further.

The problems with multiprocessing

As with threads, multiprocessing also has problems, some of which we have already discussed. Sharing data between processes is costly. As we have discussed, all communication between processes, whether by queues, OS pipes, or even shared memory, requires serializing the objects. Excessive serialization can dominate processing time. Shared memory objects can help by limiting the serialization to the initial setup of the shared memory. Multiprocessing works best when relatively small objects are passed between processes and a tremendous amount of work needs to be done on each one.

Using shared memory can avoid the cost of repeated serialization and deserialization. There are numerous limitations on the kinds of Python objects that can be shared. Shared memory can help performance, but can also lead to somewhat more complex-looking Python objects.

The other major problem with multiprocessing is that, like threads, it can be hard to tell which process a variable or method is being accessed in. In multiprocessing, the worker processes inherit a great deal of data from the parent process. This isn't shared, it's a one-time copy. A child can be given a copy of a mapping or a list and mutate the object. The parent won't see the effects of the child's mutation.

A big advantage of multiprocessing is the absolute independence of processes. We don't need to carefully manage locks, because the data is not shared. Additionally, the internal operating system limits on numbers of open files are allocated at the process level; we can have a large number of resource-intensive processes.

When designing concurrent applications, the focus is on maximizing the use of the CPU to do as much work in as short a time as possible. With so many choices, we always need to examine the problem to figure out which of the many available solutions is the best one for that problem.

 The notion of concurrent processing is too broad for there to be one right way to do it. Each distinct problem has a best solution. It's important to write code in a way that permits adjustment, tuning, and optimization.

We've looked at the two principal tools for concurrency in Python: threads and processes. Threads exist within a single OS process, sharing memory and other resources. Processes are independent of each other, which makes interprocess communication a necessary overhead. Both of these approaches are amenable to the concept of a pool of concurrent workers waiting to work and providing results at some unpredictable time in the future. This abstraction of results becoming available in the future is what shapes the `concurrent.futures` module. We'll look at this next.

Futures

Let's start looking at a more asynchronous way of implementing concurrency. The concept of a "future" or a "promise" is a handy abstraction for describing concurrent work. A **future** is an object that wraps a function call. That function call is run in the *background*, in a thread or a separate process. The `future` object has methods to check whether the computation has completed and to get the results. We can think of it as a computation where the results will arrive in the future, and we can do something else while waiting for them.

See `https://hub.packtpub.com/asynchronous-programming-futures-and-promises/` for some additional background.

In Python, the `concurrent.futures` module wraps either `multiprocessing` or `threading` depending on what kind of concurrency we need. A future doesn't completely solve the problem of accidentally altering shared state, but using futures allows us to structure our code such that it can be easier to track down the cause of the problem when we do so.

Futures can help manage boundaries between the different threads or processes. Similar to the multiprocessing pool, they are useful for **call and answer** type interactions, in which processing can happen in another thread (or process) and then at some point in the future (they are aptly named, after all), you can ask it for the result. It's a wrapper around multiprocessing pools and thread pools, but it provides a cleaner API and encourages nicer code.

Let's see another, more sophisticated file search and analyze example. In the last section, we implemented a version of the Linux grep command. This time, we'll create a simple version of the find command that bundles in a clever analysis of Python source code. We'll start with the analytical part since it's central to the work we need done concurrently:

```python
class ImportResult(NamedTuple):
    path: Path
    imports: Set[str]

    @property
    def focus(self) -> bool:
        return "typing" in self.imports

class ImportVisitor(ast.NodeVisitor):
    def __init__(self) -> None:
        self.imports: Set[str] = set()

    def visit_Import(self, node: ast.Import) -> None:
        for alias in node.names:
            self.imports.add(alias.name)

    def visit_ImportFrom(self, node: ast.ImportFrom) -> None:
        if node.module:
            self.imports.add(node.module)

def find_imports(path: Path) -> ImportResult:
    tree = ast.parse(path.read_text())
    iv = ImportVisitor()
    iv.visit(tree)
    return ImportResult(path, iv.imports)
```

We've defined a few things here. We started with a named tuple, `ImportResult`, which binds a `Path` object and a set of strings together. It has a property, `focus`, that looks for the specific string, `"typing"`, in the set of strings. We'll see why this string is so important in a moment.

The `ImportVisitor` class is built using the `ast` module in the standard library.
An **Abstract Syntax Tree (AST)** is the parsed source code, usually from a formal
programming language. Python code, after all, is just a bunch of characters; the AST
for Python code groups the text into meaningful statements and expressions, variable
names, and operators, all of the syntactic components of the language. A visitor has
a method to examine the parsed code. We provided overrides for two methods of the
`NodeVisitor` class so we will visit only the two kinds of import statements: `import x`,
and `from x import y`. The details of how each node data structure works are a bit
beyond this example, but the `ast` module documentation in the Standard Library
describes the unique structure of each Python language construct.

The `find_imports()` function reads some source, parses the Python code, visits the
`import` statements, and then returns an `ImportResult` with the original `Path` and the
set of names found by the visitor. This is – in many ways – a lot better than a simple
pattern match for `"import"`. For example, using an `ast.NodeVisitor` will skip over
comments and ignore the text inside character string literals, two jobs that are hard
with regular expressions.

There isn't anything particularly special about the `find_imports()` function, but
note how it does not access any global variables. All interaction with the external
environment is passed into the function or returned from it. This is not a technical
requirement, but it is the best way to keep your brain inside your skull when
programming with futures.

We want to process hundreds of files in dozens of directories, though. The best
approach is to have lots and lots of these running all at the same time, clogging the
cores of our CPU with lots and lots of computing.

```python
def main() -> None:
    start = time.perf_counter()
    base = Path.cwd().parent
    with futures.ThreadPoolExecutor(24) as pool:
        analyzers = [
            pool.submit(find_imports, path)
            for path in all_source(base, "*.py")
        ]
        analyzed = (
            worker.result()
            for worker in futures.as_completed(analyzers)
        )
    for example in sorted(analyzed):
        print(
            f"{'->' if example.focus else '':2s} "
```

```
            f"{example.path.relative_to(base)} {example.imports}"
        )
    end = time.perf_counter()
    rate = 1000 * (end - start) / len(analyzers)
    print(f"Searched {len(analyzers)} files at {rate:.3f}ms/file")
```

We're leveraging the same `all_source()` function shown in the *Queues* section earlier in this chapter; this needs a base directory to start searching in, and a pattern, like `"*.py"`, to find all the files with the `.py` extension. We've created a `ThreadPoolExecutor`, assigned to the `pool` variable, with two dozen worker threads, all waiting for something to do. We create a list of `Future` objects in the `analyzers` object. This list is created by a list comprehension applying the `pool.submit()` method to our search function, `find_imports()`, and a `Path` from the output of `all_source()`.

The threads in the pool will immediately start working on the submitted list of tasks. As each thread finishes work, it saves the results in the `Future` object and picks up some more work to do.

Meanwhile, in the foreground, the application uses a generator expression to evaluate the `result()` method of each `Future` object. Note that the futures are visited using the `futures.as_completed()` generator. The function starts providing complete `Future` objects as they become available. This means the results may not be in the order they were originally submitted. There are other ways to visit the futures; we can, for example, wait until all are complete and then visit them in the order they were submitted, in case that's important.

We extract the result from each `Future`. From the type hints, we can see that this will be an `ImportResult` object with a `Path` and a set of strings; these are the names of the imported modules. We can sort the results, so the files show up in some sensible order.

On a MacBook Pro, this takes about 1.689 milliseconds (0.001689 seconds) to process each file. The 24 individual threads easily fit in a single process without stressing the operating system. Increasing the number of threads doesn't materially affect the elapsed runtime, suggesting any remaining bottleneck is not concurrent computation, but the initial scan of the directory tree and the creation of the thread pool.

And the `focus` feature of the `ImportResult` class? Why is the `typing` module special? We needed to review each chapter's type hints when a new release of *mypy* came out during the development of this book. It was helpful to separate the modules into those that required careful checking and those that didn't need to be revised.

And that's all that is required to develop a futures-based I/O-bound application. Under the hood, it's using the same thread or process APIs we've already discussed, but it provides a more understandable interface and makes it easier to see the boundaries between concurrently running functions (just don't try to access global variables from inside the future!).

Accessing outside variables without proper synchronization can result in a problem called a **race condition**. For example, imagine two concurrent writes trying to increment an integer counter. They start at the same time and both read the current value of the shared variable as 5. One thread is first in the race; it increments the value and writes 6. The other thread comes in second; it increments what the variable was and also writes 6. But if two processes are trying to increment a variable, the expected result would be that it gets incremented by 2, so the result should be 7.

Modern wisdom is that the easiest way to avoid doing this is to keep as much state as possible private and share them through known-safe constructs, such as queues or futures.

For many applications, the concurrent.futures module is the place to start with designing the Python code. The lower-level threading and multiprocessing modules offer some additional constructs for very complex cases.

Using run_in_executor() allows an application to leverage the concurrent.futures module's ProcessPoolExecutor or ThreadPoolExecutor classes to farm work out to multiple processes or multiple threads. This provides a lot of flexibility within a tidy, ergonomic API.

In some cases, we don't really need concurrent processes. In some cases, we simply need to be able to toggle back and forth between waiting for data and computing when data becomes available. The async features of Python, including the asyncio module, can interleave processing within a single thread. We'll look at this variation on the theme of concurrency next.

AsyncIO

AsyncIO is the current state of the art in Python concurrent programming. It combines the concept of futures and an event loop with coroutines. The result is about as elegant and easy to understand as it is possible to get when writing responsive applications that don't seem to waste time waiting for input.

For the purposes of working with Python's async features, a *coroutine* is a function that is waiting for an event, and also can provide events to other coroutines. In Python, we implement coroutines using async def. A function with async must work in the context of an **event loop** which switches control among the coroutines waiting for events. We'll see a few Python constructs using await expressions to show where the event loop can switch to another async function.

It's crucial to recognize that async operations are interleaved, and not – generally – parallel. At most one coroutine is in control and processing, and all the others are waiting for an event. The idea of interleaving is described as **cooperative multitasking**: an application can be processing data while also waiting for the next request message to arrive. As data becomes available, the event loop can transfer control to one of the waiting coroutines.

AsyncIO has a bias toward network I/O. Most networking applications, especially on the server side, spend a lot of time waiting for data to come in from the network. AsyncIO can be more efficient than handling each client in a separate thread; then some threads can be working while others are waiting. The problem is the threads use up memory and other resources. AsyncIO uses coroutines to interleave processing cycles when the data becomes available.

Thread scheduling depends on OS requests the thread makes (and to an extent, the GIL's interleaving of threads). Process scheduling depends on the overall scheduler for the operating system. Both thread and process scheduling are **preemptive** – the thread (or process) can be interrupted to allow a different, higher-priority thread or process to control the CPU. This means thread scheduling is unpredictable, and locks are important if multiple threads are going to update a shared resource. At the OS level, shared locks are required if two processes want to update a shared OS resource like a file. Unlike threads and processes, AsyncIO coroutines are **non-preemptive**; they explicitly hand control to each other at specific points in the processing, removing the need for explicit locking of shared resources.

The asyncio library provides a built-in *event loop*: this is the loop that handles interleaving control among the running coroutines. However, the event loop comes with a cost. When we run code in an async task on the event loop, that code *must* return immediately, blocking neither on I/O nor on long-running calculations. This is a minor thing when writing our own code, but it means that any standard library or third-party functions that block on I/O must be wrapped with an async def function that can handle the waiting politely.

When working with asyncio, we'll write our application as a set of coroutines that use async and await syntax to interleave control via the event loop. The top-level "main" program's job, then, is simplified to running the event loop so the coroutines can then hand control back and forth, interleaving waiting and working.

AsyncIO in action

A canonical example of a blocking function is the `time.sleep()` call. We can't call the `time` module's `sleep()` directly, because it would seize control, stalling the event loop. We'll use the version of `sleep()` in the `asyncio` module. Used in an `await` expression, the event loop can interleave another coroutine while waiting for the `sleep()` to finish. Let's use the asynchronous version of this call to illustrate the basics of an AsyncIO event loop, as follows:

```python
import asyncio
import random

async def random_sleep(counter: float) -> None:
    delay = random.random() * 5
    print(f"{counter} sleeps for {delay:.2f} seconds")
    await asyncio.sleep(delay)
    print(f"{counter} awakens, refreshed")

async def sleepers(how_many: int = 5) -> None:
    print(f"Creating {how_many} tasks")
    tasks = [
        asyncio.create_task(random_sleep(i))
        for i in range(how_many)]
    print(f"Waiting for {how_many} tasks")
    await asyncio.gather(*tasks)

if __name__ == "__main__":
    asyncio.run(sleepers(5))
    print("Done with the sleepers")
```

This example covers several features of AsyncIO programming. The overall processing is started by the `asyncio.run()` function. This starts the event loop, executing the `sleepers()` coroutine. Within the `sleepers()` coroutine, we create a handful of individual tasks; these are instances of the `random_sleep()` coroutine with a given argument value. The `random_sleep()` uses `asyncio.sleep()` to simulate a long-running request.

Because this is built using `async def` functions and an `await` expression around `asyncio.sleep()`, execution of the `random_sleep()` functions and the overall `sleepers()` function is interleaved. While the `random_sleep()` requests are started in order of their `counter` parameter value, they finish in a completely different order. Here's an example:

```
python src/async_1.py
Creating 5 tasks
Waiting for 5 tasks
0 sleeps for 4.69 seconds
1 sleeps for 1.59 seconds
2 sleeps for 4.57 seconds
3 sleeps for 3.45 seconds
4 sleeps for 0.77 seconds
4 awakens, refreshed
1 awakens, refreshed
3 awakens, refreshed
2 awakens, refreshed
0 awakens, refreshed
Done with the sleepers
```

We can see the random_sleep() function with a counter value of 4 had the shortest sleep time, and was given control first when it finished the await asyncio.sleep() expression. The order of waking is strictly based on the random sleep interval, and the event loop's ability to hand control from coroutine to coroutine.

As asynchronous programmers, we don't need to know too much about what happens inside that run() function, but be aware that a lot is going on to track which of the coroutines is waiting and which should have control at the current moment.

A task, in this context, is an object that asyncio knows how to schedule in the event loop. This includes the following:

- Coroutines defined with the async def statement.
- asyncio.Future objects. These are almost identical to the concurrent.futures you saw in the previous section, but for use with asyncio.
- Any awaitable object, that is, one with an __await__() function.

In this example, all the tasks are coroutines; we'll see some of the others in later examples.

Look a little more closely at that sleepers() coroutine. It first constructs instances of the random_sleep() coroutine. These are each wrapped in an asyncio.create_task() call, which adds these as futures to the loop's task queue so they can execute and start immediately when control is returned to the loop.

Control is returned to the event loop whenever we call await. In this case, we call await asyncio.gather() to yield control to other coroutines until all the tasks are finished.

Each of the `random_sleep()` coroutines prints a starting message, then sends control back to the event loop for a specific amount of time using its own `await` calls. When the sleep has completed, the event loop passes control back to the relevant `random_sleep()` task, which prints its awakening message before returning.

The `async` keyword acts as documentation notifying the Python interpreter (and coder) that the coroutine contains the `await` calls. It also does some work to prepare the coroutine to run on the event loop. It behaves much like a decorator; in fact, back in Python 3.4, it used to be implemented as an `@asyncio.coroutine` decorator.

Reading an AsyncIO future

An AsyncIO coroutine executes each line of code in order until it encounters an `await` expression, at which point it returns control to the event loop. The event loop then executes any other tasks that are ready to run, including the one that the original coroutine was waiting on. Whenever that child task completes, the event loop sends the result back into the coroutine so that it can pick up execution until it encounters another `await` expression or returns.

This allows us to write code that executes synchronously until we explicitly need to wait for something. As a result, there is no non-deterministic behavior of threads, so we don't need to worry nearly so much about shared state.

> It's a good idea to limit shared state: a *share nothing* philosophy can prevent a ton of difficult bugs stemming from sometimes hard-to-imagine timelines of interleaved operations.
>
> Think of the OS schedulers as intentionally and wickedly evil; they will maliciously (somehow) find the worst possible sequence of operations among processes, threads, or coroutines.

The real value of AsyncIO is the way it allows us to collect logical sections of code together inside a single coroutine, even if we are waiting for other work elsewhere. As a specific instance, even though the `await asyncio.sleep` call in the `random_sleep()` coroutine is allowing a ton of stuff to happen inside the event loop, the coroutine itself looks like it's doing everything in order. This ability to read related pieces of asynchronous code without worrying about the machinery that waits for tasks to complete is the primary benefit of the AsyncIO module.

AsyncIO for networking

AsyncIO was specifically designed for use with network sockets, so let's implement a server using the asyncio module. Looking back at *Chapter 13, Testing Object-Oriented Programs*, we created a fairly complex server to catch log entries being sent from one process to another process using sockets. At the time, we used it as an example of a complex resource we didn't want to set up and tear down for each test.

We'll rewrite that example, creating an asyncio-based server that can handle requests from a (large) number of clients. It can do this by having lots of coroutines, all waiting for log records to arrive. When a record arrives, one coroutine can save the record, doing some computation, while the remaining coroutines wait.

In *Chapter 13*, we were interested in writing a test for the integration of a log catcher process with separate log-writing client application processes. Here's an illustration of the relationships involved:

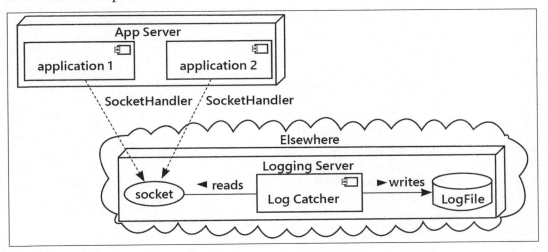

Figure 14.1: The Log Catcher in the Sky

The log catcher process creates a socket server to wait for connections from all client applications. Each of the client applications uses logging.SocketHandler to direct log messages to the waiting server. The server collects the messages and writes them to a single, central log file.

This test was based on an example back in *Chapter 12*, which suffered from a weak implementation. To keep things simple in that chapter, the log server only worked with one application client at a time. We want to revisit the idea of a server that collects log messages. This improved implementation will handle a very large number of concurrent clients because it uses AsyncIO techniques.

The central part of this design is a coroutine that reads log entries from a socket. This involves waiting for the bytes that comprise a header, then decoding the header to compute the size of the payload. The coroutine can read the right number of bytes for the log message payload, and then use a separate coroutine to process the payload. Here's the `log_catcher()` function:

```
SIZE_FORMAT = ">L"
SIZE_BYTES = struct.calcsize(SIZE_FORMAT)

async def log_catcher(
    reader: asyncio.StreamReader, writer: asyncio.StreamWriter
) -> None:
    count = 0
    client_socket = writer.get_extra_info("socket")
    size_header = await reader.read(SIZE_BYTES)
    while size_header:
        payload_size = struct.unpack(SIZE_FORMAT, size_header)
        bytes_payload = await reader.read(payload_size[0])
        await log_writer(bytes_payload)
        count += 1
        size_header = await reader.read(SIZE_BYTES)
    print(f"From {client_socket.getpeername()}: {count} lines")
```

This `log_catcher()` function implements the protocol used by the `logging` module's `SocketHandler` class. Each log entry is a block of bytes we can decompose into a header and a payload. We need to read the first few bytes, saved in `size_header`, to get the size of the message which follows. Once we have the size, we can wait for the payload bytes to arrive. Since the two reads are both `await` expressions, other coroutines can work while this function is waiting for the header and payload bytes to arrive.

The `log_catcher()` function is invoked by a server that provides the coroutine with a `StreamReader` and `StreamWriter`. These two objects wrap the socket pair that is created by the TCP/IP protocol. The stream reader (and the writer) are properly async-aware objects, and we can use `await` when waiting to read bytes from the client.

This `log_catcher()` function waits for socket data, then provides data to another coroutine, `log_writer()`, for conversion and writing. The `log_catcher()` function's job is to do a lot of waiting, and then shuttle the data from reader to writer; it also does an internal computation to count messages from a client. Incrementing a counter is not much, but it is work that can be done while waiting for data to arrive.

Here's a function, `serialize()`, and a coroutine, `log_writer()`, to convert log entries to JSON notation and write them to a file:

```
TARGET: TextIO
LINE_COUNT = 0

def serialize(bytes_payload: bytes) -> str:
    object_payload = pickle.loads(bytes_payload)
    text_message = json.dumps(object_payload)
    TARGET.write(text_message)
    TARGET.write("\n")
    return text_message

async def log_writer(bytes_payload: bytes) -> None:
    global LINE_COUNT
    LINE_COUNT += 1
    text_message = await asyncio.to_thread(serialize, bytes_payload)
```

The `serialize()` function needs to have an open file, `TARGET`, to which the log messages are written. The file open (and close) needs to be taken care of elsewhere in the application; we'll look at these operations below. The `serialize()` function is used by the `log_writer()` coroutine. Because `log_writer()` is an async coroutine, other coroutines will be waiting to read and decode input messages while this coroutine is writing them.

The `serialize()` function actually does a fair amount of computation. It also harbors a profound problem. The file write operation can be blocked, that is, stuck waiting for the operating system to finish the work. Writing to a disk means handing the work to a disk device and waiting until the device responds that the write operation is complete. While a microsecond to write a 1,000-character line of data may seem fast, it's forever to a CPU. This means all file operations will block their thread waiting for the operation to complete. To work politely with the other coroutines in the main thread, we assign this blocking work to a separate thread. This is why the `log_writer()` coroutine uses the `asyncio.to_thread()` to allocate this work to a separate thread.

Because the `log_writer()` coroutine uses `await` on this separate thread, it returns control to the event loop while the thread waits for the write to complete. This polite `await` allows other coroutines to work while the `log_writer()` coroutine is waiting for `serialize()` to complete.

We've passed two kinds of work to a separate thread:

- A compute-intensive operation. These are the `pickle.loads()` and `json.dumps()` operations.
- A blocking OS operation. This is `TARGET.write()`. These blocking operations include most operating system requests, including file operations. They do not include the various network streams that are already part of the `asyncio` module. As we saw in the `log_catcher()` function above, the streams are already polite users of the event loop.

This technique of passing work to a thread is how we can make sure the event loop is spending as much time waiting as possible. If all the coroutines are waiting for an event, then whatever happens next will be responded to as quickly as possible. This principle of many waiters is the secret to a responsive service.

The `LINE_COUNT` global variable can raise some eyebrows. Recall from previous sections, we raised dire warnings about the consequences of multiple threads updating a shared variable concurrently. With `asyncio`, we don't have preemption among threads. Because each coroutine uses explicit `await` requests to give control to other coroutines via the event loop, we can update this variable in the `log_writer()` coroutine knowing the state change will effectively be atomic – an indivisible update – among all the coroutines.

To make this example complete, here are the imports:

```
from __future__ import annotations
import asyncio
import asyncio.exceptions
import json
from pathlib import Path
from typing import TextIO
import pickle
import signal
import struct
import sys
```

Here's the top-level dispatcher that starts this service:

```
server: asyncio.AbstractServer

async def main(host: str, port: int) -> None:
    global server
    server = await asyncio.start_server(
        log_catcher,
```

```
            host=host,
            port=port,
    )

    if sys.platform != "win32":
        loop = asyncio.get_running_loop()
        loop.add_signal_handler(signal.SIGTERM, server.close)

    if server.sockets:
        addr = server.sockets[0].getsockname()
        print(f"Serving on {addr}")
    else:
        raise ValueError("Failed to create server")

    async with server:
        await server.serve_forever()
```

The `main()` function contains an elegant way to automatically create new `asyncio.Task` objects for each network connection. The `asyncio.start_server()` function listens at the given host address and port number for incoming socket connections. For each connection, it creates a new `Task` instance using the `log_catcher()` coroutine; this is added to the event loop's collection of coroutines. Once the server is started, the `main()` function lets it provide services forever using the server's `serve_forever()` method.

The `add_signal_handler()` method of a loop deserves some explanation. For non-Windows operating systems, a process is terminated via a signal from the operating system. The signals have small numeric identifiers and symbolic names. For example, the terminate signal has a numeric code of 15, and a name of `signal.SIGTERM`. When a parent process terminates a child process, this signal is sent. If we do nothing special, this signal will simply stop the Python interpreter. When we use the *Ctrl + C* sequence on the keyboard, this becomes a `SIGINT` signal, which leads Python to raise a `KeyboardInterrupt` exception.

The `add_signal_handler()` method of the loop lets us examine incoming signals and handle them as part of our AsyncIO processing loop. We don't want to simply stop with an unhandled exception. We want to finish the various coroutines, and allow any write threads executing the `serialize()` function to complete normally. To make this happen, we connect the signal to the `server.close()` method. This ends the `serve_forever()` process cleanly, letting all the coroutines finish.

For Windows, we have to work outside the AsyncIO processing loop. This additional code is required to connect the low-level signals to a function that will close down the server cleanly.

```
if sys.platform == "win32":
    from types import FrameType

    def close_server(signum: int, frame: FrameType) -> None:
        # print(f"Signal {signum}")
        server.close()

    signal.signal(signal.SIGINT, close_server)
    signal.signal(signal.SIGTERM, close_server)
    signal.signal(signal.SIGABRT, close_server)
    signal.signal(signal.SIGBREAK, close_server)
```

We've defined three standard signals, SIGINT, SIGTERM, and SIGABRT, as well as a Windows-specific signal, SIGBREAK. These will all close the server, ending the handling of requests and closing down the processing loop when all of the pending coroutines have completed.

As we saw in the previous AsyncIO example, the main program is also a succinct way to start the event loop:

```
if __name__ == "__main__":
    # These often have command-line or environment overrides
    HOST, PORT = "localhost", 18842

    with Path("one.log").open("w") as TARGET:
        try:
            if sys.platform == "win32":
                # https://github.com/encode/httpx/issues/914
                loop = asyncio.get_event_loop()
                loop.run_until_complete(main(HOST, PORT))
                loop.run_until_complete(asyncio.sleep(1))
                loop.close()
            else:
                asyncio.run(main(HOST, PORT))

        except (
                asyncio.exceptions.CancelledError,
                KeyboardInterrupt):
            ending = {"lines_collected": LINE_COUNT}
```

```
print(ending)
TARGET.write(json.dumps(ending) + "\n")
```

This will open a file, setting the global `TARGET` variable used by the `serialize()` function. It uses the `main()` function to create the server that waits for connections. When the `serve_forever()` task is canceled with a `CancelledError` or `KeyboardInterrupt` exception, we can put a final summary line onto the log file. This line confirms that things completed normally, allowing us to verify that no lines were lost.

For Windows, we need to use the `run_until_complete()` method, instead of the more comprehensive `run()` method. We also need to put one more coroutine, `asyncio.sleep()`, into the event loop to wait for the final processing from any other coroutines.

Pragmatically, we might want to use the `argparse` module to parse command-line arguments. We might want to use a more sophisticated file-handling mechanism in `log_writer()` so we can limit the size of log files.

Design considerations

Let's look at some of the features of this design. First, the `log_writer()` coroutine passes bytes into and out of the external thread running the `serialize()` function. This is better than decoding the JSON in a coroutine in the main thread because the (relatively expensive) decoding can happen without stopping the main thread's event loop.

This call to `serialize()` is, in effect, a future. In the *Futures* section, earlier in this chapter, we saw there are a few lines of boilerplate for using `concurrent.futures`. However, when we use futures with AsyncIO, there are almost none at all! When we use `await asyncio.to_thread()`, the `log_writer()` coroutine wraps the function call in a future and submits it to the internal thread pool executor. Our code can then return to the event loop until the future completes, allowing the main thread to process other connections, tasks, or futures. It is particularly important to put blocking I/O requests into separate threads. When the future is done, the `log_writer()` coroutine can finish waiting and can do any follow-up processing.

The `main()` coroutine used `start_server()`; the server listens for connection requests. It will provide client-specific AsyncIO read and write streams to each task created to handle a distinct connection; the task will wrap the `log_catcher()` coroutine. With the AsyncIO streams, reading from a stream is a potentially blocking call so we can call it with `await`. This means politely returning to the event loop until bytes start arriving.

It can help to consider how the workload grows inside this server. Initially, the `main()` function is the only coroutine. It creates the `server`, and now both `main()` and the `server` are in the event loop's collection of waiting coroutines. When a connection is made, the server creates a new task, and the event loop now contains `main()`, the `server`, and an instance of the `log_catcher()` coroutine. Most of the time, all of these coroutines are waiting for something to do: either a new connection for the server, or a message for the `log_catcher()`. When a message arrives, it's decoded and handed to `log_writer()`, and yet another coroutine is available. No matter what happens next, the application is ready to respond. The number of waiting coroutines is limited by available memory, so a lot of individual coroutines can be patiently waiting for work to do.

Next, we'll take a quick look at a log-writing application that uses this log catcher. The application doesn't do anything useful, but it can tie up a lot of cores for a long period of time. This will show us how responsive AsyncIO applications can be.

A log writing demonstration

To demonstrate how this log catching works, this client application writes a bunch of messages and does an immense amount of computing. To see how responsive the log catcher is, we can start a bunch of copies of this application to stress-test the log catcher.

This client doesn't leverage `asyncio`; it's a contrived example of compute-intensive work with a few I/O requests wrapped around it. Using coroutines to perform the I/O requests concurrently with the computation is – by design – unhelpful in this example.

We've written an application that applies a variation on the bogosort algorithm to some random data. Here's some information on this sorting algorithm: `https://rosettacode.org/wiki/Sorting_algorithms/Bogosort`. This isn't a practical algorithm, but it's simple: it enumerates all possible orderings, searching for one that is the desired, ascending order. Here are the imports and an abstract superclass, `Sorter`, for sorting algorithms:

```
from __future__ import annotations
import abc
from itertools import permutations
import logging
import logging.handlers
import os
import random
import time
import sys
```

```
from typing import Iterable

logger = logging.getLogger(f"app_{os.getpid()}")

class Sorter(abc.ABC):
    def __init__(self) -> None:
        id = os.getpid()
        self.logger = logging.getLogger(
            f"app_{id}.{self.__class__.__name__}")

    @abc.abstractmethod
    def sort(self, data: list[float]) -> list[float]:
        ...
```

Next, we'll define a concrete implementation of the abstract `Sorter` class:

```
class BogoSort(Sorter):

    @staticmethod
    def is_ordered(data: tuple[float, ...]) -> bool:
        pairs: Iterable[Tuple[float, float]] = zip(data, data[1:])
        return all(a <= b for a, b in pairs)

    def sort(self, data: list[float]) -> list[float]:
        self.logger.info("Sorting %d", len(data))
        start = time.perf_counter()

        ordering: Tuple[float, ...] = tuple(data[:])
        permute_iter = permutations(data)
        steps = 0
        while not BogoSort.is_ordered(ordering):
            ordering = next(permute_iter)
            steps += 1

        duration = 1000 * (time.perf_counter() - start)
        self.logger.info(
            "Sorted %d items in %d steps, %.3f ms",
            len(data), steps, duration)
        return list(ordering)
```

The `is_ordered()` method of the `BogoSort` class checks to see if the list of objects has been sorted properly. The `sort()` method generates all permutations of the data, searching for a permutation that satisfies the constraint defined by `is_sorted()`.

Note that a set of *n* values has *n!* permutations, so this is a spectacularly inefficient sort algorithm. There are over six billion permutations of 13 values; on most computers, this algorithm can take years to sort 13 items into order.

A `main()` function handles the sorting and writes a few log messages. It does a lot of computation, tying up CPU resources doing nothing particularly useful. Here's a main program we can use to make log requests while our inefficient sort is grinding up processing time:

```python
def main(workload: int, sorter: Sorter = BogoSort()) -> int:
    total = 0
    for i in range(workload):
        samples = random.randint(3, 10)
        data = [random.random() for _ in range(samples)]
        ordered = sorter.sort(data)
        total += samples
    return total


if __name__ == "__main__":
    LOG_HOST, LOG_PORT = "localhost", 18842
    socket_handler = logging.handlers.SocketHandler(
        LOG_HOST, LOG_PORT)
    stream_handler = logging.StreamHandler(sys.stderr)
    logging.basicConfig(
        handlers=[socket_handler, stream_handler],
        level=logging.INFO)

    start = time.perf_counter()
    workload = random.randint(10, 20)
    logger.info("sorting %d collections", workload)
    samples = main(workload, BogoSort())
    end = time.perf_counter()
    logger.info(
        "sorted %d collections, taking %f s", workload, end - start)

    logging.shutdown()
```

The top-level script starts by creating a `SocketHandler` instance; this writes log messages to the log catcher service shown above. A `StreamHandler` instance writes message to console. Both of these are provided as handlers for all the defined loggers. Once the logging is configured, the `main()` function is invoked with a random workload.

On an 8-core MacBook Pro, this was run with 128 workers, all inefficiently sorting random numbers. The internal OS `time` command describes the workload as using 700% of a core; that is, seven of the eight cores were completely occupied. And yet, there's still plenty of time left over to handle the log messages, edit this document, and play music in the background. Using a faster sort algorithm, we started 256 workers and generated 5,632 log messages in about 4.4 seconds. This is 1,280 transactions per second and we were still only using 628% of the available 800%. Your performance may vary. For network-intensive workloads, AsyncIO seems to do a marvelous job of allocating precious CPU time to the coroutine with work to be done, and minimizing the time threads are blocked waiting for something to do.

It's important to observe that AsyncIO is heavily biased toward network resources including sockets, queues, and OS pipes. The file system is not a first-class part of the `asyncio` module, and therefore requires us to use the associated thread pool to handle processing that will be blocked until it's finished by the operating system.

We'll take a diversion to look at AsyncIO to write a client-side application. In this case, we won't be creating a server, but instead leveraging the event loop to make sure a client can process data very quickly.

AsyncIO clients

Because it is capable of handling many thousands of simultaneous connections, AsyncIO is very common for implementing servers. However, it is a generic networking library and provides full support for client processes as well. This is pretty important, since many microservices act as clients to other servers.

Clients can be much simpler than servers, as they don't have to be set up to wait for incoming connections. We can leverage the `await asyncio.gather()` function to parcel out a lot of work, and wait to process the results when they've completed. This can work well with `asyncio.to_thread()` which assigns blocking requests to separate threads, permitting the main thread to interleave work among the coroutines.

We can also create individual tasks that can be interleaved by the event loop. This allows the coroutines that implement the tasks to cooperatively schedule reading data along with computing the data that was read.

For this example, we'll use the `httpx` library to provide an AsyncIO-friendly HTTP request. This additional package needs to be installed with `conda install https` (if you're using *conda* as a virtual environment manager) or `python -m pip install httpx`.

Here's an application to make requests to the US weather service, implemented using asyncio. We'll focus on forecast zones useful for sailors in the Chesapeake Bay area. We'll start with some definitions:

```python
import asyncio
import httpx
import re
import time
from urllib.request import urlopen
from typing import Optional, NamedTuple

class Zone(NamedTuple):
    zone_name: str
    zone_code: str
    same_code: str  # Special Area Messaging Encoder

    @property
    def forecast_url(self) -> str:
        return (
            f"https://tgftp.nws.noaa.gov/data/forecasts"
            f"/marine/coastal/an/{self.zone_code.lower()}.txt"
        )
```

Given the Zone named tuple, we can analyze the directory of marine forecast products, and create a list of Zone instances that starts like this:

```python
ZONES = [
    Zone("Chesapeake Bay from Pooles Island to Sandy Point, MD",
        "ANZ531", "073531"),
    Zone("Chesapeake Bay from Sandy Point to North Beach, MD",
        "ANZ532", "073532"),
. . .
]
```

Depending on where you're going to be sailing, you may want additional or different zones.

We need a MarineWX class to describe the work to be done. This is an example of a **Command** pattern, where each instance is another thing we wish to do. This class has a run() method to gather data from a weather service:

```python
class MarineWX:
    advisory_pat = re.compile(r"\n\.\.\.(.*?)\.\.\.\n", re.M | re.S)
```

```python
def __init__(self, zone: Zone) -> None:
    super().__init__()
    self.zone = zone
    self.doc = ""

async def run(self) -> None:
    async with httpx.AsyncClient() as client:
        response = await client.get(self.zone.forecast_url)
    self.doc = response.text

@property
def advisory(self) -> str:
    if (match := self.advisory_pat.search(self.doc)):
        return match.group(1).replace("\n", " ")
    return ""

def __repr__(self) -> str:
    return f"{self.zone.zone_name} {self.advisory}"
```

In this example, the run() method downloads the text document from the weather service via an instance of the httpx module's AsyncClient class. A separate property, advisory(), parses the text, looking for a pattern that marks a marine weather advisory. The sections of the weather service document really are marked by three periods, a block of text, and three periods. The Marine Forecast system is designed to provide an easy-to-process format with a tiny document size.

So far, this isn't unique or remarkable. We've defined a repository of zone information, and a class that gathers data for a zone. Here's the important part: a main() function that uses the AsyncIO tasks to gather as much data as quickly as possible.

```python
async def task_main() -> None:
    start = time.perf_counter()
    forecasts = [MarineWX(z) for z in ZONES]

    await asyncio.gather(
        *(asyncio.create_task(f.run()) for f in forecasts))

    for f in forecasts:
        print(f)
```

```
        print(
            f"Got {len(forecasts)} forecasts "
            f"in {time.perf_counter() - start:.3f} seconds"
        )

    if __name__ == "__main__":
        asyncio.run(main())
```

The `main()` function, when run in the `asyncio` event loop, will launch a number of tasks, each of which is executing the `MarineWX.run()` method for a different zone. The `gather()` function waits until all of them have finished to return the list of futures.

In this case, we don't really want the future result from the created threads; we want the state changes that have been made to all of the `MarineWX` instances. These will be a collection of `Zone` objects and the forecast details. This client runs pretty quickly – we got all thirteen forecasts in about 300 milliseconds.

The `httpx` project supports the decomposition of fetching the raw data and processing the data into separate coroutines. This permits the waiting for data to be interleaved with processing.

We've hit most of the high points of AsyncIO in this section, and the chapter has covered many other concurrency primitives. Concurrency is a hard problem to solve, and no one solution fits all use cases. The most important part of designing a concurrent system is deciding which of the available tools is the correct one to use for the problem. We have seen the advantages and disadvantages of several concurrent systems, and now have some insight into which are the better choices for different types of requirements.

The next topic touches on the question of how "expressive" a concurrency framework or package can be. We'll see how `asyncio` solves a classic computer science problem with a short, clean-looking application program.

The dining philosophers benchmark

The faculty of the College of Philosophy in an old seaside resort city (on the Atlantic coast of the US) has a long-standing tradition of dining together every Sunday night. The food is catered from Mo's Deli, but is always – always – a heaping bowl of spaghetti. No one can remember why, but Mo's a great chef, and each week's spaghetti is a unique experience.

The philosophy department is small, having five tenured faculty members. They're also impoverished and can only afford five forks. Because the dining philosophers each require two forks to enjoy their pasta, they sit around a circular table, so each philosopher has access to two nearby forks.

This requirement for two forks to eat leads to an interesting resource contention problem, shown in the following diagram:

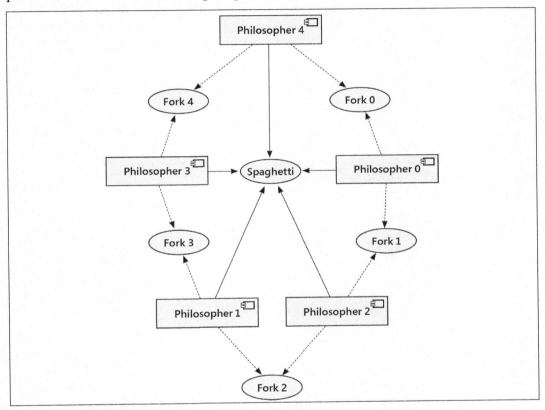

Figure 14.2: The dining philosophers

Ideally, a philosopher, say Philosopher 4, the department chairperson, and an Ontologist, will acquire the two closest forks, Fork 4 and Fork 0, required to eat. Once they've eaten, they release the forks so they can spend some time on philosophy.

There's a problem waiting to be solved. If each philosopher is right-handed, they will reach out, grab the fork on their right, and – unable to grab another fork – are stopped. The system is **deadlocked** because no philosopher can acquire the resources to eat.

One possible solution could break the deadlock by using a timeout: if a philosopher can't acquire a second fork in a few seconds, they set their first fork down, wait a few seconds, and try again. If they all proceed at the same tempo, this results in a cycle of each philosopher getting one fork, waiting a few seconds, setting their forks down, and trying again. Funny, but unsatisfying.

A better solution is to permit only four philosophers at a time to sit at the table. This ensures that at least one philosopher can acquire two forks and eat. While that philosopher is philosophizing, the forks are now available to their two neighbors. Additionally, the first to finish philosophizing can leave the table, allowing the fifth to be seated and join the conversation.

How does this look in code? Here's the philosopher, defined as a coroutine:

```python
FORKS: List[asyncio.Lock]

async def philosopher(
        id: int,
        footman: asyncio.Semaphore
) -> tuple[int, float, float]:
    async with footman:
        async with FORKS[id], FORKS[(id + 1) % len(FORKS)]:
            eat_time = 1 + random.random()
            print(f"{id} eating")
            await asyncio.sleep(eat_time)
        think_time = 1 + random.random()
        print(f"{id} philosophizing")
        await asyncio.sleep(think_time)
    return id, eat_time, think_time
```

Each philosopher needs to know a few things:

- Their own unique identifier. This directs them to the two adjacent forks they're permitted to use.

- A Semaphore – the footman – who seats them at the table. It's the footman's job to have an upper bound on how many can be seated, thereby avoiding deadlock.

- A global collection of forks, represented by a sequence of Lock instances, that will be shared by the philosophers.

The philosopher's mealtime is described by acquiring and using resources. This is implemented with the `async with` statements. The sequence of events looks like this:

1. A philosopher acquires a seat at the table from the footman, a `Semaphore`. We can think of the footman as holding a silver tray with four "you may eat" tokens. A philosopher must have a token before they can sit. Leaving the table, a philosopher drops their token on the tray. The fifth philosopher is eagerly waiting for the token drop from the first philosopher who finishes eating.

2. A philosopher acquires the fork with their ID number and the next higher-numbered fork. The modulo operator assures that the counting of "next" wraps around to zero; `(4+1) % 5` is 0.

3. With a seat at the table and with two forks, the philosopher may enjoy their pasta. Mo often uses kalamata olives and pickled artichoke hearts; it's delightful. Once a month there might be some anchovies or feta cheese.

4. After eating, a philosopher releases the two fork resources. They're not done with dinner, however. Once they've set the forks down, they then spend time philosophizing about life, the universe, and everything.

5. Finally, they relinquish their seat at the table, returning their "you may eat" token to the footman, in case another philosopher is waiting for it.

Looking at the `philosopher()` function, we can see that the forks are a global resource, but the semaphore is a parameter. There's no compelling technical reason to distinguish between the global collection of `Lock` objects to represent the forks and the `Semaphore` as a parameter. We showed both to illustrate the two common choices for providing data to coroutines.

Here are the imports for this code:

```
from __future__ import annotations
import asyncio
import collections
import random
from typing import List, Tuple, DefaultDict, Iterator
```

The overall dining room is organized like this:

```
async def main(faculty: int = 5, servings: int = 5) -> None:
    global FORKS
    FORKS = [asyncio.Lock() for i in range(faculty)]
```

```
        footman = asyncio.BoundedSemaphore(faculty - 1)
        for serving in range(servings):
            department = (
                philosopher(p, footman) for p in range(faculty))
            results = await asyncio.gather(*department)
            print(results)

    if __name__ == "__main__":
        asyncio.run(main())
```

The main() coroutine creates the collection of forks; these are modeled as Lock objects that a philosopher can acquire. The footman is a BoundedSemaphore object with a limit one fewer than the size of the faculty; this avoids a deadlock. For each serving, the department is represented by a collection of philosopher() coroutines. The asyncio.gather() waits for all of the department's coroutines to complete their work – eating and philosophizing.

The beauty of this benchmark problem is to show how well the processing can be stated in the given programming language and library. With the asyncio package, the code is extremely elegant, and seems to be a succinct and expressive representation of a solution to the problem.

The concurrent.futures library can make use of an explicit ThreadPool. It can approach this level of clarity but involves a little bit more technical overhead.

The threading and multiprocessing libraries can also be used directly to provide a similar implementation. Using either of these involves even more technical overhead than the concurrent.futures library. If the eating or philosophizing involved real computational work – not simply sleeping – we would see that a multiprocessing version would finish the soonest because the computation can be spread among several cores. If the eating or philosophizing was mostly waiting for I/O to complete, it would be more like the implementation shown here, and using asyncio or using concurrent.futures with a thread pool would work out nicely.

Case study

One of the problems that often plagues data scientists working on machine learning applications is the amount of time it takes to "train" a model. In our specific example of the *k*-nearest neighbors implementation, training means performing the hyperparameter tuning to find an optimal value of *k* and the right distance algorithm. In the previous chapters of our case study, we've tacitly assumed there will be an optimal set of hyperparameters. In this chapter, we'll look at one way to locate the optimal parameters.

In more complex and less well-defined problems, the time spent training the model can be quite long. If the volume of data is immense, then very expensive compute and storage resources are required to build and train the model.

As an example of a more complex model, look at the MNIST dataset. See http:// yann.lecun.com/exdb/mnist/ for the source data for this dataset and some kinds of analysis that have been performed. This problem requires considerably more time to locate optimal hyperparameters than our small Iris classification problem.

In our case study, hyperparameter tuning is an example of a compute-intensive application. There's very little I/O; if we use shared memory, there's no I/O. This means that a process pool to allow parallel computation is essential. We can wrap the process pool in AsyncIO coroutines, but the extra `async` and `await` syntax seems unhelpful for this kind of compute-intensive example. Instead, we'll use the `concurrent.futures` module to build our hyperparameter tuning function. The design pattern for `concurrent.futures` is to make use of a processing pool to farm out the various testing computations to a number of workers, and gather the results to determine which combination is optimal. A process pool means each worker can occupy a separate core, maximizing compute time. We'll want to run as many tests of `Hyperparameter` instances at the same time as possible.

In previous chapters, we looked at several ways to define the training data and the hyperparameter tuning values. In this case study, we'll use some model classes from *Chapter 7, Python Data Structures*. From this chapter, we'll be using the `TrainingKnownSample` and the `TestingKnownSample` class definitions. We'll need to keep these in a `TrainingData` instance. And, most importantly, we'll need `Hyperparameter` instances.

We can summarize the model like this:

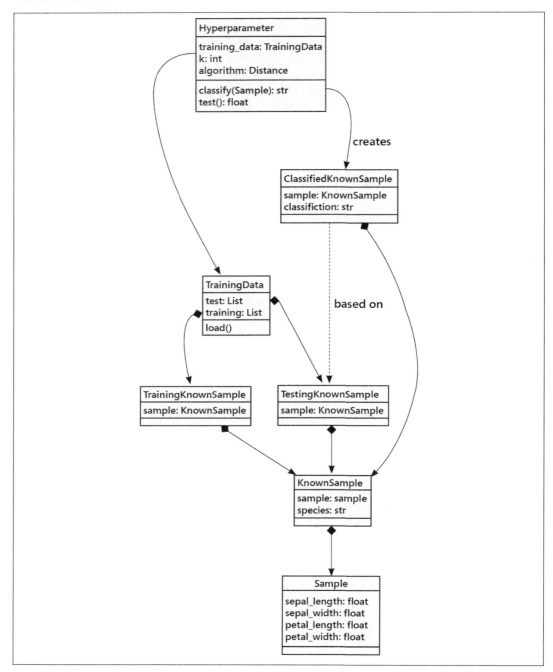

Figure 14.3: The Hyperparameter model

We want to emphasize the `KnownTestingSample` and `KnownTrainingSample` classes. We are looking at testing, and won't be doing anything with `UnknownSample` instances.

Our tuning strategy can be described as **grid search**. We can imagine a grid with the alternative values for *k* across the top and the different distance algorithms down the side. We'll fill in each cell of the grid with a result:

```
for k in range(1, 41, 2):
    for algo in ED(), MD(), CD(), SD():
        h = Hyperparameter(k, algo, td)
        print(h.test())
```

This lets us compare a range of *k* values and distance algorithms to see which combination is best. We don't really want to print the results, though. We want to save them in a list, sort them to find the highest-quality result, and use that as the preferred `Hyperparameter` configuration for classifying unknown samples.

(Spoiler alert: for this Iris dataset, they're all pretty good.)

Each test run is completely independent. We can, therefore, do them all concurrently.

To show what we'll be running concurrently, here's the test method of the `Hyperparameter` class:

```
def test(self) -> "Hyperparameter":
    """Run the entire test suite."""
    pass_count, fail_count = 0, 0
    for sample in self.data.testing:
        sample.classification = self.classify(sample)
        if sample.matches():
            pass_count += 1
        else:
            fail_count += 1
    self.quality = pass_count / (pass_count + fail_count)
    return self
```

We'll use each test sample, performing the classification algorithm. If the known result matches the species assigned by the `classify()` algorithm, we'll count this as a pass. If the classification algorithm doesn't match the known result, we'll count this as a failure. The percentage of correct matches is one way to gauge the quality of a classification.

Here's an overall testing function, `load_and_tune()`. This function loads the raw data into memory from the `bezdekiris.data` file, which can be found in the code repository for this book. The function includes the use of a `ProcessPoolExecutor` to run a number of workers concurrently:

```
def grid_search_1() -> None:
    td = TrainingData("Iris")
    source_path = Path.cwd().parent / "bezdekiris.data"
    reader = CSVIrisReader(source_path)
    td.load(reader.data_iter())

    tuning_results: List[Hyperparameter] = []
    with futures.ProcessPoolExecutor(8) as workers:
        test_runs: List[futures.Future[Hyperparameter]] = []
        for k in range(1, 41, 2):
            for algo in ED(), MD(), CD(), SD():
                h = Hyperparameter(k, algo, td)
                test_runs.append(workers.submit(h.test))
        for f in futures.as_completed(test_runs):
            tuning_results.append(f.result())
    for result in tuning_results:
        print(
            f"{result.k:2d} {result.algorithm.__class__.__name__:2s}"
            f" {result.quality:.3f}"
        )
```

We've used the `workers.submit()` to provide a function, the `test()` method of a `Hyperparameter` instance, h, to the pool of workers. The result is a `Future[Hyperparameter]` that will (eventually) have a `Hyperparameter` as a result. Each submitted future, managed by the `ProcessPoolExecutor`, will evaluate this function, saving the resulting `Hyperparameter` object as the future's result.

Is this use of the `ProcessPoolExecutor` optimal? Because we have such a small pool of data, it seems to work well. The overhead of serializing the training data for each submission is minimal. For a larger set of training and testing samples, we will run into performance problems serializing all the data. Since the samples are string and float objects, we can change the data structure to use shared memory. This is a radical restructuring that needs to exploit the Flyweight design pattern from *Chapter 12, Advanced Design Patterns*.

We used the `Future[Hyperparameter]` type hint to remind the *mypy* tool that we expect the `test()` method to return a `Hyperparameter` result. It's important to make sure the expected result type matches the result type from the function actually provided to `submit()`.

When we examine the `Future[Hyperparameter]` object, the `result` function will provide the `Hyperparameter` that was processed in the worker thread. We can collect these to locate an optimal hyperparameter set.

Interestingly, they're all quite good, varying between 97% and 100% accuracy. Here's a short snippet of the output:

```
5 ED 0.967
5 MD 0.967
5 CD 0.967
5 SD 0.967
7 ED 0.967
7 MD 0.967
7 CD 1.000
7 SD 0.967
9 ED 0.967
9 MD 0.967
9 CD 1.000
9 SD 0.967
```

Why is the quality so consistently high? There are a number of reasons:

- The source data was carefully curated and prepared by the authors of the original study.
- There are only four features for each sample. The classification isn't complex and there aren't a lot of opportunities for near-miss classifications.
- Of the four features, two are very strongly correlated with the resulting species. The other two have weaker correlations between a feature and the species.

One of the reasons for choosing this example is because the data allows us to enjoy a success without the complications of struggling with a poorly-designed problem, data that's difficult to work with, or a high level of noise that drowns out the import signal hidden in the data.

Looking at the iris.names file, section 8, we see the following summary statistics:

```
Summary Statistics:
                 Min  Max   Mean   SD    Class Correlation
   sepal length: 4.3  7.9   5.84  0.83   0.7826
    sepal width: 2.0  4.4   3.05  0.43  -0.4194
   petal length: 1.0  6.9   3.76  1.76   0.9490  (high!)
    petal width: 0.1  2.5   1.20  0.76   0.9565  (high!)
```

These statistics suggest that using only two of the features would be better than using all four features. Indeed, ignoring the sepal width might provide even better results.

Moving on to more sophisticated problems will introduce new challenges. The essential Python programming shouldn't be part of the problem anymore. It should help to craft workable solutions.

Recall

We've looked closely at a variety of topics related to concurrent processing in Python:

- Threads have an advantage of simplicity for many cases. This has to be balanced against the GIL interfering with compute-intensive multi-threading.

- Multiprocessing has an advantage of making full use of all cores of a processor. This has to be balanced against interprocess communication costs. If shared memory is used, there is the complication of encoding and accessing the shared objects.

- The concurrent.futures module defines an abstraction – the future – that can minimize the differences in application programming used for accessing threads or processes. This makes it easy to switch and see which approach is fastest.

- The async/await features of the Python language are supported by the AsyncIO package. Because these are coroutines, there isn't true parallel processing; control switches among the coroutines allow a single thread to interleave between waiting for I/O and computing.

- The dining philosophers benchmark can be helpful for comparing different kinds of concurrency language features and libraries. It's a relatively simple problem with some interesting complexities.

- Perhaps the most important observation is the lack of a trivial one-size-fits-all solution to concurrent processing. It's essential to create – and measure – a variety of solutions to determine a design that makes best use of the computing hardware.

Exercises

We've covered several different concurrency paradigms in this chapter and still don't have a clear idea of when each one is useful. In the case study, we hinted that it's generally best to develop a few different strategies before committing to one that is measurably better than the others. The final choice must be based on measurements of the performance of multi-threaded and multi-processing solutions.

Concurrency is a huge topic. As your first exercise, we encourage you to search the web to discover what are considered to be the latest Python concurrency best practices. It can help to investigate material that isn't Python-specific to understand the operating system primitives like semaphores, locks, and queues.

If you have used threads in a recent application, take a look at the code and see how you can make it more readable and less bug-prone by using futures. Compare thread and multiprocessing futures to see whether you can gain anything by using multiple CPUs.

Try implementing an AsyncIO service for some basic HTTP requests. If you can get it to the point that a web browser can render a simple GET request, you'll have a good understanding of AsyncIO network transports and protocols.

Make sure you understand the race conditions that happen in threads when you access shared data. Try to come up with a program that uses multiple threads to set shared values in such a way that the data deliberately becomes corrupt or invalid.

In *Chapter 8, The Intersection of Object-Oriented and Functional Programming,* we looked at an example that used subprocess.run() to execute a number of python -m doctest commands on files within a directory. Review that example and rewrite the code to run each subprocess in parallel using a futures.ProcessPoolExecutor.

Looking back at *Chapter 12, Advanced Design Patterns,* there's an example that runs an external command to create the figures for each chapter. This relies on an external application, java, which tends to consume a lot of CPU resources when it runs. Does concurrency help with this example? Running multiple, concurrent Java programs seems to be a terrible burden. Is this a case where the default value for the size of a process pool is too large?

When looking at the case study, an important alternative is to use shared memory to allow multiple concurrent processes sharing a common set of raw data. Using shared memory means either sharing bytes or sharing a list of simple objects. Sharing bytes works well for packages like NumPy, but doesn't work well for our Python class definitions. This suggests that we can create a SharedList object that contains all of the sample values. We'll need to apply the Flyweight design pattern to present attributes with useful names extracted from the list in shared memory. An individual FlyweightSample, then, will extract four measurements and a species assignment. Once the data is prepared, what are the performance differences among concurrent processes and threads within a process? What changes are required to the TrainingData class to avoid loading testing and training samples until they're needed?

Summary

This chapter ends our exploration of object-oriented programming with a topic that isn't very object-oriented. Concurrency is a difficult problem, and we've only scratched the surface. While the underlying OS abstractions of processes and threads do not provide an API that is remotely object-oriented, Python offers some really good object-oriented abstractions around them. The threading and multiprocessing packages both provide an object-oriented interface to the underlying mechanics. Futures are able to encapsulate a lot of the messy details into a single object. AsyncIO uses coroutine objects to make our code read as though it runs synchronously, while hiding ugly and complicated implementation details behind a very simple loop abstraction.

Thank you for reading *Python Object-Oriented Programming, Fourth Edition*. We hope you've enjoyed the ride and are eager to start implementing object-oriented software in all your future projects!

packt.com

Subscribe to our online digital library for full access to over 7,000 books and videos, as well as industry leading tools to help you plan your personal development and advance your career. For more information, please visit our website.

Why subscribe?

- Spend less time learning and more time coding with practical eBooks and Videos from over 4,000 industry professionals
- Learn better with Skill Plans built especially for you
- Get a free eBook or video every month
- Fully searchable for easy access to vital information
- Copy and paste, print, and bookmark content

Did you know that Packt offers eBook versions of every book published, with PDF and ePub files available? You can upgrade to the eBook version at www.Packt.com and as a print book customer, you are entitled to a discount on the eBook copy. Get in touch with us at customercare@packtpub.com for more details.

At www.Packt.com, you can also read a collection of free technical articles, sign up for a range of free newsletters, and receive exclusive discounts and offers on Packt books and eBooks.

Other Books You May Enjoy

If you enjoyed this book, you may be interested in these other books by Packt:

Expert Python Programming – Fourth Edition

Michał Jaworski

Tarek Ziadé

ISBN: 978-1-80107-110-9

- Explore modern ways of setting up repeatable and consistent Python development environments
- Effectively package Python code for community and production use
- Learn about modern syntax elements of Python programming, such as f-strings, dataclasses, enums, and lambda functions
- Demystify metaprogramming in Python with metaclasses
- Write concurrent code in Python
- Monitor and optimize the performance of Python application
- Extend and integrate Python with code written in different languages

Modern Python Cookbook - Second Edition

Steven F. Lott

ISBN: 978-1-80020-745-5

- See the intricate details of the Python syntax and how to use it to your advantage
- Improve your coding with Python readability through functions
- Manipulate data effectively using built-in data structures
- Get acquainted with advanced programming techniques in Python
- Equip yourself with functional and statistical programming features
- Write proper tests to be sure a program works as advertised
- Integrate application software using Python

Clean Code in Python - Second Edition

Mariano Anaya

ISBN: 978-1-80056-021-5

- Set up a productive development environment by leveraging automatic tools
- Leverage the magic methods in Python to write better code, abstracting complexity away and encapsulating details
- Create advanced object-oriented designs using unique features of Python, such as descriptors
- Eliminate duplicated code by creating powerful abstractions using software engineering principles of object-oriented design
- Create Python-specific solutions using decorators and descriptors
- Refactor code effectively with the help of unit tests
- Build the foundations for solid architecture with a clean code base as its cornerstone

Packt is searching for authors like you

If you're interested in becoming an author for Packt, please visit authors.packtpub.com and apply today. We have worked with thousands of developers and tech professionals, just like you, to help them share their insight with the global tech community. You can make a general application, apply for a specific hot topic that we are recruiting an author for, or submit your own idea.

Share Your Thoughts

Now you've finished *Python Object-Oriented Programming, Fourth Edition*, we'd love to hear your thoughts! Scan the QR code below to go straight to the Amazon review page for this book and share your feedback or leave a review on the site that you purchased it from.

https://packt.link/r/1-801-07726-6

Your review is important to us and the tech community and will help us make sure we're delivering excellent quality content.

Index

Symbols

4+1 Views technique 21

A

absolute imports 60
abstract base class 212, 224-226
  creating 207-209, 220-224
Abstract Factory pattern 545, 546
  example 547-552
  in Python 552, 553
  in UML 546
abstraction 12
Abstract Syntax Trees (ASTs) 398
access control 68
Adapter pattern 522, 523
  example 523-527
  in UML 522
advanced design patterns
  Abstract Factory pattern 545, 546
  Adapter pattern 522, 523
  case study 567-569
  Composite pattern 553-555
  Façade pattern 527, 528
  Flyweight pattern 532-534
  Template pattern 561
aggregation 15, 27
application, issues
  testing and development 612
arguments
  adding, to method 48
  unpacking 326, 327
assert statement 49
AsyncIO 650, 651
  working 652-654

AsyncIO clients 665-668
AsyncIO, for networking 655-661
  design considerations 661, 662
AsyncIO future
  reading 654
asyncio library 651
attributes 7
  dot notation 45
  specifying 6
authentication 150
authorization 150

B

basic inheritance 88
behaviors 2, 9
  adding, to class data with properties 170-173
  specifying 7
boundary value analysis 578, 611
Bray-Curtis distance 119
bug 146
built-in functions, Python 308
  enumerate() function 310-312
  len() function 308, 309
  reversed() function 309, 310
built-ins
  extending 232-235
bytes
  decoding, to text 375, 376
  text, encoding to 376-378

C

callable objects 337, 338
callback function 329-334
CapWords notation 43

case study overview **20, 21**
  context view 23-25
  development view 30-32
  key concepts 33
  logical view 26, 27
  physical view 32
  problem overview 22, 23
  process view 28, 29
case study, data validation **146**
  bad behavior 150-154
  context view 147
  CSV files, reading 157, 158
  Don't Repeat Yourself (DRY) 159
  enumerated values, validating 155, 156
  processing view 148, 149
character classes **385**
Chebyshev distance **116, 118, 613**
class **4, 37, 38**
  versus objects 47
class diagram **4, 6**
  for chess game 15
  with attributes 8, 9
  with methods 10
classification **349-352**
class variables **89**
code
  organizing, in modules 63-67
collections.abc module **213-219**
collections module **210, 211**
Column-Separated Values (CSV) **151**
Command pattern **487**
  example 488-492
  in UML 488
Comma-Separated Value (CSV) **403**
Composite pattern **553-555**
  example 555-560
  in UML 554
composition **13, 15, 27**
comprehension **428**
  dictionary comprehension 432
  set comprehension 431
  list comprehensions 428-430
concurrency **627**
  case study 673-677
concurrent processing **628, 629**
conda **41, 483**
constructor **50**

context managers **342, 346**
context view **21**
continuous integration and continuous
      deployment (CI/CD) pipeline **32**
cooperative multitasking **651**
coroutine **651**
cosine computation **369**
Counter object **275, 276**
coverage tool **576**
CSV Dictionary Reader **408-411**
CSV format designs **407, 408**
CSV List Reader **411-413**
custom formatters **372**

D

dask package
  reference link 633
data **2, 7**
  splitting 348, 349
dataclasses **261-265**
data structures **253**
  dataclasses 261
  dictionaries 265
  empty objects 253
  lists 276
  named tuples 258
  queues 290
  sets 285
  tuples 255
Decorator pattern **464**
  example 465-472
  in Python 472-476
  in UML 465
  uses 464
decorators **176, 177**
deduplication, case study **448-452**
defaultdict
  using 272-275
defaults **52**
default values **317-319**
  for parameters 314-317
Dependency Inversion **113**
deserializing **398**
design patterns **424**
  case study 509-517
  Command pattern 487, 488

Decorator pattern 464, 465
Observer pattern 476, 477
Singleton pattern 503
State pattern 493
Strategy pattern 481, 482
development view 21
diamond problem 99-105
dice-rolling abstraction
creating 221-224
dictionaries 265-270
use cases 271, 272
dictionary comprehension 432
dining philosophers benchmark 668-672
distance classes
unit testing 613-619
distance computation 368, 370
docstrings
using 53-55
doctest tool 53, 323
Don't Repeat Yourself (DRY)
principle 159, 187, 525
dot notation 45
duck typing 19, 112, 212
duplicate code
removing 185-187

E

Easier to Ask Forgiveness than Permission
(EAFP) style 152
empty objects 253, 254
encapsulation 11
enumerate() function 310-312
equivalence partitioning 578
errors 128
escaping braces 365
escaping characters 386, 387
Euclidean distance 613
event loop 651
exception hierarchy 138, 139
exceptions 128
categories 127, 128
defining 139, 141
effects 130-132
handling 132-138

raising 126-130
recommended use 142-145
existing code
reusing 187-190
Extensible Markup Language (XML) 403

F

Façade pattern 527, 528
example 528-532
in UML 528
File I/O 339-342
context managers 342-346
filesystem paths 394-398
First In First Out (FIFO) 290
Flyweight pattern 532, 534
example, in Python 534-541
in UML 533
memory optimization, via
Python's __slots__ 543, 545
multiple messages, in buffer 542, 543
format() method 373, 374
frozen dataclasses 298-301
f-strings 364, 366, 367
function objects 327-334
functions
using, to patch class 335, 336
futures 646-649

G

generator expressions 432-434
generator functions 434-439
generator stacks 441-445
generic classes 212
generic collections 93
Git 70
global interpreter lock (GIL) 633
grid search 675

H

Hyperparameter class
unit testing 620-623
Hypothesis package
reference link 611

I

immutable objects **232**
information hiding **11**
inheritance **13, 16, 88**
  applying, in practice 88-90
  built-ins, extending 90-93
  example 17, 18
  multiple inheritance 19-98
  overriding 94
  super() 95
inheritance and abstraction, case study
  logical view 114-119
  Manhattan distance 120
  Sorensen distance 119, 120
instance diagram **14**
integration tests **576**
interface **10**
Interface Segregation **113**
Internet of Things (IoT) **330, 494, 524**
iterable object
  items, yielding from 439-441
iterator protocol **425-428**
iterators **424**

J

JavaScript Object Notation (JSON) **403**
  serialization 413-415
  used, for serializing objects 403-406
  validation 416-418

K

k-NN algorithm **454**
  with bisect module 455, 456
  with heapq module 456

L

len() function **308, 309**
Lines of Code
  versus Statements 398
Liskov Substitution **113**
list comprehensions **428-430**
lists **276-279**
  sorting 279-285
logical model **294-298**

logical view **21**
log writing
  demonstration 662-665
Look Before You Leap (LBYL) style **152**

M

manager objects **180-185**
Manhattan distance **116, 117, 613**
Mapping abstractions **214, 215**
map-reduce problem **452**
matching patterns, regex **382-384**
Median Absolute Deviation
    (MAD) technique **154**
members **7**
metaclass **208, 225, 235-240**
method overloading **312-314**
Method Resolution Order (MRO)
    algorithm **20, 103, 225**
methods **9, 47**
mixin **95**
Mocks
  used, for imitating objects 599-603
modules **56-59**
  code, organizing in 63-67
  organizing 59, 60
monkey patching **336**
multiple inheritance **19, 20, 95-98**
  diamond problem 99-105
  different sets of arguments,
      managing 105-108
multiple partitions **448-451**
multiprocessing **634-636**
  issues 645, 646
multiprocessing API **634**
multiprocessing module **634**
multiprocessing package **637**
multiprocessing pools **637-640**
mutable byte strings **379**
mutable collections **232**
mypy tool **41, 42, 96, 169,**
    212, 261, 321, 330

N

NamedTuple classes **301-304**
named tuples **255-258**
  via typing.NamedTuple 258-261

name mangling 68
newline-delimited JSON 415, 416

O

OAuth
   URL 150
object diagram 14
object/instance diagram
   for chess game 14
object-oriented analysis (OOA) 2
object-oriented design (OOD) 3
object-oriented design, case study 71
   class responsibilities 80, 81
   logical view 71, 73
   samples 74
   sample states 74
   sample state transitions 75-80
   TrainingData class 81-84
object-oriented programming (OOP) 2, 3
objects 2, 4
   examples 164-169
   identifying 164
   imitating, with Mocks 599-603
   initializing 49-51
   serializing 398-400
   serializing, with JSON 403-406
   versus class 47
Observer pattern 476, 477
   example 477-481
   in UML 477
one-pass partitioning 353-356
Open/Closed Principle 113
operator overloading 226-232
overriding 94

P

package 59, 62
parameters
   default values 314-317
   types 316
partition() function 352, 353
patching
   techniques 603-606
patterns
   grouping 389, 390

patterns of characters
   repeating 387-389
physical view 21
pickles
   customizing 401-403
polymorphism 18, 19, 109, 111
print formatting 370
processing
   overview 347, 348
process view 21
properties 7
   behaviors, adding to class data 170-173
   example 174, 175
   using 177-180
property constructor 174
property function 174
protocol 96, 212
pytest
   fixtures, for setup functions 586-591
   fixtures, for teardown functions 586-591
   setup functions 583-586
   sophisticated fixtures 591-597
   teardown functions 583-586
   tests, skipping 597-599
   using, for unit testing 581-583
Python classes
   attributes, adding 44, 45
   behaviors, adding 45, 46
   creating 43, 44
Python objects
   working, core rules 38
Python Package Index (PyPI)
   URL 69
Python's __slots__
   memory, optimizing via 543, 545

Q

queues 640-645
   types 290-294

R

race condition 650
regular expressions 380, 381
   efficient, making 393, 394
   information, parsing 390-392

relative imports 61
re module
  features 392, 393
reversed() function 309, 310

S

samples, partitioning into testing and training
      subsets 191
  input partitioning 194, 195
  input validation 192-194
  property setters 200
  purpose enumeration 197-199
  repeated if statements 200
  sample class hierarchy 195-197
selection of characters
  matching 384-386
self argument 46, 47
sentinel object 606, 607
sequence types
  reference link 279
serializing 398
Set Builder background 446, 447
set comprehension 431
sets 285-290
Single Responsibility Principle 113
Singleton pattern 503
  implementing 504-508
  in UML 503
SOLID principles 113
Sorensen distance 119, 613
sorting algorithm
  reference link 662
splash radius 525
Statements
  versus Lines of Code 398
State pattern 493
  example 494-502
  in UML 493
Strategy pattern 481
  example 483-486
  in Python 486, 487
  in UML 482
  versus State pattern 502, 503

string formatting 364
string manipulation 361-364
strings 360
  Unicode 374, 375
subclass 88
super() 95
superclass 88
syntactic sugar 92

T

tagged union 279
Template pattern 561
  example 562-566
  in UML 561
test-driven development 575, 576
testing 452, 453
  capabilities 608-611
  need for 573-575
  objectives 576
  patterns 577, 578
tests
  skipping, with pytest 597-599
text
  bytes, decoding to 375, 376
  encoding, to bytes 376-378
third-party libraries 69-71
threads 629-631
threads, issues 632
  global interpreter lock 633
  shared memory 632, 633
  thread overhead 634
training data sorting, case study 241
  incremental strategy, for partitioning 246-249
  list class, extending with sublists 242, 243
  shuffling strategy, for partitioning 244-246
tuples 255-258
tuple unpacking 257
type 38
type checking 40-42
type hint annotations, for cooperative multiple
      inheritance
  reference link 108
type hints 38-41, 52, 93

U

UML diagram 4
Unified Modeling Language (UML) 4, 5, 21
unit testing
   case study, distance classes 613-619
   case study, Hyperparameter class 620-623
   with pytest 581-583
   with unittest 578-580
unit tests 576
UTF-8 360

V

variable argument lists 319-325
variadic arguments 319

Y

Yet Another Markup Language (YAML) 403

Printed in Great Britain
by Amazon

50536770R00394